Communications in Computer and Information Science   1781

Rationale

The CCIS series is devoted to the publication of proceedings of computer science conferences. Its aim is to efficiently disseminate original research results in informatics in printed and electronic form. While the focus is on publication of peer-reviewed full papers presenting mature work, inclusion of reviewed short papers reporting on work in progress is welcome, too. Besides globally relevant meetings with internationally representative program committees guaranteeing a strict peer-reviewing and paper selection process, conferences run by societies or of high regional or national relevance are also considered for publication.

Topics

The topical scope of CCIS spans the entire spectrum of informatics ranging from foundational topics in the theory of computing to information and communications science and technology and a broad variety of interdisciplinary application fields.

Information for Volume Editors and Authors

Publication in CCIS is free of charge. No royalties are paid, however, we offer registered conference participants temporary free access to the online version of the conference proceedings on SpringerLink (http://link.springer.com) by means of an http referrer from the conference website and/or a number of complimentary printed copies, as specified in the official acceptance email of the event.

CCIS proceedings can be published in time for distribution at conferences or as post-proceedings, and delivered in the form of printed books and/or electronically as USBs and/or e-content licenses for accessing proceedings at SpringerLink. Furthermore, CCIS proceedings are included in the CCIS electronic book series hosted in the SpringerLink digital library at http://link.springer.com/bookseries/7899. Conferences publishing in CCIS are allowed to use Online Conference Service (OCS) for managing the whole proceedings lifecycle (from submission and reviewing to preparing for publication) free of charge.

Publication process

The language of publication is exclusively English. Authors publishing in CCIS have to sign the Springer CCIS copyright transfer form, however, they are free to use their material published in CCIS for substantially changed, more elaborate subsequent publications elsewhere. For the preparation of the camera-ready papers/files, authors have to strictly adhere to the Springer CCIS Authors' Instructions and are strongly encouraged to use the CCIS LaTeX style files or templates.

Abstracting/Indexing

CCIS is abstracted/indexed in DBLP, Google Scholar, EI-Compendex, Mathematical Reviews, SCImago, Scopus. CCIS volumes are also submitted for the inclusion in ISI Proceedings.

How to start

To start the evaluation of your proposal for inclusion in the CCIS series, please send an e-mail to ccis@springer.com.

Deepak Garg · V. A. Narayana · P. N. Suganthan ·
Jaume Anguera · Vijaya Kumar Koppula ·
Suneet Kumar Gupta
Editors

Advanced Computing

12th International Conference, IACC 2022
Hyderabad, India, December 16–17, 2022
Revised Selected Papers, Part I

Editors
Deepak Garg
SR University
Warangal, India

P. N. Suganthan
Nanyang Technological University
Singapore, Singapore

Vijaya Kumar Koppula
CMR College of Engineering & Technology
Hyderabad, India

V. A. Narayana
CMR College of Engineering & Technology
Hyderabad, India

Jaume Anguera
Ramon Llull University
Barcelona, Spain

Suneet Kumar Gupta
Bennett University
Greater Noida, India

ISSN 1865-0929   ISSN 1865-0937 (electronic)
Communications in Computer and Information Science
ISBN 978-3-031-35640-7   ISBN 978-3-031-35641-4 (eBook)
https://doi.org/10.1007/978-3-031-35641-4

This Springer imprint is published by the registered company Springer Nature Switzerland AG
The registered company address is: Gewerbestrasse 11, 6330 Cham, Switzerland

Preface

The objective of the 12th International Advanced Computing Conference (IACC 2022) was to bring together researchers, developers, and practitioners from academia and industry working in the domain of advanced computing. The conference consisted of tracks in Advances in Machine Learning and Deep Learning, Advances in Applications of Artificial Intelligence in Interdisciplinary Areas, Reinforcement Learning, and Advances in Data Science. The conference took place on 16th and 17th December 2022 at CMR College of Engineering and Technology, Hyderabad. All editions of the series are successfully indexed in ISI, Scopus, DBLP, Compendex, SJR, and Google Scholar. The current version of the conference proceedings is published in the prestigious CCIS series of Springer.

The conference has the track record of acceptance rates of less than 20% in the last 11 years. More than 12 IEEE/ACM Fellows hold key positions of the conference committee, giving it a quality edge. In the last 11 years the conference's citation score has been consistently increasing. This has been possible due to adherence to quality parameters of review and acceptance rate without any exception, which allows us to make some of the best research available through this platform.

The conference organizers have followed the standard process for assessing papers based on the methodology & empirical study in the article, the novelty of the work, its significance, and the contribution made by the authors.

Keeping the quality benchmarks of the conference, in the 12th IACC also the acceptance rates were within our limits of 20%: 415 research papers were submitted and after single-blind review 97 papers were accepted. Out of these 97, 81 papers were registered for presentation at the conference. 6 out of 81 were selected in the short papers category and the rest in the full-length category. The final recommendation of papers was made by the general/program co-chair of IACC-2022 after receiving the review comments from the reviewers.

In the coming years, we would like to further enhance the visibility of the conference in terms of the number and quality of the papers. We are also consistently trying to reach out to under-represented regions of the world for quality papers.

Our sincere thanks to the Springer staff for their continuous support and help in taking the conference and series to the next level.

December 2022

Deepak Garg
Conference General Co-chair,
12th IACC 2022

Organization

Honorary Co-chairs

Sundaraja Sitharama Iyengar   Florida International University, USA
Sartaj Sahni   University of Florida, USA
Jagannathan Sarangpani   Missouri University of Science and Technology, USA

General Co-chairs

Deepak Garg   SR University, India
Suneet K. Gupta   Bennett University, India
Vijaya Kumar Koppula   CMR College of Engineering & Technology, India
V. A. Narayana   CMR College of Engineering & Technology, India

Proceeding Editors

P. N. Suganthan   Nanyang Technological University, Singapore
Jaume Anguera   Universitat Ramon Llull, Spain

Program Co-chairs

Kit Wong   University College London, UK
George Ghinea   Brunel University London, UK
Carol Smidts   Ohio State University, USA
Ram D. Sriram   National Institute of Standards & Technology, USA
Sanjay Madria   University of Missouri, USA
Oge Marques   Florida Atlantic University, USA
Vijay Kumar   University of Missouri-Kansas City, USA
Ajay Gupta   Western Michigan University, USA

Special Issue Co-chairs

Akansha Singh   Bennett University, India
Dilbag Singh   Gwangju Institute of Science and Technology,
                             South Korea

Technical Program Committee/International Advisory Committee

Shivani Goel   Bennett University, India
Sumeet Dua   Louisiana Tech University, USA
Roger Zimmermann   National University of Singapore, Singapore
Seeram Ramakrishna   National University of Singapore, Singapore
B. V. R. Chowdari   NUS and Nanyang Technological University,
                             Singapore
Hari Mohan Pandey   Edge Hill University, UK
Selwyn Piramuthu   University of Florida, USA
Bharat Bhargava   Purdue University, USA
Omer F. Rana   Cardiff University, UK
Javed I. Khan   Kent State University, USA
Harpreet Singh   Wayne State University, USA
Rajeev Agrawal   North Carolina A&T State University, USA
P. Prabhakaran   St. Joseph University, Tanzania
Yuliya Averyanova   National Aviation University (NAU), Ukraine
Mohammed M. Banet   Jordan University of Technology, Jordan
Dawid Zydek   Idaho State University, USA
Wensheng Zhang   Iowa State University, USA
Bal Virdee   London Metropolitan University, UK
Qun Wu   Harbin Institute of Technology, China
Anh V. Dinh   University of Saskatchewan, Canada
Lakshman Tamil   University of Texas, USA
P. D. D. Dominic   Universiti Teknologi Petronas, Malaysia
Muhammad Sabbir Rahman   North South University, Bangladesh
Zablon Akoko Mbero   University of Botswana, Botswana
V. L. Narasimhan   University of Botswana, Botswana
Kin-Lu Wong   National Sun Yat-sen University, Taiwan
Pawan Lingras   Saint Mary's University, USA
P. G. S. Velmurugan   Thiagaraja College of Engineering, India
N. B. Balamurugan   Thiagaraja College of Engineering, India
Mahesh Bundele   Poornima University, India
N. Venkateswaran   Sri Sivasubramaniya Nadar College of
                             Engineering, India

S. Sundaresh	IEEE Madras Section, India
Premanand V. Chandramani	SSN College of Engineering, India
Mini Vasudevan	Ericsson India Pvt. Ltd., India
P. Swarnalatha	VIT, India
P. Venkatesh	Thiagaraja College of Engineering, India
B. Venkatalakshmi	Velammal Engineering College, India
M. Marsalin Beno	St. Xavier's Catholic College of Engineering, India
M. Arun	VIT, India
K. Porkumaran	Dr. N.G.P. Institute of Technology, India
D. Ezhilarasi	NIT Tiruchirappalli, India
Ramya Vijay	SASTRA University, India
S. Rajaram	Thiagaraja College of Engineering, India
B. Yogameena	Thiagaraja College of Engineering, India
S. Joseph Gladwin	SSN College of Engineering, India
D. Nirmal	Karunya University, India
N. Mohankumar	SKP Institute of Technology, India
A. Jawahar	SSN College of Engineering, India
K. Dhayalini	K. Ramakrishnan College of Engineering, India
Diganta Sengupta	Meghnad Saha Institute of Technology, India
Supriya Chakraborty	Amity University, India
Mamta Arora	Manav Rachna University, India
Om Prakash Jena	Ravenshaw University, India
Sandeep Singh Sengar	University of Copenhagen, Denmark
Murali Chemuturi	Chemuturi Consultants, India
Madhu Vadlamani	Cognizant, India
A. N. K. Prasannanjaneyulu	Institute of Insurance and Risk Management, India
O. Obulesu	G Narayanamma Institute of Technology & Science, India
Rajendra R. Patil	GSSSIETW, India
Ajay Kumar	Chitkara University Institute of Engineering & Technology, India
D. P. Kothari	THDC Institute of Hydropower Engineering and Technology, India
T. S. N. Murthy	JNTUK Vizianagaram, India
Nitesh Tarbani	Sipna College of Engineering & Technology, India
Jesna Mohan	Mar Baselios College of Engineering and Technology, India
Manoj K. Patel	CSIR, India
Pravati Swain	NIT Goa, India
Manoj Kumar	University of Petroleum and Energy Studies, India

E. S. Gopi	National Institute of Technology Tiruchirappalli, India
Mithun B. Patil	NKOCET, India
Priya Saha	LPU, India
Sahaj Saxena	Thapar Institute of Engineering and Technology, India
Dinesh G. Harkut	Prof Ram Meghe College of Engineering & Management, India
Pushpendra Singh	National Institute of Technology Hamirpur, India
Nirmala J. Saunshimath	Nitte Meenakshi Institute of Technology, India
Mayank Pandey	MNNIT, India
Sudeep D. Thepade	Pimpri Chinchwad College of Engineering, India
Pimal Khanpara	Nirma University, India
Rohit Lalwani	MIT University of Meghalaya, India
Loshma Gunisetti	Sri Vasavi Engineering College, India
Vishweshwar Kallimani	University of Nottingham, UK
Amit Kumar Mishra	DIT University, India
Pawan Whig	Vivekananda Institute of Professional Studies, India
Dhatri Pandya	Sarvajanik College of Engineering and Technology, India
Asha S. Manek	RV Institute of Technology and Management, India
Lingala Thirupathi	Methodist College of Engineering & Technology, India
P. Mahanti	University of New Brunswick, Canada
Shaikh Muhammad Allayear	Daffodil International University, Bangladesh
Basanta Joshi	Tribhuvan University, Nepal
S. R. N. Reddy	IGDTUW, India
Mehran Alidoost Nia	University of Tehran, Iran
Ambili P. S.	Saintgits Group of Institutions, India
M. A. Jabbar	Vardhaman College of Engineering, India
Lokendra Kumar Tiwari	Ewing Christian College, India
Abhay Saxena	Dev Sanskriti Vishwavidyalaya, India
Kanika Bansal	Chitkara University, India
Pooja M. R.	Vidyavardhaka College of Engineering, India
Pranav Dass	Bharati Vidyapeeth's College of Engineering, India
Avani R. Vasant	Babaria Institute of Technology, India
Bhanu Prasad	Florida A&M University, USA
Barenya Bikash Hazarika	NIT Arunachal Pradesh, India
Ipseeta Nanda	Gopal Narayan Singh University, India
Satyendra Singh	Bhartiya Skill Development University, India

Sudip Mandal	Jalpaiguri Govt. Engineering College, India
Naveen Kumar	IIIT Vadodara, India
Parag Rughani	National Forensic Sciences University, India
K. Shirin Bhanu	Sri Vasavi Engineering College, India
R. Malmathanraj	NITT, India
Latika Singh	Sushant University, India
Gizachew Hailegebriel Mako	Ethio telecom, Ethiopia
Tessy Mathew	Mar Baselios College of Engineering and Technology, India
Grzegorz Chodak	Wroclaw University of Science and Technology, Poland
Neetu Verma	DCRUST, India
Sharda A. Chhabria	G.H. Raisoni Institute of Engineering & Technology, India
Neetesh Saxena	Cardiff University, UK
R. Venkatesan	Ministry of Earth Sciences, India
V. Jayaprakasan	IEEE Madras Section, India
D. Venkata Vara Prasad	SSN College of Engineering, India
Jayakumari J.	Mar Baselios College of Engineering and Technology, India
P. A. Manoharan	IEEE Madras Section, India
S. Salivahanan	IEEE Madras Section, India
P. Santhi Thilagam	National Institute of Technology Karnataka, India
Umapada Pal	Indian Statistical Institute, India
S. Suresh	NIT Trichy, India
V. Mariappan	NIT Trichy, India
T. Sentilkumar	Anna University, India
S. Chandramohan	College of Engineering, India
D. Devaraj	Kalasalingam Academy of Research & Education, India
J. William	Agnel Institute of Technology & Design, India
R. Kalidoss	SSN College of Engineering, India
R. K. Mugelan	Vellore Institute of Technology, India
V. Vinod Kumar	Government College of Engineering, India
R. Saravanan	VIT, India
S. Sheik Aalam	iSENSE Intelligence Solutions, India
E. Srinivasan	Pondicherry Engineering College, India
B. Surendiran	National Institute of Technology Puducherry, India
Varun P. Gopi	National Institute of Technology Tiruchirappal India
V. Vijaya Chamundeeswari	Velammal Engineering College, India
T. Prabhakar	GMRIT, India

V. Kamakoti	IIT Madras, India
N. Janakiraman	KLN College of Engineering, India
V. Anandakrishanan	NIT Trichy, India
R. B. Patel	MMEC, India
Adesh Kumar Sharma	NDRI, India
Gunamani Jena	JNTU, India
Maninder Singh	Thapar University, India
Manoj Manuja	NIT Trichy, India
Ajay K. Sharma	Chitkara University, India
Manjit Patterh	Punjabi University, India
L. M. Bhardwaj	Amity University, India
Parvinder Singh	DCRUST, India
M. Syamala	Punjab University, India
Lalit Awasthi	NIT Jalandhar, India
Ajay Bansal	NIT Jalandhar, India
Ravi Aggarwal	Adobe Systems, USA
Sigurd Meldal	San José State University, USA
M. Balakrishnan	IIT Madras, India
Malay Pakhira	KGEC, India
Savita Gupta	PU Chandigarh, India
Manas Ranjan Patra	Berhampur University, India
Sukhwinder Singh	PU Chandigarh, India
Dharmendra Kumar	GJUST, India
Chandan Singh	Punjabi University, India
Rajinder Nath	Kurukshetra University, India
Manjaiah D.H	Mangalore University, India
Himanshu Aggarwal	Punjabi University, India
R. S. Kaler	Thapar University, India
Pabitra Pal Choudhury	Indian Statistical Institute, India
S. K. Pal	DRDO, India
G. S. Lehal	Punjabi University, India
Rajkumar Kannan	Bishop Heber College, India
Yogesh Chaba	GJUST, India
Amardeep Singh	Punjabi University, India
Sh. Sriram Birudavolu	Oracle India Limited, India
Ajay Rana	Amity University, India
Kanwal Jeet Singh	Punjabi University, India
C. K. Bhensdadia	DD University, India
Savina Bansal	GZSCET, India
Mohammad Asger	BGSB, India
Rajesh Bhatia	PEC, India
Stephen John Turner	VISTEC, India

Chiranjeev Kumar	IIT (ISM), India
Bhim Singh	IIT Delhi, India
A. K. Sharma	BSAITM, India
Rob Reilly	MIT, India
B. K. Murthy	CDAC, India
Karmeshu	JNU, India
K. K. Biswas	IIT Delhi, India
Sandeep Sen	IIT Delhi, India
Suneeta Aggarwal	MNNIT, India
Raghuraj Singh	HBTI, India
D. K. Lobiyal	JNU, India
R. S. Yadav	MNNIT, India
Bulusu Anand	IIT Roorkee, India
R. K. Singh	KEC Dwarahat, India
Sateesh Kumar Peddoju	IIT Roorkee, India
Divakar Yadav	JIIT, India
Naveen Kumar Singh	IGNOU, India
R. S. Raw	AIACTR (NSUT East Campus), India
Vidushi Sharma	GBU, India
Sumit Srivastava	Manipal University, India
Manish K. Gupta	DAIICT, India
P. K. Saxena	DRDO, India
B. K. Das	ITM University, India
Y. Raghu Reddy	IIIT Hyderabad, India
B. Chandra	IIT Delhi, India
R. K. Agarwal	JNU, India
Basim Alhadidi	Al-Balqa' Applied University, Jordan
M. Monirujjaman Khan	North South University, Bangladesh
Emmanuel Ndashimye	University of Rwanda & CMU-Africa, Rwanda
Naveen Garg	IIT Jodhpur, India
K. S. Subramanian	IGNOU, India
Biplab Sikdar	NUS Singapore, Singapore
Sreeram Ramakrishna	NUS Singapore, Singapore
Vikas Mathur	Citrix, India
Hari Krishna Garg	NUS, Singapore
Raja Dutta	IIT Kharagpur, India
Y. V. S. Lakshmi	C-DOT, India
Vishakha Vaidya	Adobe, India
Sudipto Shankar Dasgupta	Infosys Limited, India
Atal Chaudhari	Jadavpur University, India
Gangaboraiah Andanaiah	KIMS, India
Champa H. N.	UVCE, India

Ramakanth Kumar P.	RVCE, India
S. N. Omkar	IISC Bangalore, India
Balaji Rajendran	CDAC, India
Annapoorna P. Patil	MSRIT, India
K. N. Chandrashekhar	SJCIT, India
Mohammed Misbahuddin	CDAC, India
Saroj Meher	ISI, India
Jharna Majumdar	NMIT, India
N. K. Cauvery	RVCE, India
G. K. Patra	CSIR, India
Anandi Jayadharmarajan	Oxford College of Engg., India
K. R. Suneetha	BIT Mesra, India
M. L. Shailaja	AIT, India
K. R. Murali Mohan	GOI, India
Ramesh Paturi	Microsoft, India
S. Viswanadha Raju	JNTU, India
C. Krishna Mohan	IIT Chennai, India
R. T. Goswamy	Techno International New Town, India
B. Surekha	K S Institute of Technology, India
P. Trinatha Rao	GITAM University, India
G. Varaprasad	BMS College of Engineering, India
M. Usha Rani	SPMVV, India
P. V. Lakshmi	SPMVV, India
K. A. Selvaradjou	PEC, India
Ch. Satyananda Reddy	Andhra University, India
Jeegar A. Trivedi	Sardar Patel University, India
S. V. Rao	IIT Guwahati, India
Suresh Varma	Aadikavi Nannaya University, India
T. Ranga Babu	RVR & JC College of Engineering, India
D. Venkat Rao	Narasaraopet Inst. of Technology, India
N. Sudhakar Reddy	S V Engineering College, India
Dhiraj Sunehra	Jawaharlal Nehru Technological University, India
Madhavi Gudavalli	Jawaharlal Nehru Technological University Kakinada, India
B. Hemanth Kumar	RVR & JC College of Engineering, India
A. Sri Nagesh	RVR & JC College of Engg., India
Bipin Bihari Jaya Singh	CVR College of Engg, India
M. Ramesh	JNTU, India
P. Rajarajeswari	GITAM University, India
R. Kiran Kumar	Krishna University, India
D. Ramesh	JNTU, India
B. Kranthi Kiran	JNTU, India

K. Usha Rani	SPM University, India
A. Nagesh	MGIT, India
P. Sammulal	JNTU, India
G. Narasimha	JNTU, India
B. V. Ram Naresh Yadav	JNTU, India
B. N. Bhandari	JNTUH, India
O. B. V. Ramanaiah	JNTUH College of Engineering, India
Anil Kumar Vuppala	IIIT Hyderabad, India
Duggirala Srinivasa Rao	JNTU, India
Makkena Madhavi Latha	JNTUH, India
Anitha Sheela Kancharla	JNTUH, India
B. Padmaja Rani	JNTUH, India
S. Mangai	Velalar College of Engg. & Tech., India
P. Chandra Sekhar	Osmania University, India
Chakraborty Mrityunjoy	IIT Kharagpur, India
Manish Shrivastava	IIIT Hyderabad, India
Uttam Kumar Roy	Jadavpur University, India
Kalpana Naidu	IIIT Kota, India
A. Swarnalatha	St. Joseph's College of Engg., India
Aaditya Maheshwari	Techno India NJR Institute of Tech., India
Ajit Panda	National Institute of Science and Technology (NIST), India
R. Anuradha	Sri Ramakrishna Engg. College, India
B. G. Prasad	BMS College of Engg., India
Seung-Hwa Chung	Trinity College Dublin, Ireland
D. Murali	VIT, India
Deepak Padmanabhan	Queen's University Belfast, UK
Firoz Alam	RMIT University, Australia
Frederic Andres	NII, Japan
Srinath Doss	Botho University, Botswana
Munish Kumar	Maharaja Ranjit Singh Punjab Tech. University, India
Norwati Mustapha	UPM, India
Hamidah Ibrahim	UPM, India
Denis Reilly	Liverpool John Moores University, UK
Ioannis Kypraios	De Montfort University, UK
Yongkang Xing	De Montfort University, UK
P. Shivakumara	UM, Malaysia
Ravinder Kumar	TIET Patiala, India
Ankur Gupta	Bennett University, India
Rahul Kr. Verma	IIIT Lucknow, India
Mohit Sajwan	Bennett University, India

Vijaypal Singh Rathor	Thapar University Patiala, India
Deepak Singh	NIT Raipur, India
Simranjit Singh	Bennett University, India
Suchi Kumari	Bennett University, India
Kuldeep Chaurasia	Bennett University, India
Indrajeet Gupta	Bennett University, India
Shakti Sharma	Bennett University, India
Hiren Thakkar	PDPU, India
Mayank Swankar	IIT(BHU), India
Tapas Badal	Bennett University, India
Vipul Kr. Mishra	Bennett University, India
Tanveer Ahmed	Bennett University, India
Madhushi Verma	Bennett University, India
Gaurav Singal	NSUT, India
Anurag Goswami	Bennett University, India
Durgesh Kumar Mishra	Sri Aurobindo Institute of Technology, India
S. Padma	Madanapalle Institute of Technology & Science, India
M. A. Jabbar	Vardhman College of Engineering, India
Deepak Prashar	Lovely Professional University, India
Nidhi Khare	NMIMS, India
Sandeep Kumar	IIT Delhi, India
Dattatraya V. Kodavade	D.K.T.E Society's Textile & Engineering Institute, India
A. Obulesu	Anurag University, India
K. Suvarna Vani	V.R. Siddhartha Engineering College, India
G. Singaravel	K.S.R. College of Engineering, India
Ajay Shiv Sharma	Melbourne Institute of Technology, Australia
Abhishek Shukla	R.D. Engineering College Technical Campus Ghaziabad, India
V. K. Jain	Mody University, India
Deepak Poola	IBM India Private Limited, India
Bhadri Raju M. S. V. S.	S.R.K.R. Engineering College, India
Yamuna Prasad	IIT Jammu, India
Vishnu Vardhan B.	JNTUH College of Engineering Manthani, India
Virendrakumar Bhavsar	University of New Brunswick, Canada
Siva S. Skandha	CMR College of Engineering, India
Vaibhav Anu	Montclair State University, USA
V. Gomathi	National Engineering College, India
Sudipta Roy	Assam University, India
Srabanti Maji	DIT University, India
Shylaja S.S.	PESU, India

Shweta Agrawal	SIRT, India
Shreenivas Londhe	Vishwakarma Institute of Information Technology, India
Shirin Bhanu Koduri	Vasavi Engineering College, India
Shailendra Aswale	SRIEIT, India
Shachi Natu	TSE College Mumbai, India
Santosh Saraf	Graphic Era University, India
Samayveer Singh	Ambedkar National Institute of Technology, India
Sabu M. Thampi	IIITM Kerala, India
Roshani Raut	Vishwakarma Institute of Information Technology, India
Radhika K.R.	BMSCE, India
R. Priya Vaijayanthi	Institute of Technology, India
M. Naresh Babu	NIT Silchar, India
Krishnan Rangarajan	Dayananda Sagar College of Engineering, India
Prashant Singh Rana	Thapar Institute of Engg. & Tech., India
Parteek Bhatia	Thapar Institute of Engineering & Technology, India
Venkata Padmavati Metta	BIT, India
Laxmi Lydia	VIIT, India
Nikunj Tahilramani	Dolcera IT Services Pvt. Ltd., India
Navanath Saharia	IIIT, India
Nagesh Vadaparthi	MVGR College of Engineering, India
Manne Suneetha	VR Siddhartha Engineering College, India
Sumalatha Lingamgunta	JNTU Kakinada, India
Kalaiarasi Sonai Muthu Anbananthen	Multimedia University, Malaysia
K. Subramanian	IIT Kanpur, India
Singaraju Jyothi	Sri Padmavati Mahila Visvavidyalayam, India
Vinit Jakhetiya	IIT Jammu, India
Yashwantsinh Jadeja	Marwadi University, India
Harsh Dev	PSIT, India
Yashodhara V. Haribhakta	Government College of Engineering, India
Gopal Sakarkar	GHRCE, India
R. Gnanadass	Pondicherry Engineering College, India
K. Giri Babu	VVIT, India
Geeta Sikka	B R Ambedkar National Institute of Technology, India
Gaurav Varshney	IIT Jammu, India
G. L. Prajapati	Devi Ahilya University, India
G. Kishor Kumar	RGMCET, India
Md. Saidur Rahman	Bangladesh University of Engineering and Technology, Bangladesh

Wali Khan Mashwani	Kohat University of Science & Technology, Pakistan
Krishna Kiran Vamsi Dasu	Sri Sathya Sai Institute, India
Sisira Kumar Kapat	Utkal Gaurav Madhusudan Institute of Technology, India
Kuldeep Sharma	Chitkara University, India
Zankhana H. Shah	BVM Engineering College, India
Rekha Ramesh	Shah and Anchor Kutchhi Engineering College, India
Gopalkrishna Joshi	KLE Technological University, India
Ganga Holi	AMC Engineering College., India
K. Kotecha	Symbiosis International, India
Radhakrishna Bhat	MAHE, India
Kuldeep Singh	Carnegie Mellon University, USA
Binod Kumar	JSPM's Rajarshi Shahu College of Engineering, India
Raju Kumar	Chandigarh University, India
Nitin S. Goje	Webster University in Tashkent, Uzbekistan
Pushpa Mala S.	Dayananda Sagar University, India
Ashish Sharma	GLA University, India
Ashwath Rao B.	Manipal Institute of Technology, India
Deepak Motwani	Amity University, India
V. Sowmya	Amrita School of Engineering, India
Jayashri Nair	VNR VJIET, India
Rajesh C. Sanghvi	G.H. Patel College of Engineering & Technology, India
Ashwin Dobariya	Marwadi University, India
Tapas Kumar Patra	*Odisha* University of Technology and Research, India
J. Naren	Rathinam College of Arts and Science, India
Rekha. K. S.	National Institute of Engineering, India
Mohammed Murtuza Qureshi	Digital Employment Exchange, India
Vasantha Kalyani David	Avinashilingam Institute for Home Science and Higher Education for Women, India
K. Sakthidasan	Hindustan Institute of Technology and Science, India
Shreyas Rao	Sahyadri College of Engineering and Management, India
Hiranmayi Ranganathan	Lawrence Livermore National Laboratory, USA
Sanjaya Kumar Panda	National Institute of Technology Warangal, India
Puspanjali Mohapatra	IIIT Bhubaneswar, India
Manimala Mahato	Shah & Anchor Kutchhi Engineering College, India

B. Senthil Kumar   Kumaraguru College of Technology Coimbatore,
                                India
Jyoti Prakash Singh   National Institute of Technology Patna, India
Abhinav Tomar   Netaji Subhas University of Technology, India
M. G. Sumithra   Dr. N.G.P. Institute of Technology, India

Contents – Part I

AI in Industrial Applications

Application of AI for Disease Classification and Trend Analysis

Design of Agricultural Applications using AI

Disease Classification using CNN

Contents – Part II

System Security and Communication using AI

Use of AI in Human Psychology

Use of AI in Music and Video Industries

About the Editors

Dr. Deepak Garg Vice Chancellor, SR University Director leadingindia.ai, He has been Dean, Computer Science and Engineering, Bennett University and Director, NVIDIA-Bennett Center of Research on Artificial Intelligence.

Dr. Garg is leading the largest Development, Skilling and Research initiative in AI in India with more than 1000 institutional collaborators. He is a chief consultant for algorithmguru.in. He has done his Ph.D. in efficient algorithm design in 2006. He served as chair of IEEE Computer Society, India IEEE Education Society (2013–15). He has handled funding of around INR 700 million including RAENG, UK on MOOCs, Machine Learning and AI. He has 110+ publications with 1400+ citations and Google h-index of 18. In his 24 years of experience, he has delivered 300+ invited talks and conducted 100+Workshops and 15+ Conferences across the country. He has Supervised 14 Ph.D. and 35 Students. He is a blogger in Times of India named as breaking shackles. For details please visit http://www.gdeepak.com.

Ponnuthurai Nagaratnam Suganthan (Fellow, IEEE) received the B.A. and M.A. degrees from the University of Cambridge, U.K., and the Ph.D. degree in computer science from Nanyang Technological University, Singapore. He is currently a professor with Qatar University.

Dr. Suganthan was the recipient of the IEEE Transactions on Evolutionary Computation Outstanding Paper Award in 2012 and the Highly Cited Researcher Award by the Thomson Reuters in computer science in 2015. He is currently an Associate Editor for the IEEE Transactions on Evolutionary Computation, the IEEE Transactions on SMC Systems, Information Sciences, and Pattern Recognition and the Founding Co-Editor-in-Chief for Swarm and Evolutionary Computation Journal.

Dr. Jaume Anguera IEEE Fellow, founder and CTO at the technology company Ignion (Barcelona, Spain). Associate Professor at Ramon LLull University and a member of the Smart Society research group. He is an inventor of more than 150 granted patents, most of them licensed to telecommunication companies. Among his most outstanding contributions is that of the inventor of Antenna Booster Technology, a technology that fostered the creation of Ignion. The wireless industry has adopted many of these products worldwide to allow wireless connectivity to IoT devices through a miniature component called an antenna booster that is ten times smaller than conventional antennas. Author of more than 270 widely cited scientific papers and international conferences (h-index 52). Author of 7 books. He has participated in more than 22 competitive research projects financed by the Spanish Ministry, CDTI, CIDEM (Generalitat de Catalunya), and the European Commission for an amount exceeding $13M as a principal researcher in most of them. He has taught over 40 antenna courses worldwide (USA, China, Korea, India, UK, France, Poland, Czech Republic, Tunisia, Perú, Brazil, Canada, Spain). With over 23 years of R&D experience, he has developed part of his professional experience with Fractus in South Korea in designing miniature antennas for large Korean companies such as Samsung and LG. Since 2017 he has been with Ignion in the role of CTO. He leads the company R&D activity to create new products, envisage new technologies, technical evangelism, and provide technology strategy to scale the company business. He has received several national and international awards (ex. 2004 Best Ph. D Thesis -two prizes, one given by Telefónica Mobile, 2004 IEEE New Faces of Engineering, 2014 Finalist European Patent Award). He has directed the master/doctorate thesis to more than 160 students, many of them have received awards for their thesis (COIT, COITT, Ministry of Education). His biography appears in Who'sWho in the World and Who'sWho in Science and Engineering. He is an associate editor of the IEEE Open Journal on Antennas and Propagation, Electronics Letters, and a reviewer in several IEEE and other scientific journals. He is an IEEE Antennas and Propagation Distinguished Lecturer and vice-chair of the working group "Software and Modeling" at EurAAP. More info at http://users.salleurl.edu/~jaume.anguera/.

Major Dr. V. A. Narayana is Professor in the Department of Computer Science & Engineering and Principal at CMR College of Engineering & Technology. He received his bachelor's degree in Mechanical engineering from University College of Engineering, Osmania University in 1994, Masters Degree in Computer Science and Engineering from University College of Engineering, Osmania University in 2004. He received his Ph.D. in Computer Science and Engineering from JNTU Hyderabad in 2014. He has over 28 years of experience out of which 11 years of service in the Indian Army and 17+ years of research and teaching experience. He has contributed more than 26 research papers in various Scopus Indexed and IEEE Journals. His areas of interest include Data Mining, Web Mining and Database Management Systems etc., He has provided guidance for more than 22 M.Tech student projects. He is currently guiding 3 Ph.D scholars in eminent institutes such as IIT Bombay, JNTUH, and Bennett University. He has delivered many invited talks and Guest Lectures at National and International levels and has authored four books. With the keen interest to promote and develop research, he has organized many International and National Conferences and various Workshops, Seminars etc., He has received many awards and honors for his service which include "SARVOTHAM ACHARYA PURASKAR", "Organizational Excellence in Technical Education", "Best Educationist", "DEWANG MEHTA", "Best faculty", "Best HOD" etc., He has been part of teaching, research, training and consultancy at CMRCET since 2006. With his rich academic and research experience, he has been instrumental in executing more than 25 Sponsored Research and consultancy projects funded by various funding agencies like DST, and AICTE and other renowned agencies.

Dr. Vijaya Kumar Koppula Professor & Dean (Academics), Department of CSE has completed his B.Tech with Computer Science and Systems Engineering from Andhra University, M.Tech with Computer Science & Technology from Andhra University and Ph.D with Computer Science from University of Hyderabad.

He has more than 23 years of teaching experience. He is resource person for Infosys campus program, worked as a visiting scientist for page segmentation project in CVPR Unit, ISI Kolkata. He received an award for Teaching Excellence from Indo-American Education Summit 2016. He is a paper setter for various universities, reviewer for various international conferences and guided more than 100 B.Tech and M. Tech projects. He has published papers in various International/National journals and IEEE International/National conferences. He published papers in top IEEE International conferences like ICDAR 2011 and ICPR 2012. His papers are indexed in Scopus, DBLP and IEEE xplore. PhD supervisor in eminent institutes such as JNTUH, GRIT, and Bennett University. One of the research scholar completed PhD degree under his supervision.

Suneet Kumar Gupta is Associate Professor in the Department of Computer Science Engineering at Bennett University, Gr. Noida. His current research interests are Wireless Sensor Network, Internet of Things, Natural Language Processing and Brain-Computer Interaction. Presently Dr. Gupta has completed a Wireless Sensor Network based project funded by Department of Science and Technology, Uttar Pradesh.

Dr. Gupta is also part of a project funded by the Royal Academy of Science London entitled with Leadingindia.ai. He has more than 80 research articles, authored 2 books and 3 book chapters in his account.

AI in Industrial Applications

A Smart Shopping Cart: Ezi-KART

Joe Joseph⬤, E. E. Joseph Roshan⬤, S. Krishnapriya⬤,
Riya Sara Mathew(✉)⬤, and G. Sreenu⬤

Muthoot Institute of Technology and Science, Varikoli, India
18cs116@migits.ac.in

Abstract. We often refrain from going to a supermarket, just because
we dread the long queues at the billing counters. This system makes
shopping easier, where the user just has to show the item's barcode in
front of a camera and drop it to the cart as they go. The trolley will
calculate the bill. It also comes with an interactive UI screen where the
user can login to see their purchase history and where the system recommends products based on discounts and offers, also taking into account
the purchase history of the user. Weight sensors are added to the base of
the trolley to purchase groceries whose weights are not predetermined.
These weight sensors also contribute towards theft detection by comparing the weight of the billed items to that of the current weight inside the
trolley.

Keywords: Machine learning · OpenCV · App Development · Theft
detection

1 Introduction

There are times at which people find themselves too lazy or too busy to visit
supermarkets even if it is a necessity. This lack of time or interest is mostly
triggered by the different time consuming procedures at the super markets. Our
aim is to reduce the amount of time spent by customers at supermarkets while
they take out a portion of their valuable time for the same and make their
shopping experience a lot more easier and peaceful.

Among many of the minor issues faced by people during shopping, the long
queues at the billing counters are the worst. We all have, at some point of our
lives, have been on the long queues in the billing counters of large supermarket
chains like Lulu, IKEA, etc. where we wait, after long hours of walking and
picking products in the cart, just by assuming that all that you chose might be
within your budget. We can use technology so that you can make your IKEA
experience less tiring by knowing the current total amount of all that is there in
the cart, and by self-checkout rather than crowding up at the billing counters.
The development of new technology can be utilized for removing these long
queues and helping customers to check out within a few clicks, making their
experience much more time-saving and efficient.

© Springer Nature Switzerland AG 2023
D. Garg et al. (Eds.): IACC 2022, CCIS 1781, pp. 3–16, 2023.
https://doi.org/10.1007/978-3-031-35641-4_1

Generally in supermarket chains what we see is the availability of vast products but not efficient management in the checkout process as a whole. Our product aims to reduce that context to another level by making everyday user life easy by automating the whole process of billing thus making it the whole smooth process and helping the customer save time and also ease the effort of the customer. Thus our product is believed to help the society by saving a lot of time and ease up the process.

2   Related Works

The existing systems are inefficient and open to more improvement.

In the article [1], with the help of a barcode reader, the product is validated and matched with the lookup table in the database, consisting of a list of all products in the store, and their corresponding information, including the product name, manufacturer, and price.

Billing information is calculated using ARM Cortex Controller. Whenever the trolley is moved, the LCD displays information as well as the direction of movement. Through Bluetooth6, the Android device sends signals to the microcontroller controlling the movement of the trolley. There is an external connection between the Bluetooth device and the microcontroller. Signals are sent from the Bluetooth device to the microcontroller via serial communication.

By using the conventional shopping trolley, it is tiresome and also time consuming to find the desired products in big supermarkets. This article [2] is aimed in developing a smart self-shopping trolley to solve the problems of current scenario. An IOIO microcontroller and an Android smartphone serve as sensors and controllers in this smart trolley that has two wheels. With an Android smartphone, control the robot by sending a signal to an IOIO microcontroller paired with an actuator, and capture the situation with a smartphone camera. Also included in this system is an indoor positioning system that uses Navisens (based on a gyroscope and accelerometer) to detect user location. Finally, the results of these tests on robot navigation are analyzed.

This article [3] proposes an improved version of the basic trolley. This smart trolley consists of Raspberry Pi, a barcode scanner, LCD display with Wi-Fi connection, HX711, a load cell and keypad. With the help of these modules, customer can self-scan the product and get the total cost of the bill and the overall information i.e. product name, product price, product weight displayed.

The basic concept of this article [4] is the effective time utilization of customer in shopping mall by adding the billing system to the cart itself so that customer himself/herself can scan the item and keep item into his card with the hardware and software interfaced together customer can add or remove item to or from the cart respectively with the membership card provided to the customer he can recharge the card and complete the payment for a successful and fast transaction thereby completing the waiting time of the customer near the billing counter. This uses barcode scanner which are used for product identification RFID technology for payments and IR technology for mobility of the cart.

This smart trolley [5] consists of a Raspberry Pi, a barcode scanner, and an LCD display with Wi-Fi connection. As the barcode scanner is integrated into the trolley, it is connected to the Raspberry Pi and the supermarket database through Wi-Fi. Customers can self-scan the products and view the final cost of the bill on the screen. Following shopping, the customer will only need to go to the billing counter to pay, as the customer is already aware of the overall total bill. A customer who has a limited budget can also benefit from this system.

In order for a customer to purchase intelligently [6] in a shopping mall, each and every product has to be placed with a RFID barcode to be scanned by an RFID reader. The smart trolley will consist of a RFID reader, LCD display and ZigBee transmitter. When the customer wants to purchase a product, he inserts it into the trolley which will be will scanned and the details of the product being displayed. The total cost of all the products will be added to the final bill, which will be saved in the Arduino, working as memory. These are all handled by the transmitter, whereas the wireless transmitting process takes place on the receiver side. Using a ZigBee transmitter, the product information and final bill amount of the items in the trolley will be transmitted to the billing system.

In recent years, microcontroller-based design has become one of the most in-demand fields of electronics. It is a highly technical field that is capable of integrating 1000 transistors onto a single silicon chip.

For the automation of malls in the modern era, we are developing a microcontroller-based trolley [7] that is completely automatic. The trolley follows the customer while buying items and claims to maintain a secure distance from the purchaser. The customer must only hold the barcode side of the amount cover in front of the barcode scanner. Then matching data in relation to the product will be displayed on display.

Article [8] aims to demonstrate how a smartphone and Arduino can be used to build a smart trolley. Only after the customer inserts the membership card into the trolley will it work as a smart trolley. Otherwise, it will work like a normal shopping cart. The system scans a product shown and shows its price on the LCD screen. This is implemented by using RFID Tag and RFID Reader. It is necessary that the customer inserts the membership card, which is also a RFID tag, into an RFID reader. An RFID reader will be able to recognize RFID tags and convert a shopping basket or trolley into a smart one once it detects the presence of RFID tags.

The article [9] aims at the billing automation of purchased products using Smart Shopping cart to minimize the time spent for scanning each product manually using Barcode Scanners with recommendation systems to enhance the customer's experience at supermarkets and hypermarkets. It starts with object detection applying YOLO algorithm with the camera module mounted in the e-commerce cart. First, to begin with the hardware components includes a shopping cart connected with RaspberryPi 4 model board with 4GB RAM and a SD card which acts as the ROM and the power supply is from the power bank and the Linux-based Raspbian OS specifically for the Raspberry Pi are used.

The web interface itself produce a bill which amounts to of total cost of all the shopped products put into the cart at that moment.

The system [10] is only available to those customers who have the supermarket's loyalty card. The smart trolley reads the RFID card in the customer's loyalty card. A QR scanner is available for reading the QR code of the product using image processing, which includes information such as the price, weight, etc.

Due to the Covid-19 pandemic, customers must maintain their distance, but they must also wait for their payment for a very long time. If more than five customers are lined up at the billing counter, the system will alert the customers to move to a quick checkout counter. In real-time CCTV camera capture and system alert in trolley display.

3   Objectives

This system aims at eradicating long queues by making checkout individually possible without any intervention from an outsider. It detects theft of items and to get to know about more options and discounts, it uses personalized recommendation. This system makes barcode scanning error free and hassle free.

We are planning to come up with a smart trolley called 'Ezi-KART' to integrate all the above mentioned objectives under one umbrella. People who dread the long queues can now make their shopping experience time saving and hassle free. This cart also recommends products, based on past purchase history and discounts.

4   Methodology

The cart contains cameras where the user can scan the barcode. An OpenCV algorithm is used to detect the barcode as well as the product code digits below it (just in case if the barcode is damaged in any way). After the user scans the barcode and it is detected, the product is added to the shopping list and visible on an interactive screen on the cart. The weight sensors attached to the cart keeps on monitoring the weight on the trolley, comparing it to the weight of the products presently in the list. This alerts the customer in case he or she accidentally forgets to scan a product. Also, this is a good mechanism to track theft.

Moreover, if the customer has visited the store before, based on their past purchases, they are recommended products. This also takes into account discounts that are currently active. This is done using collaborative filtering (by taking into account interests of similar users and the similar products they have choosen).

After the shopping is complete, the use can checkout using any online payment method, using the cart or they can opt for cash payment at the counter which would hardly take five minutes. In addition to all these, we will be bringing a mobile application so that users can take a look at their past purchases and transactions to the stores they have been, from the comfort of their home.

4.1 Modules Used

1. **Camera Sensor** is used to take the count of items and is shown to the display device.
2. **Weighing Sensor** is used to calculate the weight of the items added to the cart to avoid theft detection.
3. **Display Device** is used to Display the item Details in the cart.
4. The **Storage Device** used is an SD card which is used to load the OS and algorithm to the PI
5. **Barcode Detection** is done by taking snapshots of the product and using image processing algorithm to identify the product.
6. **Recommendation Engine** (Apriori Algorithm) is used to recommend products to the user depending on their previous purchase history.
7. **Mobile Application** (Flutter) to look at their purchases done earlier.
8. **Database** (MySQL) is used to store all product details and purchase history of all users.

4.2 Architecture

(See Fig. 1).

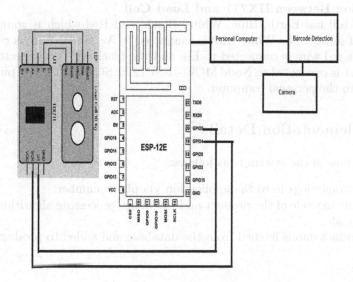

Fig. 1. Architecture

Here, we have implemented using Node MCU- ESP12-E. Which is used to connect the Load Cell and Hx711 sensor and then to the personal computer. HX711 Weighing Sensor Module is a 24 bit high precision A/D converter (Analog to digital converter). There are two analog input channels on the HX711, and a maximum gain of 128 can be achieved by programming these channels. Therefore, the HX711 module amplifies the low electric output of the load cells, and with this amplified digitally converted signal, the Arduino is able to measure the weight.

Load cells function as transducers, converting force or pressure into an electrical output that is directly proportional to its applied force. It is important to note that load cells have a strain gauge, which deforms when pressure is applied, and then the strain gauge produces an electrical signal as its effective resistance changes as a result of the deformation.

ESP-12E is a miniature Wi-Fi module that is used to establish wireless networks for microcontrollers and processors. The core of ESP-12E is ESP8266EX, a high integration wireless SoC (System on Chip). With its ability to embed Wi-Fi capabilities into systems or to function as a standalone application, it is a versatile product. IoT applications can be developed at a low cost using this solution.

Speaking about the weighing sensor it is used to prevent cheating and manipulation on products. The weigh sensor cross checks the weight of the scanned items so that there is no mismatch. The raspberry pi is generally a power hungry device so it is being powered by a direct adapter. The cart display tablet is connected using the HDMI port of the pi to display it and the SD card reader of the pi is used to load the custom softwares.

Connection Between HX711 and Load Cell
The Load cell has Earth, Blue, White, Black, and Red which is connected to the HX711 sensor. The White wire is connected to A-, Green Wire is connected to A+, the red wire is connected to E+ and the black wire is connected to E-. This Hx711 is connected to Node MCU - ESP12-E. SCK pin to, DT pin to, and ESP12-E to the personal computer.

5   Implementation Details

The basic flow of the system is as follows:

- The customer logs in to the application via phone number.
- Scans the barcode of the product and the image processing algorithm detects the barcode.
- The product info is fetched from the database and added to product list.

- Weight calculation goes on simultaneously.
- Once shopping is done, the customer can checkout out and continue with payment.

The front-end communicates with the database via APIs developed with Django REST Framework. We have a cart UI running on PyQt5 python GUI framework and database as MySQL. Initially the user login using a Mobile verification and takes to the next screen that is the barcode detection where we use Open CV Pyzbar python library. After detecting the item, item details will be retrieved from database and the weight will be cross checked for the product in the cart. For this weighing mechanism in the trolley we are using a Load Cell and HX711 sensor which is used to amplify the signals from the cell to Node Microcontroller ESP12-E. The ESP12-E is coded with Arduino IDE. Thereafter the user has the option to remove any product in the cart if not required and hence same application of weighing mechanism works. If any mismatch in the weight found it will be shown in the cart UI. Thereafter the payment for the same can be done via any online means.

Then we have an app which is developed using Flutter, it can be used by the user to get the previous billing history. The Database for the mobile app is same as MySQL.

We have a recommendation system based on previous history so that while picking each item the cart UI will be prompting whether to pick another Item based on each users purchase history, for this we use Apriori algorithm.

A. Hardware Components

HX711 Weighing Sensor Module is a 24 bit high precision(Analog to Digital converter. HX711 has two analog input channels with gain up to 128 by programming these channels. So HX711 module amplifies the low electric output of Load cells which is then fed into the Arduino to measure the weight.

ESP-12E is a Wi-Fi module giving wireless network connection for microcontrollers or processors. The core of ESP-12E is ESP8266EX, a high integration wireless SoC (System on Chip). Wi-Fi capabilities can be implanted to systems or to function as a standalone application using ESP-12E.

Load cell is a transducer that converts force or pressure into electrical output whose magnitude is directly proportional to the force applied. Load cells have a strain gauge, which deforms when pressure applied and this deformation gives out electrical signal due to the change in resistance.

Personal Computer is any PC with i5-8th gen and RAM - 8 GB. And camera that is 5MP FHD.

A. Software Components

Node MCU – ESP12-E. It is used by sensors HX711 and load cells and is programmed in C++, with HX711 Arduino Library in Arduino IDE. HX711 Arduino Library interfaces the Avia Semiconductor HX711 ADC. An Arduino library is used to interface the Avia Semiconductor HX711 24-Bit Analog-to-Digital Converter (ADC) for reading load cells/weight scales.

PyQt5. PyQt5 is a Python interface for the Qt GUI library, one of the most powerful and popular cross-platform libraries. PyQt5 is a combination of Python programming language and the Qt library. We have used this GUI for implementing the Cart UI.

Pyzbar. Pyzbar is a module that can easily read and decode 1-D barcodes and QR codes, and it requires the PIL module to function.

Django REST Framework. Django REST framework is used for building Web APIs.

Flutter. A high performance framework based on Dart language. It renders the UI directly on the operating system's canvas rather than through the native framework.

6   Results

The working of the product is also simple and easy to use as the customer logs in, scans the product and weight mismatch is calculated and once the shopping is done, the customer can proceed to checkout.

The Fig. 2 given below depicts the demonstration of how EZi-KART works. This is the prototype of the proposed system.

Fig. 2. The prototype of the proposed EZi-KART

The following images (Fig. 3, 4, 5 and 6) shows the UI of the app in the Ezi-KART.

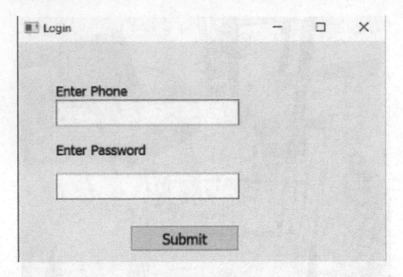

Fig. 3. Login Page

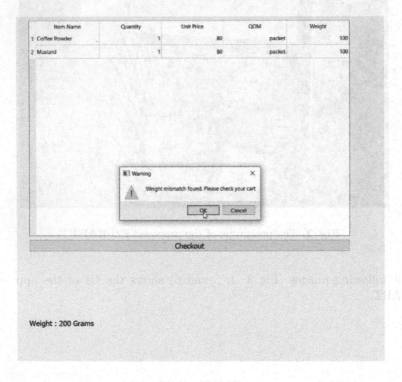

Fig. 4. Cart UI

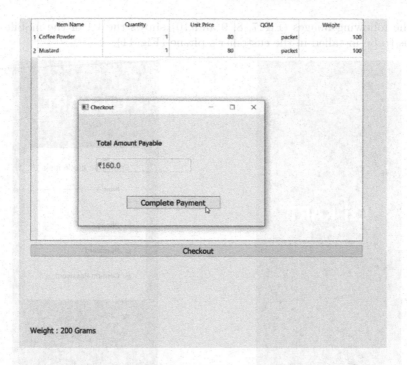

Fig. 5. Checkout

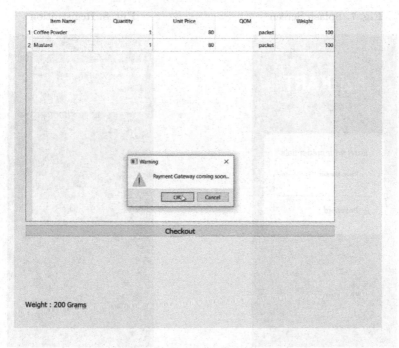

Fig. 6. Payment Gateway

The following images (Fig. 7, 8, 9 and 10) shows the UI of the mobile app that is to be installed in the customer's phone (Fig. 11).

Fig. 7. Splash Screen

Fig. 8. Registration

Fig. 9. Login

Fig. 10. Order History

Fig. 11. Order Detail

7   Future Scope

Few limitations that our system have but than can be solved in future are; Right now we are using a single camera for detecting barcode and weighing scale for theft detection, even though its not a complete solution we can solve the same by using multiple cameras inside the cart so that once the user takes an item it can be automatically read and hence we can overcome the shortcomings we have right now, Like the user need not scan the item as the item is scanned automatically as the cameras will be functioning all the time so that when a user adds an item to the cart or takes back an item it will be shown. Then also if the vegetables are packed in clean bags, we can avoid the billing of vegetables as our trolley has a weighing scale and hence the weight can be read directly from the trolley, thus making our life easy. To introduce an interactive UI, a Raspberry Pi board can be used to connect different components like the camera and the weight scale. The Pi board can be programmed with a Linux OS or Android and the PyQt5 application can be easily migrated to the same. All the features of the UI will remain same and no additional configurations are required. Usage of a microcontroller limits the portability of the entire system. A Raspberry pi module provides the flexibility of a mini computer, making integration with a interactive UI screen easier.

8   Conclusion

When shopping in a supermarket, a shopping trolley or a shopping cart is an invaluable tool for assisting in the purchase process. The long queues at the billing counter consume the majority of a customer's day after they drag the trolley all across the supermarket. Therefore, customers' shopping experience can be improved by modifying a normal trolley into a smart one with which the customer feels comfortable.

With Ezi-KART, users can use self-checkout capabilities to enable them to make easy transactions in the supermarket.

Users can be aware of the total bill amount while shopping and also make product suggestions based on previous purchases.

In the future, this system will also bring huge profits to the supermarket chain as it boosts customer satisfaction. This system would be exceptionally efficient and fully synchronized with the current structure of the supermarket. Management can reduce expenses in this way. People who despise long lines can now make their shopping experience more convenient and time-saving.

This article can be of great help to lots of supermarket chains to gain high profits and can also contribute to a digital future.

References

1. Arathi, B., Shona, M.: An elegant shopping using smart trolley. Indian J. Sci. Technol. **10**, 3–6 (2017)
2. Gunawan, A.A.S., et al.: Development of smart trolley system based on Android smartphone sensors. Procedia Comput. Sci. **157**, 629–637 (2019)
3. Abhishek, Bhumika, K.M., Chandan, G.N., Yashaswini, C., Raghu, B.R.: Automated shopping trolley for billing system. Int. J. Eng. Appl. Sci. Technol. (2021)
4. Hemalatha, Sumaiya Begum, A., Poonkuzhali, Kumar, V.V.S.P., Praveen, T.J.: Automated smart shopping cart in mega mall (2021)
5. Jogekar, R.N., Kadav, A., Ghodeswar, R., Chavhan, P., Kadu, P., Paunikar, M.: Automated shopping trolley using Raspberry Pi device. Int. J. Sci. Res. Comput. Sci. Eng. **6**(2), 126–128 (2018)
6. Sivagurunathan, P.T., Seema, P., Shalini, M., Sindhu, R.: Smart shopping trolley using RFID. Int. J. Pure Appl. Math. **118**(20), 3783–3786 (2018)
7. Awati, J.S., Awati, S.B.: Smart Trolley in Mega Mall
8. Bedi, H.S., Goyal, N., Kumar, S., Gupta, A.: Smart trolley using smart phone and Arduino. J. Electr. Electron. Syst. **06**, 1–3 (2017). https://doi.org/10.4172/2332-0796.1000223
9. Recommendation system based smart shopping cart. Int. J. Emerg. Technol. Innov. Res. **7**(5), 908–914 (2020). https://www.jetir.org. ISSN 2349-5162
10. Satheesan, P., Nilaxshan, S., Alosius, J., Thisanthan, R., Raveendran, P., Tharmaseelan, J.: Enhancement of supermarket using smart trolley. Int. J. Comput. Appl. **975**, 8887 (2021)

Underwater Image Denoising and 3D Modelling of Poompuhar Site

B. Sridevi(✉) ⒾⒹ, A. MukeshⒾⒹ, N. RakeshⒾⒹ, and G. Hari KrishnanⒾⒹ

Electronics and Communication Engineering, Velammal Institute of Technology, Thiruvallur, India
bsd@velammalitech.edu.in

Abstract. This paper proposes a method to digitally recreate an underwater heritage site, Poompuhar using a 3D model to help the ICPS division of the Department of Science and Technology (DST) of India to digitally reconstruct the underwater heritage site which is now a submerged port located 30 km away from the present Poompuhar town. To achieve 3D modeling the underwater images must be preprocessed, then mesh points, scanning process, and 3D mapping techniques are used to reconstruct a 3D model. For preprocessing one of the key factors is to reduce the noise generated by the image capture and transmission process. The existing systems use filters depending on the noise as the noises cannot be predicted because the Poompuhar images are taken at a greater depth than the normal underwater images. In this study, a combination of all the existing filters is used to nullify their individual disadvantages and to achieve a better SNR ratio.

Keywords: De-noising · Wavelet filter · Noise · Underwater Dark Channel Prior · 3D modelling · scaling process

1 Introduction

Around 3000–15000 years ago there was this great port city called Kaveri Poompattinam. In the southern part of Tamilnadu. It was once a flourishing ancient port city known as Kaveri Poompattinam, which for a while served as the capital of early Chola kings. This ancient city was destroyed by the sea around 300 AD around 1000 years ago due to sediment erosion and periodic tsunamis. Recently the Department of Science and Technology has initiated a project to digitally reconstruct the port city. The main goal of our project is to enhance the pictures of that site taken underwater and construct a 3D model using those underwater denoised and enhanced images. Generally the images taken underwater differs a lot from the images taken in air medium. Underwater images are largely affected due to attenuation which is due the absorption and scattering of the light by water medium. Also noise is introduced into the image during image transmission, acquisition, coding or processing steps. It is a process to reserve the details of an image while removing the random noise from the image as far as possible.

Different algorithms are used to eliminate low contrast, color distortion and poor visual appearance of images captured underwater. Algorithms helps in alleviating the

© Springer Nature Switzerland AG 2023
D. Garg et al. (Eds.): IACC 2022, CCIS 1781, pp. 17–32, 2023.
https://doi.org/10.1007/978-3-031-35641-4_2

color shifts, low contrast, and motion blur etc.... thus improving the quality of the image and increases the visibility of that image.

Finally after underwater image denoising and enhancing 3D Models may be created automatically or manually using appropriate softwares. The manual modeling process of preparing geometric data for 3D computer graphics is similar to plastic arts such as sculpting. The 3D model can be physically created using 3D printing devices that form 2D layers of the model with three-dimensional material, one layer at a time. Without a 3D model, a 3D print is not possible.

2 Underwater Image Noises

A key factor that decreases image resolution is the noise generated by image capture and transmission processes. Image processing typically starts with image filtering, so the type and nature of noise should be identified. From a category perspective, the main noises are:

1. Gaussian noise: This is the most common type of noise and has various unstable factors.
2. Salt and pepper noise: The gray scale value increases or decreases in a specific range. These gray pixels or areas are called salt and pepper noise.
3. Fixed mode noise: Caused by a defect in the system device.

Real image signals are often affected by correlated noise, signal-related noise, and various other distributed noises. Therefore, it is impossible to accurately determine and calculate noise.

3 Color Image Denoising Algorithm Based on Combination Algorithm

There are different de-noising abilities for different sounds, as well as their respective advantages and disadvantages for common de-noising methods. For example, The Median Filter has a better de-noising ability to impulse noise, but less effect on Gaussian noise. The Average Filter has a better de-noising ability to Gaussian noise but does not protect the edge of the image so that the image becomes indistinct. The Wiener filter is useful for preserving edges and other high-frequency parts of the image, but computationally expensive.

The following paper proposes a filtering algorithm based on the combination filter algorithm, which can not only remove the image of Gaussian and salt and pepper noise but also better preserve the image clarity better.

The algorithm is based on the use of the median filter combined with the mean filter (depending on image noises) combination, which makes the threshold selection of the algorithm easy. After de-noising, the Fourier transform and Butterworth high pass filter is used to preserve the edges of the image. The threshold functions which are divided into the hard threshold function and soft threshold function in the threshold de-noising algorithm, represent different processing strategies and estimation methods for the wavelet coefficients that exceed and fall below the threshold.

The key thing in this de-noising algorithm is how to choose the threshold and threshold function because the noise still exists in the de-noised image if the threshold is large, and important image features will be filtered out if the threshold is small. Intuitively speaking, for a given wavelet coefficient, the greater the noise, the large the threshold. So most of the threshold selection process is calculating a threshold according to the statistical characteristics of the wavelet coefficients. Therefore most of the threshold selection process is for a set of wavelet coefficients, which means a threshold is calculated according to the statistical characteristics of the group of wavelet coefficients.

4   Underwater Image Recovery

Underwater image retrieval generally creates an efficient degradation model by analyzing the underwater image mechanism and basic physics of light propagation. Next we derive the main parameters by built physics, Model some preliminary knowledge, and finally recover the restored image by reservation.

Compensation processing. Simplified IFMs are considered effective and typical. The IFM-based recovery method requires estimating two important optical parameters: BL and TM. Background light estimation is a vital step in underwater image de-noising. Most of the methods that are currently used assume a uniform background light in the underwater environment and select the brightest pixel in the dark channel as the candidate, which fails to explain the real interactions between light rays and particles in the aquatic environment and causes excessive saturation in discolored images. The transmission map depicts the portion of light that is not diffused and reaches the camera (Fig. 1).

5   Pre-based Image Recovery

The main cause of the degradation of underwater images is the absorption and dispersal of light and airborne particles. Various prior-based methods have been used or derived in water concerning optical properties or their representation of image recovery. These include a dark channel (DCP), underwater dark channel (UDCP), maximum intensity (MIP), red channel (RCP), and previous blur (BP). Underwater Light Attenuation Prior (ULAP), etc. mentioned below. Following these precedents, BL and TM (or depth maps) can be derived and used in IFM models for image reconstruction. Previously, the dark channel was based on the observation that sunny day images contain pixels with very low intensity (near zero) in at least one color channel. When using DCP directly to clean up underwater images, BL can be estimated in two steps. Select the top 0.1% of the brightest pixels in the dark channel and from those pixels select the brightest pixels in the input image. You can estimate the transmission map by minimizing both sides of the IFM model. Dark Channel Priors are prone to selective light attenuation in underwater environments, so many underwater-specific DCPs have been developed.

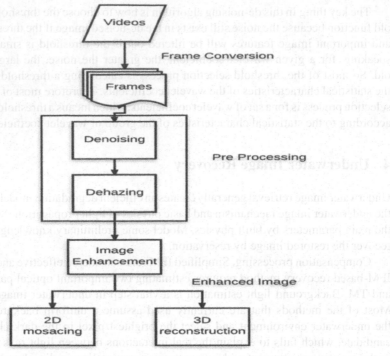

Fig. 1. Step-by-step process for de-noising, enhancing, and constructing a 3-D model of underwater images.

6 Underwater DCP-Based Image Restoration

Red light weakens much faster than green, so as blue light propagates underwater, the red channels in the underwater image dominate the dark channels. To eliminate the effects of underwater red dark channels.

On the other hand, a new method, an underwater optical model similar to UDCP, is proposed and used to estimate the scattering rate. Although the proposed UDCP can achieve more accurate TM than DCP, the restored images are still poor because these methods ignore imaging. In 2015, we found that the low pixel values in his RGB channels of muddy water were always in the blue channel, not in the purple channel, and the blue channel was the least absorbed. Therefore, they used dark dual channels (purple and blue) to estimate the coarse TM and reduced the directional TM halo and mosaic results by a weighted median filter.

In 2017, a super decision for underwater photography was proposed. This was done by taking high-determination (HR) pictures of scattered and non-scattered snapshots and using convex fusion rules to improve the final HR picture. In 2016, a UDCP-based de-cluttering across the GB channel and correction of R channel shading was proposed to recover underwater photographs. This is primarily based on the completely gray world hypothesis, according to which the estimation was done using adaptive rack cards. General stabilization sedation for restored snapshots. In 2015, automatic recovery of underwater violet channel footage was proposed, mainly based on the violet channel prior (RCP), which extracts the dark channel from the reverse violet and blue channels. On the other hand, a saturation record of fog snapshots is brought to modify the TM to effectively decorate synthetic mild spots and improve the constancy of global sedation of snapshots. However, the colors of some restored snapshots are optically incorrect and look unrealistic.

Image de-noising removes noise from a noisy image to restore the true image. However, since noise, edges, and textures are high-frequency components, it is difficult to distinguish between them when de-noising and the de-noised image can inevitably lose detail. Overall, recovering meaningful information from noisy images to obtain high-quality images in the de-noising process is an important issue today. Noise reduction is the random variation of brightness or color information in an image, an unwanted by-product of an image that obscures wanted information. Generally, noise is introduced into an image during image transmission, detection, encoding, or processing. Different types of noise in images: Gaussian noise, salt and pepper noise, and, speckle noise. Image restoration includes image noise reduction and color restoration. This article only describes the image-de-noising process. This is because a large number of images have to be processed and a full restoration is complex and time-consuming. Therefore, this will become clear in future studies.

6.1 Gaussian Noise

It is the most common kind of noise which the various unstable factors of the imaging system are often expressed. It is also called as electronic noise because it arises in amplifiers or detectors. Gaussian noise has a uniform distribution throughout the signal. A noisy image has pixels that are made up of the sum of their original pixel values plus a random Gaussian noise value. Principal sources of Gaussian noise in digital images arise during acquisition e.g. sensor noise caused by poor illumination or high temperature, or transmission e.g. electronic circuit noise (Fig. 2).

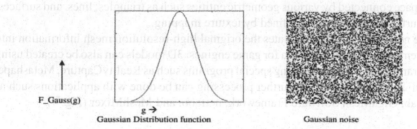

F_Gauss(g)

g →

Gaussian Distribution function   Gaussian noise

Fig. 2. Gaussian noise

6.2 Salt and Pepper Noise

A type of noise commonly seen in photographs is salt and pepper noise. It manifests as white and black pixels that appear at random intervals. The corrupted pixels are alternately set to the minimum and highest value, giving the image a "salt and pepper" appearance. In situations when quick transients, such as improper switching, occur, salt and pepper noise creeps into images.

This noise is generally caused by errors in data transmission, failure in memory cell or analog-to-digital converter errors. It takes the form of randomly occurring white and black pixels, which can significantly deteriorate the quality of an image (Fig. 3).

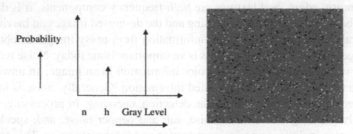

Fig. 3. Salt and pepper noise.

6.3 Speckle Noise

Unlike Gaussian or Salt and Pepper noise, speckle noise is multiplicative noise. This makes it more difficult for the observer to distinguish fine details in the images. This type of noise can be found in a wide range of systems, including synthetic aperture radar (SAR) images, ultrasound imaging, and many more.

7   3D Modeling

A three-dimensional (3D) model represents a physical body using a collection of points in 3D space connected by various geometric entities such as triangles, lines, and surfaces. Their surfaces can be further defined by texture mapping.

The new mesh usually translates the original high-resolution mesh information into displacement or normal map data for game engines. 3D models can also be created using photogrammetric techniques using special programs such as RealityCapture, Metashape, and 3DF Zephyr. Cleanup and further processing can be done with applications such as MeshLab, GigaMesh Software Framework, netfabb, and MeshMixer (Fig. 4).

7.1   Mesh Point

A 3D mesh is a structural composition of a 3D model made up of polygons. A 3D mesh defines a shape in terms of height, width, and depth using reference points on the X, Y, and Z axes. However, creating a 3D mesh approach to photorealism can require a large number of polygons.

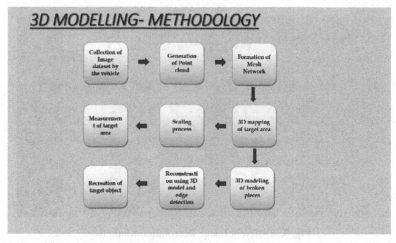

Fig. 4. 3D modelling methodology

7.2 Scaling Process

The following kind of sequences occur while performing the scaling transformations on a fixed point:

1. The fixed point is translated to the origin.
2. The object is scaled.
3. The fixed point is translated to its original position.

7.3 3D Mapping

3D mapping technology uses computer vision to profile objects in three dimensions and map them into the real world, providing modern technological methods for visualization and information gathering.

8 Evaluation Results of Typical Methods of Restoration

In this section, we evaluate and compare typical underwater image restoration and enhancement methods (Fig. 5).

The above figure is the comparison of the underwater image restoration methods. From left to right are input images, the enhanced underwater images obtained by He et al. [10], Galdran et al. [11], Drew et al. [12], Li et al. [13], Peng et al. [14], Peng et al. [15], and Berman et al. [16], respectively.

9 Comparisons of TM Estimation Models

When comparing the accuracy of transmission map (TM) estimation models, this review analyzes the correctness of TM estimation through subjective assessment due to non-reference depth/transmission map (Figs. 6, 7, 8, 9, 10, 11, 12, 13 and 14).

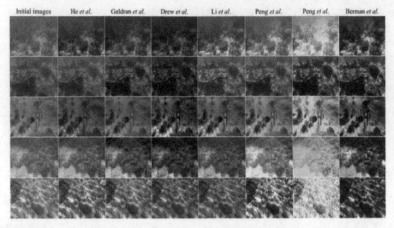

Fig. 5. Different Image Restoration Methods

Fig. 6. Original images

Fig. 7. Ref [21], DCP

Fig. 8. Ref [17], DCP

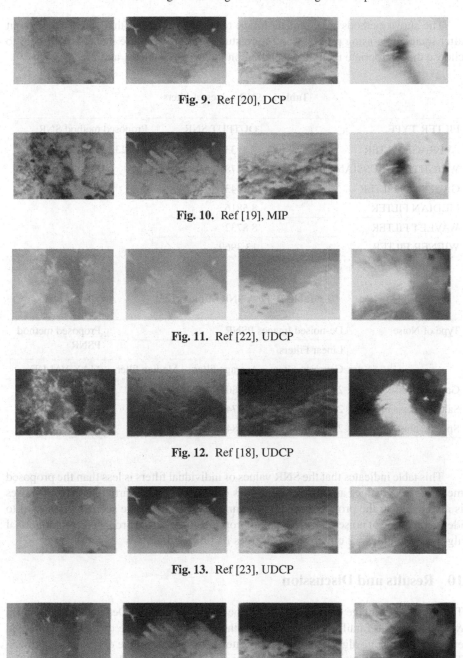

Fig. 9. Ref [20], DCP

Fig. 10. Ref [19], MIP

Fig. 11. Ref [22], UDCP

Fig. 12. Ref [18], UDCP

Fig. 13. Ref [23], UDCP

Fig. 14. Ref [24], UDCP

The above methods are complete image restoration methods that can be carried out after image de-noising process and future studies would on these methods will help to choose the appropriate method depending on the needs (Tables 1 and 2).

Table 1. SNR values of filters

FILTER TYPE	OUTPUT SNR	Proposed method SNR
AVERAGE FILTER	7.3133	**24.5233**
WEIGHTED GAUSSIAN FILTER	4.2478	
GAUSSIAN FILTER	6.4443	
MEDIAN FILTER	8.5816	
WAVLET FILTER	8.8732	
WIENER FILTER	13.3969	

Table 2. Peak SNR of filters [25]

Type of Noise	De-noised Images PSNR			Proposed method PSNR
	Linear Filters			
	Gaussian filter	Average filter	Median filter	MAX VALUE
Gaussian noise	23.5245	24.7801	24.2943	24.5233
Salt and pepper noise	21.9990	24.0744	26.9224	24.4789
Speckle noise	23.0974	24.6848	23.2255	24.5233

This table indicates that the SNR values of individual filters is less than the proposed method's SNR values and the PSNR values of these filters to particular type of noises is also less than the proposed method's psnr values. In real time scenario it is hard to identity the type of noises and apply the appropriate filters so the proposed combinational algorithm would work effectively as well as its time saving.

10   Results and Discussion

The underwater image of Poomphuar will be gathered from the Department of Science &Technology of Tamil Nadu. Our part in the research would be to find a simple and effective de-noising algorithm that has a better SNR value than the existing basic filters. These images will contain noise so the first step is preprocessing. Preprocessing includes image de-noising and enhancement, this paper focuses only on de-noising. Depending on the noises in the image filters are used. This will help in the research to create a method that can adopt characteristics of underwater light attenuation to obtain the correct depth map or TMs of R-G-B channels by building the optical imaging relationship of the R-G-B channel. The images enhanced by this method present an overwhelming red tone and amplify the noises of the original image. Both CLAHE and RGHS are based on adaptive parameters to avoid a global histogram stretching or blind pixel redistribution to reduce sharpness.

Deep-sea photos cannot be recovered using current underwater image enhancement or restoration methods. As a result, a novel imaging model for deep-sea imaging is required. Light attenuation, uneven lighting, and scattering are all issues that need to be addressed. Deep-sea photos have a lot of interference and aren't very bright, here Image realism is improved, and the halo is reduced in this method (Figs. 15, 16 and Table 3).

Fig. 15. Filtering of a grayscale underwater image

The SNR value of a noisy image is 8.9053, the SNR value of the partially filtered image is 13.0319 and the SNR value of the filtered image is 24.5233. This improvement in SNR values indicates the efficiency of the algorithm and is almost like the original image (Figs. 18 and 20).

The above series of images shows the 3D modelling process by using 3d mapping and scaling process. The first step is to add the dataset given by the Department of Science & Technology into the software then the format depending on the type of image is chosen for example urban, vertical structure, human body etc. then after processing (about 30 min) the 3D model is created. This 3D model might have some extra unwanted details which are eliminated using Meshlab software. The final 3D output is shown above.

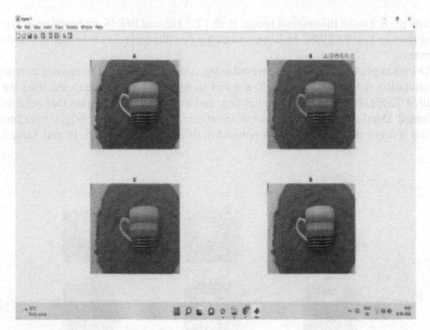

Fig. 16. De-noised images.

Table 3. SNR values of de-noised images

IMAGE	INITIAL VALUE	MIN VALUE	MAX VALUE
COLOURED IMAGE	8.0953	13.0319	24.5233
GREYSCALE IMAGE	8.0673	13.1231	24.4789

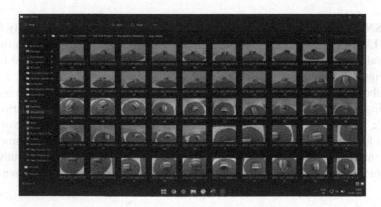

Fig. 17. Dataset of colored underwater image

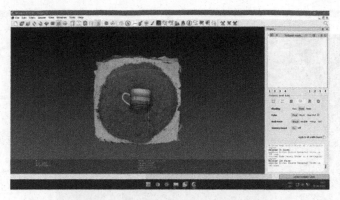

Fig. 18. 3D model of dataset in Fig. 17

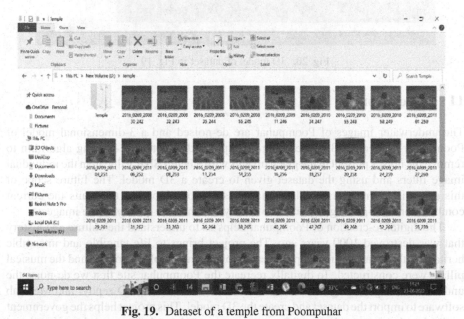

Fig. 19. Dataset of a temple from Poompuhar

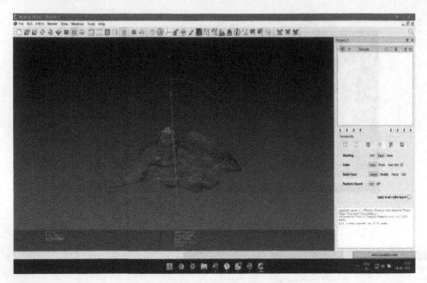

Fig. 20. 3D model of dataset in Fig. 19

11   Conclusion

The underwater images of Poompuhar are de-noised and a 3-dimensional model of Poompuhar is created. By developing a simple and effective de-noising algorithm to remove the noises present in the given images with a better SNR value than the individual image filters and using the dataset given to create a 3D model. The future scope of this paper is to create a complete image restoration algorithm that suits the current combinational de-noising algorithm to clearly enhance the quality of the images.

The digital re-creation of Poompuhar helps us to understand the culture and history that was destroyed 1000 years ago. The project brings to life tangible and intangible heritage in the area offering people a peak into how marketplaces looked and the musical pillars were constructed. To digitally recreate the Poompuhar site first we de-noise the underwater images using combination of filters. Then we use 3D zephyr and Meshlab software to import the dataset and create the 3D model. This project helps the government to display the destroyed city of Poompuhar to people and showcase the cultural and trading methods followed by ancient Tamilians and to estimate the frequency of tsunamis to be able to predict and protect the coastal areas in advance and save thousands of lives.

Acknowledgement. This project is funded by the ICPS (InterDisciplinary Cyber-Physical Systems) division of the Department of Science and Technology, Government of India.

References

1. Wang, Y., Song, W., Fortino, G., Qi, L.Z., Zhang, W., Liotta, A.: An experimental-based review of image enhancement and image restoration methods for underwater imaging. IEEE Access **7**, 140233–140251 (2019)

2. Jian, S., Wen, W.: Study on underwater image de-noising algorithm based on wavelet transform (2017)
3. Zhang, W., Dong, L., Pan, X., Zou, P., Qin, L., Xu, W.: A survey of restoration and enhancement for underwater images. IEEE Access **7**, 182259–182279 (2019)
4. Jaffe, J.S., Moore, K.D., Mclean, J., et al.: Underwater optical imaging: status and prospects. Oceanography **14**(3), 1–3 (2001)
5. Garcia, R., Nicosevici, T., Cufi, X.: On the way to solve lighting problems in underwater image. In: IEEE OCEANS Conference (OCEANS), Biloxi, Mississippi, pp. 1018–1024 (2002)
6. Portilla, J., Strela, M.W.V., Simoncelli, E.P.: Image denoising using scale mixtures of Gaussians in the wavelet domain. IEEE Trans. Image Process. **12**(11), 1338–1351 (2003)
7. McLellan, B.C.: Sustainability assessment of deep ocean resources. Procedia Environ. Sci. **28**, 502–508 (2015)
8. Lu, H., et al.: CONet: a cognitive ocean network. IEEE Wirel. Commun. **26**(3), 90–96 (2019)
9. Lu, H., Li, Y., Serikawa, S.: Computer vision for ocean observing. In: Lu, H., Li, Y. (eds.) Artificial Intelligence and Computer Vision. SCI, vol. 672, pp. 1–16. Springer, Cham (2017). https://doi.org/10.1007/978-3-319-46245-5_1
10. He, K., Sun, J., Tang, X.: Guided image filtering. IEEE Trans. Pattern Anal. Mach. Intell. **35**(6), 1397–1409 (2013)
11. Galdran, A., Pardo, D., Picón, A., Alvarez-Gila, A.: Automatic redchannel underwater image restoration. J. Vis. Commun. Image Represent. **26**, 132–145 (2015)
12. Drews, P., Jr., Nascimento, E.R., Botelho, S.S.C., Campos, M.F.M.: Underwater depth estimation and image restoration based on single images. IEEE Comput. Graph. Appl. **36**(2), 24–35 (2016)
13. Li, C., Guo, J., Guo, C., Cong, R., Gong, J.: A hybrid method for underwater image correction. Pattern Recogn. Lett **94**, 62–67 (2017)
14. Peng, Y.-T., Cosman, P.C.: Underwater image restoration based on image blurriness and light absorption. IEEE Trans. Image Process. **26**(4), 1579–1594 (2017)
15. Peng, Y.-T., Cao, K., Cosman, P.C.: Generalization of the dark channel prior for single image restoration. IEEE Trans. Image Process. **27**(6), 2856–2868 (2018)
16. Berman, D., Levy, D., Avidan, S., Treibitz, T.: Underwater single image color restoration using haze-lines and a new quantitative dataset. IEEE Trans. Pattern Anal. Mach. Intell. **43**, 2822–2837 (2020)
17. Yang, H.-Y., Chen, P.-Y., Huang, C.-C., Zhuang, Y.-Z., Shiau, Y.-H.: Low complexity underwater image enhancement based on dark channel prior. In: Proceedings of the 2nd International Conference on Innovations in Bio-inspired Computing and Applications, pp. 17–20 (2011)
18. Wen, H., Tian, Y., Huang, T., Gao, W.: Single underwater image enhancement with a new optical model. In: Proceedings of the IEEE International Symposium Circuits System (ISCAS), pp. 753–756 (2013)
19. Zhao, X., Jin, T., Qu, S.: Deriving inherent optical properties from background color and underwater image enhancement. Ocean Eng. **94**, 163–172 (2015)
20. Chiang, J.Y., Chen, Y.-C.: Underwater image enhancement by wavelength compensation and dehazing. IEEE Trans. Image Process. **21**(4), 1756–1769 (2012)
21. Chao, L., Wang, M.: Removal of water scattering. In: Proceedings of the 2nd International Conference on Computer Engineering and Technology, vol. 2, pp. V2-35–V2-39 (2010)
22. Carlevaris-Bianco, N., Mohan, A., Eustice, R.M.: Initial results in underwater single image dehazing. In: Proceedings of the MTS/IEEE SEATTLE OCEANS, pp. 1–8 (2010)
23. Drews, P., Nascimento, E., Moraes, F., Botelho, S., Campos, M.: Transmission estimation in underwater single images. In: Proceedings of the IEEE International Conference on Computer Vision Workshops, pp. 825–830 (2013)

24. Li, C., Quo, J., Pang, Y., Chen, S., Wang, J.: Single underwater image restoration by blue-green channels dehazing and red channel correction. In: Proceedings of the IEEE International Conference on Acoustics, Speech and Signal Processing (ICASSP), pp. 1731–1735 (2016)
25. Neeru, N.: Performance comparison of various image denoising filters under spatial domain (IJCA) (2014)

Formulating Mechanisms for Reduction in Greenhouse Gas Emissions at Ghatkesar

Abhiram Katuri[1]([✉]), S. Krishna Anand[2], Salugu Sindhu[3], and V. Jayaprakasan[4]

[1] Department of Electronics and Computer Engineering, Sreenidhi Institute of Science and Technology, Hyderabad, Telangana, India
katuriabhiram2002@gmail.com
[2] Department of Artificial Intelligence, Anurag University, Hyderabad, Telangana, India
[3] Department of Industrial Design, National Institute of Technology, Rourkela, Odisha, India
[4] Department of Electronics and Communication Engineering, Sreenidhi Institute of Science and Technology, Hyderabad, Telangana, India
jayaprakasanv@sreenidhi.edu.in

Abstract. The rapid growth of technology has simplified human jobs to a great extent. Jobs that used to take weeks or months are now carried out within minutes. Such has been the rapid rise in day-to-day developments that comforts which used to reach man after an arduous effort is now available at his doorstep. Going from one place to another is no longer an arduous task. With rapid rise in population and travelling being a day-to-day affair, the number of vehicles and their usage has gone up in leaps and bounds. However, the level of comfort obtained is not without its pitfalls. With vehicles crowded across the globe, the amounts of emission of greenhouse gases have also gone up. In today's world, one of the major interests of governments across the globe in the area of environmental protection is to reduce greenhouse gas (GHG) emissions and air pollutants emissions from vehicles. It has been observed that one fourth of greenhouse gas emissions have taken place owing to vehicular movements. In almost every developing and developed country, vehicular emissions have caused a serious bottleneck for global technological advancements. However, the authors have also observed that emission of greenhouse gases is not same in every part of the country. Besides, measures taken in one part of the country may not be applicable in another. With this view in perspective, the authors have focused on emissions arising from a small region named Ghatkesar located on the outskirts of a huge city. The authors have also suggested relevant ways of reducing the emissions in that region. The same measures could be extended to similar regions.

Keywords: GHG · Global warming · vehicular emissions

1 Introduction

Greenhouse gases trap heat and make the planet warmer. Human activities are responsible for almost all of the increase in greenhouse gases in the atmosphere over the last 150 years. The largest source of greenhouse gas emissions from human activities from

© Springer Nature Switzerland AG 2023
D. Garg et al. (Eds.): IACC 2022, CCIS 1781, pp. 33–44, 2023.
https://doi.org/10.1007/978-3-031-35641-4_3

burning fossil fuels for electricity, heat, and transportation. The transportation sector generates the largest share of greenhouse gas emissions. Greenhouse gas emissions from transportation primarily come from burning fossil fuel for our cars, trucks, ships, trains and planes. Over 90% of the fuel used for transportation across the globe is petroleum based, which includes primarily gasoline and diesel.

In India, it is the third most CO_2 emitting sector, and within the transport sector, road transport contributed more than 90% of total CO_2 emissions. This information has been obtained from an Indian government ministry namely Ministry of Environment Forest and Climate Change, 2018. The greenhouse gas (GHG) emissions in India consisted of 70% CO_2 and 30% non-CO_2 (methane, nitrous oxide, F-gas) emissions [14]. With economic development in India, the vehicle ownership level has increased with a growth rate of 10.4% for two-wheelers and 11% for cars from 2001 to 2015 [15], leading to an increase in emission levels on the road. An increase in vehicle population also contributed significantly to India's air pollution [16]. Serious health issues are observed due to high exposure to air pollution (PM and NOx) in India [17]. Hence, various transport policies were introduced in the past, which impacted the vehicle exhaust emission and influenced the characteristics of the vehicles present in the fleet and their activity levels. Vehicle population with fleet configuration and their activity profile have been significantly affected by the transport policies.

2 Literature Survey

Way back in the year 2006, Sally and his team [1] dealt with the manner of capturing carbon dioxide in deep geological formations. They in turn focused on aspects of low carbon economy by means of capture. In the year 2008, a research group belonging to the university of Southampton assessed the impact on human health owing to particulars like benzene, carbon monoxide, nitrogen oxides and Sulphur dioxide which in turn are emitted during various modes of transport. Special emphasis has been given to PM (2.5). Xie, Pang and Xin [2] carried out extensive research pertaining to emission of carbon dioxide in a particular area named Tianjin. They in turn evaluated the amount of greenhouse gas emissions and performed detailed analysis during the year 2010. During the same year Ali and David formulated a mixed integer program for optimizing green supply chain management. They designed a model which gave a high degree of importance to both supply chain and environmental management.

In the year 2011, Martin and Shaheen further improved the research carried out by Xie and his team by focusing on the extent of greenhouse gas emissions arising as a result of individual participating in car sharing organizations within north America. They were able to calculate the reduction in emissions as a result of car sharing. They also calculated the average greenhouse gas emissions per household. Later, in the year 2012, Ferreira and his team [3] analyzed the impact of traffic lights in enhancing the amount of carbon emissions. They made the necessary emission calculations pertaining to a particular city. During early 2015, Reto and Joeri [4] were able to investigate and find out that the temperature increase owing to carbon dioxide emissions Did not reduce despite a large amount of effort put by climate change activists after industrialization. Although a simple relationship existed between the amount of CO_2 emissions and rise in global temperature, it became a need to fix a target CO_2 budget among countries.

Formulating policies to incorporate the same became an arduous task. During the same period, Priya and her team [5] designed a fuzzy expert system to identify a list of parameters which cause a dramatic change in the amount of carbon dioxide emissions. They carried out sensitivity analysis and eliminated parameters that played an insignificant role in impacting the amount of emissions. They also analyzed parameters whose change could lead to extinction of different kinds of species. During the year 2016, Orozco and Llano [6] concentrated on reduction in CO_2 emissions by placing a special emphasis on moving vehicles. They calculated the carbon foot print arising from vehicles based on the speed of their movement and consumption of fuel. In 2017, Ciupageanu and lazaroiu [7] concentrated on reducing emissions within a short time frame. In order to analyze their findings in an objective manner, they devised an algorithm in MATLAB for estimating a number of parameters related to CO_2 emissions in Romania. They then analyzed variation in a number of parameters over a period of time. During the same period, Punam and Bhavna [8] carried out a brief literature survey on various energy efficient projects pertaining to reduction of CO_2 Emissions for wireless networks.

In the year 2019, Querishi and his team [9] monitored the amount of emissions arising due to vehicular traffic in Malaysia. They used this information for reducing the traffic congestion by designing a model based on quality of air. This information assisted them in designing mechanisms for reducing traffic congestion. During 2021, Sonali and Rajashree [10] used machine learning models for predicting the amount of CO_2 Emissions arising due to automobiles. It had been observed that a large amount of attention has been given during the last decade pertaining to CO_2 emissions, Anand and Raman [11] concentrated on impact of different greenhouse gases including SO_2 and NO_2. They calculated the amount of increase in emissions depending on the type of industry and type of gas. Research has shown that policies formulated in one region may not be applicable in all regions. With this view in focus, Eliza and Michalina [12] identified measures for implementing a municipal adaptation plan for incorporating climate change for the city Poznan. Their measures gave a larger amount of concentration on transport and bio diversity sectors. Mamatha and her team [13] made a detailed comparison of emissions occurring in different parts of country and analysed regions where amount of emissions are found to be much higher beyond the normal range. Besides, they identified that among all the sectors, transportation contributes to the highest possible extent followed by construction.

Based on studies conducted by a wide variety of researchers across the globe, it has been found that all measures taken for some regions may not be applicable for others. With this view in perspective, the authors have decided to focus on the emissions owing to vehicular traffic pertaining to Ghatkesar region. To add value to the same, they have also formulated possible actions that could be taken in the near future for controlling the same.

The parching month in set down human history was the most recent one, July of 2022. This indicates that, globally, average climate and temperatures are now increasing dependably year after year. The main starting points of this climate change phenomenon are pollution, population growth, and humankind's general disdain for the environment. However, we may particularly mention the greenhouse effect and global warming as two phenomena that cause the temperature to rise. The atmosphere is the protective layer of air that surrounds the surface of the world. The sun's infrared radiation is trapped in this atmosphere by gases, which heats the earth's surface. In a perfect world, the earth's temperature is about 15c as a result of this phenomenon. Without such an event, earth would not be able to support life. However, throughout the past few centuries, the release of greenhouse gases has multiplied due to fast industrialization and rising pollution. More radiation is subsequently trapped in the earth's atmosphere as a result of this. As a result, the planet's surface temperature continues to increase. Over a period of time, the climate change experts have succeeded in bringing types of fuel more suitable for sustainability in environment with the goal in reducing the overall carbon content. Newer technologies pertaining to green environment have come into existence. This growth has been depicted clearly in Fig. 3.

3 Effect of GHG on Mode of Transport

With advancements in technology, the amount of work to be carried out by various kinds of people has grown in leaps and bounds. To add to the fact, an exponential growth in population has not simplified day to day life. A large number of people have to commute to various places to carry out their day-to-day jobs. In most cases, the work place is situated a fair distance from their residence. This in turn facilitates the need for effective transportation. With large amount of limitations in modes of transport like railways, airways, seaways, transportation by means of roadways has become highly essential for a considerable set of population. As a result, widespread use of roadways has led to road congestion at different points in time. Studies have shown that transportation is responsible for 14% of the overall emissions. This has been depicted in Table 1.

As the government takes adequate number of steps in ensuring good serviceable roads, enough amount of effort has not been expended towards the rate of carbon dioxide emissions. The Road transport agency does make checks in levels of pollution arising as a result of usage of a number of vehicles. However, it has been done on an adhoc basis. Besides, checks are being conducted on some specific categories of vehicles. Some other categories have been conveniently omitted.

The overall emissions arising due to movement of vehicles need to be calculated. The emission levels of different vehicles are found to be different. Apart from that, the various pollutants emitted from different vehicles cannot be equated. This has been clearly highlighted in Table 1 where one particle of N_2O is equivalent to 310 particle equivalence of CO_2. For detailed analysis to be carried out, large numbers of parameters are involved. Besides, the computational complexity is very high. In most cases, it is highly infeasible in deciding an appropriate approach for reducing the emissions. With this view in perspective, this work focuses on calculating emissions within a small region. Besides, some simple implementable solution has also been suggested for controlling the emissions.

Air pollutants are substances that adversely affect the environment by interfering with climate, the physiology of plants, animal species, entire ecosystems, as well as with human property in the form of agricultural crops or man-made structures. These air pollutants in turn have a drastic effect on release of greenhouse gases which in turn affect the overall climate and life of man as a whole. This work focuses on release of

Table 1. Relationship of various Chemical elements and their GWP

GHG	Chemical Symbol	GWP
Carbon Dioxide	CO_2	1
Methane	CH_4	21
Nitrous Oxide	N_2O	310
Hydroflurocarbons	HFC - 152 a	140
	HFC - 134 a	1300
	HFC - 125	2800
	HFC - 23	11700
Perflurocarbons	CF_4	6500
	C_2F_6	9200
Sulphur Hexafluoride	SF_6	23900

greenhouse gases as a result of movement of vehicles. Different greenhouse gases have varying impact on the environment. In order to simplify computations, all gases will be converted to equivalent CO_2 values. On the other hand, climate research has linked certain compounds long recognized as air pollutants (for instance black carbon) to the warming of climate, thus providing one more reason for their control.

The region Ghatkesar has been selected as the area of study. A detailed survey had been conducted by the authors. Enough attention has been paid to identify the exact amount and type of emissions by each category of vehicle. Nine different vehicles have been identified and shown in Fig. 2. It had been found that during the survey, these vehicles have shown different levels of emissions which in turn cause large release of greenhouse gases. These values are in turn converted into equivalent CO_2 levels.

4   Incorporation of Suitable Machine Learning Algorithm

Owing to a large amount of data available for processing, steps need to be taken to ensure maximation in accuracy levels of estimation. Besides, a large number of attributes play a role in estimating the amount of equivalent CO_2 emissions. Some of them may be significant while others may have a negligible impact. In order to reduce the computational complexity, the number of dimensions must be reduced to necessary levels. Principal Component Analysis (PCA) has been found to be the most suitable machine learning algorithm. It has been implemented for data analysis.

PCA could be used to handle both small and large datasets. In this work, PCA has been effectively utilized for handling transport related data. Pandas and NumPy have been imported as PD and AP respectively. Transportation data has been loaded into a pandas data frame. The data loaded is 10 dimensional. Different transportation modes include auto, bike, bus, car, scooty, Jeep, ambulance and tempo tracker.

The region of analysis is done at the area of Ghatkesar and the map of that area is depicted in Fig. 1.

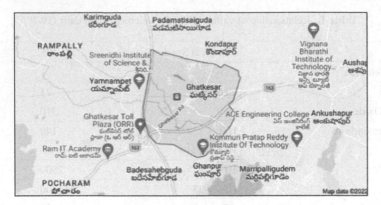

Fig. 1. Ghatkesar Map

The authors have performed a detailed analysis on the number of vehicles crossing in the region of Northern part of Ghatkesar. It has been observed that on implementation of the algorithm yields interesting results. Some of the vehicles like Tempos, Bikes and Cars result in a much larger CO_2 equivalent emissions as opposed to some other category of vehicles. However, the number of emissions resulting from a Bike (28.51 tons of equivalent CO_2) is much smaller than that of an individual Tempo (100 tons of equivalent CO_2). These results have been shown in Fig. 2.

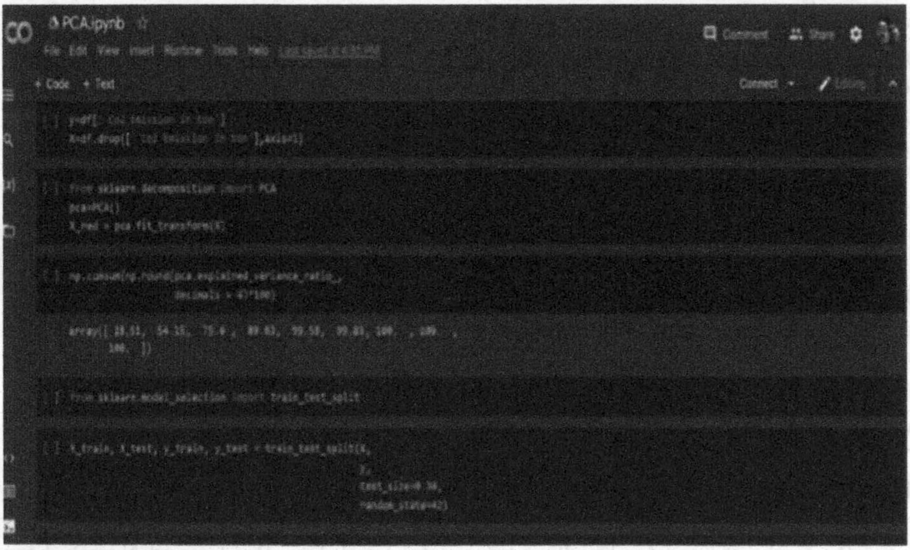

Fig. 2. Result obtained using Principal Component Analysis

In order to effectively make a significant reduction in emissions, measures have been suggested for reducing the amount of CO_2 equivalent emissions occurring as a result of transport used by Students and Faculty members belonging to Sreenidhi Institute of science and Technology which is located at Ghatkesar. The modes of transport used by each and every student and staff have been collected. This has been shown in Table 2.

Table 2. Information about Vehicles that Travel By Various Kinds of People Pertaining to SNIST (College)

Public	Travelling by	Quantity
Students	Bus	3000
	Scooter	1500
	Cycle	20
	Walk	2500
	Car	1000
Faculty	Bus	250
	Scooter	85
	Car	50
Other Staff	Bus	26
	Scooter	35
Vendors - Suppliers	Car	17
	Scooter	33
	Bus	5
Emergency Vehicle	Ambulance	29
Vacation	Business Travel	6

The overall emissions occurring as a result of each mode of transport has been shown in Table 3.

Table 3. Emissions from SNIST

Mode of Transport	Total Number of Vehicles	Capacity	Emissions	
			Total	Average
Bus	42	42 * 60	3423868	114128
Scooty	827	827 * 2	2670044	89001
Bike	1200	1200 * 2	21235005	707833
Car	271	271 * 4	26679834	889328
Ambulance	18	18 * 4	2575605	858535

In order to perform a detailed analysis, data pertaining to emissions of vehicles in Ghatkesar region has been considered. One month's data (June 1 to 30th, 2022) has been estimated. Table 4 clearly highlights the variation in emissions depending on the type of vehicle. This information has been converted into implementable form as depicted in Fig. 4a.

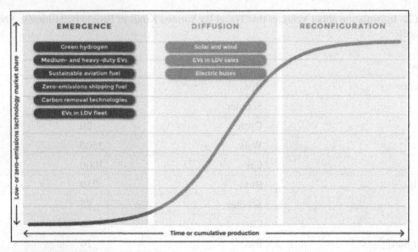

Fig. 3. Illustration of the stages of S-Curve progress for low-carbon technologies

As expected, the size and capacity of the vehicle determines the amount of emissions. However, bigger vehicles would also accommodate larger number of people which in turn reduced the average amount of emissions per person.

Results obtained during the research in Ghatkesar for nine different vehicles are 28.51, 54.15, 5.6, 89.83, 99.58, 100, 100 here $25.51CO_2$/ton being the lowest and 100 being the highest. This has been clearly shown in Fig. 4b.

The detailed list of fuels along with the amount of CO_2 emissions has been illustrated in Table 5. It can be clearly inferred that fuels like Diesel and Kerosene emit a larger amount of CO_2 as compared to LNG or compressed natural gas.

Table 4. Research in Ghatkesar Region for Nine Different Vehicles

Historic CO_2 Emissions by Transport in Ghatkesar during June 1 to June 30, 2022										
Number of Vehicles										
Date	Bike	Auto	Bus	car	Scooty	Jeep	Ambulance	Tempo	Tractor	CO_2 Emission in Ton
Jun-01	255	408	69	489	56	330	50	255	30	3456
Jun-02	456	234	66	456	23	345	50	654	20	5647
Jun-03	324	345	66	556	34	543	50	432	54	3456

(*continued*)

Table 4. (*continued*)

Historic CO_2 Emissions by Transport in Ghatkesar during June 1 to June 30, 2022

Number of Vehicles

Date	Bike	Auto	Bus	car	Scooty	Jeep	Ambulance	Tempo	Tractor	CO_2 Emission in Ton
Jun-04	453	456	67	554	43	456	50	345	34	8765
Jun-05	136	654	68	557	76	768	50	567	45	3456
Jun-06	236	432	65	667	89	765	50	765	65	6574
Jun-07	567	345	67	558	12	763	50	456	76	8756
Jun-08	435	567	65	667	37	345	50	654	23	3456
Jun-09	239	765	67	556	62	234	50	234	45	2346
Jun-10	599	456	68	556	59	456	50	987	65	6758
Jun-11	335	654	69	554	93	678	50	654	67	9457
Jun-12	245	234	64	553	47	876	50	123	87	8679
Jun-13	675	987	64	558	58	654	50	234	97	9856
Jun-14	226	654	63	228	26	345	50	345	23	3454
Jun-15	314	123	64	199	91	456	50	456	34	7658
Jun-16	567	234	64	345	49	567	50	678	32	6557
Jun-17	783	345	65	456	30	654	50	987	35	5555
Jun-18	220	456	65	678	26	456	50	543	54	4563
Jun-19	615	678	65	765	61	789	50	567	46	8756
Jun-20	234	987	67	543	72	977	50	654	61	8756
Jun-21	546	543	68	345	78	765	50	556	23	3546
Jun-22	234	567	69	543	39	763	50	556	24	5774
Jun-23	224	654	67	678	44	345	50	554	25	3452
Jun-24	564	543	68	345	67	234	50	553	65	3456
Jun-25	455	432	67	678	12	456	50	558	77	4567
Jun-26	231	432	67	234	27	678	50	228	81	9845
Jun-27	765	543	68	765	43	876	50	199	90	6574
Jun-28	554	456	67	654	37	654	50	345	84	4456
Jun-29	445	654	67	567	97	345	50	456	73	6654
Jun-30	435	765	68	234	67	123	50	678	27	4563

Table 5. Emission Factor of Transportation Fuels

Fuel Type	Kg CO_2 Per Unit	Unit
Aviation Gasoline	8.31	gallon
Bio Diesel (100%)	9.45	gallon
Compressed Natural Gas (CNG)	0.05444	scf (std.cub.ft)
Diesel	10.21	gallon
Ethanol (100%)	5.75	gallon

(*continued*)

Table 5. (*continued*)

Fuel Type	Kg CO$_2$ Per Unit	Unit
Kerosene - Type Jet Fuel	9.75	gallon
Liquefied Natural Gas (LNG)	4.5	gallon
Liquefied Petroleum Gas (LPG)	5.6	gallon
Motor Gasoline	8.78	gallon
Residual Fuel Oil	1.27	gallon

(a)

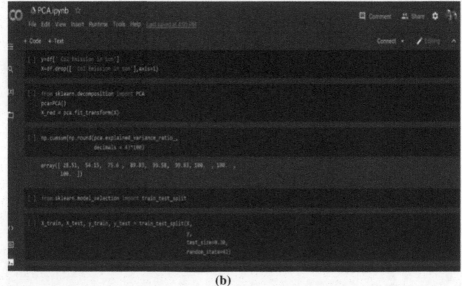

(b)

Fig. 4. (a) Data for PCA Analysis. (b) Data for PCA Analysis

Besides, literature review suggests that there is a significant degradation in the performing efficiency of vehicles over time. These vehicles need to be tested periodically over time. A series of test are conducted on each vehicle. The frequency with which tests are conducted on each type of vehicle has been shown in Table 6.

Table 6. Frequency at which the defined tests may be performed

Test Type	Vehicle Category	Frequency
Periodic Vehicle Test	Light Vehicles	Private Vehicles:
		3-1-1-1…….
		Commercial Vehicles:
		1-1-1-1…….
	Heavy Vehicles	1-1-1-1…….
New Vehicle Registration Test	Light Vehicles	Triggered Upon:
	Heavy Vehicles	1) Purchase from outside the authorised vehicle agencies in that Ghatkesar
		2) Transfer of Vehicle Ownership
		3) Re-Registration Of Vehicle
		4) Post the new registration test, the vehicles in all categories must be tested annually
Re-Test	Light Vehicles & Heavy Vehicles	Triggered within 30 days of failure of compliance to above test standards
Export Test		Triggered when exporting a vehicle outside Ghatkesar

5 Conclusion

The work carried out has effectively satisfied the twin objectives of identifying the amount of greenhouse gas emissions and also suggesting measures to mitigate the same by concentrating on a specific developing region in the outskirts of Hyderabad. Studies have shown that a large number of factors play a role in determining the overall emissions. This work has specifically focused on emissions that occur as a result of moving vehicles. With a rapid increase in population followed by the exponential increase in number of vehicles across the globe, there arose an urgent need in taking steps for reduction in emissions. This work contributed to a miniscule extent in this direction. By suitably modeling the choice of transport in an educational Institute, the amount of reduction in emissions have been found to be highly significant. With suitable measures taken in different parts of the world, overall global emissions can be reduced thus contributing to a greener planet.

References

1. Benson, S.M., Surles, T.: CO_2 capture and storage: an overview with emphasis on capture and storage in deep geological formations. Proc. IEEE **94**(10), 1795–1805 (2006)
2. Xie, Y., Pang, J., Feng, X.: Research about CO_2 Emission under the current energy structure in Tianjin. Proc. IEEE (2010)
3. Martin, E.W., Shaheen, S.A.: Greenhouse gas emission impacts of carsharing in North America. IEEE Trans. Intell. Transp. Syst. **12**(4), 1074–1086 (2011). https://doi.org/10.1109/TITS. 2011.2158539
4. Ferreira, M., d'Orey, P.M.: On the impact of Virtual traffic lights on carbon emissions mitigation. IEEE Trans. Intell. Transp. Syst. **13**(1), 284–295 (2012). https://doi.org/10.1109/TITS. 2011.2169791
5. Knutti, R., Rogelj, J.: The legacy of our CO_2 emission: a clash of scientific facts, politics, and ethics. Clim. Change **133**, 361–373 (2015). https://doi.org/10.1007/s10584-015-1340-3
6. Priya, V., Sagambari Devi, G., Krishna Anand, S.: Assessing Impact of Climate change through design of a fuzzy expert system. ARPN J. Eng. Appl. Sci. **10**(1), 193–201 (2015)
7. Orozco, O.A., LIano, G.: Optimal speed advisory: a vehicular networks application focused on decreasing CO_2 emission. IEEE Lat. Am. Trans. **14**(6), 2693–2699 (2016)
8. Ciupageanu, D.-A., Lazaroiu, G., Tirsu, M.: CO_2 emission reduction by Renewable energy employment in Romania. In: 2017 International Conference on Electromechanical and Power Systems (SIELMEN) (2017)
9. Qureshi, M.A., et al.: Modelling traffic congestion based on air quality for greener environment: an empirical study (2019)
10. Kangralkar, S., Khanai, R.: Machine learning application for automotive emission prediction. In: 2021 6th International Conference for Convergence in Technology. IEEE (2021)
11. Anand, K., Raman, S.: Incorporation of innovative mechanisms for greenhouse gas emission reduction. Environ. Earth Sci. Res. J. **8**(3), 118–124 (2021)
12. Kalbarczyk, E., Piegat, M.: Implementation of municipal adaptation plans to climate changes: case study of Poznan. Acta Sci. Pol. Administratio Locorum **20**(4), 323–334 (2021)
13. Mamatha, E., Mahadikar, A., Anand, K., Krupakara, P.V., Reddy, C.S.: Incorporation of mechanisms for providing green environment post COVID-19. Acta Sci. Pol. Administratio Locorum **21**(3), 321–334 (2022). https://doi.org/10.31648/aspal.7262
14. Olivier, P.: Trends in global CO_2 and total green house gas emissions. PBL Netherlands Environmental Assessment Agency (2020)
15. Singh, N., Mishra, T., Banarjee, R.: Emissions inventory for road transport in India in 2020: framework and post facto policy impact assessments. Research Square (2021)
16. Guttikunda, S.K., Kopakka, R.V.: Source emissions and health impacts of urban air pollution in Hyderabad, India. Air Qual. Atmos Health **7**, 195–207 (2014)
17. Goel, R., Guttikunda, S.K.: Role of urban growth, technology, and judicial interventions on vehicle exhaust emissions in Delhi for 1991–2014 and 2014–2030 periods. Environ. Dev. **14**, 6–21 (2015)

Crew Rostering Problem with Fatigue Balance

Hao Guo[1] [iD], Bin Deng[1(✉)] [iD], Weidong Li[1] [iD], Junfeng Huang[2], Jingfeng Li[2],
and Kaiyi Tang[2]

[1] Department of Mathematics and Statistics, Yunnan University, Kunming 650500, China
{gh19990221,dengbin}@mail.ynu.edu.cn
[2] China Eastern Yunnan Airlines, China Eastern Airlines, Kunming 650211, China
{hjf,lijingfeng}@ceair.com

Abstract. The crew rostering problem is one of the most important problems in
the operation of airlines. Crew rostering is the process of assigning pairings to
eligible crew members. This paper analyzes the factors to affect crew fatigue and
proposes a new optimality criterion for the crew rostering problem, which is called
fatigue balance. It is used to measure the overall fatigue level of crew members.
A linear regression model is established to predict crew fatigue and construct
a corresponding fatigue matrix. Based on the fatigue matrix, the crew rostering
problem is transformed into a matrix rearrangement problem. To find a fatigue-
balanced assignment scheme, the minimum covariance algorithm is improved to
obtain a new algorithm called the minimum covariance algorithm with fatigue.
Numerical experiments show that the new algorithm performs better than the Local
Trades algorithm and the Greedy algorithm for solving the crew rostering problem
with fatigue balance.

Keywords: Crew rostering problem · Fatigue balance · Matrix rearrangement ·
Minimum covariance algorithm with fatigue

1 Introduction

The rapid development of the civil aviation industry and the high requirements of crew
training, long training cycles, and other factors lead to crew members being scarce.
To minimize the operating burden of airlines, improve operating efficiency and reduce
operating costs, reasonable and efficient crew scheduling is very necessary. However,
the current scheduling method in China is still relatively backward. Because the manual
scheduling method takes a long time and cannot fully consider various influencing factors, the scheduling results are not ideal. Under such a background, it is meaningful to
optimize the crew scheduling.

The crew rostering problem is an important step in crew scheduling. Most studies
use mathematical programming methods to solve the crew rostering problem. It mainly

Supported by the National Natural Science Foundation of China [No. 12071417] and the
Exemption Postgraduate Research and Innovation Foundation of Yunnan University [No.
2021T093].

© Springer Nature Switzerland AG 2023
D. Garg et al. (Eds.): IACC 2022, CCIS 1781, pp. 45–63, 2023.
https://doi.org/10.1007/978-3-031-35641-4_4

transforms the crew rostering problem into a set partitioning problem (Lučic and Teodorovic [1] and Day, Ryan, and D.M et al. [2]) or a set covering problem (Moudani, Cosenza, Coligny, and Mora-Camino [3]). However, when the instance size is large, it is difficult to obtain good results with these types of methods. In fact, the crew rostering problem is a fair allocation of crew resources, so some methods to the fair allocation problem can be used to solve the problem. Heuristic algorithm is generally used in the case of large amounts of data. For example, X. Liu et al. proposed three swarm optimization algorithms [4] and a hybrid algorithm based on ant colony optimization (ACO) and Tabu Search (TS) [5]. J. Zhang et al. [6] used the classification of machine learning. And X. Zhang et al. [7] proposed a two-phase heuristic allocation algorithm etc. There are also much research on the mechanism design of fair allocation (X. Yang et al. [8], X. Zhang et al. [9], and J. Zhang et al. [10], etc.). This paper also introduces a new method to solve this problem, that is, the crew rostering problem is transformed into a matrix rearrangement problem. Through experimental verification, the new method introduced in this paper also can obtain a better result in the large instance.

The purpose of the crew rostering problem is to find a set of feasible schemes that satisfy certain optimality properties. This property is called the optimality criterion. In the past decades, many specialized papers have introduced different optimality criteria. Antosik and J. L. [11] and Byrne et al. [12] considered the preferences of employees in their study. Limlawan, Kasemsontitum, and Jeenanunta [13], Tsubasa, Tatsushi and Stefan [14], Chutima, and Arayikanon [15], and Zizhen Zhang, Mengchu Zhou, and Jiahai Wang [16] introduced fair workload. Quesnel, Alice Wu, Desaulniers, and Soumis [17] used language constraints as an optimality criterion. B. Deng [18] considered qualification constraints. Gamache, Soumis, Marquis, and Desrosiers [19] considered dead time in their paper. Dawid, König, and Strauss [20] introduced utility of rosters as an optimality criterion. Much of the literature on the crew rostering problem is based on operating costs (e.g. Kohl and Karisch [21], Maenhout and Vanhoucke [22], Medard and Sawhney [23], Moudani, Cosenza, Coligny, and Mora-Camino, and Santosa, Sunarto, and Rahman [24]). Among them, the article of Santosa mainly takes salary costs as the optimality criterion. From what we know of the literature, most of the research on crew fatigue is the monitoring and assessment of crew fatigue (Andrej, Benedikt, Andrea, and Tomasz [25]). There are few articles that consider the crew fatigue balance in the crew assignment process.

Precise control of crew fatigue will be one of the main directions to optimize crew scheduling in the future. At present, the control of fatigue of crew members is relatively unreasonable in China. Individual differences are adjusted by human beings, so refined and intelligent management cannot be achieved. But this is often the most lethal for aviation safety. In the history of civil aviation, there have been many air accidents caused by excessive fatigue of crew members. For example, the air crash of Korean Airlines flight 801 in 1997 and Continental Airlines flight 3407 in 2009.

To solve this problem effectively, this paper studies the crew rostering problem with the crew fatigue balance based on the real data provided by a Chinese airline. This section mainly describes the development status of China's civil aviation industry and points out the research significance of the crew rostering problem with the crew fatigue balance. The remainder of this paper is structured as follows. In Sect. 2, we mainly describe the crew rostering problem and divide the constraints involved in the crew rostering problem into matching constraints, horizontal constraints, and vertical constraints. The crew rostering problem is formulated and transformed into a matrix rearrangement problem. In Sect. 3, we analyze the factors to affect crew fatigue from two aspects: internal factors and external factors, put forward a new optimality criterion for crew rostering problem, which is called fatigue balance, and establish a linear regression model to predict crew fatigue according to the data provided by airlines. In Sect. 4, we improve the minimum covariance algorithm to obtain a new algorithm called the minimum covariance algorithm with fatigue (MinCovFatigue). It is used to solve the crew rostering problem with fatigue balance as an optimality criterion. The Local Trades algorithm and the Greedy algorithm are introduced to compare with the new algorithm. In Sect. 5, the numerical experiment results are presented, which proves that the new algorithm performs better than the other two algorithms. Section 6 is the conclusion of this paper.

2 Crew Rostering Problem

2.1 Restatement of Crew Rostering Problem

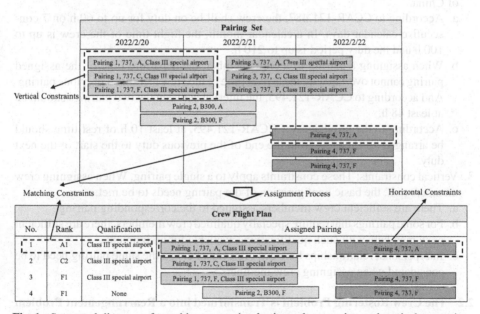

Fig. 1. Structural diagram of matching constraint, horizontal constraint, and vertical constraint.

The crew rostering problem is the assignment of the pairings to the eligible crew, that is, to make a personal flight plan for each crew. This is an important part of airline operations. Crew rostering is subject to a variety of constraints, such as regulations and rules formulated by the government, airlines, and other relevant departments, personal factors of the crew members, etc. These constraints are divided into matching constraints, horizontal constraints, and vertical constraints by using a classification method similar to that proposed by Kohl and Karisch. (The schematic diagram of the structure is shown in Fig. 1.

1. Matching constraints: These constraints determine whether the crew can perform the pairing.
   a. The rank of the crew needs to match the needs of the assigned pairing. If the mission requires, the crew can perform a lower-rank pairing.
   b. The type of aircraft that the crew can perform needs to match the aircraft type required for the assigned pairing.
   c. The base of the crew member needs to match the base of the pairing.
   d. Consider the occupancy impact of the crew, sometimes crew members occupy a certain period due to vacations, training, and other activities. When assigning pairings to crew members, it is necessary to avoid overlapping the period of the pairing with the period of such activities.
2. Horizontal constraints: This type of constraint apply to a single crew member. There are constraints between two pairings connected in a single crew flight plan. Such constraints are mainly the relevant regulations concerning crew rostering in "CCAR-121-R5/R6" [26] (abbreviated as CCAR) issued by the Civil Aviation Administration of China.
   a. According to CCAR-121.487, the crew shall be on duty for up to 60 h on 7 consecutive calendar days. In a calendar month, the flight time of the crew is up to 100 h and the duty period is up to 210 h.
   b. When assigning a pairing to a crew member, the departure time of the assigned pairing cannot overlap with the arrival time of the crew member's previous pairing. And according to CCAR-121.495, the interval between the two pairings should be at least 48 h.
   c. According to the provisions of CCAR-121.495, at least 10 h of rest time should be arranged for the crew from the end of the previous duty to the start of the next duty.
3. Vertical constraints: These constraints apply to a single pairing. When assigning crew members to it, the basic configuration of the pairing needs to be met.
   a. There are sufficient crew members assigned to the corresponding pairing.
   b. For some pairings that require specially qualified crew members, there are sufficient crew members with such qualifications available for assignment.
   c. Interpersonal relationships between crew members on the same pairing need to be considered when assigning crew members.

2.2   The Crew Rostering Problem is Transformed into a Rearrangement Problem

The configuration requirements of crew members in most pairings are often that only one crew member is required for one rank. Therefore, it is stipulated that multiple crew members of the same rank cannot jointly perform the same pairing. However, due to the particularity of the route, some pairings will require multiple crew members of the same rank to perform the pairing. Based on the above situation, when assigning crew members of this rank, a corresponding number of pseudo-pairings that are the same as the pairing are added. In practice, this operation does not change the total number of pairings, just to achieve the purpose that crew members of the same rank cannot perform the same pairing. Therefore, before proceeding with the crew assignment pairing, it is also necessary to classify the different ranks of crew members.

Through the above processing, it can be realized that the crew members of the same rank cannot jointly perform the same pairing, that is, the crew rostering problem is transformed into the fair allocation problem of indivisible goods. According to Cornilly's [27] formulation of the fair allocation problem of indivisible goods, this paper slightly adjusts its notation. Suppose $C = \{1, 2, ..., n\}$ is the set of crew members at a certain rank, $P = \{1, 2, ..., m\}$ is a set of pairings, and the matching constraints are satisfied between set C and set P, that is, the crew configuration requirements of the pairing in the set P match the qualifications of the crew members in the set C. $F = (f_{ij})$ is a $n \times m$ value matrix, which $f_{ij} > 0, i = 1, 2, \cdots, n; j = 1, 2, \cdots, m$, represents the fatigue degree of the ith crew member when performing the jth pairing (see Sect. 3.1 for the calculation method of fatigue degree). 2^P is the power set of the pairing set P, that is, the set of all subsets in P. Each element in 2^P corresponds to a flight plan. Define the map as $p : C \rightarrow 2^P$, where $p(i), i \in C$ is the flight plan is assigned to the ith crew member. To ensure that crew members of the same rank cannot jointly perform the same pairing and each pairing needs to be executed by a crew member of this rank, the map p needs to satisfy

$$p(i) \cap p(j) = \varnothing, i \neq j, \text{ and, } \bigcup_{i \in C} p(i) = P,$$

The fatigue degree $t_i(p(i))$ of the ith crew member after executing the assigned flight plan is given by

$$t_i(p(i)) = \sum_{j \in p(i)} f_{ij}. \tag{1}$$

Suppose there is an initial assignment $\pi = \{\pi_1, \pi_2, ..., \pi_m\}$. Based on the initial assignment, the matrix F can be transformed into n matrixes $F^k = (f_{ij}^k), k = 1, 2, \cdots, n$. For the sake of illustration, we provide an example of $m = 3$ pairings assigned to $n = 3$ crew members. Assume F is given by

$$F = \begin{pmatrix} f_{11} \, f_{12} \, f_{13} \\ f_{21} \, f_{22} \, f_{23} \\ f_{31} \, f_{32} \, f_{33} \end{pmatrix}. \tag{2}$$

It is assumed that the initial assignment is the first crew member to perform all pairings ($\pi_1 = \{1, 2, 3\}$), and the others do not perform any pairings ($\pi_i = \varnothing, i = 2, 3$). So according to

$$f_{ij}^k = \begin{cases} f_{kj}, i = 1, \\ 0, i \neq 1, \end{cases} \tag{3}$$

We can obtain 3 matrixes $F^k = (f_{ij}^k), k = 1, 2, 3$. They are given by

$$F^1 = \begin{pmatrix} f_{11} \, f_{12} \, f_{13} \\ 0 \quad 0 \quad 0 \\ 0 \quad 0 \quad 0 \end{pmatrix}, F^2 = \begin{pmatrix} f_{21} \, f_{22} \, f_{23} \\ 0 \quad 0 \quad 0 \\ 0 \quad 0 \quad 0 \end{pmatrix}, F^3 = \begin{pmatrix} f_{31} \, f_{32} \, f_{33} \\ 0 \quad 0 \quad 0 \\ 0 \quad 0 \quad 0 \end{pmatrix}. \tag{4}$$

Note that the elements in the kth matrix F^k are only the fatigue degrees corresponding to the kth crewmember. The ith row of the matrix F^k represents the fatigue degree caused by the kth crew member performing the pairing assigned to the ith crew member. Since crew members of the same rank cannot jointly perform the same pairing, each column of the matrix F^k has only one non-zero element.

Given a vector $\pi = \{\pi_1, \pi_2, \cdots, \pi_m\}$, where π_i represents the permutation of all elements in the ith column of all matrices F^k, that is, each π_i corresponds to a permutation order of $\{1, 2, \cdots, n\}$. Let $\mathcal{A}$ be the set of all vectors π. Here, π_i permutes the elements of the ith column, which is equivalent to reassigning the ith pairing. However, under the influence of horizontal constraints, reassignment is not allowed in some cases. See Fig. 2 for details.

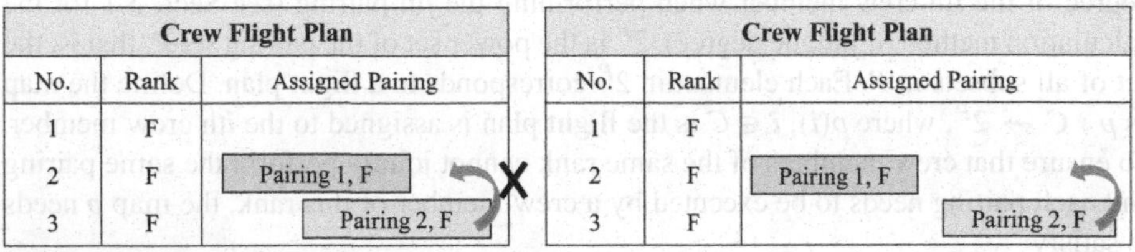

Crew Flight Plan				Crew Flight Plan		
No.	Rank	Assigned Pairing		No.	Rank	Assigned Pairing
1	F			1	F	
2	F	Pairing 1, F		2	F	Pairing 1, F
3	F	Pairing 2, F		3	F	Pairing 2, F

Fig. 2. Paired pairings violating horizontal constraints

As shown in (a) of Fig. 2, since the arrival time of pairing 1 is after the departure time of pairing 2, the non-zero elements in the 2nd column cannot be replaced to the 2nd row when replacing the elements in the 2nd column. In other words, the No. 2 crew cannot execute pairing 2 after executing pairing 1 because of the time conflict. As shown in (b) of Fig. 2, the No. 2 crew can execute pairing 2 after executing pairing 1. In the case of multiple bases, it is also necessary to consider whether the bases of the two pairings connected are consistent. When the bases are consistent, the latter pairing can be assigned to the crew executing the previous pairing.

For any $\pi \in \mathcal{A}$ that satisfies constraints, n matrices $F^k(\pi) = \left(f^k_{\pi_j(i)j}\right), k = 1, 2, \cdots, n$ can be obtained from $f^k_{ij}(\pi_j) = f^k_{\pi_j(i)j}$. According to

$$t_k(p_\pi(i)) = \sum_{j=1}^m f^k_{ij}(\pi_j) = t^k_i(\pi), i = 1, 2, \cdots, n. \tag{5}$$

It can be seen that the sum $t_k(p_\pi(i))$ of the ith row of the matrix $F^k(\pi)$ corresponds to the fatigue degree $t^k_i(\pi)$ generated by the kth crew member executing the flight plan assigned to the ith crew member under the allocation π. In particular, $t_k(p_\pi(k)) = t^k_k(\pi)$ refers to the fatigue degree generated by the kth crew member performing the flight plan assigned to oneself. Define their mean value $\bar{t}^k$ as

$$\bar{t}^k = \frac{\sum_{i=1}^n t^k_i(\pi)}{n} = \frac{\sum_{i=1}^n \sum_{j=1}^m f^k_{ij}(\pi_j)}{n} = \frac{\sum_{i=1}^n \sum_{j=1}^m f^k_{ij}}{n}. \tag{6}$$

When the vector π permutes the elements in the matrix F^k, it only changes the position of the elements in the matrix, and the value of the elements does not change. Therefore, the mean value $\bar{t}^k$ of the matrix $F^k(\pi)$ is not affected by the specific allocation π.

3 Optimality Criterion: Fatigue Balance

In this section, we mainly analyze the various factors to affect crew fatigue, establish a linear regression model to predict the fatigue degree of each crew, and propose a new optimality criterion for crew rostering problem, which is called fatigue balance.

3.1 Fatigue

Fatigue is defined by International Civil Aviation Organization [28] as a physiological state in which the ability to carry out mental or physical activities is reduced due to insufficient sleep, staying awake for a long time, circadian rhythm stage, or heavy workload. This state will reduce the alertness of crew members and their ability to safely operate aircraft.

Factors to Affect Crew Fatigue. In this section, the factors to affect crew fatigue are divided into internal factors and external factors. The structural diagram of the factors to affect crew fatigue is shown in Fig. 3.

1. Internal factors: Such factors are mainly caused by the crew's conditions, and there are individual differences.
   a. Time on duty: It indicates the energy consumed in a certain period. When the cumulative duty time reaches the upper limit specified by CCAR, it is necessary to arrange vacations for the crew members to reduce their fatigue.
   b. Physical fitness: The influencing factors are mainly quantitatively analyzed by relevant management personnel according to the regular physical examination and training assessment of crew members.
   c. Age: With the increase of age, the physical function of the crew will decline. When performing the same task, older crew members will generate more fatigue than younger crew members.
   d. Flight experience: Managers can make quantitative analyses based on the daily performance of the crew. In special circumstances, experienced flight crews will produce less fatigue than inexperienced flight crews.
   e. Behavior habits: Due to individual differences and customs, some crew members have unhealthy living habits. Such as drinking, smoking, and staying up late. These have a more or less impact on the body function, so such factors need to be considered when analyzing the fatigue of the crew.
2. External factors: It is mainly caused by the time, space, and natural conditions involved in the pairing. Because natural conditions are uncontrollable, external factors are real-time.
   a. Weather: When encountering special weather like thunderstorms, rain, and snow during the task, the crew needs to spend a lot of energy operating the aircraft,

which will increase additional fatigue. When analyzing this kind of influencing factor, it is necessary to use forecasting methods such as weather forecasts to deal with it. The influence of wind and visibility is considered in the division of special airports, so there is no additional analysis here.

b. Pairing: The impact of this factor on crew fatigue needs to be considered from many aspects. The first is the flight time required for the pairing, which needs to be analyzed together with the duty time in the internal factors to determine whether it meets the requirements of CCAR. The second is night flights. The pilot's vision is greatly affected during the night flight, which will increase additional fatigue. Finally, whether the take-off and landing airport is a special airport. Airlines classify airports according to factors such as terrain, climate, air pressure, runway length, and other factors. Airports with different degrees of difficulty will increase varying degrees of fatigue to the crew.

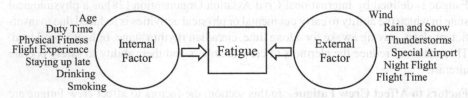

Fig. 3. Structural diagram of the factors to affect crew fatigue

Prediction of Fatigue. In this section, the linear regression model [29] is used to quantitatively evaluate the fatigue degree of the crew after performing the pairing, which provides data for the numerical experiment in Sect. 5.

It is assumed that the fatigue degree of the ith crew member when performing the jth pairing is affected by d factors. $x_{ij} = \left\{ x_{ij}^1, x_{ij}^2, \cdots, x_{ij}^d \right\}$ is defined as the set of influencing factors, where x_{ij}^m represents whether the ith crew member is affected by the mth factor when performing the jth pairing. If it is not affected by this factor, the value is 0. $\omega_{ij} = \left\{ \omega_{ij}^1, \omega_{ij}^2, \cdots, \omega_{ij}^d \right\}$ is the set of parameter values corresponding to each influencing factor, where ω_{ij}^m represents the parameter value corresponding to the mth factor when the ith crew member performing the jth pairing. Through the linear combination of each influencing factor and its corresponding parameters, the fatigue degree f_{ij} generated by the ith crew member performs the jth pairing is predicted, and its function is

$$f_{ij}(x_{ij}) = \omega_{ij} x_{ij}^T. \tag{7}$$

To determine the parameter value set ω_{ij}, the key is to estimate the error between the predicted value and the real value. The commonly used performance measure in linear regression is a mean-square error. Therefore, we collect the information on multiple flights and crew members. For n sample points $x_{ij}^1, x_{ij}^2, \cdots, x_{ij}^n$, the corresponding real fatigue degree is $f_{ij} = \left\{ f_{ij}^1, f_{ij}^2, \cdots, f_{ij}^n \right\}$, to minimize the mean square error

$$\omega_{ij}^* = \arg\min_{\omega_{ij}} \sum_{k=1}^n \left(\omega_{ij} x_{ij}^k - f_{ij}^k \right)^2, \tag{8}$$

Let us take the derivative of $E(\omega_{ij}) = \sum_{k=1}^n \left(\omega_{ij} x_{ij}^k - f_{ij}^k \right)^2$ in (8) from ω_{ij}, the outcome is

$$\frac{\partial E(\omega_{ij})}{\partial(\omega_{ij})} = 2 \left(\omega_{ij} \sum_{k=1}^n \left(x_{ij}^k \right)^2 - \sum_{k=1}^n f_{ij}^k x_{ij}^k \right), \tag{9}$$

Let (9) be equal to 0, the value of ω_{ij} can be obtained.

3.2 Fatigue Balance

The fatigue balance refers to the precise regulation of the crew fatigue to make the overall level reach a balanced state. In other words, we fully consider the factors to affect the crew of all aspects when assigning the pairing, to make the fatigue of any crew equal to that of other crew members as much as possible. This ideal is similar to the minimum inequality proposed by Cornilly. So, the crew fatigue balance by minimizing the variance of crew fatigue is measured in this section.

Under a given assignment $\pi \in \mathcal{A}$, the variance $V_i(\pi)$ of the ith crewmember fatigue is written as

$$V_i(\pi) = \frac{\sum_{j=1}^n \left(t_j^i(\pi) - \bar{t}^i \right)^2}{n}, \tag{10}$$

To make the overall level of crew fatigue level reach a balanced state, the following objective function is obtained

$$V^* = \min\{V(\pi); \pi \in A\} = \min \left\{ \frac{\sum_{i=1}^n V_i(\pi)}{n}; \pi \in A \right\} \tag{11}$$

where the variance function $V(\pi)$ represent the level of fatigue balance under the allocation π, and $V^* = V(\pi^*)$. Because the number of feasible solutions to the crew rostering problem is finite. In finite schemes, there always exists a scheme satisfying formula (11). In this paper, the assignment scheme π^* is called the assignment scheme of fatigue balance.

4 Algorithm of Crew Rostering Problem with Fatigue Balance

Since the crew rostering problem is limited by many constraints, we improved the Min-Cov algorithm proposed by Cornilly and obtained the minimum covariance algorithm with fatigue for solving the crew rostering problem in this section. To better reflect the advantages of the minimum covariance algorithm with fatigue, we introduced two algorithms: the Local Trades algorithm and the Greedy algorithm.

4.1 Minimum Covariance Algorithm with Fatigue (MinCovFatigue)

The purpose of this algorithm is to minimize the variance of crew fatigue. However, if the variance is calculated once in each iteration of the algorithm, it will increase a lot of calculations. To do this, we will split the variance formula.

Assuming that $C = \{1, 2, ..., n\}$ is the crew set, $P = \{1, 2, ..., m\}$ is the pairing set, and $F = (f_{ij}) \in \mathbb{R}^{n \times m}$ is the fatigue matrix. For a given initial assignment $\pi \in \mathcal{A}$, n matrices $F^k = (f_{ij}^k)$, $k = 1, 2, \cdots, n$ are obtained. Now all matrices F^k are rearranged through $\pi' = \{\pi_j\}$, which π_j only rearranges the elements of the jth column of all matrices F^k, and does not affect the elements of other columns in the matrix. Therefore, the row sum formula of the ith row of matrix F^k can be written as

$$t_i^k(\pi') = f_{ij}^k(\pi_j) + \sum_{l \neq j} f_{il}^k(\pi_j) = f_{ij}^k(\pi_j) + t_{i(-j)}^k(\pi_j) = f_{ij}^k(\pi_j) + t_{i(-j)}^k, \quad (12)$$

where $t_{i(-j)}^k(\pi_j)$ is the sum of the elements in the ith row of matrix F^k except the jth column. π_j just rearranges the jth column of the matrix, the change of π_j will not affect the value of $t_{i(-j)}^k(\pi_j)$, so we denote $t_{i(-j)}^k(\pi_j)$ as $t_{i(-j)}^k$.

Next, the expansion of the fatigue variance formula is obtained from (6) and (10).

$$V(\pi') = \frac{\sum_{i=1}^n V_i(\pi)}{n} = \frac{\sum_{k=1}^n \sum_{i=1}^n \left(t_i^k(\pi') - \bar{t}^k\right)^2}{n^2} = \frac{\sum_{k=1}^n \left(\sum_{i=1}^n \left(t_i^k(\pi')\right)^2 - n\left(\bar{t}^k\right)^2\right)}{n^2},$$

From the analysis in Sect. 2.2, the mean value $\bar{t}^k$ is not affected by π'. So to minimize $V(\pi')$, just minimize $\sum_{k=1}^n \sum_{i=1}^n \left(t_i^k(\pi')\right)^2$. From (12), we get

$$\sum_{k=1}^n \sum_{i=1}^n \left(t_i^k(\pi')\right)^2 = \sum_{k=1}^n \sum_{i=1}^n \left(f_{ij}^k(\pi_j) + t_{i(-j)}^k\right)^2$$

$$= \sum_{k=1}^n \sum_{i=1}^n \left[\left(f_{ij}^k(\pi_j)\right)^2 + \left(t_{i(-j)}^k\right)^2 + 2\left(f_{ij}^k(\pi_j) t_{i(-j)}^k\right)\right],$$

The first term in the last expression is to sum the elements of the jth column of the matrix F^k. π_j rearranges the jth column of the matrix F^k, it only changes the position of the elements in the jth column without changing their value, so the change of π_j does not affect the value of the first term. For the second term, in the analysis of (12), it can be obtained that the change of π_j will not affect its value. For the third term, because the change of π_j will cause $f_{ij}^k(\pi_j)$ to multiply with different $t_{i(-j)}^k$, the change of π_j affects the value of the third term. So to minimize $V(\pi')$, we just need to minimize the covariance term $C(\pi') = \sum_{k=1}^n \sum_{i=1}^n f_{ij}^k(\pi_j) t_{i(-j)}^k$. $C(\pi')$ is converted to the scalar product of two vectors $t_{(-j)} = \left\{\sum_{k=1}^n t_{1(-j)}^k, \sum_{k=1}^n t_{2(-j)}^k, \cdots, \sum_{k=1}^n t_{n(-j)}^k\right\}$ and $f_j(\pi_j) = \left\{\sum_{k=1}^n f_{1j}^k(\pi_j), \sum_{k=1}^n f_{2j}^k(\pi_j), \cdots, \sum_{k=1}^n f_{nj}^k(\pi_j)\right\}$. According to Hardy-Littlewood inequality [30], if the order of two vectors is opposite, the scalar product of two vectors can be minimized. So each iteration $V(\pi')$ can be minimized simply by reversing the sorted order of vector $t_{(-j)}$ and vector $f_j(\pi_j)$. This is the core idea of the MinCovFatigue algorithm.

The pseudocode of the MinCovFatigue algorithm is as follows. It is mainly to make the row sum of the matrix F^k as equal as possible, to achieve the purpose of the crew fatigue balance. Each iteration of this algorithm will reduce unless the pairing selected in this iteration is assigned to the correct crew. Therefore, as long as the number of iterations is set large enough, the algorithm can obtain an assignment scheme of approximate fatigue balance, and the objective function is close to the optimal solution V^*. Because the crew rostering problem is NP-hard, it is not expected that the newly proposed algorithm can find the global optimal solution, but the algorithm can find the approximate optimal solution.

Because each column of the matrix F^k has only one non-zero element and the same in the jth column, the change of π_j will only lead to the change of the row where the non-zero element f_{ij}^k of in the jth column is located. To make the overall level of crew fatigue reach the best balance state, we only need to find the component with the smallest value in vector $t_{(-j)}$ and assign the jth pairing to the crew with the corresponding smallest component under the premise of satisfying the matching constraints and horizontal constraints.

Algorithm1: MinCovFatigue

Input: Fatigue matrix $F = (f_{ij}) \in \mathbb{R}^{n \times m}$, initial assignment π.

Output: Final assignment π, and the corresponding fatigue matrix F^k.

1. According to the initial assignment π, the corresponding matrix $F^k = (f_{ij}^k), k = 1, 2,$
   $\cdots, n$ is obtained. Let the maximum number of iterations a_{iter} be a positive integer,
   and $a = 0$.

2. **While** $a \leq a_{iter}$ **do:**

3.   Randomly select $j \in \{1, 2, \cdots, m\}$, determine assignment π_j such that vector $t_{(-j)}$
          is in the reverse sort order of vector $f_j(\pi_j)$, and get the index of the position
          of the non-zero element in the jth column.

4.   **If** $V(\pi)$ is reduced **and** Matching constraints and horizontal constraints are
          satisfied between the jth pairing and the index corresponding to the crew
          then:

5.   Update π_j in assignment π and mark $F^k(\pi_j)$ as F^k.

6.   **End**

7. $a = a + 1$

8. **End**

4.2 Local Trades Algorithm

Algorithm2: Local Trades

Input: Fatigue matrix $F = (f_{ij}) \in \mathbb{R}^{n \times m}$.

Output: Final assignment π, and the corresponding fatigue matrix F^k.

1. The pairing is randomly assigned to any crew member, and the initial assignment π is obtained, it satisfies the matching constraints and horizontal constraints. According to initial assignment π, the corresponding matrix $F^k = (f_{ij}^k)$ is obtained. Let the maximum number of iterations a_{iter} be a positive integer, and $a = 0$.

2. **While** $a \le a_{iter}$ **do:**

3.   Randomly select $i \in \{1,2,\cdots,n\}$ and $j \in \{1,2,\cdots,m\}$, and then assign the jth pairing to the ith crew.

4.   **If** $V(\pi)$ is reduced **and** Matching constraints and horizontal constraints are satisfied between the jth pairing and the ith crew **then：**

5.   Update π_j in assignment π and mark $F^k(\pi_j)$ as F^k.

6.   **End**

7. $a = a + 1$

8. **End**

The Local Trades algorithm is obtained by using the local trades method. This method takes fatigue balance as the optimality criterion. The so-called local trades method is the single trade between any two crew members. If the pairing of one crew member is reassigned to another crew member, then $V(\pi)$ improved, the single trade is executed. The pseudocode of this algorithm is shown in Algorithm 2.

4.3 Greedy Algorithm

The Greedy algorithm aims the balance fatigue and adopts the greedy strategy. At each iteration, the algorithm reduces $V(\pi)$ as much as possible. The pseudocode of this algorithm is shown in Algorithm 3.

Algorithm3: Greedy
Input: Fatigue matrix $F = (f_{ij}) \in \mathbb{R}^{n \times m}$.
Output: Final assignment π , and the corresponding fatigue matrix F^k .

1. Divide fatigue matrix F into n' submatrixs $\{F_i \mid i = 1,2,...,n'\}$, where $n' < n$. The corresponding crew member set C is divided into n' subset $\{c_1, c_2, ..., c_n\}$, and the pairing set P is divided into n' subsets $\{P_1, P_2, ..., P_n\}$.

2. For each submatrix F_i , Its corresponding pairing is randomly assigned to its corresponding any crew member, and the initial assignment π_i is obtained, it satisfies the matching constraints and horizontal constraints.. According to the initial assignment π_i , the corresponding matrix F_i^k , $k = 1,2,..., |C_i|$ is obtained. Let the maximum number of iterations a_{iter} be a positive integer and $a = 0$.

3. **While** $a \le a_{iter}$ **do:**

4.   **For** $i = 1$ **to** n' **do:**

5.   On the premise of satisfying the matching constraints and horizontal constraints, all pairings in P_i are randomly assigned to any crew in C_i to obtain

        a new assignment π_i' .

6.   **If** $V(\pi_i') < V(\pi_i)$ **then:**

7.   Mark π_i' as π_i ,and mark $F^k(\pi_i')$ as F_i^k .

8.   **End**

9.   **End**

10. $a = a + 1$

11. **End**

12. Combine the assignment π_i of all submatrixes to obtain π , and the corresponding fatigue matrix F^k .

5   Numerical Experiment

In this section, we mainly show the experimental results for solving the crew rostering problem by running the three algorithms introduced in Sect. 4. In the experiment, two types of data sets are used to test the algorithm, one is randomly generated, and the other is real data provided by an airline in China.

Data preprocessing: To compare the performance of each algorithm, the number of iterations for each algorithm is fixed as $a_{iter} \in \mathbb{N}^+$ and the maximum number of iterations for the algorithm converged is $a_{cov} \in \mathbb{N}^+$ (For a given number of iterations, we run each algorithm until no improvement is observed, it indicates that the algorithm has converged.). To better reflect that the new algorithm can be used to solve high-dimensional examples. The number of pairings is a multiple of the number of crew members when randomly generating data sets. The randomly generated data set mainly randomly generates the fatigue matrix, the value depends on the uniform distribution when setting the element in the fatigue matrix. To eliminate the influence of dimension, we adjust the elements in the fatigue matrix so that the fatigue degree of each crew is normalized to 100. Before testing the algorithm with the real data set, it is necessary to classify the crew members by rank and extract the pairing of the corresponding rank in the assignment scheme.

Table 1. Parameters of influencing factors of crew fatigue

Factor	Value	Factor	Value
Time on duty	Duty time	Plateau airport	30
Physical	Percentile	Class I airport	30
Age	Proportional	Class II airport	20
Experience	Percentile	Class III airport	10
Thunderstorms	Yes: 10	General Airport	5
Rain and snow	Yes: 10	Flight time	Flight time
Smoking	Yes: 5	Night flight	Yes: 5
Drinking	Yes: 5	Staying up late	Yes: 5

According to the results predicted by the linear regression model and the summary of the usual work, we have given parameter values for the factors to affect crew fatigue. As shown in Table 1. Based on the parameter values from this table we can quantify the fatigue of the crew members in the dataset.

5.1 Algorithm Test Results Based on Randomly Generated Data Sets

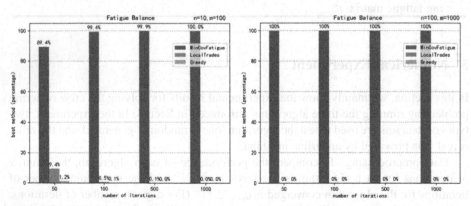

Fig. 4. For different combinations of (n, m), best method for obtaining fatigue balance allocations and the number of iterations. The number of optimal fatigue balance assignments for each algorithm are compared over 1000 different initial random assignments.

Since the crew rostering problem is NP-hard, the algorithm introduced in this paper can only find approximately optimal solutions. That is, we will get different results by running the algorithm each time. To reflect the performance of the three algorithms in solving the crew rostering problem with fatigue balance, 1000 initial assignments are randomly generated to run the algorithm. We will compare the number of optimal fatigue balance assignments for each algorithm (This paper shows in the form of percentages). As shown in Fig. 4, MinCovFatigue algorithm performs best in the case of two different combinations of crew number and pairing number of $(n, m) = (10, 100)$ and $(n, m) = (100, 1000)$. It finds the solution better than the other two algorithms in cases above 90%. The Local Trades algorithm performs relatively well and the Greedy algorithm performs worst.

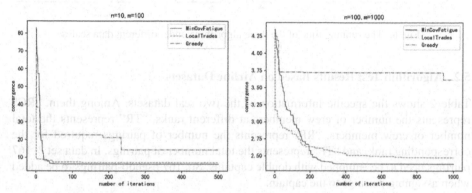

Fig. 5. For different combinations of (n, m), convergence curves of the three algorithms are used to measure the convergence level of three algorithms.

Figure 5 shows the convergence curves of the three algorithms. Figure (a) is the case of $(n, m) = (10, 100)$, and figure (b) is the case of $(n, m) = (100, 1000)$. The convergence specified in this paper is that the objective function has not been improved after a_{cov} iterations. In the case of $(n, m) = (10, 100)$ in figure (a), the MinCovFatigue algorithm performs best. It has reached the convergence level in less than 50 iterations. The Local Trades algorithm performs relatively well. It reaches the convergence level in less than 150 iterations. The Greedy algorithm performs worst. The case of $(n, m) = (100, 1000)$ in figure (b) is similar to the situation in figure (a). MinCovFatigue algorithm performs best. It reaches the convergence level around 400 iterations. The Local Trades algorithm performs relatively well. It reaches the convergence level in less than 700 iterations. The Greedy algorithm performs worst.

Figure 6 shows the running time of the three algorithms under different data scales. Figure (a) shows that the fixed number of crew is 10 and the number of pairings is changed. Figure (b) shows that the fixed number of pairings is 1000 and the number of crew members is changed. It can be seen from the figure that, the running time of each iteration of the MinCovFatigue algorithm and the Local Trades algorithm is hardly affected by the change in the number of pairings or the number of crew members except for the Greedy algorithm. But the total running time of the three algorithms is approximately linear with the scale of the data.

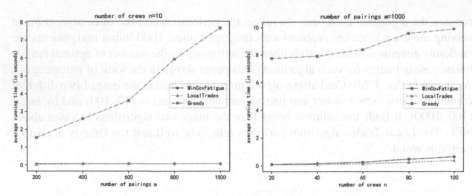

Fig. 6. The running time of the three algorithms under different data scales

5.2 Algorithm Test Results Based on Airline Datasets

Table 2 shows the specific information of the two real datasets. Among them, "RC" represents the number of crew members at different ranks, "TR" represents the total number of crew members, "RP" represents the number of pairings required for the corresponding rank, and "TP" represents the total number of pairings. In data set 2, 167 pairings need to be equipped with double captains. So, 167 pseudo-pairings to be added when assigning pairings to the captain.

Table 2. Data set information

Data Set	Rank	RC	TR	RP	TP
Data Set 1	Captain	11	21	205	205
	1st Co-pilot	10		205	
Data Set 2	Captain	371	836	1268	1268
	Line Captain	17		36	
	1st Co-pilot	335		1187	
	2nd Co-pilot	113		341	

Table 3 and Table 4 are statistical tables of the final assignment data obtained by the three algorithms to solve the crew rostering problem with fatigue balance. These results are obtained after running the algorithm 1000 times repeatedly. It can be seen from the table that the variance value obtained by the MinCovFatigue algorithm is the smallest. The results obtained by running the MinCovFatigue algorithm are more than 10 times optimized on the basis of the initial results. Compared with the other two algorithms, the MinCovFatigue algorithm has excellent performance in terms of optimization effect. The Local Trades algorithm also got relatively good results. The Greedy algorithm is not suitable for high-dimensional real instances, and its optimization effect is not ideal.

Table 3. The fatigue balance (variance) of matrix F for the initial random allocations and after using three algorithms in data set 1

Date Set	Rank	Algorithm	Fatigue Balance		
			Min	Max	Mean
Data Set 1	Captain	MinCovFatigue	3.1006	5.5717	4.2844
		Local Trades	70.6521	76.2543	74.5836
		Greedy	84.3089	211.5156	132.1731
	1st co-pilot	MinCovFatigue	2.3090	5.7870	3.6026
		Local Trades	131.8421	154.2413	140.9453
		Greedy	138.0054	287.3654	193.9844

Table 4. The fatigue balance (variance) of matrix F for the initial random allocations and after using three algorithms in data set 2

Date Set	Rank	Algorithm	Fatigue Balance		
			Min	Max	Mean
Data Set 2	Captain	MinCovFatigue	0.0074	0.0078	0.0077
		Local Trades	2.1335	2.1368	2.1348
		Greedy	3.8754	3.8770	3.8762
	Line captain	MinCovFatigue	0.4341	0.9365	0.7324
		Local Trades	2.1685	3.1378	2.8191
		Greedy	3.1398	4.3151	3.6712
	1st co-pilot	MinCovFatigue	0.0009	0.0013	0.0011
		Local Trades	2.5421	2.5437	2.5431
		Greedy	3.6919	3.6928	3.6922
	2nd co-pilot	MinCovFatigue	0.1416	0.2694	0.1774
		Local Trades	2.7214	2.9108	2.8547
		Greedy	4.9842	5.0359	4.9842

6   Conclusions

This paper mainly solves the crew rostering problem with fatigue balance, in which fatigue balance means that the overall level of crew fatigue reaches a balanced state. Based on this problem, we analyze the factors to affect crew fatigue, establish a linear regression model to predict the crew fatigue, and constructs the corresponding fatigue matrix in this paper. Based on the fatigue matrix, the crew rostering problem is transformed into a matrix rearrangement problem, and the minimum covariance algorithm is improved to obtain a new algorithm called the minimum covariance algorithm with fatigue for finding the assignment scheme of fatigue balance. It can be seen from the final experiments that the new algorithm performs better than the other algorithms in terms of optimization objective, convergence speed, and running time. The algorithm is not limited by the number of datasets and can be used in high-dimensional instances.

References

1. Teodorović, D., Lučić, P.: Metaheuristics approach to the aircrew rostering problem. Ann. Oper. Res. **155**(1), 311–338 (2007)
2. Ryan, D.M., Day, P.R.: Flight attendant rostering for short-haul airline operations. Oper. Res. **45**(5), 649–661 (1997)
3. El Moudani, W., Alberto Nunes Cosenza, C., de Coligny, M., Mora-Camino, F.: A bi-criterion approach for the airlines crew rostering problem. In: Zitzler, E., Thiele, L., Deb, K., Coello Coello, C.A., Corne, D. (eds.) EMO 2001. LNCS, vol. 1993, pp. 486–500. Springer, Heidelberg (2001). https://doi.org/10.1007/3-540-44719-9_34
4. Liu, X., Zhang, X., Li, W., Zhang, X.: Swarm optimization algorithms applied to multi-resource fair allocation in heterogeneous cloud computing systems. Computing **99**(12), 1231–1255 (2017). https://doi.org/10.1007/s00607-017-0561-x
5. Liu, X., Zhang, X., Cui, Q., et al.: Implementation of ant colony optimization combined with tabu search for multi-resource fair allocation in heterogeneous cloud computing. In: 2017 IEEE 3rd International Conference, pp. 196–201 (2017)
6. Zhang, J., Xie, N., Zhang, X., Yue, K., Li, W., Kumar, D.: Machine learning based resource allocation of cloud computing in auction. Comput. Mater. Continua **56**(1), 123–135 (2018)
7. Zhang, X., Liu, X., Li, W., Zhang, X.: Trade-off between energy consumption and makespan in the mapreduce resource allocation problem. In: Sun, X., Pan, Z., Bertino, E. (eds.) ICAIS 2019. LNCS, vol. 11633, pp. 239–250. Springer, Cham (2019). https://doi.org/10.1007/978-3-030-24265-7_21
8. Yang, X., Zhang, X., et al.: A truthful auction mechanism for cumulative resource allocation in mobile edge computing. In: The 2020 4th International Conference on High Performance Compilation, Computing and Communications, pp. 63–69 (2020)
9. Zhang, X., Li, J., Li, G., Li, W.: Generalized asset fairness mechanism for multi-resource fair allocation mechanism with two different types of resources. Clust. Comput. **25**, 3389–3403 (2022). https://doi.org/10.1007/s10586-022-03548-9
10. Zhang, J., Chi, L., Xie, N., Yang, X., Zhang, X., Li, W.: Strategy-proof mechanism for online resource allocation in cloud and edge collaboration. Computing **104**(2), 383–412 (2021). https://doi.org/10.1007/s00607-021-00962-6
11. Antosik, J.L.: Automatic monthly crew assignment: a new approach. In: Proceedings of the AGIFORS Symposium, pp. 369–402 (1978)
12. Byrne, J.: A preferential bidding system for technical aircrew. In: Proceedings of the AGIFORS Symposium, pp. 87–99 (1988)
13. Kasemsontitum, B., Jeenanunta, C., Limlawan, V.: Airline crew rostering problem using particle swarm optimization. In: The 2011 IEEE International Conference on Quality and Reliability, pp. 501–505 (2011)
14. Voß, S., Doi, T., Nishi, T.: Two-level decomposition-based matheuristic for airline crew rostering problems with fair working time. Eur. J. Oper. Res. **267**(2), 428–438 (2018)
15. Arayikanon, K., Chutima, P.: Many-objective low-cost airline cockpit crew rostering optimisation. Comput. Ind. Eng. **150**, 1–12 (2020)
16. Wang, J., Zhou, M., Zhang, Z.: Construction-based optimization approaches to airline crew rostering problem. IEEE Trans. Automat. Sci. Eng. **17**(3), 1399–1409 (2020)

17. Wu, A., Desaulniers, G., Quesnel, F., Soumis, F.: Deep-learning-based partial pricing in a branch-and-price algorithm for personalized crew rostering. Comput. Oper. Res. **138**, 1–15 (2022)
18. Deng, B.: An improved honey badger algorithm by genetic algorithm and levy flight distribution for solving airline crew rostering problem. IEEE Access **10**, 108075–108088 (2022)
19. Soumis, F., Marquis, G., Desrosiers, J., Gamache, M.: A column generation approach for large-scale aircrew rostering problems. Oper. Res. **47**(2), 247–263 (1999)
20. Strauss, C., Dawid, H., König, J.: An enhanced rostering model for airline crews. Comput. Oper. Res. **28**(7), 671–688 (2001)
21. Kohl, N., Karisch, S.E.: Airline crew rostering: problem types, modeling and optimization. Ann. Oper. Res. **127**, 223–257 (2004)
22. Maenhout, B., Vanhoucke, M.: A hybrid scatter search heuristic for personalized crew rostering in the airline industry. Eur. J. Oper. Res. **206**(1), 155–167 (2010)
23. Medard, C.P., Sawhney, N.: Airline crew scheduling from planning to operations. Eur. J. Oper. Res. **183**(3), 1013–1027 (2007)
24. Sunarto, A., Rahman, A., Santosa, B.: Using differential evolution method to solve crew rostering problem. Appl. Math. **1**(4), 316–325 (2010)
25. Novak, A., Brezonakova, A., Badanik, B., Lusiak, T.: Implications of crew rostering on airline operations. Transp. Res. Procedia **44**, 2–7 (2020)
26. China C. A. A. o. China Civil Aviation Regulations -121-R5/R6, pp. 188–196 (2020)
27. Cornilly, D., Puccetti, G., Rüschendorf, L., Vanduffel, S.: Fair allocation of indivisible goods with minimum inequality or minimum envy. Eur. J. Oper. Res. **297**(2), 741–752 (2022)
28. I.C.A. Organization. Manual for the Oversight of Fatigue Management Approaches, p. 1 (2017)
29. Zhou, Z.: Machine Learning, pp. 53–57. Tsinghua University Press, China (2016)
30. Hardy, G.H., Polya, G., Littlewood, J.E.: Inequalities, 2nd edn, pp. 261–262. Cambridge University Press, Cambridge (1952)

Data-Driven Approach for Predicting Surface Subsidence Velocity from Geotechnical Parameters

Priyanka[1] , Praveen Kumar[1]([✉]) , Pratik Chaturvedi[1] , K. V. Uday[2] ,
and Varun Dutt[1]

[1] ACS Lab, Indian Institute of Technology Mandi, Mandi 175075, Himachal Pradesh, India
bluecodeindia@gmail.com, prateek@dtrl.drdo.in,
varun@iitmandi.ac.in
[2] Geotechnical Engineering Lab, Indian Institute of Technology Mandi, Mandi 175075,
Himachal Pradesh, India
uday@iitmandi.ac.in

Abstract. The Himalayan mountains are prone to landslide disasters, which cause injury and fatalities among people. Remote sensing, particularly interferometric synthetic aperture radar (InSAR) based analyses, may help find the surface subsidence velocities, the rate of vertical movement of the Earth's surface downward. These subsidence velocities may help identify areas prone to landslides. Literature suggests that geotechnical parameters may contribute to understanding surface subsidence velocities. However, there is less research on developing data-driven algorithms that relate the geotechnical parameters with the subsidence velocities in an area. In this research, data-driven algorithms, relying upon geotechnical parameters measured across diverse locations in the Himalayan mountains, predict the subsidence velocities measured from InSAR analysis of open-source Sentinel-1 data of the same area. An InSAR-based displacement map of the study area is generated using the Small Baseline Subset (SBAS) algorithm. The ranking of geotechnical parameters is first conducted using several feature selection methods. Out of 23 parameters, 11 top-ranked features are selected for developing data-driven algorithms, including multiple regression, random forest, instance-based learner, an optimized version of support vector regression named sequential minimal optimization regression (SMOreg), multilayer perceptron (MLP), and an ensemble of MLP and SMOreg (MLP-SMO). These algorithms used the top-ranked geotechnical parameters and predicted the subsidence velocities. Results suggested that the MLP-SMO algorithm provided the best fit for data in 10-fold cross-validation with 0.94 RMSE. The MLP was the second-best model with 1.6 RMSE. Implications for developing subsidence velocity models using geotechnical parameters via data-driven approaches are discussed.

Keywords: Subsidence velocities · geotechnical parameters · InSAR · multiple regression · random forest · instance-based learner · support vector regression · multilayer perceptron

1 Introduction

Himalaya is one of the world's most seismically active and hazardous region [1]. As a result, various big landslides happened in the region, destroying infrastructure. For example, these landslides have resulted in almost 200 lives lost and $82 million in infrastructure-related losses per year [2]. Landslides mainly occur due to rainfall, earthquakes, geological, and man-made factors [3]. Given the damages caused by landslides, it is essential to closely monitor the unstable slopes to reduce the risk of landslides. A way of monitoring unstable mountain slopes is via surface subsidence velocities, the rate of vertical movement of the Earth's surface downward, evaluated using the Interferometric Synthetic Aperture Radar (InSAR) technique [4].

InSAR technique has been applied at local scales to monitor surface movements and ground subsidence [4–7]. With the advent of the Sentinel satellite program, the InSAR technique has the advantage of open-source data availability, broad area coverage, good spatial and temporal resolution, and operation under all weather conditions [4]. The small baseline subset InSAR (SBAS-InSAR) and the permanent scatterer InSAR (PS-InSAR) are the most common InSAR methods [5]. The SBAS-InSAR could be used for the measurement of geotechnical parameters and to monitor the slow deformation on the earth's surface [5]. The SBAS-InSAR interferometry technique has high accuracy in detecting broad areas of ground deformation, making it suitable for investigating surface deformation at regional and local scales [5].

In addition to the InSAR methods, the geotechnical parameters of an area may likely aid in understanding slope instabilities. The geotechnical parameters may help improve the accuracy of the physical models used to predict average subsidence velocities [8–10]. Prior research has evaluated the importance of geotechnical parameters for slope failure assessment [8–10]. For example, the geotechnical parameters, including particle size, porosity, saturated permeability, shear strength, fines content, plasticity index, liquid limit, plastic limit, and dry density, were considered to recognize slope failure modes [8–10].

Beyond physical models, an alternate way of investigating the role of geotechnical parameters in causing slope failures is by machine learning (ML) algorithms [19–21]. Thus, the ML algorithms could help in predicting slope movements and determining the effect of geotechnical parameters on slope movements [22]. Prior research has developed different ML techniques such as support vector machine (SVM), multilayer perceptron (MLP), Bayesian network (BN), decision tree (DT), and random forest (RF) for different problems in geotechnical areas [20–27]. Although various ML algorithms have been developed to predict the subsidence velocity of multiple geotechnical regions. However, the application of ML algorithms for determining an area's average subsidence velocity has received less attention in the Himalayan mountains of India.

The current study fills this knowledge gap by measuring average subsidence velocity in the Kamand valley in the Mandi region of Himachal Pradesh, India. Specifically, the current study has the following objectives: To obtain average subsidence velocity values of the study area using Sentinel-1 data and SBAS-InSAR approach; to evaluate a set of geotechnical parameters obtained in-situ and from laboratory measurements; to develop different ML algorithms to predict average subsidence velocities; and, to evaluate the relative importance of different geotechnical parameters in causing slope instability via ML algorithms. To achieve these objectives, different ML algorithms, including optimized version of support vector regression (SVR) named sequential minimal optimization regression (SMOreg), MLP, RF, instance-based learner (IBk), multiple regression, and an ensemble of MLP and SVR were developed to predict the average subsidence velocities of different sample points in the study area. Also, a rank order of different geotechnical parameters was determined by various feature-selection method.

2 Background

Remote sensing, mainly the InSAR technique, has been used at regional scales to monitor ground subsidence movement [4–7]. The two most common InSAR techniques are the permanent scatters InSAR (PS-InSAR) method and the small baseline subset InSAR (SBAS-InSAR) method [5]. In PS-InSAR, only stable pixels in the images are observed over long time intervals. Once stable pixels are detected, the line of sight (LOS) velocity can be estimated based on the displacement of the pixel in the image. The SBAS-InSAR method calculates the displacement by measuring the displacement of the slowly-decorrelating filtered phase (SDFP) pixels in the images. Hu et al. (2014) measured the average subsidence velocity in three dimensions using InSAR mapping [4]. Similarly, Milillo et al. (2018) used the multi-temporal InSAR (MT-InSAR) technique to evaluate the greenfield deformation assessment [6]. Next, Casu et al. (2006) used the SBAS-InSAR technique to investigate ground subsidence velocity using European Remote Sensing Satellite sensors in the Los Angeles (California) and Napoli Bay (Italy) test areas [7].

Apart from the InSAR methods, several researchers have detailed a field survey to find the geotechnical parameters, including dry density, porosity, saturated permeability, shear strength, and grain size parameters [8–10]. These findings suggest that geotechnical parameters play an important role in landslides. Prior research has also proposed saturated permeability, dry density, porosity, and fine content to understand various modes of slope failure [8–10]. Furthermore, prior research has assessed the significance of geotechnical and hydrological parameters (Atterberg limits, grain size, unit weight, porosity, shear strength, and in situ saturated hydraulic conductivity), which control slope failure triggering factors [9]. Moreover, the experiment discovered the correlation between selected morphometric parameters (planar curvature, profile curvature, peak distance, and slope angle) and soil types (or grain size). The geotechnical and hydrological data for this experiment were collected from 100 different locations throughout Tuscany (Italy). Results revealed that the profile, planar, and slope curvature highly correlated to the grain size classes.

Beyond physical models, prior research has developed different ML algorithms such as support vector regressor (SVR), BN, MLP, DT, and RF for problems in different geotechnical areas [11–16]. For example, the SVR and geographic information system-based multi-criteria decision analyses (MCDA) were developed by Kavzoglu et al. (2014) to produce landslide susceptibility maps [11]. The SVR and MCDA methods were trained with data from a shallow landslide in Trabzon province (Turkey). This experiment compared the SVR and MCDA algorithms with the logistic regression (LR) algorithm. The findings indicated that the SVR and MCDA algorithms had higher accuracy than LR.

Furthermore, Ali et al. (2021) investigated the performance of various ML algorithms in landslide susceptibility in the Kysuca river basin, Slovakia [12]. The RF, Nave Bayes (NB), and fuzzy decision-making analytic network process algorithms were developed to compare in this study. Results revealed that the RF formed better than the other algorithms for landslide susceptibility. Similarly, Chen et al. (2018) developed and compared several ML algorithms such as RF, radial basis function (RBF), Bayesian network (BN), and logistic model tree (LMT) for landslide susceptibility mapping in Chongren County, China [13]. The findings indicated that the RF performed better than the other algorithms. Furthermore, Hong et al. (2018) created ML algorithms like RF, Bagging, and AdaBoost for assessing landslide susceptibility using the base DT classifier [14]. Results revealed that the DT algorithm showed better accuracy for landslide susceptibility mapping.

Similarly, Kumar et al. (2019) developed autoregression (AR), conventional seasonal autoregressive integrated moving average (SARIMA), and sequential minimal optimization regression (SMOreg) algorithms for soil movement predictions [15]. The data for this experiment were taken from the Tangni landslide, Uttarakhand, India. The findings suggested that the SARIMA was the best algorithm to predict landslide movements. Furthermore, Li et al. (2019) developed an MLP, particle-swarm-optimized MLP (PSO-MLP), an information value (IV), and a backpropagation neural network (BPNN) [16]. The results revealed that the PSO-MLP algorithm outperformed the other algorithms. Although different ML techniques have been developed in diverse geotechnical areas, the application of ML techniques for InSAR-based average subsidence velocity prediction has been less explored in the Himalayan region of India.

The literature survey suggests that the InSAR techniques could estimate the subsidence velocity. Next, we found that the geotechnical parameters play an essential role in triggering the landslides. Furthermore, the ML algorithms could predict landslide displacement by inputting these geotechnical features. The major challenge is to find the crucial geotechnical parameters that affect the landslide. Thus, one needs to do feature engineering on the geotechnical parameters and find some essential features. Next, one needs to develop several ML algorithms to predict the subsidence velocity by inputting these essential features. As per the author's knowledge, this is the first kind of study for subsidence velocity prediction via ML algorithms in the Kamand valley of Himachal Pradesh, India.

3 Data Attributes

The present work uses the SBAS-InSAR approach, built over the Differential InSAR (DInSAR) technique. DInSAR is used to measure the deformation on the visible Earth's surface with high accuracy [17]. In this approach, the temporal evolution of monitored surface deformations is performed using the PInSAR and SBAS-InSAR, which properly integrate the available information from a set of multi-temporal interferograms relevant to a region of interest [18]. Sentinel-1 data stack was used for time and path prediction of landslides [19]. The surface movement was monitored using InSAR analysis on a stack of C-band SAR images (wavelength 5.6 cm, frequency 5.4 GHz) formulated by the Sentinel-1 satellite. The analysis was carried out using Sentinel-1 images acquired using the Interferometric Wide (IW) swath mode, which is the primary acquisition mode over land. The information was gathered over a 250-km swath with a spatial resolution of 5 m by 14 m. (angle and range). Images were taken along the ascending orbit at a 40.78-degree incidence angle. The Sentinel-1 archive was processed using the Small Baseline Subset (SBAS) method, which is one of the most advanced methods for analyzing multi-temporal SAR stacks. This technique uses time-series data to measure deformation through interferometric methods.

Figure 1 shows the location and the average subsidence velocity of the study area on the map by Google Earth. The average subsidence velocity values for the different points have been determined from the SBAS-InSAR between December 2014 and January 2019. SARSCAPE software was used to carry out the SBAS processing [20]. From the stack and position, a primary image was chosen. In addition, distance plots were generated for all secondary images in relation to the primary image. For each secondary image in relation to the primary image, differential interferograms were generated. The SBAS generates interferograms by selecting SAR data pairs from a network. This helps in the reduction of noise in the interferograms. During the generation of interferograms, Goldstein filtering algorithm was used to further reduce the phase noise [21]. As seen in Fig. 1, the velocity values are shown in different colors, where the red and orange colors show higher rate of average subsidence velocities (>60 mm/year), yellow color shows medium (20–50 mm/year), while green color shows smaller values of average subsidence velocity, i.e., in the range of 10–20 mm/year. Blue colored areas show upliftment. The various markers in red color shown in the Fig. 1 are indicating the locations from which soil samples were collected for laboratory-based analyses.

The soil samples data was collected from the Kamand valley in the Mandi district of Himachal Pradesh, India. The soil samples data contains twenty-three attributes like elevation of the hill, gravel (in percentage), lithology of a rock, sand (in percentage), saturated unit weight, slope angle, liquid limit (LL) of the soil, plastic limit (PL) of the soil, saturated hydraulic conductivities (ks) for gravel (in cm/s), relative compaction (in percentage), the plasticity index (IP) represents the difference between LL and PL, shear strength (C) of soil (in kPa), natural water content (in percentage), optimum moisture content (in percentage), saturated moisture content, angle of internal friction (in degrees), average subsidence velocity of soil, specific gravity, porosity, fines content (in percentage), D10, D30, D50, and D60 (in mm; where, Dxx means that xx% of the soil particles have a diameter that is smaller than the Dxx size). The average subsidence velocity was predicted from other attributes.

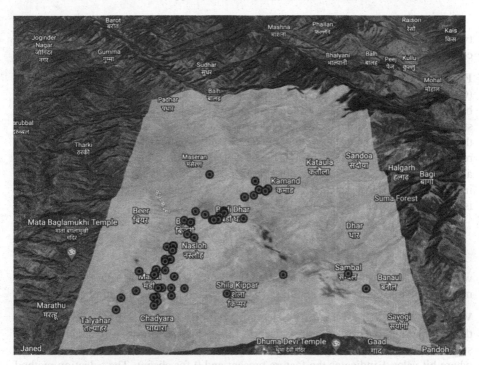

Fig. 1. Location of the Kamand valley Himachal Pradesh, India on Google Earth.

4 Methodology

4.1 Attribute Selection

Training the classification and regression algorithm may become difficult with high dimensional data because it requires high computational power. The irrelevant features in the high dimensional data could mislead the classifier, reducing the algorithm's performance. Removing the irrelevant features from the data is desirable to decrease the computational power and increase the algorithm's performance. Instead of using all the twenty-three attributes in the algorithm to classify the zonation map, we used only relevant attributes from the twenty-three attributes that best classified the zonation map. For the selection of the relevant attributes, we developed several attribute selection methods discussed as follows:

Correlation-Based Feature Selection Method. This method calculated the Pearson correlation coefficient of two attributes [22]. The correlation coefficient value could be between −1 and 1. The high correlation value is close to −1 and 1, and 0 means no correlation. The Pearson correlation coefficient between x and y attributes could be calculated as per the following equation:

$$Correlation(r) = \frac{\sum_{i=1}^{n}(x_i - \bar{x})(y_i - \bar{y})}{\sqrt{\sum_{i=1}^{n}(x_i - \bar{x})^2 \sum_{i=1}^{n}(y_i - \bar{y})^2}} \tag{1}$$

After calculating the correlation coefficient between average subsidence velocity and twenty-three attributes, we assigned the rank to all twenty-three attributes based on their correlation result.

Filter Approach for Feature Selection Method. A correlation-based feature selector (CFS) is a filter technique that ranks feature subsets using a heuristic evaluation function based on correlation [22]. The evaluation function prefers subsets with attributes that are strongly correlated with the class but uncorrelated with one another. Irrelevant features that have little to no correlation with a class should be ignored. It is critical to remove redundant features which are strongly correlated with other features. The degree to which a feature predicts classes that are not already predicted by other features in areas of the instance space determines its acceptance. The CFS's feature subset evaluation function is represented as follows:

$$H_s = \frac{n\, r_{cf}}{\sqrt{n + n(n - 1)r_{ff}}} \tag{2}$$

where r_{cf} represents the mean correlation between the class and feature, and r_{ff} is the mean correlation between the features. The value of n represents the number of features.

Wrapper Approach for Feature Selection Method. Kohavi et al. (1997) developed the wrapper approach for feature selection [23]. This algorithm searches all possible subsets of features. The algorithm's initial stage has n number of bits for n features, where bit value 1 indicates the feature present and 0 for absent. The selection method starts with the full set of attributes. In the next stage, these feature subsets pass to the induction algorithm. All subsets give to the induction algorithm with n cross-validation and estimate the accuracy of the induction algorithm. In the next stage, one more feature adds to the subsets and calculates the algorithms' accuracy via passing these subsets. After calculating the accuracy of induction algorithms via giving all possible feature sets, choose those subsets with maximum accuracy.

Figure 2 showing all possible states of the three-feature subset selection, where bit 1 indicates the feature present and 0 represents the feature absent. Every node in Fig. 2 is linked to those that have added or removed a feature. For example, the subset at level one contains no features, and the subset at level two contains the first, second, and third features. Each subset passed to the induction algorithm and estimated the accuracy for this subset.

This algorithm started with the full set of attributes and searched in the backward direction until only one attribute was left in the set. We chose the J48 DT as an induction algorithm and 10-fold cross-validation (10-CV) in this experiment.

Instance-Based Feature Selection Method. Kira and Rendell developed the Relief algorithm for feature selection in 1992 [24]. This algorithm selects the statistically relevant features in the dataset. Initially, the algorithm assigned the weights (W) to all features as zero. Later in every iteration of training, it updated the weights according to the following equation:

$$W_{i+1} = W_i - (x_i - h_i)^2 + (x_i - m_i)^2 \tag{3}$$

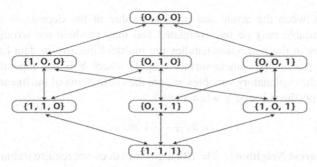

Fig. 2. All possible states for three features subset selection.

where W_i is the feature's weights, and x_i represents the training instance in the ith iteration. The h_i and m_i represent the nearest neighbor instance from the same class and opposite class of the instance x_i, respectively.

After calculating the average weights for all the features in training, the relief algorithm selects the best feature with a weight greater than the threshold (τ) value. The threshold value could be estimated with the statistical method of interval estimation. The value of the threshold should be chosen between 0 and 1.

In this algorithm, we have selected the ranker search method for the attribute search method. According to the evaluator, the ranker search method sorted the attributes by their score and discarded the attributes whose score was less than the threshold. The threshold value was set at -1 in this algorithm.

Classifier-Based Feature Selection Method. Users defined a classifier in this method and predicted the target class by placing various features in the classifier as input [22]. Next, it estimates the accuracy of the classifier based on the input features. The strength of the feature could be calculated by first measuring the classifier's accuracy by considering only one feature then calculating the accuracy of the classifier by removing it from the features set.

In this paper, we defined the ZeroR as a classifier with 10-CV. The standard deviation threshold was set at 1% to repeat the cross-validation if the standard deviation of mean accuracy exceeds this value. Furthermore, we have selected the ranker search method for the attribute search method. According to the evaluator, the ranker search method sorted the attributes by their score and discarded the attributes whose score was less than the threshold. The threshold value was set at 0.01 in this algorithm.

4.2 Machine Learning Algorithms

Random Forest. Breiman developed the RF algorithm in 2001 for classification and regression [25]. The RF creates several random DTs at the time of training. The output of the RF is the majority class (classification) or the value that is the mean of the prediction of individual trees (regression). By aggregation, the RF algorithm corrects the problem of overfitting in decision trees [25].

Multiple Regression. Multiple regression has many explanatory variables and one dependent variable [26]. Multiple regression means fitting a linear model to reduce the distance between the actual and predicted value of the dependent variable. The explanatory variable may be intercorrelated and may produce the wrong result. The ridge parameter in the regression handles the multicollinearity in data [26]. A multiple regression represents a linear surface (Eq. 4) where Y is the dependent variable, $x_1, \ldots, x_n$ are the explanatory variables, m_n are the coefficients of the linear surface, and c is the intercept (the value of Y when x = 0).

$$Y = m_1 x_1 + \cdots + m_n x_n + c \tag{4}$$

IBk (or K–Nearest Neighbor). The IBk algorithm does not require training and calculates the distance between the given data point and the k number of nearest data points [27]. The distance function could be the Euclidian or the Manhattan distance. As a result, this algorithm will yield the average of k-nearest data points. Thus, IBk has parameters k and distance function to vary.

Sequential Minimal Optimization Regression (SMOreg). The SMOreg is a variant of the SVM [28]. The run-time complexity of the SVM is very high during the training on a large dataset. The SMOreg algorithm tries to fit the data in iteration instead of providing all data simultaneously. As a result, SMOreg reduces the training time. Each iteration returns the Lagrange multiplier (alpha), which satisfies the constraints. These alphas (ai) are used to find the support vectors for the margin boundary. SMOreg has two parameters, exponent (E) of a kernel function and complexity (C) of margin. The C parameter selection allows ignoring several support vectors to select the margin lines. The E parameter is the exponential power of a kernel function. For example, E value 1 is a linear kernel. The objective function of the SMOreg is written in Eq. 4 with constraints as subject to (s.t.). Next, Eq. 5 explains the kernel functions used in the SMOreg's objective function.

$$min_\alpha \tfrac{1}{2} \sum_i^m \sum_j^m \alpha_i\alpha_j y_i y_j (X_i \cdot X_j) - \sum_i^m \alpha_i$$
$$s.t. \ 0 \le \alpha_i \le C; \ \text{for any } i = 1, 2, \ldots, m \tag{5}$$

where α_i are the Lagrange multipliers and C is the complexity parameters. The $(X_i \cdot X_j)$ is represent the kernel. The polynomial kernel (PK), radial basis function (RBF), and Pearson VII kernel (PUK) were used in SMOreg [29].

MLP. The MLP is a class of neural network mainly used for nonlinear function approximation [30]. As shown in Fig. 3, it contains three layers, input, hidden, and output layers. Each layer includes several neurons with an activation function. The input layer holds the information and passes it to the hidden layer. Next, the hidden layer transforms the input features into another dimension and provides a better feature representation to the output layer. The output layer is the final layer that does regression tasks. The backpropagation technique decreases the error of the MLP and updates the layers' weights by gradient descent [31]. Equation 6 shows the error calculation in the nth iteration at the output layer.

$$E_n = \frac{1}{2}\left(y_n - \hat{y}_n\right)^2 \tag{6}$$

where y_n and $\hat{y}_n$ are the actual and predicted value in the nth iteration. Equation 7 shows the updating in weights using the gradient descent method.

$$\Delta w_{ji} = -\eta \frac{\partial E}{\partial w_{ji}^l} v_i \tag{7}$$

where v_i is the output of the previous layer neuron, w_{ji}^l is the weight value at the jth neuron in layer l connected to the ith neuron in the previous layer, and η denotes the learning rate such that error minimizes faster. The $\frac{\partial E}{\partial w_{ji}^l}$ is a partial derivative of the error with respect to weight in a layer l.

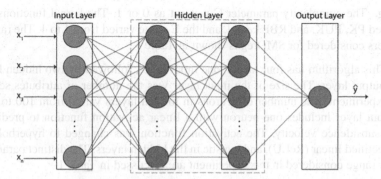

Fig. 3. An architecture of MLP algorithm.

MLP-SMO. An ensemble of MLP and SMOreg algorithms was developed where the SMOreg fitted the output of the MLP. First, the MLP network implements the global approximation, and SMOreg tries to find the local approximation in the MLP output data [32]. The parameters of the SMOreg in the MLP-SMO were recalibrated, and MLP parameters were fixed.

4.3 Optimization of the Algorithms

Random Forest. In RF, a key parameter is a number of features (nF) to consider in each split point. In this paper, we varied the nF parameter between 0 and 10 to calibrate the RF algorithm.

Multiple Regression. The ridge parameter was varied from 10 to 70. The M5 (Modeled Tree) or greedy method was used as an attribute selection method in the algorithm. The range of parameters considered for multiple regression is shown in Table 1.

IBk. The k parameter in IBk varied from 1 to 10, and the distance metric was considered Euclidean or Manhattan distance. The range of parameters considered for IBk is shown in Table 1.

SMOreg. The complexity parameter C was set as 0 or 1. The kernel functions were considered PK, PUK, and RBF kernel, and the E value varied from 1 to 4. The range of parameters considered for SMOreg is shown in Table 1.

MLP. This algorithm has four layers: one input layer, followed by two hidden layers, and an output layer. The size of the input layer was the number of attributes selected in this experiment. The number of neurons in hidden layers varied from 100 to 1500. The output layer includes one neuron with a linear activation function to predict the average subsidence velocity. The activation function was changed to hyperbolic tan (tanh), rectified linear (ReLU), and logistic in the hidden layers. The distinct parameters and their range considered in this experiment are discussed in Table 1.

MLP-SMO. The MLP parameters in the MLP-SMO were fixed as calibrated in the individual MLP algorithm. The range of SMOreg parameters in MLP-SMO was considered as specified for the individual SMOreg.

4.4 10-Fold Cross Validations (10-CV)

The performance of the ML algorithms was evaluated using the 10-CV technique [33]. The 10-CV technique randomly shuffles the dataset, then divides it into ten halves. Nine of these were selected for training and one for testing. This process is repeated ten times, with the output being the average of the ten iterations.

4.5 Error Measures

To calculate the error between actual and predicted values, the mean absolute error (MSE), root-mean-squared error (RMSE), and relative root-squared error (RRSE) in percent were used. The equations of the different errors are as follows:

$$MAE = \frac{1}{n} \sum\nolimits_{i=1}^{n} |y_i - \hat{y}_i| \qquad (8)$$

$$RMSE = \sqrt{\frac{1}{n} \sum\nolimits_{i=1}^{n} (y_i - \hat{y}_i)^2} \qquad (9)$$

Table 1. Range of parameters in the algorithms.

Parameter	Range of Parameters
	Random Forest
Bags (I)	50, 60, 70, 80, 90, and 100
Number of Features (nF)	0 to 10
	Linear Regression
Ridge	10 to 70
Attribute selection Method	M5, Greedy
	IBk
K	1 to 10
Distance function	Euclidean, Manhattan
	SMOreg
C	0 or 1
E	1 to 4
Kernel Function	PK, RBF, PUK
	MLP
Size of the input layer	11
Hidden layers	2
Neurons in hidden layers	100 to 1500
Activation	tanh, ReLU, logistic
Momentum	0.2
Learning Rate	0.3

$$RRSE = \sqrt{\frac{\sum_{i=1}^{n}(y_i - \hat{y}_i)^2}{\sum_{i=1}^{n}(y_i - \overline{y})^2}} \qquad (10)$$

where y_i is the actual data point and $\hat{y}_i$ is the predicted value by the ML algorithm. The $\overline{y}$ is the average value of the actual data points, and variable n represents the total number of data points.

5 Results

5.1 Attribute Selection Approach

The results of the attribute selection methods are reported in Table 2 across twenty-three attributes. Columns A, B, C, D, and E in Table 2 represents the instance-based, classifier-based, filter, wrapper, and correlation-based approach, respectively. The final rank column shows the total rank by the different attribute selection methods. An attribute that has the lowest final rank that is the most relevant attribute. As shown in Table 2, the elevation attribute has the lowest final rank and is the most relevant attribute to classify the soil's average subsidence velocity. The lithology attribute is the second most relevant attribute, and so on. We have chosen the top eleven relevant attributes for machine learning according to the final rank.

Table 2. The rank of all attributes by different attribute selection methods.

Attribute	Attribute Selection Method (Rank)					Final Rank
	A	B	C	D	E	
Elevation	5	8	2	9	2	26
Lithology	1	23	1	1	1	27
Gravel	11	5	2	5	5	28
Sand	8	2	7	4	10	31
D10	7	9	1	3	12	32
LL	3	7	1	2	21	34
Saturated unit weight	18	1	4	5	7	35
ks	17	13	1	2	3	36
PL	2	12	2	4	18	38
C	6	8	2	7	16	39
Slope angle	14	11	3	8	4	40
IP	4	19	1	5	17	46
D60	22	4	6	5	9	46
Relative Compaction	9	21	2	9	6	47
D50	23	6	5	6	8	48
Natural water content	20	3	1	3	23	50
D30	16	10	5	8	15	54
Specific Gravity	10	17	1	5	20	53
Saturated Moisture content	13	14	1	6	19	53
Optimum Moisture content	12	20	2	7	13	54
Angle of internal friction	15	16	6	7	11	55
Fines content	21	22	4	3	14	64
Porosity	19	15	1	8	22	65

5.2 Machine Learning Algorithms

Table 3 shows the outcomes of the various ML algorithms with the 10-CV techniques. Table 3 shows that the MLP-SMO and MLP algorithms performed the best and the second-best, respectively, compared to other algorithms.

Table 4 shows the calibrated values of distinct parameters in the RF, multiple regression, IBk, SMOreg, MLP, and MLP-SMO algorithms. For example, in Table 4, the RF has 7 number of features and 50 bags. The multiple regression parameters were the following: ridge was 30, and M5 Attribute selection Method. Next, the best k parameter value was 5, and the Euclidean distance was selected for the distance measurement for the IBk algorithm. Furthermore, the best values of C and E parameters in SMOreg were 1 and 1, respectively. The PK function chooses as a kernel function in the SMOreg algorithm. Furthermore, the MLP algorithm has 500 and 1000 neurons in the first and second hidden layers, respectively. Similarly, the minimum error of MLP-SMO was with the PK function, and the C and E value was set at 1.

Table 3. The performance of various algorithms in the 10-CV dataset.

Algorithm	Errors (mm/year)		
	MAE	RMSE	RRSE (in %)
MLP-SMO	0.52	0.94	13.52
MLP	1.32	1.60	48.07
SMOreg	4.30	6.60	95.55
Random forest	4.31	6.62	94.94
Multiple regression	4.68	7.00	102.16
IBk	5.24	7.47	108.13

Table 4. Optimized parameter for the RF, LR, IBk, SMOreg, MLP, and MLP-SMO.

Parameter	Best values
	Random Forest
Bags (I)	70
Number of Features (nF)	7
	Linear Regression
Ridge	30
Attribute selection Method	M5
	IBk
K	5

(continued)

Table 4. (*continued*)

Parameter	Best values
Distance function	Euclidean
	SMOreg
C	1
E	1.5
Kernel Function	PK
	MLP
Neurons in first hidden layers	500
Neurons in second hidden layers	1000
Activation	ReLU
Momentum	0.2
Learning Rate	0.3
	MLP-SMO
C	1
E	1
Kernel Function	PK

Figure 4 shows the fitting of the best-performing MLP-SMO algorithm in the 10-fold cross-validation datasets. As shown in Fig. 4, the blue bars are the actual average velocity, and the orange bars are the predicted average velocity.

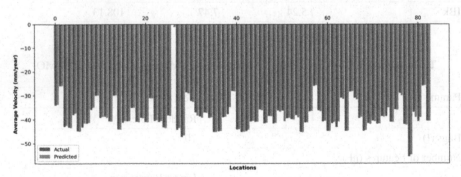

Fig. 4. Fitting of the MLP-SMO on actual and predicted average subsidence velocity in 10-CV.

6 Discussion and Conclusions

The primary focus of this research was to predict subsidence velocity at the Kamand valley in India via ML algorithms. The subsidence velocity prediction could help in this area's landslide mitigation and hazard zonation marking. In this research, the average subsidence velocity data of Kamand valley was obtained by the SBAS-InSAR technique between December 2014 to January 2019. The zonation mapping data contained twenty-three ground-based parameters (such as elevation, lithology, soil moisture, and other soil-related features), which were used as attributes to predict the average subsidence velocity. These parameters were measured by taking samples from the field and laboratory investigations.

The number of attributes was more in the dataset, and some attributes may be uncorrelated to predict the average subsidence velocity. The various attribute selection approaches (instance-based, classifier-based, filter, wrapper, and correlation-based) were developed to rank the attributes. The top eleven attributes were selected by final rank calculated by various attribute selection approaches, which were highly correlated with the subsidence velocity. The top eleven attributes were highly correlated with the subsidence velocity. The ML algorithms input these attributes to predict the average subsidence velocity.

In this research, different ML algorithms such as information gain (RF), statistical (multiple regression), lazy learner (instance-based k: IBk), and optimized version of support vector regression named sequential minimal optimization regression (SMOreg), neural network (MLP), and an ensemble of MLP and SMOreg (MLP-SMO) algorithms to predict the subsidence velocity at Kamand Valley. The 10-CV techniques were used to calculate the average error of the ML algorithms. For calculating the error, the mean absolute error (MAE), root-mean-squared error (RMSE), and the relative root squared error (RRSE) were used. This experiment's results revealed that the MLP-SMO algorithm was the best, with a 0.94 RMSE, and the MLP was the second-best algorithm with, a 1.6 RMSE. One of the reasons for the best performance of MLP-SMO could be that MLP nonlinearly transforms the data in higher space and get a global data representation. Second, SMOreg found the local approximation, fitted the polynomial kernel on the output data and minimized the error in regression.

In future work, the principal component analysis [34] and various neural network-based feature selection techniques, such as autoencoders [35], could be developed to reduce the dimension of the dataset.

Acknowledgment. We are grateful to the DST, India, and the DDMA Mandi, Kinnaur, and Kangra for providing the fund for this research grant. We are also thankful to the IIT Mandi for providing the space and computing facilities for this research work.

References

1. Nayek, P.S., Gade, M.: Seismic landslide hazard assessment of central seismic gap region of Himalaya for a Mw 8.5 scenario event. Acta Geophys. **69**(3), 747–759 (2021)
2. Parkash, S.: Historical records of socio-economically significant landslides in India. J. South Asia Disaster Stud. **4**(2), 177–204 (2011)
3. Sassa, K., Fukuoka, H., Wang, F., Wang, G.: Landslides induced by a combined effect of earthquake and rainfall. In: Sassa, K., Fukuoka, H., Wang, F., Wang, G. (eds.) Progress in landslide science, pp. 193–207. Springer, Heidelberg (2007). https://doi.org/10.1007/978-3-540-70965-7_14

4. Hu, J., Li, Z.W., Ding, X.L., Zhu, J.J., Zhang, L., Sun, Q.: Resolving three-dimensional surface displacements from InSAR measurements: a review. Earth Sci. Rev. **133**, 1–17 (2014)
5. Zhang, P., Guo, Z., Guo, S., Xia, J.: Land subsidence monitoring method in regions of variable radar reflection characteristics by integrating PS-InSAR and SBAS-InSAR techniques. Remote Sens. **14**(14), 3265 (2022)
6. Milillo, P., Giardina, G., DeJong, M.J., Perissin, D., Milillo, G.: Multi-temporal InSAR structural damage assessment: the London crossrail case study. Remote Sens. **10**(2), 287 (2018)
7. Casu, F., Manzo, M., Lanari, R.: A quantitative assessment of the SBAS algorithm performance for surface deformation retrieval from DInSAR data. Remote Sens. Environ. **102**, 195–210 (2006). https://doi.org/10.1016/j.rse.2006.01.023
8. Tofani, V., et al.: Soil characterization for shallow landslides modeling: a case study in the Northern Apennines (Central Italy). Landslides **14**(2), 755–770 (2017). https://doi.org/10.1007/s10346-017-0809-8
9. Bicocchi, G., et al.: Geotechnical and hydrological characterization of hillslope deposits for regional landslide prediction modeling. Bull. Eng. Geol. Env. **78**(7), 4875–4891 (2019). https://doi.org/10.1007/s10064-018-01449-z
10. Yalcin, A.: A geotechnical study on the landslides in the Trabzon Province, NE Turkey. Appl. Clay Sci. **52**(1–2), 11–19 (2011)
11. Kavzoglu, T., Sahin, E.K., Colkesen, I.: Landslide susceptibility mapping using GIS-based multi-criteria decision analysis, support vector machines, and logistic regression. Landslides **11**(3), 425–439 (2013). https://doi.org/10.1007/s10346-013-0391-7
12. Ali, S.A., et al.: GIS-based landslide susceptibility modeling: a comparison between fuzzy multi-criteria and machine learning algorithms. Geoscience Front. **12**(2), 857–876 (2021). https://doi.org/10.1016/j.gsf.2020.09.004
13. Chen, W., et al.: Landslide susceptibility modelling using GIS-based machine learning techniques for Chongren County, Jiangxi Province, China. Sci. Total Environ. **626**, 1121–1135 (2018). https://doi.org/10.1016/j.scitotenv.2018.01.124
14. Hong, H., et al.: Landslide susceptibility mapping using J48 Decision Tree with AdaBoost, Bagging and Rotation Forest ensembles in the Guangchang area (China). CATENA **163**, 399–413 (2018). https://doi.org/10.1016/j.catena.2018.01.005
15. Kumar, P., et al.: Predictions of weekly soil movements using moving-average and support-vector methods: a case-study in Chamoli, India. In: Correia, A.G., Tinoco, J., Cortez, P., Lamas, L. (eds.) ICITG 2019. SSGG, pp. 393–405. Springer, Cham (2020). https://doi.org/10.1007/978-3-030-32029-4_34
16. Li, D., Huang, F., Yan, L., Cao, Z., Chen, J., Ye, Z.: Landslide susceptibility prediction using particle-swarm-optimized multilayer perceptron: comparisons with multilayer-perceptron-only, BP neural network, and information value models. Appl. Sci. **9**(18), 3664 (2019)
17. Wang, L., Teng, C., Jiang, K., Jiang, C., Zhu, S.: D-InSAR monitoring method of mining subsidence based on Boltzmann and its application in building mining damage assessment. KSCE J. Civ. Eng. **26**(1), 353–370 (2021). https://doi.org/10.1007/s12205-021-1042-5
18. Cigna, F., Tapete, D.: Sentinel-1 bigdata processing with P-SBAS InSAR in the geohazards exploitation platform: an experiment on coastal land subsidence and landslides in Italy. Remote Sens. **13**(5), 885 (2021)
19. Rosen, P.A., et al.: Synthetic aperture radar interferometry. Proc. IEEE **88**(3), 333–382 (2000). https://doi.org/10.1109/5.838084
20. Sahraoui, O.H., Hassaine, B., Serief, C., Hasni, K.: Radar interferometry with Sarscape software. Photogrammetry Remote Sens. (2006)
21. Goldstein, R.M., Werner, C.L.: Radar interferogram filtering for geophysical applications. Geophys. Res. Lett. **25**(21), 4035–4038 (1998)

22. Hall, M.A.: Correlation-based feature selection for machine learning (Doctoral dissertation, The University of Waikato) (1999)

23. Kohavi, R., John, G.H.: Wrappers for feature subset selection. Artif. Intell. **97**(1–2), 273–324 (1997)

24. Kira, K., Rendell, L.A.: A practical approach to feature selection. In: Machine Learning Proceedings, pp. 249–256. Morgan Kaufmann (1992)

25. Breiman, L.: Random forests. Mach. Learn. **45**(1), 5–32 (2001)

26. Hoerl, A.E., Kennard, R.W.: Ridge regression: biased estimation for non-orthogonal problems. Technometrics **12**, 55–67 (1970)

27. Ade, R., Deshmukh, P.R.: Instance-based vs batch-based incremental learning approach for students classification. Int. J. Comput. Appl. **106**(3) (2014)

28. Platt, J.: Sequential minimal optimization: a fast algorithm for training support vector machines (1998)

29. Khan, S.R., Noor, S.: Short term load forecasting using SVM based PUK kernel. In: 2020 3rd International Conference on Computing, Mathematics and Engineering Technologies (iCoMET), pp. 1–9. IEEE (2020)

30. Rosenblatt, F.: Principles of neurodynamics. perceptrons and the theory of brain mechanisms. Cornell Aeronautical Lab Inc., Buffalo (1961)

31. Rumelhart, D.E., Hinton, G.E., Williams, R.J.: Learning internal representations by error propagation. In: Rumelhart, D.E., Mcclelland, J.L. (edn.) Parallel Distributed Processing: Explorations in the Microstructure of Cognition, vol. 1, pp 318–362 (1985)

32. Zanaty, E.: Support Vector Machines (SVMs) versus Multilayer Perception (MLP) in data classification. Egypt. Inform. J. **13**, 177–183 (2012)

33. Refaeilzadeh, P., Tang, L., Liu, H.: Cross-validation. In: Liu, L., Özsu, M.T. (eds.) Encyclopedia of Database Systems, vol. 5, pp. 532–538. Springer, Boston (2009). https://doi.org/10.1007/978-0-387-39940-9_565

34. Huang, D., Jiang, F., Li, K., Tong, G., Zhou, G.: Scaled PCA: a new approach to dimension reduction. Manag. Sci. **68**(3), 1678–1695 (2022)

35. Liou, C.-Y., Cheng, W.-C., Liou, J.-W., Liou, D.R.: Autoencoder for words. Neurocomputing **139**, 84–96 (2014)

Multi-modal Content Summarization

Shruti Mathews⬭, Simran Kucheria⬭, Jinit Sanghvi⁽⬠⁾⬭,
and Yashodhara Haribhakta⬭

College of Engineering Pune, Pune, Maharashtra, India
sanghvij18.comp@coep.ac.in

Abstract. Over the past few years, content has been generated at unimaginable rates in multiple domains such as news, education, entertainment, etc. This content takes on innumerable forms such as videos, audio clips, text based articles, etc. and becomes an important source of information to people in their day to day lives. However, consumers cannot cope with the amount of information being produced around them and are always seeking quicker and more efficient ways of consuming and understanding said content. In this paper, we present our Multi-Modal Content Summarization tool which allows you to generate concise and relevant summaries of long video lectures or information heavy content by providing visual and text summaries. While work has been done along the lines of video summarization and text summarization separately, we have been able to produce a combined summary where the visual and the audio content has been synchronized to provide the end-user a holistic summary. In status quo, work revolving around multi-modal summarization targets relatively shorter videos, whereas we attempt to summarize longer videos which are more information heavy since summaries are most relevant in such cases. We adopted an unsupervised learning approach combined with feature extraction from pre-trained models such as BERT, using which we extracted text feature vectors and ResNeXt to extract features from video frames using a 3D CNN architecture. In terms of evaluation, we performed uni-modal evaluation for both, video and text. We observed the highest ROUGE score of 37.18 for text summarization after using K-Means, Latent Semantic Analysis (LSA), and necessary context sentences. For video-summarization, we used ResNext-101 to generate feature vectors, followed by clustering on top of it. We recorded an F1 score of 69.19 after experimenting and fine-tuning.

Keywords: summarization · natural language processing · unsupervised learning · extractive summarization · video summarization

1 Introduction

Recent advances in internet connectivity and storage capacity has led to a rapid increase in multi-media content. YouTube, a primary source of video content creation allows users to create and upload videos. Studies have shown that

© Springer Nature Switzerland AG 2023
D. Garg et al. (Eds.): IACC 2022, CCIS 1781, pp. 82–97, 2023.
https://doi.org/10.1007/978-3-031-35641-4_6

YouTube serves 100 million distinct videos and 65,000 uploads daily [4]. Furthermore, Covid-19 pandemic has also given rise to generation of many online educational videos and courses around the globe. This calls for a faster way of indexing videos in order to allow consumers understand and process volumes of content easily. A good way of doing that would be to generate relevant and concise summaries that help consumers navigate through this content by providing a brief overview about the topic at hand. Along with that, these summaries can be helpful for users that need to quickly revise the content of a video that they have already seen before, especially in the context of students who can now save time by not having to rewatch entire lectures. The approach towards video summarization to generate a condensed version of the video has been gaining traction recently. Typically, video summarization techniques are of two major types: Dynamic and Static video summarization. While static video summaries have key-frames extracted from the input video, dynamic summaries constitute important clip snippets from the original video arranged continuously in a time ordered sequence. Although dynamic summaries are able to preserve the dynamic nature of videos, the extraction of static summaries or key frame extraction is important, because it provides more flexibility owing to little or no issues of synchronization [9]. Students can benefit from video summarization on instructional or information-rich videos since it would provide concise, easy-to-understand lecture notes for reference, and it could also help them in assessing the usefulness of a video at a glance without having to view full video. Such videos are generally lecture videos, seminars, online workshops, etc. However, summarising long videos while retaining most of their information is very difficult. Even if these videos are explained via slides, these slides don't capture most of the information present, since the explanation of the video is conveyed in its audio. This problem can be addressed by using the audio from the file to generate meaningful transcripts which we summarize using transformers. If content is summarized by aligning relevant key-frames with their textual explanation, viewers can quickly skim through such summaries and obtain all important information. In fact, multi-modal output increases user satisfaction by 12.4% as compared to plain text or video summaries [36]. Generating summaries of multi-media content would generate compact representations of dense information, hence providing a lot more information to the user along with the slides helping the end user consume information quickly and efficiently. Because of the subjectivity in summarising videos, there isn't a consistent evaluation metric defined in literature [9]. Our contributions in this paper are as follows:

- Implementation of a tool to generate multi-modal summaries of lengthy content
- Emphasis on problems concerning text and video summarization along with proposed methods to alleviate such problems
- In depth experimentation and hyperparameter tuning to arrive at the best results
- Uni-modal evaluation of text and video summaries using standard metrics

For evaluation, we have reported uni-modal metrics of our summary such as ROUGE - [Recall-Oriented Understudy for Gisting Evaluation] [17] along with precision and recall for video summaries. In Sect. 2, we review the literature associated with text and video summarization followed by an introduction and specification of our proposed idea in Sects. 3 and 4. We further discuss our evaluation criteria and results in Sects. 5 and 6.

2   Related Work

Most summarization work focuses solely on either text or video summarization where the objective is to present a condensed version of the input (text or video). While [36] focuses on an abstractive Multi-Modal summarization to bridge the semantic gaps between image and text, it requires a huge amount of carefully labelled data that correlates between the text and frames. Our work focuses on using an unsupervised approach and align both text and video aspects of a video in a temporal manner.

2.1   Text Summarization

Traditionally, text summarization was done by assigning numerical scores to each sentence and finding sentences with the highest rank. Multiple methods for scoring sentences include assigning scores to words and sentences for choosing relevant sentences and finding coherence between sentences [8]. Their findings reveal that the TF-IDF, sentence positioning, and Text Rank algorithm are best suited for scoring essential words, sentences, and graph similarity respectively. However recent advances in language models has led to the popularity of models such as BERT [6] and the usage of pretrained encoders [16] has led to performance gains that have achieved state of the art results in both, extractive and abstractive text summarization tasks [15,22].

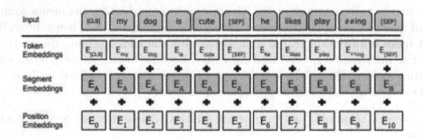

Fig. 1. BERT input representation [6]

For more domain specific approaches like summarizing scientific papers (content is more information heavy akin to lectures), RNN models that encode both the local and global contexts of the sentence along with the sentence itself achieve noteworthy results [4]. An approach which combined both extractive and abstractive summaries was proposed by [25]. Deep Q Networks were used to further improve the Rouge score and results were found to be very promising. An issue with text summarization of video lectures is its length which can lead to issues like insufficient GPU memory due to the long term dependencies in the sentences. Using local self attention units in a pre-trained model combined with aggressive content selection strategies is a better alternative as proposed by [17]. Along with that, abstractive summarization either sets limits on the number of input tokens or performs poorly for long documents since capturing long-range dependencies is tough and requires significant compute power (Fig. 2).

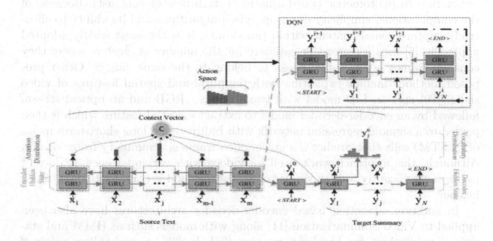

Fig. 2. Model with DQN [25]

In terms of unsupervised learning, different types of clustering techniques are used to group and select summary sentences. Graph based ranking approaches like PACSUM [Position-Augmented Centrality based Summarization] [34]. In this, they employ a BERT model to capture better sentential meaning and a directed graph structure to compute node centrality since the importance of a sentence(based on whether it should be included in the summary) is computed with respect to its relative position in the document. It performs better than data-hungry and non-positional method. Using K-Means with BERT embeddings was highly successful as shown by [18]. A method to generate abstractive summaries by combining both fusion of sentences and lexical paraphrasing was proposed by [20].

2.2   Video Summarization

Video summaries are short and succinct representations of video sequences abstracting most or all of the redundant information. Video summarization techniques are domain specific and are briefly discussed in [1]. Numerous approaches for summarizing videos have been examined and debated in literature, the most popular being the unsupervised clustering algorithms that group together similar video frames and select one or more key frames that are representative of the entire cluster [37]. Similarity between frames can be defined by any metric like color histograms, texture, motions or a combination of these features. [2] uses Zero-mean Normalized Cross (ZNCC) as its similarity metric due to its invariation to photometric transformation (brightness or contrast). Because of the computational simplicity of unsupervised algorithms and its ability to effectively capture visual content within time-limits, it is the most widely adopted approach. [5] uses a reasonable estimate for the number of clusters where they consider frames between two peaks to belong to the same cluster. Other proposed methods include exploiting both temporal and spatial features of video shots. [10] uses an I3D model with two streams - RGB and an optical stream followed by an encoder-decoder model to extract essential feature which is then passed to a sigmoid regression network with bidirectional long short-term memory(LSTM) cells that predict if a given video frame is a summary frame or not. Although, this approach works well on videos with varying scenes, it doesn't perform significantly well on similar or still scenes and is computationally much heavier.

In addition, attention based encoder-decoder architectures have also been applied to Video Summarization [11] along with models such as HMM and statistical projections for highlight creation [21]. In [35], a probability value of selection is computed for each frame using a Deep Reinforcement based learning approach which uses diversity and representation to form video summaries.

Yet another concern revolves around synchronizing video and auditory characteristics of a video to provide short yet meaningful summaries. The first breakthrough in this domain came from [13] where the objective was to produce natural language descriptions of images. Their approach was based on a novel combination of Convolutional Neural Networks over image regions, bidirectional Recurrent Neural Networks over sentences, and a structured objective that aligns the two modalities through a multi-modal embedding. This approach led to further breakthroughs involving a CNN-RNN architecture where CNN Encoders were used for obtaining video/image representations by capturing frames alongside Sequence to Sequence Model encoders to produce sentence representations. These feature vectors were then either passed directly to a Sequence to Sequence Decoder or only image vectors are passed to a Sequence to Sequence Decoder to produce a caption as done in [28].

This approach is also used to produce better video summaries as done in [3] where the relationship between important frames and captions is exploited. The video captions related to frames of images help the model to recognize which frames to retain and how to explain these frames as well. These frames were passed through a VGGNet [23] and the output vector representations are passed through a RNN in a sequence. The output of all cells are passed through an MLP layer which generate a frame-wise importance score and a weighted average of all these frames is passed to the RNN decoder. Using this hidden state, captions are generated and frames are chosen using an optimization algorithm.

Building upon the ideas of BERT, models such as VideoBERT [24] where it takes the caption and frame sequence together simultaneously and these are separated by a separator token (Fig. 3).

Fig. 3. VideoBERT [24]

30 Frame clips are taken at once and the S3D network is used to generate video vectors. These vectors are tokenized using Hierarchical K-Means which has 20,736 tokens. Thus, word and video tokens are used to train BERT according to the starting and ending timestamps of the ASR.

Despite their novelty these methods cannot be used to our advantage because of the unavailability of lengthy lecture-centric datasets. In this work, we attempt to make the most of audio and video features by synchronizing them with timestamps in the most efficient way possible.

3   Proposed Idea

Our proposed solution involves an approach that utilizes both audio and visual features of videos to generate summary sequences. The speech in audio is converted to text with the help of Automatic Speech Recognition (ASR) technologies and this text is pre-processed. Videos are divided into chunks of frames which are then passed to a 3D CNN architecture [32,33] for feature extraction. Pre-processed text is given as an input to a Sequence to Sequence model [6,27] for feature extraction. These vector representations can then be used to extract a set of key-frames and key-sentences. Finally these keyframes and key-sentences can be aligned in a temporal fashion to generate a brief report.

4   Implementation

Our approach emphasizes not only on extracting the most representative visual and audio features, but also depends upon them generating these representations in a manner such that they can be presented together in a collective fashion. A schematic of our approach is given in Fig. 4.

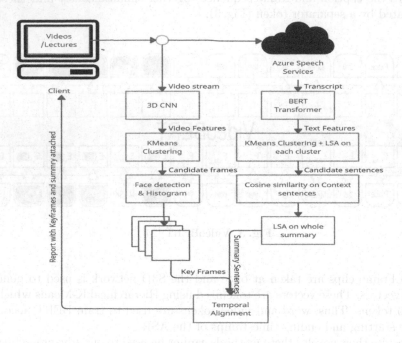

Fig. 4. Solution Workflow

When a client uploads a video, our backend uses Azure Speech Services or YouTube transcript APIs to generate transcripts along with timestamps for every spoken sentence. After transcripts are obtained, the video is passed as an input to a pre-trained 3D-CNN ResNext-101 [32] model which generates feature vectors for frames present in the video. These frames are summarized using unsupervised KMeans clustering approach and the key-frames are obtained from the corresponding cluster centres. The audio transcript is simultaneously passed to a pre-trained BERT model to generate sentence embeddings and using these embeddings, a summary is generated via clustering and topic modelling. Keyframes and summarized sentences are finally aligned with each other using timestamps and a report is generated which the client can either download or view. Implementation of individual components is explained below.

4.1   Text Summarization

To generate text summaries, we tried multiple approaches to extract the most relevant information in a most compact manner. Our attempt is to extract the most diverse sentences which wholly represent the content in conjugation with removal of redundant and irrelevant sentences. Text summarization involves multiple challenges which need to be tackled using different techniques and approaches that work well together. Deciding which sentences to retain and how to rank them is what makes this task challenging along with maintaining readability and coherence of these summaries for the end user [12,29].

Before we pass sentences for feature extraction, these sentences are preprocessed to improve the features. Sentences shorter than 3 words are removed since they do not add value to our summary. Then, these words are passed through a simple pre-processing pipeline where stopwords are removed and words are lemmatized using the WordNet lemmatizer. Once these sentences are preprocessed, they are passed to the BERT model for generating sentence embeddings. BERT takes input as shown in Fig. 1, where individual tokens are passed and special tokens are added as shown in the figure. We chose BERT for generating word embeddings since BERT considers the context a word is placed in because of its bi-directional nature along with its position in the sentence. These are important factors when generating embeddings. While BERT produces word embeddings for each individual token, our objective is to obtain a condensed embedding for the entire sentence. To do this, a simple average can be taken but this might lead to loss of information as all word embeddings are treated equally, which may be counter-productive since different words have different levels of importance in a sentence. For that reason, we take the weighted mean of all word embeddings to produce a sentence embedding. To calculate weights of each word, we used a method similar to TF-IDF Eq. 1 where we compute the weights of each word on the basis of its frequency and the number of times it occurs in different sentences. This allows us to focus on words important to a sentence and the sentence embedding is representative of such words.

$$WordWeight = TF(W) \cdot \log_{10}(\frac{S}{S_w}) \tag{1}$$

where W is the word, TF stands for term frequency, S is the total number of sentences and S_w is the number of sentences with the word w in it.

Once sentence embeddings are generated, they are passed through a clustering algorithm where similar sentences are placed in one cluster and diverse sentences are present in different clusters. We used the KMeans clustering algorithm where the number of clusters are set on the basis of metrics such as Gap Statistic [26] as per Eq. 3 using which the Within-Cluster-Sum of Squared Errors (WCSS) as in Eq. 4 is minimized to increase compactness. The number of clusters depends on how diverse the video is, meaning some videos explain a lot of different concepts whereas some videos may contain redundant content. This technique ensures that the summary is compact and diverse. The distance metric we use for our KMeans algorithm is the Euclidean Distance Eq. 2.

$$d(p, q) = \sqrt{\sum_1^n (q_i - p_i)^2} \tag{2}$$

Euclidean Distance

$$Gap_n(k) = E_n^*(\log W_k) - \log W_k \tag{3}$$

Gap Statistic

$$D_k = \sum_{x_i \in C_k} \sum_{x_i \in C_j} \|x_i - x_j\|^2 = 2n_k \sum_{x_i \in C_k} \|x_i - \mu_k\|^2 \tag{4}$$

Within-Cluster-Sum of Squared Errors (WSS)

After clustering, we extract sentences from these clusters and since we are extracting sentences from different clusters, we are able to capture the most diverse sentences leading to a representative summary. To extract the candidate sentence from a cluster, we use Latent Semantic Analysis (LSA) topic modelling algorithm using truncated Singular Value Decomposition(SVD) as Eq. 5. LSA is used to decompose document-term matrix to extract the most relevant topics from a cluster. This is done by learning TF-IDF weights for all words in a cluster followed by SVD decomposition. LSA also reduces the dimensionality of the matrix to extract significant topics.

If A represents a matrix with m documents and n unique words, it is decomposed into a matrix M with m documents and k different concepts, matrix S with k singular values, and a matrix V with n unique words and k topics.

$$A = MSV^\top \tag{5}$$

Latent Semantic Analysis with SVD

Then, LSA is used to score and rank sentences based on the 10 most important concepts or words returned for k topics. The sentences are awarded a score based on the number of keywords present in the sentence and the length of the sentence. The sentence having the highest score is extracted from the cluster. This technique enables us to rank sentences and extract the most important sentence.

Once we have our summary sentences, we have diverse sentences that explain different parts and sections of the content. These summary sentences need to be further supported and explained by context. This leads to increased human readability and coherence. For this purpose, we add context sentences which are sentences adjacent to the summary sentence. However, not all context sentences will be useful, so we compare the summary sentence and the neighbouring sentence by running similarity measures between their sentence embeddings. If the context sentence has some relation with the summary sentence, we include it.

Once sentences are extracted from clusters, we need to check whether these sentences are relevant or not. We may have multiple sentences which may be diverse from others but may not be relevant to the document. Thus, we use LSA again to get keywords for the entire document and score the sentences with respect to that and the length of the sentence. We retain a sentence only if it is above a certain threshold.

Thus, we have been able to extract the most representative and diverse sentences while maintaining relevance and compactness. Inclusion of context sentences makes the summary more readable and coherent.

4.2   Video Summarization

Our objective was to produce video summaries which captured the most information dense content related to educational videos. In content videos such as lectures, workshops and seminars, speakers deliver content by using slides for reference. Since there is a strong correlation between these slides and speech, extracting the correct slides is crucial to provide holistic summaries. Note, video summaries for activity videos are different as compared to video summaries related to educational videos since educational videos have relatively more static content. Another point of difference is that video summaries of educational videos need to cover different slides whereas activity videos focus on highlights.

Our approach was to first divide the video into chunks of frames where every chunk contains 16 frames. This helped us condense multiple frames in one entity and since educational videos have relatively more static content, most frames in a chunk are the same and hence, can be treated as one entity. For example, if a video has a frame rate of 24, a chunk represents two-thirds of a second which would mostly contain the same frames. Once we split the video into chunks, we pass this chunk to ResNext-101 to generate a feature vector of length 2048.

In such videos, a lot of frames might even contain talking heads; while this is important for engaging the audience, such frames are not relevant in summaries as they don't convey any information in themselves. We remove such frames by face detection. It is possible that there might be a talking face in the gallery view while content is being presented, our intention is not to remove such frames. Frames which exclusively have talking heads without any visual content are to be removed. We do this by calculating the average amount of area faces occupy in the frame and if the area occupied by faces in a certain frame crosses this average, we remove such frames. Along with this, we check if the face is in the center of the frame and if so, we remove these frames. We perform face detection by using Haar Cascade [30] for its ease and speed.

Once chunks are preprocessed, we pass feature vectors to a KMeans algorithm, similar to the one used for Text Summarization. The optimal number of chunks are determined using Gap Statistic. Once candidate chunks are extracted from each cluster we try to remove chunks containing frames that may be negatively correlated to rest of the frames. We do this by creating a correlation matrix between the histograms of the grey-scaled frames. This allows us to remove frames that may be outliers as compared to the rest of the frames. This is necessary because there might be unnecessary "welcome" or "thank you" slides that convey no or little information. Thus we end up with the most diverse and non redundant frames.

5 Evaluation

While Multi-Modal Summarization is a task which has been approached in innovative ways, these summaries are not well evaluated since most existing works use uni-modal metrics such as ROUGE [14] to evaluate text-summaries, while keyframes are evaluated using accuracy related metrics [9]. While we obtain these metrics for our summaries, we believe that these metrics do not consider multiple factors which are important with relation to multi-modal summaries. Since our summaries adopt the format of image-text, these metrics are uni-modal and do not consider the alignment and image-text relevance. Along with that, since our work focuses on summarization of long videos and transcripts, it is necessary for us to make these summaries coherent and human-readable for user satisfaction. Datasets such as CNN/DailyMail are shorter with an average of 30 sentences in each article, and the nature of these articles are very different from speech transcripts. These datasets focus on headline extraction or generation of summaries with 55 words on an average [31]. Our purpose is to provide summaries that are easy to read and cover as much different information as possible, which is why our work cannot be evaluated with the help of these datasets. We conducted extensive evaluation with a variety of hyperparameters to obtain not only the best possible metrics, but also to enhance readability. We experimented with hyperparameters such as cosine-similarity to choose a threshold value for similar sentences, number of context sentences attached, and the range within which the number of clusters are decided. We also experimented with hyperparameters for video-summarization such as chunk-size, range of frames, and threshold for frames with faces. Results with differing hyperparameters and techniques are elucidated in Sect. 6.

While evaluation techniques such as Multi-Modal Automatic Evaluation are suggested [36] have been proposed, these techniques require substantial manually annotated datasets [9] which currently do not exist for this domain. Metrics such as MuSQ [19] do not require ground-truth data, but these metrics only depend on coverage of content and text-image cohesiveness.

Best technique to evaluate such summaries would be via extensive human evaluations as done in [7] by the quiz method or the user-satisfaction test in [36]. Considering human evaluations can be expensive and time-consuming, we reserve this for future work.

6 Results

In lieu of all the reasons discussed above, we performed a uni-modal evaluation for summaries and keyframes each. For text summaries, we use the WikiHow extractive dataset as the summaries are longer with an average summary length of 62.5 words and cover a diverse range of topics. We decided to use a random sample of 5000 documents. Table 1 reports the F1 scores for ROUGE-1, ROUGE-2 and ROUGE-L of text summarization. While for keyframes we decided to manually annotate and derive keyframes from a collection of 25 videos taken from the National Programme on Technology Enhanced Learning (NPTEL) course **"Deep Learning in Computer Vision"**. This was compared with the generated keyframes and its recall, precision and F1 Scores were calculated as shown in Table 2.

The results for each of the techniques utilised in text summarization are very similar to each other with minute differences, this can be attributed to the lesser number of sentences in the dataset as they indicate lesser key-sentences in the summary and given the inclusion of context sentences the generated summary will be longer than the dataset's summary. This ties back into our problem with no proper dataset available for long document summarization.

While evaluating, we noticed that our model performed better for documents where the ratio of number of summary sentences to the number of sentences in the original document was higher. For example, for an article with a ratio of 0.125, the Rouge-1 Score is 0.444 while for an article with a ratio of 0.039, the Rouge-1 score is 0.264.

The F1 scores show an increase with the addition of LSA and context sentences as compared to using just clustering alone. This shows that LSA allows us to select more optimum candidate sentences and the context sentences added allow for co-reference resolution to happen more effortlessly.

Cosine Similarity was applied on the context sentences to remove sentences dissimilar to the cluster's candidate sentence. Even though it led to a slight decrease in the F1 due to a decrease in recall, it did have an increase in precision scores. The decrease in recall is explained by the fewer number of sentences in the summary.

Furthermore, two different thresholds of cosine similarities were tested with 0.8 performing better.

The results for video summarization show the highest scores for the KMeans + removing redundant frames by using face detection and removing outliers by comparing histograms. Even though this approach leads to a slight dip in recall, there is an overall increase n the precision and F1 scores which make it the most optimum strategy.

As both the summaries and the keyframes show promising results in the unimodal evaluations, their contributions to the combined report can be said to be competent. Hence we utilise the best performing strategies in each of these modes to create a combined summary that is aligned temporally, ensuring that both the text content and frame content are relevant to each other (Fig. 5).

Table 1. Text Summarization Results

Method	Rouge-1	Rouge-2	Rouge-L
KMeans	35.81	17.68	33.22
KMeans + Context	34.91	20.99	33.97
KMeans + Context + Cosine Threshold 0.95	35.97	17.92	33.40
KMeans + Context + Cosine Threshold 0.8	36.46	20.35	34.75
KMeans + LSA	37.90	19.78	35.22
KMeans + LSA + context	35.27	21.44	34.36
KMeans + LSA + context + LSA	36.97	21.52	35.66
KMeans + LSA + context + cosine threshold 0.95 + LSA	36.58	18.63	33.85
KMeans + LSA + context + cosine threshold 0.8 + LSA	37.18	20.57	35.22

Table 2. Video Summarization Results

Method	Recall	Precision	F1
KMeans (Baseline)	89.16	54.39	65.60
KMeans + Face Detector	89.71	55.62	66.60
KMeans + Face Detector + Histogram	88.30	60.06	69.19

In object detection, you go one step further and you detect all possible occurrences of the objects in your set of classes in a given image as well as localize them. In the localization task, there is only one object which you localize whereas in object detection there could be multiple objects, multiple instances of the same object, you could have a cat and a dog or two dogs and one cat all of these possibilities.

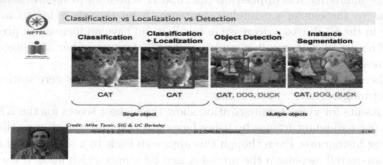

We will see what these are in the next slide and they also introduced a very powerful idea known as integral images which helps make computations of such haar-like features significantly faster as we will see.

Fig. 5. Snippet from Report generated for 'CNNs for Object Detection' by Vineeth N B

7   Conclusion

In this paper, we provide a methodology and a tool to produce Multi-Modal summaries. We focus on this task as it finds it utility for content videos which may be information heavy and while work has been done on summarization, not a lot of work has focused on multi-modal summarization of long videos such as lecture videos, workshops, etc. We propose a novel technique using an unsupervised learning approach to generate summaries for all kinds of content videos. Using ASR technologies and transcripts, we summarize the audio content of these videos using BERT [6] and the KMeans clustering algorithm by clustering individual sentences, and then we extract the most relevant ones using LSA and context. For videos, we preprocess frames to retain only the relevant ones and using the ResNext-101 [32] architecture, we generate feature vectors that are then passed to a clustering algorithm to find keyframes. At the end, we syncrhonize these frames and sentences temporally as it leads to coherence and user-readability. Our work implies that multi-modal summaries can be extremely helpful for content videos and such summaries can enhance user experience. Emphasis needs to be placed on evaluation metrics for such multi-modal summaries due to the shortcomings of uni-modal evaluation metrics. For future work, we would want to manually annotate a comprehensive dataset for multi-modal summaries along with human evaluation.

References

1. Ajmal, M., Ashraf, M.H., Shakir, M., Abbas, Y., Shah, F.A.: Video summarization: techniques and classification. In: Bolc, L., Tadeusiewicz, R., Chmielewski, L.J., Wojciechowski, K. (eds.) ICCVG 2012. LNCS, vol. 7594, pp. 1–13. Springer, Heidelberg (2012). https://doi.org/10.1007/978-3-642-33564-8_1
2. Almeida, J., Leite, N., Torres, R.: VISON: video summarization for online applications. Pattern Recogn. Lett. **33**, 397–409 (2012). https://doi.org/10.1016/j.patrec.2011.08.007
3. Bor-Chun Chen, Y.Y.C., Chen, F.: Video to text summary: joint video summarization and captioning with recurrent neural networks. In: Kim, T.-K., Stefanos Zafeiriou, G.B., Mikolajczyk, K. (eds.) Proceedings of the British Machine Vision Conference (BMVC), pp. 118.1–118.14. BMVA Press (2017). https://doi.org/10.5244/C.31.118
4. Collins, E., Augenstein, I., Riedel, S.: A supervised approach to extractive summarisation of scientific papers. CoRR abs/1706.03946 (2017). http://arxiv.org/abs/1706.03946
5. de Avila, S.E.F., Lopes, A.P.B., da Luz, A., de Albuquerque Araújo, A.: VSUMM: a mechanism designed to produce static video summaries and a novel evaluation method. Pattern Recogn. Lett. **32**(1), 56–68 (2011). https://doi.org/10.1016/j.patrec.2010.08.004, https://www.sciencedirect.com/science/article/pii/S0107865510002783. Image Processing, Computer Vision and Pattern Recognition in Latin America
6. Devlin, J., Chang, M.W., Lee, K., Toutanova, K.: BERT: pre-training of deep bidirectional transformers for language understanding (2019)

7. Erol, B., Lee, D.S., Hull, J.: Multimodal summarization of meeting recordings. In: Proceedings of the 2003 International Conference on Multimedia and Expo, ICME 2003 (Cat. No. 03TH8698), vol. 3, p. III-25 (2003). https://doi.org/10.1109/ICME.2003.1221239

8. Ferreira, R., et al.: Assessing sentence scoring techniques for extractive text summarization. Expert Syst. Appl. **40**(14), 5755–5764 (2013). https://doi.org/10.1016/j.eswa.2013.04.023. https://www.sciencedirect.com/science/article/pii/S0957417413002601

9. Jangra, A., Jatowt, A., Saha, S., Hasanuzzaman, M.: A survey on multi-modal summarization. CoRR abs/2109.05199 (2021). https://arxiv.org/abs/2109.05199

10. Jappie, Z., Torpey, D., Çelik, T.: SummaryNet: a multi-stage deep learning model for automatic video summarisation. CoRR abs/2002.09424 (2020). https://arxiv.org/abs/2002.09424

11. Ji, Z., Xiong, K., Pang, Y., Li, X.: Video summarization with attention-based encoder-decoder networks. IEEE Trans. Circuits Syst. Video Technol. **30**(6), 1709–1717 (2019)

12. Jin, F., Huang, M., Zhu, X.: A comparative study on ranking and selection strategies for multi-document summarization. In: Proceedings of the 23rd International Conference on Computational Linguistics: Posters, COLING 2010, USA. Association for Computational Linguistics (2010)

13. Karpathy, A., Fei-Fei, L.: Deep visual-semantic alignments for generating image descriptions. CoRR abs/1412.2306 (2014). http://arxiv.org/abs/1412.2306

14. Lin, C.Y.: ROUGE: a package for automatic evaluation of summaries. In: Text Summarization Branches Out, Barcelona, Spain, pp. 74–81. Association for Computational Linguistics (2004). https://aclanthology.org/W04-1013

15. Liu, Y.: Fine-tune BERT for extractive summarization. arXiv preprint arXiv:1903.10318 (2019)

16. Liu, Y., Lapata, M.: Text summarization with pretrained encoders. CoRR abs/1908.08345 (2019). http://arxiv.org/abs/1908.08345

17. Manakul, P., Gales, M.: Long-span summarization via local attention and content selection. In: Proceedings of the 59th Annual Meeting of the Association for Computational Linguistics and the 11th International Joint Conference on Natural Language Processing (Volume 1: Long Papers). Association for Computational Linguistics, Online (2021). https://doi.org/10.18653/v1/2021.acl-long.470. https://aclanthology.org/2021.acl-long.470

18. Miller, D.: Leveraging BERT for extractive text summarization on lectures. CoRR abs/1906.04165 (2019). http://arxiv.org/abs/1906.04165

19. Modani, N., et al.: Summarizing multimedia content. In: Cellary, W., Mokbel, M.F., Wang, J., Wang, H., Zhou, R., Zhang, Y. (eds.) WISE 2016, pp. 340–348. Springer, Cham (2016). https://doi.org/10.1007/978-3-319-48743-4_27

20. Nayeem, M.T., Fuad, T., Chali, Y.: Abstractive unsupervised multi-document summarization using paraphrastic sentence fusion (2018)

21. Ram, A.R., Chaudhuri, S.: Automatic capsule preparation for lecture video. In: 2009 International Workshop on Technology for Education, pp. 10–16 (2009). https://doi.org/10.1109/T4E.2009.5314119

22. Savelieva, A., Auyeung, B., Ramani, V.: Abstractive summarization of spoken and written instructions with BERT. arXiv abs/2008.09676 (2020)

23. Simonyan, K., Zisserman, A.: Very deep convolutional networks for large-scale image recognition. In: International Conference on Learning Representations (2015)

24. Sun, C., Myers, A., Vondrick, C., Murphy, K., Schmid, C.: VideoBERT: a joint model for video and language representation learning (2019)
25. Sun, G., Wang, Z., Zhao, J.: Automatic text summarization using deep reinforcement learning and beyond. Inf. Technol. Control **50**(3), 458–469 (2021). https://doi.org/10.5755/j01.itc.50.3.28047
26. Tibshirani, R., Walther, G., Hastie, T.: Estimating the number of clusters in a data set via the gap statistic. J. R. Stat. Soc. Series B (Stat. Methodol.) **63**(2), 411–423 (2001). http://www.jstor.org/stable/2680607
27. Vaswani, A., et al.: Attention is all you need. CoRR abs/1706.03762 (2017). http://arxiv.org/abs/1706.03762
28. Venugopalan, S., Rohrbach, M., Donahue, J., Mooney, R., Darrell, T., Saenko, K.: Sequence to sequence - video to text (2015)
29. Verma, S., Nidhi, V.: Extractive summarization using deep learning. CoRR abs/1708.04439 (2017). http://arxiv.org/abs/1708.04439
30. Viola, P., Jones, M.: Rapid object detection using a boosted cascade of simple features. In: Proceedings of the 2001 IEEE Computer Society Conference on Computer Vision and Pattern Recognition, CVPR 2001, vol. 1, p. I (2001). https://doi.org/10.1109/CVPR.2001.990517
31. Wang, Q., Liu, P., Zhenfang, Z., Yin, H., Zhang, Q., Zhang, L.: A text abstraction summary model based on BERT word embedding and reinforcement learning. Appl. Sci. **9**, 4701 (2019). https://doi.org/10.3390/app9214701
32. Xie, S., Girshick, R.B., Dollár, P., Tu, Z., He, K.: Aggregated residual transformations for deep neural networks. CoRR abs/1611.05431 (2016). http://arxiv.org/abs/1611.05431
33. Zhang, D., Dai, X., Wang, X., Wang, Y.F.: S3D: single shot multi-span detector via fully 3D convolutional networks (2018)
34. Zheng, H., Lapata, M.: Sentence centrality revisited for unsupervised summarization (2019)
35. Zhou, K., Qiao, Y., Xiang, T.: Deep reinforcement learning for unsupervised video summarization with diversity-representativeness reward (2018)
36. Zhu, J., Li, H., Liu, T., Zhou, Y., Zhang, J., Zong, C.: MSMO: multimodal summarization with multimodal output. In: Proceedings of the 2018 Conference on Empirical Methods in Natural Language Processing, Brussels, Belgium, pp. 4154–4164. Association for Computational Linguistics (2018). https://doi.org/10.18653/v1/D18-1448. https://aclanthology.org/D18-1448
37. Zhuang, Y., Rui, Y., Huang, T., Mehrotra, S.: Adaptive key frame extraction using unsupervised clustering. In: Proceedings 1998 International Conference on Image Processing, ICIP 1998 (Cat. No. 98CB36269), vol. 1, pp. 866–870 (1998). https://doi.org/10.1109/ICIP.1998.723655

Estimating the Water Level and Bathymetry of Lake Yahuarcocha, Ecuador Using ICESat-2/ATL13 Satellite Laser Altimetry, System Dynamics Model, and Machine Learning

Garrido Fernando[✉] and Granda Pedro[✉]

Department of Software Engineering and Artificial Intelligence, Faculty of Engineering in Applied Sciences, Technical University of the North, Avenue 17 de Julio 5-21, Ibarra, Ecuador
{jfgarridos,pdgranda}@utn.edu.ec

Abstract. Monitoring the lakes and reservoirs is crucial in managing water resources due to climate change and human interventions, where available data sets on water levels and volumes are scarce. This study aims of predicting the water level height and bathymetry of lake Yahuarcocha, Imbabura, Ecuador with the use of the NASA Ice, Cloud, and land Elevation Satellite-2 (ICESat-2) ATL13/ATL13QL since they provide observations that are suitable for water level estimation, also combining the study with System Dynamics Modelling (SD), and machine learning technique based on the extraction of points from the laser altimetry footprint at the limits of the lake vector, according to the absolute deviation method used to eliminate the outliers of the lake elevation along the orbit, and thus obtain the average values of the water level of the lake. Yahuarcocha has been seriously affected in recent years, and the anthropic activities inherent to the wetlands have been the main cause of the effects, including land use, and other watershed activities influencing surface runoff and groundwaters. Therefore, predictions of lake level are crucial for their sustainable management. In this study, the SD model simulation with the PySD library is used to have the estimation of the level of precipitation, evapotranspiration, and volume of water the lake Yahuarcocha until 2030. The results indicate that the water level estimated from ATL13 is the same as the water level trend measured in situ, with an average estimation error of 30 cm, indicating that the ICESat-2 ATL13 laser altimetry data has high precision, thus the approach of the proposed reaches more than 95.57%.

Keywords: ICESat-2 ATL13 · bathymetry · water level estimation · System Dynamics Modelling · Machine Learning

1 Introduction

Earth Observation (EO) satellites developed or operated by ESA and NASA have given users access to a large amount of data and will continue to grow as new missions further expand the routine monitoring of the land system worldwide. The Ice, Cloud, and land Elevation Satellite 2 (ICESat-2) mission is taking significant efforts to make such

© Springer Nature Switzerland AG 2023
D. Garg et al. (Eds.): IACC 2022, CCIS 1781, pp. 98–111, 2023.
https://doi.org/10.1007/978-3-031-35641-4_7

data freely available with the intention to fuel innovation and entrepreneurship. The new ATLAS/ICESat-2 L3A Along Track Inland Surface Water Data Quick Look (ATL13QL), version 5 products, now available from NSIDC DAAC (National Snow and Ice Data Center - Distributed Active Archive Center) and the Land, Atmosphere Near real-time Capability for EOS (LANCE) system, so it increases the usefulness of ICESat-2 mission data and opportunities for new user communities interested in operational decision-making and related applications [1]. ICESat-2 mission data products have applications for everything from climate change to wildlife conservation, but the data volumes are massive at up to 1 terabyte per day. Open-source tools and tutorials provide new opportunities to scale up the exploitation of big EO datasets, but researchers still face obstacles in quickly adopting them into their workflows.

Responding to both these technological and community challenges NASA is working with a consortium of international space agencies, this is helping to advance our understanding of Earth's water and energy cycles, improve forecasting of extreme events that cause natural hazards and disasters, and extend current capabilities in accurate and timely information of monitoring to directly benefit society. The results are the Tropical Rainfall Measuring Mission (TRMM), which ended collecting data on April 15, 2015 (see http:// pmm.nasa.gov/trmm/mission-end), and the Global Precipitation Measurement mission (GPM) - launched on Feb 27, 2014 (see https://gpm.nasa.gov/missions/GPM), as an Integrated Multi-satellite Retrievals for GPM data product, called IMERG, which combines all these data from 12 satellites into a single, seamless map [2].

Global Surface Water Explorer developed by the European Commission's Joint Research Centre (JRC) within the framework of the Copernicus program, was also used in the study. This maps the location and temporary distribution of water surfaces at a global scale available from 1984 to 2019 and provides statistics on the range and change of these water surfaces. Using big data techniques, as well as expert monitoring techniques, visual analysis, and evidential reasoning, the detection of water is based on multispectral aspects. Uses a web interface powered by Google Earth Engine (GEE) https://earthengine.google.com. Which allows you to execute an expert system with images of remote sensing. As well as use a virtual time machine that maps the location and temporal distribution of water surfaces at the global scale and provides statistics on their extent and change to support water-management decision-making, this is available from https://global-surface-water.appspot.com [3]. Therefore, satellite Earth observation has, like no other technology, the ability to inform, facilitate and monitor national, regional, and international developments consistently with free and open data. Particularly in regions where ground monitoring infrastructures are scarce, if not nonexistent.

According to the research we developed in 2021 using ICESat-2 ATL08 [16], we take some of the features you have in the ICESat-2 ATLAS that offer the opportunity to map lake cross-section geometry very accurately [15], according to the orbit, altitude of 500 km, this yields approximately one transmitted laser pulse every 0.7 m along ground tracks [17]. Each pulse is split by a diffractive optical element into three pairs of beams numbered by its laser spot number and orientation (GT1L/GT1R, GT2L/GT2R, and GT3L/GT3R) [18]. With a 70 m diameter footprint, the ICESat data are more suitable for calculating water levels in small lakes. However, due to the limited spatial coverage and sparse along-track footprints (with a 170 m interval), numerous small water bodies have a few observations [19]. ICESat-2 collects data through a multi-Haz photon-counting system that is sensitive at the single-photon level [20], which greatly improves data coverage density and data accuracy. The forward dispersion effect is caused by clouds in the atmosphere, aerosols, etc. It has a non despite the impact on the accuracy of the data, according to the Atlas photon counting body. To comply with the above, we combined products ATL03 and ATL13 to simulate water surface elevation, where the first map to lake cross-section geometry without the need for a rainfall-runoff model, and the second calibrates a steady-state hydraulic model to provide water surface height [27]. The classification of satellite images based on objects is one of those applications of the Convolution Neural Network (CNN), the objective is to classify each pixel, based on the pattern and texture of the neighboring pixels, for this reason in this study we use the CNN model due to a which is a supervised regression machine learning problem [16].

2 Methods and Materials

2.1 General Description of the Lake

Lake Yahuarcocha is in Ecuador in the province of Imbabura within the jurisdiction of the Ibarra canton and lies between $0°21'28''$ N and $0°22'47''$ N latitudes and $78°6'38''$ W and $78°5'25''$ W longitudes. "Laguna Yahuarcocha" in Spanish, also spelled Yawarkucha, means a lake of blood in the Kichwa language ('Yahuar' – blood, 'Cocha' – lake) and is located about 3 km (1.86 miles) from the northern city of Ibarra. It is a eutrophic lagoon, of a 12,000-year-old glacial origin, located in a strong depression of volcanic origin. Sitting at a height of 2190 m.a.s.l (7185 ft), it has around 12.7 million cubic meters of water and its temperature is around 11 °C with a depth of approximately 8 m, low rainfall in the area (up to 3000 mm per year) and an area of 2.61 km^2 [4] (see Fig. 1).

This study focuses on introducing remote sensing observations to monitor the water level of Lake Yahuarcocha; a critical component of surface water that affects the area's residential, economic, and recreational sectors. Water volumes are generally inferred from bathymetric mapping, however, as the bathymetry in Lake Yahuarcocha is shallow, ephemeral, and remote, we propose to use the new satellite-based remote sensing (ICESat-2) [25].

2.2 Analytical Methods

The role of lakes in the global hydrological and biogeochemical cycles is intimately tied to their geometric characteristics of surface area, depth, stored water volume, and shoreline length [26]. The data on the volume and depth of lakes on a global scale are scarce and inconsistent. Despite increasingly precise geopositioning technologies, combined with the current development of remote sensing technology, a series of models for lakes' water volume estimation by some researchers have been proposed [5]. The lake water volume also known as "lake water capacity balance" or "lake storage mass balance" depends on the difference in the inflow (Q_{in}) and outflow (Q_{out}) of water and can be estimated by Eq. (1) [6]

$$(Q_{in}) - (Q_{out}) = \frac{dV}{dt} = A\frac{dh}{dt} \tag{1}$$

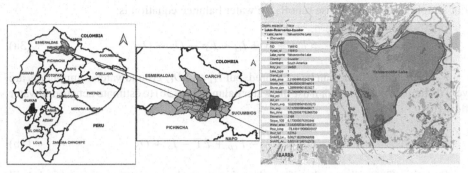

Fig. 1. Location map of lake Yahuarcocha, relative to the national, cantonal, and parish level, and your information characteristics. Source: own study.

dV: *lake water volume* (m^3)

dt: *time interval (e.g. in our case 1 year of simulation)*

$\frac{dV}{dt}$: *rate of volume change* $(m^3 y^{-1})$

A: *lake water area* (km^2)

h: *water depth* (m)

Input flux $(m^3 y^{-1})$ **Output flux** $(m^3 y^{-1})$

$P_{cp} + I_S + I_G + R$ $ET + O_G + O_S$

P_{cp}: *precipitation* ET: *evaporation & evapotranspiration*

I_S: *stream inflow* O_S: *stream outflow*

I_G: *groundwater inflow* O_G: *groundwater outflow*

R: *diffuse runoff*

SD: *snow drift (in or out)*

Evapotranspiration is defined as the loss of fresh water to the atmosphere from the ground surface, by two processes, evaporation, and transpiration. Evaporation is the loss from open bodies of water in vapor; transpiration is the loss from groundwater by plants whose roots tap the capillary fringe of the groundwater [28]. As the Yahuarcocha Lake is endorheic, the outflow is limited to evapotranspiration. The fraction (ET/P_{cp}) represents the consumption of available water (precipitation) by evapotranspiration. The land cover and the type of climate in the lake establish a way to normalize a balance of surface waters [7]. In the basin area and on the lake's surface, precipitation (P_{cp}) is controlled by orographic and atmospheric aspects. The inflows of surface water (I_S) and groundwater (I_G) due to the hydrogeological and orographic form within the drainage area are affected. Continuity Eq. (2) [8] specifies the changes in the water level (dh) of a lake which is the difference between the inputs and outputs of the water balance over the lake water surface area (A).

$$dh = \frac{(Q_{in}) - (Q_{out})}{A} = \frac{dV}{A} \qquad (2)$$

For simple lakes with diffuse runoff, the water balance equation is:

$$\frac{dV}{dt} = P_{cp} + I_S + I_G - E_T - O_S - O_G \tag{3a}$$

P_{cp}, ET, and I_s flows can be measured, but I_G and O_G groundwater components are very difficult to measure. For it use the water balance Eq. (3b) to estimate net groundwater flow [6]:

$$I_G - O_G = \frac{dV}{dt} - P_{cp} + ET - I_S + O_S \tag{3b}$$

Equation (3a) indicates that if precipitation exceeds evaporation, water levels will increase until the excess water is drained through natural drainage, in the case of the Yahuarcocha lagoon. In addition, it applies to action the man-made changes in the water balance and thus reaches the equilibrium level of the lake water. The simulation data set for our study contains the lake water level h (m) relative to a local reference point, annual precipitation P_{cp} (mm), estimated annual evaporation ET (mm), and inflow daily average I_S (m³y⁻¹), and the output flow O_S (m³y⁻¹) [6]. R, P_{cp}, and ET are currently susceptible to satellite measurement, while changes in the lake level are measured by altimetric methods, and evaporation can be estimated with the combination of satellite observations of humidity, wind, and temperature. Precipitation is measured regardless of whether the surface is land or water (see Fig. 2). I_s and O_s are not remotely measured and must be in situ measured or parameterized in terms of any observed quantity [9].

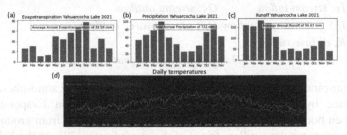

Fig. 2. Annual values for Yahuarcocha Lake for the year 2021: (a) Evapotranspiration (ET), (b) precipitation (P_{cp}), (c) runoff (R), and (d) daily temperatures. Source: own study.

With these preambles, we apply the System Dynamics (SD) method to simulate the mean annual volumes of Lake Yahuarcocha in the future period (2021–2030) [10]. With these preambles, we apply the System Dynamics (SD) method to simulate the mean annual volumes of Lake Yahuarcocha in the future period (2021–2030). We use Eq. (4) [11] to calculate the lake's mass balance

$$S_t = S_{t_0} + \int_{t_0}^{t} [Inflow(t) - Outflow(t)]d_t \tag{4}$$

where S_t is the lake's storage at time t, S_{t_0} denotes the lake's storage at time t_0, $Inflow(t)$ denotes the inflow rate, and $Outflow(t)$ outflow rate at time t (units of volume/time). The amount of water in the Yahuarcocha Lake at a time t is calculated by Eq. (5) [11]

$$V_t = V_{t_0} + \int_{t_0}^{t} [R(t) + I_S(t) + P_{cp}(t) - ET(t)]d_t \qquad (5)$$

where V_{t_0} is the water volume of the lake at time t_0 equal to 13498931.25 m^3 in 2016, V_t is water volume of the lake at time t. IG(t), OS(t), OG(t) is not considered because it is an endorheic lake [12]. For all this we use the Vensim software version 9.3.0. (see Fig. 3) along with the PySD library to run SD models in Python, to improve the integration of Big Data and Machine Learning into the SD workflow. PySD imports a Vensim (*.mdl) file and provides methods to modify, simulate, and observe those translated models [13, 29].

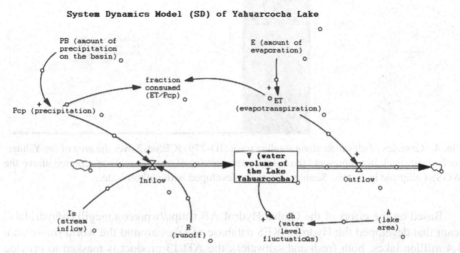

Fig. 3. Layout generalized inflow and outflow system of the Yahuarcocha lake water with System Dynamics (SD) model. Source: own study.

Research carried out in 2017 by the Technical University of the North, using a Global Water FP211 portable flow meter, showed that the amount of this lake replenished by water discharge *(IS)* is approximately 132.1 mm in the year 2016 [12]. Therefore, the stream inflow into the lake was considered this data in this simulation. An altimeter measures how high something is. Satellite radar altimeters measure water surface elevation in remote areas where in-situ data is scarce, they can be combined with hydraulic/hydrodynamic models to simulate water surface elevation and estimate discharge. Bathymetry is the study of the contour of the land underneath bodies of water and shows variations in the seafloor and lake floor depth like topographic maps on land [14]. The bathymetry of a lake describes the topography or depth within the lake and the length of the lakeside (or the length and width), they help to decide the average volume of the lake.

2.3 Data Collection

All ICESat-2 ATL13 data products were acquired from 01 January 2021 to 31 December 2021 available from the National Snow and Ice Data Center (NSIDC; https://nsidc.org/data/atl13). This data set (ATL13) download parameters include the along-track water surface height and standard deviation, subsurface signal (532 nm) attenuation, significant wave height, wind speed, and coarse depth to bottom topography [1]. The water surface level is given as the height on the WGS 84 ellipsoid of the 2008 Earth Gravitational Model (EGM2008) [17] (see Fig. 4).

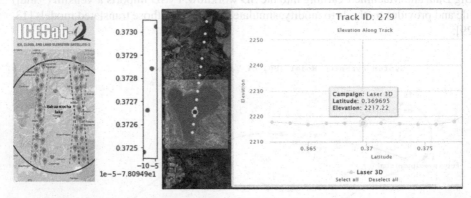

Fig. 4. Granules of elevation along satellite track (ID-279) ICESat-2 over the area of the Yahuarcocha lake. Each dot represents the height (orthometric) of a water surface reported above the WGS84 ellipsoid in meters. Source: own study developed with python code.

Based on the effort of the Global HydroLAB (http://wp.geog.mcgill.ca/hydrolab/) team that developed the HydroLAKES database of lakes around the world (more than 1.4 million lakes, both fresh and saltwater), the ATL13 product is masked to provide polygons with an area of at least 10 ha (0.10 km^2) [21]. All HydroLAKES layers were downloaded from HydroSHEDS (Hydrological Data and Maps Based on Shuttle Elevation Derivatives at Multiple Scales) [24, 30] (https://www.hydrosheds.org/pages/hydrolakes). This download was made in 2 formats: Polygons of the Lakes in an ESRI® geodatabase (Hy-droLAKES_points_v10_shp.zip of 763 MB), Lake's fluidity points in an ESRI® geodatabase (HydroLAKES_points_v10.gdb.zip of 81 MB) [21].

Therefore, in this study based on the ICESat-2 ATL13 products, with valid observations in 2021, they were filtered from the HydroLAKES database with the monthly water level changes of lake Yahuarcocha. The core HydroSHEDS layers are distributed in Raster and Vector formats at resolutions from 3 arcseconds (approximately 90 m) to 6 arcminutes (approximately 11 km) at the equator [31] and are derived primarily from elevation data of the Shuttle Radar Topography Mission (SRTM). The dataset information was obtained from the public site https://www.hydrosheds.org/downloads [22] (last access: 26 June 2022) in GeoTIFF format, and for this project, we utilized two layers of the six: void-filling of digital elevation model (DEM) (sa_dem_3s.tiff), flow direction grids (sa_dir_3s.tiff), built within a QGIS project treated with the Normalized Difference Water Index (NDWI), see Fig. 5.

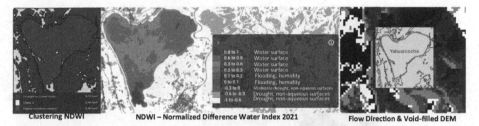

Fig. 5. HydroSHEDS layers at a resolution of 3 arcseconds and with NDWI vector data format are contains polygon information in the attribute table associated with the geodatabase of the Yahuarcocha lake for the year 2021. Source: own study developed with QGIS software.

Once lake Yahuarcocha location was verified and accepted according to the layers HydroSHEDS raster dataset to determine the lake micro-basin, proceeded to build, download, and analysis of the datasets that comprise the Global Surface Water (GSW) 1984–2020, using Google Earth Engine, the datasets were accessed in different multiband formats, to show the mapped products, the spatial distribution facets, and the surface water history of lake Yahuarcocha [3].

Figure 6 shows the occurrence of the water which provides information about the general dynamics of the water in the lake. Permanent water surfaces are represented in blue, purple-pink areas where water sometimes occurs, pale colors are areas where water occurs less frequently. Meanwhile, the occurrence intensity map provides information on where surface water increased, decreased, or remained, the bright reds showing areas with greater water loss than light green areas. The Seasonality map provides information on the behavior of the water surfaces for the year (2021), permanent water (represented in dark blue), and seasonal water (represented in lighter blue). The Recurrence map shows in blue how often the water returns from year to year, and in orange the areas that flood on an episodic basis. And finally, the Transition map presents the change in seasonality between the first and last months and captures the changes between seasonal water and permanent water [3].

3   Results and Discussion

The methodology adopted for estimating the water level of the Yahuarcocha lake involved the following steps:

1) Collection of the dataset ICESat-2 ATL13: In this step, we first create an ICESat-2 DAAC Data Access with the desired search parameters and download data from the NSIDC API [16]. To measure the water and the heights of lakes and rivers, satellite altimetry has proven to be an adequate tool [23], studies have already demonstrated the potential for ICESat-2 ATL13 (e.g., the study proposed by Xu et al. [19]). For small lakes, the estimation of the water level time series is very challenging, because the ATL13 mask of each polygon represents a 7 km wide segment, so large lakes and reservoirs are more likely to be crossed by a satellite track [23], how show Fig. 4.

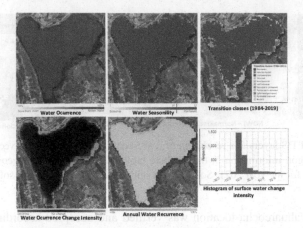

Fig. 6. Surface Water maps the Yahuarcocha Lake. Source: own study.

2) Water level extraction workflow of big EO datasets: All available Sentinel-2 L1C satellite images of Lake Yahuarcocha were downloaded from the beginning of 2020 to June 30, 2022 (provided by Sentinel Hub). NDWI index bands B03, B08, and the TRUE-COLOR visualization of the area, bands B02, B03, and B04 for CLM cloud masking. Adaptive thresholding was applied to grayscale images of NDWI. The water level was derived from a comparison of the measured to nominal water extent. An EOPatch was created and added all EO features (satellite imagery data). Nominal water extent vectorized, then proceeded to VectorToRaster task in Geopandas data frame. Defined a VALID_DATA layer: where the pixel must contain data and the cloud detector must classify it as the clear sky (CLM equals 0). In the end, the water detection algorithm was applied, filtering all the observations that have a cloud cover of more than 5% and the estimation algorithm of the water level of Lake Yahuarcocha, as shown in Fig. 7.

3) Get some SRTM30 bathymetric data: This SRTM (Shuttle Radar Topography Mission) V3 product provided by NASA JPL at a resolution of 1 arcsecond (approximately 30 m), It allowed from images to be converted into Geopandas data frames, producing 3D graphs of the bathymetry of the lake (see Fig. 8).

4) Simulation according to the SD model with PySD library: The SD model was created with Vensim software, and the advanced analysis of prediction was carried out using python with the PySD library, thus the projection statistics were found until the year 2030 on precipitation, evapotranspiration, and volume of water in Lake Yahuarcocha (see Fig. 9).

5) Applying machine learning for segmentation of the image on the water levels: the goal of these operations is to ensure precise separation between land and water. The water coverage algorithm returns a NumPy array of labels with unique values corresponding to the pixel value. Our last step is to plot to represent surface water change intensity in Yahuarcocha Lake, where each dot represents the height of a water surface short segment, this is a regression task because the target value is

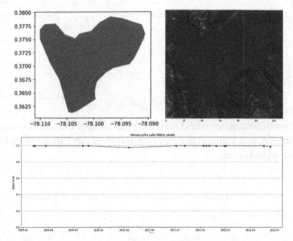

Fig. 7. The plot of results of estimating the water level of the Yahuarcocha lake from the beginning of 2020 to June 30, 2022, shows also the AOI in format vector and raster NDWI. Source: own study developed with python code.

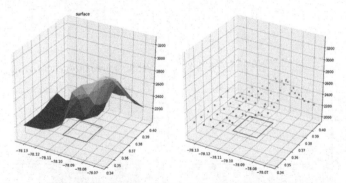

Fig. 8. The plot of results of bathymetric of the Yahuarcocha lake plotting 3D and of three-dimensional scattered points. Source: own study developed with python code.

continuous in classification, here we used TensorFlow, the icepyx software library, the Scikit-Learn module, and the regression with our SD model, see Fig. 10.

4 Conclusions

The research on lake Yahuarcocha capacity estimation can be generally summarized:

(a) This study has shown that the ICESat2 ATL13 Inland Water Body Shape Mask facilitates the identification of ICESat-2 crossings over individual water bodies, by delineating the shape and spatial distribution of contiguous individual water bodies. Being able to rely on much denser ground/bottom point and bathymetric capability, ICESat-2 data was used to obtain points along the track and generate bathymetric maps with the support of Sentinel-2 L1C products and GSW (Global Surface Water).

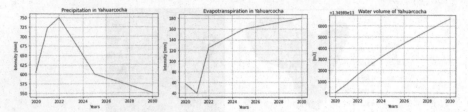

Fig. 9. The plot projection statistics found until the year 2030 of the model components (precipitation, evapotranspiration, and volume) at every timestamp of the Yahuarcocha lake. Source: own study developed with python code.

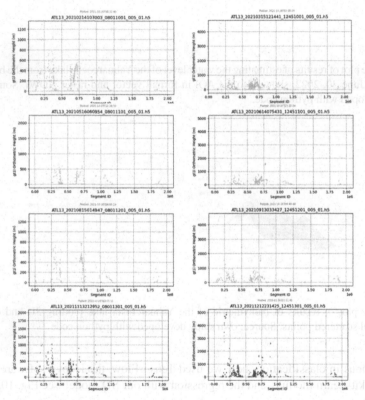

Fig. 10. ATLAS/ICESat-2 L3A Along Track Inland Surface Water Data V005, granules of Ground Track (GT1L) of the Yahuarcocha lake for the period between 01/01/2021 to 31/12/2021. Source: own study developed with python code.

These water levels are in good agreement with the in-situ water levels, which may prove that the bathymetry results from ICESat-2 are reliable.

(b) Lake level estimation in remote sensing-based research is an advanced means of real-time monitoring of changes in lakes and having historical scenarios to predict future changes, this poses a challenge for this type of investigation because the accuracy of the model is also a problem to improve the accuracy of the results.

(c) The power in research using remote sensing cloud computing platforms has provided technical support for the storage, calculation, and display of massive remote sensing data. Therefore, combined with the development of remote sensing hydrology, it has made it possible to carry out the historical reconstruction and prediction of the lake's water level and for future research work can predict the water quality of Lake Yahuarcocha.

Based on the current remote sensing research on lake Yahuarcocha water volume, can be concluded as follows:

(1) Lake Yahuarcocha has a lacustrine basin with a regular profile, presents a rapid drop in the depth of its shore, and a bottom relatively flat, concentrating the greatest spatial distribution of the water in the levels of intermediate depth (3, 4, and 5 m).
(2) Since precipitation is the natural and crucial part of the hydrological cycle, it is the variable that has been most affected by the development of anthropic activities in the micro-basin of lake Yahuarcocha varies constantly in the year of study 2021, it presents the highest level in April with 115.23 mm and the lowest level low in July with 15.07 mm, as seen in Fig. 2(b).
(3) Evaporation is the most influential variable in the system, it does not have large monthly variations, it presents the highest level in September with 79.06 mm and the lowest level in March with 11.39 mm, due to the characteristics of its location, it presents a clear dry season in June, July, August, and September with high temperatures and high solar radiation, as shown in Fig. 2(a).
(4) The surface and volumetric variation that the lake presents must be taken into account because of this prediction study until the year 2030, the precipitation decreases considerably while the evapotranspiration increases, as shown in the graphs of Fig. 10, which is the drama hydrology of Lake Yahuarcocha, where the necessary activities to be carried out by the competent entities for the comprehensive management of natural resources with a hydrographic basin approach are not provided, the icon of the city of Ibarra will become a puddle.

Crediting Photographs and Images. Imagery from the NASA ICESat-2 instrument, courtesy of NASA NSIDC DAAC.
   API from the Google Earth Engine.
   API from the Sentinel-Hub and the European Space Agency (ESA).
   The Copernicus Open Access Hub.
   The Vensim software with library PySD.

Declaration of Interests.. The authors declare that they have no known competing financial interests or personal relationships that could have appeared to influence the work reported in this paper.

References

1. Jasinski, M.F., et al.: ATLAS/ICESat-2 L3A Along Track Inland Surface Water Data Quick Look, Version 5. [Indicate subset used]. Boulder, Colorado USA. NASA National Snow and Ice Data Center Distributed Active Archive Center (2022). https://doi.org/10.5067/ATLAS/ATL13QL.005

2. Olson, W.S.: GPM Combined Radar-Radiometer Precipitation Algorithm Theoretical Ba-sis Document (Version 5). NASA/Global Precipitation Measurement Mission (2018). https://gpm.nasa.gov/resources/documents/gpm-combined-radar-radiometer-precipitation-algorithm-theoretical-basis

3. Pekel, J., Cottam, A., Gorelick, N., Belward, A.: High-resolution mapping of global surface water and its long-term changes. Nature **540**, 418–422 (2016). https://doi.org/10.1038/nature 20584

4. Imbabura Geoparque Mundial de la UNESCO. https://geoparque.imbabura.gob.ec/index.php/geoproductos/laguna-de-yahuarcocha/. Accessed 21 Jan 2022

5. Changjiang, A., Fei, Z., Ngai, W.C.H., Verner, C.J., Jingchao, S.: A review on the research progress of lake water volume estimation methods. J. Environ. Manag. **314**, 115057 (2022). https://doi.org/10.1016/j.jenvman.2022.115057. ISSN 0301-4797

6. Rosenberry, D.O., Hayashi, M.: Assessing and measuring wetland hydrology. In: Anderson, J.T., Davis, C.A. (eds.) Wetland Techniques, pp. 87–225. Springer, Dordrecht (2013). https://doi.org/10.1007/978-94-007-6860-4_3

7. Diao, H., Wang, A., Yang, H., Yuan, F., Guan, D., Wu, J.: Responses of evapotranspiration to droughts across global forests: a systematic assessment. Can. J. Forest Res. **51**(1), 1–9 (2021). https://doi.org/10.1139/cjfr-2019-0436

8. Szesztay, K.: Water balance and water level fluctuations of lakes. Hydrol. Sci. Bull. **19**(1), 73–84 (2010). https://doi.org/10.1080/02626667409493872

9. Swenson, S., Wahr, J.: Monitoring the water balance of Lake Victoria, East Africa, from space. J. Hydrol. **370**(1–4), 163–176 (2009). https://doi.org/10.1016/j.jhydrol.2009.03.008

10. Bozorg-Haddad, O., Dehghan, P., Zolghadr-Asli, B., et al.: System dynamics modeling of lake water management under climate change. Sci. Rep. **12**, 5828 (2022). https://doi.org/10.1038/s41598-022-09212-x

11. Maihemuti, B., Aishan, T., Simayi, Z., Alifujiang, Y., Yang, S.: Temporal scaling of water level fluctuations in shallow lakes and its impacts on the lake eco-environments. Sustainability **12**, 3541 (2020). https://doi.org/10.3390/su12093541

12. Revelo, J.: Evaluación del balance hidrológico y establecimiento de estrategias para la conservación del recurso hídrico del lago Yahuarcocha. Published versión (2017). http://reposi torio.utn.edu.ec/handle/123456789/7652

13. Houghton, J., Siegel, M.: Advanced data analytics for system dynamics models using PYSD. In: Proceedings of the 33rd International Conference of the System Dynamics Society (2015). https://doi.org/10.5281/senodo.5654824

14. Smith, W.H.F., Sandwell, D.T.: Conventional bathymetry, bathymetry from space, and geodetic altimetry. Oceanography **17**(1), 8–23 (2004). https://doi.org/10.5670/oceanog.200 4.63

15. Yuan, C., Gong, P., Bai, Y.: Performance assessment of ICESat-2 laser altimeter data for water-level measurement over lakes and reservoirs in China. Remote Sens. **12**, 770 (2020). https://doi.org/10.3390/rs12050770

16. Fernando, G.: Mapping the diversity of agricultural systems in the Cuellaje sector, Cotacachi, Ecuador using ATL08 for the ICESat-2 mission and machine learning techniques. In: Gervasi, O., et al. (eds.) ICCSA 2021. LNCS, vol. 12957, pp. 170–181. Springer, Cham (2021). https://doi.org/10.1007/978-3-030-87013-3_13

17. Jasinski, M.F., et al.: ATLAS/ICESat-2 L3A Along Track Inland Surface Water Data, Version 5. [Indicate subset used]. Boulder, Colorado USA. NASA National Snow and Ice Data Center Distributed Active Archive Center (2021). https://doi.org/10.5067/ATLAS/ATL13.005

18. Zhang, G., Chen, W., Xie, H.: Tibetan Plateau's Lake level and volume change from NASA's ICESat/ICESat-2 and Landsat Missions. Geophys. Res. Lett. **46**, 13107–13118 (2019). https://doi.org/10.1029/2019GL085032

19. Xu, N., Zheng, H., Ma, Y., Yang, J., Liu, X., Wang, X.: Global estimation and assessment of monthly lake/reservoir water level changes using ICESat-2 ATL13 products. Remote Sens. **13**, 2744 (2021). https://doi.org/10.3390/rs13142744
20. Wang, Ch., et al.: Ground elevation accuracy verification of ICESat-2 data: a case study in Alaska, USA. Optical Society of America under the terms of the OSA Open Access Publishing Agreement, vol. 27, no. 26 (2019). Optics Express 38168. https://doi.org/10.1364/OE.27.038168
21. Lehner, B.: Messager. HydroLAKES - Technical Documentation Version 1.0. Department of Geography, McGill University Montreal, Quebec, Canada (2016). http://www.hydrosheds.org
22. Paredes-Beltran, B., Sordo-Ward, A., Garrote, L.: Dataset of georeferenced dams in South America (DDSA). Earth Syst. Sci. Data **13**(2), 213–229 (2021). https://doi.org/10.5194/essd-13-213-2021
23. Busker, T., et al.: A global lake and reservoir volume analysis using a surface water dataset and satellite altimetry. Hydrol. Earth Syst. Sci. **23**, 669–690 (2019). https://doi.org/10.5194/hess-23-669-2019
24. Lehner, B., Verdin, K., Jarvis, A.: New global hydrography derived from space-borne elevation data. Eos Trans. Am. Geophys. Union **89**(10), 93–94 (2008). https://doi.org/10.1029/2008eo100001. Data available at https://www.hydrosheds.org
25. Neuenschwander, A.L., et al.: ATLAS/ICESat-2 L3A Land and Vegetation Height, Version 4. [Indicate subset used]. Boulder, Colorado USA. NASA National Snow and Ice Data Center Distributed Active Archive Center (2021). https://doi.org/10.5067/ATLAS/ATL08.004
26. Messager, M., Lehner, B., Grill, G., et al.: Estimating the volume and age of water stored in global lakes using a geo-statistical approach. Nat. Commun. **7**, 13603 (2016). https://doi.org/10.1038/ncomms13603
27. Coppo Frias, M., et al.: River hydraulic modeling with ICESat-2 land and water surface elevation. EGUsphere [preprint] (2022). https://doi.org/10.5194/egusphere-2022-377
28. Hanson, R.L.: Evapotranspiration and Droughts. National Water Summary 1988–89–Hydrologic Events and Floods and Droughts: U.S. Geological Survey Water-Supply Paper, vol. 2375, pp. 99–104. https://geochange.er.usgs.gov/sw/changes/natural/et/
29. Perl, I., Ward, R.: sdCloud: Cloud-based computation environment for System Dynamics models. Saint Petersburg (Russia), National Research University of Information Technologies, Mechanics and Optics (ITMO), Iowa State University (2016). https://proceedings.systemdynamics.org/2016/proceed/papers/P1164.pdf
30. Müller Schmied, H., et al.: Sensitivity of simulated global-scale freshwater fluxes and storages to input data, hydrological model structure, human water use and calibration. Hydrol. Earth Syst. Sci. **18**(9), 3511–3538 (2014). https://doi.org/10.5194/hess-18-3511-2014
31. Lehner, B.: HydroSHEDS Technical Documentation version 1.4, Data Version 1.1. World Wildlife Fund-US, Washington, DC 20037 (2022). Data is available at https://www.hydrosheds.org

Hashtag2vec: Ranking of Disaster Related Tourism Spot's Hashtag on Twitter Data

Rupesh Kumar Mishra[1], Talla Prashanthi[2], T. Susmitha[2], K. Arjun[2], and Shree Harsh Attri[3(✉)]

[1] GITAM Deemed to be University, Hyderabad, Telangana, India
rmishra3@gitam.edu
[2] CBIT(A), Hyderabad, Telangana, India
{prashanthit_cse,susmithat_cse}@cbit.ac.in,
arjun.kondabathini@gmail.com
[3] Sharda University, Greater Noida, UP, India
Shree.harsh@sharda.ac.in

Abstract. The ever expanding disasters based tourism spots industry is drawing attention of folks through social networking sites, as people are travelling to corners of the world and encouraging many to fulfill their dreams. Our work is based upon retrieving the people experiences shared on twitter's hash tag and automatically generating the rank of disasters related tourist spots in search which are safe, easily approachable and economical as per the tourist reviews. In this paper, our work is divided into data collection and filtration and then using deep learning approaches, LSTM such as word2vec, tweet2vec, hash tag2vec and NCA for feature extraction and Long Short Term Memory techniques for classification we have applied to generate results. (1) Collections of disasters based tourist spot related hashtags datasets in english and non-english language both. After that, manually classify the datasets between English and non-english languages. (2) Hash2vec has been used for making labeled datasets called Semantic-tagged tokens and (3) Apply Long Short Term Memory approach with hash2vec model have been used for representing the document and predict the rank of disasters based tourism spots hash tag. This tool will help people and travel companies to classify tourist places as per their needs and it will also help to retrieve the world's top cities chart depending on the online ratings and reviews..

Keywords: Tweet2vec · hashtag2vec · LSTM · features extraction · Polarity score · hashtag embedding

1 Introduction

In these days, the impact of social media is on decision making in all regions around the globe. According to previous papers we can see that lots of models have been introduced for making the decision based on the twitter data. Most of papers had discussed about the product rating based upon the opinion of people which is given in the social media.

© Springer Nature Switzerland AG 2023
D. Garg et al. (Eds.): IACC 2022, CCIS 1781, pp. 112–123, 2023.
https://doi.org/10.1007/978-3-031-35641-4_8

Here we want to introduce the impact of social media in the disasters based tourism spots industry. Our goal is to first identify the disasters based tourism spots via related hash tag and related tweets from the twitter. For that we are using the Twitter API and Node- XL. Using Python we are extracting the twitter data from twitter API and from Node-XL we have imported the twitter database on disasters based tourism spots industry. After that we combine all the datasets and it has completed approx. of 1000000 tweet hash tag related to disasters based tourism spots. We have to provide the rank of hash tag related to disasters based tourism spots places based upon the score which we have calculated through the hash tag representation model (HRM).

The purpose of ranking of disasters based tourism spots places is to help the tourists and also those who want to go out for a vacation or thinking about going for a vacation. We have considered multiple aspects for giving the rank to disasters based tourism spots. In our research work, we have to design an infrastructure in which the users based query can be executed and result into the predictive results which users want. So for making this tool we will use the different types of representation techniques from which this tool could give the better result.

Here we are using the word representation (word2vec), tweet representation (tweet2vec) and hash tag representation (hash tag2vec) techniques. This kind of techniques will help to make the important datasets and that datasets will use to extract the exact predictions. Our motive should be to extract output according to the users. This kind of tool will be helpful to all the users, all the responsible resource which are involved in the tourism, our government and the experts. So through these tools we can collect the status of tourist places. Through this tool we can improve the awareness about risky tourism places of the government as well as users. Using these information tourists can decide whether it is safe and fruitful to visit that place or not.

In these days, all tourists have electronic gadgets like mobile phone, tab, and laptop so they want to gather all details of tourist places and make bookings from their home and want to book that place from their home. Hence, we also have to include opinion about services of booking facility in our datasets. Here we are not using traditional method to find out the ranking of disaster based tourist places. Here we are using hash tag representation model (usingtweet2vec and hash tag2vec) and polarity to find out the ranking of tourist places. First of all we have collected all the datasets (including hash tag) which are related to disaster based tourism spots. Then the data was pre-processed, and all the noisy data was removed from the datasets. After that we have used the hash tag representation model in which all pre- processed data will be represented as a vector in continuous bag of Word using tweet2vec and hash tag2vec. On the basis of CBOW all the data will be processed and provide the single result. One key aspect to design an algorithm from this tool that can be implemented is focused upon the efficiency. In this algorithm, tweet2vec and hash tag2vec approach will be used and for training and testing Long Short Term Memory approach is used. It will be helpful for decision making for disasters based tourism spots related query. Also one block diagram or flow diagram we have used for depicting the implementation of this kind of model. We have the set of datasets which could be used to test the tool and find out how much efficient that tool is. In this paper, organization of the content is as follows. In Sect. 2, we have discussed related work. In Sect. 3, we have discussed about how to pre-process all the disasters based tourism spots related data. In Sect. 4, we have discussed about how to classify the English and non English semantic tweets. In Sect. 5, we have discussed about hash tag representation model in which we have used tweet2vec and hash tag2vec for representing tweet and hash tag vectors. In Sect. 6, we have discussed about the outcomes of this model as we needed before implementing it. In Sect. 7, we have discussed about the conclusion and future work of this current model. And at last all references have been mentioned. The goal of tool is to process the millions of twitter data based upon the hash tag recommendation or ranking decided or rank the tourist places according to positive and negative opinions of the tourists. This tool is basically executed for the Twitter API data. At present we are manually taking twitter data. Through this tool when user will search about tourist places then he/she can see which tourist places are good or bad for his/her selection. Also this tool will help government in enhancement of the facility and making a good layout for that particular place. The main novelty of this paper is the collection of hash tag based twitter data manually after using twitters API. Also we can focus upon the English based tweets only. If we take all the language based tweets then we will have to apply the language translator and that translator will convert all non-English word or sentences into the English sentences. Also another thing which we have to focus upon is the datasets. If something is written in English but semantics are not in English then we will also have to think about that aspect in the model. Our model will be beneficial for the government and for all users on the basis of economic and safety purpose. Also this is beneficial for those private or public industries which are involved in the disasters based tourism spots.

2 Related Work

In the area of word representation, document representation and opinion mining, many researchers have given their contributions in order to recommend the hash tags in twitter. Some papers have more information about the recommendation of hash tags of twitter data. But no paper talks about the ranking of hash tag for tourist data with the help of tweet2vec and hash tag2vec both in our knowledge. Previously we have discussed about the HRM which we are going to develop for the twitter hash tag data that will be useful for all to find out the rank of disaster based tourist places. This will be popular because with the help of these tools we can improve the awareness about secure tourist places all over the world. In many papers, the tourist data has been compiled to get the recommendation of hash tags based on twitter data but this has not been done for all types of data which we want for tourists. However they are not ideal for the ranking of hash tag of tourist data. In turn, we have revised some relevant papers related to this subject.

In [1], authors show that a distributed memory model of paragraph vector (PV-DM) taking account into the word vector and paragraph vector to put in context into the result analysis. In this model, through BOW which finds several text classification and sentiment classification through paragraph vector and word vector approaches not the traditional approaches. Through this model all the paragraph vector and word vectors are trained using stochastic gradient descent and the gradient via back propagation. In this paper also introduce Distributed Bag- of-word version of Paragraph Vector (PV-DBOW) as opposed to Distributed Memory version of Paragraph Vector (PV-DM).

In [2], authors show that a word representation model taking the account into word vector to put in context into the result analysis. In this model, the word vector provides state-of-the-art performance on the measuring of syntactic and semantic word similarities. In this paper, try to maximize accuracy of word vector operations by developing this model that preserves the linear regularities among word. Here also mentioned about training time and accuracy depends on the dimensionality of the word vectors. This model has given better accuracy then the using previous word representation LSA and LDA.

In [3], authors shows that twitter blogging applications the account into the recommendation of hash tag in context into the result analysis. In this model how to different types of hash tag taken from the twitter and identify for a particular problem and define into as a recommendation. The presented algorithm is based on the analysis of similar tweets and the hash tags contained in these tweets. Basically these models used for evaluation of self-crawled data set which is consisting of 12 million tweets.

In [4], authors show that a Predictive Text Embedding through large scale heterogeneous network in which this application gives the result on both supervised and unsupervised learning concepts. Also in this application accuracy of information retrieval and information representation are more accurate than others like word representation, paragraph representation and document representation. In this paper the network used word to word, word to document and word to label. Through bipartite network embedding predict the next word, document. PTE has worked for long length document but CNN works for short length document. PTE works both on labelled and unlabeled data but CNN only works for labelled data.

In [5], authors shows that a character Composition Model, tweet2vec, which finds vector-space representations of whole tweets by learning complex, non-local dependencies in character sequences. The proposed model outperforms a word-level baseline at predicting user annotated hash tags associated with the posts, doing significantly better when the input contains many out-of-vocabulary words or unusual character sequences. All the data has been taken through twitter API and removed infrequent hash tags. In this paper, for the future scopes are tweet2vec embedding can be used in domains, where there is a need for semantic understanding of social media, such as tracking of infection diseases.

In [6], authors shows that a skip gram model which is efficient for learning high-quality distributed vector representation that capture a large number of precise syntactic and semantic word relationships. In this model it's identified an important word and on the basis of that word it defines the size of word embedding and on the basis of important word and word embedding give the target words and documents. Basically used a hierarchical soft max method to find out the target data. In this model basically the choice of training algorithm and the hyper-parameter selection is a task specific decision and the choice of model architecture is the size of the vectors, the sub sampling rate and the size of the training window.

In [7], authors shows that a Paragraph vector Model in which build the vector matrix on the basis of paragraph not on the basis of word. The proposed model has given better performance in comparison to other BOW and LDA or other unsupervised models. This Model has work on two tasks: benchmark paragraph vectors on the task of Wikipedia browsing and ar-Xiv browsing. Through this model paragraph vectors can effectively be used for measuring semantic similarity between long pieces of text.

In [8], author's shows that a Latent Dirichlet Allocation (LDA) Hash tag Recommendation model which works on unsupervised and context based hash tag recommendation of tweets. This model underlying topic assignment of language classified tweets. This model is used for short text classification. In this model Binary classification algorithm in which it is used for classifies between English and non-English language tweets. LDA is a hidden topic model in which it is selecting keyword for hash tag recommendation. In the paper, designed a binary language classifier for tweets based on the Naïve Baye's method and Expectation Maximization. The LDA can recommend the hash tag for tweets in a fully unsupervised manor. Advantage over existing work is the suggestion of general hash tag instead of sparse existing hash tag which enables effective categorization and search of tweets.

3   Sampling and Pre-processing

In order to build a representative of twitter datasets manually using python code on twitter API and import data in excel sheet from Node-XL sheet. On day by day data collected manually approximate of 60 days data which is 10,33,000 tweets related to disasters based tourism spots. Using python code on the retrieved datasets, apply pre-processing techniques to remove all the noisy data and make a tweet vector and hash tag vector.

4   Unsupervised Language Classification

When we collect and preprocessed all datasets, we can see there is lots of a tweet which is related to disasters based tourism spots but not in English language. There are all in unsupervised datasets so all those different types of language are classified between English and non-English. Here we have used only English language datasets. We have applied binary classification techniques (BCT) [8] to do this above classification. Also we can use the google translator machine for converting non-english tweets into English tweets.

5   Hashtag Representation Model (HRM)

In the Hash tag Representation Model (HRM), both the hash tag vector of disasters based tourism spots and tourist has to interlink with its own tweets which are related to disasters based tourism spots and tourist. In this model basically we are implementing a network of hash tag, which will help to easily retrieve different types of disasters based tourism spots related tweet in a minimum time frame. This model will work after pre-processed data which we are filtering from the applied methods. With the help of this model we have interconnect hash tag2vec with tweet2vec representation model.

In the Fig. 1, how we have processed the data and find out the result has been mentioned. In the previous paper I have applied KNN approach for classification. Also find out the Rank of the disaster based tourism spot.

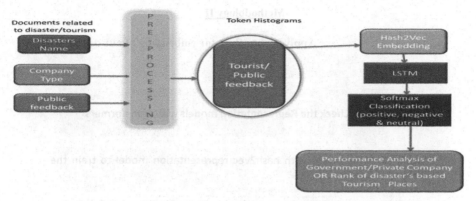

Fig. 1. HASH TAG REPRESENTATION MODEL (HRM)

Methodology I

Collected manually all thefeedback data related to disaster from online newsand social media post.

Classification manually between English and Spanish languages based feedback between non-Engli and non-Spanish language

Using pre-processing, remove all the un-necessary noisy data from manually classified data

Construct histogram   for   capturingfrequent meaningful words

Assign the polarity score in the pre- processed feedback data by comparingwith the manually assigned polarity scores

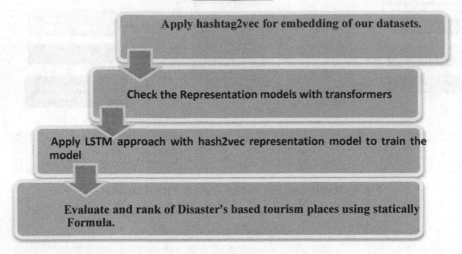

Methodology II

Apply hashtag2vec for embedding of our datasets.

Check the Representation models with transformers

Apply LSTM approach with hash2vec representation model to train the model

Evaluate and rank of Disaster's based tourism places using statically Formula.

6   Methodology

We have proposed steps for pre processing content of hash tag based disasters based tourism spots data. Sequence has been maintained for find out the rank of hash tag related to disasters based tourism spots for the proposed problem. The sequences are follows:

   i) Collect all disasters based tourism spots related hash tags from twitter and manually classify between English and non-English.
  ii) Pre-process all the content inside the hash tag in the twitter and remove all noisy data from it.
 iii) Apply senti-net-word for giving the polarity score of retrieved noisy free keywords either positive, neutral or negative.
  iv) Apply Hash2vec approach for embedding the processed datasets.
   v) Compare with transformer based embedded systems.
  vi) Apply LSTM on the trained model to organize the rank of disasters related tourist spots hash tags.

Here, we have introduced three flow diagram related to tourist places for achieving the goal. We have designed the combined model of three opinion based tokens. we applied a soft-max function on the semantic-tagged tweets to compute posterior hash tag probabilities (Figs. 2 and 3).

$$\text{Softmax } \sigma(\vec{z})i = \frac{e^{z_i}}{\sum_{j=1}^{K} e^{z_j}}$$

Finally, the semantic-tagged tweets are passed through a linear layer formula [5] to compute posterior hash tag probabilities.

$$\text{linear layer formula} = P(y = j|e) = \frac{\exp(W_j^T e + b_j)}{\sum_{i=1}^{L} \exp(W_j^T e + b_j)}$$

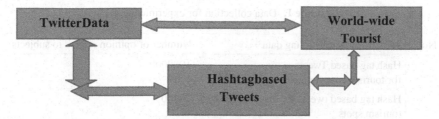

Fig. 2. Three semantic perspectives for characterizing performance context.

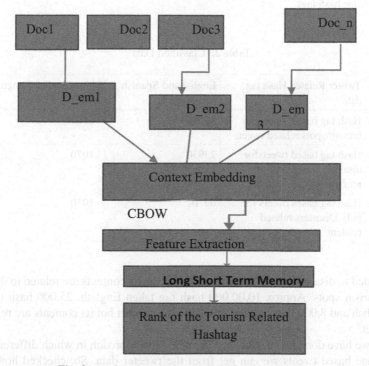

Fig. 3. Hashtag2vec(X1) and CNN for Classification

7 Result Analysis

We will test our tool on twitter based hash tag related to disasters based tourism spots for English and Non- English tweets. The statistics summarization for the datasets in Table 1 (Table 2).

• Hash tag based tweets:

All the hash tag which is based on disasters based tourism spots related content taken from Social media (Twitter) as an input for ranking to hash tags. Here we have considered English and Non-English based hash tag and also we are considering that hash tag which

Table 1. Data collection for experiments

S. No	Twitter Related Hash tag data	Number of opinion related to subjects
1	Hash tag based Tweets for tourism spots related tweets	1000000
2	Hash tag based tweets for disasters based tourism spots	25000
3	Hash tag bases tweets for only Disasters related content with different name hash tags	8000

Table 2. Classified Data

S. No	Twitter Related Hash tag data	Englishand Spanish Language	Non-English Language
1	Hash tag based Tweetsfor tourismspots related tweets	84970	15030
2	Hash tag based tweetsfor disasters based tourism spots	23930	1070
3	Hash tag bases tweets for only Disasters related content	6970	1030

is not related to disasters based tourism spots but the its contents are related to disasters based tourism spots. Approx 10,00,000 hash tag taken English, 25,000 hash tag as a Non-English and 8,000 hash tag not related to the subject but its contents are related to the subject.

Here we have done language based classification approach in which different types of language based tweets we can get from the tweeter data. So, checked how many of English based tweets and how many of other than English based. We have to first translate all the non English language based tweets into in English because this tool is working only in the English based tweets.

In this Table 3, we have to interconnect between the public opinion with tourism places and disasters because we have to rank of all the tourism places which is affected with different types of disasters. That will be designed the histogram with the help of hash2vec method before applying the long short term memory deep learning approach.

In the Table 4, we have found the rank of hash tag based tweets which are related to disasters based tourism spot. On the basis of public opinions the ranking of different countries which effects or related to disasters. Here +1 shown the country's most regularly effected tourism place. −1 shown the less effected but not regularly.0 shown not affected. This ranking has been given on the basis of prediction scores. The formula we

Table 3. Histogram for Interconnected between of Public Opinion, Tourism Places and Disasters

Public Opinion	Tourism Places	Disaster's Name
#KEDARNATH	India	FLOOD
#BHUJ&KACHCH H	India	EARTHQUAKE
#CORONA	US	COVID 19
#SAAS DISEASE	China	SAAS
#AIDS DISEASE	Africa	AIDS
#REFUGEE	Nepal	WAR
#HUMANITARIAN	Sri Lanka	ZIKA Virus

Table 4. Ranking of different organization during disasters

Tourism Places	Disasters Name	Hash tagbased Tweets	Score s	Rank of Hash tag based tourim spot
India	FLOOD	#KEDARNATH	0.85	+ 1
India	EARTHQU AKE	#BHUJ&KACHCH H	0.82	+ 1
US	COVID 19	#CORONA	0.87	+ 1
China	SAAS	#SAAS DISEASE	0.77	+ 1
Africa	AIDS	#AIDS DISEASE	0.60	0
Nepal	WAR	#REFUGEE	0.51	− 1
Sri Lanka	ZIKA Virus	#HUMANITARIAN	0.49	-1

have used for ranking this hash tag is:

$$\frac{\sum_{k=1}^{n} (P_k - N_k) * 5/TF}{n}$$

Where P and N is a positive and negative feedback.

TF = Total no of feedback of the individual tourism spot n = Different types of feedback questions. On the basis of feature extraction, system has predicted the score of all different tourism places who is effected from disasters. Also here we have keep in minds that which places are manmade or natural disasters and how many times it occurs during a month or year. So based upon this we have given rank. We know that the persons do plan for vacation either in a year or two times in a year. So month wise data we have taken and analyze that data and provide the rank.

8　Conclusions and Future Work

In the present work we have described a set of experiments with convolution neural network on top of tweet2vec and hash tag2vec. The contribution of our work has given impact on social media to retrieve a effective results for tourists. The model HRM, which Rank the hash tag for only tourist places and Rank those tourist places based upon different aspects. From this experiment, we get an evidence for unsupervised pre-training of hash tag vector and tweet vector to apply an important ingredient in Deep learning for NLP.

References

1. Mikolov, T.: Distributed representation of sentences and documents. In: International Conference on Machine Learning, vol. 32. JMLR: W&CP. Beijing (2014)
2. Mikolov, T.: Efficient estimation of word representation in vector space. CoRR, abs/1309.4168 (2013b)
3. Zangerle, E., Gassler, W., Specht, G.: Recommending hash tags in Twitter. In: Proceeding of the Workshop on Semantic Adaptive Social web (2011)
4. Tang, J., Qu, M., Mei, Q.: PTE:Predictive text embedding through large scale hetrogenious text networks. In: KDD 2015, 10–13 August 2015, Sydney (2015)
5. Dhingra, B., Zhou, Z., Fitz, D., Muehl, M., Cohen, W.: Tweet2vec: character-based distributed representación for social media. In: ACL (2016)
6. Mikolov, T., Sutskever, I., Chen, K., Carrado, G., Dean, J.: Distributed representations of words and phrases and their compositionality In: NIPS, pp. 3111–3119 (2013)
7. Dai, A.M., Olah, C., Le, Q.V.: DocumentEmbeddingwithParagraphVectors, arXiv:1507.079 98v1 [cs.CL] (2015)
8. Godin, F., Slavkovikj, V., De Neve, W., Schrauwen, B.: UsingTopicModelsfor Twitter Hashtag Recommendation. 13–17 May 2013 Rio de JaneiroACM (2013). 978–1–4503–2038–2/13/05
9. Walle, R.V.D.: UsingTopicModelsfor Twitter Hash tag Recommendation. 13–17 May 2013 Rio de Janeiro, Brazil, ACM (2013). 978–1–4503–2038–2/13/05
10. Mishra, R., Berlanga, L., Srinathan, K.: Automatic Tracking of Tourism Spots for Tourists Using Social Media, pp. 777–783 (2019)
11. Berlanga, R., García-Moya, L., Nebot, V., Aramburu, M.J., Sanz, I., Llidó, D.M.: SLOD-BI: an open data infrastructure for enabling social business intelligence. Int. J. Data Warehouse. Min. (IJDWM) 11(4), 1–28 (2015)
12. Schnebele, E., Cervone, G., Kumar, S., Waters, N.: Real time estimation of the calgary floods using limited remote sensing data. Water 6(2), 381–398 (2014)
13. Kumar, S., Hu, X., Liu, H.: A behavior analytics approach to identifying tweets from crisis regions. ACM (2014.) ISBN: 978–1–4503–2954–5
14. Mandel, B., Culotta, A., Boulahanis, J., Stark, D., Lewis, B., Rodrigue, J.: A demographic analysis of online sentiment during hurricane Irene (2012)
15. Nagy, A., Stamberger, J.A.: Crowd sentiment detection during disasters and crises. In: Proceedings of the 9th International ISCRAM Conference-Vancovuver (2012)
16. Mishra, R., Saini, K.: Automatic detection of interlinked events for better disaster management. In: IEEE, IACC-2014, ITM Gurgaon (2014)
17. Kim, Y.: Convolutional neural network for sentence classification. arXiv:1408.5882v2 (2014)
18. Weston, J., Bordes, A., Yakhnenko, O., Usunier, N.: Connecting language and knowledge bases with embedding models for relation extraction. In: Proceeding of the Conference on Empirical Methods in Natural Language Processing (EMNLP) (2013)

19. Sainath, T.N., Vinyals, O., Senior, A., Sak, H.: Convolutional, long short term memory, fully connected deep neural networks. In: 2015 IEEE International Conference on Acoustics, Speech and Signal Processing (ICASSP), pp. 4580–4584. IEEE (2015)
20. Mishra, R., Berlanga, L., Srinathan, K.: Sentiment and Semantic Embeddings for Disaster Decision Making. In: IEEE Indiacom Conference, New Delhi (2018)
21. Kolla, M., Mishra, R.K.: CNN-based brain tumor detection model using local binary pattern and multilayered SVM classifier. Int. J. (Comput. Intell. Neurosci. Hindawi), Scopus, Web of Science, SCIE, UGC (2022). https://www.hindawi.com/journals/cin/2022/9015778/
22. Kolla, M., Mishra, R.K.: Design and implementation of brain tumor segmentation and detection using a novel Woelfel filter and morphological segmentation. Int. J. (Complexity Hindawi), Scopus, Web of Science, SCIE, UGC (2022). https://www.hindawi.com/journals/complexity/2022/6985927/29

Vision Transformer and Bidirectional RoBERTa: A Hybrid Image Captioning Model Between VirTex and CPTR

Khang Nhut Lam[1]([envelope]) [iD], Diem-Kieu Thi Le[1] [iD], Truong Dinh Ngo[1] [iD], and Jugal Kalita[2] [iD]

[1] Can Tho University, Can Tho, Vietnam
{lnkhang,ltdkieu}@ctu.edu.vn
[2] University of Colorado, Colorado Springs, USA
jkalita@uccs.edu

Abstract. Image captioning neural networks are trained simultaneously on image recognition sub-models and natural language processing sub-models to generate description sentences for images. This paper presents several image captioning models based on the encoder-decoder framework. We change the neural sub-models used for the encoder as well as the decoder, and make comparisons. First, we experiment with several ResNet architectures (viz., ResNet-50, ResNet-101, and ResNet-152) as encoders, and Transformer or bidirectional Transformer models as decoders. Second, we use the combination of the Vision Transformer as a visual encoder, and the standard Transformer or RoBERTa as the language decoder. Finally, we propose an image captioning model using Vision Transformer for encoding images and bidirectional Transformer for predicting image captions. The models are trained on the Flickr8k dataset in English and Vietnamese and evaluated using the BLEU metric. The combination model between the Vision Transformer and the bidirectional RoBERTa model outperforms the existing image captioning models, including VirTex and CPTR models. The BLEU-1, BLEU-2, BLEU-3, and BLEU-4 scores of our best image captioning model are 0.870, 0.661, 0.443, and 0.331 on the English dataset, and 0.829, 0.647, 0.483, and 0.387 on the Vietnamese dataset.

Keywords: Image captioning · ResNet · Transformer · bidirectional Transformer · RoBERTa · bidirectional RoBERTa · Vietnamese

1 Introduction

An image captioning model based on an encoder-decoder framework consists of a neural network model for understanding and extracting image features, which are then fed to a language model for generating image description sentences. The visual encoder is usually a type of convolutional neural network (CNN) such as VGG, Inception, and ResNet. The language decoder is a neural network language model (NNLM) such as RNN, LSTM, and GRU. A vanilla combination of CNN

© Springer Nature Switzerland AG 2023
D. Garg et al. (Eds.): IACC 2022, CCIS 1781, pp. 124–137, 2023.
https://doi.org/10.1007/978-3-031-35641-4_9

and NNLM leads to incorrect object detection and thus inappropriate caption generation [29]. Therefore, several approaches have been introduced to improve the quality of image captioning, such as applying attention and introducing geometric object relations.

Chen and Zitnick [4] generate image caption sentences using a bidirectional RNN for mapping between images and caption sentences. The model creates not only sentences from the visual observations or image features, but also the visual features from sentences. To improve the quality of description sentences, attention mechanisms have been applied to image captioning models. Huang et al. [15] propose an encoder-decoder model with a conventional attention mechanism, called an Attention on Attention (AoA), for constructing image captions. The AoA module generates information vectors from the context and the attention result, creates an attention gate from the query and the attention result, adds another attention by applying the attention gate to information vectors, and obtains attended information. The image captioning model using a CNN-based network for an encoder and an LSTM [13] for a decoder with the AoA module outperforms existing encoder-decoder models such as CNN-LSTM, self-critical sequence training [27] using the reinforcement learning, and a scene graph auto-encoder [36] applied to both encoder and decoder.

Early image captioning models often did not detect objects well; therefore, much research has been devoted to overcome this issue. Yang et al. [37] introduce a multi-model neural network to automatically generate image captions. Faster R-CNN [26] is used to extract the objects and their locations in the image. The object detection model is used to detect N objects in the image, each of which is represented as a feature vector. Then, each object with its corresponding bounding box is considered a new image and fed to VGG16 [30] to extract a feature vector for it. An object is represented by two feature vectors describing the content of the image and the object location in the image. These feature vectors are fed to an LSTM model with an attention mechanism to build caption sentences. Li et al. [20] propose a global-local attention (GLA) method to handle incorrect detection of objects in an image captioning model. The global and local image features are extracted from the fc7 layer of VGG16 and the top-n detected objects recognized by Faster R-CNN, respectively. Through the attention mechanism, the GLA method integrates local representation at object level with global representation at the image level. Finally, LSTM is used to create image caption sentences. The GLA model, with a beam size of 3, achieves the best performance. Al-Malla et al. [1] also improve the quality of captions by using object detection features. The encoder block consists of a pre-trained image classification Xception CNN [5] model and a pre-trained object detection YOLOv4 [2]. The CNN features and object features are concatenated and fed to a language generation model to decode captions.

Herdade et al. [12] propose a spatial attention-based encoder-decoder model that integrates information about the spatial relationship between objects detected through geometric attention. Object detection and feature extraction are performed by using Faster R-CNN with ResNet-101, while description generation is performed using the Object Relation Transformer, which discovers spatial relationships among objects. He et al. [11] propose an image captioning model using an image Transformer architecture. The model uses Faster-RCNN for detecting regions, 3 sub-Transformer layers for discovering spatial relationships, and LSTMs and a Transformer for decoding captions. Geometric relationships among objects for improving the quality of captions is also explored by Wang et al. [34]. They propose a Geometry Attention Transformer comprising a geometry self-attention refiner encoder to detect geometric object relations and represent objects detected and a position-LSTM decoder to generate captions.

Feng et al. [9] construct caption sentences for images using an unsupervised method. Their model comprises an image encoder, a sentence generator, and a sentence discriminator. Inception-V4 is used to extract image features, which are then fed to the LSTM to generate image captions. The discriminator is used to decide whether an image caption sentence should be generated from the model or extracted from the corpus. For experiments, images are extracted from the MS COCO dataset, while the caption sentences are extracted from Shutterstock[1]. Bidirectional generative adversarial networks are used to construct image descriptions. Wang and Cook [35] introduce a model, including a caption generator for constructing image caption sentences and a caption discriminator for evaluating the quality of captions. The generator model consists of a CNN and a BiLSTM with attention to extract image features and generate image captions, respectively. Similar to the generator model, the discriminator model also comprises CNN and BiLSTM, along with a scoring system for measuring the similarity between output vectors of LSTM and CNN.

Staniūtė and Šešok [31] observe that although ResNet has fewer parameters, it outperforms other variant CNN models, while Dosovitskiy et al. [8] claim that Vision Transformer outperforms CNN models "without pre-training or strong augmentation" [3] in computer vision tasks. Transformer [33] is currently state-of-the-art language model. In this paper, we explore the effectiveness of an encoder based on various ResNet architectures and Vision Transformer, and a decoder based on Transformers for the image captioning. We perform experiments on the Flickr8k [14] dataset in both English and Vietnamese. The contributions of our work are enumerated below.

- We explore several ResNet architectures to extract image features, and Transformer or bidirectional Transformer to create image captions.
- We experiment with image captioning models using a Vision Transformer as encoder, and Transformer or RoBERTa as decoder.
- We introduce a hybrid image captioning model which encodes image features using a Vision Transformer and produces image description sentences using a bidirectional RoBERTa model.
- We create a Flickr8k dataset in Vietnamese, which may be used to train other image captioning models in Vietnamese.

The remaining sections of our paper are structured as follows. Image captioning models, including our approach proposed, are presented in Sect. 2. Experimental results are discussed in Sect. 3. Section 4 concludes the paper.

---

[1] https://www.shutterstock.com/.

2   Image Captioning Models

In this work, we create description sentences for images using the encoder-decoder framework. The image captioning model consists of a visual encoder for encoding image features and a language model for predicting captions. The visual encoder may be a CNN-based model, combinations of a CNN-based model and an attention mechanism over grids or regions, a graph-based method with attention mechanisms and region relations, and a self-attention method based on Transformer [32]. The decoder may be a language model based on neural networks with or without attention mechanisms. This section presents image caption models using several types of ResNet architectures and Vision Transformer for encoders, and Transformer and bidirectional Transformer for decoders.

2.1   ResNet and Transformer

The encoder-decoder framework using ResNet and Transformer for image captioning is presented. ResNet [10], using CNN blocks, was introduced to handle the problems of vanishing gradient of traditional CNN networks by building residual learning blocks with the skip connection technique. The ResNet visual encoder receives raw image pixels, computes the visual features of images, and outputs a spatial grid of image features. Image features are a matrix of shape $N_I D_i$ giving a D_I-dimensional vector for each of the $N_I = 7 \times 7$ positions in the final layer of the visual encoder. In particular, the model accepts a 224×224 image and produces a 7×7 grid of 2,048-dimensional features after the final convolutional layer. A linear projection layer is applied to the visual features before passing them to the language model to facilitate decoder attention over visual features. The traditional Transformer decoder receives image features and generates captions for images. In particular, the description sentence is segmented into tokens $c_0, c_1, \ldots, c_T, c_{T+1}$, where $c_0 = [SOS]$ is a start-of-sentence token and $c_{T+1} = [EOS]$ is an end-of-sentence token. The decoder receives embeddings of $c_0, c_1, \ldots, c_T, c_{T+1}$ tokens with the corresponding positional embeddings as inputs and predicts tokens.

2.2   ResNet and Bidirectional Transformer

An interesting image captioning model, called VirTex [6], uses ResNet-50 for a visual encoder and bidirectional Transformer or bi-Transformer for a decoder. In VirTex, the decoder predicts captions in forward and backward directions by using 2 original Transformer decoders. Additionally, the Transformer decoder running forward as presented in the previous method, VirTex uses another Transformer decoder running backward which receives embeddings of $c_{T+1}, c_T, \ldots, c_1, c_0$ tokens and corresponding positional embeddings as inputs. Finally, they are jointly trained to maximize the log-likelihood of the correct caption tokens using the following formula.

$$
L(\theta, \phi) = \sum_{t=1}^{T+1} log\left(p\left(c_t | c_{0:t-1}, I; \phi_f, \theta\right)\right) + \sum_{t=0}^{T} log\left(p\left(c_t | c_{t+1:T+1}, I; \phi_b, \theta\right)\right), \quad (1)
$$

where θ, ϕ_f, ϕ_b are parameters of the encoder, forward and backward Transformer models, respectively.

2.3 Vision Transformer and Transformer

An image captioning model based on Transformer, called CPTR [21] uses a Vision Transformer for encoder and a standard Transformer for decoder. The given images are resized and partitioned into non-overlapped patches of fixed sizes. These patches are then flattened, reshaped and linearly embedded into vectors, added to the positional embeddings, and fed to the Transformer encoder. The Transformer encoder and decoder have a stack of N_e and N_d identical layers, respectively. The Transformer decoder receives output of the encoder and the previous decoder output to predict the next words. CPTR minimizes the cross entropy loss using the following formula.

$$L(\theta) = - \sum_{t=0}^{T} log\left(p_\theta\left(c_t|c_{0:t-1}\right)\right), \qquad (2)$$

where $c_{1:T}, c_t, \theta$ are ground truth sentence, image description sentence generated, and a parameter of the model, respectively.

2.4 Vision Transformer and Bidirectional Transformer

A hybrid model between VirTex and CPTR, as presented in Fig. 1, uses a Vision Transformer to encode the images and a bidirectional Transformer to decode image captions. This model encodes images using the same method as the CPTR model. The given images are partitioned, flattened, reshaped, embedded, enhanced with positional embeddings, and fed to the Transformer encoder. To predict the description sentences, this model uses two Transformer models running backward and forward, similar to the decoder in VirTex. Currently, RoBERTa [22], a robustly optimized BERT [7] which uses only Transformer encoder, has achieved state-of-the-art results in many natural language processing tasks. The main difference between RoBERTa and BERT is that BERT uses static masking patterns, whereas RoBERTa uses dynamic masking patterns. Therefore, we improve the image captioning model by using Vision Transformer as encoder and bidirectional RoBERTa as decoder.

3 Experiments

Our experiments are performed in the Google Colaboratory environment, Pro version, 1 GPU (16 GB VRAM), Python version 3.9. We use the Flickr8k [14] dataset consisting of 8,091 photos and 40,455 captions in English. We perform experiments on the Flickr8k dataset in Vietnamese, which is obtained by translating from the original Flickr8k using the googletrans[2] library. The datasets are split into two parts with a ratio of 80% for training and 20% for testing.

[2] https://pypi.org/project/googletrans/.

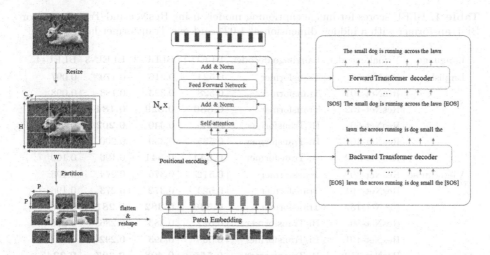

Fig. 1. Vision Transformer and bidirectional Transformer for image captioning inspired from VirTex [6] and CPTR [21].

The caption sentences are pre-processed by converting sentences to lower-cases, removing special characters, and punctuation marks. We tokenize captions with SentencePiece [16] using the BPE algorithm [28], and lowercase words. We obtain an English vocabulary set with 20,000 tokens and a Vietnamese vocabulary set with 9,000 tokens. The BLEU (Bilingual Evaluation Understudy) [23] metric is used to evaluate image captioning models.

3.1 ResNet and Transformer-Based Language Decoders

In this section, we discuss experiments with (i) several ResNet architectures, including RestNet-50, ResNet-101 and ResNet-152, as encoders to find the most effective ResNet for extracting image features, (ii) Transformer and bidirectional Transformer models as decoders, and make comparison. The combined models are trained with a batch size of 128 images for 20,000 iterations (392 epochs). We use the same learning rates as the work of Desai and Johnson [6]. In particular, the maximum learning rate values for the visual encoder and the decoder are 2×10^{-1} and 2×10^{-3}, respectively. We perform experiments with different parameters settings. Let H be the width of each Transformer layer, and L be the number of Transformer layers used to control the depth of language model. Initially, we use the same parameters for Transformers with H = 1024, L = 1, beam size of 5, and the Adam optimizer. The BLEU scores of the models on the Flickr8k dataset in English and Vietnamese are presented in Table 1.

We notice that the image captioning model using ResNot and bidirectional Transformer outperforms the model using ResNet and Transformer in all cases. In other words, the bi-Transformer model helps achieve better BLEU scores in both English and Vietnamese Flickr8k datasets than using the Transformer model. Therefore, we stop further experiments with ResNet and Transformer. In

Table 1. BLEU scores for image captioning models using ResNet and Transformer or Bi-Transformer with a hidden dimension of 1,024 and one Transformer layer.

Language	Visual encoder	Language decoder	BLEU-1	BLEU-2	BLEU-3	BLEU-4
English	ResNet-50	Transformer	0.524	0.316	0.179	0.097
	ResNet-101	Transformer	0.528	0.323	0.183	0.098
	ResNet-152	Transformer	**0.530**	**0.329**	**0.184**	**0.101**
	ResNet-50	Bi-Transformer	0.533	0.340	**0.202**	**0.116**
	ResNet-101	Bi-Transformer	0.535	0.339	0.200	0.114
	ResNet-152	Bi-Transformer	**0.544**	**0.341**	0.196	0.100
Vietnamese	ResNet-50	Transformer	0.512	0.376	0.274	0.196
	ResNet-101	Transformer	0.523	0.372	0.273	0.196
	ResNet-152	Transformer	**0.536**	**0.382**	**0.281**	**0.203**
	ResNet-50	Bi-Transformer	0.522	0.383	0.286	0.208
	ResNet-101	Bi-Transformer	0.539	0.393	0.292	0.211
	ResNet-152	Bi-Transformer	**0.555**	**0.408**	**0.307**	**0.224**

the next experiments, we only use ResNet and bidirectional Transformer with different parameters, as presented in Table 2 and Table 3.

The results in Table 2 and Table 3 show that using deeper L and wider H, bidirectional Transformers achieve better results. Moreover, higher-capacity visual encoders potentially improve the models' performance. The models using ResNet-152 for extracting image features achieve higher BLEU scores than models using ResNet-50 and ResNet-101.

3.2 Vision Transformer and Transformer-Based Language Decoders

We train the model with a batch size of 20 images for 46,500 iterations (30 epochs). Both Greedy and Beam searches of size of 5 are used. The learning rate is 2×10^{-5} as suggested by Liu et al. [22]. The number of layers in the encoder and decoder are 12 and 4, respectively, and the attention head number is 12, as suggested of Liu et al [21]. We experiment with Adam, RMSprop, and SGD optimizers. We notice that the Adam optimizer converges faster then the others. Therefore, the following experiments use the Adam optimizer to improve performance. Table 4 presents BLEU scores for image captioning models using Vision Transformer as encoder and Transformer or RoBERTa as decoder on the Flickr8k dataset in English. In this table, the column called "Images resized" means the size of images after the step of pre-processing. The images resized are partitioned into fixed patches of 32×32 pixels.

The visual encoder using Vision Transformer with the capability of "modeling global context at every encoder layer" [21] improves the image captioning model much better than ResNet. In addition, the RoBERTa model generates better captions for images. Therefore, we use RoBERTa as a decoder in the next set of experiments. The size of the images after pre-processing has little impact on the image captioning model. To facilitate comparison, images after the step of pre-processing

Table 2. BLEU scores for image captioning models using ResNet and Bi-Transformer on the Flickr8k dataset in English.

Visual encoder	Language decoder	L	H	BLEU-1	BLEU-2	BLEU-3	BLEU-4
ResNet-50	Bi-Transformer	1	512	0.418	0.248	0.132	0.071
		1	768	0.527	0.332	0.189	0.100
		1	1024	0.533	0.340	0.202	0.116
		2	1024	0.551	0.336	0.191	0.107
		3	1024	0.550	0.337	0.190	0.107
		4	1024	0.550	0.349	0.207	0.123
		1	2048	0.555	0.343	0.206	0.122
		2	2048	0.555	0.369	0.237	0.149
		3	2048	**0.568**	**0.378**	**0.245**	**0.153**
ResNet-101	Bi-Transformer	1	512	0.444	0.269	0.1447	0.080
		1	768	0.503	0.321	0.182	0.096
		1	1024	0.535	0.339	0.200	0.114
		2	1024	0.550	0.339	0.197	0.106
		3	1024	0.555	0.355	0.215	0.131
		4	1024	0.564	0.368	0.229	0.144
		1	2048	**0.570**	0.347	0.206	0.113
		2	2048	0.561	0.364	0.225	0.134
		3	2048	0.558	**0.370**	**0.239**	**0.154**
ResNet-152	Bi-Transformer	1	512	0.446	0.269	0.141	0.074
		1	768	0.516	0.325	0.182	0.097
		1	1024	0.544	0.341	0.196	0.100
		2	1024	0.558	0.344	0.198	0.108
		3	1024	0.558	0.349	0.208	0.123
		4	1024	**0.578**	0.368	0.223	0.134
		1	2048	0.560	0.326	0.192	0.112
		2	2048	0.544	0.341	0.202	0.116
		3	2048	0.555	**0.361**	**0.225**	**0.136**

are resized to 224 × 224, the same size as fed to the image captioning model using ResNet and Transformer. Table 5 shows the BLEU scores for image captioning using Vision Transformer and RoBERTa on the Flickr8k dataset in Vietnamese.

Finally, we evaluate the image captioning models using Vision Transformer and bidirectional RoBERTa or bi-RoBERTa in the Flickr8k dataset in both English and Vietnamese, as presented in Table 6. Some examples of image description sentences created using Vision Transformer and bi-RoBERTa are shown in Fig. 2.

3.3 Discussion

Experimental results show that the higher capacity visual encoders potentially improve the model's performance, and the backward and forward Transformer

Table 3. BLEU scores for image captioning models using ResNet and Bi-Transformer on the Flickr8k dataset in Vietnamese.

Visual encoder	Language decoder	L	H	BLEU-1	BLEU-2	BLEU-3	BLEU-4
ResNet-50	Bi-Transformer	1	512	0.426	0.305	0.225	0.162
		1	768	0.499	0.350	0.254	0.183
		1	1024	0.522	0.383	0.286	0.208
		2	1024	0.565	0.419	0.317	0.233
		3	1024	0.568	0.430	0.329	0.245
		4	1024	0.570	0.424	0.335	0.253
		1	2048	0.571	0.427	0.372	0.247
		2	2048	0.588	0.451	0.353	0.271
		3	2048	**0.588**	**0.452**	**0.354**	**0.273**
ResNet-101	Bi-Transformer	1	512	0.462	0.333	0.246	0.178
		1	768	0.523	0.373	0.276	0.200
		1	1024	0.539	0.393	0.292	0.211
		2	1024	0.572	0.431	0.329	0.245
		3	1024	0.570	0.433	0.333	0.250
		4	1024	0.574	0.441	0.343	0.260
		1	2048	0.593	0.452	0.352	0.268
		2	2048	0.597	0.457	0.356	0.273
		3	2048	**0.599**	**0.461**	**0.361**	**0.277**
ResNet-152	Bi-Transformer	1	512	0.425	0.304	0.224	0.161
		1	768	0.526	0.380	0.279	0.201
		1	1024	0.555	0.408	0.307	0.224
		2	1024	0.586	0.444	0.340	0.253
		3	1024	0.578	0.443	0.343	0.259
		4	1024	0.577	0.445	0.346	0.263
		1	2048	0.603	0.455	0.351	0.265
		2	2048	0.603	0.474	0.372	0.276
		3	2048	**0.614**	**0.468**	**0.368**	**0.285**

decoders predict better image captions than using only a forward Transformer decoder. In addition, Vision Transformer with the capacity of modeling global context at each layer of the encoder notably improves the image captioning model. Moreover, RoBERTa helps decode much better image captions than the standard Transformer model. The combination of Vision Transformer and bi-RoBERTa helps create the best image description sentences in Vietnamese. Interestingly, on the Flickr8k dataset in English, the BLEU scores of image captioning models using Vision Transformer and RoBERTa are very close to the scores of models using Vision Transformer and bi-RoBERTa.

For the sake of comparison, we compare our work with the work of Lam et al. [17]. Lam et al. construct image caption sentences in Vietnamese using VGG16 for extracting image features and LSTM for creating image captions. The authors improve the model by performing color recognition on the color of

Table 4. BLEU scores for image captioning models using Vision Transformer and a language model based Transformer on the Flickr8k dataset in English.

Images resized	Language decoder	Selection	BLEU-1	BLEU-2	BLEU-3	BLEU-4
224 × 224	Transformer	Greedy	0.859	0.754	0.638	0.555
224 × 224	Transformer	Beam	0.824	0.749	0.615	0.528
384 × 384	Transformer	Greedy	0.818	0.537	0.293	0.193
384 × 384	Transformer	Beam	0.822	0.540	0.296	0.190
224 × 224	Roberta base	Greedy	0.874	0.674	0.465	0.356
224 × 224	Roberta base	Beam	0.862	0.687	0.508	0.404
224 × 224	Roberta large	Greedy	0.882	0.711	0.526	0.420
224 × 224	Roberta large	Beam	0.870	0.696	0.519	0.384
384 × 384	Roberta base	Greedy	0.869	0.638	0.413	0.302
384 × 384	Roberta base	Beam	0.874	0.713	0.540	0.440
384 × 384	Roberta large	Greedy	0.882	0.720	0.542	0.440
384 × 384	Roberta large	Beam	0.872	0.707	0.535	0.433

Table 5. BLEU scores for image captioning models using Vision Transformer and RoBERTa on the Flickr8k in Vietnamese.

Language decoder	Selection	BLEU-1	BLEU-2	BLEU-3	BLEU-4
RoBERTa base	Greedy	0.801	0.609	0.435	0.333
RoBERTa base	Beam	0.814	0.628	0.439	0.318
RoBERTa large	Greedy	0.808	0.613	0.443	0.344
RoBERTa large	Beam	0.814	0.628	0.439	0.317

objects using YOLOv5 [25]. The BLEU scores from BLEU-1 to BLEU-4 of their model on the Flickr8k dataset in Vietnamese are 0.629, 0.426, 0.281, and 0.175, respectively. Currently, the BLEU-1, 2, 3 and 4 scores of the best model using ResNet-152 and bi-Transformer with L = 3 and H = 2048, are 0.614, 0.468, 0.368, and 0.285; whereas the scores of the best model using Vision Transformer and bi-RoBERTa are 0.829, 0.647, 0.486, and 0.387, respectively. Both Lam's models [17] and the models reported in this paper can construct captions for images, each of which has one object or person, very well. A drawback of their proposed approach is that the model using vanilla CNN and LSTM [17] cannot generate image caption sentences to describe groups of objects in the images. The captions generated by using ResNet or Vision Transformer and Transformer or bi-Transformer models can not only describe one object but also a group of objects including attributes, spatial arrangement, and actions of objects.

In addition, for generating image caption sentences in Vietnamese, our proposed models using ViT and Bi-RoBERTa outperform all image captioning models using VGG-16 and ResNet as image encoders and LSTM as a decoder, proposed by Lam et al. [18]. The BLEU-1, 2, 3, and 4 of their best model [18] are 0.710, 0.575, 0.476, and 0.394, respectively.

Table 6. BLEU scores for image captioning models using Vision Transformer and Bi-RoBERTa on the Flickr8k dataset.

Language	Encoder	Decoder	Selection	BLEU-1	BLEU-2	BLEU-3	BLEU-4
English	ViT	Bi-RoBERTa base	Greedy	0.865	0.633	0.406	0.295
English	ViT	Bi-RoBERTa base	Beam	0.835	0.612	0.390	0.281
English	ViT	Bi-RoBERTa large	Greedy	0.870	0.661	0.443	0.331
English	ViT	Bi-RoBERTa large	Beam	0.829	0.623	0.414	0.307
Vietnamese	ViT	Bi-RoBERTa base	Greedy	0.829	0.647	0.483	0.387
Vietnamese	ViT	Bi-RoBERTa base	Beam	0.817	0.617	0.446	0.345
Vietnamese	ViT	Bi-RoBERTa large	Greedy	0.822	0.641	0.479	0.382
Vietnamese	ViT	Bi-RoBERTa large	Beam	0.804	0.609	0.441	0.340

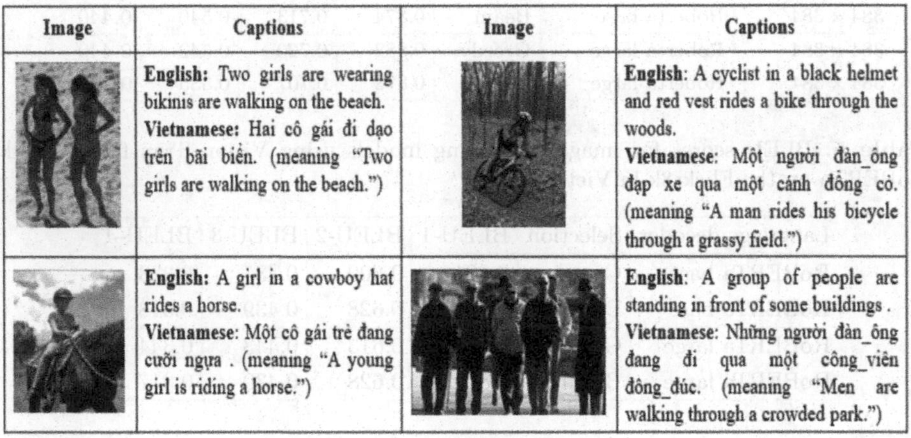

Image	Captions	Image	Captions
	English: Two girls are wearing bikinis are walking on the beach. **Vietnamese:** Hai cô gái đi dạo trên bãi biển. (meaning "Two girls are walking on the beach.")		**English:** A cyclist in a black helmet and red vest rides a bike through the woods. **Vietnamese:** Một người đàn_ông đạp xe qua một cánh đồng cỏ. (meaning "A man rides his bicycle through a grassy field.")
	English: A girl in a cowboy hat rides a horse. **Vietnamese:** Một cô gái trẻ đang cưỡi ngựa . (meaning "A young girl is riding a horse.")		**English:** A group of people are standing in front of some buildings . **Vietnamese:** Những người đàn_ông đang đi qua một công_viên đông_đúc. (meaning "Men are walking through a crowded park.")

Fig. 2. Examples of image description sentences created by using Vision Transformer and bidirectional RoBERTa.

4   Conclusion

In this paper, we experiment with several image captioning models using different values of parameters. Our image captioning model using Vision Transformer to encode the image and bidirectional RoBERTa to predict the image description sentence achieves better BLEU scores than the other models including VirTex and CPTR. Especially, when generating image description sentences in Vietnamese, the combination model between ViT and Bi-RoBERTa outperforms all existing models. For future work, we plan to integrate other models, such as a color recognition model, age and gender detection models, into the existing models, experiment with different models for extracting image features and models for generating captions such as BART [19] and T5 [24] to improve the quality of image captions. We also plan to experiment with a better quality datasets consisting of more images and captions, to generate captions having higher accuracy.

References

1. Al-Malla, M.A., Jafar, A., Ghneim, N.: Image captioning model using attention and object features to mimic human image understanding. J. Big Data **9**(1), 1–16 (2022)
2. Bochkovskiy, A., Wang, C.Y., Liao, H.Y.M.: YOLOv4: optimal speed and accuracy of object detection. ArXiv abs/2004.10934 (2020)
3. Chen, X., Hsieh, C.J., Gong, B.: When vision Transformers outperform ResNets without pre-training or strong data augmentations. arXiv preprint arXiv:2106.01548 (2021)
4. Chen, X., Zitnick, C.L.: Learning a recurrent visual representation for image caption generation. arXiv preprint arXiv:1411.5654 (2014)
5. Chollet, F.: Xception: deep learning with depthwise separable convolutions. In: 2017 IEEE Conference on Computer Vision and Pattern Recognition (CVPR), pp. 1800–1807 (2017)
6. Desai, K., Johnson, J.: Virtex: learning visual representations from textual annotations. In: Proceedings of the IEEE/CVF Conference on Computer Vision and Pattern Recognition, pp. 11162–11173 (2021)
7. Devlin, J., Chang, M.W., Lee, K., Toutanova, K.: BERT: Pre-training of deep bidirectional Transformers for language understanding. arXiv preprint arXiv:1810.04805 (2018)
8. Dosovitskiy, A., et al.: An image is worth 16x16 words: Transformers for image recognition at scale. arXiv preprint arXiv:2010.11929 (2020)
9. Feng, Y., Ma, L., Liu, W., Luo, J.: Unsupervised image captioning. In: Proceedings of the IEEE/CVF Conference on Computer Vision and Pattern Recognition, pp. 4125–4134 (2019)
10. He, K., Zhang, X., Ren, S., Sun, J.: Deep residual learning for image recognition. In: Proceedings of the IEEE Conference on Computer Vision and Pattern Recognition, pp. 770–778 (2016)
11. He, S., Liao, W., Tavakoli, H.R., Yang, M., Rosenhahn, B., Pugeault, N.: Image captioning through image Transformer. In: Proceedings of the Asian Conference on Computer Vision (2020)
12. Herdade, S., Kappeler, A., Boakye, K., Soares, J.: Image captioning: transforming objects into words. In: Advances in Neural Information Processing Systems, vol. 32 (2019)
13. Hochreiter, S., Schmidhuber, J.: Long short-term memory. Neural Comput. **9**, 1735–1780 (1997)
14. Hodosh, M., Young, P., Hockenmaier, J.: Framing image description as a ranking task: data, models and evaluation metrics. J. Artif. Intell. Res. **47**, 853–899 (2013)
15. Huang, L., Wang, W., Chen, J., Wei, X.Y.: Attention on attention for image captioning. In: Proceedings of the IEEE/CVF International Conference on Computer Vision. pp. 4634–4643 (2019)
16. Kudo, T., Richardson, J.: Sentencepiece: a simple and language independent subword tokenizer and detokenizer for neural text processing. arXiv preprint arXiv:1808.06226 (2018)
17. Lam, K.N., Nguyen, K.N.T, Nguy, L.H., Kalita, J.: Facial expression recognition and image description generation in Vietnamese. In: Fuzzy Systems and Data Mining VII, pp. 63–69. IOS Press (2021)

18. Lam, Q.H., Le, Q.D., Nguyen, V.K., Nguyen, N.L.-T.: UIT-ViIC: a dataset for the first evaluation on Vietnamese image captioning. In: Nguyen, N.T., Hoang, B.H., Huynh, C.P., Hwang, D., Trawiński, B., Vossen, G. (eds.) ICCCI 2020. LNCS (LNAI), vol. 12496, pp. 730–742. Springer, Cham (2020). https://doi.org/10.1007/978-3-030-63007-2_57
19. Lewis, M., et al.: BART: denoising sequence-to-sequence pre-training for natural language generation, translation, and comprehension. In: Association for Computational Linguistics (2020)
20. Li, L., Tang, S., Deng, L., Zhang, Y., Tian, Q.: Image caption with global-local attention. In: Thirty-first AAAI Conference on Artificial Intelligence (2017)
21. Liu, W., Chen, S., Guo, L., Zhu, X., Liu, J.: CPTR: full Transformer network for image captioning. arXiv preprint arXiv:2101.10804 (2021)
22. Liu, Y., et al.: RoBERTa: a robustly optimized BERT pretraining approach. arXiv preprint arXiv:1907.11692 (2019)
23. Papineni, K., Roukos, S., Ward, T., Zhu, W.J.: BLEU: a method for automatic evaluation of machine translation. In: Proceedings of the 40th Annual Meeting of the Association for Computational Linguistics, pp. 311–318 (2002)
24. Raffel, C., et al.: Exploring the limits of transfer learning with a unified text-to-text Transformer. ArXiv abs/1910.10683 (2020)
25. Redmon, J., Divvala, S., Girshick, R., Farhadi, A.: You only look once: unified, real-time object detection. In: Proceedings of the IEEE Conference on Computer Vision and Pattern Recognition, pp. 779–788 (2016)
26. Ren, S., He, K., Girshick, R., Sun, J.: Faster R-CNN: towards real-time object detection with region proposal networks. In: Advances in Neural Information Processing Systems, vol. 28 (2015)
27. Rennie, S.J., Marcheret, E., Mroueh, Y., Ross, J., Goel, V.: Self-critical sequence training for image captioning. In: Proceedings of the IEEE Conference on Computer Vision and Pattern Recognition, pp. 7008–7024 (2017)
28. Sennrich, R., Haddow, B., Birch, A.: Neural machine translation of rare words with subword units. arXiv preprint arXiv:1508.07909 (2015)
29. Sharma, H., Agrahari, M., Singh, S.K., Firoj, M., Mishra, R.K.: Image captioning: a comprehensive survey. In: 2020 International Conference on Power Electronics & IoT Applications in Renewable Energy and its Control (PARC), pp. 325–328. IEEE (2020)
30. Simonyan, K., Zisserman, A.: Very deep convolutional networks for large-scale image recognition. arXiv preprint arXiv:1409.1556 (2014)
31. Staniūtė, R., Šešok, D.: A systematic literature review on image captioning. Appl. Sci. 9(10), 2024 (2019)
32. Stefanini, M., Cornia, M., Baraldi, L., Cascianelli, S., Fiameni, G., Cucchiara, R.: From show to tell: a survey on deep learning-based image captioning. IEEE Trans. Pattern Anal. Mach. Intell. 45(1), 539–559 (2022)
33. Vaswani, A., et al.: Attention is all you need. In: Advances in Neural Information Processing Systems, vol. 30 (2017)
34. Wang, C., Shen, Y., Ji, L.: Geometry attention Transformer with position-aware LSTMs for image captioning. Expert Syst. Appl. 201, 117174 (2022)
35. Wang, Y., Cook, D.: Brain: a bidirectional generative adversarial networks for image captions. In: 2020 3rd International Conference on Algorithms, Computing and Artificial Intelligence, pp. 1–6 (2020)

36. Yang, X., Tang, K., Zhang, H., Cai, J.: Auto-encoding scene graphs for image captioning. In: Proceedings of the IEEE/CVF Conference on Computer Vision and Pattern Recognition, pp. 10685–10694 (2019)
37. Yang, Z., Zhang, Y.-J., Rehman, S., Huang, Y.: Image captioning with object detection and localization. In: Zhao, Y., Kong, X., Taubman, D. (eds.) ICIG 2017. LNCS, vol. 10667, pp. 109–118. Springer, Cham (2017). https://doi.org/10.1007/978-3-319-71589-6_10

ANN Model to Predict Religiosity Based on Social Online Behaviors and Personality Traits

Marta R. Jablonska[1,2]([⊠]) [iD] and Smruti Rekha Das[3] [iD]

[1] Research Advisory Board of Gandhi Institute for Education and Technology, Baniatangi, Bhubaneswar, Odisha, India
marta.jablonska@uni.lodz.pl
[2] Faculty of Economics and Sociology, University of Lodz, Łódź, Poland
[3] Gandhi Institute for Education and Technology, Baniatangi, Bhubaneswar, Odisha, India

Abstract. Social online behaviors include religiosity manifestations. This paper studies religiosity in the context of social online behaviors and personality traits. Data from 1358 participants were used to build artificial neural network model. Respondents, invited with a snowball sampling technique, filled a questionnaire consisting of personality traits measures, religiosity, and selected online behaviors, particularly about social media activities. A set of multilayer perceptron models was developed to asses a classification according to religiosity of respondents. The best fitting network was able to classify correctly between being a theist or atheist more than 84% of cases by assigning them to one of these two groups. Conducted global sensitivity analysis proved the importance of each input variable, showing that selected online social behaviors and personality traits may be used to predict religiosity. The model analyzed religiosity from the view of online support, behaviors, social media expectations, and the Big Five personality traits presenting its importance in behavior studies on the social media.

Keywords: sociology · religion · artificial neural networks · learning algorithms · the Big Five · social media

1 Introduction

Artificial neural networks (ANNs) are defined as learning algorithms, statistical methods created to automatically carrying out categorization, prediction or pattern recognition through automated learning on labeled data, with limited or no human intervention [1–3]. ANNs combine basic mathematical methods in a myriad of combinations leading to efficiency beyond manual computation [4]. During an iterative process, network's nodes are estimated from data by minimizing the dispersion between the predicted actually observed values [4]. Still it is important to have in mind that ANNs also have some limitations. Learning algorithms may be trained to mirror existing classifications which may be affected by human error. It may result in reinforced discrimination, just by finding patterns and excessively employing them to boost results [5]. They also may be missing transparency and intelligibility, raising difficulty to measure exactly this discrimination and its sources [6]. They are developed for data mining tasks hard and complicated to program explicitly, and seen as one of the most powerful techniques, especially appropriate at gathering advanced data patterns and trends [2, 4]. Although ANNs were primarily more often implemented in clinical studies [7], the generation of huge amount of data in social sciences shows the essentiality to profit from data mining, including learning algorithms [1].

Religiosity carries on to be studied in a growing number of scientific research areas [1]. Still, as it includes an inherent belief beyond individuals' description, it is difficult to evaluate and requires new approaches to measure and analyze these data [5]. Due to the complexity of religiosity, it is important to include the social and individual differences into these studies [1]. Religiosity expresses the importance and a degree of belief and commitment to religion and is an active process of transferring to life beliefs and teachings by persons and society with various outlooks and behaviors. It expresses the core role that belief plays in everyday life, and displays the intensity of belief and commitment to religious activities [1]. Religiosity adverts to thoughts and deeds related to the overall religious values, it adds courage and confidence to a believer, thus, improving attitudes and behaviors and that playing crucial role in wellbeing and self-development [8]. Religious individuals are more expected to be decent, hardworking, devoted, keen, as well as dedicated to achieve excellence [9–11]. Religiosity may provide a framework for understanding emotional and physical states, research human behavior, as it harmonizes personality [8]. So, it is used in both, sociological and psychological studies.

The fact that people more often are using social media for spiritual support is proven by a huge amount of current studies [12]. Social media may be used for activities of religious nature, lowering sense of feeling lonely, isolated, and disconnected from others [13].

Studies conducted by Turan [14], Keating [12], Kleman [15], Cantone [16] argue that online deeds may be affected by religiosity, thus different for theists and atheists, simultaneously pointing out research examining atheists group remains scarce. As social media plays important role in communication in all societies and limited research is available on religiosity and online media [17, 18], the research on manifestations of religiosity on social media should be broadened. We hope that our study will help to enlarge the knowledge on ANNs role in predicting religiosity in social media.

Learning algorithms have been already implemented into some studies in the context of religiosity but their number remains still limited. Religiosity has been predicted with ANNs to predict the future status of religiosity due to gender [1], religious coping situations [2], and religious piety [8]. ANNs are also able to predict in areas of social science, i.e. forecasting changes in the intentions and behaviors [19, 20], to evaluate the mental health [21], and self-esteem [22].

To summarize the above, our paper aims at contributing to the current state of art by:

1. Presenting a role of ANNs in social science for diagnosis and future predictions;
2. Broaden religious studies scope by implementing ANNs as a predictor of religiosity based on social online behaviors and personality traits.

ANNs are perceived as a encouraging method to provide a diagnostic classification of various measures of mental health [23, 24], that is why we decided to use it in our study to evaluate importance of religiosity basing on social attitudes, selected personality traits and social media behaviors. To the best of our knowledge, any study has researched religiosity with online behaviors and personality traits at the same scope as we did using ANNs.

The paper is structured as follows. The subsequent section describes materials and methods. Here we thoroughly explain sample, procedure, measures, and data analysis methods. This part is then followed by the section in which we present and discuss the results. This paper ends with concluding thoughts, limitations, and future studies possibilities.

2 Materials and Methods

2.1 Sample and Procedure

Participants were recruited primarily via social media and snowball sampling. The sample was 1358 respondents 18–66 years (M = 29.64, SD = 12.40; including 869 females, 489 males; 891 theists and 467 atheists) completed questionnaire related to: their religiousness, social media habits, and scales: social media usage intensity, online social support, social media expectations, the Big Five inventory (see Table 1). The study was approved by the Ethics Committee of the University of Lodz (8(II)/KBBN-UŁ/II/2020–21). The respondents weren't rewarded in any form and were informed on voluntary nature of the study.

2.2 Measures

Religiosity was assessed with a question regarding theist/atheist option (the Cronbach's α 0.86). We measured the intensity of social media activities with adopted 13-item, 5-point Likert scale Facebook Intensity Scale [25, 26] with the Cronbach's α 0.81. The Online Social Support Scale (OSSS) [27] assessed online social support on 4-point Likert scale including four subscales esteem and emotional support (by providing acceptance, intimacy, care, respect, empathy, or compassion), social companionship (a feeling of belonging), informational (help in dealing with difficulties), and finally instrumental support (means financial aid, material resources, and required services). Calculated Cronbach's α was 0.83 for esteem/emotional, 0.82 for social companionship, 0.85 for informational, and 0.82 for instrumental support. To measure social media expectations an adopted 40-item, 5-point Likert scale Expected Effects of Internet Usage measure [28] was used. It has four subscales: interpersonal (the optimization and enrichment of social relations; the Cronbach's α 0.74), pragmatic (the facilitation of communication; the Cronbach's α 0.73), hedonistic (mood improvement and entertainment; the Cronbach's α 0.79), and compensatory (freeing from complexes and low self-esteem; the Cronbach's α 0.73) expectations. The Big Five was assessed with BFI-44 on 5-point Likert scale [29] using five subscales Agreeableness (the Cronbach's α 0.81), Conscientiousness (the Cronbach's α 0.80), Extraversion (the Cronbach's α 0.78), Neuroticism (the Cronbach's α 0.79), and Openness (the Cronbach's α 0.81).

Table 1. Behavior and personality variables in theists and atheists groups.

Variable	Theists N = 891		Atheists N = 467	
	M	SD	M	SD
Social Media Intensity	1.589	0.984	2.204	0.924
OSS—Esteem/Emotional Support	1.143	0.737	1.569	0.767
OSS—Social Companionship	1.226	0.771	1.679	0.721
OSS—Informational Support	1.258	0.759	1.679	0.724
OSS—Instrumental Support	0.852	0.675	1.190	0.798
SME—Interpersonal expectations	1.849	1.101	2.422	0.994
SME—Pragmatic expectations	2.245	1.089	2.831	0.760
SME—Hedonistic expectations	1.827	1.057	2.369	0.902
SME—Compensatory expectations	1.497	1.013	1.962	1.084
Posting selfies	0.975	1.163	1.657	1.543
Using non-face avatars	1.195	1.222	1.075	1.233
Social media annoying	1.418	1.090	1.433	1.095
Social media mood decreasing	1.165	0.999	1.120	0.969
Social media self-esteem decreasing	1.264	1.157	1.206	1.118
Social media life satisfaction decreasing	1.226	1.138	1.236	1.137
Hater	0.363	0.786	0.441	0.763
Using vulgar language	0.790	1.144	1.094	1.265
Big5_Extraversion	2.080	0.778	2.264	0.800
Big5_Agreeableness	2.205	0.692	2.284	0.744
Big5_Conscientiousness	2.455	0.775	2.305	0.803
Big5_Neuroticism	2.231	0.840	2.247	0.826
Big5_Openness to Experience	2.513	0.853	2.380	0.834

Note. OSS - Online Social Support; SME - Social Media Expectations

2.3 Data Analysis

We used the Statistica 13.3.0 software (Tibco Software Inc., Palo Alto, CA, USA). An initial data check presented no missing or extreme values. ANNs models were implemented and trained to create a classification theist/atheist model. Various learning algorithms with different configurations of settings were done on three subsets of data: training (70%), testing (15%), and validation (15%) and two algorithms were implemented: multilayer perceptron (MLP) that is built of input, hidden (at least single), and output layers, and radial basis function (RBF) with similar structure but possessing a single hidden layer [30]. In our calculation process, network architecture consisted of three layers: input (22 nodes for input with all attainable variants), hidden (automatically selected), and output (2 neurons: atheist, theist). To protect our models form underfitting or overfitting, we have used a mechanism built in automated ANNs generator in our software to manage the number of epochs (iterations of learning cycles) and we also used a method where a minimal number of nodes is automatically set to prevent underfitting [31]. It is crucial as excessive amount of iterations makes a model vulnerable to overfitting and, on the other hand, too little epochs may cause underfitting [32].

3　Results

The network MLP 22-98-2 showed the best fit with testing quality at 84.91%. The construction of this model included: BFGS (Broyden–Fletcher–Goldfarb–Shanno) algorithm with 11 epochs to improve network's weights; tanh as a hidden layer's activation function; Softmax as an activation output function, and entropy error function for training.

Then, we conducted a global sensitivity analysis (GSA) to check the architecture of MLP 22-98-2 network by displaying the significance of each input and verifying the model's error behavior in reaction to changes in input values. Scores above 1 indicate a variable improving ANN performance but they can't be interpreted directly in a way that a high score suggests significant usefulness, and vice versa. The network MLP 22-98-2 resulted above 1 for each input (Table 2).

Table 2. MLP 22-98-2 GSA results.

Variable	MLP 22-98-2
SM Intensity	1.068
SME—Pragmatic expectations	1.049
SME—Hedonistic expectations	1.019
Posting selfies	1.013
Big5_Conscientiousness	1.012
SM annoying	1.011
Vulgar language	1.011
OSS—Social Companionship	1.011
Big5_Openness to Experience	1.008
OSS—Informational Support	1.007
Big5_Extraversion	1.006
SM mood decreasing	1.005
SM life satisfaction decreasing	1.004
OSS—Instrumental Support	1.003

(*continued*)

Table 2. (*continued*)

Variable	MLP 22-98-2
SME—Compensatory expectations	1.003
OSS—Esteem/Emotional Support	1.002
SM self-esteem decreasing	1.002
Non-face avatars	1.002
SME—Interpersonal expectations	1.001
Big5_Neuroticism	1.001
Big5_Agreeableness	1.001
Hater	1.000

Our ANNs classified 84.91% cases. By comparing to other studies, for example 64% accuracy described in [2, 4] these results seem to appear satisfactory in the area of social sciences.

4 Discussion

In the field of social science, learning algorithms are considered to have the potential to strive towards more predictive models [33]. As ANNs are capable of leveraging knowledge on cognitive processes, emotional states, and social identity, to better understand behavior [34] and researchers point to the lack of research into social behaviors and personality traits in relation to religion in online media [35], we decided to merge these two areas and conduct a study of possibility to predict religiosity with ANNs using social online behaviors and personality traits.

Our study responded to the call to broaden religious research in the social media context [12, 16, 36] by exploring the relationship between religiosity, social support, the Big Five, social media habits for the ANNs model. Our model classified correctly almost 85% of data, assigning respondents to theists or atheists classes. This network may be used for farther classification of new datasets, either directly in the Statistica software or as an external script.

We used learning algorithms to confront the studied variables as predictors of religiosity, presenting that religiosity may be influenced by online behaviors and personality traits. An analysis of the current research showed the requirement of extending studies on online habits with religiosity, especially concerning atheists. Thus, a next step of our study was to evaluate theists and atheists, and embrace an advance of analysis to the personality traits and online behaviors recommended in current literature.

Among limitations, following can be mentioned. First, its cross-sectional nature. A longitudinal approach would make it possible to draw long term conclusions and provide sturdy evidence for the patterns found by our ANN model. Second, a non-probabilistic approach allows inference only for the studied sample. Still, we shall remark that existing past studies used a very much alike studies methodology providing useful information for the scientific society [37, 38].

Future avenues to draw a deeper picture on religiosity influence to online social behaviors, would add longitudinal data, increased social and internal sample diversity enrichment, such as adding intergenerational issues, sexual orientation, or political views.

References

1. Kızılgeçit, M., Çinici, M., Tuysuz, E.: Religiosity prediction by gender with artificial intelligence in 2020–2025 in Turkey. J. Ilahiyat Res. **56**, 283–307 (2021). https://doi.org/10.29288/ilted.993560
2. Kızılgeçit, M., Çinici, M.: Prediction of individuals' religious coping levels in the coronavirus (Covid-19) process by using artificial neural networks. J. Ilahiyat Res. **54**, 45–65 (2020). https://doi.org/10.29288/ilted.774693
3. Kotsiantis, S.B., Zaharakis, I., Pintelas, P.: Machine learning: a review of classification and combining techniques. Artif. Intell. Rev. **26**, 159–190 (2006). https://doi.org/10.1007/s10462-007-9052-3
4. de Saint Laurent, C.: In defence of machine learning: debunking the myths of artificial intelligence. Europe's J. Psychol. **14**(4), 734–747 (2018). https://doi.org/10.5964/ejop.v14i4.1823
5. Rusu, P., Turliuc, M.: Ways of approaching religiosity in psychological research. J. Int. Soc. Res. **4**, 361 (2011)
6. Hacker, P.: Teaching fairness to artificial intelligence: existing and novel strategies against algorithmic discrimination under EU law. Common Mark. Law Rev. **55**, 1143–1186 (2018)
7. Mirchi, N., et al.: Decoding intracranial EEG with machine learning: a systematic review. Front. Hum. Neurosci. **16**, 913777 (2022). https://doi.org/10.3389/fnhum.2022.913777
8. Bhatti, O.K., Öztürk, A.O., Maham, R., Farooq, W.: Examining Islamic piety at workplace via an artificial neural network. Cogent Psychol. **8**(1), 1907038 (2021). https://doi.org/10.1080/23311908.2021.1907038
9. Bhatti, O.K., Alam, M.A., Hassan, A., Sulaiman, M.: Islamic spirituality and social responsibility in curtailing the workplace deviance. Humanomics **32**(4), 405–417 (2016). https://doi.org/10.1108/H-03-2016-0022
10. Kamil, N.M., Sulaimam, M., Selladurai, S., Khalid, N.: The impact of spirituality and social responsibility on organizational citizenship behavior from the Islamic perspective: empirical investigation of Malaysian businesses. J. Komunikasi: Malays. J. Commun. **31**(1), 59–80 (2015). https://doi.org/10.17576/JKMJC-2015-3101-04
11. Sulaiman, M., Selladurai, S., Kamil, N.M., Mukred, N.R.: The influence of spirituality and responsibility on business leadership effectiveness: an empirical analysis. J. Soc. Sci. Hum. **10**(2), 310–334 (2015)
12. Keating, D.M.: Spirituality and support: a descriptive analysis of online social support for depression. J. Relig. Health **52**, 1014–1028 (2013). https://doi.org/10.1007/s10943-012-9577-x
13. Titgemeyer, S.C., Schaaf, C.P.: Facebook support groups for rare pediatric diseases: quantitative analysis. JMIR Pediatr. Parenting **3**, e21694 (2020). https://doi.org/10.2196/21694
14. Turan, Y.: Coping with loneliness: loneliness, religious coping, religiosity, life satisfaction and social media usage. Cumhuriyet Theol. J. **22**, 395–434 (2018). https://doi.org/10.18505/cuid.406750
15. Kleman, E.E., Everett, M.K., Egbert, N.: Social support strategies among women of faith. J. Commun. Relig. **32**, 157–193 (2009)

16. Cantone, J.A., Walls, V., Rutter, T.: Self-referencing affects perceptions of workplace discrimination against atheists. Psychol. Relig. Spiritual. **14**, 381–385 (2022). https://doi.org/10.1037/rel0000466
17. Brubaker, P.J., Haigh, M.M.: The religious Facebook experience: uses and gratifications of faith-based content. Soc. Media + Soc. **3**, 2056305117703723 (2017). https://doi.org/10.1177/2056305117703723
18. Jafarkarimi, H., Saadatdoost, H., Sim, A.T.H., Hee, J.M.: Behavioral intention in social networking sites ethical dilemmas: an extended model based on theory of planned behavior. Comput. Hum. Behav. **62**, 545–561 (2016). https://doi.org/10.1016/j.chb.2016.04.024
19. Catellani, P., Carfora, V., Piastra, M.: Connecting social psychology and deep reinforcement learning: a probabilistic predictor on the intention to do home-based physical activity after message exposure. Front. Psychol. **12**, 696770 (2021). https://doi.org/10.3389/fpsyg.2021.696770
20. Kang, Z.: Artificial intelligence network embedding, entrepreneurial intention, and behavior analysis for college students' rural tourism entrepreneurship. Front. Psychol. **13**, 843679 (2022). https://doi.org/10.3389/fpsyg.2022.843679
21. Liang, L., Zheng, Y., Ge, Q., Zhang, F.: Exploration and strategy analysis of mental health education for students in sports majors in the era of artificial intelligence. Front. Psychol. **12**, 762725 (2022). https://doi.org/10.3389/fpsyg.2021.762725
22. Martínez-Ramón, J.P., Morales-Rodríguez, F.M., Ruiz-Esteban, C., Méndez, I.: Self-esteem at university: proposal of an artificial neural network based on resilience, stress, and sociodemographic variables. Front. Psychol. **13**, 815853 (2022). https://doi.org/10.3389/fpsyg.2022.815853
23. Xue, K., Bradshaw, L.P.: A semi-supervised learning-based diagnostic classification method using artificial neural networks. Front. Psychol. **11**, 618336 (2021). https://doi.org/10.3389/fpsyg.2020.618336
24. Edwards, D.J., Lowe, R.: Associations between mental health, interoception, psychological flexibility, and self-as-context, as predictors for alexithymia: a deep artificial neural network approach. Front. Psychol. **12**, 637802 (2021). https://doi.org/10.3389/fpsyg.2021.637802
25. Drageset, J., Eide, G.E., Ranhoff, A.H.: Anxiety and depression among nursing home residents without cognitive impairment. Scand. J. Caring Sci. **27**, 872–881 (2013). https://doi.org/10.1111/j.1471-6712.2012.01095.x
26. Ellison, N.B., Steinfield, C., Lampe, C.: The benefits of Facebook "Friends:" social capital and college students' use of online social network sites. J. Comput.-Mediat. Commun. **12**, 1143–1168 (2007). https://doi.org/10.1111/j.1083-6101.2007.00367.x
27. Nick, E.A., Cole, D.A., Cho, S.J., Smith, D.K., Carter, T.G., Zelkowitz, R.L.: The online social support scale: measure development and validation. Psychol. Assess. **30**, 1127–1143 (2018). https://doi.org/10.1037/pas0000558
28. Poprawa, R.: Expectations of the effects of using the Internet and its problematic use [Oczekiwania efektów korzystania z internetu a problematyczne jego używanie]. Qual. Life Psychol. [Psychologia Jakości Życia] **8**, 21–44 (2009)
29. Cai, L., Liu, X.: Identifying Big Five personality traits based on facial behavior analysis. Front. Public Health **10**, 1001828 (2022). https://doi.org/10.3389/fpubh.2022.1001828
30. Fath, A.H., Madanifar, F., Abbasi, M.: Implementation of multilayer perceptron (MLP) and radial basis function (RBF) neural networks to predict solution gas-oil ratio of crude oil systems. Petroleum **6**, 80–91 (2018). https://doi.org/10.1016/j.petlm.2018.12.002
31. Ruppert, H., Krug, A., Shardt, Y.A.W.: Method to design a neural network with minimal number of neurons for approximation problems. IFAC-PapersOnLine **55**(7), 568–573 (2022). https://doi.org/10.1016/j.ifacol.2022.07.504
32. Lee, C.P., Lim, K.M.: COVID-19 diagnosis on chest radiographs with enhanced deep neural networks. Diagnostics **12**(8), 1828 (2022). https://doi.org/10.3390/diagnostics12081828

33. Yarkoni, T., Westfall, J.: Choosing prediction over explanation in psychology: lessons from machine learning. Perspect. Psychol. Sci. **12**(6), 1100–1122 (2017)
34. Mariani, M.M., Perez-Vega, R., Wirtz, J.: AI in marketing, consumer research and psychology: a systematic literature review and research agenda. Psychol. Mark. **39**, 755–776 (2022). https://doi.org/10.1002/mar.2161
35. Davidson, T., Farquhar, L.K.: Correlates of social anxiety, religion, and Facebook. J. Media Relig. **13**, 208–225 (2014). https://doi.org/10.1080/15348423.2014.971566
36. Sedlar, A.E., Stauner, N., Pargament, K.I., Exline, J.J., Grubbs, J.B., Bradley, D.F.: Spiritual struggles among atheists: links to psychological distress and well-being. Religions **9**, 242 (2018). https://doi.org/10.3390/rel9080242
37. Morales-Rodríguez, F.M., Martínez-Ramón, J.P., Méndez, I., Ruiz-Esteban, C.: Stress, coping, and resilience before and after COVID-19: a predictive model based on artificial intelligence in the university environment. Front. Psychol. **12**, 647964 (2021). https://doi.org/10.3389/fpsyg.2021.647964
38. Ozamiz-Etxebarria, N., Idoiaga, N., Dosil, M., Picaza, M.: Psychological symptoms during the two stages of lockdown in response to the COVID-19 outbreak: an investigation in a sample of citizens in Northern Spain. Front. Psychol. **11**, 1491 (2020). https://doi.org/10.3389/fpsyg.2020.01491

Concrete Crack Detection Using Deep Convolutional Generative Adversarial Network

Biswajit Padhi[1] , Motahar Reza[1](✉) , Md. Salman Shams[2] , and Arcot Navya Sai[3]

[1] Department of Mathematics, GITAM Deemed to be University,
Hyderabad 502329, India
motaharreza90@gmail.com
[2] Department of Mechanical Engineering, Jamia Millia Islamia Central University,
New Delhi 110025, India
[3] Department of Computer Science and Engineering,
GITAM Deemed to be University, Hyderabad 502329, India

Abstract. To solve the problems related to the small sample extent in intelligent crack detection, we are using the synthetic image sets generation method for concrete cracks are expected based on DCGANs. Since the initial dataset of the crack image is significantly less, that makes a bottleneck to building a deep learning model for better accuracy. DCGANs help generates massive synthetic data for the crack image. This GANS classifier can perform better using this synthetic data and improve the crack features recognition. DCGAN model hyper-parameters are optimized. Subsequently, we are using Adam optimizer to optimize the loss function. The projected technique has the compensations of DCGANs. Finally, a concrete crack classifier detection model based on the CNN is used to classify whether the image is crack or not. In the results, our model has an average accuracy of more than 90%, which is higher than any other method which is proposed before, to estimate using the similar test dataset. This method generates non-real crack images that are nearly similar to real images. That's why solving the issue of lacking image datasets of cracks in specific concrete surface sections is not an issue. And one more thing, this system provides the data guarantee for the intelligent of concrete crack detection and decrease in concrete surface maintenance & crack detection costs.

Keywords: Generative Adversarial · GANS · DCGANS · Crack image · CNN · deep learning · image generation

1 Introduction

Condition valuation of concrete plays a crucial role in maintaining any building's health and reliability. It has involved the devotion of researchers because establishments have experienced hurrying deterioration because of environmental and

D. Garg et al. (Eds.): IACC 2022, CCIS 1781, pp. 147–161, 2023.
https://doi.org/10.1007/978-3-031-35641-4_11

load effects, and structural health monitoring (SHM) cannot be Overvalue. The structures which have warped in current times is due to aged and unsuitable monitoring and maintenance. Early detection of small cracks on a concrete structure is an essential maintenance task. They were spending Millions of dollars to monitor structural health across the world. Many concrete structures collapse in the early stages of construction. As we all know, whenever cracks appear on the structure, the paths are open for water and corrosive agents, and it causes the subsurface rods and steel reinforcements. Hence, developing automated and reliable inspection methods are necessary (Fig. 1).

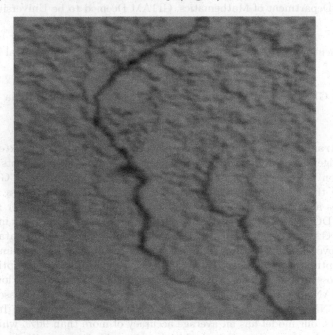

Fig. 1. Typical micro-cracking in concrete

The current method is very time and money-consuming. On the site, Skilled inspectors measure the structure condition by marking the cracks on a surface, which is difficult for inspectors and inconvenient to local people as the process requires a large area. And traditional human-based crack detection processes [1] are highly needed on trained humans, requiring years for inspection. Automatic and accurate assessment of surface conditions requiring minimal area is highly needed for fast, extensive inspection. To lessen human mistakes in the inspection structure, many researchers have done with a lot of image processing-based methods [2]. With the use of the video and GPS (Global Positioning Method) data Chen et al. [3] collected during the driving test, an automatic crack detecting system for pavement was proposed. Each frame of the received video data is transformed for image processing. The image is then improved to differentiate the fracture from the image of ordinary pavement using grayscale processing, filtering, and histogram equalisation.

One of the most widely used techniques for producing images today is generative adversarial networks (GANs). Deep learning is the favored method for dealing with image datasets as it has the advanced pixel-level target detection technique. It needs a massive amount of primary data, including our target, to gain the accurate method training [4]. If the datasets are not large, the method can not work as it will suffer from the overfitting phenomenon [5]. It can be resolved by using generative models [6]. Shmelkov et al. [7] contend that the ones that are now in use are insufficient and must be adequate for the work at hand. They provide two image classification-based metrics, GAN-train and GAN-test, which roughly represent the recall (diversity) and precision (image quality) of GANs, respectively. Based on these two metrics, they assess a number of recent GAN methods and show a noticeable performance difference.

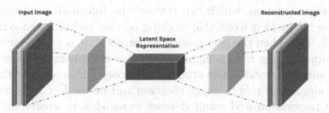

Encoder: compress input into a latent-space of usually smaller dimension. h = f(x)
Decoder: reconstruct input from the latent space.   r = g(f(x)) with r as close to x as possible

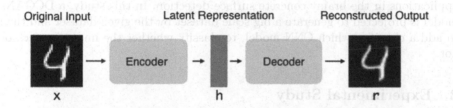

Fig. 2. Auto encoding and decoding processes.

Generally, GANs models contain automatic encoders and variational autoencoders (VAEs) [8]. In [9], given the idea of (GANs), which familiarized the idea of the training process of the network, the GANs model lastly generates good quality truthful images which are hard to discriminate from the real images. Auto-Encoder: Autoencoders are designed to reproduce their input, especially for image (See Fig. 2). A joint GAN model and the VAE are called as Zero-VAE-GAN [10]; as a result of enhancing the class stage discrimination skill and generate good characteristic hidden attributes. Hou et al. [11] describe a novel technique for enhancing variational autoencoder performance (VAE). We implement a generative adversarial training technique to drive the VAE to create realistic and natural images in addition to enforcing the deep feature consistency principle, which ensures that the VAE output and its related input images have similar deep features.

In [12], the author used the deep convolutional GANs (DCGANs) for the identification of home address number, for a usual road. This can also be used to improve the resolution of uncertain data (images) to extract healthy data features, further used in the training dataset, and accurately identify the numbers on natural roads. In [13], the author advanced DCGANs for extensive data fluid modeling, in that discrete cosine transform (DCT) is applied, predicting the spatiotemporal nonlinear fluid flow. The technique completed decent results.

GANs discovered a few applications in different types of concrete structure maintenance. In [14], used a GANs model for detecting the field of crack segmentation to explain the problem of the breakdown of cracks in the surface. By that, a division structure is contributed to the discriminator and the generative and the division shape to form a complete model with super-resolution rebuilding and division functions simultaneously. In recently it is proposed a GANs-based model for crack image restoration, which can remove the information of any difficult place to get the image as it fixed. [15] working on this technique to generate the images of crack. But when the background is not good, it is tough for the model to learn the aim features from a significantly less sized sample, thus resulting in less quality aim generation. The studies mentioned above specify that GANs can perform a significant role in image creation and be used in applications that needful image restoration and small dataset expansion to create images with required features.

In summary, the GANs model is very considerable progress, some how several issues are still exist, which we cannot overlooked. GANs have the restricted applications in the brainy concrete surface detection. In this study, a DCGANs model is projected to generate a big scale dataset by the given dataset and then to add a classifier which CNN model, to classify whether the image is crack or not.

2   Experimental Study

The work has done in Python including some libraries such as Keras, OpenCV, TQDM and TensorFlow. The steps involved at first to creating a discriminator and then generator for data argumentation and train the generator to fool the discriminator are implemented by GANs represented in (Fig. 3). For the classification we added CNN model to classify the images.

– Image pre-processing.
– Applying GANs model for data augmentation.
– Applying CNN model for classification.

2.1   Data Collection

For our projected methodology, the dataset which we are using is contains dissimilar images which are occupied from some concrete surfaces. For the gaining

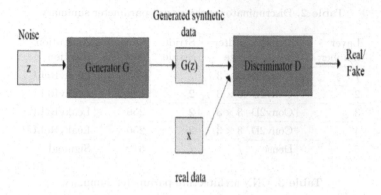

Fig. 3. Basic structure of GANs model.

of images, they are clicked by using of high resolution camera under different lighting conditions for the different surface locations having both non-crack (Negative) and crack (Positive) images.

Dataset with 20,001 images labeled as Positive and 20,020 images labeled as Negative, and the dimension of each images are (227 × 227). The results shows the effectiveness of the proposed methodology. The image pre-processing steps are as follows:

- Change into greyscale.
- For noise removal and edge detection we used median filtering.
- For removal of imperfections we used binarisation and morphological operations.

3 Proposed Method

(See Table 3).

Table 1. Generator architecture parameter summary

Layer number	Type	Filter size	Stride Stride	Output channels	Activation fn.
0	Dense	/	/	512	LeakyReLU
1	Conv2DTrans	4 × 4	2	256	LeakyReLU
2	Conv2DTrans	4 × 4	2	256	LeakyReLU
3	Conv2DTrans	4 × 4	2	128	LeakyReLU
4	Conv2DTrans	4 × 4	2	128	LeakyReLU
5	Conv2DTrans	4 × 4	2	128	LeakyReLU
6 (out put)	Conv2D	3 × 3	/	3	tanh

Table 2. Discriminator architecture parameter summary

Layer number	Type	Filter size	Stride Stride	Output channels	Activation function
1	Conv2D	3 × 3	/	64	LeakyReLU
2	Conv2D	3 × 3	2	128	LeakyReLU
3	Conv2D	3 × 3	2	256	LeakyReLU
4	Conv2D	3 × 3	2	256	LeakyReLU
5	Dense	/	/	512	Sigmoid

Table 3. CNN architecture parameter summary

Layer number	Type	Filter size	Stride Stride	Output channels	Activation function
1	Conv2D	3 × 3	/	64	ReLU
2	Conv2D	3 × 3	2	64	ReLU
3	Conv2D	3 × 3	2	128	ReLU
4	Conv2D	3 × 3	2	126	ReLU
5	Conv2D	3 × 3	2	256	ReLU
6	Conv2D	3 × 3	2	512	ReLU
7	Conv2D	3 × 3	2	512	ReLU
8	Dense	/	/	1024	ReLU
9	Dense	/	/	512	ReLU
10	Dense	/	/	128	Sigmoid

GANs model is used by creating the generator and discriminator Networks which is used in data augmentation (Fig. 5 and Fig. 6).

The generator network used in here has five layers. which continuously increasing the dataset and get the crack image as the output. Details of the generator parameters and activation functions which are used for each layers are in Table 1.

Generated crack images are the input of the discriminator. And the probability of judging the authenticity of the images are the output. Initially, the image goes under four consecutive down samplings in this manner so that the image can be strictly reduced. At the end, by the layers, a probability value representing the genuineness of the input image is gained. Facts of every layers for the discriminator are in Table 2.

3.1 Optimizing the Model

Weights are modernized as to capitalize on the probability that any real data which we are using as input x, is classified as fit in to real dataset, while minimizing the probability of that the fake image is classified as fitting to the real dataset. In technical language, the loss/error function are used to maximizes the function D(x) and at the same time it also minimizes D(G(z)) (Fig. 4).

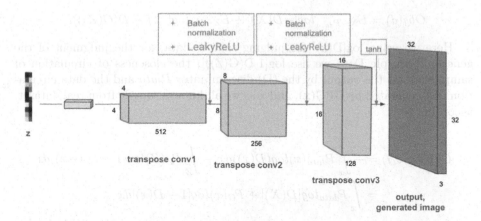

Fig. 4. Structure of DCGAN Generator.

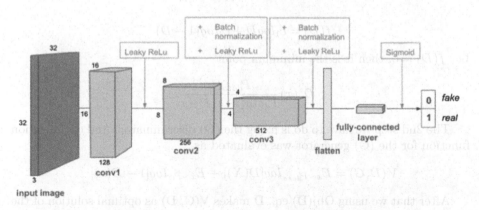

Fig. 5. Structure of DCGAN Discriminator.

Later, the generator function maximizes D(G(z)). Because, during training both we are annoying with opposite loss functions, which can be assumed of two players playing a minimax game with the value function V(G, D). X is the circulation of the real dataset we call it as sample image data, P_Z denotes arbitrarily distributed noise, Z couriers number of the random vectors in the P_Z. The first step that we need to do is finding the minimum cross entropy of the (D) discriminator with the condition where the (G) generator is given. We can calculate the objective function by using

$$\min_{G} \max_{D} V(D, G) = \min_{G} \max_{D} E_{X \sim p_{data}} log[-D(X)] + E_{Z \sim P_Z} log[-(1 - D(G(Z)))]$$

where

$$Obj(d) = E_{X \sim P_{data}} log[-D(X)] + E_{Z \sim P_Z} log[-(1 - D(G(Z)))]$$

Here we using $log[D(x)]$ for judging sample data, for the judgment of the generated sample Data we use $log[1\text{-}D(G(Z))]$, the closeness of circulation of sample data as the output by the (D) discriminator P_data and the data circulation (G) generated by $GPG(x)$, and x as we all know a sample from real dataset, according to

$$Obj(\theta_D, \theta_G) = -\int_x P_{data}(x) log(D(x)) dx - \int_Z P_Z(Z) log(1 - D(G(x)) dx$$

$$= \int_x P_{data} log[D(X)] + P_G(x) log[1 - D(x)] dx$$

As data and generator is given, those can considered as constant. Assuming that generator and data are replaced, so then we will get

$$f(D) = c_1 log D + c_2 log(1 - D)$$

Let $f(D) = 0$, then it is the minimum point

$$D^*(x) \frac{P_{data}(x)}{P_data(x) + P_G(x)}$$

The 2nd step we have to do is fixing the (D) discriminator. And optimization function for the (G) generator was evaluated as

$$V(D, G) = E_{x \sim P_{data}} log[D(X)] + E_{x \sim P_G} log[1 - D(x)]$$

After that we using Obj(D) eq., D makes V(G, D) as optimal solution of the (G) generator, that can be evaluated as

$$\min_{G} V(G, D) = V(G, D^*)$$

$$= E_{x \sim P_{data}} \left[log \frac{P_{data}(x)}{P_data(x) + P_G(x)} \right]$$

$$+ E_{x \sim P_G} \left[log \frac{P_{data}(x)}{P_data(x) + P_G(x)} \right]$$

For the practical training (D) discriminator is trained at 1st. Then, the (D) discriminator is secure and the (G) generator is trained. After that, we can continue to fix (G) generator and train the (D) discriminator, execution iterative optimization training till then $P_data = P_G$, at which the point of global optimization is reached.

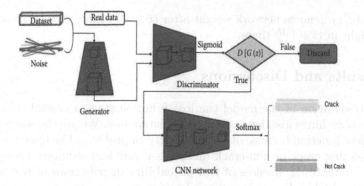

Fig. 6. DCG-CNN framework.

3.2   Addition of Classifier

The DCG - CNN network planning has been projected, combination of GANs and CNN to classify between crack and not crack image more broadly. In Fig. 6, the DCG - CNN framework is there. The images from dataset were laid into the GANs model to generate the crack images with several shapes and textures. Also, the false causing images detection were also created.

CNN contains the convolutional and pooling layers. Convolutional layers abstract crack features by layers of studying crack images. The pooling layers reduce the feature dimension by compressing the images without disturbing the feature of images. The fully connected layer then fit in limited feature map to comprehend the classification function. And for the last layer contains two neurons which signify crack image. We are adjusting network structure limitations for the network can have a good detection rate and a less false alarm rate for the crack which seems in definite scenes.

3.3   Network Training

In our model, GANs is uses Adam optimizer. For maintaining balance between generated data-set and quality of crack images, we are regulating the amount of crack images which have a variation of shapes and textures during the GANs model training process. We are setting 10 epochs and then detect the created crack images after every 10 epochs for the more fit crack images.

Now the model is updated constructed on mini batch in its place of sole sample, so we can update the change to make the convergence steady. The learning rate can regulate the rate of convergence combines gradient and modernized weight of earlier repetition can update network model weight, which can be articulated as:

$$V_{t+1} = \mu V_t + \alpha \nabla L(W_t),$$
$$W_{t+1} = W_t - V_{t+1}$$

Here W_{t+1} denotes network weight after $(t+1)^{th}$ times, $Vt+1$ denotes network weight in $(t+1)^{th}$ times.

4   Results and Discussions

In the presentation of the model the loss function stage a crucial role. As loss functions have hinge loss, log loss and contrastive loss. We are choosing the cross entropy loss function because of the suitability of problems like binary classification. Detecting crack or non-crack images is a problem of binary classification. It use to evaluate the likeness of two probability distributions of the real label and predicted label. For cross-entropy loss function equation are:

$$H(p,q) = -\sum_x p(x)log(q(x))$$

Here q(x) and p(x) denotes output and input labels, respectively.

By the use of training-related hyper-parameters, also by setting mini batch. Settings of various hyper-parameters play a important influence on the model. In summary, for the overlapped max pooling which attains improved presentation as compare to non overlapped max pooling layers. Correctly reducing the quantity of neurons in layers not only reduce the merging time but also increase the recognition skill for detection.

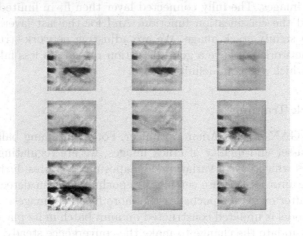

Fig. 7. Image generated from our GAN Model after 10 epoch.

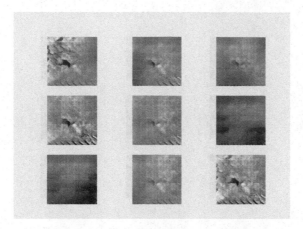

Fig. 8. Image generated from our GAN Model after 20 epoch.

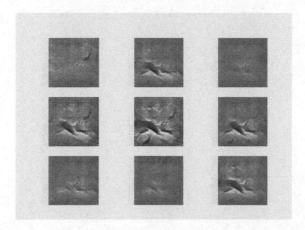

Fig. 9. Image generated from our GAN Model after 30 epoch.

From Fig. 7, 8, 9, 10, 11 and 12, it shows the generated images from our GANs model. As we can see that, for the beginning epoch (i.e., from 10 to 30 epoch) the images quality is not good. But as our model learns and epoch (i.e., from 140 to 150 epoch) the images quality is getting good. After generating the synthetic data, we used whole data for classify using CNN classifier. The accuracy of GANs classifier give 91.25%. It is observed that with using the synthetic data the accuracy level is below 90%.

In this study we have used some dataset which files are calculated to estimate the eminence and range of the non real produced image. At the same time, the produced image sets are use in concrete crack detection. Assessment pointers of assessment sets are use to critic the excellence of produced image, the meaning of the image generation research can be used in civil business. Figure 13 and 14 show the accuracy of the training and loss of the model.

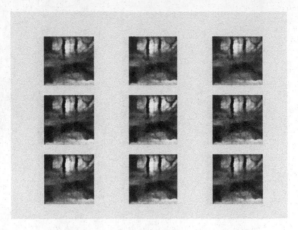

Fig. 10. Image generated from our GAN Model after 140 epoch.

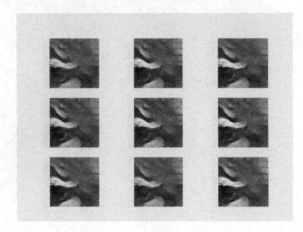

Fig. 11. Image generated from our GAN Model after 150 epoch.

Table 4 compares the accuracy of CNN using the initial, extended, and hybrid DCGAN datasets. It displays the accuracy results when compared with and without GANs. It demonstrates that the GANS classifier outperforms the traditional CNN classifier in terms of results. The generation of data samples by GANS aids in more accurate network learning.

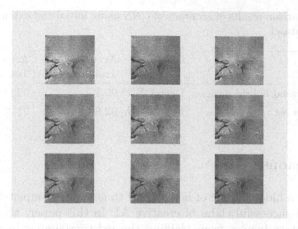

Fig. 12. Image generated from our GAN Model after 200 epoch.

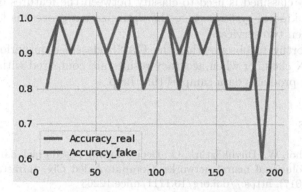

Fig. 13. Accuracy.

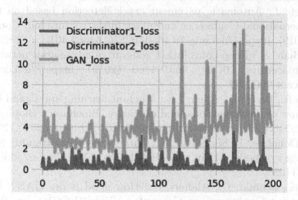

Fig. 14. Training loss.

Table 4. Comparison results of accuracy of CNN using initial and extended/ DCGAN-based hybrid dataset

Data Set	Classifier	Accuracy on Training data	Accuracy on Testing data
DCGAN-based hybrid dataset	Deep CNN	95.1%	92.8%
Initial data set	Deep CNN	92.8%	91.4%

5   Conclusions

Selection from a hidden space of images and to generate completely new images is popular and successful claim of creative AI. In this paper, we demonstrated a way to generate images from training the existing similar images to create synthetic image.

Then CNN classified is used to classify between the features of the images. GANs is that kind of system where the optimization process is looking for an balance between two services.

It's noteworthy to observe that the GANS classifier outperforms the conventional CNN classifier when accuracy results are compared with and without GANs. GANS produces data samples that help.

References

1. Cha, Y., Choi, W., Büyüköztürk, O.: Deep learning-based crack damage detection using convolutional neural networks. Comput.-Aided Civ. Infrastruct. Eng. **32**, 361–378 (2017). https://doi.org/10.1111/mice.12263
2. Denton, E.L., Chintala, S., Szlam, A.D., Fergus, R.: Deep generative image models using a laplacian pyramid of adversarial networks. In: NIPS, pp. 1486–1494 (2015)
3. Chen, C., et al.: Automatic pavement crack detection based on image recognition. In: International Conference on Smart Infrastructure and Construction 2019 (ICSIC) (2019). https://doi.org/10.1680/ICSIC.64669.361
4. Wang, J., Bian, Y.: Deep convolution generative adversarial network (DCGAN). Mol. Pharmaceutics **16**(11), 4451–4460 (2019). https://doi.org/10.1021/acs.molpharmaceut.9b00500
5. Ellingson, S.R., Davis, B., Allen, J.E.: Machine learning and ligand binding predictions: a review of data, methods, and obstacles. Biochimica Biophys. Acta Gener. Subjects 129545. (2020). https://doi.org/10.1016/j.bbagen.2020.129545
6. Brock, A., Donahue, J., Simonyan, K.: Large scale GAN training for high fidelity natural image synthesis. ArXiv, abs/1809.11096 (2018). https://doi.org/10.48550/arXiv.1809.11096
7. Shmelkov, K., Schmid, C., Alahari, K.: How good is my GAN?. In Proceedings of the European Conference on Computer Vision (ECCV), pp. 213–229 (2018). https://doi.org/10.1007/978-3-030-01216-8_14
8. Duan, X., Liu, J., Zhang, E.: Efficient image encryption and compression based on a VAE generative model. J. Real-Time Image Process. **16**(3), 765–773 (2018). https://doi.org/10.1007/s11554-018-0826-4

9. Goodfellow, I., Pouget-Abadie, J., Mirza, M., Xu, B., Warde-Farley, D., Ozair, S., Bengio, Y.: Generative adversarial networks. Commun. ACM **63**(11), 139–144 (2020). https://doi.org/10.1145/3422622
10. Gao, R., et al.: Zero-VAE-GAN: generating unseen features for generalized and transductive zero-shot learning. IEEE Trans. Image Process. **29**, 3665–3680 (2020). https://doi.org/10.1109/TIP.2020.2964429
11. Hou, X., Sun, K., Shen, L., Qiu, G.: Improving variational autoencoder with deep feature consistent and generative adversarial training. Neurocomputing **341**, 183–194 (2019). https://doi.org/10.1016/j.neucom.2019.03.013
12. Zhong, J., Gao, J., Chen, R., Li, J.Y.: Digital recognition of street view house numbers based on DCGAN. In: Proceedings of the 2nd International Conference on Image and Graphics Processing (2019). https://doi.org/10.1145/3313950.3313963
13. Cheng, M., Fang, F., Pain, C.C., Navon, I.M.: Data-driven modelling of nonlinear spatio-temporal fluid flows using a deep convolutional generative adversarial network. ArXiv, abs/2004.00707 (2020). https://doi.org/10.1016/j.cma.2020.113000
14. Li, L., Hu, M.: Method for small-bridge-crack segmentation based on generative adversarial network. Laser Optoelectron. Progr. (2019). https://doi.org/10.3788/lop56.101004
15. Sun, Z., Pei, L., Li, W., Xueli, H., Yao, C.: Pavement encapsulation crack detection method based on improved faster R-CNN. J. South China Univ. Technol. (Nat. Sci. Edn.) **48**(2), 84–93 (2020)

Chlorophyll Prediction System with Machine Learning Algorithms in Lake Titicaca (Peruvian Sector)

Antonio Arroyo Paz[1]($\boxtimes$) (iD) and Yalmar Ponce[2] (iD)

[1] Postgraduate School, Universidad Nacional del Altiplano, Puno, Perú
arroyopaz@unap.edu.pe

[2] Universidad Nacional de Juliaca, Juliaca, Perú
ytponcea.doc@unaj.edu.pe

Abstract. Water is a fundamental resource, eutrophication is an important factor in determining water quality, and chlorophyll-a is an indicator of this degree. Artificial intelligence offers important tools to help improve classification and prediction for inland water studies such as lakes. This study evaluated the water quality in the Lake Titicaca basin (Peruvian sector), using the monitoring results of the Instituto del Mar del Perú (IMARPE), between 2011 and 2021. The dataset used in the study included 579 samples and their meta-data collected over eleven years. A program was designed to compare the performance of four machine learning models as follows, linear regression model, decision tree, random forest, and XGBoost. The result of the research showed that the XGBoost model performed better, with an r^2 of 0.5455, MAPE of 25.8168, and RMSE of 0.6509, compared to the other algorithms. The findings strengthen the argument that ML models, especially XGBoost, can be used for chlorophyll prediction in lakes.

Keywords: Water Quality · Machine Learning · Random Forest · XGBoost · Chlorophyll

1 Introduction

Water is one of the natural resources necessary for life in general and the maintenance of ecosystems. it is a limited, scarce, and vulnerable resource, and at the same time strategic for the socioeconomic development of the people.

Because of the significance of inland lakes to socio-economic development, the preservation of biodiversity, and the tourism industry, it is essential to monitor the water quality of these lakes [1]. For no more than fifteen years, urban growth in the Titicaca basin has been sustained as a result of the vegetative increase of the urban population and as a consequence of population migration from rural areas, a situation that constitutes one of the factors of greatest pressure on the quantity and quality of water [2]. Recent studies have shown that 45% of the monitoring points in the Lake Titicaca basin have a higher mesotrophic level, classified as acceptable water quality, and 55% have a eutrophic level, classified as poor water quality [3, 4, 12].

D. Garg et al. (Eds.): IACC 2022, CCIS 1781, pp. 162–170, 2023.
https://doi.org/10.1007/978-3-031-35641-4_12

Chlorophyll a (Chl-a) in lakes has been widely used to assess the trophic status and is a common indicator of phytoplankton biomass. The influence of spatial and seasonal variations in chlorophyll on lake management is crucial. Climate, morphology, ecology, and anthropogenic factors influence the variability of Chl-a between and within lakes [17].

Machine learning, also known as ML, is an essential component of artificial intelligence (AI) since it enables a system to automatically learn and grow from experience without being expressly designed to do so [5]. Machine learning and its algorithms have been applied to different studies [19–21].

Extreme Gradient Boosting, also known as XGBoost, is a technique for gradient boosting that makes use of a framework that is built on decision trees. In addition to being able to solve regression problems, XGBoost may also be used to tackle classification difficulties, user-defined prediction challenges, and classification problems. The significance of XGBoost has been extensively acknowledged across a variety of machine learning and data mining problems, one of which is the classification of water [7, 8].

The objective of this study is to predict chlorophyll by comparing the performance of four machine learning models: linear regression model, decision tree, random forest, and XGBoost, based on data collected on water quality parameters of Lake Titicaca, during the period from 2011 to 2021.

2 Materials and Methods

2.1 Study Area

Lake Titicaca is a body of water. It occupies the northern part of the Peruvian-Bolivian altiplano plain. It is the second largest lake in South America, with an area of 8400 km^2 (variable depending on the intensity of rainfall), of which 55% corresponds to the Republic of Peru and 45% to the Plurinational State of Bolivia. Irregular and elongated in shape, it has a volume of approximately 891.1 km^3, of which Lake Mayor or Lago Grande occupies a volume of 878.7 km^3 (94.5% of the total), and Lake Huiñaymarca or Lago Menor, 12.36 km^3 [16]. It is one of the most important freshwater bodies in the Peruvian highlands and one of the most fragile ecosystems from an ecological and environmental point of view, unique in the world due to its geographical location ($15°13'19''–16°35'37''$ S; $68°33'36''–70°02'13''$ W) (Fig. 1 and Table 1).

2.2 Dataset

The dataset used for this research has been obtained from the Instituto del Mar del Perú (IMARPE) and includes records of temperature, pH, dissolved oxygen, electrical conductivity, PO$_4$, NO$_3$, and chlorophyll-a of Lake Titicaca, corresponding to the Peruvian side, from 2011 to 2021. This dataset consists of 579 rows. The data are appropriate for the present research project since the necessary characteristics for water quality are available in this dataset (Table 2).

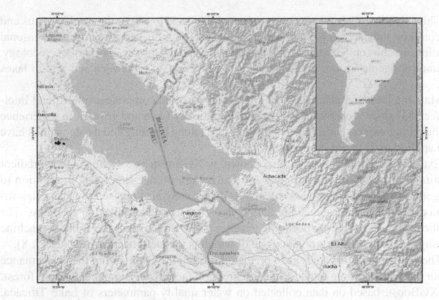

Fig. 1. Location of Lake Titicaca in South America between Peru and Bolivia

Table 1. Characteristics of Lake Titicaca.

Characteristics	Values	Water Quality	Average values
Altitude	3812 m.s.n.m	Water temperature	13.9°
Area	8562 km^2	pH	8.52
Volume	893 km^3	Total Dissolved Solids	12.59 mg/L
Average depth	107 m	Turbidity	12 NTU
Maximum depth	283 m	Chlorophyll-a	7 mg/m^3

Table 2. Dataset

Temperature °C	pH	Dissolved oxygen (mg/L)	Conductivity (μm/cm)	WQWERQPO$_4$ (mg/L)	NO$_3$ (mg/L)	Chlorophyll (mg/m^3)
13.90	8.12	6.75	1419	0.145	0.106	5.63
13.60	8.35	5.92	1401	0.027	0.182	1.19
13.50	8.33	6.76	1416	0.027	0.298	1.71
...	...	...	...	...	...	...
13.90	8.74	6.27	1589	0.017	0.037	0.87

2.3 Data Preprocessing

Before using the data for training, the data must undergo data preprocessing, which means identifying and correcting errors in the dataset that may adversely affect the prediction model. The most common errors in the database are missing columns and duplicate rows. The data preprocessing step is essential to improve data quality. The use of raw data from the dataset in classification can generate incorrect results. Therefore, data cleaning is essential [8].

2.4 Machine Learning Methods

The concept of linear regression is essential to the process of statistical modeling [9]. The statistical technique known as regression can be categorized as a form of supervised machine learning. The field of regression classification includes a great number of different algorithms, one of which is linear regression. Classification models and regression models are the two broad types that make up supervised learning models. In classification, an attempt is made to forecast a label, whereas, in regression, a quantity is anticipated [10].

The decision tree algorithm is one of the earliest and most effective machine learning algorithms, and it is the foundation upon which the majority of other machine learning algorithms are built. A rooted tree is a type of graph that is used to represent decision trees. A tree graph is a type of graph in which each edge (or path) is connected to at least two leaves (also referred to as vertices or nodes). A decision tree is represented by a rooted tree. A tree graph is a type of graph in which each edge (or path) is connected to at least two leaves [11].

Random Forest is a machine-learning algorithm that ensembles multiple decision trees [13]. Its accuracy can be increased by applying a split data sequence called bootstrap aggregation, and it allows continuous evaluation of the generalization of a set of combined trees [13].

XGBoost is an algorithm that creates many shallow decision trees and high prediction accuracy is achieved by combining all the trees [14]. The decision trees generated by the XGBoost algorithm are used not only to minimize the objective function by considering the loss function but also to protect the tree from overfitting through the regularization process [15].

2.5 Algorithm Development

The first step ordered the chlorophyll values of the dataset from lowest to highest, we found that the minimum value is 0.08 mg/m^3 and the maximum value is 7.96 mg/m^3, then we proceed to divide into 3 levels assigning a classification of low, medium and high for each of the ranges, we assign the value 1 for the first range, value 2 for the second range and value 3 for the third range. These new values are part of the dataset representing chlorophyll. Table 3 shows the range of chlorophyll classification.

The data set is into two separate sets: a training set and a test set. The training set consists of the data used in training the model. That is, it consists of n percent of the rows or observations in the data set. Normally this percentage is around 70–90%. On the

Table 3. Chlorophyll classification range

Value	Initial Range	Final Range	Classification
1	0.08 mg/m^3	0.95 mg/m^3	under
2	0.96 mg/m^3	1.83 mg/m^3	medium
3	1.85 mg/m^3	7.96 mg/m^3	high

other hand, the test set consists of the remaining percentages of the set of rows and is used to validate the model. In other words, it is used to verify that the model is properly trained (Fig. 2).

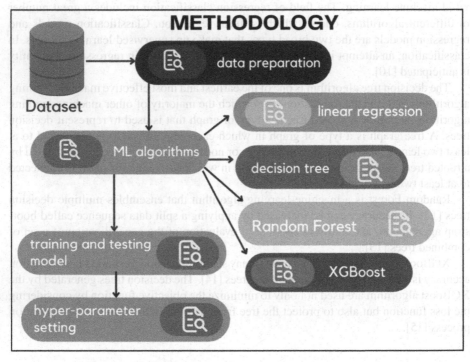

Fig. 2. Flow chart of the methodology used.

Before applying ML models to perform the analysis of the data, preparatory work had to be done to get the data ready to be fed into the model. As part of this process, the data were separated into training and testing sets so that the 4 models could be trained and their performance evaluated. In addition, the dataset was cleaned by removing incorrect values and populating empty cells with the median of the dataset's input variables. This was done to make the dataset as accurate as possible.

Before training the model, it is necessary to convert the data to an XGBoost compatible format using the xgb.DMatrix() function. Once this is done, the model can be trained using XGBoost. For this, the xgboost() function is used, which is passed the training set and the number of repeated impulse iterations is set to 100, which is often used.

To carry out these simulations, the Python programming language was run through the Jupyter environment using the Anaconda navigator. The machine that was used contained a processor of the Intel i7 core 7th generation and had 12 gigabytes of RAM.

3 Results and Discussion

This paper explores four machine learning algorithms, linear regression, decision tree, random forest, and XGBoost. The main objective is to compare the performance of the supervised algorithms. The data have been divided into 90% for training and 10% for testing. Chlorophyll values have been classified into 3 ranges, the XGBoost algorithm has improved its performance, with the use of hyperparameters such as n_estimators, learning_rate, subsample, colsample_bytree, max_depth, and gamma as shown in Table 4.

Table 4. Values of XGBoost used in code.

Parameter	Value
n_estimators	1000
learning_rate	0.08
subsample	0.75
colsample_bytree	1
max_depth	7
gamma	0

After running the algorithms in Python, using the sci-kit-learn library, and defining the hyperparameters for XGBoost in Table 4, the following results have been obtained, showing that the XGBoost algorithm has a better performance, with an r2 of 0.5455, MAPE of 25.8168 and RMSE of 0.6509, in comparison with the other algorithms (Table 5).

Table 5. Results of machine learning algorithms

Algorithm	R^2	MAPE	RMSE
Linear regression	−0.0205	51.0601	0.8602
Decision tree	−0.1595	29.1666	0.9170
Random Forest	0.3538	33.3636	0.6845
XGBoost	0.5455	25.8168	0.6509

A graph has been made comparing the test and predicted values, finding a not-so-significant difference, as we can see in Fig. 3, which will help us to predict future chlorophyll values.

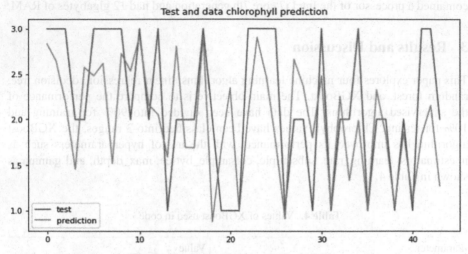

Fig. 3. Test data and chlorophyll prediction.

Figure 4 shows that the high chlorophyll values do not exceed 8 mg/m^3, and the minimum values do not fall below 0 mg/m^3, indicators that inform us that the predictive model using XGBoost is within the expected ranges.

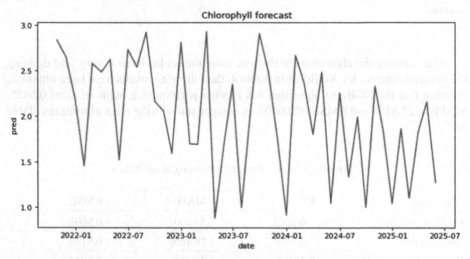

Fig. 4. Chlorophyll forecast from October 2021 to July 2025

4 Conclusion

This research focused on predicting chlorophyll values using machine learning techniques and evaluated four algorithms, from which the following conclusions can be drawn. The dataset included more than 500 samples collected between 2011 and 2021 from the Peruvian sector of Lake Titicaca. The dataset parameters consisted of temperature, pH, dissolved oxygen, electrical conductivity, PO4, NO3, and chlorophyll. A classification of the chlorophyll values was made, dividing them into 3 ranges, assigned 1 for low values, 2 for medium values, and 3 for high values. A Python program was run which initially did not obtain good metrics, then with the change of hyperparameters the results improved. The ML algorithms used in the study were linear regression, decision trees, random forest, and XGBoost. In terms of metrics, the order of the algorithms was as follows: XGBoost with an r2 of 0.5455 and RMSE of 0.6509, followed by random forest with an r2 of 0.3538 and RMSE of 0.6845, decision tree with an r2 of -0.1595 and RMSE of 0.9170 and linear regression with an r2 of -0.0202 and RMSE of 0.8602. Therefore, XGBoost has a better performance for chlorophyll prediction. We suggest making improvements in the hyperparameter values for the metrics to improve, also a larger number of samples is required.

Acknowledgments. Instituto del Mar del Perú (IMARPE), Laboratorio Continental de Puno.

References

1. Khan, R.M., Salehi, B., Mahdianpari, M., Mohammadimanesh, F: Water quality monitoring over finger lakes region using sentinel-2 imagery on google earth engine cloud computing platform. ISPRS Ann. Photogramm. Remote Sens. Spatial Inf. Sci. (3), 279–283 (2021)
2. Ocola Salazar, J.J., Laqui Vilca, W.F.: Fuentes Contaminantes en la Cuenca del Lago Titicaca: Un aporte al conocimiento de las causas que amenazan la calidad del agua del maravilloso lago Titicaca. Lima: Autoridad Nacional del Agua (2017)
3. Beltrán Farfán, D.F., Palomino Calli, R.P., Moreno Terrazas, E.G., Peralta, C.G., Montesinos-Tubée, D.B.: Calidad de agua de la bahía interior de Puno, lago Titicaca durante el verano del 2011. Rev. Peru. Biol. **22**(3), 335–340 (2015)
4. Vasquez, Y.F.: Efectos de la eutrofización en el hábitat de la bahía de Puno, en la diversidad y abundancia de avifauna del lago Titicaca. Rev. Inv. (Puno)-Escuela Posgrado UNA PUNO, **6**(1), 1–10 (2017)
5. Sun, A.Y., Scanlon, B.R.: How can big data and machine learning benefit environment and water management: a survey of methods, applications, and future directions. Environ. Res. Lett. **14**(7), 073001 (2019)
6. Zhiquan, C., Zhanfu, L., Huihuang, X., et al.: Performance optimization of the elliptically vibrating screen with a hybrid MACO-GBDT algorithm. J. Part. (Engl. Ed.) **56**(3), 193–206 (2021)
7. Chen, T., Guestrin, C.: XGBoost: A scalable tree boosting system. In: Proceedings of the ACM SIGKDD International Conference on Knowledge Discovery and Data Mining, vol. 13–17, pp. 785 794 (2016)
8. Yusri, H.I.H., Ab Rahim, A.A., Hassan, S.L.M., Halim, I.S.A., Abdullah, N.E.: Water quality classification using SVM and XGBoost method. In: 2022 IEEE 13th Control and System Graduate Research Colloquium (ICSGRC), pp. 231–236 (2022). https://doi.org/10.1109/ICS GRC55096.2022.9845143

9. Su, X., Yan, X., Tsai, C.L.: Linear regression. Wiley Interdiscip. Rev. Comput. Stat. **4**, 275–294 (2012)
10. Teoh, T.T., Rong, Z.: Classification. In: Artificial Intelligence with Python. Machine Learning: Foundations, Methodologies, and Applications, pp. 183–211. Springer, Singapore (2022). https://doi.org/10.1007/978-981-16-8615-3_11
11. Abraham, A., Livingston, D., Guerra, I., Yang, J.: Exploring the application of machine learning algorithms to water quality analysis. In: 2022 IEEE/ACIS 7th International Conference on Big Data, Cloud Computing, and Data Science (BCD), pp. 142–148 (2022). https://doi.org/10.1109/BCD54882.2022.9900636
12. Delgado, A., et al.: Assessment of water quality in Titicaca Lake, Peru using the grey clustering method. Eng. Lett. **30**(2), 847–853 (2022)
13. Breiman, L.: Random forests. Mach. Learn. **45**(1), 5–32 (2001)
14. Singha, S., Pasupuleti, S., Singha, S.S., Singh, R., Kumar, S.: Prediction of groundwater quality using efficient machine learning technique. Chemosphere **276**, 130265 (2021). https://doi.org/10.1016/j.chemosphere.2021.130265
15. Garabaghi, F.H.: Performance evaluation of machine learning models with ensemble learning approach in classification of water quality indices based on different subset of features (2021). https://doi.org/10.21203/rs.3.rs-876980/v1
16. Wirrmann, D., Ybert, J.P., Mourguiart, P., Ybert, J.P.: Paleohydrology. In: Dejoux, C., Iltis, A. (eds.) Lake Titicaca. Monographiae Biologicae, vol. 68, pp. 40–62. Springer, Dordrecht (1992). https://doi.org/10.1007/978-94-011-2406-5_3
17. Cao, Z., Melack, J.M., Liu, M., Duan, H., Ma, R.: Spatial and seasonal variability of chlorophyll a in different-sized lakes across eastern China. Inland Waters **12**(2), 205–214 (2022). https://doi.org/10.1080/20442041.2021.1970462
18. Carpio Vargas, E.E.: Modeling of relationships between physicochemical and microbiological parameters in waters of the interior bay of lake Titicaca-Puno (Peru) using prediction trees. Rev. Téc. Fac. Ing. Univ. Zulia. **44**(3), 154–168 (2021). https://doi.org/10.22209/rt.v44n3a02
19. Calderon-Vilca, H.D., Wun-Rafael, W.I., Miranda-Loarte, R.: Simulation of suicide tendency by using machine learning. In: 2017 36th International Conference of the Chilean Computer Science Society (SCCC), pp. 1–6 (2017). https://doi.org/10.1109/SCCC.2017.8405128
20. Torres-Cruz, F., et al.: Comparative analysis of high-performance computing systems and machine learning in enhancing cyber infrastructure: a multiple regression analysis approach. In: 2022 2nd International Conference on Innovative Practices in Technology and Management (ICIPTM), pp. 69–73 (2022). https://doi.org/10.1109/ICIPTM54933.2022.9753839
21. Goyzueta, C.A.R., De la Cruz, J.E.C., Machaca, W.A.M.: Advantages of assembly machine learning models for predicting employee productivity in a garment manufacturing company. In: 2021 IEEE Engineering International Research Conference (EIRCON), pp. 1–4 (2021). https://doi.org/10.1109/EIRCON52903.2021.9613559

Application of AI for Disease Classification and Trend Analysis

The Perceived Impact of Correlative Relationship between Depression, Anxiety, and Stress among University Students

Sharayu Dosalwar(✉) [iD], Ketki Kinkar [iD], Aditi Baheti [iD], and Shilpa Sonawani [iD]

School of CET, MITWPU, Pune, India
sharayudosalwar6@gmail.com

Abstract. Living in the 21st century, mental stress is something which everyone is concerned about. University students face a plethora of issues related to anxiety, stress and depression. But most of them are unaware of what they are facing, or are not ready to accept it. Youngsters beginning their college or university education face a variety of pressures related to their life stage and new surroundings. According to recent studies, symptoms associated with crucial mental health issues such as depression, stress, and anxiety are prevalent. However, university students have a poor understanding of the factors that influence these issues. In this paper, our main aim is to detect these problems in college going students with the help of questionnaires such as Perceived Stress Scale (PSS), Hamilton Anxiety Rating Scale and Beck's Depression Inventory. The purpose of the study was to see how contextual variables affected students' self-answered mental health and how these impacts vary by depression, anxiety, and stress. Through this, we come to know about the main factors which lead to such issues and in future can additionally implement methods to avert it. We have used various Machine Learning Algorithms to detect anxiety, stress and depression in students from sundry educational backgrounds.

Keywords: Stress · Anxiety · Depression · University Students · Machine Learning · Preventive Measures

1 Introduction

Mental health issues are frequently a barrier to academic performance. Students' motivation, attentiveness, and relationships with people, mental illness may have an impact on all of these factors, which are all important factors in academic achievement. The COVID-19 epidemic has raised awareness of those whose mental health has been affected. Epidemics are well-known intensify or produce new stressors, such as anxiety and get concerned about oneself or loved ones, get limited means of physical exercise and social contact as well as outgoing due to quarantine, and sudden and dramatic lifestyle changes.

There is essentially no evidence that the current pandemic has had any psychological or mental health consequences for college students, who are a susceptible demographic.

© Springer Nature Switzerland AG 2023
D. Garg et al. (Eds.): IACC 2022, CCIS 1781, pp. 173–182, 2023.
https://doi.org/10.1007/978-3-031-35641-4_13

As stated in several recent correspondences, there is an urgent need to research the impact of the current pandemic on the mental health and well-being of university students. University students are at a significant risk for depression and anxiety symptoms, and they are exposed to a variety of stresses that are particular to this stage of life, highlighting the need for mental health interventions. Despite the fact that the prevalence of psychological conditions in young adults is higher regardless of whether they attend post-secondary school, campus-based preventive programming has some inherent advantages for large-scale implementation due to students' proximity to campus services and the availability of campus services.

The terms stress, anxiety, and depression are often used interchangeably when referring to bad life situations or occurrences. Analytical research on anxiety and pressure offers a number of viewpoints on the subject. As seen by the increasing speed of living, as well as rushed and concentrated lifestyles, stress is an inextricable part of human life. In a man who is adapting to strain, conduct resistances can be noticed. As a result, one's psychological operations shift, and an exciting situation emerges. Anxiety, stress, and depression can be debilitating on their own. It also affects how we react to nature and how we get ideas. There could be considerable harm as a result of the pressure measures.

1.1 Causes of Stress in Undergraduate Studies

Stress is one of the many challenges that college students experience. Short-term stress may aid students in improving grades, refining an essay, or pursuing their dream career. On the other hand, if long-term stress is not addressed, it might have harmful implications. More than half of degree seekers' coursework is affected by stress, and unmanaged stress can have health consequences such as a weaker immune system. Aside from the harmful consequences of stress, more university students than ever before report spending considerable amounts of time under it. While coursework is the most common source of stress, other factors such as family, friends, and employment can all contribute to stress, resulting in poor academic and emotional outcomes. Students may experience emotional and psychological issues such as:

A. Anxiety about aspects of their studies, such as exams and presentations;
B. Depression; and general stress and anxiety
C. Bereavement and parental separation
D. Isolation and homesickness
E. Low self-esteem or loss of self-confidence
F. Making tough decisions
G. Alcohol or drug problems
H. Suicidal thoughts

2 Related Study

The interview with the patient takes at least 20 to 30 min to conduct in order to explore and diagnose the patient with an anxiety condition. Furthermore, diagnosis based on a specific scale necessitates the patient filling out a questionnaire with a thorough grasp of the contents of the questionnaire. Identifying the risks of an anxiety illness early on may lead to earlier intervention and simpler therapy. As a result of advancements in the field of machine learning and its successful application in a variety of sectors, researchers were drawn to employ machine learning algorithms for the diagnosis of anxiety disorders. Interrelationships between indices of stress, anxiety, depression, and physical sickness were investigated in [7] in a proportionate sample of college freshmen (N = 184). Significant associations were discovered between stress and sickness, anxiety and illness, depression and illness, and anxiety and depression.

Research work in [19] discovered that huge demand for employment was connected with the occurrence of new depression and anxiety disorders in those who had no prior diagnosis or treatment for either illness. [14] showed that the research mainly focused on the prediction of five severity levels of anxiety, depression, and stress with the use of eight different machine learning models, with the RBNF model predicting the best results.

In [8], the greatest indicators of distress were identified using a random forest machine learning technique. Regression trees were created to chalk out people who are predisposed to anxiety, depression, and post-traumatic stress disorder. Greater distress was related with somatization and reduced reliance on adaptive defense mechanisms. These findings emphasize the need of measuring individuals' physical experiences of psychological distress as well as emotion management mechanisms in order to assist mental health clinicians in tailoring evaluations and treatment amid a global health crisis.

3 Dataset and the Scaling System

The dataset was compiled from 263 students from a variety of universities and domains. The information came from the PSS exam, the Hamilton Anxiety Rating Scale, and Beck's Depression Inventory, and it includes questions from all three questionnaires, as well as the enormous emotional inquiry. The questions were graded in one of five ways: a) Never, b) Almost Never, c) Sometimes, d) Fairly Often, and e) Very Often. The weighted average approach is then implemented, with each question being prioritized.

Students from the university contributed to the data set. They were asked basic questions on how they felt and reacted to circumstances they had encountered in the previous month. Their responses are assigned a number of weights, which are used to create a score that can be used to assess an individual's stress, anxiety and depression level. To assess the weights and determine final scores, the dataset was pre-processed. To improve the performance of our model, we used K-fold cross-validation.

Stress: The Perceived Stress Scale is one of the most widely used psychological measures for assessing stress perception (PSS). The conditions were created to demonstrate how unexpected, chaotic, and upsetting the respondents' lives are. For use in community samples, the PSS was designed with at least a junior high school education in mind. The questions and answers are rather simple and broad in nature. The scale for each question is 0–4.

Anxiety: The HAM-A rating scale was developed to evaluate anxiety symptoms and is now widely used in clinical practice and research. The 14-item scale assesses both psychic and somatic anxiety and provides a list of symptoms that are evaluated in this system. Each item is graded on a scale of 0 (not present) to 4 (severe), for a total score range of 0–56, with 17 denoting light severity, 18–24 denoting mild to moderate severity, and 25–30 denoting moderate to severe severity.

Depression: The Beck Depression Inventory (BDI, BDI-1A, BDI-II) was created by Aaron T. Beck and consists of a 21-question multiple-choice self-report inventory. Its creation indicated a shift in mental health experts' opinions on depression, which had previously considered it as a psychodynamic problem rather than one founded in the patient's own thinking.

4 Methods/Algorithms Used to Detect Accuracy

4.1 Logistic Regression

Statistical analysis is used to solve and analyze issues in a wide range of industries and businesses. The effects of independent variables on the outcome variables are estimated as probability using logistic regression.

4.2 Support Vector Machine

SVM is a classification and regression prediction algorithm that uses machine learning techniques to improve predictive accuracy while automatically limiting overfitting of data.

4.3 Decision Tree Classifier

The algorithm creates rules using training data that can be represented as a tree structure.

4.4 Naive Bayes

The classifier assumes that characteristics are independent within a specific class, and hence significantly simplifies learning. Regardless of the fact that independence is a terrible assumption in general, naive Bayes frequently beats more sophisticated classifiers in reality. A subset of Bayesian decision theory is Naive Bayes. Because the formulation contains some naive assumptions, it's labeled naive.

4.5 Random Forest Classifier

This algorithm makes use of a collection of decision trees to create a classification model, and also proves to be a better approach to reduce overfitting. The goal is to use an averaging technique to combine the predictions of numerous decision trees and construct a final result (majority voting).

4.6 XGBoost Classifier

Gradient boosted decision trees are implemented using XGBoost, which is a high-speed and high-performance implementation.

4.7 XGB Classifier with Parameter Tuning

XGBoost offers a number of parameters that can be tweaked to improve model accuracy or generalization. XGBoost writers split the whole XGB classifier with parameter tweaking parameters into three categories: 1. General parameters: These parameters serve as a guide for the overall operation. 2. Booster Parameters: At each phase, guide the specific booster (tree/regression). 3. Learning Task Parameters: Use these to direct the optimization process.

4.8 K-Nearest Neighbors

The k-most proximate neighbors (KNN) algorithm is a data classification approach that estimates the chances that a data point will belong to either one of two groups based on the data points closest to it.

5   Methodology

The study's aim was to identify how common depression, anxiety, and stress were among graduate students, as well as the relationship between depression, anxiety, and stress and certain variables like gender, age, and domain. The goal is also to examine the impact of contextual variables on students' self-answered mental health and how these impacts vary by depression, anxiety, and stress.

In this research, we used machine learning techniques to detect rising stress, anxiety, and depression levels in students and to predict their levels in advance, allowing us to prevent substantial harm to their lives. During the test, we assess students in a variety of circumstances. The undertaking execution authorized the level of stress, anxiety, and depression. The suggested model covers PSS dataset collection, preprocessing, feature extraction, and machine learning models such as Logistic Regression, KNN, SVM, Decision Tree Classifier, Naive Bayes, Random Forest Classifier, XGBoost Classifier and comparison on three performance metrics as given in Fig. 1.

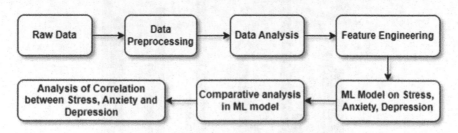

Fig. 1. Implemented Methodology in General

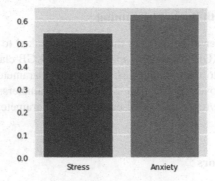

Fig. 2. Correlation of Depression with Stress and Anxiety

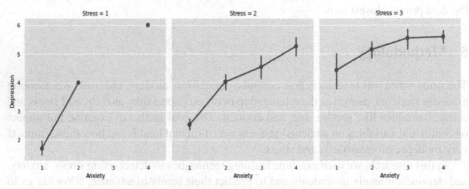

Fig. 3. Variation in Depression and Anxiety on basis of Stress Level

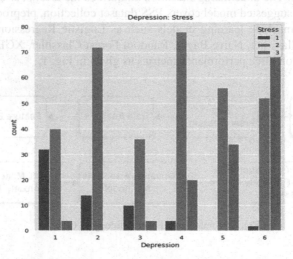

Fig. 4. Count for Stress levels in each Depression level

6   Result and Discussion

Figure 2 depicts the relationship between Depression and Stress; Depression and Anxiety. It has been observed that Anxiety, which is concerned with physical changes in the body, has a greater impact on Depression than Stress, which is concerned with changes in the mental state of mind. Figure 3 depicts a factorplot for Depression versus Anxiety for an individual's stress level. The first graph in Fig. 3 is for regular stress levels, where Anxiety and Depression both begin at the basic stage, not much variation is observed. The second graph in Fig. 3 is for moderate stress levels, in which depression begins after stage 2 depression and continues to rise linearly until stage 5 depression as anxiety levels rise. The key observation in graph 3 of Fig. 3 is that with high stress levels, depression levels begin above stage 4 and gradually grow as anxiety levels increase. In Fig. 4, we can observe and correlate the variation of different levels of stress with different levels of depression. As we can see, moderate level stress is present with all levels of depression, and high level of depression clearly concludes high levels of stress in the individual.

From our model implementation, we have predicted the stress, depression, anxiety level of a person based on the questionnaire data. For stress level detection, best accuracy was obtained from Logistic Regression that is 92.8%. For anxiety level detection, best accuracy was obtained by Logistic Regression again with 87.9% accuracy. Again, for depression level detection, best accuracy was obtained by KNN with 90% accuracy (XGBoost Classifier model is overfitting). In paper, [2, 15, 16] describes how higher stress levels affect students, in our research work we have evaluated how higher stress levels and high anxiety might lead to higher degrees of depression. It has been observed that stress, anxiety, and depression are correlated, thus a rise in one parameter might raise the other, substantially disrupting an individual's mental well-being.

6.1   Stress

Model Used	Accuracy
Logistic Regression	0.923
Support Vector Machine	0.829
Decision Tree Classifier	0.753
Naïve Bayes	0.502
Random Forest Classifier	0.829
XGBoost Classifier	0.848
XGB classifier with parameter tuning	0.720

6.2 Anxiety

Model Used	Accuracy
Logistic Regression	0.879
Logistic Regression using K-fold cross-validation	0.829
Support Vector Machine	0.816
Decision Tree Classifier	0.645
KNN	0.778
Random Forest Classifier	0.702
XGB classifier	0.689

6.3 Depression

Model Used	Accuracy
Logistic Regression	0.824
Support Vector Machine	0.630
Decision Tree Classifier	0.881
KNN	0.900
Random Forest Classifier	0.715
XGB classifier	0.985

7 Preventive Measure

A. Raise public awareness among university students about the need of seeking mentoring or therapy from a student counseling center if they are experiencing academic or emotional difficulties.
B. Research should be conducted to discover whether or not there are any psychological issues at the respective universities.
C. Counseling organizations should address the issue of identifying students with psychological disorders early on. Organizing seminars and workshops for graduate school professors on how to recognise and treat psychiatric illnesses in students.
D. Student counseling centers can be built in all universities with the help of mental health specialists, and counseling can be provided as an early intervention.
E. Students should be offered monthly workshops on stress management, planning skills, and language skills.
F. University meditation activities for students should be held on a regular basis, additionally raising public awareness among university students to seek mentorship or therapy from a student counseling center if they encounter any academic or emotional issues.

8 Conclusion

The current study is a pioneer in the investigation of anxiety, stress, and depression among academic students. Because of their heightened psychological discomfort, students require extra treatment, according to the findings of the study. Students should be encouraged to learn in a friendly and effective setting. Stress, anxiety and depression must be diagnosed early and dealt with effectively, thus support and coaching are essential. According to our research, maintaining a high level of stress and anxiety for an extended period of time can lead to higher stages of depression, which is both mentally and physically detrimental. We can also conclude from our visualizations that higher stages of depression could be avoided if anxiety and stress are managed more effectively at lower levels. For predicting Stress and Anxiety levels, Logistic regression gives best accuracy of 92% and 87% resp., whereas for predicting Depression, XGBoost Classifier gives the best accuracy of 98%. By carrying out this research, the community will become more aware of mental health issues and how students are dealing with them, and therefore will begin to take mental health more seriously in the future. In this paper, we have studied correlation between Stress, Depression and Anxiety at a higher level. In future, Correlation between parameters of individuals questionnaires of stress, depression and anxiety could be studied to get a lower-level understanding of the cause.

References

1. Jung, Y., Yoon, Y.I.: Multi-level assessment model for wellness service based on human mental stress level. Multimed. Tools Appl. 76(9), 11305–11317 (2016). https://doi.org/10.1007/s11042-016-3444-9
2. Adnan, N., et al.: University students stress level and brainwave balancing index: Comparison between early and end of study semester. In: Research and Development (SCOReD), 2012 IEEE Student Conference on. IEEE (2012)
3. Khosrowabadi, R., Quek, C., Ang, K.K., Tung, S.W., Heijnen, M.: A brain-computer interface for classifying EEG correlates of chronic mental stress. In: IJCNN, pp. 757–762 (2011)
4. Subahni, A.R., Xia, L., Malik, A.S.: Association of mental stress with video games. In: Intelligent and Advanced Systems (ICIAS) 2012 4th International Conference on, vol. 1. IEEE (2012)
5. Ghaderi, A., Frounchi, J., Farnam, A.: Machine learning-based signal processing using physiological signals for stress detection. In: 2015 22nd Iranian Conference on Biomedical Engineering (ICBME), pp. 93–98 (2015)
6. Xu, Q., Nwe, T.L., Guan, C.: Cluster-based analysis for personalized stress evaluation using physiological signals. IEEE J. Biomed. Health Inform. 19(1), 275–281 (2015)
7. Rawson, H.E., Bloomer, K., Kendall, A.: Stress, anxiety, depression, and physical illness in college students. J. Genet. Psychol. 155(3), 321–330 (1994)
8. Prout, T.A., et al.: Identifying predictors of psychological distress during COVID-19: a machine learning approach. Front. Psychol. 11, 3063 (2020)
9. Bjorksten, O., Sutherland, S., Miller, C., Stewart, T.: Identification of medical student problems and comparison with those of other students. J. Med. Educ. 58(10), 759–767 (1983)
10. Bourne, E.J.: The Anxiety and Phobia Workbook, 3rd ed. New Ham Binger Publication, Oakland, USA (2004)
11. Firth, J.: Levels and sources of stress in medical students. BMJ 292, 1177–1180 (1986)

12. Delene, L.M., Brogowicz, A.A.: Student health needs attitudes & behavior marketing implication for college health centers. **38**(4), 157–164 (1990)
13. Kumaraswamy, N., Ebigbo, P.O.: A comparative study of somatic complaints of Indian and Nigerian second year medical students, Indian. J. Clin. Psychol. **11**, 79–86 (1984)
14. Kumar, P., Garg, S., Garg, A.: Assessment of anxiety, depression and stress using machine learning models. Procedia Comput. Sci. **171**, 1989–1998 (2020)
15. Dixon, S.K., Kurpius, S.E.R.: Depression and college stress among university undergraduates. J. Coll. Stud. Dev. **49**(5), 412–424 (2008)
16. Acharya, L., Jin, L., Collins, W.: College life is stressful today—emerging stressors and depressive symptoms in college students. J. Am. Coll. Health **22**, 1–10 (2018)
17. Ibrahim, A.K., Kelly, S.J., Adams, C.E., Glazebrook, C.: A systematic review of studies of depression prevalence in university students. J. Psychiatr. Res. **47**(3), 391–400 (2013)
18. Hamaideh, S.H.: Alexithymia among Jordanian university students: its prevalence and correlates with depression, anxiety, stress, and demo-graphics. Perspect. Psychiatr. Care **54**(2), 274–280 (2018)
19. Melchior, M., Caspi, A., Milne, B.J., Danese, A., Poulton, R., Moffitt, T.E.: Work stress precipitates depression and anxiety in young, working women and men. Psychol. Med. **37**(8), 1119–1129 (2007)
20. Karasek, R., Theorell, T.: Healthy Work: Stress, Productivity, and the Reconstruction of Working Life. Basic Books, New York (1990)

Machine Learning Approach for Predicting the Maladies of Humans

Chalapathiraju Kanumuri[1]([⊠]), Ravichandra Torthi[2], Yadavalli S. S. Sriramam[1], D. Kumara Swamy[2], and Pavani Maganti[1]

[1] S.R.K.R Engineering College, Bhimavaram, AP, India
chalapathirajuk@gmail.com
[2] Ellenki College of Engineering and Technology, Hyderabad, TS, India

Abstract. Health plays a key role in everyone's life for that we try all the necessary things to be healthy but what if we can't find the problem that we are facing in our body which sickens our health and every time we are not in a situation to reach a medic for the treatment. In every sector, we observe that technology is playing its role to make work easier. In the medical sector, we have also seen technology and how it makes diagnosis easier. Considering that, in the proposed model also we are taking the help of one modern technology like Machine Learning.

As we know in the medical sector every disease or any health problem is confirmed or analyzed through symptoms. So, considering that, a model is built utilizing machine learning algorithms to foretell a person's health issue. So, using this model the health problem faced by a person is accurately analyzed through the symptoms before approaching a doctor. By using multiple algorithms response, we can give precise results when compared to using a single algorithm of machine learning technology. The proposed model attained good accuracy in discovering the correct disease based on the symptoms provided to the model.

Keywords: Machine Learning · Maladies · SVM · K-nearest neighbor · Naïve Bayes · Random Forest · Logistic regression

1 Introduction

The goal of this study is to use symptoms to forecast health issues, which helps us accurately know the exact issues the person is facing in his/her body. Along with this if we take the assistance of technology, we can raise the accuracy effectively in predicting the health issue. So, we are using Machine Learning algorithms and classifiers to predict health problems. Because Machine Learning algorithms can help in giving accurate results when it comes to predictions.

We make use of Machine Learning to predict health problems because using this modern technology we can easily train the model with the data we are using from the dataset. Here by we do not lose much time and the model can be trained accurately.

We have used machine learning technology since it can improve over time. This technology typically increases efficiency and it provides accuracy if the data expands

© Springer Nature Switzerland AG 2023
D. Garg et al. (Eds.): IACC 2022, CCIS 1781, pp. 183–191, 2023.
https://doi.org/10.1007/978-3-031-35641-4_14

too. The main notion of this project is to get the awareness of the problem. That a person is facing in his/her body when the person is, not in a situation to consult a doctor. This project will be a helping hand to the people who can't approach a doctor in a necessary situation. To build this model we utilized certain techniques called Support Vector Machine (SVM), Naive Bayes, and Random Forest classifiers for machine learning. Which gives results with higher accuracy compared to other classifications in prediction.

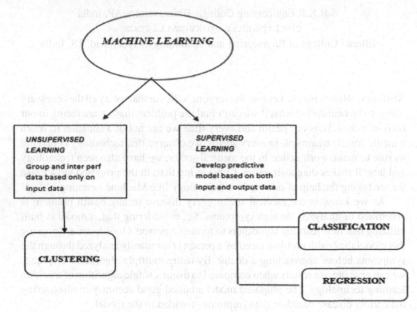

Fig. 1. Model graph of Machine Learning

From Fig. 1 we can observe the two forms of learning we utilize in machine learning: unsupervised and supervised learning. Unsupervised learning is a Machine learning paradigm for problems where the available data consists of unlabelled examples. The goal of unsupervised learning algorithms is to learn useful patterns or structural properties of data. We observe clusters in unsupervised data because it deals with finding a structure in a collection of unlabelled data. Where supervised learning is a machine learning paradigm for problems where the available data consists of labelled data, we observe classification and regression in supervised learning both problems have the goal of constructing a succinct model that can predict the value of the dependent attribute from the attribute variables. Our model comes under supervised learning where we use classifications and regression. The algorithms which are used in this model are based on classifications and our model is based on developing a predictive model based on both input and output data. This serves as the training and testing sets of data that we utilize to develop the model, respectively.

2 Literature Survey

Machine learning techniques are now becoming crucial for predicting problems in medical systems. As we can see, these models can make reliable predictions for a variety of serious illnesses, such as diabetes, fatty liver disease, Parkinson's disease, chronic kidney disease, Brain tumor, and heart disease. Cancer is one of the most frightening diseases to mankind and thanks to doctors and technology we are trying to fight it one of the research we have studied recently is predicting the prognosis of cervical cancer using modern technology which is Machine learning. The authors called Masatoyo Nakajo et al. have done this research in 2021. They have done this research to examine the usefulness of machine learning in predicting the prognosis of cervical cancer. This retrospective study included 50 cervical cancer patients who underwent 18F-FDG-PET/CT before treatment. They have used 6 machine learning algorithms like a neural network, K-nearest neighbor, Naïve Bayes, Random Forest, Logistic regression, and Support vector machine. Of all the algorithms Naïve Bayes gave the highest accuracy of all.

Author Senthil Kumar et al. also used hybrid ml algorithms like LR, hybrid random forest, KNN, NN, and SVM to improve the accuracy of the model and he gained an 88.7% correctness in foretelling the cardiovascular disease. Classifiers like Nave Bayes and decision trees of machine learning are among the most popularly used classifiers. Author Sonam Nikah also used decision trees and Naïve Bayes classifiers to predict heart disease. These models allow us to see how machine learning classifiers are crucial in disease prediction [1–5].

In the area of dermatological disorders also machine learning approaches are proposed through image-processing which was addressed by author Hasija et al. Uddin et.al in his approach made a comparison with different Supervised Ml models for comparison and decision-making in medical Informatics. Similarly, Raju et al. in their review of brain tumor detection discussed various models involved in Medical Imaging. Serekh et al. suggested a model predict chronic kidney disease using classifiers including NB, RF, and KNN classifiers. The F-measure, precision, and accuracy of their performance are evaluated. In terms of accuracy and F measure, RF performed better according to analysis, whereas NB produced superior precision. Utilizing NB and SVM, author Vijaya Vani sought to identify kidney disorders. Acute Nephritic Syndrome, Acute Renal Failure, Chronic Glomerulonephritis, and Chronic Kidney Disease (CKD) were the categories of kidney disorders that the classifiers used to differentiate. In a similar manner to Brain tumor detection also machine learning algorithms are used a review report of it was proposed by Raju [6–8].

Md Mohamoud Islam and Chie Chen Wu created a model utilizing machine learning to predict fatty liver disease (FLD). To predict the disease, they employed classification models including Random Forest (RF), Naive Bayes (NB), Artificial Neural Networks (ANN), and Logistic Regression using data from individuals who had an initial fatty liver screening (LR) [12].

Using machine learning and classifiers that have never been used before, such as Multilayer Perceptron, Bayes Net, Random Forest, and Boosted Logistic Regression, the researcher's Kamal Nayan, Bobita Majhi, and Ganapati Panda have developed a model of an improved approach for the prediction of Parkinson's disease (PD) [13].

To categorize and forecast diabetic disease, Md Maniruzzaman, Md Rahman, Benoir Ahamed, and Md Abedin developed a model utilizing the machine learning paradigm. The team has employed classifiers including Logistic regression (LR), Nave Bayes (NB), Decision Tree (DT), Ada Boost (AB), and Random Forest to determine the risk variables for diabetes disease based on p-value and odds ratio (OR),(RF)[15]. The proposed models were only created by the authors to forecast serious illnesses like the diseases mentioned above. However, the algorithm we are putting forth is thought to be able to forecast more than just one disease based on the data collected.

3   Proposed Method

Methodology:
DATA USED IN MODEL: Dataset used in this project is taken from the Kaggle website which contains symptoms of a particular disease. The training and testing portions of the dataset are separated. Data used for testing is 20%, and training data is 80%.

Training:
The graph in Fig. 2 shows the dataset has been successfully trained to the model after the dataset has been fed into the model. The y-axis and x-axis of graphs are counts and diseases respectively.

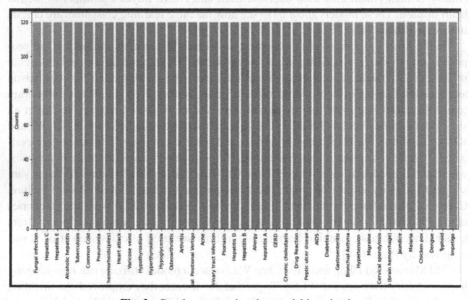

Fig. 2. Graph representing that model is trained

Graph that represents that the model is successfully trained. In this graph on the x-axis, we have 42 diseases with 120 samples on the y-axis.

Flowchart:
(See Fig. 3).

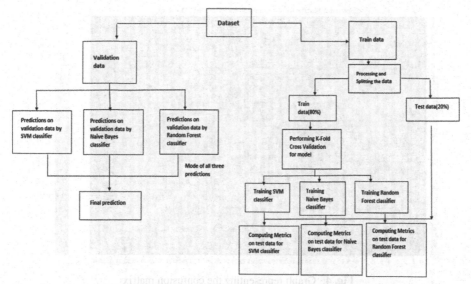

Fig. 3. Flow Chart Representation for Proposed Method

4 Procedure to Apply Methodology

The dataset's data is split into train and test sets, with the train set being subjected to K-fold cross-validation. We utilized k-fold cross-validation to categorize the classifiers, which helps divide the input dataset into k groups of samples of equal sizes. Three classifiers are now allowed access to the data. Regression analysis and classification are the foundations of the SVM classifier. Regression is a method for examining the correlation between independent and dependent variables.

Based on probabilistic classifiers, the Naive Bayes classifier offers high levels of accuracy. A probability distribution over several classes can be predicted using a probabilistic classifier. Many different decision trees are built throughout the operation of the random forest classifier. To consider a multitude of decision trees is to do so to obtain the best results. We track and evaluate the model's performance using computing metrics after providing test data to the classifiers. Now, we employ validation data as the model's last check, as it offers a preliminary assurance that the model can produce valuable predictions in a real-world situation, something that training data cannot. By using multiple algorithms we have a high chance of accuracy so trying multiple algorithms over a single algorithm to predict will be more helpful.

5 Evaluation and Result

Confusion matrix:
The performance of the classification models for a certain set of test data is assessed using the confusion matrix. As a result, it chooses the caliber of models (Fig. 4).

Applying a confusion matrix to the dataset will give us the quality of the models. So, when we give testing data to the model each classifier tests the data in its way and

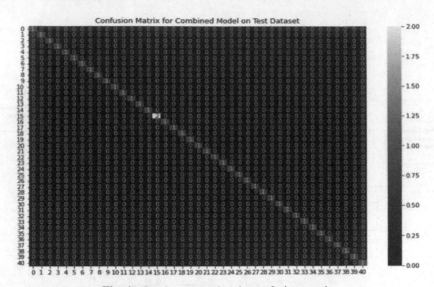

Fig. 4. Graph representing the confusion matrix

gives the prediction separately. By considering the predictions of three classifiers a final prediction is considered using a confusion matrix. Figure 5, Fig. 6, and Fig. 7 represent the confusion matrix of the SVM, Nave Bayes' and Random forest Classifiers.

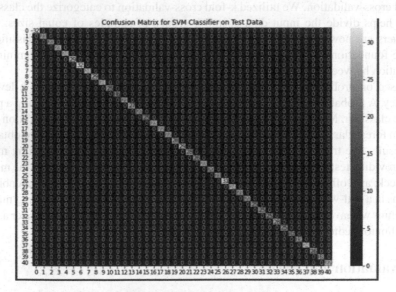

Fig. 5. SVM confusion matrix

By giving the symptoms as input, we get a predicted output of a person's disease in his body depending on the three classifiers we used in the approach for prediction. In

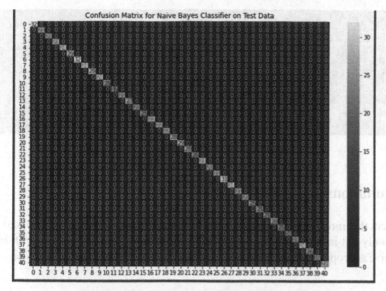

Fig. 6. Nave Bayes' confusion matrix

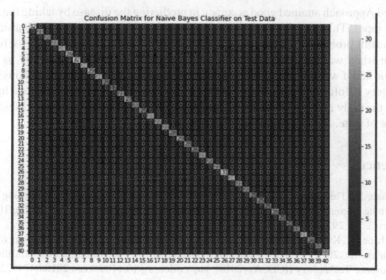

Fig. 7. Confusion matrix of Random Forest

the above diagrams, we observe that the graph has zeros and ones which represent false and true respectively of the data provided to it (Fig. 8).

Fig. 8. Output got for the given input symptoms

6   Limitations and Future Scope

At present this model can only predict the diseases through the symptoms based on the dataset only but in the future, we try to implement this model to interact with humans and to give appropriate medication suggestions to the person according to the prediction.

7   Conclusion

Proposed Approach attained good accuracy in predicting the disease by taking the symptoms as input. This model will become a helping hand to people to get the awareness of the health problem they have before approaching a doctor and will be useful in a situation when we can't consult a medic. This type of situation is faced by us in the pandemic and if we face this type of circumstance again we can be ready and this model can be very helpful. We know how dangerous the situation becomes when we have an issue in the body and we do not know the reason. Proposed model will be a lifesaver in that type of state.

References

1. Mohan, S., Thirumalai, C., Srivastava, G.: Effective heart disease prediction using hybrid machine learning techniques. IEEE Access **7**, 81542–81554 (2019). https://doi.org/10.1109/access.2019.2923707
2. Gavhane, A., Kokkula, G., Pandya, I., Devadkar, K.: Prediction of heart disease using machine learning. In: 2018 Second International Conference on Electronics, Communication and Aerospace Technology (ICECA) (2018). https://doi.org/10.1109/iceca.2018.8474922
3. Katarya, R., Srinivas, P.: Predicting heart disease at early stages using machine learning: a survey. In: 2020 International Conference on Electronics and Sustainable Communication Systems (ICESC) (2020). https://doi.org/10.1109/icesc48915.2020.9155586
4. Ismaeel, S., Miri, A., Chourishi, D.: Using the extreme learning machine (ELM) technique for heart disease diagnosis. In: 2015 IEEE Canada International Humanitarian Technology Conference (IHTC2015) (2015). https://doi.org/10.1109/ihtc.2015.7238043
5. Gonsalves, A.H., Thabtah, F., Mohammad, R.M., Singh, G.: Prediction of coronary heart disease using machine learning. In: Proceedings of the 2019 3rd International Conference on Deep Learning Technologies - ICDLT 2019 (2019). https://doi.org/10.1145/3342999.3343015

6. Hasija, Y., Garg, N., Sourav, S.: Automated detection of dermatological disorders through image processing and machine learning. In: 2017 International Conference on Intelligent Sustainable Systems (ICISS) (2017). https://doi.org/10.1109/iss1.2017.8389340
7. Uddin, S., Khan, A., Hossain, M.E., Moni, M.A.: Comparing different supervised machine learning algorithms for disease prediction. BMC Med. Inform. Decis. Making **19**(1) (2019). https://doi.org/10.1186/s12911-019-1004-8
8. Kanumuri, C., Madhavi, C.H.R.: A survey: Brain tumor detection using MRI image with deep learning techniques. In: Smart and Sustainable Approaches for Optimizing Performance of Wireless Networks, pp. 125–138 (2022). https://doi.org/10.1002/9781119682554.ch6
9. Kohli, P.S., Arora, S.: Application of machine learning in disease prediction. In: 2018 4th International Conference on Computing Communication and Automation (ICCCA) (2018). https://doi.org/10.1109/ccaa.2018.8777449
10. Patil, M., Lobo, V.B., Puranik, P., Pawaskar, A., Pai, A., Mishra, R.: A proposed model for lifestyle disease prediction using a support vector machine. In: 2018 9th International Conference on Computing, Communication and Networking Technologies (ICCCNT) (2018). https://doi.org/10.1109/icccnt.2018.8493897
11. Yuan, F.Q.: Critical issues of applying machine learning to condition monitoring for failure diagnosis. In: 2016 IEEE International Conference on Industrial Engineering and Engineering Management (IEEM) (2016). https://doi.org/10.1109/ieem.2016.7798209
12. Wu, C.-C., et al.: Prediction of fatty liver disease using machine learning algorithms. Comput. Methods Programs Biomed. **170**, 23–29 (2019). https://doi.org/10.1016/j.cmpb.2018.12.032
13. Challa, K.N., Pagolu, V.S., Panda, G., Majhi, B.: An improved approach for prediction of Parkinson's disease using machine learning techniques. In: 2016 International Conference on Signal Processing, Communication, Power and Embedded Systems (SCOPES) (2016). https://doi.org/10.1109/scopes.2016.7955679
14. Dinesh, K.G., Arumugaraj, K., Santhosh, K.D., Mareeswari, V.: Prediction of cardiovascular disease using machine learning algorithms. In: 2018 International Conference on Current Trends towards Converging Technologies (ICCTCT) (2018). https://doi.org/10.1109/icctct.2018.8550857
15. Maniruzzaman, M., Rahman, M.J., Ahammed, B., Abedin, M.M.: Classification and prediction of diabetes disease using machine learning paradigm. Health Inf. Sci. Syst. **8**(1), 1–14 (2020). https://doi.org/10.1007/s13755-019-0095-z
16. Kanumuri, C., Madhavi, C.H.R., Ravichandra, T.: Novel approach in classification and prediction of COVID-19 from radiograph images using CNN. Int. J. Adv. Comput. Sci. Appl. **13**(9) (2022). https://doi.org/10.14569/ijacsa.2022.0130966
17. https://www.geeksforgeeks.org/disease-prediction-using-machine-learning/amp/

Forecasting Futuristic COVID-19 Trend Using Machine Learning Models

Korimilla Yashwanth Reddy[✉] and V. A. Narayana

CMR College of Engineering and Technology, Hyderabad, India
yashwanthrk96@gmail.com

Abstract. Machine learning-based perioperative forecasting models have shown to be crucial for predicting outcomes to support the decision-making on the long-term course of Machine learning models have been employed for a long time in numerous applications that called for the identification of danger-related factors and identity authentication. To overcome forecasting challenges, a wide variety of prediction approaches are often used. This study demonstrates that machine learning algorithms can forecast how many people may eventually contract COVID-19, a condition that is currently thought to pose a threat to humanity. Four widely used forecasting models—linear regression (LR), least absolute shrinkage and selection operator (LASSO), support vector machine (SVM), and exponential smoothing—are used in this study to predict the terrifying COVID-19 components (ES). The number of newly infected cases, the number of fatalities, and the number of recoveries over the next several days are each predicted using a different mode 75% of the dataset was used to train the models, while the remaining 25% was used to test them. The results of the study demonstrate that using these methods in the context of the ongoing COVID-19 epidemic is a promising methodology. The results show that the ES surpasses all other models, with LR and LASSO coming in second and third. These models are good at forecasting new confirmed cases, mortality rates, and recovery rates. In contrast, with the available data, SVM performs poorly in all prediction situations.

Keywords: COVID-19 · Machine Learning · Linear Regression · Loss Function · Disease classification

1 Introduction

Machine learning has become a significant area of study during the past ten years as a result of the numerous incredibly difficult and complex real-world problems it has been able to successfully solve. One of the most crucial areas of machine learning is forecasting, which has numerous applications in prognostication, disease forecasting, securities market forecasting, and disease prediction. The longer-term course of action is guided in this area by a number of popular machine learning algorithms. Numerous studies using machine learning techniques have been carried out to predict various diseases, including coronary artery disease, disorder prediction, and cancer prediction. The most noticeable symptoms of COVID-19 are fever (98%), cough (76%), and diarrhea (3%), which are typically less common in many older persons with chronic illnesses [16]. A lot of patients have also mentioned having trouble breathing. 2019- nCoV has spread quickly throughout the world since it was first identified in late 2019 [18], with many cases mimicking flu symptoms [17]. The epidemic has had an influence on more than 209 nations and territories around the world as well as nearly two international transportations.

1.1 Objective

The study also focuses on the forecast of the COVID-19 outbreak and early reaction because the research article is intended for live forecasting of COVID-19 confirmed, recoveries, and death cases. The decision-making process for handling this scenario and directing early actions to properly control this type of disease or virus is greatly aided by these prediction algorithms.

2 Related Work

Numerous studies have previously been conducted utilizing different AI to diagnose and forecast COVID-19 infection and recovery. Four data processing techniques were used to create a predictive model for COVID-19 patient recovery as part of data mining; however, the decision tree model had the highest accuracy of all of them, at 99.85%. Convolutional neural networks were created in the work to forecast new coronavirus using x-ray pictures. The automated prediction of 2019-nCoV patients uses the deep learning technique, one of many disciplines of machine learning that is inspired by the structure of the human brain. Pre-trained models like InceptionV3, ResNet50, and Inception ResNetV2 were trained and tested on a dataset containing chest x-ray pictures.

The ResNet pre-trained model provided the best accuracy of the three models, according to the study's performance results, at 98%. This demonstrates how the model can support clinical practise decisions made by medical professionals with high performance accuracy and possibly even detect 2019-nCoV in its early phases of infection. A modified susceptible-exposed- infectious-removed (SEIR) model and machine learning model were created as part of the endeavour to anticipate the trajectory of the 2019-nCoV pandemic in China. The pandemic peaks and size could be accurately predicted by the models. The SEIR Model was used to estimate the pandemic curve using updated 2019-nCoV epidemiology data as well as population migration data before and after January 23, 2020.

To forecast the epidemic, the machine learning method was trained on 2003 SARS data. It was common practise to estimate the number of 2019-nCoV positive cases using long STM and linear regression models. The models were assessed using 10 folds of cross-validation and the root mean square error (RMSE) measure, respectively. Long immediate memory models' root mean square errors (RMSE) were 27.187 and 7.562, respectively. In addition, the research forecast the trend of the 2019-nCoV outbreak. By properly planning, allocating, and deploying healthcare resources, such projections can support healthcare administrators and policymakers. Reference used an orientation-free method based on machine learning to identify an intrinsic 2019-nCoV genomic signature. This strategy integrated digital signal analysis of the genome under the management of machine learning, enhanced decision-making, and Spearman's rank correlation analysis for validation outcomes. The study's findings support the research theory that a bat is where the 2019-nCoV pandemic originated, and as a result, the study further categorises the pandemic as being caused by the Sarbeco virus within the beta coronavirus family. With over 90% accuracy, over 5000 different genomic sequences with a combined length of 61.8 million base pairs were evaluated from the dataset.

3 Novel Model

The research report discusses COVID-19 predictions for a novel coronavirus. COVID-19 has demonstrated that it could pose a threat to human life. Tens of thousands of people die as a result of it, and the death rate is rising globally every day. This study seeks to forecast the death rate, the number of daily confirmed infected cases, and the number of recovery cases for the next several days in order to aid in the control of the current pandemic scenario. Four machine learning techniques that are relevant to the current situation were used for the predicting. Data from the Git Hub registry, provided by the Systems Science and Engineering Center at Johns Hopkins University, were gathered. With assistance from the ESRI Living Atlas Team, the university mostly made the archive for the Novel Corona Virus visual dashboard available in 2019. The files used for data gathering are stored in a file called a Git Center repository (cssecovid19). The daily statistic summary tables used in the study's dataset include information on the number of confirmed cases, fatalities, and recoveries for the last number of days since the pandemic began. The dataset was initially preprocessed for this study to look up global statistics on the number of deaths, confirmed cases, and recoveries on a daily basis. The resulting statistics have been extracted from the reported data, the samples of the resulting dataset are shown below (Table 1).

Table 1. Samples of the resulting time-series dataset

	Country Name	No. of confirmed cases	No. of deaths	No. of recoveries	No. of active cases	Mortality rate
0	US	3507562	137170	1075882	2294510	0.039107
1	Brazil	1973933	75604	1350098	548231	0.038301
2	India	968857	24914	612768	331175	0.025715
3	Russia	745197	11753	522375	211069	0.014772
4	Peru	337751	46300	226400	65051	0.137083
5	Chile	321205	7186	292085	21934	0.022372
6	Mexico	317635	36906	252368	28361	0.116190

The dataset has been split into two subsets after the initial data preprocessing step: a training set to guide the models and a testing set. In this work, training models like SVM, LR, LASSO, and ES are used [19]. These models are trained using historical data and patterns related to newly confirmed cases, recovery, and mortality. After that, the educational models were assessed and supported by significant metrics including the R2-score, R2-adjusted score, MSE, RMSE, and MAE, and the results were published. A graphic illustrating the suggested methodology used in the study has been provided (Fig. 1).

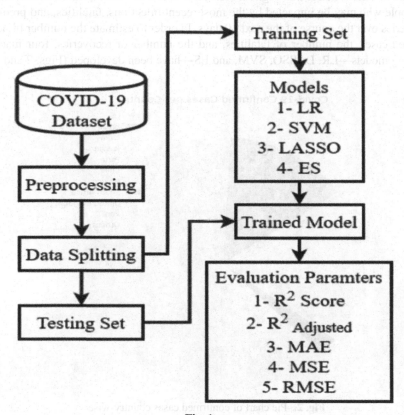

Fig. 1. .

4   Experimental Results and Outputs

In this study, machine learning techniques are used to create a system for the longer-term forecasting of the number of COVID-19 instances. Data from daily reports on the number of newly infected cases, the number of recoveries, and the number of deaths attributable to COVID-19 are included in the dataset utilized for the analysis. Due to the fact that the death rate and the number of confirmed cases are rising daily, which is a worrying situation for the world. It is unknown how many people the COVID-19 pandemic has affected in various nations throughout the world. This study aims to estimate the number of people who may be impacted by the most recent infections, fatalities, and predicted recoveries over the course of the next 10 days. In order to estimate the number of newly infected cases, the number of fatalities, and the number of recoveries, four machine learning models—LR, LASSO, SVM, and ES—have been developed (Figs. 2 and 3).

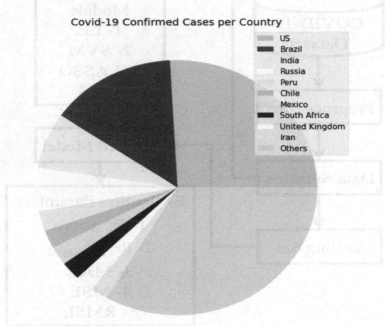

Fig. 2. Pie chart of confirmed cases country-wise

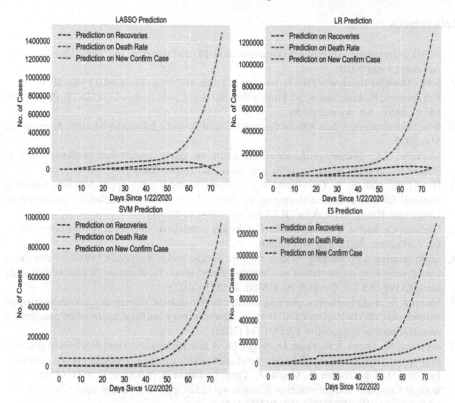

Fig. 3. Predictions of confirmed, death & recoveries using Machine Learning models

5   Experimental Results and Outputs

I The COVID-19 pandemic's vulnerability has the potential to spark a severe world-wide calamity. There are concerns among certain experts and government organisations around the world that the epidemic may affect a disproportionately large number of people. In this study, a machine learning-based prediction approach for estimating the likelihood of COVID-19 outbreaks worldwide was developed. The system uses machine learning techniques to analyse the dataset comprising the day-by-day actual previous data and anticipate future days. Given the nature and amount of the dataset, the study's findings demonstrate that ES performs best within the current forecasting area. To a certain extent, LR and LASSO also excel in forecasting mortality rates and confirming cases. The outcomes of those two models predict that in the next days, the death rates will rise and the rate of recovery would stall. Because of the fluctuations in the dataset values, SVM delivers subpar results for all cases. Overall, we draw the conclusion that model predictions made based on the current environment are accurate and can be used to anticipate future events. Thus, the study's forecasts can also be of tremendous use to the authorities in helping them decide what to do and when to do it in order to handle the COVID-19 crisis. One of the first areas of emphasis in future development will be real-time live forecasting.

References

1. WHO. Naming the Coronavirus Disease (Covid-19) and therefore the Virus That Causes it. Accessed 1 Apr 2020
2. Johns Hopkins University Data Repository. Cssegis and data. Accessed 27 Mar 2020
3. Petropoulos, F., Makridakis, S.: Forecasting the novel coronavirus COVID-19. PLoS ONE **15**(3) (2020). Art. no. e0231236
4. BBC. Coronavirus: Up to 70% of Germany Could Become Infected—Merkel. Accessed 15 Mar 2020
5. Mediaite, N.C.: Harvard professor sounds alarm on 'likely' coronavirus pandemic: 40% to 70% of world could be infected this year. Accessed 18 Feb 2020
6. Han, J.-H., Chi, S.-Y.: Consideration of manufacturing data to apply Machine Learning methods for predictive manufacturing. In: Proceedings of 8th International Conference on Ubiquitous Future Networking (ICUFN), pp. 109–113 (2016)
7. Grushka-Cockayne, Y., Jose, V.R.R.: Combining prediction intervals in the m4 competition. Int. J. Forecast. **36**(1), 178–185 (2020)
8. Eight pruning deep learning models for low storage and high-speed COVID-19 computed tomography lung segmentation and heatmap-based lesion localization: A multicenter study using COVLIAS 2.0. Comput. Biol. Med. 105571 (2022)
9. Munjral, S., et al.: Cardiovascular risk stratification in diabetic retinopathy via atherosclerotic pathway in COVID-19/Non-COVID-19 frameworks using artificial intelligence paradigm: a narrative review. Diagnostics **12**(5), 1234 (2022)
10. Agarwal, M., Gupta, S.K., Garg, D., Singh, D.: A novel compressed and accelerated convolution neural network for covid-19 disease classification: a genetic algorithm based approach. In: Garg, D., Jagannathan, S., Gupta, A., Garg, L., Gupta, S. (eds.) IACC 2021. Communications in Computer and Information Science, vol. 1528, pp. 99–111. Springer, Cham (2021). https://doi.org/10.1007/978-3-030-95502-1_8
11. Inter-variability study of COVLIAS 1.0: hybrid deep learning models for COVID-19 lung segmentation in computed tomography. Diagnostics **11**(11) (2022)
12. Systematic review of artificial intelligence in acute respiratory distress syndrome for COVID-19 lung patients: a biomedical imaging perspective. IEEE J. Biomed. Health Inform. (2022) **25**(11), 4128–4139
13. COVLIAS 1.0: lung segmentation in COVID-19 computed tomography scans using hybrid deep learning artificial intelligence models. Diagnostics **11**(8), 1405 (2022)
14. Saba, L., et al.: Six artificial intelligence paradigms for tissue characterization and classification of non-COVID-19 pneumonia against COVID-19 pneumonia in computed tomography lungs. Int. J. Comput. Assist. Radiol. Surg. **16**(3), 423–434 (2022)
15. Zhang, Y., Jiang, B., Yuan, J., Tao, Y.: The impact of social distancing and epicenter lockdown on the COVID-19 epidemic in mainland China: a data-driven SEIQR model study. medRxiv (2020)
16. Huang, C., et al.: Clinical features of patients infected with 2019 novel coronavirus in Wuhan, China. Lancet (2020)
17. Lisa, E.G., Vineet, D.M.: Return of the coronavirus: 2019-nCoV. Viruses **12**(2), 135 (2020). https://doi.org/10.3390/v12020135
18. Muhammad, L.J., Usman, S.S.: Power of artificial intelligence to diagnose and prevent further COVID-19 outbreak: a short communication (2020). arXiv:2004.12463 [cs.CY]
19. Tuli, S., et al.: Next generation technologies for smart healthcare: challenges, vision, model, trends and future directions. Internet Technol. Lett. e145 (2020)

Machine Learning Techniques in Cardiovascular Disease Prediction

Rajat Srivastava(✉) (iD), Srabanti Maji(✉) (iD), and Trinath Panda(iD)

DIT University, Dehradun, Uttarakhand, India
rj.raaj321@gmail.com, srabantiindia@gmail.com

Abstract. The heart is the crucial organ of the human body that aids in the coursing and filtering of blood to every one of the parts of the body and the heart itself. In the world, millions of deaths are due to cardiovascular diseases each year. Some of cardiovascular diseases include Heart failure, cardiomyopathy, cardiac dysrhythmia, hypertension, Stroke, and pulmonary heart disease. Some common indications or symptoms are dyspnea, palpitation, dizziness, fatigue, angina, sweating, and nausea. This review includes a brief in-depth analysis of machine learning (ML) techniques for the prediction of heart diseases that are available in the literature. The machine learning techniques that are discussed are Random Forest, Support Vector Machine (SVM), Artificial neural network (ANN), Naïve Bayes (NB), Decision Tree (DT) and K-nearest neighbor (KNN). Furthermore, all these mentioned techniques are compared on basis of their features.

Keywords: Unsupervised learning · Machine learning · Supervised learning · Naïve bias · Heart disease · K-NN · SVM · Artificial neural network · cardiovascular diseases

1 Introduction

Cardiovascular diseases (CVD) are the most mortal diseases in the world, causing danger to the life of both young people and old ones. In the whole world, more than eighty million people suffer from a form of cardiovascular disease, with a mortality rate of seventeen million people every year. This translates to the deaths that occur, higher than the deaths caused by the other five leading killer diseases. It is more common in people over 50 and the risk increase with an increase in age. There are various forms of cardiovascular disease, and the most common of them is hypertension known as, heart failure, coronary heart disease, arrhythmia, stroke, congenital cardiovascular defects, rheumatic heart disease, vascular disease, heart valve disease, and other vascular diseases. Most deaths are caused due to Myocardial infarction.

Sreeniwas Kumar A predictably, up to 90% of cardiovascular diseases can be prevented. Anticipation of CVD involves reducing risks by completing healthy diet habits, exercising, and avoiding tobacco, smoking, and alcohol consumption. Giving other danger factors, such as diabetes, high blood pressure, and blood lipid are also helpful in preventing. Raising awareness among people about techniques to prevent CVD can also help in preventing death due to CVD [1].

© Springer Nature Switzerland AG 2023
D. Garg et al. (Eds.): IACC 2022, CCIS 1781, pp. 199–211, 2023.
https://doi.org/10.1007/978-3-031-35641-4_16

There are different types of cardiovascular diseases:

Pulmonary-heart diseases: A disease where there is a dysfunction of the right side of the heart with the involvement of the respiratory system.

Cardiomyopathy: A disease where the muscle of the heart cannot be capable to supply blood to other areas of the human body.

Cardiac arrhythmia: A condition when the electric impulse to the heart doesn't coordinate properly resulting in a beating heart too fast or slow or also sometimes irregular.

Coronary heart disease: Diseases caused due to narrowing of the blood vessels that supply blood to the heart itself, resulting in chest pain and dyspnea due to shortness of oxygen-carrying blood to the heart. The main cause of the narrowing of blood vessels are deposition of cholesterol and/or plaques in the walls of blood vessels.

Hypertension: A serious medical condition where the blood vessels that carry the blood to all parts of the body from the heart have high pressure of blood flow. This is a vital sign if not controlled early can lead to life-threatening diseases like stroke, heart failure, and other kinds of heart diseases.

In this paper, we have discussed several machine learning techniques for using cardiovascular disease predictions. Presently a day there are excesses of modern methods to identify the coronary illness like information mining, AI, supervised learning, and so on.

2 Literature Review

Amanda H. Gonsalves, Fadi Thabtah used ancient scientific information to predict CHD with the application of Machine Learning (ML) technology. The possibility of their studies is constrained to the use of three supervised learning methods particularly Support Vector Machine (SVM), Naïve Bayes (NB), and Decision Tree (DT) to find the association in coronary heart disease info that would assist in enhancing the forecast percentage. Using the dataset from South African Heart Disease (SAHD) of 462 instances, intelligent models were derived through the taken into consideration of Machine Learning strategies and the use of 10-fold cross-validation. Empirical consequences of the use of different overall performance assessment measures file that probabilistic models derived through Naïve Bayes are suggesting in identifying coronary heart diseases [2].

G. Parthiban, S.K. Srivatsava predicted heart disease using diabetic diagnosis attributes. Classifiers used helped in the early detection of heart disease in diabetic patients, which will warn the patients to change their lifestyle, resulting in cost-effectiveness as well as less mortality rates. SVM is a classification technique with excellent predictive performance. With the help of the ROC curve, this has also been investigated for testing data and training data. Therefore, the classification of the diabetic dataset SVM model can be recommended [3].

Fadoua Khennou, Charif Fahim suggested a decision-based system and ML to foresee cardiovascular diseases and validated the gathering of datasets of heart diseases from the repository of UCI ML. The author united and also trained the Cleveland, Hungarian, and Switzerland datasets using SVM algorithms and NB algorithms. Then it was compared and analyzed with other models for the accuracy of around 86% for NB and 87% for SVM, which shows good and high data compare to already existing methods using small subset data and no imputation technique [4].

Youness Khourdifi, and Mohamed Bahaj for improving the condition of heart disease classification used a procedure known as Fast Correlation-Based Feature Selection (FCBF) to sort out unnecessary characteristics. Later they used numerous categorization algorithms like Multilayer Perception, Support Vector Machine, Random Forest, Naïve Bayes, and K-Nearest Neighbor to perform classifications. A mixed approach of Artificial Neural Network optimized by Particle Swarm Optimization (PSO) combined with Ant Colony Optimization (ACO) is applied to the dataset of heart disease. Max precision of 99.65% with the use of optimized model proposed by Fast Correlation Based Features, Particle Swarm Optimization, and Ant Colony Optimization. The results for the proposed system showed that the performance is better than that of the classification technique presented [5].

Hager Ahmed, Eman M.G. Younis proposed a real-time heart disease prediction system that describes the current health status of the patients. The main goal was to find the ideal ML algorithm that attains high precision used for predicting heart disease. They used two kinds of features selection algorithms, Relief feature selection, and univariate feature selection, and also compared four types of ML algorithms; Logistic Regression Classifier, Random Forest Classifier, Support Vector Machine, and Decision Tree to enhance accuracy they applied hyperparameter tuning and cross-validation. By integrating Apache Kafka with Apache Spark as the fundamental foundation of the method it's done. The outcomes showed that the peak accuracy of 94.9% is achieved by random forest classifiers as compared to other models [6].

Halima EL HAMDAOUI, Saïd BOUJRAF suggested a heart disease predicting support system applying ML Algorithms like Random Forest, KNN, SVM, DT, and Naive Bayes applied in the study with the help of data of risk factors that is gathered from the medical records. After conducting multiple experiments, they found that Naïve Bayes with validation techniques such as cross-confirmation and train-test split showed a precision of 82.17% and 84.28% respectively. They also found that by applying cross-validation techniques to all the algorithms such as Random Forest, KNN, SVM, DT, and Naive Bayes, the accuracy of these algorithms decreases [7].

Senthilkumar M, Chandrasegar T. proposed heart disease predicting novel method that focus on gathering the significant features by the application of ML techniques that help in improving the precision of heart disease prediction. In their model they introduced and used a technique called Hybrid Random Forest with Linear Model (HRFLM) that combines the features of Random Forest and Linear Method. Using this hybrid prediction model, they able to get a better accuracy of 88.7% for the cardiovascular disease [8].

Samiksha M., Mahesh M. they concentrate on pathophysiology of DR, retinal and CAD imaging, as well as the function of substitute biomarkers for CVD because CAD risk assessment is costly for low-income countries. This study also emphasizes on comprehending how DR, which is brought on by atherosclerotic disease and diabetes, worsens CVD, as it is seen in diabetic patients, Diabetic Retinopathy is linked to an increasing risk of cardiovascular events. They provide a fix for the problem of how AI may assist in identifying CVD risk [9].

Luca Saba, Skandha S. Sanagala performed a study whose goals are to (a) develop a collection of artificial intelligence (AI)-based tissue characterization and classification (TCC) systems utilizing ultrasound-based carotid artery plaque images gathered from various sites, and (b) assess the performance of the AI. According to their theory, symptomatic plaque is dispersed more than asymptomatic plaque. As a result, the AI system can automatically identify, describe, and classify them. Four machine learning (ML) systems, one transfer learning (TL) system, and one deep learning (DL) architecture with various layers make up our six different types of AI systems. There are two kinds of plaque characterization used by Atheromatic 2.0: A bispectrum analysis and an AI-based mean feature strength (MFS). Data on London, Lisbon, and combined (London + Lisbon) were all gathered. To do 3D optimization for the ideal amount of AI layers vs folds, they balanced and then enhanced five folds. In contrast to Atheromatic 1.0, AI paradigms for London and Lisbon demonstrated improvements of 10.41% and 3.32%, respectively. For applications involving carotid plaque tissue categorization and characterization in vascular surgery, Atheromatic 2.0 demonstrated steady and reliable results [10] as shown in the Table 1.

3 Methodology

Naive Bayes:- This is a probabilistic AI calculation because of the Bayes Hypothesis, utilized in a wide assortment of grouping undertakings. In this article, we will comprehend the Gullible Bayes calculation and all fundamental ideas so there is no space for questions in understanding. The equation is mentioned below

$$P(A|B) = P(B|A)P(A)/P(B) \tag{1}$$

P(A|B) = posterior probability, P(B|A) = likelihood probability, P(A) = prior probability, and P(B) = marginal probability.

K-Means Clustering:- This is a bunching calculation that processes centroids and retrospections until the ideal centroid is set up. It's hypothetically known the number of groups that are right there. It's else called the position bunching computation. The volume of bunches set up from information by the technique is signified by the letter 'K' in K-implies. In this technique, records focuses are relegated to organizations in order that the quantum of the squared distances among the records of hobby and the centroid is every round as low as may be anticipated. It's pivotal to observe that diminished variety inside bunches activates similarly indistinguishable record of hobby internal a analogous group [23] As shown in Fig. 1.

Table 1. Accuracy measures of various techniques

Year	Author	Manuscript Title	Technique used	Accuracy
2019	A. H. Gonsalves [2]	Prediction of Coronary Heart Disease using Machine Learning: An Experimental Analysis	Data Mining, SVM, DT, Naïve bias Supervised Learning	95%
2019	Khennou F [4]	A Machine Learning Approach: Using Predictive Analytics to Identify and Analyse High Risks Patients with Heart Disease	ML, prediction, SVM, Naïve Bayes	SVM-87%, NB-86%
2019	Khourdifi Y [5]	Heart Disease Prediction and Classification Using Machine Learning Algorithms Optimized by Particle Swarm Optimization and Ant Colony Optimization	ANN, K-NN, SVM, NB, Random Forest, Feature selection, Classification Ant colony optimization, Particle swarm optimization, ML	FCBF, PSO, ACO-96.65% KNN-96%
2020	Hamdaoui H [7]	A Clinical support system for Prediction of Heart Disease using Machine Learning Techniques	Clinical decision systems, machine learning, cross-validation technique	NB-84.28%
2016	Dangi G [11]	A Smart Approach to Diagnosing Heart Disease through Machine Learning and Springleaf Marketing Response	ML, Data Analysis, DM, Multinomial Regression	XGBOOST-79.32% NB-74.24%
2016	Miao K [12]	Diagnosing Coronary Heart Disease Using Ensemble Machine Learning	Adaptive Boosting algorithm, classifier, classification error, ML, precision	CCF-80.14 LBMC-77.78 HIC- 89.12 SUH- 96.72

(*continued*)

Table 1. (*continued*)

Year	Author	Manuscript Title	Technique used	Accuracy
2019	Mohan S [8]	Effective Heart Disease Prediction Using Hybrid Machine Learning Techniques	ML, feature selection, prediction model, classification algorithms	HRFLM-88.70%
2020	Sharma V [13]	Heart disease prediction using machine learning techniques	ML, K-NN, Random Forest	K-NN-86.88% Random Forest algorithm -81.967%
2020	Garg A [14]	Heart Disease Prediction using Machine Learning Techniques	ML, ANN, SVM, Classification	Random Forest algorithm-99% DT-85.00%
2020	Rajdhan A [15]	IJERT, Heart Disease Prediction using Machine Learning	DT, NB, Logistic Regression, Random Forest	Random Forest algorithm-90.16%
2018	Vijayashree J [16]	A Machine Learning Framework for Feature Selection in Heart Disease Classification Using Improved Particle Swarm Optimization with Support Vector Machine Classifier	Particle Swarm Optimization, Support Vector Machine, fitness function, ROC analysis	PSO-SVM-84.36%
2020	Rani S [17]	Predicting congenital heart disease using machine learning techniques	ANN, weighted Random Forest, SVM, NB	ANN-99.60%

(*continued*)

Table 1. (*continued*)

Year	Author	Manuscript Title	Technique used	Accuracy
2020	Du Z [18]	Accurate Prediction of Coronary Heart Disease for Patients with Hypertension from Electronic Health Records with Big Data and Machine-Learning Methods: Model Development and Performance Evaluation	ML	XGBOOST-94.30% K-NN-90.80%
2020	Choudhary G [19]	Prediction of Heart Disease using Machine Learning Algorithms	ML, Classification, DT, Ada-Boost	Ada-boost algorithm-89.88%
2021	Rani P [20]	A decision support system for heart disease prediction based upon machine learning	ML	Random Forest-86.60%
2021	Ghosh P [21]	Use of Efficient Machine Learning Techniques in the Identification of Patients with Heart Diseases	K-NN, DT, Random Forest	5-fold Cross Validation (CV)-99.33%
2018	Nashif S [22]	Heart Disease Detection by Using Machine Learning Algorithms and a Real-Time Cardiovascular Health Monitoring System	Data Mining, ML, Internet of Things, Patient Monitoring Systems, Heart Disease Detection, and Prediction	SVM-97.53%

K-Nearest Neighbors: - The K-Nearest neighbors' computation, else called K-NN, is a non-parametric, directed learning classifier, which utilizes vicinity to make characterizations or prospects about the gathering of a singular data of interest. While it very well may be utilized for one or the other relapse or characterization issues, it is regularly utilized as a grouping calculation, working off the presumption that comparative focuses can be viewed as close to each other [23]. As shown in Fig. 2.

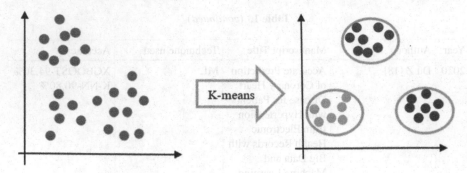

Fig. 1. K-means

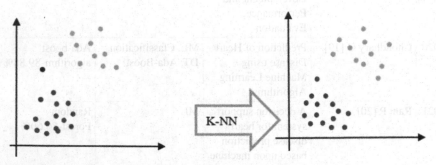

Fig. 2. K-Nearest Neighbor (KNN)

Random Forest:- This is an adaptable, simple to-use AI computation that produces, indeed without hyperactive-boundary tuning, an inconceivable outgrowth more frequently than not. It's likewise relatively conceivably the most-utilized computation,

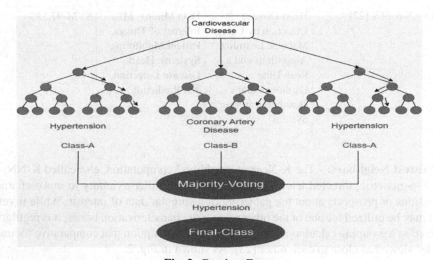

Fig. 3. Random Forest

because of its effortlessness and variety, it tends to be employed for both order and relapse undertakings [24]. As shown in Fig. 3.

Artificial Neural Network (ANN):- Artificial neural networks are computational models and are roused by the human mind. A significant number of new headways have been made in the field of Man-made brainpower, including Voice Acknowledgment, Picture Acknowledgment, and Mechanical technology utilizing Fake Brain Organizations. They are the naturally enlivened re-enactments performed on the PC to play out specific explicit errands [25]. As shown in Fig. 4.

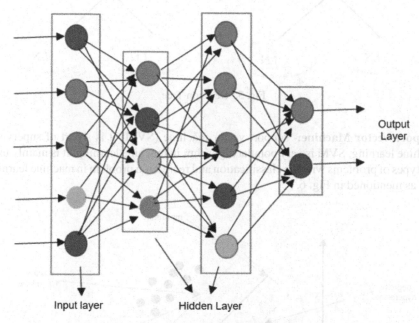

Output Layer

Input layer   Hidden Layer

Fig. 4. Artificial neural network (ANN)

Decision Tree:- This is a supervised learning method it's a part of machine learning it is able to be employed for each grouping and relapse issues, yet generally it's liked for diving bracket issues. It's a tree-prepared classifier, in which interior capitals address the highlights of a dataset, branches cope with the selection tips and every leaf capital addresses the end result. In a DT, there are two capitals, which might be the desire hub and Leaf capital. Preference hub are applied to go together with any preference and feature exclusive branches, though Leaf capitals are the end result of these desire and include no further branches. The options or the check are achieved primarily based totally on factors of the given dataset. It's a graphical depiction for getting every one of the implicate answers for an issue choice in light of given conditions. It's referred to as a desire tree because, like a tree, it start with the root capitals, which develops in addition branches and builds a tree-like design. To assemble a tree, we use the Tree computation, which represents Order and Relapse Tree computation. A desire tree poses an inquiry, and due to the response (Yes/No), it in addition resolves the tree into subtrees [26]. As shown in Fig. 5.

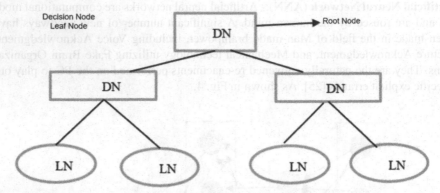

Fig. 5. Decision Tree

Support Vector Machine:- support vector machine (SVM) it is a part of supervised machine learning. SVM is very popular algorithm in machine learning. It is mainly used two types of problems with the classification and recreation problem in machine learning [16] as mentioned in Fig. 6.

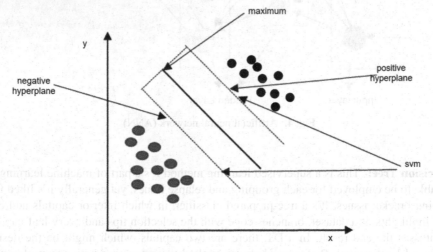

Fig. 6. Support vector machine

4　Identified Gaps

Thus, this studies depicts that the use of machine learning techniques in the field of bioinformatics produces notable variety with inside the result. Such techniques assist us in early prediction of cardiovascular disease. Though meticulous work has been completed over the previous few years and exceptional fulfillment has been completed, there are various areas that have been discovered as gaps or boundaries withinside the study work.

Many abilities have been eliminated at some point of implementation of machine learning techniques. Exclusion of worldwide datasets over language boundaries have become discovered with much less use of hybrid algorithms over dataset.

5 Conclusion and Future Work

We are an analysis of machine learning methods for the prediction of cardiovascular diseases (CVD). Machine Learning methods have been mentioned within side the medical area and specifically for the prediction of CVD. The end of the set of rules has been determined, the proposed gadget can be used within side the patient in the medical field. More precise function choice procedures are used to enhance the set of rules' precision so that dependable effects may be obtained. If a selected form of coronary disease is diagnosed. In destiny, we can recommend an approach for initial prediction of coronary heart disease along with excessive accurateness and minimal fee and complication.

The future challenges that could be confronted are working on algorithms which use hybrid machine learning techniques on global dataset. Another intention is achieving excessive accuracy while implementing machine learning algorithms on diverse dataset. Use of more machine learning algorithms to check the performance of model predicted.

References

1. Sreeniwas Kumar, A., Sinha, N.: Cardiovascular disease in India: a 360 degree overview. Med. J. Armed Forces India **76**, 1–3 (2020)
2. Gonsalves, A.H., Thabtah, F., Mohammad, R.M.A., Singh, G.: Prediction of coronary heart disease using machine learning: an experimental analysis. In: ACM International Conference Proceeding Series. Association for Computing Machinery, pp. 51–56 (2019)
3. Parthiban, G., Srivatsa, S.K.: Foundation of Computer Science FCS (2012). ISSN: 2249-0868
4. Khennou, F., Fahim, C., Chaoui, H., Chaoui, N.E.H.: A machine learning approach: using predictive analytics to identify and analyze high risks patients with heart disease. Int. J. Mach. Learn. Comput. **9**, 762–767 (2019). https://doi.org/10.18178/ijmlc.2019.9.6.870
5. Khourdifi, Y., Bahaj, M.: Heart disease prediction and classification using machine learning algorithms optimized by particle swarm optimization and ant colony optimization. Int. J. Intell. Eng. Syst. **12**, 242–252 (2019). https://doi.org/10.22266/ijies2019.0228.24
6. Ahmed, H., Younis, E.M.G., Hendawi, A., Ali, A.A.: Heart disease identification from patients' social posts, machine learning solution on Spark. Future Gener. Comput. Syst. **111**, 714–722 (2020). https://doi.org/10.1016/j.future.2019.09.056
7. El Hamdaoui, H., Boujraf, S., Chaoui, N.E.H., Maaroufi, M.: A clinical support system for prediction of heart disease using machine learning techniques. In: 2020 International Conference on Advanced Technologies for Signal and Image Processing (ATSIP 2020). Institute of Electrical and Electronics Engineers Inc. (2020)
8. Mohan, S., Thirumalai, C., Srivastava, G.: Effective heart disease prediction using hybrid machine learning techniques. IEEE Access **7**, 81542–81554 (2019). https://doi.org/10.1109/ACCESS.2019.2923707

9. Munjral, S., et al.: Cardiovascular risk stratification in diabetic retinopathy via atherosclerotic pathway in COVID-19/non-COVID-19 frameworks using artificial intelligence paradigm: a narrative review. Diagnostics **12**(5), 1234 (2022)
10. Saba, L., et al.: A multicenter study on carotid ultrasound plaque tissue characterization and classification using six deep artificial intelligence models: a stroke application. IEEE Trans. Instrum. Meas. **70**, 1–12 (2021). https://doi.org/10.1109/TIM.2021.3052577
11. Dangi, G., Choudhury, T., Kumar, P.: A smart approach to diagnose heart disease through machine learning and Springleaf Marketing Response. In: 2016 International Conference on Recent Advances and Innovations in Engineering (ICRAIE 2016). Institute of Electrical and Electronics Engineers Inc. (2016)
12. Miao, K.H., Miao, J.H., Miao, G.J.: Diagnosing coronary heart disease using ensemble machine learning (2016)
13. Sharma, V., Yadav, S., Gupta, M.: Heart disease prediction using machine learning techniques. In: Proceedings - IEEE 2020 2nd International Conference on Advances in Computing, Communication Control and Networking (ICACCCN 2020). Institute of Electrical and Electronics Engineers Inc., pp 177–181 (2020)
14. Garg, A., Sharma, B., Khan, R.: Heart disease prediction using machine learning techniques. In: IOP Conference Series: Materials Science and Engineering. IOP Publishing Ltd. (2021)
15. Rajdhan, A., Agarwal, A., Sai, M.: Heart disease prediction using machine learning
16. Vijayashree, J., Sultana, H.P.: A machine learning framework for feature selection in heart disease classification using improved particle swarm optimization with support vector machine classifier. Program. Comput. Softw. **44**, 388–397 (2018). https://doi.org/10.1134/S0361768818060129
17. Rani, S., Masood, S.: Predicting congenital heart disease using machine learning techniques. J. Discret. Math. Sci. Cryptogr. **23**, 293–303 (2020). https://doi.org/10.1080/09720529.2020.1721862
18. Du, Z., et al.: Accurate prediction of coronary heart disease for patients with hypertension from electronic health records with big data and machine-learning methods: model development and performance evaluation. JMIR Med. Inform. **8**(7), e17257 (2020). https://doi.org/10.2196/17257
19. Choudhary, G., Narayan Singh, S.: Prediction of heart disease using machine learning algorithms. In: Proceedings of the International Conference on Smart Technologies in Computing, Electrical and Electronics (ICSTCEE 2020). Institute of Electrical and Electronics Engineers Inc., pp. 197–202 (2020)
20. Rani, P., Kumar, R., Ahmed, N.M.O.S., Jain, A.: A decision support system for heart disease prediction based upon machine learning. J. Reliab. Intell. Environ. **7**(3), 263–275 (2021). https://doi.org/10.1007/s40860-021-00133-6
21. Ghosh, P., Azam, S., Karim, A., Jonkman, M., Hasan, M.Z.: Use of efficient machine learning techniques in the identification of patients with heart diseases. In: ACM International Conference Proceeding Series. Association for Computing Machinery, pp. 14–20 (2021)
22. Nashif, S., Raihan, M.R., Islam, M.R., Imam, M.H.: Heart disease detection by using machine learning algorithms and a real-time cardiovascular health monitoring system. World J. Eng. Technol. **06**, 854–873 (2018). https://doi.org/10.4236/wjet.2018.64057
23. Triguero, I., García-Gil, D., Maillo, J., Luengo, J., García, S., Herrera, F.: Transforming big data into smart data: an insight on the use of the k-nearest neighbors algorithm to obtain quality data. Wiley Interdiscip. Rev. Data Min. Knowl. Discov. **9**(2), e1289 (2019)
24. Rustam, Z., Saragih, G.S.: Prediction schizophrenia using random forest. TELKOMNIKA (Telecommun. Comput. Electron. Control) **18**, 1433–1438 (2020). https://doi.org/10.12928/TELKOMNIKA.v18i3.14837

25. Yin, C., Rosendahl, L., Luo, Z.: Methods to improve prediction performance of ANN models. In: Simulation Modelling Practice and Theory, pp. 211–222 (2003)
26. Maji, S., Arora, S.: Decision tree algorithms for prediction of heart disease. In: Fong, S., Akashe, S., Mahalle, P.N. (eds.) Information and Communication Technology for Competitive Strategies. LNNS, vol. 40, pp. 447–454. Springer, Singapore (2019). https://doi.org/10.1007/978-981-13-0586-3_45

Comparative Analysis of Various Machine Learning Algorithms for Detection of Malware and Benign

Saika Mohi ud din$^{(\boxtimes)}$, Fizza Rizvi, Nonita Sharma, and Deepak Kumar Sharma

Department of Information Technology, Indira Gandhi Delhi Technical University for Women, Kashmere Gate, Delhi, India
{saika017mtit21,fizza006mtit21,nonitasharma,
deepaksharma}@igdtuw.ac.in

Abstract. The expansion of the cyberspace world has paved the way for numerous attacks and misuses of online resources and networks. For instance, malware is the prime cause of data loss and data theft, which is the source of capital loss for many corporations and institutes. Therefore, it becomes imperative to identify whether the data or a file is malicious or not. The methods for malware and benign detection in this study are different machine learning algorithms like Random Forest, XG Boost, Gradient Boost, Decision Tree, Logistic Regression, K-nearest neighbours (KNN), and Naive Bayes (NB). The main objective of this study is to find the best algorithm which gives the best accuracy in the detection of malware. A comparison was made among seven machine learning algorithms, with the accuracy (99%), precision (0.99), recall (1) and F1 score (0.99) of Random Forest being the best.

Keywords: Malware · Benign · Malware Detection · Random Forest · XG Boost · Gradient Boost · Logistic Regression · K-Nearest Neighbours (KNN) · Naive Bayes (NB)

1 Introduction

Malware variations are routinely and automatically produced in vast numbers, and as such spreading at an exponential rate, thus posing significant threat to our daily lives [1]. The main method that hackers employ to attack a network is malware assaults in particular, for instance, malicious cyber activity cost the US economy USD 109 billion in 2016, due to various online attacks carried out by hackers, including DDOS attacks, man-in-the-middle attacks [2, 3]. Without being dominated by one infostealer, the United States area was subjected to more varied attacks [4].

The word "malware" refers to a range of unwanted, dangerous software programmes that are developed for evil intentions and installed on a system or network without the owner's consent [5]. Hackers have created destructive programmes that are incredibly difficult to crack and notice, along with clever programming, meanwhile, a new method transformation trademark carried out by malware researchers created a damaging code, which sparked the massive growth of malware [6].

© Springer Nature Switzerland AG 2023
D. Garg et al. (Eds.): IACC 2022, CCIS 1781, pp. 212–218, 2023.
https://doi.org/10.1007/978-3-031-35641-4_17

Kernel level drivers created to mask the existence of the virus, malware client and server components to provide proxy services through an infected machine, and other components are frequently included by malware authors in a single malicious payload [7].

Every time a malicious file is launched on a device or a network, it compromises the security and privacy of the system. Data availability, secrecy, and integrity—the CIA triad—are all under risk.

In the context of data analysis and computers, machine learning, which often enables the applications to perform in an intelligent manner, has evolved quickly in recent years [8, 9]. A bewildering array of applications, including data evaluation and security diagnostics, have been made possible by machine learning [10]. The "Signature Method," which recognises attacks based on the trail of evidence left in the network by the attackers, is the main focus of conventional approaches to malware detection but it becomes very challenging to control all the signatures that are attacking the network with the latest versions because there are so many dangerous signatures, therefore to identify malicious and good files in the network, the most recent machine learning techniques are applied [11]. Signature Method is the static analysis technique, this technique analyse the suspicious code without running it; they are the simplest and lowest-risk examination procedures and because the virus identity is not disclosed, it becomes the downside of static analysis [12].

The two main categories of machine learning are supervised learning and unsupervised learning, where supervised learning is more specific than its counterparts because the system is given a set of training data and how that data is classified, and the algorithm is able to classify new input by learning from the training set that it was provided with, whereas in unsupervised learning, the system is given only with data and no classification keys, and the idea of unsupervised learning is that the system learns from the training set that it was provided with [13].

A labelled dataset of samples or instances is used in supervised learning to build the predictive model, which is frequently employed to address classification or regression issues, it is a regression problem when the output is predicted using a continuous variable, and a classification problem when the output is predicted using a discrete variable [14].

On the basis of labelled and unlabelled data, respectively, the supervised and unsupervised machine learning approaches are applied where in supervised machine learning, dangerous and benign files are separated from one another using a labelled dataset, additionally, the data is subjected to the feature visualisation, which categorises the data as either benign or malicious and the dataset is then trained and tested to create a model, which in turn recognises the malicious data.

In this study, malware and benign files are detected using supervised machine learning techniques, where a model is taught to recognise and distinguish between the two types of files. To obtain the highest accuracy, various machine learning algorithms are applied to the dataset and then compared.

2   Methodology

The main goal of this study is to examine the accuracy of various machine learning algorithms used to identify malware and benign files in order to determine which method has the highest accuracy, recall and F1 score. In this study, a model is created using seven machine learning algorithms to identify malicious and benign files, and a comparison analysis of these seven methods is performed to determine which algorithm has the highest accuracy. Random Forest, XG Boost, Gradient Boost, Decision Tree, Logistic Regression, K-nearest Neighbors (KNN), and Naive Bayes are the seven machine learning methods employed in this study (NB).

2.1   Objectives

The goal of this study was to identify the optimum detect method by using and comparing several machine learning techniques Fig. 1 depicts every step taken during the current study's processes. The dataset, which includes benign and malicious files, was obtained from Kaggle [15]. After performing a feature visualisation as part of data preparation, the data was then divided into train and test data. Various machine learning models were created for comparison. Finally, the outcomes were assessed via a comparative study of several algorithms.

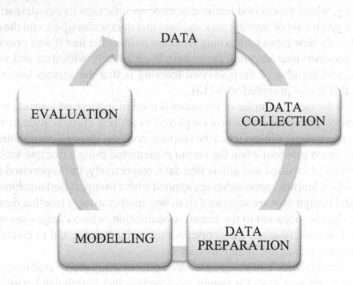

Fig. 1. Methodology.

2.2   Data Collection

The data is divided into training and test datasets and contains roughly 19611 entries between the range index of 0–19610 with a total of 79 data columns. The test data is used to verify the model's accuracy while the training data is utilised to train the machine learning model. The dataset includes samples of both harmful and helpful data from PE files. The number of sections, the time and date stamp, the pointer to the number symbols, the number of symbols, and other details are all included in each observation. Figure 2 displays the dataset's header information. Figure 3 displays the details about the data.

▷ | data.head()

[3]:

	Name	e_magic	e_cblp	e_cp	e_crlc	e_cparhdr	e_minalloc	e_maxalloc
0	VirusShare_a878ba26000edaac5c98eff4432723b3	23117	144	3	0	4	0	65535
1	VirusShare_ef9130570fddc174b312b2047f5f4cf0	23117	144	3	0	4	0	65535
2	VirusShare_ef84cdeba22be72a69b198213dada81a	23117	144	3	0	4	0	65535
3	VirusShare_6bf3608e60ebc16cbcff6ed5467d469e	23117	144	3	0	4	0	65535
4	VirusShare_2cc94d952b2efb13c7d6bbe0dd59d3fb	23117	144	3	0	4	0	65535

5 rows × 79 columns

Fig. 2. Header Information.

data.info()

```
<class 'pandas.core.frame.DataFrame'>
RangeIndex: 19611 entries, 0 to 19610
Data columns (total 79 columns):
 #   Column               Non-Null Count  Dtype
---  ------               --------------  -----
 0   Name                 19611 non-null  object
 1   e_magic              19611 non-null  int64
 2   e_cblp               19611 non-null  int64
 3   e_cp                 19611 non-null  int64
 4   e_crlc               19611 non-null  int64
 5   e_cparhdr            19611 non-null  int64
 6   e_minalloc           19611 non-null  int64
 7   e_maxalloc           19611 non-null  int64
 8   e_ss                 19611 non-null  int64
 9   e_sp                 19611 non-null  int64
 10  e_csum               19611 non-null  int64
 11  e_ip                 19611 non-null  int64
 12  e_cs                 19611 non-null  int64
 13  e_lfarlc             19611 non-null  int64
 14  e_ovno               19611 non-null  int64
 15  e_oemid              19611 non-null  int64
 16  e_oeminfo            19611 non-null  int64
 17  e_lfanew             19611 non-null  int64
 18  Machine              19611 non-null  int64
 19  NumberOfSections     19611 non-null  int64
 20  TimeDateStamp        19611 non-null  int64
 21  PointerToSymbolTable 19611 non-null  int64
 22  NumberOfSymbols      19611 non-null  int64
 23  SizeOfOptionalHeader 19611 non-null  int64
 24  Characteristics      19611 non-null  int64
```

Fig. 3. Data Information.

2.3 Data Preparation

The gathered information is shown visually and split into train and test data.

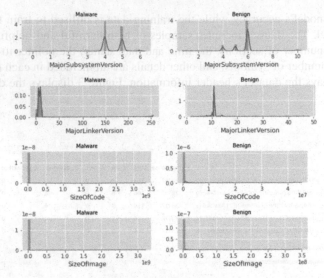

Fig. 4. Class Distribution.

Feature Visualisation: Fig. 4 illustrates the feature visualisation process used during data preparation, which reveals how the data appears.

Splitting the Data: There are training datasets and test datasets for the data. The test data is used to verify the model's accuracy while the training data is utilised to train the machine learning model.

3 Model Description

In this study, malware and benign data are identified from the dataset using supervised machine learning models. The following machine learning methods were applied to the dataset in order to identify malware: Random Forest, XG Boost, Gradient Boost, Decision Tree, Logistic Regression, K-nearest Neighbors (KNN), and Naive Bayes (NB). To determine the data's accuracy, precision, recall, and F1 score, each classifier is employed. Each classifier is compared after detection, and the best one is chosen.

4 Experimental Results and Comparison

The effectiveness of each malware detection algorithm will be shown in this part, along with a comparison of them all.

4.1 Results

The effectiveness of malware detection has been assessed using the four distinct evaluation metrics, namely precision, accuracy, recall and F1 Score. The different machine learning models and the outcomes are shown in Table 1.

Table 1. The outcome of different machine learning algorithms

Class	Accuracy	Recall	Precision	F1 Score
Results of Random Forest				
Malware	99%	1.00	0.99	0.99
Benign	99%	0.96	0.99	0.97
Results of XG Boost				
Malware	99%	0.99	0.99	0.99
Benign	98%	0.97	0.98	0.97
Results of Gradient Boost				
Malware	99%	0.99	0.99	0.99
Benign	98%	0.97	0.98	0.97
Results of Decision Tree				
Malware	99%	0.99	0.99	0.99
Benign	98%	0.97	0.98	0.97
Results of Logistic Regression				
Benign	7%	0.00	0.00	0.00
Malware	13%	1.00	0.26	0.41
Results of K-nearest neighbours (KNN)				
Benign	96%	0.98	0.97	0.98
Malware	95%	0.92	0.94	0.93
Results of Naïve Bayes(NB)				
Benign	81%	0.09	0.99	0.17
Malware	63%	1.00	0.27	0.43

4.2 Comparison

The greatest method for malware detection, according to a comparison of each algorithm, is random forest, which has the highest accuracy (99%), recall (1), precision (0.99), and F1 score (0.99). And logistic regression, with an accuracy of just 7%, produced the least accurate findings.

5 Conclusion

Malware development has had an economic and financial impact on the world. In order to detect malware, this work has employed a supervised machine learning approach. Random Forest has surpassed the other algorithms among all seven methods. The findings showed that random forest performed remarkably well, with an accuracy of 0.99, while logistic regression and naive bayes performed poorly. These findings show that random forest increases detection accuracy and correctly identifies malware by leveraging relevant attributes.

Pavithra and Josephin (2020) found that their study's random forest model had the best accuracy, which was 99.43%. Pavithra and Samy (2022) revealed similar findings in their investigation, where they found that a random forest classifier had the greatest accuracy of 0.9947 [16].

In the future, we will use the Bias-Variance Tradeoff to balance the bias and tradeoff in order to balance the uneven data.

References

1. Xiao, F., Lin, Z., Sun, Y., Ma, Y.: Malware detection based on deep learning of behavior graphs. Math. Probl. Eng. **2019**, 1–10 (2019). https://doi.org/10.1155/2019/8195395
2. Akhtar, Z.: Malware detection and analysis: challenges and research opportunities (2021)
3. Faruki, P., Bharmal, A., Laxmi, V., et al.: Android security: a survey of issues, malware penetration, and defenses. IEEE Commun. Surv. Tutor. **17**, 998–1022 (2015). https://doi.org/10.1109/comst.2014.2386139
4. Sharma, R., Sharma, N., Mangla, M.: An analysis and investigation of InfoStealers attacks during COVID'19: a case study. In: 2021 2nd International Conference on Secure Cyber Computing and Communications (ICSCCC) (2021). https://doi.org/10.1109/icsccc51823.2021.9478163
5. Gavrilut, D., Cimpoesu, M., Anton, D., Ciortuz, L.: Malware detection using machine learning. In: Proceedings of the International Multiconference on Computer Science and Information Technology, vol. 4, pp. 735–741 (2009). https://doi.org/10.1109/IMCSIT.2009.5352759
6. Pavithra, J., Josephin, F.: Analyzing various machine learning algorithms for the classification of malwares. In: IOP Conference Series: Materials Science and Engineering, vol. 993, p. 012099 (2020). https://doi.org/10.1088/1757-899X/993/1/012099
7. Bhojani, N.: Malware analysis (2014). https://doi.org/10.13140/2.1.4750.6889
8. Sarker, I.H.: Machine learning: algorithms, real-world applications and research directions. SN Comput. Sci. **2**(3), 1–21 (2021). https://doi.org/10.1007/s42979-021-00592-x
9. Sarker, I.H., Furhad, M.H., Nowrozy, R.: AI-driven cybersecurity: an overview, security intelligence modeling and research directions. SN Comput. Sci. **2**(3), 1–18 (2021). https://doi.org/10.1007/s42979-021-00557-0
10. Mangla, M., Shinde, S.K., Mehta, V., et al.: Handbook of Research on Machine Learning: Foundations and Applications. Apple Academic Press, Milton (2022)
11. Khan, M.D., Shaikh, M.T., Ansari, R., et al.: Malware detection using machine learning algorithms. Int. J. Adv. Res. Comput. Commun. Eng. (2017). ISO 3297:2007
12. Roseline, A., Subbiah, G.: Intelligent malware detection using oblique random forest paradigm (2018).https://doi.org/10.1109/ICACCI.2018.8554903
13. Yang, R., Kang, V., Albouq, S., Zohdy, M.: Application of hybrid machine learning to detect and remove malware (2015). https://doi.org/10.14738/tmlai.34.1436
14. Liu, K., Xu, S., Xu, G., et al.: A review of android malware detection approaches based on machine learning. IEEE Access **8**, 124579–124607 (2020). https://doi.org/10.1109/access.2020.3006143
15. Mauricio: Benign & malicious PE files. In: Kaggle (2018). https://www.kaggle.com/datasets/amauricio/pe-files-malwares
16. Pavithra, J., Samy, S.: A comparative study on detection of malware and benign on the internet. Math. Probl. Eng. **2022** (2022). https://doi.org/10.1155/2022/4893390

XACML: Explainable Arrhythmia Classification Model Using Machine Learning

S. Nithya[ID] and Mary Shanthi Rani[✉][ID]

The Gandhigram Rural Institute (Deemed to be University), Gandhigram 624 302, Tamilnadu, India
drmaryshanthi@gmail.com

Abstract. Cardiac arrhythmia, an irregular heart rhythm has a high mortality rate. Early diagnosis may redeem the patient from death. Many reliable decision support systems have recently been built as "black boxes," or systems that conceal their internal logic from the user. This absence of justification raises both ethical and practical problems. The literature describes a variety of strategies for resolving this significant flaw, often, accuracy is sacrificed for interpretability. Trust among clinical experts, particularly in medicine, can be established through the justification of decisions provided by automated medical expert systems. This work aims to integrate explainability with the Boosting model in the classification of cardiac arrhythmia diagnosis. The reasons behind the model's output are explained using the familiar explainable AI tool LIME in a simple and comprehensible manner.

Keywords: Arrhythmia · Explainable AI (XAI) · Explaination · Model Agnostic · Machine Learning · LIME

1 Introduction

Clinical trials could benefit from machine learning by being more effective, generalizable, patient-centered, and successful. There are numerous machine learning (ML) techniques available for managing massive and heterogeneous data sources, spotting complicated and elusive patterns, and forecasting complex outcomes.

In the last decade, there has been an abrupt increase in interest in devising ML models for healthcare. Although ML has been a domain of study since the middle of the 20th century, advances in data accessibility, computing power, new techniques, and an expanding range of applications and technical expertise have greatly influenced the use of ML in medical care [1].

Preclinical exploration and observational studies lead to traditional trials and trials with pragmatic components, which in turn stimulate clinical registries and additional implementation work. Clinical research is a broad and essential spectrum area for enhancing healthcare but it is currently conducted in a complex, labor-intensive, expensive manner that may occasionally be vulnerable to unanticipated biases and errors, endangering its successful application, adoption, and acceptability [2].

© Springer Nature Switzerland AG 2023
D. Garg et al. (Eds.): IACC 2022, CCIS 1781, pp. 219–231, 2023.
https://doi.org/10.1007/978-3-031-35641-4_18

Numerous high-accuracy machine-learning techniques have been presented [3–5]. On the account of the lack of model interpretability, which is indispensable for ensuring the reliability of the results, the implementation of these models into clinical practice is constrained [6].

The electrocardiogram is one of the quick and easy medical tests used to detect abnormalities in the heart by measuring the electrical activity produced by the heart as it contracts. This medical test plays a key role in detecting cardiac arrhythmia the deadlier disease due to abnormal sinus rhythm [7–9].

Interpretability and explainability are domain dependent. The explanations can be full or partial. Complete explanations are provided by fully interpretable models in a transparent manner. Partially, interpretable models shed light on key aspects of the processes such as measures of variable importance. Local models that roughly resemble global models at some locations, and saliency maps are a few examples of partial explanations [10].

With enormous development in the field of machine learning, yet another crucial challenge remains in the interpretability of results produced by the algorithm. Detection of arrhythmia and its classification is a tedious task. Exactly finding the important feature that supports the detection of arrhythmia is strenuous. This research work focuses on the classification of cardiac arrhythmia with boosting algorithms.

The motivation behind the work is multi-fold: i) lack of adequate explainable machine learning models for arrhythmia classification, ii) identification of significant features that contribute to the decision through feature selection techniques, and iii) to enhance the prediction accuracy boosting algorithms have been implemented in this work.

This research paper is structured as follows; a review of related research is presented in Sect. 2. The novel explainability of boosting algorithm results is given in Sect. 3 followed by the discussion on experimental results in Sect. 4. Eventually, the conclusion is presented in Sect. 5.

2   Related Works

ML and Deep Learning (DL) techniques play an indispensable role in the detection of cardiac arrhythmia for a long time. The literature of the related works is presented below. Conventional ML algorithms, despite being transparent regarding the classification process, can also be tedious and costly tasks, such as feature engineering, etc. This section reviews key concepts and techniques in the field of explainable AI techniques.

Global techniques attempt to explain the model as a whole; the justification should hold for each record in the dataset. Instead, local approaches aim to provide a high level of knowledge for a small subset of records. The ensuing review takes into account both global and local strategies created in a model-agnostic manner to apply to any type of ML model by design. A common strategy is to take a feature, or set of features, out of the model and assess the loss in terms of model goodness [11]. The notion was first created by Breiman [12] using Random Forest. Leave One Covariate Out (LOCO) inference was proposed for a model-free notion of variable importance [13].

The predictive capability of the ML models has been broken down into single variable contributions based on variable exclusion as partial Dependence Plots (PDP) [14],

Individual Conditional Expectation (ICE) [15], and Accumulated Local Effects (ALE) [16] plots based on the various premises of the ML model.

A similar concept is used in SHapley Additive exPlanations (SHAP), where the decomposition is gained through a game-based environment, for local explanations as well. The objective of these techniques is to fairly assess the feature importance as the correlation among features has a great impact on the findings. Several approaches have been suggested to address the correlation issues based on their theoretical properties [17].

Another frequent strategy is to train a surrogate model that mimics the ML model's behaviour. In this approach, estimation of the whole input space is provided in some of the research works [18, 19] in some of the approaches LIME is used to explain the model [20–22] where it relies on local approximation.

Surrogate models have an advantage over feature attribution approaches in that they permit what-if analysis, which is a benefit of utilizing a prediction model. The what-if analysis can be relatively approximate because global procedures typically only provide a rough estimate of the ML model; in contrast, local methods only provide excellent approximations for a small portion of the input variables, therefore the scenario we evaluate should only involve minor changes.

This proposed work implements the key concepts of explainable Machine learning techniques used to diagnose arrhythmia. The major goal of this research work is to unravel the black box approach to the final decision on arrhythmia diagnosis through the responsible AI.

3 Materials and Methods

3.1 Description of the Dataset

The dataset used in this work is openly available from the UCI ML repository. The arrhythmia dataset has details of 452 patients with 279 features in it. The features hold linear as well as categorical data. 206 features are linear valued data and the remaining are categorical data. Personal information of the cardiac patients is represented in the first four features, 275 features are extracted from the ECG Signal [23].

3.2 Methods

The proposed methodology is implemented with the following modules, i. preprocessing, ii. Feature Selection, iii. Classification iv. Explainability. The algorithm for the proposed model XACML is presented in Algorithm 1 and the proposed workflow is presented in Fig. 1.

Algorithm 1. Algorithm for model XACML

Algorithm:
Phase: I *Preprocessing*
Class Labeling and Data Normalization
Phase: II *Feature Selection with two Pipelines*
Feature Selection with SRC and MI
Phase: III *Classification of Cardiac Arrhythmia*
Phase: IV *Explaination of the Models using LIME*

The dataset has been labeled as a normal and abnormal class and it is normalized since it has a lot of missing values was done in phase I, and then the features are selected with the help of two feature selection algorithms namely, Mutual Information (MI) and Spearman Ranking Coefficient (SRC) in Phase II. The classification of cardiac arrhythmia is performed in Phase III, and the explainability of the model is done in Phase IV.

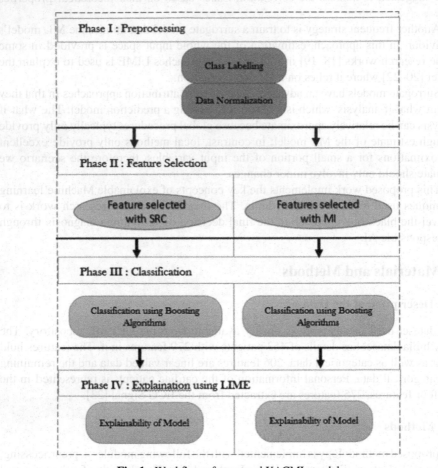

Fig. 1. Workflow of proposed XACML model.

Feature Selection

Spearman Ranking Coefficient

Spearman Ranking Coefficient is a filter-based feature selection method. It is a non-parametric technique for measuring the relationship between the two variables. Typically, the feature selection can be done by the correlation coefficient. It can be calculated by using the following formula.

$$\rho = 1 - \frac{6\Sigma d_i^2}{m(m^2 - 1)} \tag{1}$$

where 'm' is the total number of observations and 'di' is the difference between ranks in paired items as shown in Eq. (1) [24].

Mutual Information

The statistical dependence between random variables can be calculated with the application of mutual information (MI). MI is quite skilled at managing both linear and non-linear dependencies. Picking pertinent attributes for predicting the target class the MI is best suited for feature selection. The dependencies within two discrete random variables are measured by MI using Eq. (2) [5].

$$I(X; Y) = \sum_{y \in Y} \sum_{x \in X} p(X, Y)(x, y) \log \frac{p(X, Y)(x, y)}{pX(x)pY(y)} \tag{2}$$

where X, Y and pX and pY are considered as marginal probability mass functions of X and Y, and p(X, Y) is as joint probability respectively. Continuous variable formulas in Eq. (3) are used [25].

$$I(X;Y) = \int_Y \int_X p(X, Y)(x, y).\log \frac{p(X, Y)(x, y)}{pX(x)pY(y)} dxdy \tag{3}$$

Classification Using Boosting Algorithms

Adaboost

This Boosting technique is known as AdaBoost or Adaptive Boosting, which is used as an Ensemble Method in ML. For supervised learning, boosting is used to lower bias and variance. The power of the algorithm lies in the conversion of weak learners to strong learners [26].

Gradient Boosting

Gradient Boosting (GB) trains the model in a sequential and additive manner. The differentiation between AdaBoost and GB is GB that the latter accomplishes the same task by utilizing gradients in the loss function, but the AdaBoost model detects weak learners by using high-weight data points [27].

Extreme Gradient Boost

Extreme Boost (XGBoost) can perform parallel computation. Normally, it is 10 times faster than gradient boosting. It accepts sparse input for both linear booster and tree booster. This is optimized for sparse input. It has better performance on several different datasets [28].

CatBoost
CatBoost name is derived from the word "Category" and "Boosting". It uses statistics to transform categorical values into numbers automatically. It decreases the likelihood of overfitting and the requirement for significant hyper-parameter tuning, both of which result in more generalized models [29].

LightGBM
Light Gradient Boosting Machine (LightGBM), is a framework with high performance which uses a decision tree for ranking, regression, and classification. It has vertical level-wise growth in contrast with XGBoost which has less loss and higher accuracy [30].

Explainability Using LIME
The Local Interpretable Mode-agnostic Explanations is an explainable AI method that explains the model's predictions. It tries to illuminate machine learning models to make comprehensible predictions individually. This technique explains every single instance hence it is suitable for local explanations [20].

Black-box models, or models whose internal logic is obscure and difficult to comprehend, can be explained using LIME. By closely approximating the behaviour of the original model.

LIME is one of the tools for local explainability because of this feature. Lime is an excellent tool to explain what machine learning models are performing. It is simple, uncomplicated, easy to understand, and effortless to execute [31].

The model-agnostic method examines the connections between trained model I/O pairs. They are independent of the model's internal architecture. These techniques can be useful when there is no theory or other mechanism to account for what is occurring in the model. Figure 2 shows how the LIME works.

4 Results and Discussion

The proposed work is carried out with UCI Arrhythmia Dataset. As a first step in pre-processing, the dataset's missing values are replaced with mean values. Some of the instances with more missing values are eliminated. The second step is labeling the class, the target class 1 is considered to be normal, and the remaining 15 classes are considered to be abnormal. The process is performed as a Binary classification. Finally, data normalization is performed. The class distribution of the dataset is shown in Fig. 3.

The motivation behind the use of feature selection methods in this research work is to reduce the number of input features which significantly minimizes the complexity of the network. Furthermore, the reduction in the parameters expedites the training process as well.

The preprocessed dataset is further subjected to 20-fold cross-validation for training, testing, and validation. Two best-suited filter-based feature selection methods namely, SRC and MI are used for testing individually. Among the total 279 features, the 88 features selected by SRC and MI separately are fed as input to five boosting algorithms

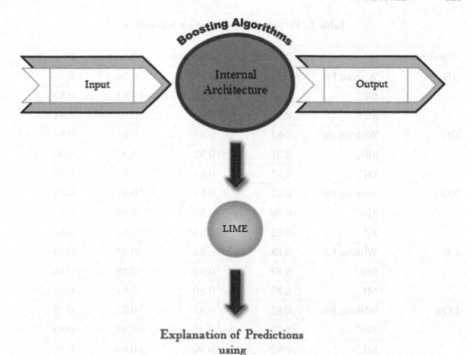

Fig. 2. Explanation of Boosting Algorithms using LIME

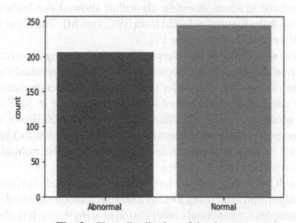

Fig. 3. Class distribution of the dataset

namely, Adaboost, Gradient boost, XGboost, Catboost, and LightGBM which are discussed in the previous section. The results of boosting algorithms with feature selection methods are shown in Table 1.

Table 1 demonstrates that the accuracy is superior for classification with feature selection than without feature selection. It is also worth noting that the LightGBM

Table 1. Performance of Boosting Algorithms

Algorithm		Accuracy	Precision	Recall	F1-score
AB	Without FS	0.76	0.75	0.76	0.76
	SRC	0.82	0.81	0.83	0.82
	MI	0.91	0.90	0.92	0.91
GB	Without FS	0.82	0.83	0.81	0.81
	SRC	0.91	0.92	0.91	0.90
	MI	0.82	0.81	0.82	0.82
XGB	Without FS	0.82	0.83	0.81	0.81
	SRC	0.96	0.96	0.98	0.97
	MI	0.82	0.83	0.81	0.81
CB	Without FS	0.88	0.86	0.85	0.79
	SRC	0.87	0.89	0.88	0.86
	MI	0.82	0.80	0.81	0.82
LGB	Without FS	0.82	0.83	0.81	0.79
	SRC	0.91	0.92	0.88	0.93
	MI	0.92	0.90	0.89	0.91

performed well for features selected by MI and reached the highest accuracy of 92%. Similarly, the extreme gradient boosting algorithm showed the highest performance accuracy of 96% with the features selected from SRC than MI. The accuracy comparison of the boosting algorithms is depicted in Fig. 4.

The research work focuses on the interpretability of boosting algorithms after applying feature selection techniques. The boosting algorithm that reached the highest accuracy in each feature selection is chosen for interpretability. As demonstrated in the accuracy comparison chart, XGBoost showed its highest accuracy in SRC and LightGBM attained the top accuracy for MI. The interpretability of the XGBoost algorithm after applying SRC for two normal and abnormal test cases is shown in Fig. 5. The figure depicts the top 10 features that significantly contribute to the normal and abnormal classification of arrhythmia respectively.

Figure 5a) and b) illustrates the two sample cases for normal classification classified by the XGBoost algorithm after using SRC as a feature selection method. Figure 5c), and d) show the two samples for abnormal classification of arrhythmia. It is observed from the Fig. 5 which presents the top 10 attributes crucial for two normal and abnormal prediction respectively. It is worth noting that among the top 10 features in the above prediction Heart rate, T-wave linear, and of channel V1:.3 overlap in all the 4 plots, revealing the significance in the prediction outcome of model for SRC based classification.

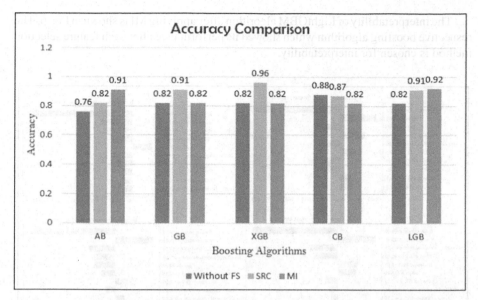

Fig. 4. Classification Accuracy Comparison of Boosting Algorithms with SRC and MI.

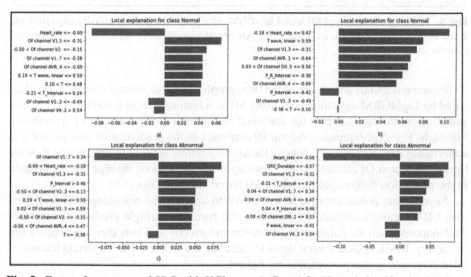

Fig. 5. Feature Importance of SRC with XGboost. a). Case 1 for Normal classification b). Case 2 for Normal classification. c). Case 1 for Abnormal classification. d). Case 2 for Abnormal classification.

The interpretability of LightGBM algorithm after applying MI is shown in Fig. 6. The respective boosting algorithm which showed its performance after each feature selection method is chosen for interpretability.

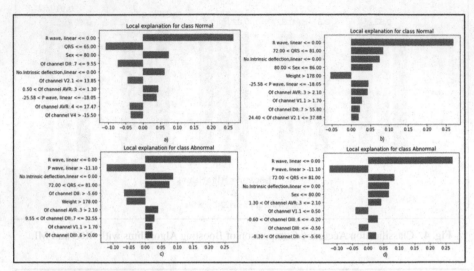

Fig. 6. Feature Importance of MI with LightGBM. a). Case 1 for Normal classification b). Case 2 for Normal classification. c). Case 1 for Abnormal classification d). Case 2 for Abnormal classification.

Figure 6a) and b) demonstrates the two sample cases for normal classification classified by LightGBM algorithm after using MI as a feature selection method. Figure 6c), and d) show the two samples for abnormal classification of prediction of arrhythmia. Similarly, Fig. 6 also presents the top 10 attributes in the prediction of two normal and abnormal classes respectively. Among the top 10 features in the above prediction R-wave linear, QRS, and Of channel AVR.:3 overlap in all the 4 plots, divulge the importance in the prediction outcome of model for MI based classification.

Several data points are used to test LIME to uncover the reasoning behind it. Various LIME settings are used to show how the parameters might produce inconsistent explanations when the parameters are chosen incorrectly and how they can identify the instability. LIME is used several times to calculate the indices. The important feature of false diagnosis is also presented in the figures.

5   Conclusion

This paper presents a responsible ML model for arrhythmia classification using the best performing classification pipelines XGB and Lightgbm. The proposed approach includes the optimal filter based feature selection methods, SRC and MI. It selects only 88 features amongst 279 attributes. Those features are classified with boosting algorithms, and the best performed algorithms XGBoost in SRC and LightGBM in MI are selected for interpreting normal and abnormal classes. Explainability of disease identification and classification helps clinicians to understand the major risk factors that lead to mortality. This explainable binary arrhythmia classification model through LIME is typically used to determine which variables are crucial for the arrhythmia prediction of a certain individual. The future direction of this work would be to extend the explainability for different classes of arrhythmia with different architectures as well.

References

1. Battina, D.S.: The role of machine learning in clinical research: transforming the future of evidence generation. Future **4**(12) (2017)
2. Michelson, M., Reuter, K.: The significant cost of systematic reviews and meta-analyses: a call for greater involvement of machine learning to assess the promise of clinical trials. Contemp. Clin. Trials Commun. **16**, 100443 (2019)
3. Alfaras, M., Soriano, M.C., Ortín, S.: A fast machine learning model for ECG-based heartbeat classification and arrhythmia detection. Front. Phys. **7**, 103 (2019)
4. Bulbul, H.I., Usta, N., Yildiz, M.: Classification of ECG arrhythmia with machine learning techniques. In: 2017 16th IEEE International Conference on Machine Learning and Applications (ICMLA), pp. 546–549. IEEE (2017)
5. Karthikeyan, N., Rani, M.S.: ECG classification using machine learning classifiers with optimal feature selection methods. In: Suma, V., Fernando, X., Du, K.-L., Wang, H. (eds.) Evolutionary Computing and Mobile Sustainable Networks. LNDECT, vol. 116, pp. 277–289. Springer, Singapore (2022). https://doi.org/10.1007/978-981-16-9605-3_19
6. Vellido, A., Martín-Guerrero, J.D., Lisboa, P.J.: Making machine learning models interpretable. In: ESANN, vol. 12, pp. 163–172 (2012)
7. Bennett, P.B., Yazawa, K., Makita, N., George, A.L.: Molecular mechanism for an inherited cardiac arrhythmia. Nature **376**(6542), 683–685 (1995)
8. Nithya, S., Rani, M.S.: Deep learning model for arrhythmia classification with 2D convolutional neural network. In: Garg, D., Kumar, N., Iqbal, R., Gupta, S. (eds.) Innovations in Information and Communication Technologies. Algorithms for Intelligent Systems, pp. 1–11. Springer, Singapore (2023). https://doi.org/10.1007/978-981-19-3796-5_1
9. Nithya, S., Rani, M.S.: Stacked variational autoencoder in the classification of cardiac arrhythmia using ECG signals with 2D-ECG images. In: IEEE Xplore (In Press)
10. Gunning, D., Stefik, M., Choi, J., Miller, T., Stumpf, S., Yang, G.Z.: XAI—explainable artificial intelligence. Sci. Robot. **4**(37), eaay7120 (2019)

11. Guidotti, R., Monreale, A., Ruggieri, S., Turini, F., Giannotti, F., Pedreschi, D.: A survey of methods for explaining black box models. ACM Comput. Surv. **51**(5), 1–42 (2018)

12. Breiman, L.: Random forests. Mach. Learn. **45**(1), 5–32 (2001)

13. Lei, J., G'Sell, M., Rinaldo, A., Tibshirani, R.J., Wasserman, L.: Distribution-free predictive inference for regression. J. Am. Stat. Assoc. **113**(523), 1094–1111 (2018)

14. Friedman, J.H.: Greedy function approximation: a gradient boosting machine. Ann. Stat. 1189–1232 (2001)

15. Goldstein, A., Kapelner, A., Bleich, J., Pitkin, E.: Peeking inside the black box: visualizing statistical learning with plots of individual conditional expectation. J. Comput. Graph. Stat. **24**(1), 44–65 (2015)

16. Apley, D.W., Zhu, J.: Visualizing the effects of predictor variables in black box supervised learning models. J. R. Stat. Soc. B Stat. Methodol. **82**(4), 1059–1086 (2020)

17. Lundberg, S.M., Lee, S.-I.: Advances in neural information processing systems. In: 31st Annual Conference on Neural Information Processing Systems (NIPS 2017), Long Beach, United States, 4–9 December, vol. 2017, pp. 4765–4774 (2017)

18. Craven, M., Shavlik, J.: Extracting tree-structured representations of trained networks. Adv. Neural Inf. Process. Syst. **8** (1995)

19. Zhou, Y., Hooker, G.: Interpreting models via single tree approximation. arXiv preprint arXiv: 1610.09036 (2016)

20. Ribeiro, M.T., Singh, S., Guestrin, C.: "Why should i trust you?" explaining the predictions of any classifier. In: Proceedings of the 22nd ACM SIGKDD International Conference on Knowledge Discovery and Data Mining, pp. 1135–1144 (2016)

21. Ribeiro, M.T., Singh, S., Guestrin, C.: Anchors: high-precision model-agnostic explanations. In: Proceedings of the AAAI Conference on Artificial Intelligence, vol. 32, no. 1, (2018)

22. Magesh, P.R., Myloth, R.D., Tom, R.J.: An explainable machine learning model for early detection of Parkinson's disease using LIME on DaTSCAN imagery. Comput. Biol. Med. **126**, 104041 (2020)

23. Newman, D., Hettich, S., Blake, L., Merz, C.J.: UCI repository of machine learning databases. Dept. of Information and Computer Sciences, University of California, Irvine (1998). http://www.ics.uci.edu/mlearn/MLRepository.html

24. Xu, J., Mu, H., Wang, Y., Huang, F.: Feature genes selection using supervised locally linear embedding and correlation coefficient for microarray classification. Comput. Math. Methods Med. (2018)

25. Beraha, M., Metelli, A.M., Papini, M., Tirinzoni, A., Restelli, M.: Feature selection via mutual information: new theoretical insights. In: 2019 International Joint Conference on Neural Networks (IJCNN), pp. 1–9. IEEE (2019)

26. Ying, C., Qi-Guang, M., Jia-Chen, L., Lin, G.: Advance and prospects of AdaBoost algorithm. ActaAutomaticaSinica **39**(6), 745–758 (2013)

27. Beygelzimer, A., Hazan, E., Kale, S., Luo, H.: Online gradient boosting. arXiv preprint arXiv: 1506.04820 (2015)

28. Chen, T., et al.: XGBoost: extreme gradient boosting. R package version 0.4-2, 1(4), 1-4 (2015)

29. Hancock, J.T., Khoshgoftaar, T.M.: CatBoost for big data: an interdisciplinary review. J. Big Data **7**(1), 1–45 (2020). https://doi.org/10.1186/s40537-020-00369-8
30. Ke, G., et al.: Lightgbm: a highly efficient gradient boosting decision tree. Adv. Neural Inf. Process. Syst. **30** (2017)
31. Visani, G., Bagli, E., Chesani, F., Poluzzi, A., Capuzzo, D.: Statistical stability indices for LIME: obtaining reliable explanations for machine learning models. J. Oper. Res. Soc. **73**(1), 91–101 (2022)

Intelligent Analytical Randomization of Clinical Trials

Vandana Sharma[1]([⊠]) [iD] and Shalini Singh[2] [iD]

[1] Computer Science, ABES Engineering College, Ghaziabad, UP, India
vandana.kuhu@gmail.com
[2] Computer Science and Engineering, Quantum University, Roorkee, Uttarakhand, India
shalinisingh@abes.ac.in

Abstract. Patients are assigned randomly to treatment groups in clinical studies. Artificial intelligence is proving to be an excellent instrument that has a significant impact on clinical trials for traditional random drugs. The common problems in random trials, such as cohort patient recruiting, patient monitoring, cost, and time, are escalating quickly as the number of patients' data continues to grow. The utilization of big data and Deep Learning (DL), a machine learning technology, has altered how clinical trials and drug development are conducted. For effective trials, a variety of tools are employed, including patient selection, patient compliance, AI/ML-based software that is used in healthcare, and drug discovery. Compared to conventional RCTs, AI systems can operate more efficiently and with more statistical power. One Meagre Issue Clearly Sufficient (OMICS) data, which includes imaging, laboratory, and many other complexities, can be combined by machine learning. Endpoints created by AI can improve measurement accuracy and conduct data analysis without the aid of a person.

Keywords: Randomized Clinical Trials (RCTs) · healthcare · Drug discovery · Patient selection · Patient compliance · Imaging · Laboratory

1 Introduction

The industry has recently made large expenditures in digitizing operations, improving workflow, and moving to the cloud. But there are numerous difficulties today. First, the major factor in time and expense to get medications to market continues to be clinical trials, with cost effects increasing practically everywhere. Secondly, manual procedures, poorly integrated systems, and the flow of the primary clinical data from beginning to end can all be blamed for a substantial portion, though not all, of the cost and efficiency in clinical trials. To minimize potential biases, the random assignment of RCT participants to specific groups is regarded as "best practice" [1]. Artificial Intelligence and Machine learning can help provide smart recommendations and suggestions based on data from past studies. As data moves from protocols to the case report form, to programming, and reporting, each step of the process has disparate tools that don't have common metadata. Metadata-driven technologies can help us to get a better outcome.

© Springer Nature Switzerland AG 2023
D. Garg et al. (Eds.): IACC 2022, CCIS 1781, pp. 232–241, 2023.
https://doi.org/10.1007/978-3-031-35641-4_19

Data will be streamlined, completely networked, and integrated in the future. Full traceability is provided by AI and metadata applications. The capability of AI also makes it possible to automate and streamline the process of incorporating modifications into the data life cycle. Thanks to systematically organized huge datasets that comprise clinical and multimodal imaging, the natural history of each study item can be anticipated using sophisticated statistical techniques, and study endpoints can be assessed using a data-driven methodology. This eliminates the need for expensive manual reviews. AI has the potential to completely transform crucial phases of clinical trial design, from test creation to execution, to increase trial success rates.

The clinical study protocol is too large. A digitized protocol can be created using contemporary technologies and improvements in standards. Based on previous research, artificial intelligence and machine learning can help generate insightful recommendations and ideas. One can speed up the establishment of a fully digital protocol by using tags in conjunction with biological principles that are being defined as part of serious standards and a common protocol template. The ability to learn and change is provided by machine learning. Assistive systems utilizing these AI approach subgroups could link patients to clinical trials and find new volunteers by autonomously analyzing HER (Electronic Health Record) and clinical trial eligibility databases.

The class of ML algorithms still has several drawbacks. The accessibility of vast, categorized data, which may be difficult to be faultless in terms of measurement, is crucial for the quality of algorithms. So, by employing more objective training targets, the algorithms that ignore manual labeling will become more significant. Another drawback is the nature of the "black box". Techniques that look into the genesis of an Artificial Intelligence decision tree, including class activation maps [2] and occlusion testing [3, 4], will be crucial for the integration of AI into RCTs.

Hariry and others demonstrate further AI-based innovations. They talked about a few clinical research studies that predicted patient outcomes using ML, TREWScore, reinforcement learning agents, and deep neural networks. For the best decision-making, multifunction prediction, risk assessment, and sickness modeling, these AI techniques were employed.

2 Literature Review

The systematic review tries to provide a recent sketch of the current principles of Machine learning and deep learning for the development of clinical applications. Preferably, the implementation of these applications would be done in two main steps. First, well-regulated and well-described forming and validation studies. Second, well-regulated and unambiguous reported randomized clinical trials [5–8].

ML framework can upgrade the recruiting process of the patients at a huge level, thus improving the quality of separate screening and the need for big test data. Recruiting patients who meet unambiguous recruiting criteria is important to avoid favorable misclassifications. To improve recruitment efficiency, multi-channeled data, such as laboratory, imaging, and other complex-omics data, can be merged. This is one of the areas where the Intelligent Research in Sight (IRIS) data from the American Academy of Ophthalmology will be applied to RCT recruiting [9].

Several RCTs require a large sample size [10]. AI applications have the capability to select "the potential" participants for RCTs, who are "quickly proceeding" with the disease based on the AI's predicted algorithm. Compared to how they are now measured, primary research endpoints can be measured with greater care by AI applications. For instance, central macular thickness from Optical Coherence Tomography devices has been a significant result in numerous RCTs, but it has been shown that its reliability and correlation vary among various methods of measurement [11, 12].

The outcome imaging data can be used directly with ML models. Clinical imaging labels from the treatment and control arms may be mixed up in any scenario, similar to Monte-Carlo permutation techniques [13], and ML models would then be directed to further decide whether the items were from the control or treatment arm.

It has been determined that randomized participant allocation is a crucial step in minimizing significant biases in the selection and placement of patients. The environment surrounding the ordinance is ambiguous because there are no universally acknowledged technical standards. In their study, the authors described a service that allows patients to be randomly assigned to RCT groups. They made the case that having two channels of communication may be essential because RCTs may leverage ICT technologies to manage patients in a less methodical fashion.

Clinicians can greatly benefit from readily available imaging technology in clinical settings, such as chest X-rays and thoracic CT scans [14–19]. The international war against COVID-19 was greatly aided by medical imaging techniques like computed tomography (CT) and X-rays, whereas freshly created artificial intelligence (AI) technologies are boosting the capability of imaging equipment and helping medical practitioners. The authors examined the medical imaging community's frequent responses to COVID-19 (driven by AI).

The fight against COVID-19 has greatly benefited from artificial intelligence (AI), a relatively new method in the field of medical imaging [20]. AI enables the development of imaging systems that are safer, more accurate, and more productive than the conventional imaging workflow, which primarily relies on human labour. One of the most recent AI-powered applications is the COVID-19 imaging platform.

Many restrictions, including social withdrawal and travel restrictions, were necessary for society to adhere to during the COVID-19 pandemic. All of these factors considerably decreased trial participants' and staff's ability and/or willingness to visit clinical sites that directly impacted data collecting. Nevertheless, information was obtained in various ways, such as remotely rather than physically. The COVID-19 public health emergency was acknowledged by FDA as having the potential to affect how clinical trials for medicinal goods were conducted. Even before symptoms appeared, the illness was contagious. Even some infected people showed no signs. All of these worries likely caused issues that complicated the interpretation of clinical trial results and affected study data.

Between 33.6% and 52.4% of all Phase I, II, and III drug development clinical trials failing to proceed to the next trial phase, there is an overall 13.8% possibility that a medicine investigated in Phase I will be authorized. When the trial phase is considered, this number decreases to around 10% [21]. The typical price of research and development to produce a drug is estimated to be $1.3 billion [22], after failure studies are taken into consideration, which has a substantial impact on drug development costs. Researchers now have access to vast amounts of medical data, particularly from Electronic Health Records (EHRs) and wearable technology, which has allowed for the development of advanced machine learning and deep learning algorithms.

According to the PROBAST(Prediction model Risk Of Bias Assessment Tool) technique for evaluating prediction model risk of bias, 58 of 81 (72%) research were categorized as high risk due to the general threat of bias. The analytical domain has consistently been rated as having a high bias risk as compared to domains for participant or outcome ascertainment. The following inquiries Was the participant count sufficient? Every enrolled person is included in the analysis, correct? Accurate assessments of important model performance indicators? Did you account for overfitting and overly optimistic model results? All had significant issues.

3 State of Art

A systematic search of the literature was conducted to find relevant articles published from the inception of each database. The goal of this study was to demonstrate how various uses of AI and metadata have altered public perceptions and the pharmaceutical industry's view of clinical trial randomization. However, using carefully crafted huge datasets, without the requirement for costly manual assessment, AI models can be trained to pick potential study participants, to predict each study participant's natural history using cutting-edge statistical techniques, and to evaluate study endpoints using a data-driven approach. However, the COVID-19 pandemic period presented a significant problem for pharmaceutical companies.

3.1 Clinical Trial Process

Every clinical trial performed by AI applications has to go through two clinical trial stages: 1. Discovery Stage 2. Clinical Trials (see Fig. 1).

Step 1: The preponderance of particle and biological drugs strive for their effects by agitating protein targets. The recognition of such objects is therefore focal of drug discovery.

Step 2: Numerous combinations may be viable candidates for development as a medical treatment at this crucial stage. However, only a few combinations appear promising after preliminary testing and are taken into consideration for further study.

Step 3: FDA-approved clinical medication molecules are used at this time to identify innovative curative treatments. Promoting drug candidates with novel pharmacological activity or curative potential have been found to be effective.

Step 4: Before experimenting any drug on human beings, researchers must find out whether it can cause some serious harm. Vitro and Vivo are the two subtypes of preclinical research. A drug developer must submit all preclinical data through Phase 3 trial data in a New Drug Application (NDA). Developers are required to incorporate all inquiry, data, and analysis reports

Step 5: Even while clinical studies give important information regarding a drug's efficacy and safety, it is impossible to know everything about a drug's safety at the time of licensure.

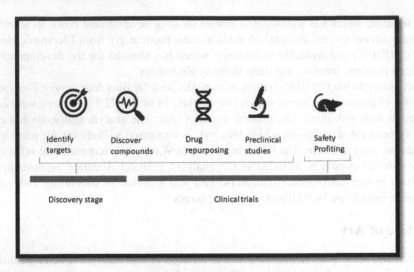

Identify targets   Discover compounds   Drug repurposing   Preclinical studies   Safety Profiting

Discovery stage   Clinical trials

Fig. 1. Clinical Trial Process

3.2 Randomized Clinical Trials

[23] only 12 records have been used for a review and comparative study using deep learning randomised clinical trials (see Table 1). Only one is a non-random trial, one has been completed (with low risk of bias, and high adherence to reporting standards), one will be completed by November 2023, and one can be completed by Oct'2022, and nine are ongoing. Only three of the twelve trials are recruiting, and only one has progressed to phase 2. Only seventeen of the 100 randomized clinical studies were tested as non-retrospective, and 83 were retrospective. There was very little access to all datasets and code. The overall risk of bias was minimal, and the reporting guidelines were not always followed. More than 60% of studies claimed that the performance of artificial intelligence was at least on par with (or even superior to) that of medical professionals.

Only 17 out of 100 studies (17%) indicated that additional prospective research or clinical trials were necessary (See Table 1). (Source: World Health Organization trial registry). A comparative study of randomized and non-randomized clinical trials has been provided based on the Table 1 (See Fig. 2).

The method prescribed by law for cohort equivalence in nonrandomized observational data, probability summing followed by match using propensity scores, is one that the authors have employed [24]. The triplet "Y, T, X" stands for a binary output, a binary exposure, and a set of p-dimensional variables. The conditional probability of the treatment assignment $P(T = 1|X)$ is all that the propensity score is.

In most cases, logistic regression is used to estimate it. Logistic regression is insufficient due to high complexity and probable collinear variables. Therefore, any CI approach must make the necessary modifications to the model of high-dimensional data in order to produce accurate or consistent estimates of the average treatment impact [25].

In Fig. 3, a framework tailored for several use case types is depicted. Comparative research has been conducted using the Real World Data.

Table 1. Summarizes the 12 trial registrations

TrialID	Date reg	Recruitment Status	Inc. agemin	Inc. agemax	Inc. gender	Normalized Trg size	Study type
ISRCTN14065615	06-10-22	Recruiting			Both	1	Interventional
ISRCTN87061146	06-10-22	Recruiting			Both	0.0048	Interventional
NCT05571657	06-10-22	Not recruiting	12 Yrs	17 Yrs	All	0.2866	Interventional
NCT05571735	05-10-22	Not recruiting	18 Yrs	N/A	All	0.0067	Observational
NCT05571683	05-10-22	Recruiting	18 Yrs	80 Yrs	All	0.0048	Observational
NCT05571553	05-10-22	Not recruiting	65 Yrs	N/A	All	0.0128	Interventional
ACTRN12622001287729	04-10-22	Not recruiting	18 Yrs	No limit	Both	0.0395	Interventional
NCT05569421	04-10-22	Not recruiting	18 Yrs	60 Yrs	All	0.0067	Interventional
NCT05569252	04-10-22	Not recruiting	18 Yrs	75 Yrs	All	0.0037	Interventional
NCT05569408	04-10-22	Not recruiting	12 Yrs	N/A	All	0.3997	Observational
NCT05567510	03-10-22	Not recruiting	18 Yrs	55 Yrs	Male	0	Interventional
NCT05567874	03-10-22	Not recruiting	18 Yrs	N/A	All	0.0139	Observational

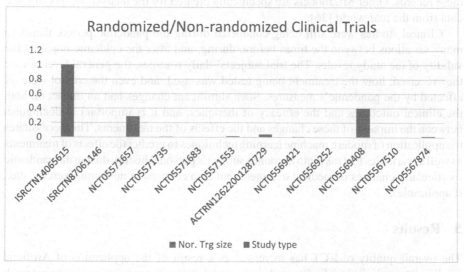

Fig. 2. A comparative study of randomized and non-randomized clinical trials

Fig. 3. A framework tailored for several use case types

4 Comparative Analysis of Data from Ongoing Clinical Trials

Missing data will result from fewer frequent on-site patient assessments during the pandemic. Additionally, potential variations in visit frequency before, during, and after the pandemic may prevent the typical intervals for sampling patient data. Both of these problems could be solved using current ML techniques.

ML algorithms created expressly to impose missing data in streams of data from the real world may be used to dictate missing data [26]. These techniques made it feasible to draw conclusions about the patient's condition at the time when on-site monitoring was less frequent. On this task, ML tools significantly outperform traditional techniques, such as Multiple Imputation by Chained Equations, Matrix Completion, and Expectation Maximization on a variety of datasets. These techniques use Multi-Dimensional Recurrent Neural Networks and Generative Adversarial Imputation Nets (from the online UCI repository). All of these techniques are predicated on the idea that missing data occur randomly. Variables that are affected by cancelled visits are probably going to be reported. On the other hand, if sufficient and reliable information is not obtained, the estimation will continue to be problematic [27]. It could be necessary to combine patient data from the study with site-level operational data in order to access these records. Other ML models are specifically created for the analysis of sporadic test data from the real world [26].

Clinical studies were still being conducted during the pandemic period, therefore many variations between the times before, during, and after the epidemic impaired the validity of the study results. The trial subjects' daily routines, the general level of care they received, how the treatment being tested was used, and even the control were all affected by the pandemic's measures. Such significant changes had an impact on both the clinical outcomes and the efficacy of therapies, and it is important to distinguish between the impacts of these changes and the effects of the treatments. This necessitates the application of modern machine learning techniques to predict the effects of treatments as well as variables that take into account a subject's personal history during the pandemic (particularly changes in medical treatment, but also changes in nutrition, exercise, etc., if applicable).

5 Results

The overall quality of RCT has increased as a result of the application of Artificial Intelligence in clinical trials. The study indicated that over the previous ten years, research interest in this field has increased. In this comparative study of RCT using AI tools and standard methods, patients, who received the complete intervention of AI tools, had statistically significantly higher distinction of a better clinical status distribution than those receiving standard observation.

Although most articles were "overview" studies, several concentrated on particular elements such as patient matching, eligibility, and recruiting. Weissler and colleagues described the significant areas of clinical trial design where ML provides particular promise in a commentary on machine learning (ML) use in clinical research with a heavy emphasis on ML.

In the scientific literature, there are presently very few examples of Artificial Intelligence use in randomized clinical trials. In the review of the paper, a scoping review has been considered to address this gap. The purpose was to draw attention to the aspects of the random clinical trial design that were most problematic, were impacted by this innovation, the efficacy of such AI tools, and how these factors impacted the success of overall clinical trials.

The severity of these difficulties will depend on factors like the length of the current COVID-19 pandemic, the number of affected subjects, the disease condition under investigation, and different aspects of the trial design, and they could lead to the suspension of numerous ongoing clinical trials. It could be challenging to obtain and record the knowledge that was anticipated in the trial design due to the unequal clinical trial and the subsequent lack of data, particularly if the experiment was stopped early on.

Therefore, Different artificial intelligence techniques, such as machine learning, deep learning, and natural language processing, are being implemented by educational researchers as well as professionals in the pharmaceutical industry to improve clinical trials. This comparative study will help in finding out the gaps in AI-based RCTs and developing more efficient, result-oriented, statistically powerful Machine Learning tools.

6 Conclusions

A recent and promising area is the use of artificial intelligence in clinical studies. However, there is not much research that looks at the quantitative impact of AI technologies on clinical trial design and execution. Trials could be made more efficient in their initial stages, saving time and money. Key principles and best practices could encourage the utilization of artificial intelligence in studies and clinical trials by establishing integrated networks of research and development with the participation of all key parties. The results of a comparative analysis that was done to find and highlight the gaps in the literature provide a broad picture of the areas of application and the prospects for future engagement between legislators, businesses, people, and patients. Implementing digital innovation can help alter healthcare and improve the effectiveness and caliber of healthcare systems. The implementation of AI-based tools in the design of clinical trials shows favorable results in all research. Applications based on AI offer a lot of potentials, but additional research is required to support and test these technologies.

References

1. Lim, C.Y., In, J.: Randomization in clinical studies. Korean J. Anesthesiol. 72(3), 221–232 (2019)
2. Zhou, B., Khosla, A., Lapedriza, A., Oliva, A., Torralba, A.: Learning deep features for discriminative localization. In: Proceedings of the IEEE Conference on Computer Vision and Pattern Recognition, pp. 2921–2929 (2016)

3. Lee, C.S., Baughman, D.M., Lee, A.Y.: Deep learning is effective for the classification of OCT images of normal versus age-related macular degeneration. Ophthalmol. Retina. **1**, 322–327 (2017)

4. Zeiler, M.D., Fergus, R.: Visualizing and understanding convolutional networks. In: Fleet, D., Pajdla, T., Schiele, B., Tuytelaars, T. (eds.) ECCV 2014. LNCS, vol. 8689, pp. 818–833. Springer, Cham (2014). https://doi.org/10.1007/978-3-319-10590-1_53

5. Kappen, T.H., van Klei, W.A., van Wolfswinkle, L., Kalkman, C.J., Vergouwe, Y., Moons, K.G.M.: Evaluating the impact of prediction model: learned, challenges and recommendation. Diagn. Progn. Res. **2**, 1–11 (2018)

6. Psaty, B.M., Furberg, C.D.: COX-2 inhibitors—lessons in drug safety. N. Engl. J. Med. **352**(11), 1133–1134 (2005)

7. Schulz, K.F., Altman, D.G., Moher, D., CONSORT Group: CONSORT 2010 statement: updated guidelines for reporting parallel group randomised trials. BMJ. **340** (2015)

8. Wallace, E., et al.: Framework for the impact analysis and implementation of Clinical Prediction Rules (CPRs). BMC Med. Inform. Decis. Mak. **11**(1), 1–7 (2011)

9. Pershing, S., Lum, F.: The American Academy of Ophthalmology IRIS Registry (Intelligent Research in Sight); current and future state of big data analytics. Curr. Opin. Ophthalmol. **33**, 394–398 (2022)

10. Stolberg, H.O., Norman, G., Trop, I.: Randomized controlled trials. AJR Am. J. Roentgenol. **183**, 1539–1544 (2004)

11. Wells, J.A., Glassman, A.R., Ayala, A.R., et al.: Aflibercept, bevacizumab, or ranibizumab for diabetic macular edema: two-year results from a comparative effectiveness randomized clinical trial. Ophthalmology **123**, 1351–1359 (2016)

12. Browning, D.J., Glassman, A.R., Aiello, L.P., et al.: Optical coherence tomography measurements and analysis methods in optical coherence tomography studies of diabetic macular edema. Ophthalmology **115**, 1366–1371 (2008)

13. Tusher, V.G., Tibshirani, R., Chu, G.: Significance analysis of microarrays applied to the ionizing radiation response. Proc. Natl. Acad. Sci. USA **98**, 5116–5121 (2001)

14. Kanne, J.P.: Chest CT findings in 2019 novel coronavirus (2019-nCoV) infections from Wuhan, China: key points for the radiologist. Radiology **295**, 16–17 (2020)

15. Bernheim, A., et al.: Chest CT findings in coronavirus disease-19 (COVID-19): relationship to duration of infection. Radiology (2020). Art. no. 200463

16. Xie, X., Zhong, Z., Zhao, W., Zheng, C., Wang, F., Liu, J.J.R.: Chest CT for typical 2019-nCoV pneumonia: relationship to negative RT-PCR testing. Radiology (2020). Art. no. 200343

17. Narin, A., Kaya, C., Pamuk, Z.: Automatic detection of coronavirus disease (COVID-19) using X-ray images and deep convolutional neural networks. arXiv:2003.10849 (2020)

18. Apostolopoulos, I.D., Bessiana, T.: COVID-19: automatic detection from X-ray images utilizing transfer learning with convolutional neural networks. arXiv:2003.11617 (2020)

19. Wang, L., Wong, A.: COVID-net: a tailored deep convolutional neural network design for detection of COVID-19 cases from chest radiography images. arXiv:2003.09871 (2020)

20. Joseph, L.A.B., Hoffmann, P.K., Cynthia, L., Miguel, A.L.-O.: Mapping the landscape of artificial intelligence applications against COVID-19. arXiv:2003.11336 (2020)

21. Wong, C.H., Siah, K.W., Lo, A.W.: Estimation of clinical trial success rates and related parameters. Biostatistics **20**, 273–286 (2019)

22. Wouters, O.J., McKee, M., Luyten, J.: Estimated research and development investment needed to bring a new medicine to market, 2009–2018. JAMA **323**, 844–853 (2020)

23. BMJ 368 (2020). https://doi.org/10.1136/bmj.m689

24. Prasad, T., Rashed, S.: Real world data for clinical trials designs using machine learning. In: IEEE International Conference on Big Data (Big Data), pp. 5991–5993 (2021)

25. Hastie, T., Tibshirani, R., Wainwright, M.: Statistical Learning with Sparsity: The Lasso and Generalizations. Taylor & Francis, Boca Raton, Florida (2015)

26. Zame, W.R., et al.: Machine learning for clinical trials in the era of COVID-19. Stat. Biopharm. Res. **12**(4), 506–517 (2020)
27. Akacha, M., et al.: Challenges in assessing the impact of the COVID-19 pandemic on the integrity and interpretability of clinical trials. Stat. Biopharm. Res. **12**(4), 419–426 (2020)

Optimizing Beat Management System Using Soft Biometrics

N. Kaushik[1]([✉]) [iD], Chandrakala G. Raju[1] [iD], Sumalatha Aradhya[2] [iD], Ishaan Joshi[1] [iD], M. Indramma[1] [iD], and K. R. Radhika[1] [iD]

[1] Department of ISE, BMS College of Engineering, Bangalore, India
{kaushikn.is19,Chandrakalagraju.ise,ishaanj.is19,indira.cse,
rkr.ise}@bmsce.ac.in
[2] Department of CSE, Siddaganga Institute of Technology, Tumkur, India
sumalatha@sit.ac.in

Abstract. In the Police Department, officials need to carry out regular beats in prescribed areas and monitor their attendance in real time. Marking attendance regularly at appropriate beat location at a prescribed time becomes challenging. The motive of the paper is to implement a Beat Management System using the deep metric learning algorithm for the Police Department to collaborate with the community within the assigned territory. The Deep metric learning algorithm in facial recognition systems does an excellent job in addressing the nonlinearity and scalability in comparison to the conventional algorithms. A novel solution is proposed in the form of an end-to-end application in order to overcome the challenges faced by the Police Department in registering attendance. This serves as a concrete solution to the problem with the amount of data that can be generated in the form of facial images from Police Officers along with the precision-based geolocation tracking. The result obtained shows that the model supports even smaller sample sizes of 4–5 images of everyone. Incremental dataset uses the concept of self- learning in order to train the model on more images captured, analyzed and processed continuously in real time. The system recognizes the person by matching the features with an accuracy of 99.38% for a constrained sample size.

Keywords: Soft Biometrics · Face Recognition · Deep Metric Learning · Beat Management System

1 Introduction

Identification of a genuine user is important based on the bio metrics which make the authentication more secure and robust. Non-biometric methods like edge-driven and token-driven methods have quite several security flaws as tokens can be easily accessed by a middleman. Even in smartphones users tend to unlock phones using biometrics rather than manually typed passwords due to speed irregularities. Face Recognition is the ability of the computer to recognize a person by matching the facial features and encodings. This soft biometric method is useful in many sectors such as Institutes,

D. Garg et al. (Eds.): IACC 2022, CCIS 1781, pp. 242–253, 2023.
https://doi.org/10.1007/978-3-031-35641-4_20

universities, manufacturing units, and in many other industries. In the public sector, such as the Police Department, the officials need to carry out regular beats in prescribed areas and there is a need to monitor their attendance in real time.

The dataset that can be acquired from the police officials in terms of a focused image of their face in various angles is hard to acquire because of availability and most importantly the sensitivity of such data. Beat in police terms means that a police officer patrolling task within the given territory and beat policing task maintains a good relationship and connection to collaborate with the community within the assigned territory to ensure a safer society. Our proposed work is implemented as end-to-end solution and shall be scalable to any sector where bio metric is needed. The innovation feature of the proposed concepts imbibes AIoT based framework with the support of i) Industry qualified RFID sensor for data acquisition, ii) continuous monitoring with GPS tracking and navigations, and iii) Data analytics for visualizing beat activity using Deep Metric algorithm.

2 Related Work

There are many algorithms and techniques for facial recognition system. The core is with accuracy and nature of application. The key factors are the application nature and Accuracy. Sehra et al. [1] proposed a HOG feature using Viola Jones method. The researchers used AT&T and Yale faces data sets. Chang et al. [2] established a facial recognition system based on HOG features but achieved lower computation time than Gabor Features on FRGC v2.0 dataset and CAS-PEAL dataset. Bhatia et al. [3] proposed Local Binary System Histograms (LBPH) algorithm.

Xiang et al. [4] proposed a method driven by a dense grid HOG features and the face recognition on raspberry pi implementation was discussed by Singh et al. [5] proposed a facial recognition system implemented using Microsoft Face API. Though hosted on cloud, the platform needs paid services. MQTT-based weather monitoring system was proposed by Kudali et al. [6]. Perrone et al. [7] have used open-source tools to work on security features. Hassaballah et al. [8] analyzed facial recognition with multiple data sets.

Thakur et al. [9] used a sign language recognition system with natural language synthesis. Jacob et al. [10] mentioned that one can use Image modification and PCA techniques to extract the features. Omoyiola et al. [11] performed analysis on biometric identification using features such as hand geometry, facial features, and retinal scans. Sunaryono et al. [12] proposed an attendance system using facial recognition and an accuracy of 97.29% was achieved using linear discriminant analysis algorithm. The implementation of eye tracking analysis, though unique, may not be faster in night mode vision systems. The biometric measures are supported by mapping and statistical analysis of features, contours, and tracing distances [13] and require the training of multiple data using neural networks. In this paper, the deep neural network using deep metric algorithms is proposed. The emotional computing approach to analyze a person's behavior is done by using Pseudo Zernike Moments method and increases the accuracy of facial recognition using fuzzy logic [14]. As the logic involves extra computation for emotional analysis, the method may not be useful for the beat management system.

An intelligent system method to access the face through mobile application is suggested by L. Niu et al [15] and it uses a ResNet based neural network to recognize facial landmarks. However, there might be misused and misplaced diagnosis. Enormous facial data set is available as open source and only few research analyses are accomplished and there is a research gap in facial recognition especially in beat management systems [16]. In Nigeria, to recognize a person ethnic group, an acceptance model framework is used for biometric [17] and it requires a selective biometric identification. The policies for surveillance are adding values to the existing face recognition system in the global south and such surveillance may be needed for security aspects [18]. The proposed beat management system framework in the paper has such multidimensional feature support that is sensor based. As the technology is progressing, a student attendance system is getting enhanced support for GPS and Near Field Communication technologies [19]. The methods such as Contourlet transform, local derivative ternary feature extraction algorithm is applied on the extracted traits by Gunashekan et. al [20]. It is suggested that long wave Infrared based image processing on face recognition systems yields better accuracy [21] and it requires thermal based signatures. There are many methods for implementing the facial recognition system using different algorithms out of which some algorithms are KLT Algorithm [22] and, Viola-Jones Algorithm face limitations etc. [23]. A secure force algorithm to secure biometric data by applying an active appearance model is proposed by Ziaul Haque Choudhury et. al and 93. 06% of accuracy is achieved [24]. With the references and reviews of Intelligence systems using deep neural network, a face recognition system along with RFID communication framework is proposed as a solution in the paper. An end-to-end solution to recognize physiological behavioral traits is implemented and further, analysis of computer vision data is performed by using deep metric algorithm and an accuracy of 99.38% is achieved in real time.

3 Proposed Work

The proposed framework helps to record and monitor multiple parameters of the Beat process. The system is integrated with RFID sensor reader, GPS, Mobile Camera that can record the path, time, Police Officer information, Beat status and other parameters as needed by the Police department. The Beat Management System is an end-to-end mobile application that can avoid all the paperwork, update the data to the server automatically and provide live information of Beat status to appropriate senior officers. Figure 1 shows the functionality of the proposed framework.

The Beat Management flow is depicted in Fig. 2. The control room monitoring station communicates with Police Department Server through an authenticated cloud platform. Beat locations are installed with RFID sensors and each time the beat police officer visits the place the path is tracked using geolocation, and an alert is triggered with navigation update. Higher authorities receive the notification on successful and unsuccessful beat attempts.

The Beat Management System has the multimodal biometric solution. The face recognition feature further assists the biometric functionality. The image captured through the camera is processed further by using Deep Metric Learning algorithm. The images from the dataset along with the names were recorded, resized, and bounding

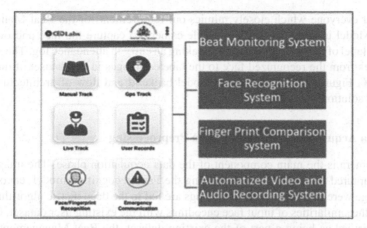

Fig. 1. Beat Management System

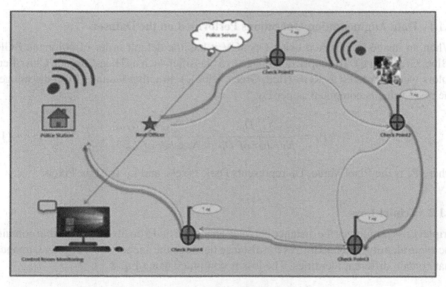

Fig. 2. Beat Management Flow

boxes were constructed around the faces. These bounding boxes narrow down the number of encodings from the entire image to the face of the person. Encodings and names were mapped and stored. These mapped values were given as input to the Haar-cascade Classifier. Once a new input image outside the training data is given as input to the model, it tries to look for similarities with the images in the training data to give a result based on the classification. If the tested face does not have similarities of a certain threshold with the labeled faces in training data, the test image was labeled as "unknown".

The proposed model is deployable on mobile applications using TensorFlow lite. The model has been trained using the LFW (Labeled Faces in the Wild) dataset as it has 3–5 images of everyone which closely mimics our requirement for the Beat Management dataset. Model is tested by using a mobile camera to capture the face and output the resulting label of the person's name like making an entry in attendance log. The accuracy of features from the recognized face to the labeled images in the dataset of the person is 99.38%. Figure 3 shows the entire model backend and flow of architecture of the proposed solution.

3.1 Data Acquisition Followed by Data Preprocessing

Phone camera is the main component of the data acquisition phase. The image of the user is captured by a phone camera. Using the Face recognition model, encodings of each image were captured. These encodings are fed to the deep metric algorithm which matches the similarities of input face encodings with the existing user dataset. Once the user is verified as being a part of the existing dataset, the Beat Management System application records the presence of that user.

3.1.1 Data Augmentation Operations Performed on the Dataset

When an image is imported using OpenCV it has the default order of colors as BGR (Blue, Green, Red). To supply that image to a classifier such as Haar Cascade Classifier, colors were reordered as RGB (Red, Green, Blue). Extracting features from the image, the pixel value is computed as per Eq. 1

$$P_v = \frac{\sum_p^1 D_p}{Number\ of\ D_p} - \frac{\sum_p^1 L_p}{Number\ of\ L_p} \tag{1}$$

where P_v is the Pixel Value, D_P represents Dark Pixels, and L_P is Light Pixels

3.1.2 Triplet Loss

Triplet Loss minimizes the distance between an anchor and a positive, images that contain the same identity, and maximizes the distance between the anchor and a negative, images that contain different identities. The loss is computed using Eq. 2

$$Loss = \sum_{i=1}^{N} [|\|f_i^a - f_i^p|2\,2 - \|f_i^a - f_i^n\|2\,2\| + \alpha] \tag{2}$$

Here,

f^a- the output encoding of the anchor.

f^p - the output encoding of the positive.

f^n - the output encoding of the negative.

α- used to make sure that the network does not try to optimize towards

$$f^a - f_i^p = f^a - f_i^n = 0$$

sum is equal to max (0, sum)

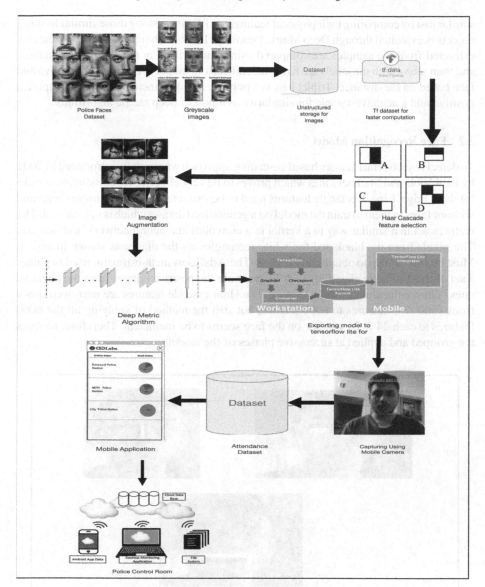

Fig. 3. End to End Beat Management System

Face Similarity Calculation Based on Euclidean Distance and is done as per Eq. 3

$$AB = x1 - y12 + x2 - y22 + \ldots + x128 - y1282 \qquad (3)$$

AB signifies the Euclidean Distance between two points given by Eq. 3. The sole objective of incorporating nascent deep learning techniques into every aspect of technology is to replicate what humans can do and achieve that at a much higher pace and accuracy. In this paper the stimulus of the human brain to recognize two objects to be similar just by comparing their physical features and distinguishing those similar looking objects is exploited through Deep Metric Learning. In this technique, simply put features extracted from the samples are compared using similarities, in this case face distance, and then along with the labels are fed to an embedding model to classify each individual face based on the distance. Triplet loss is a popular and convincing metric to compare a positive and a negative sample for similarity as a part of deep metric algorithms.

3.2 Face Recognition Model

To detect objects, Haar feature based cascading approach was initially introduced in 2001 by Paul Viola and Michael Jones which proves to be very effective for classification tasks till date. Edge, Line, Rectangle features need to be extracted from both images with and without faces in them to train the model on a generalized dataset which is not skewed. The features act in a similar way to a kernel in a convolutional neural network architecture. The pixels from the black and the white rectangles on the diagrams shown in Fig. 4. Must be summed up to obtain each feature. The AdaBoost meta-estimator used to gather a set of most suitable classifiers that differentiate the positive images from the negative ones. Thus, enhancing model accuracy. The Haar cascade features are narrowed down from 160000 + features to 6000 features but still the method of applying all the 6000 features to each 24 × 24 window on the face seems to be inefficient. Therefore, features are grouped and applied at successive phases of the model.

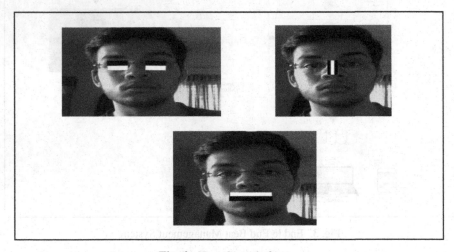

Fig. 4. Haar Cascade feature

Deep Metric Learning Algorithm uses similarity metrics between various features generated by the Haar Cascade model and uses them to classify images under the same name or label to identify the person in question. The model is separated into two phases, forward propagation, and backward propagation, during forward propagation, activation functions are used to be generated outputs from the hidden layers and during backward propagation also known as gradient descent the weights and biases are computed and optimized such that the predict the output as accurately as possible for the given input image based on the data that the model is built on. The similarity measure is based on a distance between the features for the faces that are labelled already in the dataset and the input dataset, in this case the Euclidean distance is used to calculate similarity metric. The activation function used in the hidden CNN layers in the Rectified Linear Unit and in the output layer SoftMax activation is used along with cross entropy loss function used for multiclass classification. In this technique, simply put features extracted from the samples are compared using similarities, in this case face distance, and then along with the labels are fed to an embedding model to classify each individual face based on the distance.

3.3 Hardware and Software Requirements

Android Studio framework and java Language to build the Application which is an industry used tool for building android applications developed by Google. The usage of Android Studio helps in integration of models in a smooth way. Google Jupyter Notebook has been used to train the model and fetch the images from dataset using TensorFlow Datasets, this is the most efficient way of loading the datasets into the memory and the compression challenges for image-based datasets are reduced significantly. Models written and executed using python libraries are key in recognition of faces. Intel I5 processor and above with 4 cores and more to run the model locally, GPU based execution was also done for faster model training.

4   Results and Conclusions

The Beat Management Solution is tested in real time at Tumkur. The beat officer is provided with two modes of logins namely List Mode and GPS Mode. In List Mode, all the Beat Points of a particular police station will be listed in the tabular format and also the status balls with the color options. The User to confirm the completion of any beat point, he/she must double tap the respective row to get confirmed and the status will change to Green as shown in the Fig. 5.

The GPS mode is an improved solution from the existing approach. The sensor is enabled along with GPS for fine tuning the accuracy of location. The result of GPS mode is shown in Fig. 6.

The proposed model trained on the Labeled Faces in Wild Dataset having 4–5 images of each celebrity closely replicating our Police Officers Dataset shows an accuracy of 99.38%. The same model has been trained and tested with 10 images of a single person giving an accuracy of 96.4%. The algorithm thus performs well in abundance of training data and can cross the face distance threshold of 0.6 more consistently and accurately as shown in Fig. 7. As the application classifies the new image it also saves the images in the dataset to train the model for the next time hence improving the accuracy further.

The confidence score here refers to the accuracy in calculation of the face distance (similarity metric) between the two faces in consideration when a classification must be done. These two faces are as follows, first one, the input face from the camera and the second is the one stored in the labeled dataset. The threshold value is the level up to which the similarity should be so that the classification is accurate.

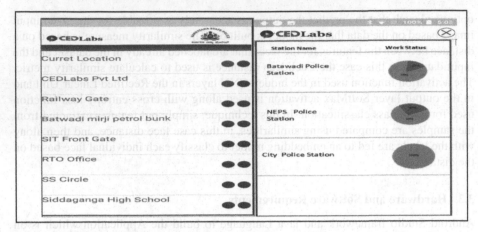

Fig. 5. List Mode - Beat Management Status and Reporting Statistics

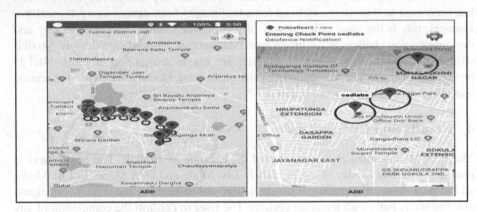

Fig. 6. GPS Mode – Beat Management Status

4.1 Accuracies of Similar Work

Figure 8 shows a comparison of the maximum accuracies obtained in similar work with different algorithms by several other researchers. LBPH stands for Local Binary Pattern Histogram algorithm and HOG stands for Histogram of Oriented Gradients algorithm.

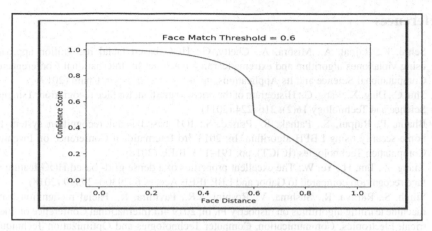

Fig. 7. Face Match Threshold

Researchers	Year of Publication	Method	Accuracy(%)
Julian et al	2017	HOG	90.2
Xiang et al	2018	HOG	92.6
Bhatia et al	2018	LBPH	90.0
Singh et al	2019	Haar-Cascade	50.0
Sehra et al	2019	Viola-Jones	96.1

Fig. 8. Accuracies Comparison of similar work the accuracy of our proposed model is 99.38%

5 Future Works

In the future, an implementation of this model on images that have multiple faces and the distance from the camera is higher will be considered by fine tuning the existing model to achieve similar results for those images. Authentication can also be achieved by using other means of soft biometrics such as iris recognition. The model is trained on images which have high quality resolution.

Acknowledgment. The work is done in real time to assist the Beat Management at Tumkur region. We are thankful to Rudraradhya P, Managing Director, CEDLabs Pvt Ltd, Tumkur for the support and technical guidance in carrying out the work. We are thankful for the support of TEQIP-III, BMS college of Engineering, ISE Research Center for sponsoring the environment to carry out the research work.

References

1. Sehra, K., Rajpal, A., Mishra, A., Chetty, G.: HOG based facial recognition approach using viola jones algorithm and extreme learning machine. In: International Conference on Computational Science and Its Applications, pp. 423–435. Springer, Cham (2019)
2. Shu, C., Ding, X., Fang, C.: Histogram of the oriented gradient for face recognition. Tsinghua Science and Technology **16**(2), 216–224 (2011)
3. Bhatia, P., Rajput, S., Pathak, S., Prasad, S.: IOT based facial recognition system for home security using LBPH algorithm. In: 2018 3rd International Conference on Inventive Computation Technologies (ICICT), pp. 191–193. IEEE (2018)
4. Xiang, Z., Tan, H., Ye, W.: The excellent properties of a dense grid- based HOG feature on face recognition compared to Gabor and LBP. IEEE Access **6**, 29306–29319 (2018)
5. Singh, S., Ramya, R., Sushma, V., Roshini, S.R., Pavithra, R.: Facial recognition using machine learning algorithms on raspberry Pi. In: 2019 4th International Conference on Electrical, Electronics, Communication, Computer Technologies and Optimization Techniques (ICEECCOT), pp. 197–202. IEEE (2019, December)
6. Kodali, R.K., Gorantla, V.S.K.: Weather tracking system using MQTT and SQLite. In: 2017 3rd International Conference on Applied and Theoretical Computing and Communication Technology (iCATccT), pp. 205–208. IEEE (2017, December)
7. Perrone, G., Vecchio, M., Pecori, R., Giaffreda, R.: The Day After Mirai: A Survey on MQTT Security Solutions After the Largest Cyber-attack Carried Out through an Army of IoT Devices. In: IoTBDS, pp. 246–253 (2017, April)
8. Hassaballah, M., Aly, S.: Face recognition: challenges, achievements and future directions. IET Computer Vision **9**(4), 614–626 (2015)
9. Thakur, A., Budhathoki, P., Upreti, S., Shrestha, S., Shakya, S.: Real time sign language recognition and speech generation. Journal of Innovative Image processing (JIIP) **02**(02), 65–76 (2020). https://www.irojournals.com/iroiip/, https://doi.org/10.36548/jiip.2020.2.001, ISSN: 2582- 4252 (online)
10. Jacob, J., Darney, P.E.: Design of deep learning algorithm for IoT application by image based recognition. Journal of ISMAC **03**(03), 276–290 (2021). http://irojournals.com/iro ismac/ https://doi.org/10.36548/jismac.2021.3.008
11. Omoyiola, B.O.: Overview of biometric and facial recognition techniques. IOSR Journal of Computer Engineering (IOSR-JCE), **20**(4), 01–05 (Jul - Aug 2018). Ver. I, e-ISSN: 2278-0661, p-ISSN: 2278-8727. www.iosrjournals.org
12. Sunaryono, D., Siswantoro, J., Anggoro, R.: An android based course attendance system using face recognition. Journal of King Saud University – Computer and Information Sciences **33**, 304–312 (2021)
13. Mahbub, U., Rahman Ahad, M.A.: Advances in human action, activity and gesture recognition. Pattern Recognition Letters **155**, 186–190 (2022). ISSN 0167-8655
14. Bernardini, F., et al.: Facial recognition pattern before and after lower eyelid blepharoplasty: an eye tracking analysis. Facial Plastic Surgery Clinics of North America **30**(2), 271–276 (2022). ISSN 1064-7406, ISBN 978032384922
15. Sivapriyan, R., Pavan Kumar, N., Suresh, H.L.: Analysis of facial recognition techniques. Materials Today: Proceedings **57**(Part 5), 2350–2354 (2022). ISSN 2214-7853, https://doi.org/10.1016/j.matpr.2022.01.296
16. Ahmady, M., et al.: Facial expression recognition using fuzzified Pseudo Zernike Moments and structural features. Fuzzy Sets and Systems **443**(Part B), 155–172 (2022). ISSN 0165-0114, https://doi.org/10.1016/j.fss.2022.03.013
17. Niu, L., Xiong, G., Shen, Z., Pan, Z., Chen, S., Dong, X.: Face image based automatic diagnosis by deep neural networks. In: 2021 IEEE 16th Conference on Industrial Electronics

and Applications (ICIEA), pp. 1352–1357 (2021). https://doi.org/10.1109/ICIEA51954.2021. 9516294

18. Ullah, N., Javed, A., Ghazanfar, M.A., Alsufyani, A., Bourouis, S.: A novel DeepMaskNet model for face mask detection and masked facial recognition. Journal of King Saud University - Computer and Information Sciences (2022). ISSN 1319-1578, https://doi.org/10.1016/j.jks uci.2021.12.017

19. Irhebhude, M.E.K., Uche, A.O., Dupe, A.C., Adeleye, V.: Perception of government employees on the use of biometric technology in determining a person's ethnic group in Nigeria. African Journal of Science, Technology, Innovation and Development (June, 2022). https://doi.org/10.1080/20421338.2022.2072793

20. Dauvergne, P.: Facial recognition technology for policing and surveillance in the Global South: a call for bans. Third World Quarterly (2022). https://doi.org/10.1080/01436597.2022. 2080654

21. Chiang, T.-W., et al.: Development and evaluation of an attendance tracking system using smartphones with GPS and NFC. Appl. Artif. Intell. **36**, 1 (2022). https://doi.org/10.1080/08839514.2022.2083796

22. Raja, K.J., Pitchai, R.: Deep multimodal biometric recognition using contourlet derivative weighted rank fusion with human face, fingerprint and iris images. Automatika **60**(3), 253-265 (2019). https://doi.org/10.1080/00051144.2019.1565681

23. Rodríguez-Pulecio, C.G., Benítez-Restrepo, H.D.B., Conrad, A.: Making long-wave infrared face recognition robust against image quality degradations. Quantitative InfraRed Thermography Journal, Taylor & Francis, pp. 1768–6733 (October 2019). https://doi.org/10.1080/176 86733.2019.1579020

24. Choudhury, Z.H., Munir Ahamed Rabbani, M.: Facial blemishes detection and encryption with secure force algorithm into HCC2D code for biometric-passport. Information Security Journal: A Global Perspective **30**(6), 342-358 (2021). https://doi.org/10.1080/19393555. 2020.1846823

Towards Better Gait Predictions: Sensor-Based Detection of Flexion and Extension of Human Lower Limb Joints During Walking

Chaitanya Nutakki[1], Abhijith Balachandran[1], Akhil Kuchimanchi[2],
Vagdevi Maddineni[2], Meghana Reddy[2], Ganesh Avugaddi[2], and Shyam Diwakar[1,2]([✉])

[1] Amrita Mind Brain Center, Amrita Vishwa Vidyapeetham, Amritapuri Campus, Clappana
P.O., Kollam, Kerala 690525, India
shyam@amrita.edu

[2] Department of Electronics and Communications Engineering, School of Engineering, Amrita
Vishwa Vidyapeetham, Amritapuri Campus, Clappana P.O., Kollam, Kerala 690525, India

Abstract. Lower limb joint kinetics and dynamics are necessary for the efficiency of walking. As the gait behavior changes, lower body joints like lumbar, knee and ankle undergo constant changes in accordance with the walking environment, physiological and structural changes. These changes can be monitored by the external system and provide a balance mechanism to accomplish the gait pattern. In this study we used low-cost mobile phone accelerometer sensors to extract the data from lower body joints like lumbar, knee and ankle to analyze the kinetic and dynamic behavior in terms of joint velocities, angles during flexion and extension across people with different weight groups. The extracted data has also been classified using different machine learning algorithms to understand the data inhomogeneities and develop a model for better gait prediction. Joint angles varied across the people with different weight groups, where ankle and hip showed modified angular velocities with respect to flexion and extension. Compared to the joint angle data, angular velocity data was better able to discriminate between the gait patterns of the healthy people and provide interventions during gait disorders especially hip related disorders.

Keywords: Joint Angle · Angular Velocity · Accelerometer · Gyroscope · Flexion · Extension · LibSVM · Simple Logistic · J48

1   Introduction

Gait analysis refers to the study of locomotion and involves the assessment of kinematic and dynamic behavior of joints that characterize locomotion. Advancements in wearable sensor technologies (WST) have raised the ability to monitor the parameters that describe mobility impairment [1, 2]. Development of gait sensor techniques and analysis helps in health monitoring, easy analysis of kinematic and dynamic behavior of joints, analyzing movement precision, detection of fall risk and allows physicians in decision making and treatment.

D. Garg et al. (Eds.): IACC 2022, CCIS 1781, pp. 254–262, 2023.
https://doi.org/10.1007/978-3-031-35641-4_21

Some of the gait analysis approaches based on the motion capturing system using 3-dimensional motion cameras force plate system measuring the ground reaction forces with respect to walking was successfully developed and used in many gait laboratories. Gait analysis using different variable sensors attached to the joints may include accelerometers, goniometers, force plates can measure various kinematic and dynamic characteristics of gait [3]. Gait shoe wearable system contains accelerometer, gyroscope, force sensors was used to detect the position and orientation of foot and detecting gait phases like toe-off and heel-strike [4]. In context of mobile gait analysis system with inertial sensor units were used to detect the joint angles velocities flexion and extension after knee arthroplasty [5].

The limbic system is dysfunctional when it comes to walking, which results in asymmetrical gait cycle fluctuations, decreased cadence, and gait speed. Inconsistent gait cycles raise the risk of stumbling because of unstable postural support [6, 7]. The qualitative and quantitative gait parameters like stance/swing phase, heel strike, toe-off angle, stride variations were analyzed using wearable inertial sensor-based system as a diagnosing tool helps to understand the disease progression of Parkinson's disease [8, 9]. However, standard gait analyses require expensive equipment and experimental setup. Therefore, an alternative approach has been made based on wearable sensors which can be made available for many clinicians and researchers particularly in low-income countries. Accelerometers within smartphones were employed to analyze the gait kinematic parameters like cadence, stride length, step length and detecting stance swing phases helps in detecting abnormal gait [10] Using low-cost mobile phone accelerometers, the joint kinematic and dynamic behavior in terms of joint angles, torques across the gender and people with different weight groups were classified and modelled during progressive and gait cycles [11, 12].

In this study, we used mobile phone accelerometer data to simulate the joint velocities, joint angles during flexion and extension phases of lower body joints such as lumbar, knee and ankle contribution towards balance regulation and movement initiation with respect to weight. Also, the extracted velocities were classified using different machine learning algorithms to understand how data inhomogeneities are and build a model for gait prediction.

2 Methods

Healthy human volunteers (n = 9) mean age between 19–25, were recruited for gait data extraction and classified the whole data into three groups based on subjects' weight. Subjects with weights of 40- 50 kg were categorized into group I, 50- 60 kg as group II and 60- 70 kg as group III. The data collection and methods were approved by the institutional ethical review board and an open consent was collected from the participants prior to gait recordings [13].

2.1 A Data Acquisition

A low-cost mobile phone-based accelerometer and gyroscope was mounted to the joints (Lumbar (L5)), Femur (Knee) and Tarsus (Ankle) to measure changes in the body's position and speed while walking (Fig. 1A). The participants were instructed to walk 5 m with an average stride length and width of 50 cm and 45 cm (Table 1). Everyone was instructed to complete 3 trials of 4 cycles each, for a total of 12 cycles that were measured. An accelerometer app for Android enabled text export of the gait data (Fig. 1B).

2.2 Data Preprocessing

High-frequency noise and the latency experienced during the collection of gait data are both included in the derived acceleration data. Third-order Butterworth low-pass filter was (Eq. 1) employed with a passband frequency curve that can be described as in order to preserve the spatiotemporal information of the activity and feature extraction in the lower-frequency portion of the data.

$$|\mathrm{H}(\omega)|^2 = \frac{1}{1 + (\omega/\omega_c)^{2n}} = \frac{1}{1 + \varepsilon^2 (\omega/\omega_p)^2} \tag{1}$$

For the lower body joints of the lumbar (L5), knee, and ankle during stance and swing in a sagittal plane, the peak amplitude changes of joint angles and joint velocities were mathematically modelled (Eq. 2). Additionally, the accelerometer and gyroscope were used to derive joint angles as data was being recorded.

$$V = U + At \tag{2}$$

where 'V' is the joint velocity, 'U' is the initial velocity and 'A' is the acceleration with respect to time 't'.

Table 1. List of gait parameters.

Gait Parameter (unit)	Description
SD (s)	Stride Duration
Sw (%)	Swing phase
St (%)	Stance phase
DLS (%)	Double leg Support
V (m/s)	Joint velocity

2.3 Machine Learning for Gait Categorization

Using machine learning algorithms, we classified the gait spatiotemporal data based on foot- and body-related parameters, such as joint acceleration, joint angles, flexion and extension, and joint mobility with a dataset of 15 features and 6750 data points. The data was classified using LibSVM, Simple Logistic, J48, Random Forest, and OneR algorithms implemented in WEKA Percentage split validation with 60–40% and 70–30% train-test validation split was used. By supplying training and test data, a support vector

Table 2. Local maxima and local minima of the joint angle (L5, Knee and Ankle) for group I weight of 40–50 kg, group II 50–60 kg and group III 60–70 kg respectively

Joints						
	Lumbar (L5)		Knee		Ankle	
Weights (Kg)	Local maximum	Local minimum	Local maximum	Local minimum	Local maximum	Local minimum
40–50	36.97	−62.35	24.88	−8.57	8.15	−12.27
50–60	23.04	−23.39	13.91	−9.30	8.85	−11.72
60–70	22.50	−55.40	11.442	−9.20	5.24	−5

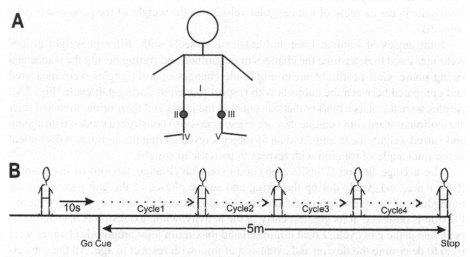

Fig. 1. Extracting gait data **A** Cartoon representation of the joints mounted with accelerometer sensors (positions I-lumbar, II-right knee, III- left knee, IV-right ankle, V-left ankle). **B**. Measuring gait. The Go cue starts the cycle with the left (first stance) and right (first swing), which involves cycle 1. These movements were then immediately repeated one after the other.

machine (SVM) classifier with a linear kernel was employed to categorize the nonlinearly separable data. Whereas J48 primarily uses C4.5 mainly for data classification on a tree structure with various nodes serving as branches to represent each tuple in the dataset. The data that divides into subgroups most efficiently and enriches one class based on normalized information gain that determines the nodes of the tree. The decision to create a model will be based on the amount of information gained [14].

3 Results

3.1 Comparison of Joint Velocities and Joint Angles During Gait Cycle with Respect to Subject Weight Groups

The average joint velocity amplitude and variation amplitude during the stance and swing phase of a gait cycle were calculated and compared across the subjects with different weight groups. Joint velocities are mainly dependent on the mathematical integral of angular velocity, stride duration and acceleration with respect to time. Mean lumbar, knee and ankle joint velocities for the subjects with 40–50 kg of weight shown 8.3, 1.2, 12.21 where the subjects with 50–60 kg and 60–70 kg of weight shown the mean joint velocities of 12.02, 3.30, 9.41 and 14.55, 3.58, 12.54. Only ankle and lumbar velocities demonstrated the changes during whole gait cycle. Particularly the lumbar and ankle shown the linear increase of joint angular velocity as the weight of the person increases (Fig. 2B).

Joint angles of lumbar, knee and ankle of subjects with different weight groups were measured to determine the changes in magnitude and timing during the stance and swing phase. Gait profile of mean amplitude changes of joint angles were measured and compared between the subjects with respect to weight during gait cycle (Fig. 2A). Angles were taken as a marker that can connect the joints and their orientation and their attributions towards how unique they are in each person to construct a model, with ageing and varied weight, mean angular data of subjects revealed that the significant decrement in the joint angle of rotation with respect to increase in weight.

The average flexion (Dorsiflexion) and extension (Plantar flexion) of the Lumbar (L5), Knee, and Ankle during the swing and stance phases of the gait patterns of the individuals of various weights were used to characterize and identify key the gait patterns. Flexion is observed at its greatest early in the activity, while extension is detected at its peak late in the gait cycle. Local minimum and maximum joint amplitude changes were used to determine the flexion and extension of joint with respect to age. All the subjects walked for 5 m at selected speed with a minimum of two trails processed and averaged. As the subjects varied in weight all the comparisons were averaged among the subjects according to the body weight. The subjects with weights between 40–50 kg showed a maximum and minimum acceleration of 36.97 and −62.35 for Lumbar, 24.88 and −8.7 for knee and 8.15 and −12.27 for the ankle. For the subjects with weight between 50–60 kg shown a maximum and minimum acceleration of 23.04 and −23.39 for lumbar, 13.91 and −9.30 for knee and 8.85 and −11.72 for the ankle whereas for the subjects with weight between 60–70 kg shown a maximum and minimum acceleration of 22.50 and −55.40 for lumbar, 11.42 and −9.20 for knee and 5.24 and −5 for the ankle.

3.2 Machine Learning Based Categorization of Flexion/Extension in Gait

Along with SVM and decision tree classifiers, logistic and rule based supervised learning algorithms were also used to classify the gait spatiotemporal data. The model's predictive ability was tested by changing the learning rate and training parameters, using percentage split method, the dataset has been divided into training and testing set with different split ratio of 60%, 70%. The decision tree models explicitly illustrate the feature contribution

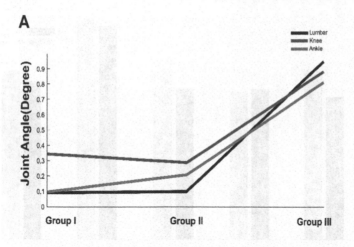

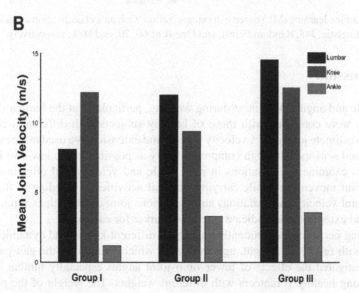

Fig. 2. Body weight and joint velocities during gait. A Joint Angles (m/sec) of L5, Knee and Ankle group I weight of 40–50 kg, group II 50–60 kg and group III 60–70 kg respectively **(B)** Joint Velocities (m/sec) of L5, Knee and Ankle group I weight of 40–50 kg, group II 50–60 kg and group III 60–70 kg respectively

that determines the attribute relation to the class label. From the analysis it was identified that random forest, J48 and LibSVM (linear kernel) produced the most predictive model with highest accuracy. When the dataset is nonlinear and multifeatured, SVM(Linear), random forest and J48 showed good commitment in terms of accuracy compared to the other algorithms (Fig. 3).

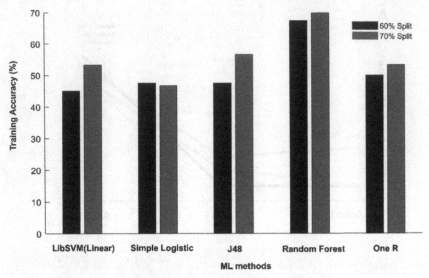

Fig. 3. Machine learning (ML) based gait categorization. Gait data classification accuracy showed LibSVM, Logistic, J48, Random Forest, and One-R at 60, 70, and 80%, respectively.

4   Discussion

Joint angle and angular velocities during walking, particularly at the lumbar (L5), knee and ankle were compared with those of healthy subjects with different weight categories. To estimate joint angle, velocity flexion and extension, we used more basic smart phone-based sensors. Although comprehensively as possible, these low-cost kinematic techniques examine the variations in joint angle and velocity and offer insights into various joint movements while carrying out gait activities. According to the individual, the joint velocity and variations among various joint combinations throughout the flexion and extension may indicate a new biomarker for each joint.

Walking performance frequently undergoes different kinetic and dynamic behavior changes with respect to weight, age and speed which could alter the gait pattern. We have investigated the effects of lower limb joint angles especially lumbar, knee and ankle among healthy volunteers with different weights. The weight of the person has a direct effect on the angle of rotation of the lower limb joints and their variability during progressive gait. The ankle, lumbar and knee engage more during walk and joint angle increase with respect to weight that can provide firm base support to the skeletal system. The angular velocity of the ankle and hip are significantly different. Moreover, we observed the peak values of the joint angular velocities of Lumbar (L5) and ankle were associated with an increase in the weight of a person and speed of walking. The decrement in the joint angular velocity may reflect the joint flexion movement that reflects the muscle contractile system. The increment and decrement of joint angular velocity may be dependent on the muscle-tendon extensibility. However, Lumbar (L5) and Knee joint velocities were not changed by muscle-tendon lengthening even though it involved flexion and extension. The modelled positive velocities, joint angles, positive flexion especially at the Lumbar (L5), knee and ankle would help us to develop models that can classify the spastic gait and dysplasia of hip. The classification approach aimed to build an appropriate model that can classify gait kinetic and dynamic features during stance and swing. Classification results indicated linear classifiers and the learning algorithms can be employed predictively for analyzing the human gait data. Based on the attribute evaluation, our proposed models based on SVM, random forest and J48 performed well in terms of accuracy and mean squared error. The design and implementation of ML models helps to detect the gait patterns using various qualitative accuracy metrices to classify the various gait unknown patterns on test samples.

5 Conclusion

In this paper, we have demonstrated an alternative approach to flexion-extension categorization and a method to calculate body-joint velocity maps using low-cost sensors (mobile phone accelerometers), even though there are numerous approaches combining machine learning and feature recognition for other approaches in gait analysis. This exploratory investigation weight-dependent changes in velocity between different joints that support posture maintenance and progressive gait. Since the data included heterogeneities, we estimate that more data may be needed for determining optimal classifiers. A mobile-based mapping tool can be created through more detailed analysis to assess movement problems by linking posture control and progressive gait to brain activations related to gait failures and normal circumstances.

Acknowledgement. This study derives direction and ideas from the Chancellor of Amrita Vishwa Vidyapeetham, Sri Mata Amritanandamayi Devi. This study was supported by the Department of Science and Technology grant DST/CSRI/2018/3 (G) from Government of India, and by Amrita Vishwa Vidyapeetham and by Embracing the World research for a cause initiative.

References

1. Youn, K.W., Youn, J., Scheffler, J.: Wearable Sensor-Based Biometric Gait Classification Algorithm Using WEKA **14**(1), 45–50 (2016)
2. Muro-de-la-Herran, A., García-Zapirain, B., Méndez-Zorrilla, A.: Gait analysis methods: an overview of wearable and non-wearable systems, highlighting clinical applications. Sensors (Switzerland). (2014). https://doi.org/10.3390/s140203362
3. Bonato, P.: Wearable Sensors/Systems and Their Impact on Biomedical Engineering. IEEE Eng. Med. Biol. Mag. **22**(3), 18–20 (2003). https://doi.org/10.1109/MEMB.2003.1213622. May
4. Bamberg, S.J.M., Benbasat, A.Y., Scarborough, D.M., Krebs, D.E., Paradiso, J.A.: Gait analysis using a shoe-integrated wireless sensor system. IEEE Trans Inf Technol Biomed **12**(4), 413–423 (2008). https://doi.org/10.1109/TITB.2007.899493. Jul.
5. Calliess, T., Bocklage, R., Karkosch, R., Marschollek, M., Windhagen, H., Schulze, M.: Clinical evaluation of a mobile sensor-based gait analysis method for outcome measurement after knee arthroplasty. Sensors (Basel) **14**(9), 15953–15964 (2014). https://doi.org/10.3390/ S140915953. Aug.

6. "Accelerometer based Gait Analysis - Multi Variate Assessment of Fall Risk with FD-NEAT. I Request PDF." https://www.researchgate.net/publication/221334617_Accelerometer_b ased_Gait_Analysis_-_Multi_Variate_Assessment_of_Fall_Risk_with_FD-NEAT, accessed 11 Nov. 2022

7. Mannini, A., Trojaniello, D., Cereatti, A., Sabatini, A.: A machine learning framework for gait classification using inertial sensors: application to elderly, post-stroke and huntington's disease patients. Sensors 16(1), 134 (2016). https://doi.org/10.3390/s16010134. Jan.

8. Ye, Q., Xia, Y., Yao, Z.: Classification of gait patterns in patients with neurodegenerative disease using adaptive neuro-fuzzy inference system. Comput Math Methods Med 2018, 1–8 (2018). https://doi.org/10.1155/2018/9831252. Sep.

9. Schlachetzki, J.C.M., et al.: Wearable sensors objectively measure gait parameters in Parkinson's disease. PLoS One 12(10) (Oct. 2017). https://doi.org/10.1371/JOURNAL.PONE.018 3989

10. Yodpijit, N., Tavichaiyuth, N., Jongprasithporn, M., Songwongamarit, C., Sittiwanchai, T.: The use of smartphone for gait analysis. In: 2017 3rd International Conference on Control, Automation and Robotics, ICCAR 2017, pp. 543–546 (Jun. 2017). https://doi.org/10.1109/ ICCAR.2017.7942756

11. Balachandran, A., Nutakki, C., Bodda, S., Nair, B., Diwakar, S.: Experimental recording and assessing gait phases using mobile phone sensors and EEG. In:2018 International Conference on Advances in Computing, Communications and Informatics (ICACCI), pp. 1528–1532 (Sep. 2018). https://doi.org/10.1109/ICACCI.2018.8554790

12. Nutakki, A., Narayanan, J., Anchuthengil, A.A., Nair, B., Diwakar, S.: Classifying gait features for stance and swing using machine learning. In: 2017 International Conference on Advances in Computing, Communications and Informatics (ICACCI), pp. 545–548 (Sep. 2017). https://doi.org/10.1109/ICACCI.2017.8125896

13. Nutakki, A., Bodda, S., Diwakar, S.: Correlations of gait phase kinematics and cortical EEG: modelling human gait with data from sensors. Advances in Neural Signal Processing (2020). https://doi.org/10.5772/INTECHOPEN.88465. Sep.

14. Hall, M., Frank, E., Holmes, G., Pfahringer, B., Reutemann, P., Witten, I.H.: The WEKA data mining software. ACM SIGKDD Explorations Newsl 11(1), 10 (2009). https://doi.org/ 10.1145/1656274.1656278. Nov.

A Comparative Study of Stroke Prediction Algorithms Using Machine Learning

Manu Singh[1]([✉]) [iD], Sonia Verma[1,2] [iD], and Pooja Singhal[3] [iD]

[1] Department of Computer Science, ABES Engineering College, Ghaziabad 201204, India
drmanuajaykumar@gmail.com
[2] Department of Computer Science and Engineering, SRM IST Delhi-NCR Campus Delhi,
Meerut Road, Modinagar, Uttar Pradesh 201204, India
[3] Banasthali Vidyapith, Banasthali, Rajasthan, India

Abstract. A brain stroke, in some cases also known as a brain attack, happens when anything prevents blood flow to a part of the brain or when a blood vessel within the brain ruptures. Parts of the brain either ended up dying or being injured in either scenario. A stroke can result in permanent brain damage, permanent disability, or even death. While relatively few studies have looked at the risk of brain attacks, the majority of research has concentrated on forecasting heart attacks. To predict the probability of a brain stroke, various machine learning models have been developed. Several physiological variables and machine learning algorithms, including Logistic Regression (LR), Decision Tree Classification (DTC), Random Forest Classification (RFC), K-Nearest Neighbors (K-NN), Support Vector Machine (SVM), Naive Bayes Classification (NBC), and ADABoost (AB), were used in this study to train seven different models for accurate prediction. The best strategy for this problem was the SVM approach since it had a higher accuracy metric. The fact that this model was trained on text data rather than real brain images is a disadvantage. The study demonstrates the use of seven machine learning classification techniques. The scope of this study may be increased to cover all current machine learning methodologies.

Keywords: Brain Stroke · Machine Learning · Support Vector Machine · Naïve Bayes classification

1 Introduction

Many of us are unaware of the symptoms and events associated with "brain strokes" or "brain attacks," yet we can all prevent and recognise them. The brain's ability to function properly is jeopardised when it is deprived of blood and the oxygen it transports, or when bleeding floods surrounding tissue and causes the brain to expand. Both instances have the potential to result in long-lasting eyesight issues, seizures, exhaustion, speech loss, memory loss, and paralysis, among other negative effects [11]. They can even be fatal if they are severe enough. Over 11 million strokes are reported to occur annually in low- and middle-income nations, including those in the WHO South-East Asia Region. Each

© Springer Nature Switzerland AG 2023
D. Garg et al. (Eds.): IACC 2022, CCIS 1781, pp. 263–274, 2023.
https://doi.org/10.1007/978-3-031-35641-4_22

year, this results in 4 million fatalities and 30% or more gravely injured survivors. The chance of having another stroke is significantly raised for the 70% of survivors who make a full recovery. A brain stroke can happen to anyone who has high blood pressure, high cholesterol, heart disease, diabetes, or high blood sugar. The same goes for those who are overweight, smoke, drink a lot, or are sedentary physically. Males are more likely to get a stroke than females, and the risk of stroke rises with age. To avoid brain stroke, the majority of lifestyle-related hazards can be decreased. Smokers should stop smoking, and heavy drinkers should stop. The risk of stroke is multiplied by numerous factors. ML may now be used to forecast the likelihood of having a brain stroke thanks to advancements in medical technology. ML algorithms are helpful in giving accurate analysis and making correct forecasts. Most previous research on stroke has focused on cardiac stroke prediction. The study of brain strokes has not received much attention. The likelihood of a subsequent algorithm is forecasted in this study using ML [1].

Logistic Regression: Based on a collection of independent variables, logistic regression calculates the likelihood that an event will occur, such as voting or not voting. Given that the result is a probability, the dependent variable's range is 0 to 1.

Naive Bayes Classifier: The features are presumed to be independent by the Naive Bayes classifier. This indicates that even though we are still assuming class-specific covariance matrices (as in QDA), they are diagonal matrices instead. The notion that the features are independent is to blame for this.

Random Forest Classifier: Decision tree classifiers can be replaced by the random forest classifier, which is more accurate. A random forest classifier, which is based on ensemble learning [8, 9], uses a number of decision trees on different subsets of the provided dataset and averages the results to increase the dataset's predicted accuracy. In general, more trees in the forest produce higher accuracy and mitigate the overfitting issue.

The K-nearest Neighbours: K-nearest neighbours are: Using proximity, the K-nearest neighbours (KNN) classifier can categorise or forecast data points that are independent of one another. The results of this technique will differ depending on whether it is applied in a classification or regression scenario. When it comes to classification, decisions are made by majority vote, which means that the class that is given to a new data point is assumed to be the one that is most frequently observed nearby. Since a model is not learned, KNN is often referred to as a lazy learner technique. Instead, if a prediction is required, the raw data is retained and used.

Decision Tree Classifier: Classification and regression problems can be solved using supervised learning methods called decision trees. There are internal nodes that represent the features of the dataset, branches that represent the decision-making process, and leaves that represent the classification result [7]. Based on a training dataset of N input variables x and corresponding target variables t, (Gaussian) Naive Bayes assumes that the class-conditional densities are normally distributed.

Support Vector Classifier: Both classification and regression can be accomplished using SVM, which is a popular algorithm for supervised learning. The vast majority of its applications are in ML Classification. In order to quickly classify fresh data points in the future, the SVM algorithm tries to define the best line or decision boundary into classes in the n-dimensional space, thereby dividing n-dimensional space into classes. These optimal decision boundaries are called hyper-planes [2]. As part of the hyper-plane creation process, SVM selects extreme vectors and points.

AdaBoost Classifier: In a multi-level decision tree set, or a decision tree with AdaBoost, the most widely used algorithm is AdaBoost, which is also known as Adaptive Boosting. Basically, this algorithm builds a model and weighs all the data points equally. It then assigns higher weights to points that are wrongly classified. Now all the points which have higher weights are given more importance in the next model. It will keep training models until and unless a low error is received.

2 Literature Survey

Eight machine learning models are used in [1] to estimate the green time based on the volume and classification of passenger car units. The models are evaluated based on several performance measures. The results showed that when traffic categorization was used as the input, all of the selected models properly predicted green splits with 91% accuracy, but only with 85% accuracy when PCU was used. Using five machine learning algorithms, the Cardiovascular Health Study (CHS) dataset was used in [2] to predict strokes. The authors combined the Decision Tree with the C4.5 algorithms, Principal Component Analysis, Artificial Neural Networks, and Support Vector Machine to provide the best result. The CHS Dataset, however, which was used for this work, has fewer input parameters.

Through analysis of user-posted social media content, [3] performed stroke prediction. The DRFS method has been employed by the writers of this particular paper to identify the various stroke syndrome signs. Natural Language Processing is used to extract text from social media posts, but this increases the model's overall execution time, which is not optimal. By utilizing an improvised random forest method, the authors of [4] completed the objective of stroke prediction. Analysis of the hazards associated with strokes was done using this. This method supposedly outperformed the already available algorithms, as claimed by the authors. Future stroke kinds cannot be treated with the results of this particular study because it is only applicable to a small number of stroke types.

According to research publication [5], the model was trained to predict strokes using decision trees, random forests, and multi-layer perceptron's. The three approaches' obtained accuracies were remarkably similar, with only minor variations. Decision Tree's accuracy was calculated to be 74.31%, Random Forest's accuracy to be 74.53%, and Multi-Layer Perceptron's accuracy to be 75.02%.

This study contends that Multi-Layer Perceptron outperforms the other two techniques in terms of accuracy. The only performance metric that would not always produce favorable results was accuracy score. Research conducted in [6] demonstrates the use of a machine learning algorithm to predict cardiac attacks. They built the model using a variety of machine learning approaches, including Decision Tree, Naive Bayes, and SVM, and then compared the results. The methods they utilized yielded a maximum accuracy of just 60%, which is quite low. In [7], the researchers forecast the likelihood of a stroke using several data mining categorization approaches. The Ministry of National Guards Health Affairs Hospitals in the Kingdom of Saudi Arabia provided the dataset. C4.5, Jrip, and multi-layer perceptron were the three classification methods employed (MLP). With these techniques, the model was approximately 95% accurate. Even though the research claims to achieve an accuracy of 95%, the training and prediction times are longer since the authors used several sophisticated algorithms.

Three distinct methods may be used, according to research published in [8], to forecast the likelihood of having a stroke. These algorithms include Neural Networks, Decision Trees, and Naive Bayes. This study found that, among the three algorithms, the decision tree has the highest accuracy (about 75%). Nevertheless, based on the results from the confusion matrix, this model could not account for the examples from the real world. The researchers used the Cardiovascular Health Study (CHS) dataset to do stroke prediction in [9]. On the basis of their suggested conservative mean, they introduced a unique automatic feature selection technique that chooses robust features. For further effectiveness, they paired this approach with the Support Vector Machine technique. However, this led to the creation of a number of vectors that have the tendency to make the model perform worse.

The prediction of thrombo-embolic stroke disease using artificial neural networks is suggested by research in [10]. The Back-propagation algorithm was employed as the prediction approach. The accuracy achieved by this model was about 89%. However, because of their complicated structure and growing number of neurons, neural networks take longer to train and demand more processing time.

3   Research Methodology

3.1   Dataset Description

To continue with this work, a dataset picked from Kaggle is displayed in Table 1 with a variety of physiological features as its properties. There are 12 columns and 5110 rows in this particular dataset. These elements are later examined and utilised for the final forecast. Data pre-processing is done to balance the data for higher accuracy. The dataset's Range Index has 5110 entries with a range of 0 to 5109 and data columns (total 12 columns).

The research comes to a conclusion about which algorithm is best for stroke prediction after thorough analysis. Figure 1 displays the methodology of the suggested system in a flow chart format.

3.2   Exploratory Data Analysis

The most crucial phase in any data-driven study has been thought to be exploratory data analysis (EDA) and data preprocessing. While data preparation works with duplicate and unbalanced data, highly correlated and low variance features in the dataset, missing values, outliers in the dataset, etc., EDA deals with improving comprehension of the data by visualising various elements of it. Following EDA [17, 18], it was discovered that the

Table 1. Dataset Description

SNo	Column	Non-Null	Count	Dtype
0	P_id	5110	non-null	int64
1	P_gender	5110	non-null	object
2	P_age	5110	non-null	float64
3	P_hypertension	5110	non-null	int64
4	P_heart_disease	5110	non-null	int64
5	P_ever_married	5110	non-null	object
6	P_work_type	5110	non-null	object
7	P_Residence_type	5110	non-null	object
8	P_avg_glucose_level	5110	non-null	float64
9	P_bmi	4909	non-null	float64
10	P_smoking_status	5110	non-null	object
11	P_stroke	5110	non-null	int64

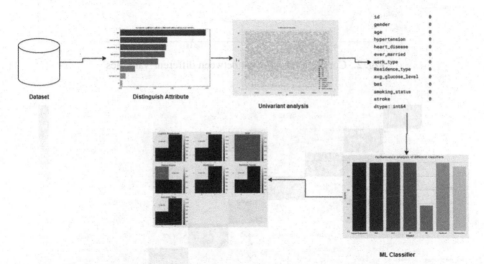

Fig. 1. Model for The Comparison of Algorithms

PIDD includes a large number of missing values, outliers, and attribute values that are not normalised. As a result, the preprocessing methods used in the current study, which are briefly explained as follows, include outlier rejection (OR), filling missing values (MV), and normalisation (N): We used a variety of graph formats, such as the following, to study the data and determine the best approach to use these features: Histogram: to examine how the various qualities are distributed.

3.3 Correlation Coefficient

A statistical indicator of the strength of the association between the relative movements of two variables is the correlation coefficient. The values are in the −1.0 to 1.0 range. There was a measurement error in the correlation if the estimated value was larger than

1.0 or lower than −1.0. Perfect negative correlation is shown by a correlation of −1.0, and perfect positive correlation is shown by a correlation of 1.0. A correlation of 0.0 indicates that there is no linear relationship between the two variables' movements (Figs. 2, 3 and 4).

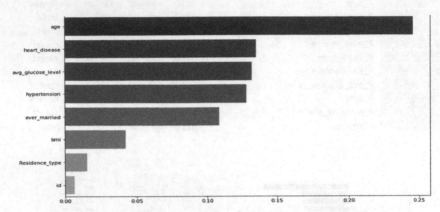

Fig. 2. Correlation coefficient between different Variables

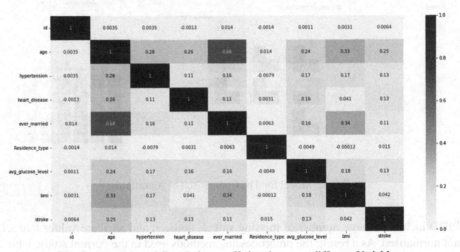

Fig. 3. Heat Map of Correlation coefficient between different Variables

3.4 Data Pre-processing

This process handles missing values, balances data that are out of balance, and performs label encoding specific to this dataset. The pre-processed data is now ready for model construction [3]. The dataset is divided into train and test data following data pre-processing.

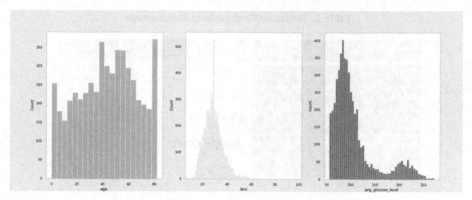

Fig. 4. Age Factor affecting the occurrence of stroke

3.5 Data Imputation

It refers to the process of substituting missing data with a different value in order to retain the majority of information and data in the dataset. The reason for using these methods is that it would not be feasible to remove data from a dataset on a regular basis. Furthermore, it would substantially reduce the size of the dataset, making analysis more difficult and raising concerns about bias.

3.6 One-Hot Encoding

Data can be converted using one hot encoding as a means of getting a better prediction and preparing the data for an algorithm [19–21]. With one-hot, we create a new categorical column for each categorical value and give it a binary value of 1 or 0. A binary vector is used to represent each integer value.

4 Result and Discussion

4.1 Environment Setup

Some resources were required to carry out this research. The materials used to create this suggested model are listed in Table 2 and include.

The suggested system has undergone testing and training on, respectively, 30% and 70% of the data. Different machine learning classifiers, including LR, DTC, RFC, K-NN, SVM, NBC, and AB, are used to determine which model is the best. The best machine learning model is found among these eleven classifiers utilising performance metrics including accuracy, recall, precision, and f1-score [4]. The environmental setup, confusion matrix for individual classifiers, and accuracy are all covered in this section. A model is then built utilising the pre-processed data and a number of classification algorithms [14–16]. To find the best accurate prediction model, the accuracy of each of these methods is calculated and compared (Table 3).

Using five accuracy metrics—Accuracy Score, Precision Score, Recall Score, and F1 Score—seven distinct models are built. When the models are compared [5], the model with the highest accuracy metrics is chosen to move on to the deployment stage.

Table 2. Hardware Configuration Requirement

Resource	Details
CPU	Intel®
RAM	12 GB
GPU	K80
Experimental tool	Google Colab

Table 3. F1-Score Table for various Algorithm

	Model	Score
0	LogisticRegression	0.998695
1	KNN	0.994781
2	SVC	1.000000
3	RF	0.996086
4	NB	0.370515
5	AdaBoost	0.994781
6	DecisionTree	0.940639

4.2 Confusion Matrix

The N*N matrix, where N is the total number of target classes, is used to measure machine learning classification [11–13] and is known as a confusion matrix. By using this technique, it is possible to observe which machine learning classifiers work best by summarising the number of accurate and incorrect predictions. This section evaluates and compares the classifiers that were employed in the study [10]. Each classifier's performance is displayed in the Fig. The confusion matrix contains four outcomes that measure each classifier's performance on positive and negative classes separately; two types of the outcomes—true positive (TP), true negative (TN), false positive (FP), and false-negative—give correct predictions, while the other two types give inaccurate ones (Fig. 5).

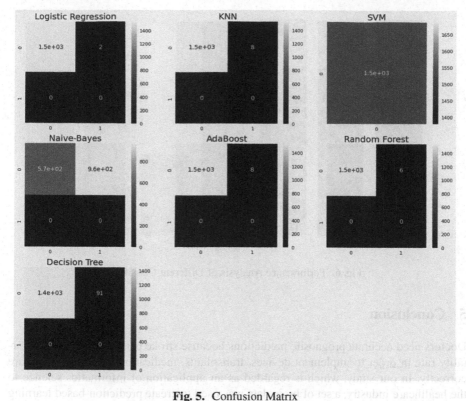

Fig. 5. Confusion Matrix

4.3 Performance Analysis of Different Classifier

Various classification algorithms are then used to create models based on the pre-processed data. For each of these methods, accuracy is calculated and compared to obtain the most accurate prediction model. When the models are compared, the model with the highest accuracy metrics is chosen to move on to the deployment stage. The paper comes to a conclusion about which algorithm is best for stroke prediction after thorough analysis. The Fig. 6 shows that the support vector classifier is the best classifier for such type of data.

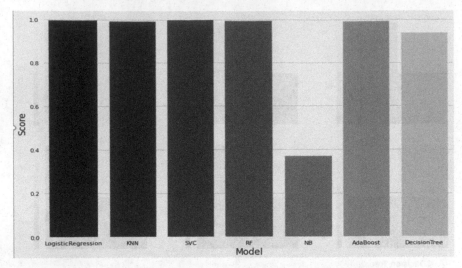

Fig. 6. Performance Analysis of Different Classifier

5 Conclusion

Doctors need accurate prognostic predictions because stroke patients have a high mortality rate in order to implement devices, transplants, medications, and palliative care correctly. In our study, which is regarded as an application of informatics science to the healthcare industry, a set of brain data was used to create prediction-based learning models and decision support systems that learn from data. By using these models to assess the risk of losing a human life, it aims to advance science. In this study, machine learning techniques were used to accurately predict all of the features in the data set for a controlled classification problem involving the mortality-survival prediction due to brain failure. In this regard, our study has demonstrated that the dual classification of stroke patient health records using machine learning can be done successfully. Comparatively, classification accuracy was attained between 35 and 100% using a variety of machine learning techniques and modifications. The performances of the machine learning techniques SVM and Logistic regression have been found to be at their peak. The small size of the data set (5110 patients) and its imbalance for classification should not be disregarded as a limitation of the current study. Additionally, information not included in the data set about the patients' physical characteristics, such as their body mass index, environment, blood type, and genotype, may be helpful in identifying additional risk factors for diseases.

References

1. Savithramma, R.M., Sumathi, R., Sudhira, H.S.: A comparative analysis of machine learning algorithms in design process of adaptive traffic signal control System. J. Phys.: Conf. Series **2161**(1), 012054 (2022). https://doi.org/10.1088/1742-6596/2161/1/012054

2. Sheetal Singh, M., Choudhary, P., Thongam, K.: A comparative analysis for various stroke prediction techniques. In: Nain, N., Vipparthi, S.K., Raman, B. (eds.) Computer Vision and Image Processing: 4th International Conference, CVIP 2019, Jaipur, India, September 27–29, 2019, Revised Selected Papers, Part II, pp. 98–106. Springer Singapore, Singapore (2020). https://doi.org/10.1007/978-981-15-4018-9_9

3. Pradeepa, S., Manjula, K.R., Vimal, S., Khan, M.S., Chilamkurti, N., Luhach, A.K.: DRFS: detecting risk factor of stroke disease from social media using machine learning techniques. Neural Process. Lett. (2020)

4. Bandi, V., Bhattacharyya, D., Midhunchakkravarthy, D.: Prediction of brain stroke severity using machine learning. Rev. d'Intelligence Artif. **34**(6), 753–761 (2020)

5. Nwosu, C.S., Dev, S., Bhardwaj, P., Veeravalli, B., John, D.: Predicting stroke from electronic health records. In: 41st Annual International Conference of the IEEE Engineering in Medicine and Biology Society IEEE (2019)

6. Alotaibi, F.S.: Implementation of machine learning model to predict heart failure disease. Int. J. Adv. Comput. Sci. Appl. **10**(6), 261–268 (2019)

7. Almadani, O., Alshammari, R.: Prediction of stroke using data mining classification techniques. Int. J. Adv. Comput. Sci. Appl. **9**, 457–460 (2018)

8. Kansadub, T., Thammaboosadee, S., Kiattisin, S., Jalayondeja, C.: Stroke risk prediction model based on demographic data. In: 8th Biomedical Engineering International Conference (BMEiCON) IEEE (2015)

9. Khosla, A., et al.: An integrated machine learning approach to stroke prediction. In: Proceedings of the 16th ACM SIGKDD International Conference on Knowledge Discovery and Data Mining (2010)

10. Shanthi, D., Sahoo, G., Saravanan, N.: Designing an artificial neural network model for the prediction of thrombo-embolic stroke. Int. J. Biometric Bioinform. (IJBB) **3**, 10–18 (2009)

11. Saba, L., et al.: Six artificial intelligence paradigms for tissue characterisation and classification of non-COVID-19 pneumonia against COVID-19 pneumonia in computed tomography lungs. Int. J. Comput. Assist. Radiol. Surg. **16**(3), 423–434 (2021)

12. Suri, J.S., et al.: A narrative review on characterization of acute respiratory distress syndrome in COVID-19-infected lungs using artificial intelligence. Comput. Biol. Med. **130**, 104210 (2021)

13. Agarwal, M., et al.: A novel block imaging technique using nine artificial intelligence models for COVID-19 disease classification, characterization and severity measurement in lung computed tomography scans on an Italian cohort. J. Med. Syst. **45**(3), 1–30 (2021)

14. Suri, J.S., et al.: Systematic review of artificial intelligence in acute respiratory distress syndrome for COVID-19 lung patients: a biomedical imaging perspective. IEEE J. Biomed. Health Inform. **25**(11), 4128–4139 (2021)

15. Suri, J.S., et al.: COVLIAS 1.0: lung segmentation in COVID-19 computed tomography scans using hybrid deep learning artificial intelligence models. Diagnostics **11**(8), 1405 (2021)

16. Suri, J.S., et al.: Inter-variability study of COVLIAS 1.0: hybrid deep learning models for COVID-19 lung segmentation in computed tomography. Diagnostics **11**(11), 2025 (2021). https://doi.org/10.3390/diagnostics11112025

17. Agarwal, M., et al.: Eight pruning deep learning models for low storage and high-speed COVID-19 computed tomography lung segmentation and heatmap-based lesion localization: a multicenter study using COVLIAS 2.0. Comput. Biol. Med. **146**, 105571 (2022)

18. Munjral, S., et al.: Cardiovascular risk stratification in diabetic retinopathy via atherosclerotic pathway in COVID-19/Non-COVID-19 frameworks using artificial intelligence paradigm: a narrative review. Diagnostics **12**(5), 1234 (2022)

19. Agarwal, M., et al.: A novel compressed and accelerated convolution neural network for COVID-19 disease classification: a genetic algorithm based approach. In: Garg, D., Jagannathan, S., Gupta, A., Garg, L., Gupta, S. (eds.) Advanced Computing: 11th International

Conference, IACC 2021, Msida, Malta, December 18–19, 2021, Revised Selected Papers, pp. 99–111. Springer International Publishing, Cham (2022). https://doi.org/10.1007/978-3-030-95502-1_8

20. Rani, P., et al.: Simulation of the lightweight blockchain technique based on privacy and security for healthcare data for the cloud system. Int. J. E-Health Med. Commun. **13**(4), 1–15 (2022)

21. Rani, P., et al.: An implementation of modified blowfish technique with honey bee behavior optimization for load balancing in cloud system environment. Wirel. Commun. Mob. Comput. **2022**, 1–14 (2022). https://doi.org/10.1155/2022/3365392

Design of Agricultural Applications using AI

Intelligent Crop Recommendation System Using Machine Learning Algorithms

Swapnil Desai[1]($\boxtimes$) (iD), Manuj Joshi[1], and Pradip Mane[2] (iD)

[1] PAHER University, Udaipur, India
swapnildesai2022@gmail.com
[2] VPPCOE&VA, Mumbai, India
pradip.mane@pvppcoe.ac.in

Abstract. Agriculture is a foremost provider to the Indian financial system. The widespread dilemmas accessible among the Indian farmers are they don't opt the accurate crop based on their soil necessities. As a result, they get to face a solemn impede in final yield. This crisis of the farmers is presented via precision agriculture. Precision agriculture is a contemporary agricultural practice which utilizes research data of soil distinctiveness, type of soil, gathered data of yielded crop and directs the farmers the precise crop based on their parameters of site. This lowers down the incorrect selection on a crop and enhances the final output.

In current article, we are using an intelligent system, which has the capability to aid the Indian farmers in taking a well-versed choice about which crop they should be growing by keeping the factors into the consideration such as sowing season, geographical location and soil features. Additionally, the system will also aid the farmer, the prediction about the yield if he plants the suggested crop.

Keywords: Precision Agriculture · Yield prediction · Machine learning

1 Introduction

A farmer's decision about which crop to make is everything seen as obfuscated by his sense and other senseless parts like making second gains, nonattendance of care about market pay, befuddling a soil's capacity to help a particular crop, and so on. An astoundingly misled decision concerning the farmer could overburden his family's money related condition. Perhaps this could be one of the many reasons adding to the unending breakdown occasions of farmers that we hear from media constantly.

In a country like India, where agriculture and related region adds to normally 20.4% of its Gross Value Added (GVA) [2], such an off track judgment would have negative repercussions on the farmer's family, yet the entire economy of a district. In this way, we have seen a farmer's trouble about which crop to make during a particular season, as an incredibly grave one.

The need essential is to design a system that could give speedy encounters to the Indian farmers, as such helping them with settling on an informed decision about which crop to make. Considering this, we propose a system, an intelligent system that would

© Springer Nature Switzerland AG 2023
D. Garg et al. (Eds.): IACC 2022, CCIS 1781, pp. 277–289, 2023.
https://doi.org/10.1007/978-3-031-35641-4_23

analyze ordinary limits (temperature, rainfall, geographical area regarding state) and soil characteristics (pH value, soil type and upgrades center) before recommending the most sensible crop to the client.

Machine learning is a use of artificial intelligence (artificial intelligence) that attracts systems to get and make truly without being inconceivably unique by the programmer thus. The most prominent method for managing learning begins with perceptions or data, similar to models, direct data, or bearing, to look for plans in data and settle on better decisions later on considering the models that we give. The essential clarification for machine learning is to allow computers to progress subsequently and change their exercises to chip away at the accuracy and handiness of the program, with no human mediation or help. Standard relationship of activities for a PC can be portrayed as robotizing the strategies to be performed on input data to make yield old-fashioned pieces.

There are a wide degree of programming tools open to create machine learning models and to apply these models to new, covered data. There are furthermore endless clear machine learning algorithms open. These tools conventionally contain libraries completing obviously the most well-known machine learning algorithms.

A reliably developing number of experts have begun to see this issue in Indian agriculture and are effectively committing their time and endeavors to help with diminishing the issue. Different works harden the use of Regularized Greedy Forest to wrap up an appropriate crop development at a given time stamp. Another methodology proposes a model that includes certifiable records of meteorological data as training set.

Model is ready to see atmospheric circumstances that are impediment for the making of apples. It then, profitably predicts the yield of apples considering month to month weather patterns. The use of a few algorithms like Artificial Neural Network, K Nearest Neighbors, and Regularized Greedy Forest is displayed in [5] to pick a crop considering the measure yield rate, which, along these lines, is impacted by various endpoints. Additional components related with the system are pesticide measure and web trading pondering common things.

2 Problem Statement

Frustration of farmers to settle on the best crop for his space using standard and non-sensible methods is a dead troublesome issue for a country where generally half of everybody is gotten with making. Both straightforwardness and accessibility of right and cutting edge data blocks expected experts from working on arising country relevant assessments. With assets inside our show up at we have proposed a system which can conclude this issue by giving fast scraps of data on crop value and recommendations considering machine learning models coordinated thinking about essential standard and money related limits.

3 Proposed System

We to discard the actually alluded to detriments, we propose an Intelligent Crop Recommendation system-which thinks about beyond what many would consider possible in general, including temperature, rainfall, region and soil condition, to expect crop sensibility. This system is on an unquestionably urgent level stressed over filling the fundamental control of AgroConsultant, which is, giving crop recommendations to farmers algorithms.

We moreover give the advantage evaluation on crops filled in different states which gives the client an immediate and strong data to pick and plan the crops. The paper presents a solution that uses different pretrained machine learning models and traditional approaches as well and applies them on a dataset in order to provide recommender.

4 Related Work

Kumar et al. (2015) proposed a method named Crop Selection Method (CSM) to manage crop selection issue, and lift net yield speed of crop over season and in this manner achieves most extraordinary financial improvement of the country. The proposed method could additionally energize net yield speed of crops [1].

Lee et al. (2014) analyzed about the assessment and the arrangement of a reasonable country yield studying system thinking about propelling month to month environment. It is endeavoring to expect the provincial crop creation because of the peculiar environment that happens constantly and convenient nearby ordinary change considering a risky atmospheric devation. The improvement of agrarian yield finishing up system that utilization it is frantically expected to propelling environment data [2].

Doshi et al. (2015) proposed and did an intelligent crop recommendation system, which can be easily used by farmers all over India. This system would help the farmers in settling on an informed decision about which with cropping to support dependent upon a variety of customary and geographical parts. We have similarly completed an associate system, called Rainfall Predictor, which predicts the rainfall of the going with a year [6].

Ramanujam et al. (2013) proposed a recommendation system through a social event model with larger part projecting a majority rule structure method using Random tree, CHAID, K-Nearest Neighbor and Genuine Bayes as understudies to recommend a crop for the site express limits with high exactness and viability [7].

Paul et al. (2015) presented a system, which consolidates data mining methods to predict the class of the disconnected soil datasets. The class, as such expected will show the yielding of crops. The issue of expecting the crop yield is formalized as a technique rule, where Direct Bayes and K-Nearest Neighbor methods are used [8].

5 Dataset

For the system, we are using different datasets all downloaded for government site page and kaggle.

An insignificant portrayal of the datasets:

1. Yield Dataset: This dataset contains yield for 16 essential crops made across all of the states in kg per hectare. Yield of 0 shows that the crop isn't made in the specific state.
2. Cost of Cultivation dataset: This dataset gives the cost of cultivation to each crop in Rs. per hectare.
3. Assessed cost of crops: This dataset gives the standard market costs for those crops generally through a period of two months
4. Standard expense of crops: This dataset gives the steady business district cost of the crops in Rs per hectare.
5. Soil supplement content dataset: This dataset has five segments with the characteristics in the business State, Nitrogen content, Phosphorous substance, Potassium content and customary ph.
6. Rainfall Temperature dataset: This dataset contains crops, max and min rainfall, max and min temperature, max and min rainfall and ph values.

6 Machine Learning Algorithms

Machine Learning algorithms used in the recommendation system are:

Linear Regression: Linear regression is a linear method for supervising modeling the connection between a scalar response (or ward variable) and something like one sensible parts (or independent elements). Linear regression is used for finding linear relationship among target and something like one predictors. It fits a linear model with coefficients $w = (w1,..., wp)$ to restrict the holding up extent of squares between the saw natural surroundings in the dataset, and the goals expected by the linear measure. Linear regression is used for finding linear relationship among target and something like one predictors (Fig. 1).

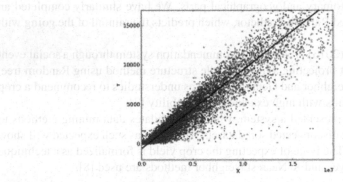

Fig. 1. Linear regression example

Logistic Regression: Logistic Regression is the veritable regression evaluation to lead when the dependent variable is dichotomous (same). The logistic model (or logit model) is used to model the probability of a particular class or event existing like pass/crash and burn with a vengeance, win/lose, alive/dead or strong/got out. This can be loose to model a few classes of events, for instance, singling out the remote possibility that an image contains a catlike, canine, lion, etc. Everything being seen in the image would be named a probability a couple of spot in the degree of 0 and 1 and the through and through adding to one.

Neural Network: Neural networks are a set of algorithms, modeled straightforwardly after the human brain, that should see plans. They decipher obvious data through a kind of machine wisdom, venturing or assembling rough data. The models they see are numerical, contained in vectors, into which each credible datum, be it pictures, sound, text or time series, ought to be deciphered. Neural networks help us pack and portray. Neural Networks are themselves general limit approximations, which is the explanation they can be applied to essentially any machine learning issue about learning a stunning preparation from the commitment to the outcome space (Fig. 2).

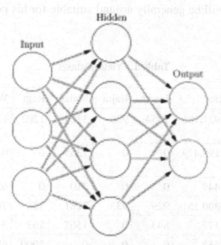

Fig. 2 Neural network example

7 System Configuration

H/W Configuration:

Processor: 2 gigahertz (GHz) or faster processor or SoC.
RAM: 6 gigabyte (GB) for 32-bit or 8 GB for 64-bit.
Hard disk space: = 16 GB.

8 Software Configuration

O.S: Windows XP/7/8/8.1/10, Linux and Mac.
Coding Language: Python.
Tools: Pandas, Numpy, Tensorflow, Keras and Sickitlearn.

9 Data Analysis

Maybe the earliest progression we perform during execution is an evaluation of the data. This was done by us trying to see the presence of any connection between the various characteristics present in the dataset.

Getting of Training Dataset: The accuracy of any machine learning algorithm depends on how much limits and the rightness of the training dataset. In this attempt destroyed extraordinary datasets assembled from Government site – https://data.gov. in/and Kaggle and meticulously picked the limits that would give the best results.

Many works done in this field have considered normal limits to expect crop sensibility some have involved yield as standard issue where as in unambiguous works fundamentally cash related parts are mulled over. We have attempted to join both regular endpoints like rainfall, temperature, ph, supplements in soil, soil type, region and money related limits like creation, and yield to give unmistakable and reliable recommendation to the farmer on which crop will be generally around suitable for his property (Tables 1, 2, 3 and 4).

Table 1. Yield Dataset

S.NO	State	Rice	Jowar	Bajra	Maize	Ragi	Wheat	Barley	Gram
1	Andhra Pradesh	2921.186	1054	906	3328	1202	1139	0	567
2	Arunachal Pradesh	1190.479	0	0	1365	0	0	160	127
3	Assam	1449	0	0	710	0	657	781	651
4	Bihar	1300.151	929	933	2281	784	789	269	120
5	Chattisgarh	1177	843	0	1567	263	345	543	908
6	Goa	2652	0	0	0	1000	689	431	120
7	Gujarat	1610	901	1152	1300	1876	123	908	983
8	Haryana	2894	296	1313	2228	996	569	678	567
9	Himachal Pradesh	1447	0	0	2251	0	908	441	431
10	Jammu & Kashmir	1960	589	571	1535	2451	0	214	239
11	Jharkhand	1413	988	1253	1465	3979	458	3680	710
12	Karnataka	2561	845	626	2654	1482	347	753	550
13	Kerala	2197	490	0	0	1543	781	174	840
14	Madhya Pradesh	862	985	1244	1525	1682	1341	349	419

(*continued*)

Table 1. (*continued*)

S.NO	State	Rice	Jowar	Bajra	Maize	Ragi	Wheat	Barley	Gram
15	Maharashtra	1594	812	695	1835	736	234	870	727
16	Manipur	2315	0	0	2495	0	891	90	631
17	Meghalaya	1692	0	0	1452	1630	479	231	871
18	Mizoram	1501	0	0	1814	1320	528	655	238
19	Nagaland	1556	1246	1269	1609	0	381	44	65
20	Orissa	1366	608	559	1412	1699	380	89	91
21	Punjab	3686	0	984	2702	0	0	901	54

Table 2. Temperature Rainfall and Nutrients dataset

1	Bajra	3	18	30	6.5	8	350	750	L	L	M
2	Banana	4	15	35	3	8.5	450	750	M	VL	VL
3	Barley	4	12	32	5.5	8	800	1100	VL	VL	M
4	Bean	2	14	32	5.5	6.5	300	500	L	VL	M
5	Black Peper	6	23	33	5	6.5	1200	2500	H	VL	M
6	Black Gram	2	23	35	6.5	7	500	750	L	VL	VL
7	Bottle Gound	2	24	27	5.5	7.5	400	650	VL	VL	VL
8	Brinjal	3	15	32	5.5	6.5	600	1000	VL	H	M
9	Cabbage	4	12	30	4.5	6.5	300	600	M	VL	H
10	Cardamon	8	18	35	5.5	7	1200	4000	H	L	M
11	Carrot	4	7	23	5	7	350	1000	M	VL	M
12	Castor	6	20	30	6	7	500	800	VL	M	VL
13	Cauliflower	4	12	30	5.5	8.5	100	300	M	H	M
14	Chilly	3	18	40	6	7	625	1500	VL	H	L
15	Coriander	3	15	30	6	7	750	1000	L	M	M
16	Cotton	4	15	35	5	8.5	500	1100	M	VL	VL
17	Cowpea	5	22	35	6	7	700	1100	VL	L	M
18	Drum Stick	4	20	30	6	7	750	2000	M	VL	VL
19	Garlic	4	10	30	5	10	500	800	VL	VL	VL
20	Ginger	8	15	35	5	8	1200	1800	VL	VL	H
21	Gram	4	20	30	6.5	7	600	900	VL	VL	H
22	Grapes	4	15	35	5	7	650	850	VL	VI	VL
23	Groundnuts	3	20	35	5	7	600	750	VL	VL	H

Table 3. Regression model training dataset

	Rainfall	Temperature	pH	Crop	Production
1	400.1508	20	3	Bajra	0.0069
2	400.1633	20	3.2	Bajra	0.00747
3	400.1639	20	3.2	Bajra	0.00749
4	400.1797	20	3.2	Bajra	0.00822
5	400.1958	20	3.2	Bajra	0.00895
6	400.2905	20	3.2	Bajra	0.01328
7	400.3887	20	3.2	Bajra	0.01777
8	400.3989	20	3.2	Bajra	0.01824
9	400.4159	20	3.2	Bajra	0.01902
10	400.4561	20	3.2	Bajra	0.02085
11	400.4604	20	3.2	Bajra	0.02105
12	400.4672	20	3.2	Bajra	0.02136
13	400.5277	20	3.2	Bajra	0.02413
14	400.542	20	3.2	Bajra	0.02478
15	400.5644	20	3.2	Bajra	0.02581
16	400.5686	20	3.2	Bajra	0.026

Table 4. Soil Nutrients distribution as per state (Nitrogen, Phosphorous, Potassium)

1	Andaman	L	VL	L	6.5
2	Andhra Pradesh	H	VH	M	6.3
3	Arunachal Pradesh	H	M	M	5.6
4	Assam	M	L	VL	6.5
5	Bihar	VL	VH	H	6
6	Goa	M	VL	M	5.4
7	Gujarat	L	VH	H	6
8	Haryana	VL	M	H	6
9	Himachal Pradesh	M	M	H	6.5
10	Jammu & Kashmir	H	M	M	6
11	Jharkhand	L	M	M	6.2
12	Kerala	H	VH	M	6.2

(continued)

Table 4. (*continued*)

1	Andaman	L	VL	L	6.5
13	Madhya Pradesh	L	M	M	6.2
14	Maharashtra	H	H	H	6
15	Manipur	M	VH	M	5.7
16	Meghalaya	L	M	L	5.9
17	Mizoram	M	M	M	5
18	Nagaland	M	M	M	5.1

10 Data Preprocessing

Happening to disengaging and envisioning the data, the going with stage is preprocessing. Data preprocessing is a colossal stage as it helps in cleaning the data and making it sensible for use in machine learning algorithms. Most of the fixation in preprocessing is to take out any eccentricities or worked up data, as well as managing any missing values. First we changed over the data into pandas all around data and from that point on conveyed codes for crops and states autonomously we than added these and made detached datasets.

The means are illustrated under.
profit data ['state'] = profit data ['state'].
as type ('categ').
prof data ['crop'] = prof data ['crop'].
as type ('categ').
st encod. csv ("data/st_no.csv", index = False).
crop encod.csv ("data/crop code.csv", index = False).
ds [col].csv ("data/encoded ds.csv", index = False, header = False).

Further to reduce how much data going into the linear regression model we separated the crops considering the crucial interminably supplements present in the soil. Enduring the improvement content of the soil was under that common by the crops, then, at that point, that crop was discarded, in this way we had the choice to decrease the training time a ton.

for row:
n_crop = con (r[8])
p_crop = con (r[9])
k_crop = con (r[1 0])

if (n_area >= n_crop and p_area >= p_crop and k_area >= k_crop);
n_mon = int (r [1])
sum = r[0]+","+str (rainfall final [n_mon − 1]) + "," + str (temp final [n_mon − 1])+","+ph + "\n" m_crops./n (total)

11 Results

For the inspirations driving this attempt we have used three surprising algorithms: Linear regression, Logistic regression and Neural network. All of the algorithms rely on coordinated learning.

Output of profit analysis (Table 5):

Table 5. Profit on crops per state

No	State	Crop	Profit
1	Andhra Pradesh	Rice	6.39E+04
2	Andhra Pradesh	Jwor	1.10E+04
3	Andhra Pradesh	Bajra	7.40E+03
4	Andhra Pradesh	Maize	3.13E+04
5	Andhra Pradesh	Ragi	5.63E+04
6	Andhra Pradesh	Wheat	1.00E+04
7	Andhra Pradesh	Barley	−1.00E+04
8	Andhra Pradesh	Gram	5.05E+04
9	Andhra Pradesh	Tur	1.00E+02
10	Andhra Pradesh	Groundnut	7.63E+03
11	Andhra Pradesh	Mustard	9.72E+03
12	Andhra Pradesh	Soyabean	1.00E+02
13	Andhra Pradesh	Sunflower	−1.00E+03
14	Andhra Pradesh	Cotton	1.60E+04
15	Andhra Pradesh	Jute	8.91E+05
16	Andhra Pradesh	Mesta	9.99E+04
17	Arunachal Pradesh	Sugarcane	−1.00E+04
18	Arunachal Pradesh	Rice	1.00E+04

In above analysis, we get the profit data for each crop developed in all the states. This presents an obvious approaching on which crop to be chosen.

Output for Crop recommender (Fig. 3, Table 6):

The Crop proposal model lists the crops in an order where the 1st crop would have the uppermost efficiency directed by the enduring in the group (Table 7).

```
pred = model.predict_proba(Choices)
df2 = pd.DataFrame (pred, columns = ["Rice", "Wheat", "Coton", "SugarCane", "Tea",
"Coffee", "Rubber", "Coconut"])
print (df2)
df2.shape
```

Table 6. Regression model output

Barley	Bottle Gourd				
−13.77759935					
−0.81033561					
−5.14828826					
−2.21432874					
−4.81342706					
−59.6094					
−2.8407					
−75.81					
0.699					
Barley	Bottle Gourd	Groundnut			
0.70479237					
Barley	Bottle Gourd	Groundnut	Jowar		
0.61912891					
Barley	Bottle Gourd	Groundnut	Jowar	Khesari	
−9.91352					
−0.2852					
−1.76					
4.1188					
Barley	Bottle Gourd	Groundnut	Jowar	Khesari	Orange
−262.25					
8.456					
Accuracy Score:	**88.2634**				

print('Recommend crop for the month of '+Numtomonth [month]+' in '+state+' is/are: \n' +final_crop)
Recommend crop for the month of May in Bihar is/are:
Potato, Bottle Groud, Orange, Barley, Jowar, Khesri

Fig. 3. Crop recommendation

Here, we notice the prophecy value of sustainability for each crop provided 3 inputs. Therefore, from these values we can get the best idea on which crop will give superior yield.

Table 7. Crop Sustainability prediction values

Rice	Wheat	Cotton	Sugarcane	Tea	Coffee	Cashew
0.495	0.2027	0.236	0.184	0.43	0.035	0.0046
Rubber	Coconut	Oil seed	Ragi	Maize	Ground nut	Millet
0.002973	0.05	0.067	0.087	0.137	0.754	0.1257
Barley						
0.043136						

12 Conclusion

The proposed method helps the farmer with picking the correct crop by giving encounters that standard farmers don't screen as needs be decreasing the normal aftereffects of crop disillusionment and growing capacity. It nearly gets them far from causing setbacks. The method can be related with the web and can be gotten to by a noteworthy number of farmers the nation over. We could receive a result of 89.88% from the neural network and an accuracy of 88.26% from the linear regression model.

Future development is to undertake the crop recommendation system with another subsystem, yield predictor that would similarly give the farmer with an extent of creation enduring the fans out the proposed crop.

References

1. Kumar, R., Singh, M.P., Kumar, P., Singh, J.P.: Crop selection method to maximize crop yield rate using machine learning technique. In: 2015 International Conference on Smart Technologies and Management for Computing, Communication, Controls, Energy and Materials (ICSTM), pp. 138–145 (2015)
2. Lee, H., Moon, A.: Development of yield prediction system based on real-time agricultural meteorological information. In: 16th International Conference on Advanced Communication Technology, pp. 1292–1295 (2014)
3. Lekhaa, T.R.: Efficient crop yield and pesticide prediction for improving agricultural economy using data mining techniques. Int. J. Modern Trends Eng. Sci. (IJMTES) 03(10), 134–139 (2016)
4. Gholap, J., Ingole, A., Gohil, J., Gargade, S., Attar, V.: Soil data analysis using classification techniques and soil attribute prediction. Int. J. Comput. Sci. Issues 9(3), 347–352 (2012)
5. Savla, A., Israni, N., Dhawan, P., Mandholia, A., Bhadada, H., Bhardwaj, S.: Survey of classification algorithms for formulating yield prediction accuracy in precision agriculture. In: 2015 International Conference on Innovations in Information, Embedded and Communication Systems (ICIIECS), pp. 1–7 (2015)
6. Doshi, Z., Nadkarni, S., Agrawal, R., Shah, N.:AgroConsultant: intelligent crop recommendation system using machine learning algorithms. In: 2018 Fourth International Conference on Computing Communication Control and Automation (ICCUBEA), pp. 1–6 (2018)

7. Pudumalar, S., Ramanujam, E., Rajashree, R.H., Kavya, C., Kiruthika, T., Nisha, J.:Crop recommendation system for precision agriculture. In: 2016 Eighth International Conference on Advanced Computing (ICoAC), pp. 32–36 (2017)
8. Savla, A., Dhawan, P., Bhadada, H., Israni, N., Mandholia, A., Bhardwaj, S.: Survey of classification algorithms for formulating yield prediction accuracy in precision agriculture. In: Innovations in Information, Embedded and Communication systems (ICIIECS) (2015)

Plant Disease Detection Using Multispectral Imaging

Malithi De Silva(✉) ⓘ and Dane Brown ⓘ

Rhodes University, Drosty Rd, Grahamstown, Makhanda 6140, South Africa
g22d5181@campus.ru.ac.za

Abstract. People worldwide are undergoing many challenges, including food scarcity. Many pieces of research are now focused on improving agriculture to increase the harvest and reduce the cost. Identifying plant diseases and pests in the early stages helps to enhance the yield and reduce costs. However, most plant disease identification research with computer vision has been done with images taken in controlled environments on publically available data sets. Near-Infrared (NIR) imaging is a favourable approach for identifying plant diseases. Therefore, this study collected NIR images of healthy and diseased leaves in the natural environment. The dataset is tested with eight Convolutional Neural Network (CNN) models with different train-test splits ranging from 10:90 to 90:10. The evaluated models attained their highest training and test accuracies from the 70:30 split onwards. Xception outperformed all the other models in all train-test splits and achieved 100% accuracy, precision and recall in the 80:20 train-test split.

Keywords: Plant Diseases · Image Classification · Near Infrared Imaging · Disease Identification

1 Introduction

Food scarcity and global hunger are among world-leading problems today. Due to radical growth in the world's population, gradual rising income levels in developing countries, global warming and other environmental hazards, the food industry has been unable to control the demand-supply chain. Hence, increasing harvest production using existing and new agricultural trends is a primary concern to mitigate the above issues. Soil monitoring, pest and disease monitoring, and fertilizer management are among the topics of smart farming that direct towards the growth in the harvest. These topics heavily rely on Computer Vision. Out of the smart farming topics, early identification of plant diseases and pests boosts

This work is carried out with the support of the Organization for Women in Science for the Developing World (OWSD) and the Swedish International Development Cooperation Agency (Sida). This work was undertaken in the Distributed Multimedia CoE at Rhodes University.

© Springer Nature Switzerland AG 2023
D. Garg et al. (Eds.): IACC 2022, CCIS 1781, pp. 290–308, 2023.
https://doi.org/10.1007/978-3-031-35641-4_24

the harvest and reduces the cost of fertilizers, fungicides, and pesticides. Therefore, computer vision techniques can use to identify plant diseases at their early stages as it plays a crucial role.

Hence, this research uses NIR images with multiple deep learning models to identify plant diseases. NIR is part of the infrared band of the electromagnetic spectrum ranging from the wavelength of 780 nm to 2500 nm [22]. This wavelength includes frequencies beyond the human's visible range and provides beneficial unseen information to supplement the wavelength of human eyes.

Deep learning plays a significant role in computer vision. Therefore, multiple CNN models were tested with the gathered NIR images to determine which models performed well in identifying plant diseases in the natural environment.

Several studies identify plant diseases using different spectral images [19]. The majority of the works are based on Visible RGB images. Research works performed with thermal or hyperspectral images were performed in laboratory conditions. Therefore, those research works can be improved to represent real-world data with non-trivial environmental conditions and natural backgrounds. Further, some research used manual disease classification, which is labour-intensive and expensive.

The contributions of this work are mentioned as follows,

- A new NIR dataset of ten agricultural plants was collected in realistic environmental conditions.
- Identified plant diseases using NIR images with state-of-the-art CNN classification models.
- Eight popular deep-learning models were trained and tested to identify the best-performing CNN architecture on the NIR dataset.
- Different train-test splits ranging from 10:90 to 90:10 were tested to find the best train-test split for the data set.
- The performance of each architecture was compared by analyzing the model's overall training, testing accuracies, precision and recall.

The rest of the paper is organized as follows. Section 2 reviews related work, and Sect. 3 explains the detailed methodology used. Section 4 describes the experiments and results, and finally, Sect. 5 concludes with future work.

2 Related Work

The precision of plant disease identification is largely based on the way image data were collected. Many studies attempt to determine which imaging techniques are appropriate for high classification accuracy of plant diseases. Among popular imaging techniques, hyperspectral imaging is becoming prevalent in agriculture [12] as it contains useful details that are not available in the visible spectrum range [22] as shown in Fig. 1.

Singh et al. [19] published a review paper based on the literature available for image capturing techniques used for plant disease identification. Magnetic Resonance Imaging, Photoacoustic Imaging, Tomography, Thermography, Multispectral Imaging, and Thermal Imaging are some image capturing methods discussed

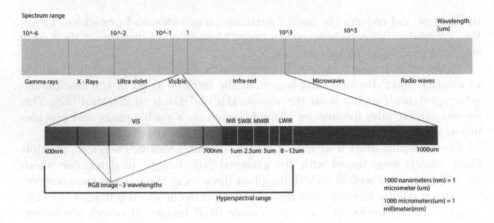

Fig. 1. Hyperspectral range in electromagnetic spectrum [11]

in this paper. The paper examined the current trends and challenges in detecting plant disease using computer vision and advanced imaging techniques. They further stated the importance of integrating advanced imaging techniques and computer vision algorithms to identify plant diseases better. Moreover, this work mentioned the need for further research on different variations in surrounding conditions and Expert Systems for plant disease detection. The review showed that the majority of research focuses on plant disease identification using thermal and hyperspectral image-capturing techniques.

The study was done by Saleem et al. [16] also showed that hyperspectral imaging technology is favoured in disease identification research and that Deep Learning can be effective means for plant disease detection.

Lowe et al. [11] and Pineda et al. [15]reviewed articles on plant stress identification using hyperspectral images in 2017 and 2021, respectively. Both discussed the positives and the limitations of hyperspectral imaging technology, especially when gathering outside images with sunlight, illumination, shadows, and reflection. Some plants do not visibly indicate stress for some time and during drought periods. However, the potential yield and quality of the crop may decline as plant development is affected. They concluded that hyperspectral imaging technology could be used for early plant stress detection before human observation and that proper water management and other necessary precautions are key to saving and maintaining plants.

A technical study was conducted by Bauriegel et al. [2] to identify Wheat plant Fusarium infections using a hyperspectral imaging mechanism. This study categorized healthy and unhealthy plant areas with Principal Component Analysis (PCA) by analyzing wavelengths. Experimental Wheat plants were grown under laboratory conditions, and they concluded that this visualization algorithm is ineffective outdoors as direct sunlight affects the wavelengths.

In 2021, Nguyen et al. [13] combined hyperspectral imaging with deep learning to identify grapevine vein-clearing virus (GVCV) . This research was conducted at the University of Missouri South Farm Research Center, Columbia, and during the data collection stage, average temperature and precipitation were near-constant. Data were collected in four cycles and two categories, healthy and GVCV-Infected Vines. However, this research was conducted with minimal data, i.e., 40 hyperspectral images comprising 20 healthy and 20 infected vines.

Yang et al. [24] has conducted a study to detect rice blast disease using hyperspectral imaging with PCA. This research used two hundred rice seedlings under laboratory conditions. The results showed that the changes in spectral characteristics extracted from the full spectrum of 950 to 1650 nm nm caused by rice blast disease could be represented with the first 5 principal components score images with 92% accuracy.

Other than hyperspectral imaging technology, another popular technology for plant disease detection is thermal imaging technology. The human eye can only capture specific limited light ranges. This limitation can be overcome by infrared and thermal imaging technology. Every living creature, including plants, emits heat that can be captured using thermal technology, and this valuable information can be used in identifying abnormal conditions [6].

In 2016, Buitrago et al. [3] investigated the effect of plant stress on the spectral properties in the thermal part of the electromagnetic spectrum using two plant types. They measured the Leaf Water Content (LWC) and cuticle thickness of plants to see any connection to the changes in the spectral properties. The experiment was conducted considering eight samples per leaf, and 520 scans per sample. These measurements were averaged per leaf. Five leaves per plant were measured in the same way for 75 leaves for the experiment. When exposed to water or temperature stress, the results demonstrated that both species showed notable differences in their Thermal Infrared (TIR) spectra. The TIR spectrum change is identical within a species and varies between species. TIR spectral modifications have a relationship with the microstructure and biochemistry of leaves. The authors proposed a detailed assessment of cuticle change to investigate the effect of microstructure on TIR spectra.

In 2019, research was done by Yang et al. [23] using TIR images to detect tea disease areas in a field. They used image processing techniques on thermal images and manually selected infected areas using them. The results were then verified with an expert observation which showed a regression analysis value of 0.97. This approach is very labour-intensive and requires the physical presence of experts for evaluation.

Awad et al. [1] have made an early identification of disease using TIR images of wheat. They artificially infected the wheat leaves with a fungus for experimental purposes under greenhouse conditions. Subsequently, the temperature difference was monitored in healthy and infected leaves under different states. The disease symptoms were observed with a laboratory test five days after the infection, and its severity increased up to 30.9% in 21 days after infection. However, with thermal imaging, they observed the temperature difference of leaves hours after infection.

The TIR imaging technology was used to identify Scab disease in apple plants by Oerke et al. [14]. Changes in temperature and maximum temperature difference of apple plant leaves were monitored and calculated periodically. It noted that increments of maximum temperature difference strongly correlate with the infected locations and the disease severity. Thermographically, the first indication of disease was identified six days after incubation, and it showed visible symptoms only after eight days of incubation.

Zhu et al. [25] produced a system to identify tomato mosaic disease and wheat leaf rust using TIR imaging technology. The temperature information of the two crops was regularly observed during the incubation period. The study has concluded that detecting disease earlier than the naked eye is possible. For tomato mosaic disease and wheat leaf rust, early identification was made by five days and seven days, respectively, before showing any visible symptoms of diseases.

In 2022 **De Silva** and **Brown** [5] conducted a research work on visible and NIR plant images in natural environment. Four CNN models were used, and the accuracies of the two datasets were compared. They concluded that the visible dataset performed marginally better with the tested CNNs but that the performance on the NIR dataset can be improved with more complex CNN models using different train-test splits.

All the above works found that using hyperspectral and thermal imaging technologies for classifying plant diseases have much room for improvement with deep learning. Most of the above-mentioned literature was conducted in controlled environmental conditions. Thermal imaging technology showed promising results when identifying diseases before plants show physical symptoms in laboratory conditions.

3   Methodology

The process followed in this work is shown in Fig. 2. Each step is described in the succeeding subsections.

3.1   Data Collection

The dataset contained twenty target classes of ten plants of the farmable crops, as shown in Table 1.

The NIR images were captured using a Canon EOS 800D with a removed internal visible wavelength filter. Kolari Vision K850 external NIR filter was used for data gathering, allowing NIR wavelengths of 850–1000 nm to reach the camera's sensor. The NIR images were taken to reflect real-world data with complex backgrounds and a series of images of various plant species. Figure 3 shows sample NIR images of healthy and diseased leaves taken in natural environmental conditions. During image capturing, sunlight is the light source utilized in the field. As per the availability of plants and healthy and diseased leaves, the number of samples for each species is different, as shown in Table 1. It is rare

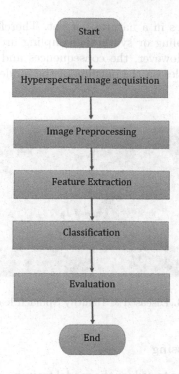

Fig. 2. Methodology

Table 1. Dataset distribution

Species	Healthy	Diseased
Borage	58	71
Kale	59	77
Lemon	79	79
Nasturtium	43	75
Peach	75	19
Potato	30	216
Pumpkin	39	67
Spinach	61	99
Sunflower	47	41
Tomato	53	80

to have equal sample sizes in a natural dataset. Therefore, techniques such as undersampling, oversampling or synthetic sampling are not used in this work to balance the classes. However, the consequences and impact of the ratio of healthy to diseased samples on the outputs of the models are mentioned where appropriate.

Fig. 3. Diseased & Healthy Spinach leaves

3.2   Image Preprocessing

Image pre-processing helps to reduce the model training and validation time. The NIR image dataset was initially resized to 256×384. However, the proposed system evaluates eight CNN models with different input dimensions. AlexNet model input expects 227×227 images and VGG 19, Resnet50V2, Densnet121 and MobileNetV2 use 224×224 images. InceptionResnet, Inceptionv3 and Xception models use 299×299 dimension input images.Therefore, all the images are resized and centre-cropped to accommodate multiple CNN models.

Some classes contain a small number of samples. Hence, data augmentation is vital to improve the model's generalization ability and prevent over-fitting of the network caused by inadequate training data. Data augmentation is thus only performed on training data, and it includes horizontal and vertical random flipping, random rotation within the range of [0,45] degrees, horizontal and vertical random shift and random zoom within the range of 20%.

3.3   Feature Extraction and Classification

CNN models can support both feature extraction and classification, as shown in Fig. 4. Eight popular CNN architectures were considered for this work, namely AlexNet, Xception VGG19, DenseNet121, Resnet50V2, MobilenetV2, and InceptionV3, InceptionResnet. The architecture for the final model was selected by analysing literature and comparing each architecture's ability on multiclass plant disease identification problems.

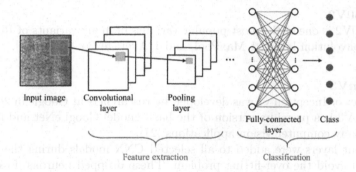

Fig. 4. CNN feature extraction and classification [10]

AlexNet
AlexNet won the ImageNet Large Scale Visual Recognition Challenge (ILSVRC) in 2012 [9]. It has been shown to impact image recognition and classification tasks significantly, and it is the most used CNN model in plant disease identification literature [16]. Hence, AlexNet is implemented in this research to check the model's performance with NIR plant images in natural environment images.

Xception
Xception is a 71-layer deep convolutional neural network architecture that applies Depthwise Separable Convolutions [4].

VGG19
VGG stands for Visual Geometry Group, and this variant has 19 convolution layers. VGG19 pre-trained model has trained with a wide variety of images. Hence, it can be used for different image classification tasks [18].

DenseNet121
A DenseNet is a CNN that uses dense connections between layers via Dense Blocks. It connects all layers with matching feature-map sizes directly with each other [8]. Moreover, each layer accepts additional inputs from all prior layers and passes its feature maps to all succeeding layers.

MobileNetV2
MobileNet is a lightweight, faster CNN model [7]. It contains a new depthwise separable convolution layer, causing the model to be light and faster.

Inception-ResNetV2
Inception-ResNetV2 is a CNN model based on the Inception family of architectures that integrate residual connections. These residual connections improve the accuracy and increase the original Inception model's convergence speed [20].

ResNet50V2

ResNet-50V2 is one of the most popular variants of many variants of ResNet. It has 48 Convolution layers, 1 MaxPool, and 1 Average Pool layer [17].

InceptionV3

GoogLeNet or Inception v1 was developed by researchers at Google in 2014. The inception V3 is a premium version of the basic model GoogLeNet and is widely used in many computer vision applications [21].

Dropout layers were added to all selected CNN models during the training process to avoid the over-fitting problem. These dropped neurons do not contribute to the forward or back propagation during the training phase, reducing the over-fitting of the model. Moreover,hyper-parameters were tuned to find the best set. The input data was provided to the various pre-trained networks, and different combinations of hyper-parameters were tested. Batch size, number of epochs, steps, and learning rate are some of the tuned hyper-parameters.

This paper used 32 batch size with Adam optimizer during the training procedure. The initial learning rate of 1e−04 (beta 1 = 0.9, beta 2 = 0.999 and epsilon = 1e−07) and 300 epochs were used with early stopping, monitoring the validation accuracy and restoring best weights.

3.4 Evaluation

The dataset is split into two partitions, train, and test sets, with different ratios starting from a minimum split of 10:90 up to maximum train and test split of 90:10.

Training data is used to train the model, and testing data is used to evaluate the trained model. Different train-test splits ratios were used to identify the most appropriate split for the NIR dataset other than the standard 80:20 train-test split. The performance of the models was mainly calculated using accuracy. Accuracy is the most reflexive measurement of the performance of models. It defines the ratio of corrected observations to the total observations.

$$Accuracy = \frac{\text{number of correct classifications}}{\text{total number of classifications attempted}}$$

Furthermore, precision and recall for each class are calculated. Precision measures the correctness of all positive classifications per class, whereas True positive refers to correct classifications.

$$Precision = \frac{\text{True Positives}}{\text{True Positives} + \text{False Positives}}$$

The recall metric counts how many classifications of a particular class were found out of all the samples for that class again. True positive refers to correct classifications, and negative refers to incorrect classifications.

$$Recall = \frac{\text{True Positives}}{\text{True Positives} + \text{False Negatives}}$$

4   Results

This study used multiple CNN models for classification, and thus, respective results obtained on different train-test splits are as follows.

In the first split, 10% of the data set was selected for training, and the remaining 90% was used for testing. According to the results shown in Table 2, DenseNet121, MobileNetV2, and VGG19 have inadequate training and test accuracies. All three classifiers suffer underfitting as they were stuck in local minima, possibly due to low starting weights. The remaining models achieved training and test accuracies of around 90% and 70%, respectively, on limited training data. This is a promising result especially given the difficulty in obtaining and lack of NIR data.

Table 2. Performance of different models on NIR images with minimum (10:90) train-test split.

Model	Training		Testing	
	Loss	Accuracy	Loss	Accuracy
AlexNet	0.9485	89.41%	1.1599	71.12%
Xception	0.0029	100.00%	0.5087	87.17%
VGG19	1.6392	50.75%	2.7883	21.78%
DenseNet121	3.1649	12.87%	2.9037	17.71%
MobileNetV2	2.9704	15.84%	2.9739	15.18%
Inception-ResNetV2	0.3179	98.56%	0.9693	70.33%
ResNet50V2	0.1665	94.06%	1.1729	73.47%
InceptionV3	0.2116	95.05%	0.9005	74.35%

In this division, the highest performing classifier is Xception, and the confusion matrix for the Xception model is shown in Fig. 5. It is also apparent that all the classes have misclassifications except Peach Diseased. The Potato Diseased type has the most misclassifications. This can be attributed to a large number of diverse samples in the Potato Diseased class, and thus, the limited training is data not enough to represent all unseen diseases and complex backgrounds.

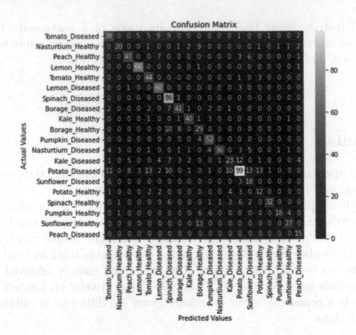

Fig. 5. Confusion matrix of Xception model for minimum (10:90) train-test split.

The training sample percentage continued to increase during this work while decreasing the test sample percentage. Figure 6, shows that during the process, training and testing accuracies gradually increase for most models from the minimum train-test split. In the 30:70 train-test split, a significant increase in test accuracy is observed for VGG19, DenseNet121 and MobileNetV2 models, which substantially benefit from more training data. The highest spike is indicated by DenseNet121, which gradually improves its accuracy until the maximum train-test split. This may be caused by the layer propagation in DenseNet121, which is more efficient assuming sufficient training data.

For the 70:30 split, all the training accuracies were above 80%, and all the models except VGG19 (67.65%) and MobileNetV2 (74.15%) achieved greater than 80% test accuracy at this split. Table 3 shows the superior performance of the Xception model with 100% training and 98.27% test accuracy.

According to the confusion matrix of the Xception model as illustrated in Fig. 7, the misclassifications are a healthy Kale sample classified as a diseased Kale leaf and a diseased Sunflower leaf classified as a diseased Potato leaf.

Xception again yields the highest accuracy while VGG19 underperformed with the lowest accuracy of 67.65%. Figure 6 shows that AlexNet, Inception-ResNetV2 and InceptionV3 achieve higher training and test accuracies on 70:30

train-test split than all the other splits. Moreover, DenseNet121, Inception-ResNetV2 and InceptionV3 models produced similar testing accuracies ranging from 88.64% to 90.62%.

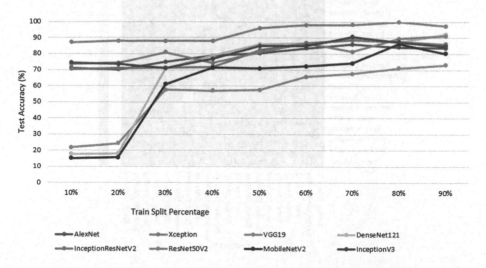

Fig. 6. Model test accuracy for different train-test splits.

Table 3. Performance of different models on NIR images with 70:30 train-test split.

Model	Training		Testing	
	Loss	Accuracy	Loss	Accuracy
AlexNet	0.5633	95.39%	0.6664	85.93%
Xception	0.0028	100.00%	0.1095	98.27%
VGG19	0.5723	80.08%	1.0087	67.65%
DenseNet121	0.4027	91.86%	0.3490	89.40%
MobileNetV2	0.6826	89.08%	0.8085	74.15%
Inception-ResNetV2	0.1826	94.70%	0.3943	88.64%
ResNet50V2	0.5569	83.70%	0.5302	81.44%
InceptionV3	0.2085	94.49%	0.2872	90.62%

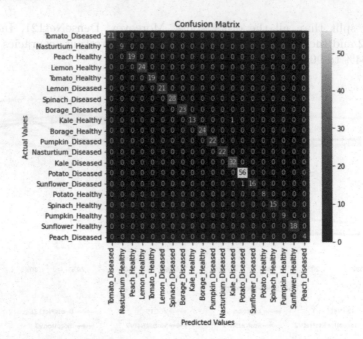

Fig. 7. Confusion matrix of Xception model for 70:30 train-test split.

Regarding the training and test accuracy gap, MobileNetV2 showed 89.08% training accuracy, and it performed with 74.15% test accuracy with a difference of nearly 15%, followed by VGG19 with a 12.5% gap for 70:30 split.

In the precision and recall tables of healthy and diseased plants, the top results are emphasised in grey, and the lowest results are highlighted in blue. Concerning the precision and recall values of 70:30 split in Table 4 and 5, most CNN models showed high precision and recall in classifying Lemon healthy and Lemon diseased leaves. Table 1 shows that the Lemon diseased and healthy leaves have balanced data. That may be one of the reasons for the similarly high precision and recall. Potato marked the lowest precision and recall for the healthy class and Kale for the disease class. Moreover, the Xception model obtained the highest precision and recall, outperforming all the other models, while VGG19 performed poorly in both healthy and diseased plants.

In the standard train-test split, 80% of the data is allocated for training and 20% assigned for testing. According to Fig. 6, Xception and MobileNetV2 performed better than all the train-test splits for both train and test accuracies in this split.

Moreover, similar to other splits, in this split also, the Xception model exceeded all the other models with 100% training and test accuracy. The confusion matrix for the Xception model in the Fig. 8 clearly showed its ability to accurately classify the NIR plant disease dataset (Table 6).

Table 4. Precision vs Recall of healthy plants in 70:30 train-test split.

Species	AlexNet		Xception		VGG19		DenseNet121		MobileNet V2		Incp-ResV2		ResNet-50V2		Inception-v3	
	Precision	Recall	Precision	Recall	Precision	Recall	Precision	Recall	Precision	Recall	Precision	Recall	Precision	Recall	Precision	Recall
Borage	70%	100%	100%	100%	68%	81%	100%	100%	100%	73%	90%	95%	95%	95%	100%	94%
Kale	85%	100%	93%	100%	84%	73%	87%	81%	100%	100%	84%	100%	79%	95%	80%	75%
Lemon	96%	100%	100%	100%	91%	100%	97%	97%	100%	100%	96%	100%	97%	100%	97%	91%
Nasturtium	60%	100%	100%	100%	53%	50%	80%	80%	830%	80%	100%	89%	85%	100%	80%	80%
Peach	95%	81%	100%	100%	75%	92%	87%	100%	82%	73%	95%	91%	97%	100%	78%	90%
Potato	62%	71%	100%	100%	50%	86%	84%	100%	83%	75%	78%	73%	75%	100%	45%	100%
Pumpkin	100%	81%	100%	100%	38%	86%	100%	100%	75%	80%	100%	90%	65%	69%	33%	50%
Spinach	92%	92%	100%	100%	82%	88%	91%	100%	67%	890%	84%	100%	94%	94%	82%	82%
Sunflower	82%	75%	100%	100%	69%	56%	100%	83%	83%	70%	100%	67%	100%	100%	100%	100%
Tomato	76%	100%	100%	100%	71%	77%	100%	84%	100%	100%	75%	100%	96%	100%	96%	94%

Table 5. Precision vs Recall of diseased plants on NIR images in 70:30 train-test split.

Species	AlexNet		Xception		VGG19		DenseNet121		MobileNet V2		Incp-ResV2		ResNet-50V2		Inception-v3	
	Precision	Recall	Precision	Recall	Precision	Recall	Precision	Recall	Precision	Recall	Precision	Recall	Precision	Recall	Precision	Recall
Borage	52%	92%	100%	100%	68%	65%	100%	96%	70%	87%	85%	89%	97%	97%	92%	88%
Kale	83%	83%	100%	97%	45%	41%	90%	84%	83%	73%	79%	66%	90%	90%	59%	68%
Lemon	100%	96%	100%	100%	90%	89%	100%	100%	100%	100%	100%	100%	100%	100%	94%	100%
Nasturtium	100%	54%	100%	100%	65%	92%	91%	91%	78%	83%	83%	90%	93%	93%	95%	81%
Peach	100%	84%	100%	100%	50%	60%	100%	83%	100%	100%	100%	75%	100%	100%	80%	57%
Potato	69%	81%	100%	98%	83%	75%	95%	86%	92%	81%	88%	79%	95%	87%	88%	72%
Pumpkin	94%	94%	100%	100%	80%	48%	93%	87%	100%	81%	95%	100%	92%	81%	86%	80%
Spinach	83%	100%	100%	100%	33%	56%	93%	97%	100%	100%	96%	96%	100%	97%	90%	96%
Sunflower	100%	73%	94%	100%	50%	67%	60%	86%	60%	100%	87%	76%	83%	88%	50%	83%
Tomato	80%	79%	100%	100%	59%	59%	87%	87%	90%	83%	81%	76%	91%	83%	70%	88%

Table 6. Performance of different models on NIR images with standard (80:20) train-test split.

Model	Training		Testing	
	Loss	Accuracy	Loss	Accuracy
AlexNet	0.0926	91.04%	0.4321	84.20%
Xception	0.0016	100.00%	0.0081	100.00%
VGG19	0.4539	80.25%	0.5231	71.11%
DenseNet121	0.0712	90.56%	0.0978	87.40%
MobileNetV2	0.0626	90.80%	0.2521	86.44%
Inception-ResNetV2	0.0830	92.50%	0.2069	87.65%
ResNet50V2	0.0539	90.12%	0.1352	89.63%
InceptionV3	0.0912	88.56%	0.1781	87.41%

Besides the Xception model for highest and VGG19 model for lowest training and test accuracies in 80:20 split, all the other models showed more or less similar results. Training accuracies varied from 88.56%–91.04%, and test accuracies varied in the range of 84.20%–89.63%.

DenseNet121, MobileNetV2, and ResNet50V2 models produced approximately 90% training accuracy with an insignificant difference. Almost similar testing accuracy of 87.5% was obtained for DenseNet121, Inception-ResNetV2 and InceptionV3.

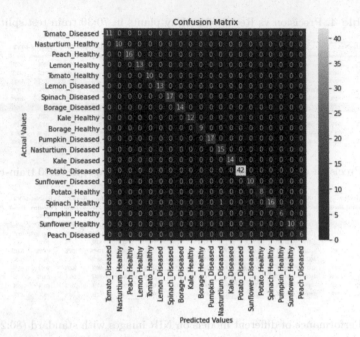

Fig. 8. Confusion matrix of Xception model for 80:20 train-test split.

Table 7. Precision vs Recall of Healthy Plants in 80:20 train-test split.

Species	AlexNet		Xception		VGG19		DenseNet121		MobileNet V2		Incp-ResV2		ResNet-50V2		Inception-v3	
	Precision	Recall	Precision	Recall	Precision	Recall	Precision	Recall	Precision	Recall	Precision	Recall	Precision	Recall	Precision	Recall
Borage	75%	100%	100%	100%	100%	67%	75%	100%	100%	73%	91%	100%	100%	86%	100%	100%
Kale	75%	100%	100%	100%	25%	100%	100%	100%	100%	100%	100%	100%	100%	100%	75%	100%
Lemon	100%	100%	100%	100%	100%	83%	100%	90%	100%	100%	80%	100%	100%	100%	100%	90%
Nasturtium	33%	100%	100%	100%	36%	75%	67%	100%	82%	100%	88%	73%	100%	82%	100%	86%
Peach	88%	100%	100%	100%	78%	75%	75%	86%	100%	89%	100%	100%	100%	100%	100%	89%
Potato	73%	100%	100%	100%	83%	100%	86%	100%	83%	75%	100%	80%	75%	75%	100%	100%
Pumpkin	80%	100%	100%	100%	75%	82%	100%	80%	75%	100%	100%	100%	75%	100%	100%	100%
Spinach	67%	100%	100%	100%	67%	100%	67%	100%	67%	100%	67%	100%	56%	100%	100%	100%
Sunflower	100%	83%	100%	100%	100%	71%	100%	100%	100%	100%	100%	67%	100%	100%	100%	100%
Tomato	100%	100%	100%	100%	100%	100%	73%	89%	100%	100%	100%	100%	100%	100%	100%	100%

Table 8. Precision vs Recall of Diseased Plants on NIR images in 80:20 train-test split.

Species	AlexNet		Xception		VGG19		DenseNet121		MobileNet V2		Incp-ResV2		ResNet-50V2		Inception-v3	
	Precision	Recall	Precision	Recall	Precision	Recall	Precision	Recall	Precision	Recall	Precision	Recall	Precision	Recall	Precision	Recall
Borage	60%	100%	100%	100%	100%	71%	100%	83%	100%	100%	88%	88%	100%	100%	73%	100%
Kale	83%	62%	100%	100%	67%	57%	100%	56%	83%	73%	91%	77%	83%	71%	50%	50%
Lemon	100%	100%	100%	100%	100%	100%	100%	100%	100%	100%	100%	100%	100%	100%	100%	90%
Nasturtium	100%	100%	100%	100%	50%	75%	80%	67%	100%	83%	100%	100%	100%	83%	67%	100%
Peach	100%	100%	100%	100%	100%	100%	100%	90%	100%	100%	100%	67%	100%	100%	100%	73%
Potato	78%	74%	100%	100%	75%	73%	86%	100%	100%	81%	94%	88%	100%	81%	91%	83%
Pumpkin	100%	67%	100%	100%	67%	44%	89%	100%	100%	81%	100%	100%	100%	81%	100%	100%
Spinach	67%	100%	100%	100%	66%	55%	100%	100%	100%	100%	85%	100%	100%	100%	100%	100%
Sunflower	100%	83%	100%	100%	67%	75%	100%	100%	60%	100%	50%	88%	60%	100%	100%	100%
Tomato	45%	83%	100%	100%	38%	57%	73%	89%	100%	100%	91%	91%	100%	100%	73%	83%

Concerning the precision and recall values as per Table 7 and Table 8, healthy plant leaves were classified with higher precision and recall than diseased plant leaves during the standard train-test split. Of the healthy category, the majority of the CNN models precisely identified and showed the highest correctly classified positive samples of the Tomato class and the lowest with the Nasturtium class. Regarding the diseased category, Lemon plants showed the highest precision and recall, whereas Kale marked the lowest. Similar to the 70:30 train-test split, the 80:20 separation also the Xception model obtained the highest precision and recall for both healthy and diseased plants, surpassing all the other models, and the VGG19 model gained the lowest.

90:10 train and test is the highest training data split evaluated in this work. Like the other partitions, Xception produced the highest train and test accuracy, as shown in Table 9.

Table 9. Performance of different models on NIR images with maximum (90:10) train-test split.

Model	Training		Testing	
	Loss	Accuracy	Loss	Accuracy
AlexNet	0.4828	96.95%	0.6442	83.70%
Xception	0.0064	99.88%	0.1103	97.41%
VGG19	0.5129	81.58%	0.8984	73.04%
DenseNet121	0.2203	94.31%	0.2799	92.22%
MobileNetV2	0.8226	87.80%	0.7095	80.15%
Inception-ResNetV2	0.2505	91.94%	0.4063	86.11%
ResNet50V2	0.1620	94.23%	0.5174	91.11%
InceptionV3	0.5581	85.15%	0.6004	84.81%

The Xception model started with 87.74% test accuracy in the 10:90 split, gradually improved accuracy and reached its highest point in the 80:20 split with 100% showing the lowest gap around 13% between the minimum and maximum accuracies. Similarly, AlexNet, InceptionResNetV2, ResNet50V2, and InceptionV3 initiated with higher accuracy (above 70%) in the 10:90 division and topped in the 70:30 split marking the gap between maximum and minimum test accuracies below 18%. Therefore, the above models appear to have satisfactory accuracy with minimum data requirements.

In contrast, the DenseNet121 model showed 17.71% in the minimum split and topped with 92.22% in the maximum division, with an interval of 74.51%. Like the DenseNet121, VGG19 and MobileNetV2 started with the insufficient test accuracy and indicated gaps for their maximum test accuracy with 51.26% and 71.26%, respectively. These three models clearly showcase their dependency on adequate training data for higher results.

On the whole, the evaluated eight CNN models marked their highest training and test accuracies from the 70:30 train-test split onwards. AlexNet, Inception-ResNetV2, and InceptionV3 scored the top test accuracy in 70:30 division. Xception and MobileNetV2 achieved their best test accuracy in the 80:20 split, and the rest of the models (VGG19, DenseNet121, ResNet50V2) gained the highest test accuracy in 90:10 separation, suggesting greater data dependence.

5   Conclusion

Most previous research worked on openly available data sets, such as the Plant Village dataset, Mendeley dataset, or data collected in controlled environments. Therefore, this study introduced a natural environment image dataset for future researchers.

Furthermore, as per the literature, AlexNet is the most commonly selected deep learning model for plant disease detection research despite its age. Hence, this study experimented with seven different CNN models other than AlexNet and compared their results. In the standard train-test split, all the models achieved around 90% training accuracy except VGG19, which showed the lowest training accuracy of 80.25%.

Training and test accuracies increased for most models, from the minimum training data (10:90) to 70:30. However, increasing it to 80:20, AlexNet, InceptionResNetV2, and InceptionV3 dropped in accuracy while the rest of the models improved.

This research identified plant diseases using NIR images. Xception was the top-performing classifier for all splits, whilst VGG19 was the worst-performing classifier for most of the splits.

Evaluating the diseased category, in both 70:30 and 80:20 splits, the highest precision and recall were obtained for the Lemon diseased plants. Top precision and recall were obtained for Lemon in the 70:30 split and Tomato in the 80:20 split in the healthy category.

In future, this work can be extended by keeping a constant number of samples per species using different techniques and observing whether sample balance affects the outcome. Moreover, there is an excellent potential for future research to focus on identifying the diseases in the early stages of the plants before showing any visible symptoms to the naked eye. This research direction can allow the disposal of unrecoverable plants early without allocating further costs for replacements of nearby susceptible healthy plants or treatments and other nutrition.

References

1. Awad, Y.M., Abdullah, A.A., Bayoumi, T.Y., Abd-Elsalam, K., Hassanien, A.E.: Early detection of powdery mildew disease in wheat triticum aestivum l. using thermal imaging technique. In: Filev, D., et al. (eds.) Intelligent Systems'2014. AISC, vol. 323, pp. 755–765. Springer, Cham (2015). https://doi.org/10.1007/978-3-319-11310-4_66
2. Bauriegel, E., Giebel, A., Geyer, M., Schmidt, U., Herppich, W.: Early detection of fusarium infection in wheat using hyper-spectral imaging. Comput. Electron. Agric. **75**(2), 304–312 (2011)

3. Buitrago, M.F., Groen, T.A., Hecker, C.A., Skidmore, A.K.: Changes in thermal infrared spectra of plants caused by temperature and water stress. ISPRS J. Photogramm. Remote. Sens. **111**, 22–31 (2016)
4. Chollet, F.: Xception: deep learning with depthwise separable convolutions. In: Proceedings of the IEEE Conference on Computer Vision and Pattern Recognition, pp. 1251–1258 (2017)
5. De Silva, M., Brown, D.: Plant disease detection using deep learning on natural environment images. In: 2022 International Conference on Artificial Intelligence, Big Data, Computing and Data Communication Systems (icABCD), pp. 1–5 (2022). https://doi.org/10.1109/icABCD54961.2022.9855925
6. Hashim, I., Shariff, A., Bejo, S., Muharam, F., Ahmad, K., Hashim, H.: Application of thermal imaging for plant disease detection. In: IOP Conference Series: Earth and Environmental Science, vol. 540,1, p. 012052. IOP Publishing (2020)
7. Howard, A.G., et al.: Mobilenets: efficient convolutional neural networks for mobile vision applications. arXiv preprint arXiv:1704.04861 (2017)
8. Huang, G., Liu, Z., Van Der Maaten, L., Weinberger, K.Q.: Densely connected convolutional networks. In: Proceedings of the IEEE Conference on Computer Vision and Pattern Recognition, pp. 4700–4708 (2017)
9. Krizhevsky, A., Sutskever, I., Hinton, G.E.: Imagenet classification with deep convolutional neural networks. In: Advance in Neural Information Processing System, vol. 25, pp. 1097–1105 (2012)
10. Lee, S.Y., Tama, B.A., Moon, S.J., Lee, S.: Steel surface defect diagnostics using deep convolutional neural network and class activation map. Appl. Sci. **9**(24), 5449 (2019)
11. Lowe, A., Harrison, N., French, A.P.: Hyperspectral image analysis techniques for the detection and classification of the early onset of plant disease and stress. Plant Methods **13**(1), 1–12 (2017)
12. Lu, B., Dao, P.D., Liu, J., He, Y., Shang, J.: Recent advances of hyperspectral imaging technology and applications in agriculture. Remote Sens. **12**(16), 2659 (2020)
13. Nguyen, C., Sagan, V., Maimaitiyiming, M., Maimaitijiang, M., Bhadra, S., Kwasniewski, M.T.: Early detection of plant viral disease using hyperspectral imaging and deep learning. Sensors **21**(3), 742 (2021)
14. Oerke, E.C., Fröhling, P., Steiner, U.: Thermographic assessment of scab disease on apple leaves. Precis. Agric. **12**(5), 699–715 (2011)
15. Pineda, M., Barón, M., Pérez-Bueno, M.L.: Thermal imaging for plant stress detection and phenotyping. Remote Sens. **13**(1), 68 (2021)
16. Saleem, M.H., Potgieter, J., Arif, K.M.: Plant disease detection and classification by deep learning. Plants **8**(11), 468 (2019)
17. Sarwinda, D., Paradisa, R.H., Bustamam, A., Anggia, P.: Deep learning in image classification using residual network (ResNet) variants for detection of colorectal cancer. Procedia Comput. Sci. **179**, 423–431 (2021)
18. Simonyan, K., Zisserman, A.: Very deep convolutional networks for large-scale image recognition. arXiv preprint arXiv:1409.1556 (2014)
19. Singh, V., Sharma, N., Singh, S.: A review of imaging techniques for plant disease detection. Artif. Intell. Agric. **4**, 229–242 (2020)
20. Szegedy, C., Ioffe, S., Vanhoucke, V., Alemi, A.A.: Inception-v4, inception-resnet and the impact of residual connections on learning. In: Thirty-first AAAI Conference on Artificial Intelligence (2017)

21. Szegedy, C., Vanhoucke, V., Ioffe, S., Shlens, J., Wojna, Z.: Rethinking the inception architecture for computer vision. In: Proceedings of the IEEE Conference on Computer Vision and Pattern Recognition, pp. 2818–2826 (2016)
22. Vasefi, F., MacKinnon, N., Farkas, D.: Hyperspectral and multispectral imaging in dermatology. In: Imaging in Dermatology, pp. 187–201. Elsevier (2016)
23. Yang, N., Yuan, M., Wang, P., Zhang, R., Sun, J., Mao, H.: Tea diseases detection based on fast infrared thermal image processing technology. J. Sci. Food Agric. **99**(7), 3459–3466 (2019)
24. Yang, Y., Chai, R., He, Y.: Early detection of rice blast (pyricularia) at seedling stage in nipponbare rice variety using near-infrared hyper-spectral image. Afr. J. Biotech. **11**(26), 6809–6817 (2012)
25. Zhu, W., Chen, H., Ciechanowska, I., Spaner, D.: Application of infrared thermal imaging for the rapid diagnosis of crop disease. IFAC-PapersOnLine **51**(17), 424–430 (2018)

Whale Optimization Based Approach to Compress and Fasten CNN for Crop Disease and Species Identification

Mohit Agarwal[1], Simar Preet Singh[1(✉)], Rohit Kaliyar[1],
Suneet Kumar Gupta[1], Deepak Garg[1], and Mani Jindal[2]

[1] Bennett University, Gr. Noida 201310, India
{simarpreet.singh,deepak.garg}@bennett.edu.in
[2] Christ Deemed to be University Delhi NCR, Mariam Nagar,
Ghaziabad 201003, India

Abstract. In recent years deep learning and machine learning have been widely researched for image based recognition. This research proposes a simplified CNN with 3 layers for classification from 39 classes of crops and their diseases. It also evaluates the performance of pre-trained models such as VGG16 and ResNet50 using transfer learning. Similarly traditional Machine Learning algorithms have been trained and tested on the same dataset. The best accuracy using proposed CNN was 87.67% whereas VGG16 gave best accuracy of 91.51% among Convolution Neural Network models. Similarly Random Forest machine learning method gave best accuracy of 93.02% among Machine Learning models. Since the pre-trained models are having huge size hence in order to deploy these solutions on tiny edge devices compression is done using Whale Optimization. The maximum compesssion was obtained with VGG16 of 88.19% without loss in any performance. It also helped betterment of inference time of 44.13% for proposed CNN, 56.76% for VGG16 and 63.23% for ResNet50.

Keywords: CNN · Deep neural network · Crop disease · Cnn compression

1 Introduction

Farming is a vital occupation of India and country's economy is dependant on agriculture. These days image based recognition is vital for many applications such as medical, automobile, etc. Hence a need is felt for identification of crops and its diseases from images of plants. Since leaves are clear indicator of crops and any disease present in the crop, a leaf dataset was used to classify crop alongwith its diseases from the leaf images. PlantVillago [1] is a dataset of leaves with 39 classes having 14 types of crops and different diseases in each crop. Several research work have been published for classification of different diseases from one of crops in this dataset such as Apple, Grapes, Tomato, Potato, Corn,

© Springer Nature Switzerland AG 2023
D. Garg et al. (Eds.): IACC 2022, CCIS 1781, pp. 309–320, 2023.
https://doi.org/10.1007/978-3-031-35641-4_25

etc. This research is to classify from all the 39 classes to identify the type of crop and disease both. The leaves in this dataset are already with a plain background hence not much pre-processing is needed. To create similar images for testing leaf images were taken by placing on a white paper and it was found that trained deep learning and machine learning models were correctly able to identify the correct crop from 1 of its 14 crops and disease also.

The major contributions of this research are:

- Development of a light weight CNN model for classifying 1 of 39 classes of PlantVillage dataset.
- Comparison of pre-trained models with Machine Learning models for classification accuracy.
- Compression of pre-trained models using Whale Optimization for deployment on edge computing devices.

The further layout of article comprises of background literature in Sect. 2 followed by Dataset in Sect. 3 and Proposed Model in Sect. 4. These sections are followed by results in Sect. 5 and finally conclusion in Sect. 6.

2   Background Literature

Image based plant disease identification can be greatly assisted by computer vision based techniques. To extract image characteristics, LBP [2], SIFT [3], sparse codes [4], and various features [5] such as color,and texture can be extracted using plant leaves images and pooled using Fisher vector encoding (FVE) [2] and bag-of-words (BOW) to obtain image-level characteristics.

In recent years, a large number of leaf disease identification studies [6–8] have been conducted utilizing transfer learning. However, these methods differences [6–8] are negligible because the utilized architectures are not novel. Consequently, a region-aware DCNN architecture is proposed in this paper.

Several recent research work were able to use Convolution Neural Networks (CNN) for classifying images into various output classes in various domains [9–15]. Similarly some research work have shown the usage of meta heuristic algorithms for compression of semantic segmentation models such as SegNet and UNet [16,17]. CNN usage have not been limited to any particular domain and their usage can also be seen in medical domain images of various body organs [18–20].

Some latest research work also show different meta heuristic based approaches for CNN model compression [21–27].

3   Dataset

The PlantVillage dataset [1] used had 39 classes of 14 different crops and diseases affecting those crops. Some crops images from dataset are shown in Fig. 1. Since number of samples in each class were not same, hence augmentation techniques were used to make the number of images in each class same. Hence if images were 789, 211 augmented images were created by rotation, flipping, cropping, zooming, etc. Similarly if 1234 images were in a class, first 1000 images were taken from the class. Finally like this each class had 1000 images. The dataset was split at run time in 80:10:10 train, validation and testing ratio.

a) Apple Scab   b) Corn Common Rust   c) Grape Black Rot

d) Peach Bacterial Spot   e) Potato Late Blight   f) Tomato Mosaic Virus

Fig. 1. Sample Images of PlantVillage dataset.

4 Proposed Algorithm

The proposed CNN comprises of a input convolution layer with 64 filter followed by a max pooling layer. This is followed by a convolution layer comprising of 32 filters and a max pooling layer. After this another convolution layer with 16 filters is present with a max pooling layer. These convolution layers take 2-D input and also provides 2-D output, however the output layer is 1-D with 39 elements corresponding to 39 classes. Hence after convolution layer a Flatten layer is added which is followed by a Dense layer of 256 nodes and finally an output layer of 39 nodes is present with softmax activation function. Other convolution and Dense layers have ReLU as activation function. The proposed CNN is shown graphically in Fig. 2.

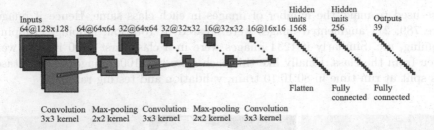

Fig. 2. Architecture of proposed CNN.

The pre-trained models are compressed using Whale Optimization algorithm which mimics hump back whales behaviour of catching its prey. Whales encircle the prey in a spiral fashion and few number of whales learn from each other to reach final prey position. The Whale position vector is created randomly consisting of 0 and 1, where 0 is denoted for a node being dropped in Convolution Neural Network (CNN) and 1 means node is kept. Depending on the fitness function the best position vector of whales is obtained which corresponds to the prey position. Based on best position vector nodes corresponding to 0 elements are dropped from CNN and it is further trained by copying weights from original CNN model to compressed model. This process is iteratively carried by taking compressed models as base model and applying Whale Optimization on it again till the performance degrades by more than 8%.

4.1   Whale Optimization

Whale Optimization algorithm comprises of mainly three steps:

– Step 1) Encircling Prey
– Step 2) Bubble-net attacking method (exploitation phase)
– Step 3) Search for prey (exploration phase)

Depending on the equations for these steps the algorithm for Whale Optimization is as given in Algorithm 1.

5   Results and Discussion

A simple CNN with 3 convolution layers, VGG16 and ResNet50 were trained for 39 classes of PlantVillage dataset [1]. These models were further compressed and accuracy was recorded of compressed models. This process can help to deploy the model on tiny edge devices having limited memory and computing power. The results of size and accuracy of original and compressed models is given in Table 1.

Algorithm 1 : The iterative process for Whale Optimization

1: **procedure** WHALEOPTIMIZATION
2:   ▷ Initialize the Whale Population randomly
3:     $X_i(i = 1, 2 \dots, n)$
4:   ▷ Calculate fitness of each agent
5:     $X_{best} = best\ search\ agent$
6:     $t \leftarrow 0$
7:     **while** $t < max\_iter$ **do**
8:         **for all** $Search\ Agents$ **do**
9:             $Update\ constants\ a,\ A,\ C,\ l\ and\ p$
10:            **if** $p < 0.5$ **then**
11:                **if** $|A| < 1$ **then**
12:                    $Update\ Curr\_agent\ by\ Step\ (1)\ above$
13:                **else**
14:                    $Update\ Curr\_agent\ by\ Step\ (3)\ above$
15:            **else**
16:                $Update\ Curr\_agent\ by\ Step\ (2)\ above$
17:   ▷ Calculate fitness of each agent
18:            $X_{best} = best\ search\ agent$
19:            $t \leftarrow t + 1$
20:     $return\ X_{best}$

Table 1. Comparison of size and accuracy of original and compressed models.

Model	Size (KB)	Accuracy (%)
CNN	855	87.67
Compressed CNN	271	80.55
VGG16	94568	91.51
Compressed VGG16	11165	93.36
ResNet50	105004	53.45
Compressed ResNet50	21615	82.75

Thus as seen from Table 1 the maximum accuracy was achieved with compressed VGG16 equal to 93.36%. Also the percent compression of CNN was 68.30%, VGG16 was 88.19% and ResNet50 was 79.41%.

The comparison of accuracy of different models is shown in Fig. 3.

The compression process as seen was able to increase accuracy for VGG16 and ResNet50 as redundant neurons were removed from the trained model to enhance the accuracy. The comparison of validation loss *vs.* accuracy is shown in Fig. 4, 5, and 6 for proposed CNN, VGG16 and ResNet50 respectively. As seen in these figures the loss tends to decrease with epochs and accuracy increases and saturates at a given level near to 100%.

The comparison of inference times of different models is shown in Table 2 which clearly shows the acceleration of models alongwith model compression.

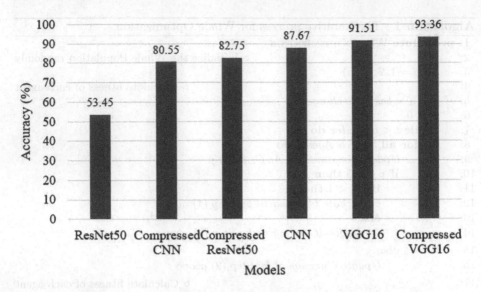

Fig. 3. Comparison of accuracy for different CNN models.

Table 2. Comparison of inference time of original and compressed models.

Model	Original inference time (sec)	Final inference time (sec)
CNN	20.23	11.30
VGG16	78.35	34.00
ResNet50	142.11	52.25

5.1 Machine Learning Models

The Machine Learning (ML) models such as Logistic Regression, Linear Discriminant Analysis, k-NN, Decision Trees and Random Forest were also used to train and test the plants classification problem of 39 classes of species and diseases. The results of ML models is given in Table 3. The features used for ML methods were Haralick features, HSV histogram and Hu-moments. The ROC-AUC curve for ML models is given in Fig. 7 which shows best area under curve (AUC) value for Random Forest. The ML methods need handcrafted features hence Haralick features (based on image texture and calculated using Gray Level Co-occurence matrix (GLCM)), Hu-moments and Hue Saturation Intensity Value (HSV) historgram are concatenated to form a feature vector. This feature vector is passed to the ML models by splitting dataset in 80:20 ratio for training and testing.

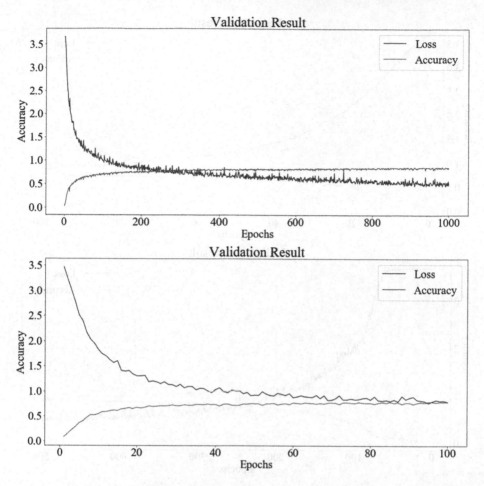

Fig. 4. Comparison of validation loss and accuracy curve for simple CNN in top row and compressed CNN in bottom row.

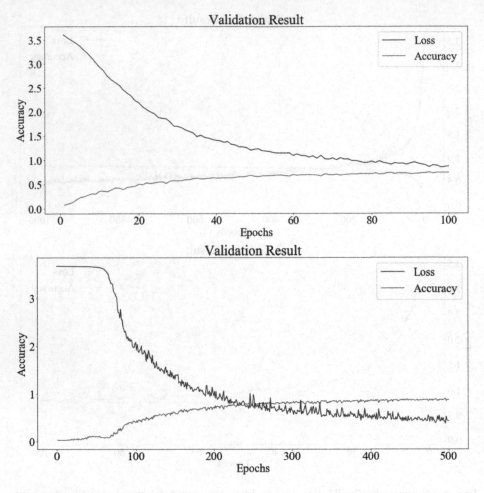

Fig. 5. Comparison of validation loss and accuracy curve for VGG16 in top row and compressed VGG16 in bottom row.

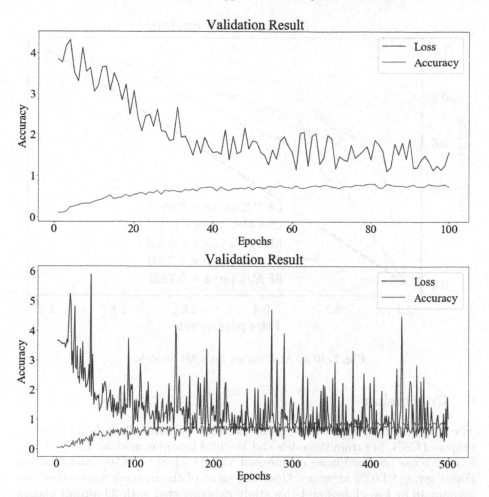

Fig. 6. Comparison of validation loss and accuracy curve for ResNet50 in top row and compressed ResNet50 in bottom row.

Table 3. Comparison of performance of different ML models.

Model	TP	FP	TN	FN	Precision	Recall	Accuracy	F1-score	Sensitivity	Specificity
Logistic Regression	2083	639	122	21	0.765246	0.990019	0.769634	0.863241	0.990019	0.160315
LDA	1690	1032	88	55	0.620867	0.968481	0.620593	0.75666	0.968481	0.078571
k-NN	2220	502	99	44	0.815577	0.980565	0.809424	0.890493	0.980565	0.164725
Decision Tree	1884	838	102	41	0.692138	0.978701	0.693194	0.810846	0.978701	0.108511
Random Forest	2529	193	136	7	0.929096	0.99724	0.930192	0.961963	0.99724	0.413374

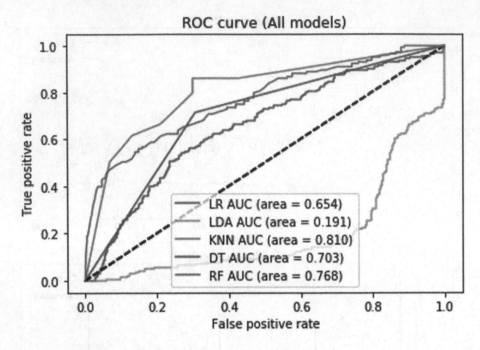

Fig. 7. ROC-AUC curves for 6 ML models.

6 Conclusion

The proposed study was able to classify 39 classes of PlantVillage dataset using a proposed CNN, pre-trained models and Machine Learning models. The best performance was obtained using compressed VGG16 equal to 93.56% and Random Forest giving 93.02% accuracy. Generally most of the research work takes into account 10 or less classes and this study experimented with 39 output classes with a high accuracy. The compression of models also lead to their size reduction and acceleration for their easy deployment on edge devices. This process can help in developing IoT based devices having Raspberry-pi or Jetson Nano embedded in them. As a future work this study could explore more pre-trained models such as MobileNet, InceptionV3, DenseNet etc.

References

1. Hughes, D., Salathé, M., et al.: An open access repository of images on plant health to enable the development of mobile disease diagnostics. arXiv preprint arXiv:1511.08060 (2015)
2. Guo, Z., Zhang, L., Zhang, D.: A completed modeling of local binary pattern operator for texture classification. IEEE Trans. Image Process. **19**(6), 1657–1663 (2010)
3. Lowe, D.G.: Distinctive image features from scale-invariant keypoints. Int. J. Comput. Vis. **60**(2), 91–110 (2004)

4. Yang, J., Yu, K., Gong, Y., Huang, T.: Linear spatial pyramid matching using sparse coding for image classification. In: 2009 IEEE Conference on Computer Vision and Pattern Recognition, pp. 1794–1801. IEEE (2009)
5. Singh, V., Misra, A.K.: Detection of plant leaf diseases using image segmentation and soft computing techniques. Inf. Process. Agric. 4(1), 41–49 (2017)
6. Yu, H.J., Son, C.H.: Leaf spot attention network for apple leaf disease identification. In: Proceedings of the IEEE/CVF Conference on Computer Vision and Pattern Recognition Workshops, pp. 52–53 (2020)
7. Fuentes, A., Yoon, S., Kim, S.C., Park, D.S.: A robust deep-learning-based detector for real-time tomato plant diseases and pests recognition. Sensors 17(9), 2022 (2017)
8. Ferentinos, K.P.: Deep learning models for plant disease detection and diagnosis. Comput. Electron. Agric. 145, 311–318 (2018)
9. Agarwal, M., Singh, A., Arjaria, S., Sinha, A., Gupta, S.: ToLeD: tomato leaf disease detection using convolution neural network. Procedia Comput. Sci. 167, 293–301 (2020)
10. Agarwal, M., Gupta, S.K., Biswas, K.K.: Grape disease identification using convolution neural network. In: 2019 23rd International Computer Science and Engineering Conference (ICSEC), pp. 224–229. IEEE (2019)
11. Agarwal, M., Kaliyar, R.K., Singal, G., Gupta, S.K.: FCNN-LDA: a faster convolution neural network model for leaf disease identification on apple's leaf dataset. In: 2019 12th International Conference on Information & Communication Technology and System (ICTS), pp. 246–251. IEEE (2019)
12. Agarwal, M., Sinha, A., Gupta, S.K., Mishra, D., Mishra, R.: Potato crop disease classification using convolutional neural network. In: Somani, A.K., Shekhawat, R.S., Mundra, A., Srivastava, S., Verma, V.K. (eds.) Smart Systems and IoT: Innovations in Computing. SIST, vol. 141, pp. 391–400. Springer, Singapore (2020). https://doi.org/10.1007/978-981-13-8406-6_37
13. Agarwal, M., Bohat, V.K., Ansari, M.D., Sinha, A., Gupta, S.K., Garg, D.A.: A convolution neural network based approach to detect the disease in corn crop. In 2019 IEEE 9th International Conference on Advanced Computing (IACC), pp. 176–181. IEEE (2019)
14. Agarwal, M., Gupta, S.K., Biswas, K.K.: Development of efficient CNN model for tomato crop disease identification. Sustain. Comput. Inf. Syst. 28, 100407 (2020)
15. Agarwal, M., Gupta, S., Biswas, K.K.: A new conv2d model with modified ReLU activation function for identification of disease type and severity in cucumber plant. Sustain. Comput. Inf. Syst. 30, 100473 (2021)
16. Agarwal, M., Gupta, S.K., Biswas, K.K.: A compressed and accelerated SegNet for plant leaf disease segmentation: a differential evolution based approach. In: Karlapalem, K., et al. (eds.) PAKDD 2021. LNCS (LNAI), vol. 12714, pp. 272–284. Springer, Cham (2021). https://doi.org/10.1007/978-3-030-75768-7_22
17. Agarwal, M., Gupta, S.K., Biswas, K.K.: Plant leaf disease segmentation using compressed UNet architecture. In: Gupta, M., Ramakrishnan, G. (eds.) PAKDD 2021. LNCS (LNAI), vol. 12705, pp. 9–14. Springer, Cham (2021). https://doi.org/10.1007/978-3-030-75015-2_2
18. Agarwal, M., et al.: Wilson disease tissue classification and characterization using seven artificial intelligence models embedded with 3D optimization paradigm on a weak training brain magnetic resonance imaging datasets: a supercomputer application. Med. Biol. Eng. Comput. 59(3), 511–533 (2021)

19. Agarwal, M., et al.: A novel block imaging technique using nine artificial intelligence models for COVID-19 disease classification, characterization and severity measurement in lung computed tomography scans on an Italian cohort. J. Med. Syst. **45**(3), 1–30 (2021)
20. Saba, L., et al.: Six artificial intelligence paradigms for tissue characterisation and classification of non-COVID-19 pneumonia against COVID-19 pneumonia in computed tomography lungs. Int. J. Comput. Assist. Radiol. Surg. **16**(3), 423–434 (2021)
21. Agarwal, M., et al.: Eight pruning deep learning models for low storage and high-speed COVID-19 computed tomography lung segmentation and heatmap-based lesion localization: a multicenter study using covlias 2.0. Comput. Biol. Med. **146**, 105571 2022
22. Agarwal, M., Gupta, S.K., Biswas, M., Garg, D.: Compression and acceleration of convolution neural network: a genetic algorithm based approach. J. Ambient Intell. Humanized Comput. 1–11 (2022)
23. Agarwal, M., Gupta, S.K., Garg, D., Singh, D.: A novel compressed and accelerated convolution neural network for COVID-19 disease classification: a genetic algorithm based approach. In: Garg, D., Jagannathan, S., Gupta, A., Garg, L., Gupta, S. (eds.) IACC 2021. Communications in Computer and Information Science, vol. 1528, pp. 99–111. Springer, Cham (2021). https://doi.org/10.1007/978-3-030-95502-1_8
24. Agarwal, M., Gupta, S.K., Garg, D., Khan, M.M.: A partcle swarm optimization based approach for filter pruning in convolution neural network for tomato leaf disease classification. In: Garg, D., Jagannathan, S., Gupta, A., Garg, L., Gupta, S. (eds.) IACC 2021. Communications in Computer and Information Science, vol. 1528, pp. 646–659. Springer, Cham (2021). https://doi.org/10.1007/978-3-030-95502-1_49
25. Yar, H., Hussain, T., Agarwal, M., Khan, Z.A., Gupta, S.K., Baik, S.W.: Optimized dual fire attention network and medium-scale fire classification benchmark. IEEE Trans. Image Process. **31**, 6331–6343 (2022)
26. Skandha, S.S., Agarwal, M., Utkarsh, K., Gupta, S.K., Koppula, V.K., Suri, J.S.: A novel genetic algorithm-based approach for compression and acceleration of deep learning convolution neural network: an application in computer tomography lung cancer data. Neural Comput. Appl. **34**, 1–23 (2022)
27. Agarwal, M., Kaliyar, R.K., Gupta, S.K.: Differential evolution based compression of CNN for apple fruit disease classification. In: 2022 International Conference on Inventive Computation Technologies (ICICT), pp. 76–82. IEEE (2022)

Few-Shot Learning for Plant Disease Classification Using ILP

Dany Varghese(✉), Uzma Patel, Paul Krause, and Alireza Tamaddoni-Nezhad

University of Surrey, Guildford GU2 7XH, UK
{dany.varghese,up00039,p.krause,a.tamaddoni-nezhad}@surrey.ac.uk

Abstract. Plant diseases are one of the main causes of crop loss in agriculture. Machine Learning, in particular statistical and neural nets (NNs) approaches, have been used to help farmers identify plant diseases. However, since new diseases continue to appear in agriculture due to climate change and other factors, we need more data-efficient approaches to identify and classify new diseases as early as possible. Even though statistical machine learning approaches and neural nets have demonstrated state-of-the-art results on many classification tasks, they usually require a large amount of training data. This may not be available for emergent plant diseases. So, data-efficient approaches are essential for an early and precise diagnosis of new plant diseases and necessary to prevent the disease's spread. This study explores a data-efficient Inductive Logic Programming (ILP) approach for plant disease classification. We compare some ILP algorithms (including our new implementation, PyGol) with several statistical and neural-net based machine learning algorithms on the task of tomato plant disease classification with varying sizes of training data set (6, 10, 50 and 100 training images per disease class). The results suggest that ILP outperforms other learning algorithms and this is more evident when fewer training data are available.

Keywords: Few-shot Learning · Data Efficient Machine Learning · ILP · Inverse Entailment · Plant Disease Classification

1 Introduction

Crop cultivation and production play a crucial role in the field of agriculture. The primary cause of agriculture losses is infected crops, which in turn reduces the production rate. Thus, plant diseases have become a significant threat to global food security. Also, sustainable farming can play a vital role in our climate and the earth's ecosystems. Agriculture needs biodiversity and vice versa. Livestock and other crops nourish themselves and originate from existing crops, whilst biodiversity maintains and provides environments necessary for the production of crops. Therefore, plant diseases pose a considerable threat to the global economy and the codependent relationship between agriculture and biodiversity [44]. Diseases can affect whole crops and cause 100% losses. It is essential to determine what is wrong as fast as possible before it has spread or ripened.

© Springer Nature Switzerland AG 2023
D. Garg et al. (Eds.): IACC 2022, CCIS 1781, pp. 321–336, 2023.
https://doi.org/10.1007/978-3-031-35641-4_26

Moreover, the lack of access to technology in some areas means that management of these issues may be poor, and farmers could lack access to knowledge on how to deal with the illnesses. Therefore, an effective plant disease detection system could cut the cost and time spent on the issue while providing enough knowledge to understand the impact on crops better. Several systems for plant disease detection have been introduced in recent years—the fast progress in machine vision and artificial intelligence speeds up the research interest in this area [8,31,32]. Deep Neural Networks (DNNs) have demonstrated state-of-the-art results in plant disease detection [47,53]. Also, several mobile-based platforms were introduced to help the farmers, such as Plantix [16]. However, existing learning algorithms require extensive sets of training examples, e.g. we need hundreds or thousands of images to train DNNs for image classification.

However, we might only have a small number or even only one training example in some applications. For example, an early and precise diagnosis of new plant diseases may be essential in preventing the spread of the disease. Machine learning algorithms that work with a few training examples (one-shot learning, few-shot learning) would make a significant contribution to risk mitigation for the industry. Also, according to Algorithmia's "2020 State of Enterprise Machine Learning" [2], 50% of respondents said it took 8–90 days to deploy one model, with only 14% saying they could deploy in less than a week [18]. Furthermore, a recent study on life cycle assessment of large AI models shows that the process can emit more than 626,000 pounds of carbon dioxide equivalent-nearly five times the lifetime emissions of the average American car [50]. It is thus imperative to reduce the effort needed to train models as their use becomes more prevalent.

Since the rules and the knowledge in traditional expert systems are defined and formulated by human experts, these rules and knowledge are easy for humans to understand and interpret. In this scenario, Inductive Logic Programming (ILP) has several advantages over most machine learning approaches. Because logic resembles natural language, it can be easily read by humans. Also, ILP systems can perform well with very small amounts of data [36], even succeeding with one-shot(single) data [55,56]. This efficiency is enhanced further by the inclusion of background knowledge in the form of logic rules. ILP [37] is a machine learning formalism that induces a hypothesis that generalizes examples. ILP uses a first-order logic program as data, whereas most forms of ML use vectors or tensors to represent data. ILP models are more data-efficient, explainable, and can incorporate human knowledge more easily compared to other forms of machine learning. In this paper, we introduce a data-efficient machine learning approach which can learn from small amounts of data. We illustrate its use on plant disease detection, and show that it can outperform more traditional algorithms; especially in cases where limited training data is available.

2   Related Work

Plenty of works have been devoted to detection and classification using image processing in history, and still, it continues to attract researchers to this field.

We present the literature study in three parts. Part one explains few-shot learning and its importance in the machine learning community, whereas, in part two, we reviewed plant disease classification. Part 3 will give an overview of different feature extraction techniques.

2.1   Few-Shot Learning

In order to learn from a limited number of examples with supervised information, a new machine learning paradigm called Few-Shot Learning (FSL) was proposed. The seminal work toward few-shot learning dates back to the early 2000 s with work by Li Fei-Fei et al. [29]. The authors developed a variational Bayesian framework for image classification, using the premise that previously learned classes could be leveraged to help forecast future ones when very few examples are available from a given class [12,30]. More recently, Lake et al. approached the problem of one-shot learning as an instance of few-shot, addressing one-shot character recognition with a method called Hierarchical Bayesian Program Learning (HBPL) [27]). A detailed study on FSL can be found in [58].

According to Mitchell [1], a learning approach can be considered as a program that can learn from experiences (E) related to the task (T) to improve performance(P). Following this definition, we can define FSL as a machine learning problem that takes the tuple $< T, P, E >$; E contains only a limited number of examples with supervised information for the target T. FSL can relieve the burden of large scale data collection and reduce the data gathering effort for data-intensive applications. Several learning approaches have been introduced for FSL, and they can be mainly classified into 4 categories:

1. Weakly supervised learning
   (a) Semi-supervised learning [21,42,59]
   (b) Active learning [13,39]
2. Transfer learning [60,61]
3. Meta-learning [45,61]
4. ILP/MIL based methods [10,55,56]

Focusing on the research concept of this paper, Li et al. [28] proposed a semi-supervised few-shot learning approach to solve the plant leaf disease recognition problem. They have used the transfer learning concepts and implemented them using deep learning methods. Extensive comparison experiments considering the domain split and few-shot parameters (N-way, k-shot) were carried out to validate the correctness and generalization of proposed semi-supervised few-shot methods.

Chen et al. [7] used local feature matching conditional neural adaptive processes (LFM-CNAPS) based on meta-learning that aims at detecting plant diseases. They have applied intense training on datasets like 20,000 training iterations. David et al. [3] presented the FSL approach to plant disease classification using transfer learning and the Siamese network.

2.2   Plant Disease Classification Methods

Sunil et al. [17] used multiple descriptors such as Discrete Wavelet Transform (DWT), Principal Component Analysis (PCA) and Grey-Level Co-occurrence Matrix (GLCM) to extract informative features of leaves. Before feature extraction, they also applied K-means clustering and histogram equalization on 256 × 256 data items. They have done experiments on the village database of tomato leaves and compared it with Support Vector Machine (SVM), Convolutional Neural Network (CNN) and K-Nearest Neighbor (K-NN), reporting the accuracy of the resulting models as 88%, 99.6% and 97% respectively.

Kalpesh et al. [25] have experimented on tomato, apple, potato, and grape leaves from the Plant-Village dataset. They used GLCM to shape and texture features and applied feature engineering mechanisms to find highly correlated features. The database was divided into two sets during the experiment: the training set, which contained 70%, and the testing set, which comprised 30%. A 93% accuracy rate has been reported using the Random Forest model.

G. Saradhambal et al. [26] proposed an approach to produce a system for automatic plant disease detection. The research was done to predict the infected area of the leaves by applying a k-means clustering algorithm and Otsu's classifier. Both the shape and texture features were extracted in the proposed work. The shape-oriented features extracted in this work included area, colour axis length, eccentricity, solidity and perimeter. In contrast, the texture oriented features were contrast, correlation, energy, homogeneity, and mean. The classification in this research was done using a neural network.

Irfan et al. [41] have performed some experiments on rice plant disease images by using the Probabilistic Neural Network (PNN), one of the Artificial Neural Networks (ANN) models. First, the images were pre-processed with the median filtering method, and then the OTSU method was used for segmentation. Later, they applied GLCM for feature extraction. The accuracy rate of this system was 76.8%.

2.3   Feature Extraction

Accuracy is the main parameter used to calculate the performance of a model. The classifier's accuracy depends primarily on the extracted features. So, feature extraction plays a vital role in identifying disease and improves diagnostic accuracy. Hand-crafted feature engineering and deep learning feature extraction are the two main types of feature extraction. Hand-crafted feature engineering from images can be mainly divided into three types, shape, texture, and colour. In this paper, we only consider the hand-crafted feature engineering methods.

The shape of an object is an essential and fundamental visual feature for describing image content [5, 19]. It can be considered a silhouette of the object, invariant to rotation, scale and translation. Shape features are less developed than their colour and texture counterparts because of the inherent complexity of representing shapes.

Among the visual features, colours are the most vital, reliable, and widely used features. The colour feature descriptor of images has been used widely, showing its robustness to background complication and independence over image size and orientation. Colour feature extraction methods broadly fall into global and local methods [40]. In global methods, the feature extraction process considers the complete image, including global colour histogram, intersection, and image bitmap. On the other hand, local methods consider a portion of the image, including local colour histogram, colour correlogram, and colour difference histogram.

Texture is the primary term used to define objects or concepts of a given image. Tactile texture directs the natural feel, and visual texture refers to seeing the image's shape or contents [4]. In image processing, texture can be defined as a function of spatial variation of the brightness intensity of the pixels. Texture analysis is vital in computer vision cases such as object recognition, surface defect detection, pattern recognition, and medical image analysis.

Hu Moments. Moments and the related invariants have been extensively analyzed to characterize the patterns in images in a variety of applications. We use Hu Moments (or rather Hu moment invariants), a set of 7 numbers calculated using central moments invariant to image transformations [22]. The first six moments have been proved invariant to translation, scale, rotation, and reflection. While the seventh moment's sign changes for image reflection. Hu firstly introduces moment invariants. In [20], Hu derived six absolute orthogonal invariants and one skew orthogonal invariant based upon algebraic invariants, which are not only independent of position, size and orientation but also independent of parallel projection

Haralick Texture. Haralick texture features are estimated from a Grey Level Co-occurrence Matrix (GLCM), a matrix that counts the co-occurrence of neighbouring grey levels in the image [18]. The GLCM is a square matrix with the dimension of the number of grey levels N in the region of interest (ROI). The GLCM functions characterize an image's texture by calculating how often pairs of pixels with distinct values and specified spatial relationships appear in an image, composing a GLCM, and then pulling statistical estimates from this matrix.

3 Methodology

The basic methodology of the developed system is presented schematically in Fig. 1.

3.1 Image Data

The image data were collected from a well-known dataset, "PlantVillage" [23,43]; freely available in [35]. The dataset contains 50,000 RGB images of 14 crops.

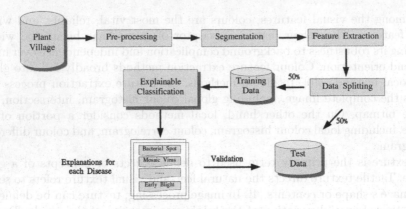

Fig. 1. System Description

The current paper focuses on tomato images which contain ten classes as explained in Table 1, including healthy images. To address the unbalance in the dataset, we created new instances which contain 50 images from each class.

Leaf Diseases and Symptoms. Over a thousand different fruit, vegetable and herb species are cultivated worldwide. The growth process for them all is not the same, and neither are the diseases that affect them. In an ideal world, we would be able to quickly identify each of these species and all the diseases that affect them, to eliminate and reduce any possible problems. To reach this ideal, we must find the most efficient method to design an application or system to identify the diseases. Identification must be carried out at a high level of accuracy since this is the deciding factor on what to do next. We begin this process by gaining some background knowledge on each disease in our chosen dataset.

In this study, we have taken the following nine plant diseases, illustrated in Fig. 2, for the experiments, where a summary of the symptoms of each disease can be found in Table 1:

1. Bacterial Spot
2. Mosaic Virus
3. Late Blight
4. Yellow Leaf Curl
5. Target Spot
6. Sectorial Leaf Spot
7. Spider Mites
8. Leaf Mould
9. Early Blight

3.2   Pre-processing

There are 3 main stages during pre-processing:

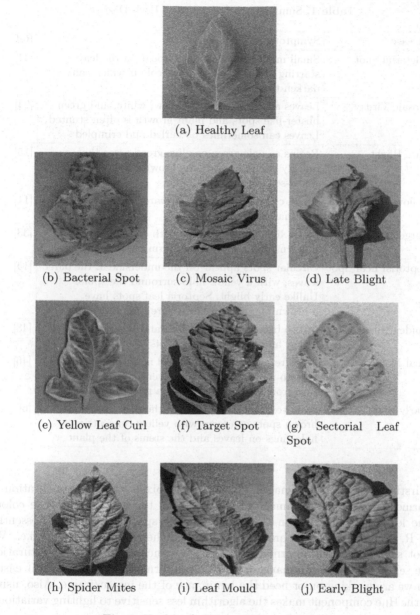

(a) Healthy Leaf

(b) Bacterial Spot   (c) Mosaic Virus   (d) Late Blight

(e) Yellow Leaf Curl   (f) Target Spot   (g) Sectorial Leaf Spot

(h) Spider Mites   (i) Leaf Mould   (j) Early Blight

Fig. 2. Healthy & Disease Effected Leaves

1. Resizing
2. Image Segmentation
3. Colour Space Conversion

Table 1. Summary of Symptoms of Each Disease

Disease	Symptoms	Ref.
Bacterial Spot	Small moist circular areas appear on the leaves, starting off as a yellow-green colour which can darken to brown-red	[34]
Mosaic Virus	Leaves are mottled with yellow, white, and green blister-like spots and plant growth is often stunted. Leaves can sometimes be curled and crimpled	[24]
Late Blight	Begins as pale-green or olive-green areas that quickly enlarge to become brown-black, water-soaked, and oily-looking	[15]
Yellow Leaf Curl	small, crumpled and curl upwards. Leaves are also marginal yellowing	[11]
Target Spot	small, light brown lesions, with concentric patterns and a yellow halo form on the leaves	[33]
Septorial Leaf Spot	Circular spots appear on the underside of the older leaves, with a yellow halo surround the spots. Unlike early blight, Septoria leaf spots have a brown margin and lighter grey-tan centres	[14]
Spider Mites	leaf to become speckled, dull and botchy with pale yellow and reddish-brown spots	[48]
Leaf Mould	Pale green spots can be found near the tips of the tomato plants leaves which eventually enlarge and turn from green to brown to a purplish black	[46]
Early Blight	Start towards the bottom of the plant where dark brown spots can form with yellow concentric halo rings on leaves and the stems of the plant	[6]

Firstly, we resized all images to 256×256 pixels. Then, segmentation is performed to separate the image of the leaf from the background. The colour of the leaf is extracted from the image. Colour space conversion is essential since R, G, and B in RGB are all co-related to the colour luminance, i.e., We cannot separate colour information from luminance. HSV or Hue Saturation Value separates image luminance from colour information. This makes it easier when we are working on or need the luminance of the image/frame. Also, using only the Hue component makes the algorithm less sensitive to lighting variations.

3.3   Feature Extraction and Scaling

Feature extraction is the process of reducing dimensionality in the dataset by using various methods to combine existing features to create new features. The new features summarize what the original features tell us without losing essential information or knowledge. Overfitting can occur when a dataset's dimensionality is high, an issue we look to avoid through feature extraction. Other benefits include better accuracy, a reduction in training time, better data visualization and simpler explanations of our model. Feature extraction also allows our model to understand what it is looking for and subsequently indexes and retrieves relevant information. This information is then used to mathematically describe various attributes, such as colours, textures, or shapes. As explained in Sect. 2.3, we mainly extract 13 Haralick features using Grey Level Co-occurrence Matrix.

Feature scaling is an essential step in standardizing the independent features present in the data to a common range. In this stage, we normalise the highly varying magnitudes or values or units. If feature scaling is not performed, then a machine learning algorithm will be biased by features with higher numerical values and reduce the influence of features with smaller values, regardless of the unit of the values. As part of the normalisation process, we have rounded all the feature values to 5 decimal points.

4   Empirical Evaluation

This section empirically evaluates ILP systems against other machine learning approaches using four differently sized datasets.

4.1   Materials and Methods

We have created four chunks of images from the original dataset. The first two chunks contain 100 and 50 images per class. The third and fourth chunks contain 10 and 6 images per class. During the experiments, we followed the hold-out learning strategy. We have split the data in the ratio of 1:1. Since an ILP architecture always considers the learning problem as a binary classification, we have followed a new execution strategy to have a fair comparison of both rule-based and machine learning approaches. We have run the experiment "10" times (equal to the number of classes; nine diseased plus one healthy), and in each run, examples from one class will be considered as a positive example/class and all others as a negative example/class.

It is vital to generate background knowledge using first-order logic rules since we are doing experiments using ILP. In [55], it is explained that the categorical value method is an excellent mechanism for dealing with numerical data. We have divided each feature into three categorical classes/ranges: low, medium, and high, according to the local population of feature points. We will use the feature names as predicates in the background knowledge.

We have developed our experiment using a novel ILP system, PyGol[1], based on meta inverse entailment(MIE), which is motivated by Mode-directed inverse entailment [36] but never uses mode to generate the bottom clause. The significant merit of this system is that the training phase is fully implemented in Python, and to have a fair comparison during the test phase, PyGol uses a Prolog interpreter. During the test phase, PyGol used a python-based approach

---

[1] Available from: https://github.com/danyvarghese/PyGol.

from the system PyILP [57], which uses PySwip [52] in the back-end. PyGol can automatically generate the first-order logic database, i.e. background knowledge, from relational data. A schematic diagram of generating the logic rules from the relational dataset is shown in Fig. 3.

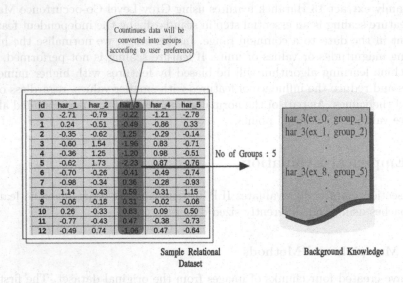

Fig. 3. Automatic generation of logical rules from relational dataset

PyILP is a novel, user-friendly Python interface for Inductive Logic programming(ILP) systems for teaching relational machine learning and comparing different algorithms, whereas PySwip act as the bridge between python and Prolog. PyGol enables us to do every experiment in a single platform called Jupyter Notebook. We have compared PyGol with two other state-of-the-art ILP systems, seven statistical machine learning approaches and two neural network approaches.

Aleph [49] is a state-of-the-art ILP algorithm that has been used for several real-time applications and is one of the ILP systems we are considering for empirical evaluation. Like PyGol, Aleph also uses the advantage of inverse entailment, but mode-directed inverse entailment.

The second system for our consideration is Metagol [9] which is developed based on the concept of meta-interpretive learning (MIL) [38] and has been successfully trialled in several applications [36, 10]. Learning recursive rules and predicate invention is the major contribution of MIL to the ILP community, but they cannot deal with noisy input, a significant disadvantage. In order to overcome this issue, a noise-tolerant version of metagol is introduced as metagol_nt [36,51]. During the empirical evaluation, we use the python version of metagol_nt, which is available from [54]. Other approaches used for evaluation are listed below;

1. Statistical Machine Learning
   (a) Decision Tree (DT)
   (b) Naive Bayes (NB)
   (c) Support Vector Machines (SVM)
   (d) Logical Regression (LR)
   (e) Latent Dirichlet Allocation (LDA)
   (f) K-Nearest Neighbors (KNN)
   (g) Random Forest (RF)
2. Artificial Neural Network Learning
   (a) Perceptron (Per.)
   (b) Multi-Layer Perceptron (MLP)

5   Results and Discussion

Figures 4, 5, 6 and 7 will provide an overall idea about each model on four different datasets. We have plotted overall performance and average F1-Score obtained
on each run and an execution time comparison on different ILP systems. In each
figure, the subplot 'a' indicates the system's overall performance in each run.
The sub-plot 'b' indicates the F1 score during the classification. The F1 score is
more important than accuracy in this scenario, since each run can be considered
an imbalanced classification and will also sum up the predictive performance of
a model.

While analysing each box plot, it is clear that machine learning approaches
other than ILP systems respond differently with each dataset, but the ILP system
responds almost consistently. In almost all cases, the accuracy of the ILP system
lies between 80%–100%, which shows its efficiency compared to other models for
classification. Also, from the box plot, it is clear that the median of accuracies
from each run for typical machine learning approaches is always around 90%
which is the default accuracy. From the plots related to the F1 score, other than
the decision tree, none of them could achieve an average value of 0.5, meaning
the predictive performance of those systems is worse than random.

Focusing on the ILP systems, as the number of examples in each class
increases, Aleph's performance improves. However, for metagol_nt, it deterio-
rates. Both PyGol and Aleph outperform all the statistical approaches, with a
large-scale difference. We have done some experiments with CNN, but it couldn't
perform well (just giving predictive accuracy always) since our dataset is imbalanced w.r.t. to the concept of a binary classification problem. That is the reason
why we did not report the results from CNN. We also noticed that the average
response time of PyGol is just 7 s.

Aleph's learning procedure depends on the order of examples given and also
follows a greedy approach while learning. During the learning cycle, a seed sample will be chosen then a candidate hypothesis will be generated from the bottom
clause, and examples covered by the theory are removed, and the process continues. But PyGol follows a global theory generation procedure in which the system
generates all the possible candidate hypotheses from all the examples.

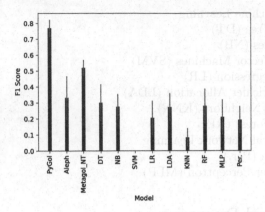

Fig. 4. Performance comparison on Dataset with 6 images per class

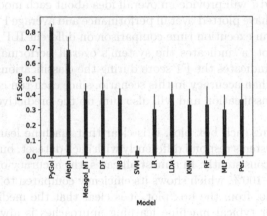

Fig. 5. Performance comparison on Dataset with 10 images per class

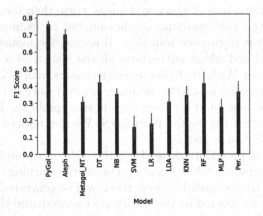

Fig. 6. Performance comparison on Dataset with 50 images per class

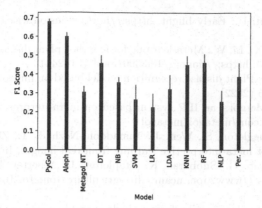

Fig. 7. Performance comparison on Dataset with 100 images per class

6   Conclusion

The objective of this study is to introduce a few-shot model using ILP for plant disease classification. In order to evaluate the data efficiency of each system, we have divided the image dataset into four chunks containing 6, 10, 50 and 100 images per class and experiments on individual chunks. As discussed, the ILP approaches significantly outperform all the machine learning approaches selected, even a convolutional neural network. It is also evident from the performance evaluation that machine learning approaches struggled to learn from the small datasets of 6 or 10 images per class. However, ILP approaches perform well in this scenario too. This shows that the proposed approach of using ILP is data-efficient with respect to other statistical machine learning approaches. Furthermore, the proposed PyGol approach can reduce user interaction compared to other ILP systems since it does not use mode declarations and meta-rules as in Aleph and MIL, respectively. It shows the potential of PyGol for automated data science.

References

1. Machine Learning. McGraw Hill (1997)
2. Algorithmia': 2020 state of enterprise machine learning. https://algorithmia.com/state-of-ml
3. Argüeso, D., et al.: Few-shot learning approach for plant disease classification using images taken in the field. Comput. Electron. Agric. **175**, 105542 (2020)
4. Armi, L., Fekri-Ershad, S.: Texture image analysis and texture classification methods - a review (2019). https://doi.org/10.48550/ARXIV.1904.06554. https://arxiv.org/abs/1904.06554
5. Babapour Mofrad, F., Valizadeh, G.: A comprehensive survey on two and three-dimensional Fourier shape descriptors: biomedical applications. Arch. Comput. Methods Eng. **29**(7), 4643–4681 (2022)

6. Brian Hudelson, U.: Early blight. https://hort.extension.wisc.edu/articles/early-blight/
7. Chen, L., Cui, X., Li, W.: Meta-learning for few-shot plant disease detection. Foods **10**, 2441 (2021). https://doi.org/10.3390/foods10102441
8. Chen, Z., et al.: Plant disease recognition model based on improved yolov5. Agronomy **12**(2), 365 (2022)
9. Cropper, A.: Metgol - an ILP system based on meta-iterpretive learning (2016). https://github.com/metagol/metagol
10. Dai, W.Z., Muggleton, S., Wen, J., Tamaddoni-Nezhad, A., Zhou, Z.H.: Logical vision: one-shot meta-interpretive learning from real images. In: ILP (2017)
11. Davis, R., Miyao, G., Subbarao, K., Stapleton, J., Aegerter, B.: Tomato yellow leaf curl. https://www2.ipm.ucanr.edu/agriculture/tomato/Tomato-Yellow-Leaf-Curl/
12. Fink, M.: Object classification from a single example utilizing class relevance metrics. In: Advances in Neural Information Processing Systems, vol. 17 (2004)
13. Garcia, V., Bruna, J.: Few-shot learning with graph neural networks. arXiv preprint arXiv:1711.04043 (2017)
14. Garden, M.B.: Septoria leaf spot of tomato. https://www.missouribotanicalgarden.org/gardens-gardening/your-garden/help-for-the-home-gardener/advice-tips-resources/pests-and-problems/diseases/fungal-spots/septoria-leaf-spot-of-tomato.aspx
15. Gevens, A., Seidl, A., Brian Hudelson, U.: Late blight. https://hort.extension.wisc.edu/articles/late-blight/
16. GmbH, P.: Plantix : a mobile crop advisory app for farmers, extension workers and gardeners (2015). https://plantix.net/en/
17. Harakannanavar, S.S., Rudagi, J.M., Puranikmath, V.I., Siddiqua, A., Pramodhini, R.: Plant leaf disease detection using computer vision and machine learning algorithms. Glob. Trans. Proc. **3**(1), 305–310 (2022)
18. Hinek, J.P.: How long does it take to build an ml model?. https://m.mage.ai/how-long-does-it-take-to-build-an-ml-model-d68b8afa50a5
19. Hong, T.C.K., Economou, A.: What shape grammars do that cad should: the 14 cases of shape embedding. Artif. Intell. Eng. Des. Anal. Manuf. **36**, e4 (2022). https://doi.org/10.1017/S0890060421000263
20. Hu, M.K.: Visual pattern recognition by moment invariants. IRE Trans. Inf. Theory **8**(2), 179–187 (1962)
21. Huang, H.P., Puvvada, K.C., Sun, M., Wang, C.: Unsupervised and semi-supervised few-shot acoustic event classification. In: ICASSP 2021–2021 IEEE International Conference on Acoustics, Speech and Signal Processing (ICASSP), pp. 331–335. IEEE (2021)
22. Huang, Z., Leng, J.: Analysis of Hu's moment invariants on image scaling and rotation, vol. 7, pp. V7–476 (2010)
23. Hughes, D.P., Salathe, M.: An open access repository of images on plant health to enable the development of mobile disease diagnostics (2015)
24. Iseli, M.: Mosaic virus - is my plant infected? identification & treatment. https://plantophiles.com/plant-care/mosaic-virus-symptoms-and-treatments/
25. Joshi, K., Awale, R., Ahmad, S., Patil, S., Pisal, V.: Plant leaf disease detection using computer vision techniques and machine learnings. In: ITM Web of Conferences (2022)
26. KSaradhambal, G., D.R.L.S.R.R.: Plant disease detection and its solution using image classification. Int. J. Pure Appl. Math. **119** (2018). https://doi.org/10.1051/itmconf/20224403002

27. Lake, B., Salakhutdinov, R., Tenenbaum, J.: One-shot learning by inverting a compositional causal process. In: Advances in Neural Information Processing Systems (2013), 27th Annual Conference on Neural Information Processing Systems, NIPS 2013, 05–10-December-2013 (2013)
28. Li, Y., Chao, X.: Semi-supervised few-shot learning approach for plant diseases recognition. Plant Methods 17, 1–10 (2021)
29. Li Fe-Fei, Fergus, Perona: A bayesian approach to unsupervised one-shot learning of object categories. In: Proceedings Ninth IEEE International Conference on Computer Vision, vol. 2, pp. 1134–1141 (2003)
30. Fei-Fei, L., Fergus, R., Perona, P.: One-shot learning of object categories. IEEE Trans. Pattern Anal. Mach. Intell. 28(4), 594–611 (2006)
31. Lu, J., Ehsani, R., Shi, Y., De Castro, A., Wang, S.: Detection of multi-tomato leaf diseases (late blight, target and bacterial spots) in different stages by using a spectral-based sensor. Sci. Rep. 8, 2793 (2018)
32. Lu, J., Zhou, M., Gao, Y., Jiang, H.: Using hyperspectral imaging to discriminate yellow leaf curl disease in tomato leaves. Precis. Agric. 19, 1–16 (2018)
33. McAvoy, G.: Take the right aim to tame target spot of tomato. https://www.growingproduce.com/vegetables/take-the-right-aim-to-tame-target-spot-of-tomato/
34. Michelle Marks, U.: Bacterial spot of tomato. https://hort.extension.wisc.edu/articles/bacterial-spot-of-tomato/
35. Mohanty, S.: Plantvillage-dataset. https://github.com/spMohanty/PlantVillage-Dataset
36. Muggleton, S., Dai, W.Z., Sammut, C., Tamaddoni-Nezhad, A.: Meta-interpretive learning from noisy images. Mach. Learn. 107, 1097–1118 (2018)
37. Muggleton, S., de Raedt, L.: Inductive logic programming: theory and methods. J. Logic Program. 19–20, 629–679 (1994). Special Issue: Ten Years of Logic Programming
38. Muggleton, S., Lin, D., Tamaddoni-Nezhad, A.: Meta-interpretive learning of higher-order dyadic datalog: predicate invention revisited. Mach. Learn. 100, 49–73 (2015)
39. Müller, T., Pérez-Torró, G., Basile, A., Franco-Salvador, M.: Active few-shot learning with fasl. arXiv preprint arXiv:2204.09347 (2022)
40. Narwade Manoorkar, J., Kumar, D.B.: Local and Global Color Histogram Feature for Color Content-Based Image Retrieval System, pp. 293–300 (2016)
41. Ökten, İ, Yüzgeç, U.: Rice plant disease detection using image processing and probabilistic neural network. In: Seyman, M.N. (ed.) Electrical and Computer Engineering, pp. 82–94. Springer International Publishing, Cham (2022). https://doi.org/10.1007/978-3-031-01984-5_7
42. Qi, A., Gryaditskaya, Y., Xiang, T., Song, Y.Z.: One sketch for all: one-shot personalized sketch segmentation. IEEE Trans. Image Process. 31, 2673–2682 (2022)
43. Radovanović, D., Ukanovic, S.: Image-based plant disease detection: a comparison of deep learning and classical machine learning algorithms. In: 2020 24th International Conference on Information Technology (IT), pp. 1–4 (2020)
44. Reganold, J.P., Papendick, R.I., Parr, J.F.: Sustainable agriculture. Sci. Am. 262(6), 112–121 (1990)
45. Ren, M., et al.: Meta-learning for semi-supervised few-shot classification. arXiv preprint arXiv:1803.00676 (2018)
46. RHS: Tomato leaf mould. https://www.rhs.org.uk/disease/tomato-leaf-mould

47. Sharma, P., Berwal, Y., Ghai, W.: Performance analysis of deep learning CNN models for disease detection in plants using image segmentation. Inf. Process. Agric. **7**, 566–574 (2019)

48. Spengler, T.: What are two-spotted spider mites - two-spotted mite damage and control insects. https://www.gardeningknowhow.com/plant-problems/pests/insects/two-spotted-spider-mite-control.htm

49. Srinivasan, A.: A learning engine for proposing hypotheses (aleph) (2001). https://www.cs.ox.ac.uk/activities/programinduction/Aleph/aleph.html

50. Strubell, E., Ganesh, A., McCallum, A.: Energy and policy considerations for deep learning in NLP. CoRR (2019)

51. Tamaddoni-Nezhad, A.: Metagol_nt. https://github.com/atnezhad/Metagol_NT

52. Tekol, Y., contributors: PySwip v0.2.10 (2020). https://github.com/yuce/pyswip

53. Türkoğlu, M., Yanikoglu, B., Hanbay, D.: Plantdiseasenet: convolutional neural network ensemble for plant disease and pest detection. Signal Image Video Process. **16**(2), 301–309 (2022)

54. Varghese, D.: Metagol_nt. https://github.com/danyvarghese/Metagol_NT

55. Varghese, D., Bauer, R., Baxter-Beard, D., Muggleton, S., Tamaddoni-Nezhad, A.: Human-like rule learning from images using one-shot hypothesis derivation. In: Katzouris, N., Artikis, A. (eds.) Inductive Logic Programming, pp. 234–250. Springer, Cham (2022). https://doi.org/10.1007/978-3-030-97454-1_17

56. Varghese, D., Tamaddoni-Nezhad, A.: One-shot rule learning for challenging character recognition. In: Proceedings of the 14th International Rule Challenge, Oslo, Norway, vol. 2644, pp. 10–27 (2020)

57. Varghese, D., Tamaddoni-Nezhad, A.: Pyilp (2022). https://github.com/danyvarghese/PyILP/

58. Wang, Y., Yao, Q., Kwok, J.T., Ni, L.M.: Generalizing from a few examples: a survey on few-shot learning. ACM Comput. Surv. **53**(3), 1–34 (2020)

59. Ying, Z.: Weakly-supervised diagnosis with attention models (2022)

60. Yu, Z., Chen, L., Cheng, Z., Luo, J.: Transmatch: a transfer-learning scheme for semi-supervised few-shot learning. In: Proceedings of the IEEE/CVF Conference on Computer Vision and Pattern Recognition, pp. 12856–12864 (2020)

61. Zhu, P., Zhu, Z., Wang, Y., Zhang, J., Zhao, S.: Multi-granularity episodic contrastive learning for few-shot learning. Pattern Recognit. **131**, 108820 (2022)

Deep Learning-Based Multiclass Classification of Cotton Leaf Images Using ResNet and Transfer Learning

Sengathir Janakiraman[ID] and Ranga Pravallika Rayapudi[✉][ID]

Department of Information Technology, CVR College of Engineering, Mangalpally, Vastunagar, Hyderabad, Telangana, India
20b81db012@cvr.ac.in

Abstract. In this study, a deep learning model is proposed to classify the cotton leaf images into multiple classes. There are five steps in the entire procedure. At the first step of this process, images are acquired from the dataset. Next, in pre-processing, the image sizes are reduced to 200×200. After that, data augmentation takes place, which entails modifying the original data in order to produce new data points. Later, features are extracted using CNN. As the final step, the deep learning model Res-Net is used to classify the images. The performance of the classifier can be measured using the F1-score, recall, and precision as well. The dataset used for this research consists of five different classes: healthy and diseased. In the diseased class, there are subclasses of four types of diseased leaves, namely Alternaria, Cercospora, Grey Mildew, and Bacterial Blight. As a result, this Res-Net model has provided individual accuracy of 100% for healthy and Cercospora classes, 88.2% and 87.5% for Grey Mildew and Bacterial blight and 82.35% for Alternaria.

Keywords: Cotton Leaf Images · Deep Learning · Image Classification · Performance Validation · Transfer Learning

1 Introduction

In India, cotton is one of the main crops. A reduction in cotton productivity is largely a result of cotton diseases 80–90% of diseases that attack cotton plants commonly occur on the leaves, like Alternaria leaf spot and Bacterial Blight. Agarwal et al. [1] studied that Agricultural losses are the result of failing to identify plant diseases at the right time, which feeds the country. In other nations, like Africa and India, low food yields cause starvation. A recent study sheds some light on the value of deep learning and machine learning in detecting diseases at an early stage. In deep learning, the mathematical perceptual approach makes identifying and classifying objects more straightforward [2]. The diversified development and advancement of deep learning models across many different industries through the incubation of pre-formed models. Geetharamani et al.

© Springer Nature Switzerland AG 2023
D. Garg et al. (Eds.): IACC 2022, CCIS 1781, pp. 337–349, 2023.
https://doi.org/10.1007/978-3-031-35641-4_27

[3] observed that Deep learning has become an avid technique for predicting and categorizing because of the compatibility of neural networks and mathematical calculus. There are different diseases of cotton, some of which are described below.

1) **Grey Mildew Disease**: The organism often attacks older leaves, producing irregular, rakish, pale, and dull patches. They are often under or above the cut piece of the leaf and are joined by the veinlets. On the surface of the leaf, it is common to see a few dots that might number in the hundreds. When there is a serious disease, the leaves drop off early and turn a yellowish-brown tint.

2) **Bacterial Blight Disease:** Mohit Agarwal et al. have visualized that there may be several phases of the condition [4]. The worst one, though, appears on the leaves 45 to 60 days after sowing. There may be tiny, uneven, pale-brown dots on the leaves that range in size from 0.5 to 6 mm. A core lesion is present in each site, which is encircled by concentric rings. Many places converge to generate blighted zones. The impacted leaves wilt and weaken. Rarely are stem lesions seen. However, in rare circumstances, these dots may show up on bracts and bolls.

3) **Vascular Wilt Disease:** This illness will be influenced by soils with pH levels between 6 and 8.00. Nearly every component of the plant is impacted. At the seedling stage, cotyledons begin to yellow, petioles begin to sauté, and dry leaf filling begins. But Suneeth Kr Gupta et al. [5] analysed that the absence of bloating, hanging leaves, fragile shoots and, finally, the death of plants occurs in young and mature plants, by contrast.

4) **Cercospora:** The disease mostly damages mature plants' older leaves. During the early stages of illness, these leaves will develop reddish lesions. The lesions expand and turn white to light brown or grey in the middle, with a purple, dark brown, or blackish edge as the condition develops. Lesions are round or irregular, and their size varies according to when they are infected. The dots are concentric, with alternating dark and light brown or red edges. Affected leaves gradually turn pale in colour and fall off.

The objective of this study is to classify the cotton leaf images by using deep learning algorithm named ResNet. This paper is further comprised as follows: In Sect. 2, various DL architectures and its process were described and modified techniques for visualizing plant diseases. Section 3 describes the workflow of the whole experiment and elaborates upon the methodology used for the proposed model. Section 4 discusses the results and analysis, and Sect. 5 concludes with a description of the model for better visualization, classification and detection of plant diseases.

2   Literature Survey

Chohan et al. [6] described a method for identifying plant diseases using CNN. The collected dataset is first subjected to augment as pre-processing. Augmentation is done to increase the dataset's size, which helps to train the model better. Then, the image size is reduced by 256 × 256. Next, these are sent as input to the convolution network layer for prediction. There are two main functions: convolution and pooling. Convolution is utilised to detect the edges in an image. Pooling is utilised to reduce the image size. The different CNN architectures involved in this are simply CNN, VGG, and Inception V3. A total of five convolutional layers that have a 3×3 filter and five maximum pooling layers with a 2×2 filter are used. Then, batch normalisation is performed to scale the data. Then the classifier can categorise the given image into unhealthy and healthy. To detect plant diseases, two datasets are employed. 38 classes are included in the second data set, compared to 15 classes in the first. This model has an accuracy of 95%. Then, the model is evaluated using the parameters like accuracy.

Ramacharan [7] developed a three-stage method for disease detection. This research was done on cotton leaves using the CNN Algorithm. As its name suggests, this model consists primarily of three steps: image acquisition, convolution layers and disease forecasting. In image acquisition, an image is taken as input by the user and converted into a greyscale image by resizing it to 128×128. After that, the images are preprocessed and passed through the hidden layers where feature extraction, pooling, dense, dropout, activation, and flattening are done. Then, disease prediction can be done using the Soft-Max layer after applying CNN. Accuracy can be increased by increasing the number of epochs. In this process, a total of 500 epochs were adopted. An accuracy of 96.6% was obtained.

Balambigai Subramanian [8] introduced a disease detection model in the lemon leaf using image processing techniques. The standard image processing procedures, such as picture capture, pre-processing of the image, image segmentation, and feature extraction, are the first ones carried out in this process. Once the photos have been gathered, they are converted into digital images and sent for pre-processing in the image acquisition process. Next, in pre-processing, the improvement of an image can be done by applying different techniques like cropping, colour space conversion, smoothing, and image enhancement. Then, after pre-processing, all the images are sent to the segmentation process. It divides the image into different regions. Later, features are extracted using GLCM features. Both colour and texture features are extracted, and they were calculated using mean, median, and standard deviation. After that, the images are sent to the classification step. At classification, CNN and SVM are compared. It starts with an input image and then a feature map is created using four filters. Next, apply the ReLU function, pooling layer, and flattening. After that, insert the vector into the completely linked layer, which offers the necessary class vote. Hence, the accuracy was 93.8% by using CNN in class, which showed better results.

Islam et al. [9] suggested an automated network-based neuronal convolution method for categorizing and identifying photos of diseased rice leaves. In total, four models that come under deep CNN are analysed for this research. They are Xception, ResNet-101, Inception-Resnet-V2, and VGG-19. After the image acquisition, the images are sent for pre-processing. The pre-processing step includes resizing, rotation, zooming, flipping, and shuffling. Then, CNN can be used for feature extraction and segmentation. The classification technique makes use of ANN-based fully connected layers, while transfer learning can also be used. For this, Deep, CNN applications such as Kera's are used. It contains multiple convolutional layers, pooling and dense layers. Additionally, it consists of several layer blocks that extract characteristics from the input data image. The feature parameters the model learns may be portable. Dense layers are included in Kera's' final block to help classify the images. Finally, this model was tested with 4 CNN deep learning Kera algorithms and the highest accuracy of 92% was obtained by using Inception ResNet-V2. The data set used in this model contains 984 images collected from the UCI machine learning repository and Kaggle. The performance of all the algorithms was compared with the values of accuracy, recall, precision, and F1-Score.

Pankhuri Pragya et al. [10] presented a Senet CNN-based model for the detection of tomato leaf disease. A hybrid procedure is described in this approach, which builds on the Senet and CNN layer concepts for better categorization. To begin, an input dataset is chosen from among the available resources and analysed for disease prediction. Following that, the image was pre-processed using grayscale conversation before being binarized. Then, the characteristics are quantified using the characteristic extraction as a histogram of oriented gradients (HOG) and the appropriate segmentation selection. The block is then normalised after the colour and intensity data are filtered by using a filter kernel. Then, the standard CNN technique is used for data classification. In this case, removing less frequently used data can speed up the process. So, it tries to give more weight to each feature map in the layer. As a result, SE combined with CNN will function as a recommended solution for a quick and accurate procedure. The confusion matrix is calculated, and the comparison analysis result parameter is returned.

Obrien et al. [11] proposed a model for the identification of Mango leaf disease using CNN. The input images resized to 256×256. Then, these images are sent as input to the CNN layer. In this model, there are 4 convolutional operations and it is made up of 32,64,64,128 after every convolution. Later, the output is sent to the max-pooling layer. When the stride is 1, The sizes of filters for all the max pooling and convolution layers were 5×5. In the previous model, there are 2 fully connected layers. The first one had 1×512 dimensions whereas the output layer had 1×4 dimensions. To improve network speed and training process, the Adam optimizer and ReLU layer have been deployed. Adam's method is an efficient way of computing learning rates for very noisy gradients; It determines each unique learning rate for various parameters. The ReLu layer conducts a linear operation to avoid the vanishing gradient problem. The dataset consists of 2080 images used for this process.

Srivastava et al. [12] put up a system for categorizing plant diseases. First, the images are subjected to a preprocessing technique, which generally consists of removing low-recurrence, eliminating reflections, veiling segments of images, and normalizing the power of small particulars displayed on the images. After preprocessing, the images are sent to the CNN model for training. Then, classification can also be done using CNN. A CNN is a 2D convolution layer that develops a convolution core by weaving inlet layers and facilitates the production of an outlet tensor. It also includes different steps like the Maxpooling layer, which chooses the best element from the region; Flattening to convert the 2D matric features to vector; Image Data Generator to generate batches from image files; and Epoch, which determines the count of passes. Later, after all these steps, the last stage is the validation stage, which categorizes the testing set images into healthy and diseased. The Plant Village dataset, which is available in a public repository called Kaggle, is used in this process. The best accuracy achieved is 88% for this model.

Rao et al. [13] defined a new hybrid approach that is introduced in three steps for classifying leaf diseases. The experiment is done in two modes by dividing the training and test data into two different ratios. In model 1, the ratio of training to testing is 50%–50%, whereas it is 70%–30% for the second model. At the initial stage, image improvement and conversion techniques are used to solve problems caused by insufficient illumination and noise. For image enhancement, the histogram equalization technique is used. Hence, image preprocessing stages are applied. Then, in the next step, feature extraction can be done by combining GLCM, Gabor, and Curve let feature extraction models. Different features such as texture, color, and shape are extracted in that phase. Then, these extracted features are sent as input to the classifier. In this step, the input data is processed and feature-wise data is gathered. The Fuzzy membership function is used to fuzzify the appropriate feature values. This classification process is again divided into 3 phases: 1) Fuzzification 2) Building a neural network classifier 3) Defuzzification. Lastly, the image class is classified as healthy or unhealthy using a neuro-blur classifier formed with the collected characteristics. In terms of accuracy, the performance of the classifiers is calculated. This approach was implemented using the MATLAB tool and obtained an accuracy of 90%.

Rai [14] uses a deep convolution neural network to automatically classify damaged cotton leaves. Initially, data augmentation is done, which is the process of creating datasets from existing datasets. So, the enlarged dataset is carried out in this process. The dataset is then partitioned into three pieces at random: validation, training, and testing. After that, the classification process can be done with the help of convolution neural networks. CNN's design includes fully interconnected layers, four convolutional layers, and four pooling layers. Each max-pooling is 2×2, and the convolutional layer is 3×3 in size. The feature map and the size of the input image differ. The last layer is used as an output layer while computing the SoftMax activation function. The training was done using three different epochs: 100, 300, and 500. The dataset was collected from the online platform called Kaggle, which consists of 2293 images of cotton leaves. The suggested model has the best test and training precision of 99.73% and 97.98%, respectively. The F1-score, recall, and precision is used to gauge performance.

Azath. M et al. [15] offered a CNN-based methodology for categorising photos of cotton leaves. The first step of the process starts with image collection. Then, these images are pre-processed using vectorization, normalization, resizing and increasing image, and then the features are extracted using CNN. After that, data partitioning can be done using k-fold cross-validation followed by classification. At this classification step, the images are sent to the input layer after data partitioning. The weights are taken into account for each picture with the addition of neurons. All output from the hidden layer is supplied to the input-output layer. The name of the foliar disease to which it belongs appears in the exit provided by that exit layer. Numerous tests were done during the experimental process to modify different parameters that led to a variety of results to create an effective model. The variables are the dataset's colour, the number of epochs, the augmentation, the optimizer, and the dropout. The dataset used consists of 2400 leaf images that were captured using digital cameras and smartphone cameras in the southern part of Ethiopia. Finally, the overall accuracy obtained is 96.4 percent, as demonstrated in the confusion matrix. This deep learning model was created using Jupyter as a development environment and the Python Keras library.

These studies show that CNNs have achieved acceptable outcomes in identifying plant diseases. As CNN technology advanced, deep CNN architectures with a variety of pre-trained models, including ResNet, AlexNet, GoogleNet, DenseNet, ImageNet, and VGGNet were developed. Furthermore, most application-oriented image recognition algorithms are based on transfer learning strategies. Thus, a CNN-based image identification model for cotton leaf diseases is proposed in this study.

3   Proposed Workflow and Methodology

The acquired cotton plane dataset is first pre-processed to convert the image size to 200 * 200 * 3 as the image sensor input to our network input. Monitoring the process of increasing the pre-processing data is applied to broaden the data set for better training (data augmentation). The augmented dataset is used as input to the proposed network. Using transfer learning and net image weights, the Res-Net classifier will be able to categorise the images by processing each layer. After the fully connected layers are applied to the Res-Net model, the final layer is the SoftMax activation layer, which produces output. As a result, cotton leaf images are classified as shown in below Fig. 1.

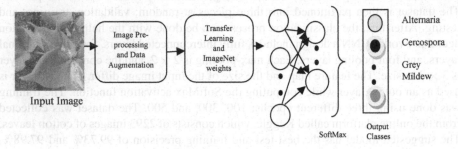

Fig. 1. Process of the proposed model

3.1   Dataset

The dataset acquired is the cotton leaf dataset, where the cotton leaf images are taken using a digital camera. The original raw image size of the data was 6000 × 4000 × 3, which was reduced to 384 × 256 × 3. The dataset consists of five classes: one for healthy cotton leaf images, and the remaining four are for different types of diseased images, namely Alternaria, Bacterial Blight, Cercospora, and Grey Mildew. Phases of testing and training are applied to the entire data collection. While only 30% of the data is used for training, the remaining 70% is used for validation. The dataset used for this experiment's sample photographs is shown below in Fig. 2.

3.2   Image Pre-processing

Convolutional neural networks use pre-processed image data for training by converting the input image data into meaningful floating-point tensors. In the case of the 64 × 64 image, the tensor will have the following dimensions: (64, 64, 3).

| Alternaria | Bacterial Blight | Cercospora |

Grey Mildew   Healthy

Fig. 2. Sample images of the Input Dataset

In this proposed dataset, there are images with a resolution of 384 * 256 * 3 pixels for which the model is trained. A possible solution is to resize images to smaller dimensions to simplify the model training process. So, images can be reduced to 200 * 200 * 3 as the image sensor input to the network. The size of the image after pre-processing can be shown in Fig. 3.

Fig. 3. Sample image after pre-processing

3.3 Data Augmentation

The task of collecting and analysing data can be time-consuming. Augmentation technique which includes several operations like rotations, zooming, and cropping are used. In this study, the following collection of techniques are used to do the data augmentation: The Rotation range is 15, the horizontal flip is true, the vertical flip is true, the shear range is 0.1, the brightness range is [0.5, 1.5], the width shift range is 0.2, height shift range is 0.1.

3.4   Transfer Learning and ImageNet Weights

According to the WordNet database, images are hierarchically arranged in ImageNet. To aid, academics working in the area of image and vision research, including students and other researchers.

Researchers from all across the world are competing in ImageNet's Large-Scale Visual Recognition Challenge to create systems that have the lowest top-1 and top-5 error rates (ILSVRC). 1.2 million images make up the 1,000-class training set, 50,000 images make up the validation set, and 150,000 images make up the test set.

3.5   Architecture

In this research, ResNet50 is used, which means that it has 50 layers to process based on the number near Res-Net, which indicates the number of deep layers. It incorporates skip connections, thus solving the problem of vanishing gradient descent. ResNet50 takes the input as 200 dimensions, and its main advantage is its support for 200-dimensional input. Convolution and max-pooling are performed by each ResNet, followed by stacked convolutions. Due to the stacked convoluted, this fix for vanishing gradients is possible. In this experiment, batches are 8 and the loss function is a cross-entropy loss function. A learning rate scheduler is set, with a momentum of 0.9. Figure 4 demonstrates the ResNet50 architecture overall and the final average pooling layer with two labels: diseased or fresh leaf. The ResNet50 architecture showed below step by step.

- In the first step, Images are sent as input to the classifier.
- Convolution with 64 distinct kernels with strides of size 2 and a kernel size of 7 * 7 making 1 layer.
- The next step is to the max pool with strides of size 2.
- After that, perform a 1 * 1,64 kernel and a 3 * 3,64 kernel, followed by a 1 * 1,256 kernel, which results in a total of nine layers in this stage after being repeated three times.
- Four times through this process, a total of 12 layers were added. The kernel of 1 * 1,128 is next, followed by 3 * 3,128 and 1 * 1,512.
- This is followed by a kernel of 1 * 1,256, followed by another one of 3 * 3,256, followed by a final one of 1 * 1,1024. This has a total of 18 layers after being repeated six times.
- In total, nine layers are there composed of three 1 * 1,512 kernels, then three 3 * 3,512 kernels, and two 1 * 1,2048 kernels.
- The next step is an average pool, followed by 1000 fully connected nodes, and finally, perform a SoftMax function to produce 1 layer. The calculation does not include the activation functions or the maximum/average pooling layers.
- This is accomplished by using a Deep Convolutional Network with $1 + 9 + 12 + 18 + 9 + 1 = 50$ layers

3.6   Adam Optimizer

Gradient descent is an optimization technique based on adaptive moment estimation. When dealing with large problems with many variables or data, the method is very

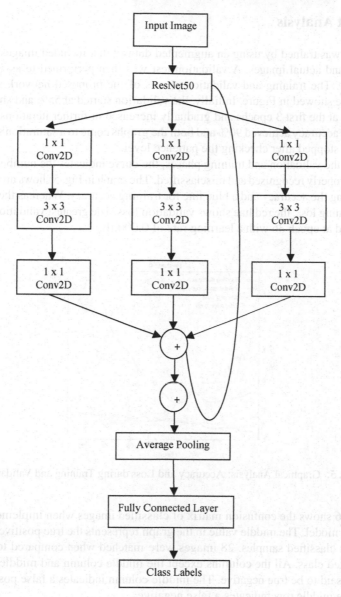

Fig. 4. Architecture of ResNet50

efficient. Memory is consumed less and the method is more efficient. It is a method that was designed by combining ADAGrad, root mean square propagation, and the algorithm for gradient descent with momentum with Adam, gradient descent is combined with one of two methods: y taking into account the "exponentially weighted average" of the gradients, this method is utilised to accelerate the gradient descent process. The algorithm converges towards minima faster by using averages.

4 Result Analysis

The model was trained by using an augmented dataset that included images from augmentation and actual images. A validation test was then performed to assess its generalizability. The training and validation phases of the proposed network show good convergence showed in Figure. Initially, the validation started at 55% and showed little uncertainty at the first 3 epochs and gradually increased in further iterations. Whereas, the training accuracy achieved 90% and both the graphs come to a saturation state where the process stopped after checking the patience level.

During the validation and training phases, the curve indicates the number of photos that were properly recognised and misclassified. The graph in Fig. 5 shows an orange line for validating the accuracy and a blue line for training accuracy. Whereas the green line reflects training loss, the red line shows validation loss. The greatest validation accuracy was attained at epoch 36 with a learning rate of 0.00001.

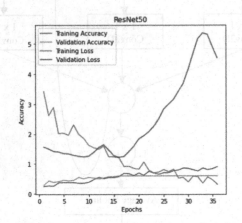

Fig. 5. Graphical Analysis: Accuracy and Loss during Training and Validation

Figure 6 shows the confusion matrix of classified images when implemented using the ResNet model. The middle value in the graph represents the true positive rate which is correctly classified samples. 28 images were matched when compared to the actual and predicted class. All the columns except the middle column and middle row of the matrix are said to be true negative. The middle column indicates a false positive value, whereas the middle row indicates a false negative.

This above 5 × 5 confusion matrix gives the results of all five class labels. The below Fig. 7 illustrates the comparison of performance metrics for all classes. As shown in the figure, the maximum individual classification accuracy of 100% is obtained for Cercospora and Healthy classes. Grey Mildew and Bacterial Blight classes got an accuracy of 88.2% and 87.5%. The remaining Alternaria class achieved an accuracy of 82.35%.

The ROC curve graphs and AUC values for each class are displayed below in Fig. 8. The graph's dotted line indicates the Comparison of TPR and FPR (False Positive Rate) at various categorization criteria.

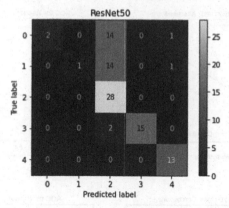

Fig. 6. Confusion matrix of output class labels

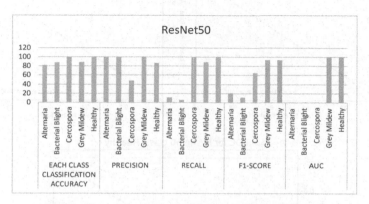

Fig. 7. Comparison of performance metrics for all classes

The terms "True Positive Rate" and "False Positive Rate" are defined as follows:

$$TPR = \frac{TP}{TP + FN}$$

$$FPR = \frac{FP}{FP + TN}$$

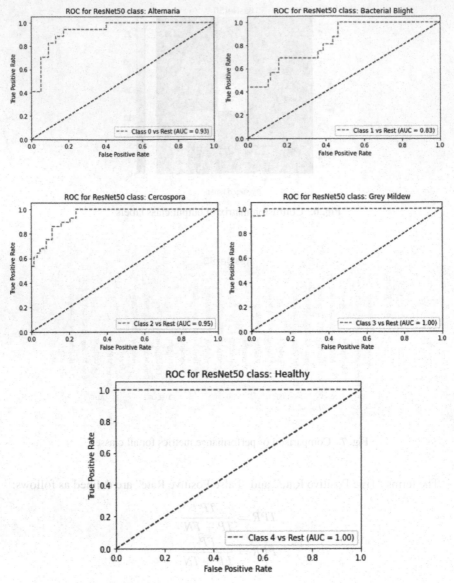

Fig. 8. ROC curve for each class with AUC values

5   Conclusion

An automated prediction model for identifying and categorizing plant leaf diseases based on image processing and classification techniques has been developed in the above-mentioned research. Several other transfer learning models were compared with the model performances along with graphs.

For the classes Cercospora and Healthy, the suggested model attained a maximum individual classification accuracy of 100%. Grey Mildew and Bacterial Blight classes got an accuracy of 88.2% and 87.5%. The remaining Alternaria class achieved an accuracy of 82.35%. This classifier model performs better at classifying Alternaria, Bacterial Blight, Healthy classes with 99% precision and the F1-Score with 98% compared to other models. The greatest validation accuracy was attained at epoch 36 with a learning rate of 0.00001. Python and the Keras library were utilised for the implementation, and Jupyter was used as the development environment.

References

1. Agarwal, M,, et al.: FCNN-LDA: a faster convolution neural network model for leaf dise ase identification on apple's leaf dataset. In: 2019 12th International Conference on Information & Communication Technology and System (ICTS). IEEE (2019)
2. Agarwal, M., et al.: A partcle swarm optimization based approach for filter pruning in convolution neural network for tomato leaf disease classification. In: International Advanced Computing Conference (2021)
3. Geetharamani, G., Arun Pandian, J.: Identification of plant leaf diseases using a nine-layer deep convolutional neural network. Comput. Electr. Eng. **76**, 323–338 (2019)
4. Agarwal, M., et al.: ToLeD: Tomato leaf disease detection using convolution neural network. Procedia Comput. Sci. **167**, 293–301 (2020)
5. Agarwal, M., Gupta, S.K., Biswas, K.K.: Plant leaf disease segmentation using compressed UNet architecture. In: Gupta, M., Ramakrishnan, G. (eds.) Trends and Applications in Knowledge Discovery and Data Mining: PAKDD 2021 Workshops, WSPA, MLMEIN, SDPRA, DARAI, and AI4EPT, Delhi, India, May 11, 2021 Proceedings, pp. 9–14. Springer International Publishing, Cham (2021). https://doi.org/10.1007/978-3-030-75015-2_2
6. Chohan, M., Khan, A., Chohan, R., Katpar, S.H., Mahar, M.S.: Plant disease detection using deep learning. Int. J. Recent Technol. Eng. (IJRTE) **9**(1), 909–914 (2020)
7. Ramacharan, S.: A 3-Stage method for disease detection of cotton plant leaf using deep learning CNN algorithm. Int. J. Res. Appl. Sci. Eng. Technol. **9**(VII), 2503–2510 (2021)
8. Subramanian, B., Jayashree, S., Kiruthika, S., Miruthula, S.: Lemon leaf disease detection and classification using SVM and CNN. Int. J. Recent Technol. Eng. (IJRTE) **8**(4), 11485–11488 (2019)
9. Islam, M.A., Nymur, M., Shamsojjaman, M., Hasan, S., Shahadat, M., Khatun, T.: An automated Convolutional neural network-based approach for Paddy leaf disease detection. Int. J. Adv. Comput. Sci. Appl. **12**(1), 280–288 (2021)
10. Pragya, P.: A Senet CNN-based tomato leaf disease detection. Int. J. Innovative Technol. Exploring Eng. **8**(11), 773–777 (2019)
11. Orbien, C.T.: Identification of Carabao mango leaf disease using Convolutional neural network. J. Adv. Res. Dyn. Control Syst. **12**(01-Special Issue), 152–158 (2020)
12. Srivastava, P., Mishra, K., Awasthi, V., Kumar Sahu, V., Kumar Pal, P.: Plant disease detection using convolutional neural network. Int. J. Adv. Res. **9**(01), 691–698 (2021)
13. Rao, A., Kulkarni, S.: A hybrid approach for plant leaf disease detection and classification using digital image processing methods. The Int. J. Electr. Eng. Educ. **12**, 002072092095312 (2020)
14. Rai, C.K.: Automatic classification of real-time diseased cotton leaves and plants using a deep-convolutional neural network (2022)
15. Azath, M.A., Zekiwos, M., Bruck, A.: Deep learning-based image processing for cotton leaf disease and pest diagnosis. J. Electr. Comput. Eng. **2021**, 9981437 (2021)

Identification of Potato Leaf Diseases Using Hybrid Convolution Neural Network with Support Vector Machine

Tasleem Sultana[1,2] and Motahar Reza[2(✉)]

[1] Department of Mathematics, JBIET, Hyderabad, India
[2] Department of Mathematics, GITAM Deemed to be University,
Hyderabad 502329, India
motaharreza90@gmail.com

Abstract. Agriculture has long been a vital source of sustenance. More over 60% of the world's population relies mostly on agricultural sources for food, according to linked statistics. Plant infections, however, are a catastrophic issue that seriously hampers agriculture productivity. Plant diseases cause a loss of agriculture productivity of about 25% per year. Potato crops have many benefits for human life. One of the most valuable benefits of potatoes for humans is their carbohydrate content; carbohydrates are the leading food for humans. The development of potato crop agriculture is significant for the sustainability of human life. There are several obstacles to developing potato farming, including a disease that attacks potato leaves. Infestans only the diseases early Blight (Alternia Solani) and late Blight (Phytophthora infestans de Bary) are among the most harmful to potato crops. However, the percentage of crops that fail to grow grows due to the erroneous and tardy identification of plant diseases. Using a diagnostic and detection system based on the Hybrid CNN (Convolutional neural network) with SVM (Support vector machine) presently deep learning (DL) technology, we offer an efficient and accurate way to identify early plant illnesses to reduce the plant output losses. Potato leaf disease detection issues can be resolved with the use of informatics technology and digital image processing. From the input photos of the supported training dataset, we utilised CNN to extract best feature of the illness characteristics, and then we used SVM to those features to do classification. 1900 photos of potato leaves were used to train the deep learning model, and about 950 images were utilised for testing.

We suggested the CNN model and trained a strong accuracy data set. In addition, we employed ResNET50, a transfer learning model, and obtained accuracy that was superior to our suggested CNN model. It's interesting that the accuracy of our suggested Hybrid CNN (ResNet 50) with SVN is 97.3% and that it was trained using the same Potato lead picture dataset and test data accuracy is 95.6.

Keywords: Plant disease detection · Potato leaf image · Deep Learning · CNN · ResNet50 · SVM

© Springer Nature Switzerland AG 2023
D. Garg et al. (Eds.): IACC 2022, CCIS 1781, pp. 350–361, 2023.
https://doi.org/10.1007/978-3-031-35641-4_28

1 Introduction

In India, for economic development, agriculture is a valuable source. To increase the production of food, the agriculture industries keep on searching for efficient methods to protect crops from damages. This makes researchers search for new efficient, and precise technologies for high productivity. The diseases on crops give low production and economic losses to farmers and agricultural industries [1,2]. In India 70%of population depends on agriculture and contributes 17% towards the GDP of country. For a successful farming system, one of the essential things is disease identification. In general, the naked eye observations of experts is the traditional approach, this method can be time consuming, expensive and inaccurate, a farmer observes symptoms of disease in plants that need continuous monitoring.

Different types of disease kill leaves in a plant. For identifying these diseases, farmers get more difficulties. For disease detection, the image processing methods are suitable and efficient with the help of plant leaf images. Though continuously monitoring of health and disease detection of plant increases the quality and quantity of the yield, it is costly. Machine learning algorithms are experimented due to their better accuracy. However, selection of classification algorithms appears to be a difficult task as the accuracy varies for different input data [3]. The objectives are to detect leaf disease portion from the image, extract features of an exposed part of the leaf, and recognize diseased leaf through SVM. Further, Convolutional Neural Network (CNN) model is evaluated and compared for accuracy.

The paper is arranged into five sections: the first section gives the introduction, the second section presents the literature survey, the third section discusses methodologies like feature extractions of images, SVM and CNN, the fourth section shows the result of classification, and the fifth section is about the conclusion and future scope.

2 Literature Survey

Shruthi et al. [1] presented the stages of general plant diseases detection system and study of machine learning techniques for plant disease detection. They showed that a convolutional neural network (CNN) detects many diseases with high accuracy. Vaishnnave et.al. [2] at reviewed of various types of plant diseases and different classification techniques in machine learning that are used for identifying diseases in different plant leaves along with the pros and cons. This paper summaries different algorithms used for classifying and detecting bacterial, fungal and viral plant leaf diseases [3]. Hossain et al. [4] used eleven statistical features and the Support Vector Machine classifier (SVM) to recognize the diseases. The advantages of this increase the efficiency of the detection, identification, and classification process. It gives 93% accurate results in disease classification. Islam et al. [5] integrated image processing and machine learning to allow diagnosing diseases from leaf images of potato plants. It gave 95% of the accuracy of disease classification using Color thresholder, GLCM and multiclass SVM [6]. They describe methods of an image processing and neural network for disease detection and classification. The color images preprocessed and k-means clustering is used for segmentation. The texture features are extracted using a gray level co-occurrence matrix (GLCM) method and given to the artificial neural network. The overall accuracy of this method is 90%.

For the detection and classification of tomato leaf disease, Sardoğan et .al [7] studied a Convolutional Neural Network (CNN) model and Learning Vector Quantization (LVQ) algorithm-based method. For automated feature extraction and categorization, they created a model of a CNN. The output feature vector from the convolutional component was input into the LVQ to train the network using straightforward leaf photos of healthy and ill plants, Ferentinos citedeep built the convolutional neural network models to perform plant disease identification and diagnosis. The model's extremely high success rate makes it an excellent advising or early warning tool, and it is a strategy that might be developed further to provide an integrated plant disease diagnosis system that can function under actual cultivation conditions. The challenge of illness diagnosis in the wild has been addressed by Johannes et al. [9] with the development of a novel image processing technique based on candidate hot-spot detection in conjunction with statistical inference approaches. A novel method for identifying rice diseases is put out by Lu et al. [10] and is based on deep convolutional neural network (CNN) methods. The suggested CNNs-based model obtains an accuracy of 95.48% when using the 10-fold cross-validation method. Compared to traditional machine learning models, this accuracy is far higher. The simulation results for identifying rice diseases demonstrate the viability and efficiency of the suggested approach. Saleem et al. [11] saleem give a thorough discussion of how DL models are used to depict different plant diseases. Additionally, several research holes are found that might be filled to increase transparency for identifying plant diseases even before their symptoms are plainly visible. Liu et al. [12,13] suggests a novel model called Leaf GAN, which is based on generative adversarial networks (GANs), to produce images of four different grape leaf diseases for training identification models, focusing on the shortage of training photos of grape leaf diseases. The dense connectivity strategy and instance normalisation are combined into an effective discriminator to distinguish between real and fake disease images by utilising their excellent feature extraction capabilities on grape leaf lesions. A generator model with degressive channels is first designed to generate images of grape leaf disease.

3   Dataset

The best deep learning model was created for this project using the publicly available PlantVillage dataset found at https://data.mendeley.com/datasets/tywbtsjrjv/1. By species and illness, the 54303 images of healthy and diseased leaves in the PlantVillage collection are divided into 38 groups. The data structure of the PlantVillage dataset comprises Labels are saved in a tensor that contains the labels for the linked photos, while pictures are stored in a tensor that contains the pictures. The images span 14 crop species: Apple, Blueberry, Cherry, Corn, Grape, Orange, Peach, Bell Pepper, Potato, Raspberry, Soybean, Squash, Strawberry, Tomato. In contains images of 17 fungal diseases, 4 bacterial diseases, 2 mold(oomycete) diseases, 2 viral disease, and 1 disease caused by a mite. 12 crop species also have images of healthy leaves that are not visibly affected by a disease. For our analysis we consider only Potato leaf dataset. Sample Potato data set is displayed in Fig. 5.

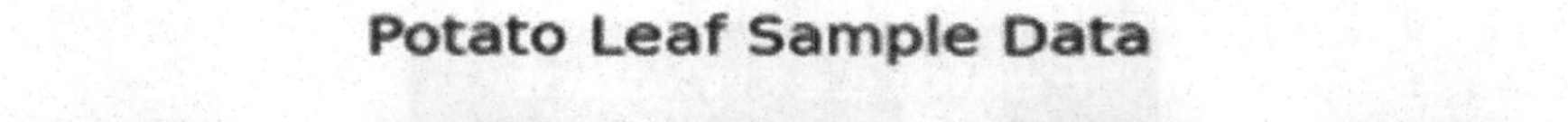

Potato Leaf Sample Data

Fig. 1. Potato Leaf Sample data

4 Methodology

Image acquisition is the first step of a plant disease detection system. By using digital cameras, scanners, or lounger, high quality plant images can be captured. The images can also be taken from the web. Large numbers of image samples were collected from PlantVillage dataset, which consists of diseased and healthy leaves. Image Preprocessing is used to increase the quality of leaf image and eliminate the unwanted noise. The segmentation process is used to partition the plant image in various segments to separate the diseased portion of the leaf. In general image proccesing technique is used to extract the feature (see Fig. 1). They any classifier is used to classify. But our case instead of image processing we used advance Convolution Neural Network (CNN) deep learning technique to reduce the features. Then we used the Support Vector Machine (SVM) classifier to classify.

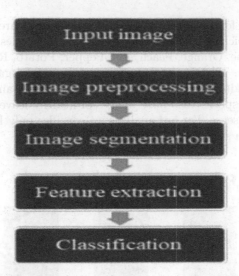

Fig. 2. Flowchart for Leaf Disease Recognition Fig. 1 shows the flow chart of operations involved in leaf disease recognition

4.1 Support Vector Machine (SVM) Classifier

To classify the various diseases in plants any of the machine learning techniques can be used. The classification phase suggested deciding if the input image is healthy or diseased. In this paper Support Vector Machine (SVM) classifier has been used because it has some advantages over other classifiers such as effective in high dimensional spaces also in cases where the number of dimensions is greater than the number of samples. It is memory efficient as it uses a subset of training points in the decision function (called support vectors) [5]. SVM is a supervised machine learning algorithm used for both classification and regression. SVM is a discriminative classifier. In this problem, for classification, the SVM technique has been applied. In SVM, each data item is plotted as a point in n-dimensional space; the number of dimensions corresponding to the number of features being classified. The classification is obtained by discovering the hyper-plane that uniquely distinguishes between different groups of scattered data points [6]. By finding the hyper-plane the classification is performed. Hyper-plane differentiates two classes very well. This is shown in Fig. 2. Suppose training data satisfy following constrains also.

$$W^T X^{(i)} + b \geq +1 \; for \; Y^{(i)} = +1 \tag{1}$$
$$W^T X^{(i)} + b \leq -1 \; for \; Y^{(i)} = -1 \tag{2}$$

Combining Eq. 1 and 2, the reduced equation can be written as

$$Y^{(i)}(W^T X^{(i)} + b) \geq 1 \; for \; \forall i \tag{3}$$

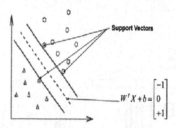

Fig. 3. Support Vector Machine recognition

Our objective is to find Hyperplane (W,b) with maximal separation between it and closest data points while satisfying the above constrains

$$Max\ W, b = \frac{2}{||W||} \tag{4}$$

such that

$$Y^{(}i)\,(W^T\,X^{(}i) + b) \geq 1\,\forall i \tag{5}$$

all so we know

$$||W|| = \sqrt{W^T W} \tag{6}$$

4.2 Convolutional Neural Network (CNN)

CNN is a class of deep neural networks. The CNN model comprises an input layer, convolution layer, pooling layer, a fully connected layer, and an output layer shown in Fig. 3. To classify the disease in plants in a precise manner the images are provided as input. The convolution layer is used for extracting the features from the images. The pooling layer computes the feature values from the extracted features. Depending on the complexity of images, the convolution and pooling layer can be further increased to obtain more details. A fully connected layer uses the output of previous layers and transforms them into a single vector that can be used as an input for the next layer. The output layer finally classifies the plant disease [6].

1. Convolution is a point-wise multiplication of two functions to produce a third function
2. Primary purpose of convolution in CNN is to extract features from the input image.
3. Matrix formed by sliding the filter over the image and computing the dot product is called the a Convolved Feature or ~Activation Map or the ~Feature Map
4. CNNs do a little pre-processing, that means the network learns the filters before doing the real classification. Vertical edge detection is shown in Fig. 4.

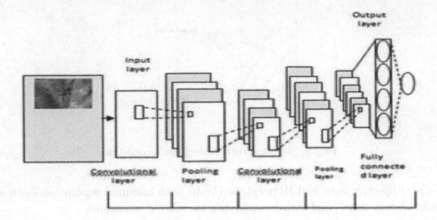

Fig. 4. CNN MODEL

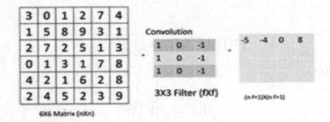

Fig. 5. Detecting Vertical edges

4.3 Propose CNN Model

The Deep Convolutional Neural Networks' training dataset was the dataset from potato leaves (Fig. 6). The purpose of this CNN was to train the data for feature reduction and classification utilising fully connected layers (ANN) for the detection of illnesses affecting potato leaves. A proper kernel size and the number of convolution layers are considered while building the best-fit model. The batch size, number of epochs, regularisation, dropout, and the appropriate optimizer are all taken into account while modifying the hyper tuning parameters.

Model: "sequential"

Layer (type)	Output Shape	Param #
module_wrapper (ModuleWrapper)	(None, None, None, 64)	1792
module_wrapper_1 (ModuleWrapper)	(None, None, None, 64)	0
module_wrapper_2 (ModuleWrapper)	(None, None, None, 128)	73856
module_wrapper_3 (ModuleWrapper)	(None, None, None, 128)	0
module_wrapper_4 (ModuleWrapper)	(None, None, None, 256)	295168
module_wrapper_5 (ModuleWrapper)	(None, None, None, 256)	0
batch_normalization (BatchNormalization)	(None, None, None, 256)	1024
module_wrapper_6 (ModuleWrapper)	(None, None, None, 512)	1180160
module_wrapper_7 (ModuleWrapper)	(None, None, None, 512)	0
flatten (Flatten)	(None, None)	0
dense (Dense)	(None, 1024)	33555456
dropout (Dropout)	(None, 1024)	0
batch_normalization_1(BatchNormalization)	(None, 1024)	4096
dense_1 (Dense)	(None, 128)	131200
dense_2 (Dense)	(None, 4)	516

Total params: 35,243,268
Trainable params: 35,240,708
Non-trainable params: 2,560

Fig. 6. The summary of proposed Convolution Neural Network

Next that tomato Leaf picture dataset was used as a feature extractor for the convolution layers of the ResNet 50 pre-trained deep neural networks, which are publicly available in the Keras toolkit, to train fully connected (FC) layers from scratch. The architechure of ResNet50 is displayed in Fig. 7. The summary of ResNet50 model is displayed in Fig. 8.

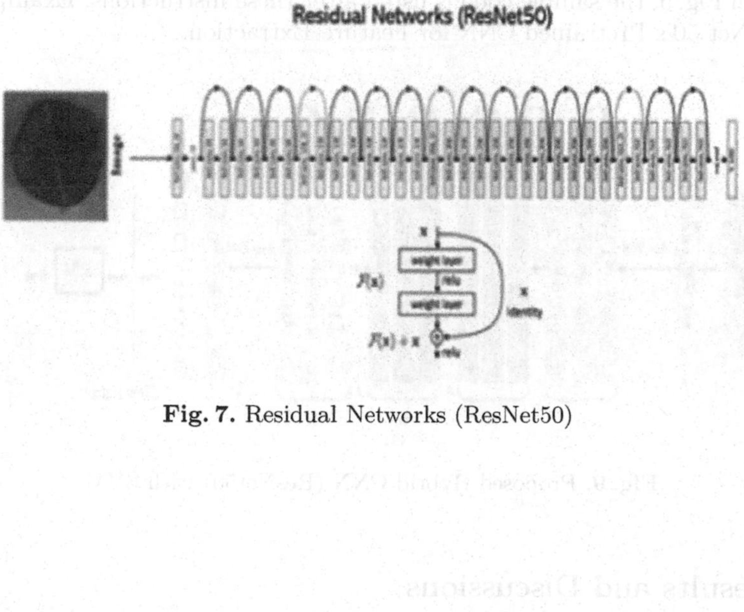

Residual Networks (ResNet50)

Fig. 7. Residual Networks (ResNet50)

Resnet 50 Model: "sequential"

Layer (type)	Output Shape	Param #
resnet50 (Functional)	(None, 2048)	23587712
flatten (Flatten)	(None, 2048)	0
dense (Dense)	(None, 256)	524544
dense_1 (Dense)	(None, 256)	65792
dense_2 (Dense)	(None, 4)	1028

Total params: 24,179,076
Trainable params: 591,364
Non-trainable params: 23,587,712

Fig. 8. The summary of RestNet50 Architecture

4.4   Proposed Hybrid CNN Model (ResNet50) with SVM

We proposed the hybrid CNN model (Resnet50) with SVM. The architecture of this proposed model is displayed in Fig. 9. In order to extract the feature from the dataset of potato leaf image data, we utilised pre-trained CNN Model ResNet 50 (see Fig. 9). The flattened image array is created using the ResNet 50 model. The feature vector is converted into a data frame for the SVM classifier's input. In Fig. 9, the sample code is listed after these instructions. Example code for ResNet 50's Pretrained CNN for Feature Extraction.

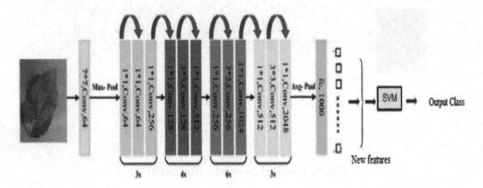

Fig. 9. Proposed Hybrid CNN (ResNet50) with SVM

5   Results and Discussions

The dataset of potato leaf images was divided between training and testing groups at a ratio of 70:30. To detect the potato lead illnesses, we trained the Deep Convolutional Neural Network (see Fig. 6). With batch size set to 20, we utilised the ADAM optimizer with epoch 50. The suggested CNN architecture has 35,243,268 total parameters. The accuracy on the test data set is 91.2% and the accuracy on the training data is 93.2%. This understanding can be accepted. However, it can be further boosted by performing hyperparameter fine tweaking. We also notice variations in the loss function, accuracy, and recall value with respect to epochs. The learning rate is set at 0.001.

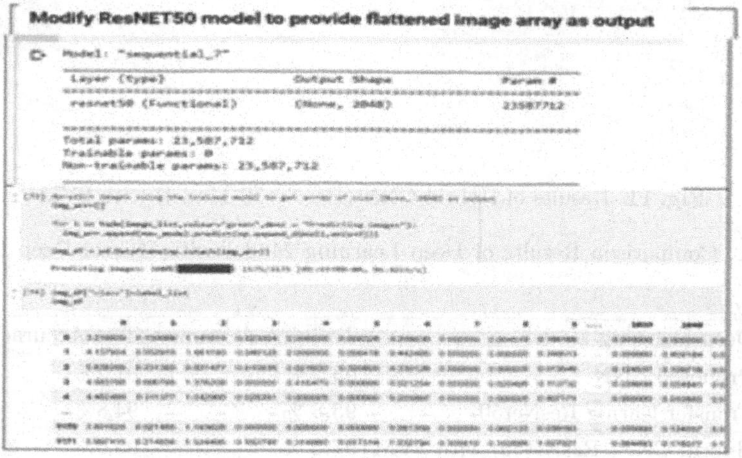

Fig. 10. Modify ResNet50 Model to provide flattened image array as output

We used pre-trained CNN Model ResNet 50 (see Fig. 9) to extract the feature from the potato leaf image data set. This ResNet 50 model is used to produce flattened image array. The feature vector convert in data frame which is used as input of SVM classifier. The sample code is mentioned below this steps in Fig. 10 Sample code for Feature extraction using Pretrained CNN: ResNet 50. The performance of the hybrid CNN (ResNet 50) with SVM classifier gives the accuracy 95.6% for test data . It is good agreement and acceptable. The confusion matrix of this Hybrid deep learning model: ResNet50 with SVM is shown in Fig. 11. Performance matric: Confusion matrix for hybrid CNN (ResNet50) with SVM.

5.1   Comparison Results

Details comparison results on accuracy on training and test data set for different deep learning model are shown in Table 1. We considered CNN model and Hybrid CNN (ResNet50) with SVM for analys the results. It is found that Hybrid CNN (ResNet50) with SVM gives better accuracy.

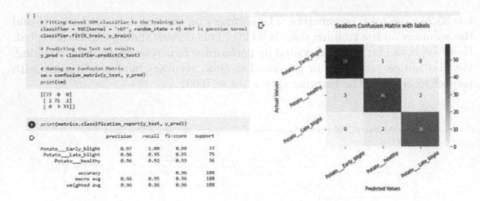

Fig. 11. Results of Hybrid CNN (ResNet50 Model) with SVM

Table 1. Comparison Results of Deep Learning Model with Hybrid Deep Learning Model

Deep Learning Model	Training Accuracy	Test Accuracy
Proposed CNN	93.2%	91.2%
Transfer learnig ResNet50	95.8 %	94.8%
Hybrid CNN(ResNet50) with SVM	97.3 %	95.6%

6   Conclusion

Disease detection and identification is done by using an Deep Learning. The data is collected from PlantVillage website. The Potato leaf data set is used to detection the disease by using an Hybrid Deep learning algorithm CNN with SVM. We proposed CNN model and train the data set good accuracy. We also used transfer learning model ResNET50 and got more better accurcy than our proposed CNN model. It is interesting that our proposed Hybrid CNN (ResNet 50) with SVN is trained using the same Potato lead image dataset and the accuracy is 97.3% and accuracy for test data is 95.6%.

It is concluded that Hybrid CNN with SVM is giving better accuracy.

References

1. Shruthi, U., Nagaveni, V., Raghavendra, B. K.: A review on machine learning classification techniques for plant disease detection. In: 2019 5th International Conference on Advanced Computing & Communication Systems (ICACCS), pp. 281–284 (2019). https://doi.org/10.1109/ICACCS.2019.8728415
2. Vaishnnave, M. P., Suganya, D. K., Srinivasan, P., ArutPerumJothi, G.: Detection and classification of groundnut leaf diseases using KNN classifier. In: 2019 IEEE International Conference on System, Computation, Automation and Networking (ICSCAN), pp. 1–5 (2019). https://doi.org/10.1109/ICSCAN.2019.8878733

3. Puspha Annabel, L.S., Annapoorani, T., Deepalakshmi, P.: Machine learning for plant leaf disease detection and classification - a review. In: 2019 International Conference on Communication and Signal Processing (ICCSP), pp. 0538–0542 (2019). https://doi.org/10.1109/ICCSP.2019.8698004

4. Hossain, M.S., Mou, R.M., Hasan, M.M., Chakraborty, S., Razzak, M.A.: Recognition and detection of tea leaf's diseases using support vector machine. In: 2018 IEEE 14th International Colloquium on Signal Processing & Its Applications (CSPA), pp. 150–154 (2018). https://doi.org/10.1109/CSPA.2018.8368703

5. Islam, M., Dinh, A., Wahid, K.A., Bhowmik, P. : Detection of potato diseases using image segmentation and multiclass support vector machine. In: 2017 IEEE 30th Canadian Conference on Electrical and Computer Engineering (CCECE), pp. 1–4 (2017). https://doi.org/10.1109/CCECE.2017.7946594

6. Dhakate, M., IngoleA., B.: Diagnosis of pomegranate plant diseases using neural network. In: 2015 Fifth National Conference on Computer Vision, Pattern Recognition, Image Processing and Graphics (NCVPRIPG), pp. 1–4 (2015). https://doi.org/10.1109/NCVPRIPG.2015.7490056

7. Sardoğan, M., Tuncer, A., Ozen, Y. Plant leaf disease detection and classification based on CNN with LVQ algorithm. In: 2018 3rd International Conference on Computer Science and Engineering (UBMK), pp. 382–385 (2018). https://doi.org/10.1109/UBMK.2018.8566635

8. Ferentinos, P.K.: Deep learning models for plant disease detection and diagnosis. Comput. Electron. Agric. 145, 311–318 (2018). https://doi.org/10.1016/j.compag.2018.01.009

9. Johannes, A., et al.: Automatic plant disease diagnosis using mobile capture devices, applied on a wheat use case. Comput. Electron. Agric. 138, 200–209 (2017). https://doi.org/10.1016/j.compag.2017.04.013

10. Lu, Y., Yi, S., Zeng, N., Liu, Y., Zhang, Y.: Identification of rice diseases using deep convolutional neural networks. Neurocomputing 267, 378–384 (2017). https://doi.org/10.1016/j.neucom.2017.06.023

11. Saleem, M.H., Potgieter, J., Arif, K.M.: Plant disease detection and classification by deep learning. Plants 8, 468–476 (2019). https://doi.org/10.3390/plants8110468

12. Liu, B., Tan, C., Li, S., He, J., Wang, H.: A data augmentation method based on generative adversarial networks for grape leaf disease identification. IEEE Access 8, 102188–102198 (2020). https://doi.org/10.1109/ACCESS.2020.2998839

13. Fawakherji, M., Potena, C., Prevedello, I., Pretto, A., Bloisi, D.D., Nardi, D.: Data augmentation using GANs for crop/weed segmentation in precision farming. In: 2020 IEEE Conference on Control Technology and Applications (CCTA), pp. 279–284 (2020). https://doi.org/10.1109/CCTA41146.2020.9206297

A Substantial Deep Learning Approach for Classification of Local and Coastal Fish

Sajal Das[✉][iD], Shumaiya Akter Shammi[iD], and Dewan Mamun Raza[iD]

Daffodil International University, Dhaka, Bangladesh
{sajal15-12381,shumaiya15-12179,dewan.cse}@diu.edu.bd
https://daffodilvarsity.edu.bd/

Abstract. Fish is a popular food all around the world Because of its excellent nutritional content. Furthermore, fish is low in fat and high in protein. The nutritional value of various fish varies. Fish are essential experimental animals in a variety of fields of biological and medical research. A solid foundation for understanding the more adaptable behavior of higher vertebrates has been established by research on fish. This article focused on the classification of two types of fish: local and coastal fish. This will aid in identifying fish, and this article will also provide knowledge of numerous fish species identifications, allowing researchers to study the nutritional value of fish. The local and coastal fish categories contain twelve different fish species: Catla, Cyprinus Carpio, Grass Carp, Mori, Rohu, Silver, Black Sea Sprat, Gilt Head Bream, Red Sea Bream, Horse Mackerel, Sea Bass, and Trout. Moreover, there are 13,176 fish shots in the dataset used in this article. In addition, to identify the species, fish are labeled with unique integer values. A deep learning based approach has been applied to classify the fish species in this article. A Convolutional Neural Network (CNN) technique has been used in this research work as CNN provides high-quality performance in the field of image segmentation. Hence, the proposed model achieves a satisfactory result of 98.33%.

Keywords: Computer Vision · Deep Learning · Image Processing · Machine Learning · Image Classification

1 Introduction

Image segmentation is becoming a more popular study topic [2,3,8]. Researchers have worked on a variety of photographs to identify various objects, including human disease detection, animal and plant disease detection, flower recognition, fish detection, and so on. Because of the prominence of artificial intelligence, this research topic is quickly expanding. Furthermore, fish categorization is currently one of the most important research fields that leads academics to learn more about fish species and their significance [6].

© Springer Nature Switzerland AG 2023
D. Garg et al. (Eds.): IACC 2022, CCIS 1781, pp. 362–373, 2023.
https://doi.org/10.1007/978-3-031-35641-4_29

This article examines several research gaps that should be filled in order to absorb the knowledge of fish and its nutritional worth so that biologists and the general public can get sufficient proficiency and add adequate nutritional value to their diets. This article noted that some work on local fish classification has been done in a number of countries [2–4]. Despite this, there is a scarcity of coastal fish classification study. Coastal fish, on the other hand, have a nutritional advantage over local fish because they are raised in the sea.

Furthermore, the classification of both local and coastal fish is the topic of this article [4,7]. The focus of this study is on the identification of six common local fish in Bangladesh. The coastal fish dataset, on the other hand, included six different types of fish. Furthermore, our aim is to take a raw snapshot of data and supplement it using our own augmentation technique, resulting in a new dataset. This paper discusses a complex enhancement procedure that yielded a total of 13,176 pictures. Another goal of this study is to collect a wide range of data in order to train the proposed model. Following that, this study used our enhanced dataset to train our proposed model, which performed admirably. However, this article will address the following research question regarding fish classification:

- Why is data augmentation necessary?
- What can be the output of before and after augmentation?
- How does CNN perform for image classification?

We have demonstrated an inclusion and exclusion criteria in Fig. 1 which indicates that some dataset building research work, fish species classification based work and survey in this field to understand the present situation of this field have been selected for this research purpose.

The rest of the article is structured as follows: some literature works have been illustrated in Sect. 2. Section 3 defines the methodology part consist of data preprocessing, augmentation and the implementation of proposed model. Section 4 evaluates the performance of the model and finally Sect. 5 concludes the final outcome.

2   Literature Review

Having a good deal of nutritious value, fish plays a vital role in a human food diet. As fish is the source of high-quality protein, it is important to have knowledge of fish. For this reason, the domain of fish classification research and finding other nutritious values is becoming popular day by day. Many people don't recognize fish [4] along with the nutritional value of fish in Bangladesh. Consequently, some work has been done for fish classification and its dataset. In article [5], researchers prepared a dataset consisting of six local fish species where they constructed their dataset by the fishes i.e. Catla, Cyprinus Carpio, Grass Carp, Morl, Rohu, Silver [4,5]. The name of their dataset is Fish-Pak: an image dataset of 6 different fish species encapsulated by a single camera. Their dataset contains 915 images. As Convolutional Neural Network is familiar for image processing,

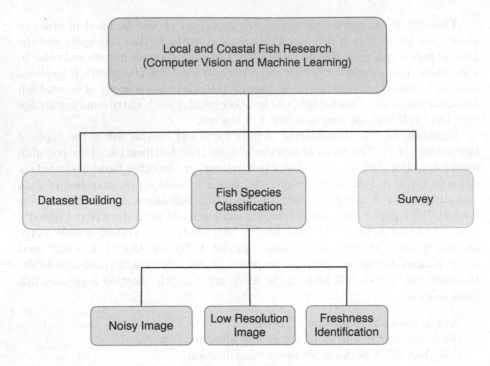

Fig. 1. Visualization of inclusion criteria

this approach is used in the article [4]. Here, CNN achieves a satisfactory result with 88.96% accuracy. On the other hand, Machine Learning-based approaches have been applied in the article [2] such as Support Vector Machine (SVM), k-nearest neighbors (KNN), and Ensemble methods where SVM gave the highest accuracy of 94.20%.

Oguzhan Ulucan et al. have also used Support Vector Machine [7] to detect nine sea fish species. Their dataset contains 1000 images of fish. They used Bag of Words (BoF) and CNNsF with their SVM model and got 81.55%, and 93.25% accuracy for BoF and CNNsF respectively. However, few of them used Naive Bayesian fusion-based deep learning [6] for fish classification. They used two datasets named FishPak and BYU. The volume of their dataset is 273 and 630 for FishPak and BYU respectively. They classified 6 fish from the FishPak dataset and 4 fish from the BYU dataset. Using the transfer learning approach, AlexNet is trained for each fish segmentation. They got an accuracy of 98.64% for the FishPak dataset, and 98.94% for the BYU dataset. Fish identification along with fish freshness determination has been done on paper [3]. They categorized three fish species for instance milkfish, round scad, and tilapia. Their dataset contains 800 images and they labeled the freshness of fish into five levels.

Convolutional Neural Network (CNN) is one of the most widely used models for image classification. There are three types of layers used in CNN which have the multiple convolutional filters working and scanning the complete feature matrix and carry out the dimensionality reduction. This enables CNN to be a very apt and fit network for image classifications and processing[1]. In article [13], CNN achieved a remarkable validation accuracy of 90% and 92% respectively where the networks derived from the VGGNet. On the contrary, Deep CNN has been used in the context of noise in images where the training model synthesizes more data with random noise, in the article [10]. Dhruv Rathi et al. [1] have worked on classifying underwater fish species from the dataset containing 27,142 images. They have classified the fish species based on 21 classes with the CNN and Deep Learning models and their model gave an accuracy of 96.29% which showed an improvement from the previous proposed classification models. Moreover, another fish classification has been implemented with a huge dataset containing 22,443 images of 15 different fish species but their concern was to classify the low-resolution images. CNN with 2 convolutional layers combined with dropout and data augmentation achieved 99.7% accuracy on testing data [9].

AlexNet is used for deep CNN for classifying 6 fish species from the dataset of 1334 images and their proposed model customized layered AlexNet achieved 90% testing accuracy in the article [11]. Moreover, In the article [15], brown trout (Salmo trutta) and European grayling (Thymallus thymallus) images extracted from videos for classification without prior pre-processing and the high accuracy of above 99% showing the dominance of AlexNet. On the other hand, VGG16 Network also gave an immersive result on the article [14], their model achieved 99% of accuracy for three different fish species from a small dataset of 530 images.

Moreover, surveys on fish classification techniques are also a part of gathering knowledge about fish. The study on preprocessing methods features extraction techniques and classifiers from recent works have also been done in this domain [8,12]. After studying the preprocessing methods, feature extractions and classification techniques, a fish classification architecture was proposed by [8]. They also showed the dataset available in this domain and their description. Another article made a review on recent advances in machine vision technology for fish classification [12]. They represented an overview of machine vision models applied in the field of fish classification. They produced an elaborate description of this field and discussed the advantages of applied techniques.

3   Methodology

This article has worked on classifying the local and coastal fish species and evaluating the proposed model on these data. The functionality of the whole process regarding this research is illustrated in Fig. 2. However, a CPU of AMD Ryzen 7 3700X 8-Core Processor 3.59 GHz has been used for data augmentation and model implementation in this study. Accordingly, the RAM size of this hardware is 16 GB and GPU is NVIDIA 1660 Super 6 GB. For coding, implementation jupyter notebook has been used in this article.

---

[1] https://medium.datadriveninvestor.com/why-are-convolutional-neural-networks-good-for-image-classification-146ec6e865e8.

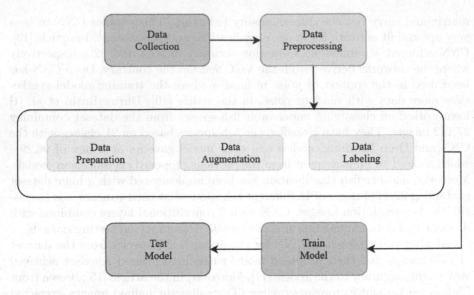

Fig. 2. Workflow Diagram

3.1 Dataset

This article has worked on two different fish datasets: Local fish and coastal fish. The name of the local fish dataset is "Fish-Pak: Fish Species Dataset from Pakistan for Visual Features Based Classification" [6] and the coastal fish dataset name is "A Large Scale Fish Dataset" [8]. There are 915 images in the local fish dataset where the images contained the body, head, and scale of a fish. But this article selected only body part images as we will train our model by the full image of each fish species. We selected 269 full-body images in the local fish dataset and the ratio of the images was 3:2. This dataset contains six species of fish for instance Catla, Cyprinus Carpio, Grass Carp, Mori, Rohu, and Silver. On the other hand, the coastal fish dataset contains 9 different fish species collected from a supermarket in Izmir, Turkey. The dataset includes gilt head bream, red sea bream, sea bass, red mullet, horse mackerel, black sea sprat, striped red mullet, trout, and shrimp image samples. From these species, we selected only six species as our local fish has six fish species. We have selected black sea sprat, gilt head bream, red sea bream, horse mackerel, sea bass, and trout. The reason behind choosing these species is these fish species look similar to the local fish we have selected. This will help to evaluate our proposed model more accurately. In addition, there are 280 images in the coastal fish dataset after selecting the several six species and the image ratio was 4:3. The number of images for each species of fish is represented in Table 1 and Table 2. Accordingly, some samples of local and coastal fish are visualized in Figs. 3 and 4 from our dataset.

Table 1. Number of Data (images) for Local fishes

Fish Name	Number of images
Catla	18
Cyprinus Carpio	50
Grass Carp	11
Mori	70
Rohu	73
Silver	47

Table 2. Number of Data (images) for Coastal fishes

Fish Name	Number of images
Black Sea Sprat	50
Gilt Head Bream	50
Horse Mackerel	50
Red Sea Bream	50
Sea Bass	50
Trout	30

3.2 Data Preprocessing

Data Preparation. There are some discrepancies in the data. Since two distinct datasets have been taken to evaluate the proposed model in this research work. The pictures in the dataset had diverse aspect ratios. So, this difficulty must be addressed in order to obtain effective results. As a consequence, all of

Fig. 3. Sample Images for Local Fish (Rohu)

Fig. 4. Sample Images for Coastal Fish (Sea Bass)

the data has been reduced to 100 by 100 pixels in order to keep the same aspect ratio.

Additionally, an RGB image is made up of pixels, each of which has three numeric values that correlate to the color intensity. And the range of the numeric values is 0 to 255. Thus, all of the features have been separated into 255 to assist speed up the learning process by reducing the scatteredness.

Data Augmentation. This article used augmentation to turn one image into 24 images. This artificial data augmentation resulted in a dataset with 6,456 images for local fish and 6,720 images for coastal fish. As a result, data augmentation has produced a total of 13,176 images. The following is the augmentation procedure: Rotate images at positive 15°, 30°, 45°, 60°, 75°, 90°, 105°, 120°, 135°, 150°, 165°, and flip each image horizontally.

Data Labeling. To label each of the fish species in the dataset, this article employed unique integer values. The fishes are designated by 12 integer values such as 0–11. There are 12 fish species in the local and coastal fish taxonomy. Table 3 lists the fish species that have been labeled:

Table 3. Corresponding Labels of Different Classes

Fish Name	Label
Catla	0
Cyprinus Carpio	1
Grass Carp	2
Mori	3
Rohu	4
Silver	5
Black Sea Sprat	6
Gilt Head Bream	7
Horse Mackerel	8
Red Sea Bream	9
Sea Bass	10
Trout	11

3.3 Proposed Model

Convolutional Neural network (CNN) is very familiar in the field of Deep Learning as it performs very well for image segmentation [4]. This article classifies 12 different fish species where six species are local fish and the rest of the part is coastal fish. As there are two datasets that have been used, this article combines these two datasets to build a new one. After combining them, the whole dataset contains 13,176 data.

The dataset was split by 80:20 to train the data and we trained the dataset on several multilayer convolutional neural networks. There were two dense layers and a flatten layer that performed best. Different filters for different layers were used where the first layer had 64 layers, second layer had 128 and third had 256 layers. To implement the model, 3×3 size was used for each convolutional kernel size and there was an activation function called "relu". And the maxpooling layer has the pool size of 2×2.

Flatten layer was used to feed the data into dense layers. There were 128 hidden units in the first dense layer, 64 hidden units in the second layer and 12 hidden units in the output layer which denoted the number of labels or the number of fish species. Softmax activation function was used in the output layer. In addition, this article used 20% dropout after every layer to avoid the overfitting problem. However, the flatten layer and the output layer were not used dropouts. In "adam" optimizer 0.001 value was set for learning rate. An illustration of our CNN model is shown in Fig. 5. This proposed model has got 98.33% accuracy on testing dataset.

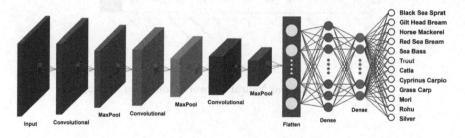

Fig. 5. Convolutional Neural Network model architecture.

4   Performance Evaluation

This article has made a comparison between the proposed model and the other existing model's performance based on the volume of the dataset and the number of classes they have dealt with. The table below shows the circumstances as well.

The suggested model clearly outperformed the other existing techniques, as shown in Table 4. Furthermore, certain approaches 6, 14, 15 produced findings that are almost identical to our proposed method. However, the size of the dataset and the number of classes are not comparable to our study. This article contains a large number of class variations 12, when most only have 2–6 class variations. However, when compared to other datasets, the volume of this arti cle's dataset is quite large. This post has used a unique augmentation approach to help increase the number of data as well as the image quality.

This article has examined the result before and after augmentation which is described in Table 5. Before augmentation of data, the result was too poor.

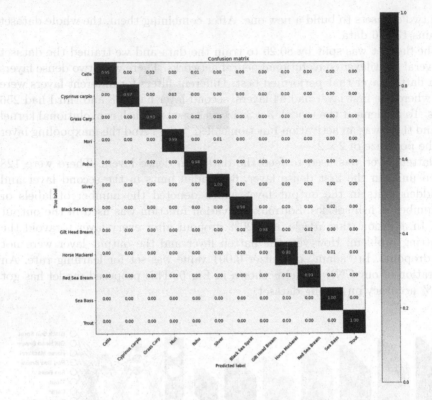

Fig. 6. Convolutional Neural Network Confusion Matrix

Table 4. Performance Evaluation of Different Existing Works with Proposed Model

Method	Dataset Volume	No of Classes	Classifier	Accuracy
Israt Sharmin et al.	180	6	SVM	94.20%
Shumaiya Akter Shammi et al.	4575	6	CNN	88.96%
Abinaya N.S. et al.	273 (FishPak), 630 (BYU)	6, 4	Naive Bayes	98.64%, 98.94%
Oguzhan Ulucan et al.	1000	9	SVM	93.2%
Adamu Ali-Gombe et al.	3777	8	Deep CNN	N/A
Muhammad Ather Iqbal et al.	1334	6	Deep CNN	90.48%
B. S. Rekha et al.	3777	8	CNN	92%
Francis Jesmar P. Montalbo et al.	530	3	CNN (VGG16)	99%
Thitinun Pengying et al.	9220	2	CNN	99%
Proposed Method	**13,176**	**12**	**CNN**	**98.33%**

Table 5. Comparison of performance before and after augmentation

Before Augmentation	After Augmentation
Data structure is inconsistent for which model cannot learn properly from these variable size of data	Data is properly organized and structured that enhances the learning capability of model
Performance is significantly poor: 40.91% accuracy	Performance is satisfactory: 98.33%

40.91% accuracy was achieved before the augmentation of data. Because, data were inconsistent before augmentation and the model cannot learn properly from the huge number of inconsistent data. On the other hand, augmentation is necessary to prepare the variation of data. This article have done this variation with several types of angular position of the data that helps to create the variation and helps model to learn the features. The confusion matrix, as well as the train and validation of the model's performance, have previously been shown in the methodology part, which determines the satisfactory performance.

Performance visualization of our proposed model and the performance before augmentation is shown in Fig. 6 by confusion matrix. Accordingly, the accuracy and loss during the training and validation phase has been given in Fig. 7.

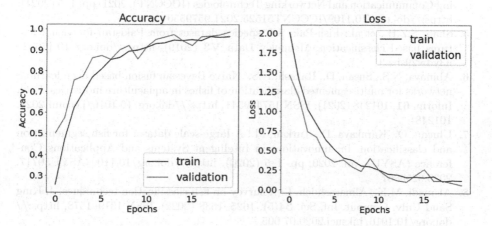

Fig. 7. Accuracy and Loss during the training and validation phase

The accuracy and loss during the training and validation phase has been given in Fig. 7.

5   Conclusion

This article has attempted to create a wide variety of fish species datasets, which has been done well in this study. Local fish species and coastal fish species are represented in two categories of fish photographs gathered from various sources. There are six fish species in each group. All of the fish shots were preprocessed and scaled to the same ratio using excellent preprocessing techniques. Multiple representations of fish have been created using a rich augmentation technique. Finally, to obtain a successful outcome, a convolutional neural network-based technique was used. Using the proposed model, this article has a 98.33% accuracy, which is highly satisfactory.

References

1. Rathi, D., Jain, S., Indu, S.: Underwater fish species classification using convolutional neural network and deep learning. In: Ninth International Conference on Advances in Pattern Recognition (ICAPR), vol. 2017, pp. 1–6 (2017). https://doi.org/10.1109/ICAPR.2017.8593044
2. Sharmin, I., Islam, N.F., Jahan, I., Ahmed Joye, T., Rahman, M.R., Habib, M.T.: Machine vision based local fish recognition. SN Appl. Sci. **1**(12), 1–12 (2019). https://doi.org/10.1007/s42452-019-1568-z
3. Navotas, I., Santos, C., Balderrama, E.J., Candido, F.E., Villacanas, A.J., Velasco, J.: Fish identification and freshness classification through image processing using artificial neural network. J. Eng. Appl. Sci. **13**, 4912–4922 (2018)
4. Shammi, S.A., Das, S., Hasan, M., Noori, S.R.H.: FishNet: fish classification using convolutional neural network. In: 2021 12th International Conference on Computing Communication and Networking Technologies (ICCCNT), 2021, pp. 1–5 (2021). https://doi.org/10.1109/ICCCNT51525.2021.9579550
5. Shah, S.Z.H., et al.: Fish-Pak: fish species dataset from Pakistan for visual features based classification. Mendeley Data **V3** (2019). https://doi.org/10.17632/n3ydw29sbz.3
6. Abinaya, N.S., Susan, D., Rakesh, K.S.: Naive Bayesian fusion based deep learning networks for multisegmented classification of fishes in aquaculture industries. Ecol. Inform. **61**, 101248 (2021). ISSN 1574–9541, https://doi.org/10.1016/j.ecoinf.2021.101248
7. Ulucan, O., Karakaya, D., Turkan, M.: A large-scale dataset for fish segmentation and classification. In: Innovations in Intelligent Systems and Applications Conference (ASYU), vol. 2020, pp. 1–5 (2020). https://doi.org/10.1109/ASYU50717.2020.9259867
8. Alsmadi, M.K., Almarashdeh, I.: A survey on fish classification techniques. J. King Saud Univ. Comput. Inf. Sci. **34**(5), 1625–1638 (2022). ISSN 1319–1578, https://doi.org/10.1016/j.jksuci.2020.07.005
9. Rachmatullah, M.N., Supriana, I.: Low resolution image fish classification using convolutional neural network. In: 2018 5th International Conference on Advanced Informatics: Concept Theory and Applications (ICAICTA), 2018, pp. 78–83 (2018). https://doi.org/10.1109/ICAICTA.2018.8541313
10. Ali-Gombe, A., Elyan, E., Jayne, C.: Fish classification in context of noisy images. In: Boracchi, G., Iliadis, L., Jayne, C., Likas, A. (eds.) EANN 2017. CCIS, vol. 744, pp. 216–226. Springer, Cham (2017). https://doi.org/10.1007/978-3-319-65172-9_19
11. Iqbal, M.A., Wang, Z., Ali, Z.A., Riaz, S.: Automatic fish species classification using deep convolutional neural networks. Wirel. Pers. Commun. **116**(2), 1043–1053 (2019). https://doi.org/10.1007/s11277-019-06634-1

12. Li, D., Wang, Q., Li, X., Niu, M., Wang, H., Liu, C.: Recent advances of machine vision technology in fish classification. ICES J. Mar. Sci. **79**(2), 263–284 (2022). https://doi.org/10.1093/icesjms/fsab264
13. Rekha, B.S., Srinivasan, G.N., Reddy, S.K., Kakwani, D., Bhattad, N.: Fish detection and classification using convolutional neural networks. In: Smys, S., Tavares, J.M.R.S., Balas, V.E., Iliyasu, A.M. (eds.) ICCVBIC 2019. AISC, vol. 1108, pp. 1221–1231. Springer, Cham (2020). https://doi.org/10.1007/978-3-030-37218-7_128
14. Montalbo, F.J.P., Hernandez, A.A.: Classification of fish species with augmented data using deep convolutional neural network. In: 2019 IEEE 9th International Conference on System Engineering and Technology (ICSET), 2019, pp. 396–401 (2019). https://doi.org/10.1109/ICSEngT.2019.8906433
15. Pengying, T., Pedersen, M., Hardeberg, J.Y., Museth, J.: Underwater fish classification of trout and grayling. In: 2019 15th International Conference on Signal-Image Technology & Internet-Based Systems (SITIS), 2019, pp. 268–273 (2019). https://doi.org/10.1109/SITIS.2019.00052

Intelligent & Smart Navigation System
for Visually Impaired Friends

Merugu Suresh[2] (iD), Abdul Subhani Shaik[1,2](✉) (iD), B. Premalatha[2] (iD),
V. A. Narayana[3] (iD), and George Ghinea[4] (iD)

[1] Department of ECE, NIT Silchar, Silchar, Assam, India
abdul_rs@ece.nits.ac.in
[2] Department of ECE, CMR College of Engineering and Technology, Hyderabad, Telangana,
India
[3] Department of CSE, CMR College of Engineering and Technology, Hyderabad, Telangana,
India
[4] Mulsemedia Computing, Brunal University London, Wilfred Brown Building 215, London,
UK

Abstract. The objective of this paper is to provide the low-cost assistive device
with localization and mapping of the visually-impaired people. This can be used as
plug and play device low power consumption and economical solution to visually-
impaired. Further, the smart assistive device will be an integration of computer
vision techniques and sensors network which can be validate the sturdiness and
consistency of the obstacle recognition and detection modules. Need to test the
obstacle detection data and the module is reliant on the collected data from both
the smartphone camera and ultrasonic sensors, which will be nourished to the
recognition unit to categorize the existing things of the scene. "Humans are not
disabled. A person can never be broken. This inbuilt environment, technologies,
is broken and disabled and the people need not accept the limitations, but can
transfer disability through technological Innovation".

Keywords: Assistive device · GPS · Machine learning · Image processing and
computer vision

1 Introduction

Numerous technologies have approached for various assistive aids for visually impaired
people. Initially, technology based on ultrasound was simple and less accurate, arrang-
ing these sensors on human body plays vital role because placing when these sensors
are placed on repositioning body parts can be led to wrong information to assistive
device triggering to irritation of users [1], similar these another research work [2] made
convenient to user by making their device more portable to hold in hand for detection
of obstacles. Many blind people are habituated to have a long wooden stick or a cane
rod in their hand, having a sensor at the tip of stick for depth and manhole detection
is effective but constantly hitting on ground and to other obstacles leads to damage of

© Springer Nature Switzerland AG 2023
D. Garg et al. (Eds.): IACC 2022, CCIS 1781, pp. 374–383, 2023.
https://doi.org/10.1007/978-3-031-35641-4_30

sensors, moreover single purpose assistive device cannot meet the needs of the visually impaired people [3]. Conversely, most research have worked on RGB sensors and depth sensors for detecting the obstacles in environment [4], this paper gives knowledge about obstacles such as staircase, walls and open area (all within indoor environment) to blind person using Fast Artificial Neural Network (FANN). Path detection for blind people plays essential role for avoiding obstacles [5] can be implemented using Artificial Intelligence (AI) for prominent results.

2 Literature Review

Over the past three decades, the population has increased substantially, as people seek a higher quality of life [6]. To achieve quality life for visually impaired friends' cutting-edge technology, need to be introduced for them. Visually impaired friends require continuous support for navigating from one position to another, to achieve these various algorithms are used [7] for reducing the probability of obstacle [8]. Depth and edge detection of environment can also be retrieved from an image by using various filtering methods [9].

Globally maximum number of visually impaired friends use white canes devices to drive from one location to another. Due to their impaired vision, they are not able to distinguish their environments. So, the mobility of the visually impaired people is limited [10–12].

Now there are many numbers of visually impaired friends in India. Out of 37 million visually impaired persons across the globe, concluded 15 million are from India only. All of these are from weaker section and economically backward people and they should depend on others or to roam around, some may be using white canes. This means an important portion of persons through distinct requirements living right between us [13]. It's not only the worsening of visualization that they have to suffer from; the complete eminence of their lives declines too, also distressing their level of individuality [14]. The respectable update is that health care collective with technical progression is enlightening with each ephemeral day [15].

Consequently, the smart device absorbed on notifying the operator complete ability to speak response. This innovative assistive device is intended for serving the visually impaired persons to navigate from place to place safely [16, 17]. Operator organizes not essential to move the white cane from place to place to perceive difficulty like they do generally. Consequently, operator can simply walk and continuously get data around complications from one place to another with the help of camera involved [18, 19]. Numerous examinations are being directed on construction of a direction-finding device for the visually impaired persons. Some scholars discourse this test in inside and outside environment. However, greatest of these methods consume boundaries, since this test include numerous subjects (e.g., precision, handling, serviceability) [20, 21]. State-of-the-art of low vision resolutions consume collected up latterly, submission dissimilar kinds of topographies and purposes catered towards a complete choice of visual disabilities. Progression, few of them are improved than others in the way they are intended and for some purpose.

3 Methodology

Assistive technologies are intended to progress the practical capabilities of people with various disabilities. Some are relatively low-tech and well-known, such as such as reading glasses and mobility aids. Other devices are more advanced with internet of things, using cutting edge engineering technology, with smart assistive technologies under various developments that could have a huge impact on all our livelihood. Inopportunely, most of these assistive technologies are restricted in their capabilities. Technology-based plug-n-play systems with narrow focus on the user requirements is one of the major drawbacks in the development of the assistive systems. This work systematically reviews the assistive technology solutions for visual impaired people and exposes that most of the existing solutions address a specific part of the travel problems. This proposal deals with the prototyping of assistive device with sensor technology and processing methods are being used to capture scene details of the visually impaired friends neighboring locations.

3.1 Real-Time Testing

Smart assistive user-friendly devices developed with multiple activities such as typing text, navigation, object-detection, and travel. Devices are as diverse as the technology used and the location for visually impaired.

A user friendly portable assistive device is developed by using bleeding-edge technology with absolute requirement of user. The device is capable of detection of obstacles, signs, poster, and provide novel path for user in volatile environment. In additional to it can also help the user to type text message, make a call with ease. The user-friendly interaction and with persists audio command from device helps in monitoring blind person. The detailed process is given in flow chart below in Fig. 2 and Fig. 3 deals with basic elements required for building of this device. For user interface a user handset is developed to adapt the mode of requirement, it can be wired or wireless according to user's choice.

3.2 Machine Learning

This section is significant for processing the input image, mainly the taken pictures, for the persistence of objects arrangement. The processing procedure is established using machine learning approaches and can be separated into some steps, specifically feature extraction, machine learning approaches, model training and estimate. The proposed system is divided into two phases: collection of input imagery, feature extractions for training the machine learning algorithm, and evaluating performance including spatial inputs such as photography or visual content. The input images are collected and pre-processed and it consists of two main parts: feature extraction and a language prediction model built with two deep learning techniques.

4 Design and Working

Design of our product includes selection of the hardware which it starts with processor, camera, ultrasonic mems, GPS and buttons leds power source following is the block diagram representation of our product (Fig. 1).

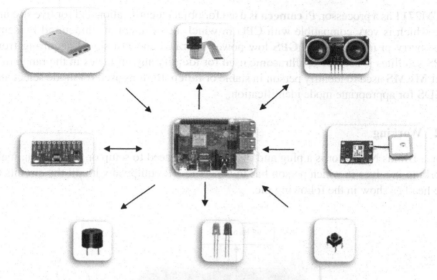

Fig. 1. Assistive System Design

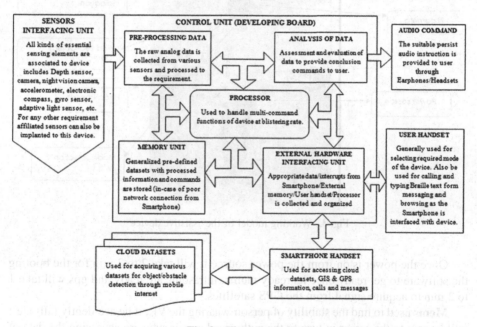

Fig. 2. Block Design

4.1 Processor

In this work Linux operated device is used which is not only supports multitasking but also used to run OpenCV which is machine learning software that's why we choose

BCM2711 as a processor, Pi **camera** is used for object identification and for live streaming which is very compatible with CPU in which this camera manufactured by same Raspberry pi manufacturers **GPS** low power operated and fast signal acquiring from GPS satellites is used here, Ultrasonic used for identify any obstacles in the range of 3 feet **MEMS** used to identify person in stable or fallen. Buttons used for mode select and LEDS for appropriate mode identification.

4.2 Working

Since Blinds Navigator is a plug and play device no need to setup or installation, main working involves in which person has to wear the VR equipped with all the circuits to the head as show in the following pic.

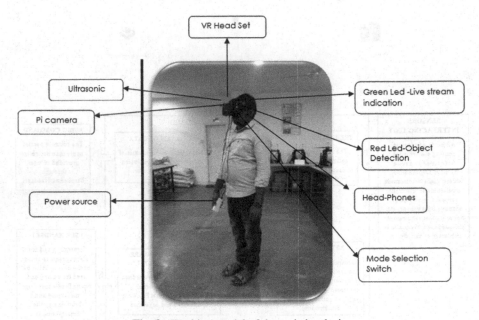

Fig. 3. Working model of the assistive device

Once the power is on from the power source it will take 2 to 3 min for the booting the software to get ready once its ready mems, ultrasonic are ready and gps will take 1 to 2 min to acquire signal from the GPS satellites,

Mems used to find the stability of person wearing the VR, if he accidently falls alert will be sent to the server in turn to the authorised person who are accessing the data of the disabled person in turn, he can be get alerted.

Ultrasonic used to find the objects above 3 feet, alerts the disabled person using beep sound from the buzzer installed.

GPS used to find the location by acquiring signal from the GPS satellites signal consists of latitude, longitude, speed and altitude as the latitude and longitude with some standard formats are sent to user in the form of link, so the user by clicking on the link the exact location can be obtained on Google maps. Thus, live tracking of the person is obtained.

Pi Camera, Now comes the Camera part which is a standard pi camera which installed in the front and middle portion of VR head set clearly seen in above Picture as used for two modes.

1. Live streaming
2. Object detection

When we press a button on the left side of the VR Head Set green led will glow and at same time voice will be heard by saying *"Pls check live streaming started"*, hence from the remote place we can observe the person live stream through camera.

In the same manner if we press the button once again the RED led will glow and the same time voice will heard by saying *"Pls check object detection started"*, thus with help of computer version software, camera starts identifying the object appeared or seen by camera and object identified is spoken out as *"person","chair","table" "car"* etc. is heard by the head phones connected to the processor board with 3.5mm audio jack.

The main data such as GPS data and live stream data are uploading to the server and each and every person are assigned by unique id for log in, once login the details will be shown the details of the person shown as screen shots as follows. Application opened in client side is shown as follows:

Main Page

On clicking on the image it routes to new page contains person details such as stable or fallen and followed by GPS data.

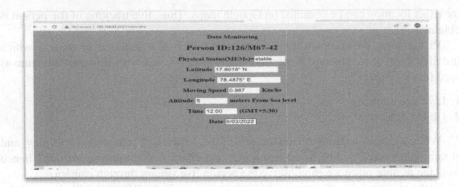

When clicking on **main page** link named **"live controls"** routes to the new page contains.
Live Stream and Live Location.

When clicking on live Stream it automatically streams the live video as follows.

On clicking on **live location** with help of the Google maps and the GPS coordinates obtained by GPS modules with Google maps api linking we get the live location as follows as we have taken the live location in CMR college (Table 1).

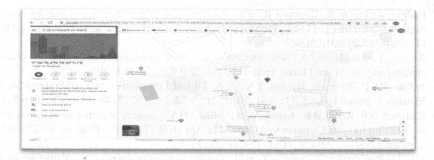

Table 1. Showing the Survey Details of various problems facing by the beneficiaries in Medchal mandal

Region – Medchal

Ages (in years)	Population	Blind	Visually Impaired	Low Vision	Bad Vision
0–14	40	10	10	15	5
15–49	80	10	30	30	10
> = 50	30	5	10	10	5
All Ages	**150**	**25**	**50**	**55**	**20**

5 Conclusion

It is concluded that a visually impaired person can easily walk any-where. This developed assistive device for visually impaired was taken to complete with the inspiration and the knowledge to resolve complications of visually impaired in both indoor and outdoor. There were many traditional methods to solve this same issue but not up to the mark, this research paper helped to solve these issues by using computer vision and image processing techniques with the help of OpenCV. The developed assistive device can be taken by them all the time and their live location can be monitored by their family members from anywhere. Hence, it uses computer vision and image processing technique that is used in recognizing the objects in the environments and gives an audio output. The hearing ability of the user tries to fulfil his/her seeing ability.

References

1. World Health Organization: World Report on Vision. https://www.who.int/publications-det nil/world-report on vision
2. National Programme for Control of Blindness & Visual Impairment (NPCBVI), Government of India "The National Blindness & Visual Impairment Survey India 2015–2019" https://npc bvi.gov.in/writeReadData/mainlinkFile/File341.pdf

3. Badave, A., Jagtap, R., Kaovasia, R., et al.: Android based object detection system for visually impaired. 2020 Int Conf Ind 40 Technol I4Tech 2020, 34–38 (2020). https://doi.org/10.1109/I4Tech48345.2020.9102694

4. Anitha, J., Subalaxmi, A., Vijayalakshmi, G.: Real time object detection for visually challenged persons. Int J Innov Technol Explor Eng **8**, 312–314 (2019)

5. Jadhav, P.S.P., Tomy, S., Jayswal, S.S., et al.: Object Detection in Android Smartphone for Visually Impaired Users **5**, 332–334 (2016). https://doi.org/10.17148/IJARCCE.2016.51171

6. Khairnar, D.P., Karad, R.B., Kapse, A., et al.: PARTHA: a visually impaired assistance system. In: 2020 3rd Int Conf Commun Syst Comput IT Appl CSCITA 2020 – Proc, pp. 32–37 (2020). https://doi.org/10.1109/CSCITA47329.2020.9137791

7. Sait, U., Ravishankar, V., Kumar, T., et al.: Design and development of an assistive device for the visually impaired. Procedia Comput Sci **167**, 2244–2252 (2020). https://doi.org/10.1016/j.procs.2020.03.277

8. Kuriakose, B., Shrestha, R., Sandnes, F.E.: Tools and technologies for blind and visually impaired navigation support: a review. IETE Tech Rev (Institution Electron Telecommun Eng India) 0, 1–16 (2020). https://doi.org/10.1080/02564602.2020.1819893

9. Merugu, S., Jain, K., Mittal, A., Raman, B.: Sub-scene Target Detection and Recognition Using Deep Learning Convolution Neural Networks - ICDSMLA 2020. Lecture Notes in Electrical Engineering, pp. 1082–1101. Springer, Singapore (2020)

10. Manjari, K., Verma, M., Singal, G.: A survey on Assistive Technology for visually impaired. Internet of Things **11**, 100188 (2020). https://doi.org/10.1016/j.iot.2020.100188

11. Merugu, S., Ghinea, G.: A review of some assistive tools and their limitations for visually impaired. Helix - The Scientific Explorer | Peer Reviewed Bimonthly International Journal **12**(1), 1–9 (2022)

12. Chen, L.B., Su, J.P., Chen, M.C., et al.: An implementation of an intelligent assistance system for visually impaired/blind people. IEEE Int Conf Consum Electron ICCE **2019**, 4–5 (2019). https://doi.org/10.1109/ICCE.2019.8661943

13. Lin, Y., Wang, K., Yi, W., Lian, S.: Deep learning based wearable assistive system for visually impaired people. In: Proc - 2019 Int Conf Comput Vis Work ICCVW 2019, pp. 2549–2557 (2019). https://doi.org/10.1109/ICCVW.2019.00312

14. Syed, S.M., Kumar, V.: Augmented Reality on Sudoku Puzzle Using Computer Vision and Deep Learning, - Advances in Cybernetics, Cognition, and Machine. In: Lecture Notes in Electrical Engineering, pp. 567–578. Springer, Singapore (2020)

15. Devi, R.A., Uthaman, I., Shanthanam, R.R.: An IOT Security Based Electronic Aid for Visually Impaired detection with Navigation Assistance System. 0–6 (2020)

16. Bhatnagar, V., Chandra, R., Jain, V.: IoT Based Alert System for Visually Impaired Persons. Springer Singapore (2019)

17. Merugu, S., Reddy, M.C.S., Goyal, E., Piplani, L.: Text message classification using supervised machine learning algorithms. In: Kumar, A., Mozar, S. (eds.) ICCCE 2018. Lecture Notes in Electrical Engineering, vol. 500. Springer, Singapore (2019). ISSN 1876-1100

18. Anand, S., Kumar, A., Tripathi, M., Gaur, M.S.: Human face detection enabled smart stick for visually impaired people. Springer Singapore (2019)

19. Jain, S., Sushanth, D., Varsha, V., et al.: Design and implementation of the smart glove to aid the visually impaired. In: Proc 2019 IEEE Int Conf Commun Signal Process ICCSP 2019, pp. 662–666 (2019). https://doi.org/10.1109/ICCSP.2019.8698009

20. Shaik, A.S., Karsh, R.K., Suresh, M., Gunjan, V.K.: LWT-DCT Based Image Hashing for Tampering Localization via Blind Geometric Correction. In: Kumar, A., Senatore, S., Gunjan, V.K. (eds.) ICDSMLA 2020. LNEE, vol. 783, pp. 1651–1663. Springer, Singapore (2022). https://doi.org/10.1007/978-981-16-3690-5_156
21. Kumar, D.R., Thakkar, H.K., Merugu, S., Gunjan, V.K., Gupta, S.K.: Object Detection System for Visually Impaired Persons Using Smartphone. In: Kumar, A., Senatore, S., Gunjan, V.K. (eds.) ICDSMLA 2020. LNEE, vol. 783, pp. 1631–1642. Springer, Singapore (2022). https://doi.org/10.1007/978-981-16-3690-5_154

Digitized Smart Farming Technology for Urban Agriculture for Future Sustainability

S. Sai Kumar[1], K. Subba Shankar[2], E. Sunil[2], P. Saidulu[3], N. Rajeswaran[4(✉)], and G. Venkata Hari Prasad[5]

[1] Department of Information Technology, PVP Siddhartha Institute of Technology, Vijayawada, Andhra Pradesh, India
[2] Department of Computer Science and Engineering, Malla Reddy Engineering College, Secunderabad, Telangana, India
[3] Department of Information Technology, Malla Reddy Engineering College, Secunderabad, Telangana, India
[4] Department of Electrical and Electronics Engineering, Malla Reddy Institute of Engineering and Technology, Secunderabad, Telangana, India
rajeswarann@gmail.com
[5] Department of Electronics and Communication Engineering, CMR College of Engineering and Technology, Hyderabad, Telangana, India

Abstract. The world is experiencing rapid urbanization, and its effects on society, the economy, and the environment are of vital concern. India is gradually acquiring experience with the use of drones for crop protection. Crop health is closely monitored in real time using drone and Artificial Intelligence (AI) technology. The usage of drones is also employed for variable rate technologies. Urban Agriculture (UA) is involved in the production of food grains, fruits, flowers, vegetables, and livestock products in urban environments like cities and towns. In addition to the issue of the expanding urban population, it addresses the question of sustainable development. Along with the aforementioned objectives, UA must also support the Sustainable Development Goals set forth by the UNO by recycling urban trash, using efficient water resources, conserving energy, reducing air pollution and soil erosion, and making cities more beautiful. The main focus of this paper is on implementing a multi-faceted approach to support the UA, which includes raising production through the development of resources for better irrigation, using inputs effectively, lowering post-harvest losses, adding value and reforming agriculture.

Keywords: Smart Farming · Urban Agriculture · Artificial Intelligence · Drone · Sustainability

1 Introduction

In India, urban farming has not yet taken root, but there is great potential for growth in the years to come [1, 2]. In September 2021, the Indian Council of Agricultural Research (ICAR) began a network initiative where research on the use of drones and Artificial Intelligence (AI) for timely monitoring of crop development and health as

© Springer Nature Switzerland AG 2023
D. Garg et al. (Eds.): IACC 2022, CCIS 1781, pp. 384–390, 2023.
https://doi.org/10.1007/978-3-031-35641-4_31

well as management with improved input use efficiency were taken up [3–5]. In fact, research on ecosystem services has mostly emphasised the ability of urban agriculture to produce food. India is still taking baby steps in this area while only a very small number of nations, like the United States, Singapore, and a few countries in the European Union, have adopted urban farming [6, 7]. The government has implemented a number of reforms, programmes, initiatives, and policies aimed at improving farmer incomes. Drone technology use in farming has the potential to change Indian agriculture [8]. Managing farms with IoT, robotics, drones, and AI is referred to as "smart farming" (Shown in Fig. 1), and it aims to increase product quality and quantity while reducing the need for human labour [9]. Nearly every business imaginable has benefited from the Internet of Things (IoT) [10–12]. Nearly every business imaginable has benefited from the Internet of Things (IoT) [13, 14]. IoT in agriculture is not just solving time-consuming and tiresome activities that are frequently involved, but it is also fundamentally altering how we view agriculture [15, 16].

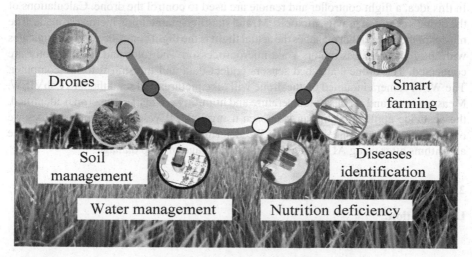

Fig. 1. Smart Farming Technology.

Drones are excellent tools for gathering meaningful information about the soil's quality at the start or end of a crop cycle [17]. In order to understand any concerns with the soil's quality, including the nutrients or any dead zones. The best planting strategies and enhanced crop management can both be made with the help of all this information. Drones can also be used to more accurately identify and monitor water resources across areas. In comparison to other agricultural uses for drones, seed planting is a relatively young application of drone technology. Crop spraying is another application for drones in the agricultural sector. Monitoring crops across large swathes of land using drone technology is another crucial application in the agriculture sector. Farmers have historically had to do this manually, which is extremely time-consuming and ineffective. Recently, IT companies have surveyed and mapped crop fields using satellite or airborne photography, but this comes at a significant expense. Drones with AI capabilities have recently taken over farming's surveying and mapping functions, enabling farmers to efficiently keep an eye on the crop in real-time [18].

Irrigation management and monitoring have been another issue for farmers in the past. With an irrigation system that is many miles long, problems might always occur. Drones with thermal imaging systems are now widely utilised to efficiently monitor the entire irrigation network and identify any problems in real time [19]. Farmers are better able to maximise drainage and create backup plans for problems when they have access to real-time information via drones. This proposed paper is structured as follows, the experimental framework described in Sect. 2 is used to assess the effectiveness of the drone control, and the conclusion of the planned work with regard to future scope is described in Sect. 3.

2 Results and Discussion

In this idea, a flight controller and remote are used to control the drone. Calculations of the drone's centre of gravity, motor RPM, and stability-maintaining inertia are made. The master of the system that manages the actual flight is the flight controller. It communicates with the four brushless motors via a microprocessor. The rotor and BLDC motor are connected. The drone's attached sensors collect data and transmit it to the computer. The Wi-Fi camera mounted on the drone will take pictures and send them to LabVIEW. Measurements and graphs of temperature and humidity are made. The crop is identified, the pesticide application timing is chosen using LabVIEW, and the sensor values we obtained from the drone are plotted. We determine when to spray depending on the algorithms after using AI to determine the percentage of crop damage.

2.1 Drone Control

Lift Equation:

$$C_L = \text{Coefficient of Lift} \rho = \text{Density of Air}$$
$$v = \text{Velocity}$$
$$A = \text{Surface area} L = \text{Lift}$$
$$L = 1/2 \, \rho \, v2 \, A \, CL \qquad (1)$$

Force of Gravity Equation:

$$g = \text{gravity} \left(9.8 \text{ m/s}^2\right)$$
$$m = \text{mass}$$
$$\text{Force of Gravity} = mg \qquad (2)$$

Thrust Equations:

$$\Delta P = \text{Change in Pressure} A = \text{area of propeller disks}$$
$$\rho = \text{Density of air} \approx 1.2 \, \text{kg/m}^3$$

$$Vf = \text{Final Velocity}$$
$$Vi2 = \text{Initial Velocity}$$
$$Fthurst = A \, \Delta P$$
$$Fthurst = 1/2 \, A \, \rho \, (Vf2 - Vi2) \tag{3}$$

Drag Equation:

$$D = Drag$$
$$\rho = \text{Density of Air} \approx 1.2 \, \text{kg/m}^3 \, v = \text{Velocity}$$
$$A = \text{Surface area}$$
$$CD = \text{Coefficient of drag}$$
$$D = 1/2 \, \rho \, v2 \tag{4}$$

Voltage Equations:

$$V = \text{Voltage}$$
$$P = \text{Power}$$
$$I = \text{Current}$$
$$V = I \, R \tag{5}$$

or

$$V = P/I \tag{6}$$

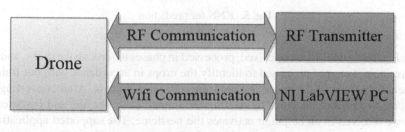

Fig. 2. Remote link between drone and system

In Fig. 2, the RF transmitter transmits an RF signal to the drone's RF receiver, which then relays it to the flight control kk 2.1.5, which decides the drone's speed and activates the BLDC motor based on the programme and input signal (Shown in Fig. 3).

2.2 AI Algorithms to Train

After receiving the live footage, it is put through various phases of processing to forecast the crops. Images of crops in various states must be entered in order to train the classifier to recognise crops that are partially, minimally, and completely damaged. To speed up

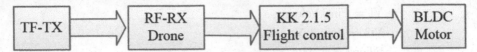

Fig. 3. Transmission control

training, the photographs are scaled to a particular size. To distinguish the same image in any colour, RGB images are turned into grayscale. Using Machine Learning algorithms, categorization and prediction are being done. The picture is then stored as a classifier file (Shown in Fig. 4).

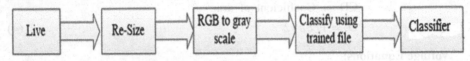

Fig. 4. Categorization and classification of Image

In classification, the picture threshold is changed to turn it into a binary image, and then the little item is removed using advanced morphology to make the prediction even clearer. In Fig. 5, the image is trained and classified using the KNN algorithm, and after labelling the samples for each class, the image is stored as a classifier file.

Fig. 5. KNN for prediction

In Fig. 6, the live video is received, processed in phases to forecast the crops, and then the live images are pre-processed to identify the crops in accordance with our training. To accurately forecast the image, we are using the same process. After converting it to grayscale, we predict the crops by reading the trained classifier file, and based on the score we received as an output, it activates the pesticide. The supported application of this techniques is presented in Table 1. It can be further extended by different application of smart farming.

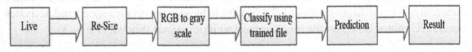

Fig. 6. Classification of Image

Table 1. Urban Agriculture supported by digitization.

Partial Spoiled	Spoiled maximum	Spoiled Minimum
This UI represents that if the crop is partially spoiled and the status of spraying pesticide. The temperature and humidity are represented as a thermometer with a digital display. You can also know the climate whether it's raining or the sun shines. You can also watch the live telecast captured by the drone using a camera	This UI represents that if the crop is fully spoiled and the status of spraying pesticide. The temperature and humidity are represented as a thermometer with a digital display. You can also know the climate whether it's raining or the sun shines. You can also watch the live telecast captured by the drone using a camera	This UI represents that if the crop is spoiled less and the status of spraying pesticide. The temperature and humidity are represented as a thermometer with a digital display. You can also know the climate whether it's raining or the sun shines. You can also watch the live telecast captured by the drone using a camera

3 Conclusion

The world's population growth in general and the concentration of people in metropolitan areas in particular are major causes for concern. Every year, more and more people move to urban areas because of the improved educational opportunities, employment opportunities, access to quality healthcare, and living conditions. By 2030 and 2050, respectively, studies project a staggering 5 billion and 9 billion people will live in metropolitan areas. Urban population growth of this magnitude will undoubtedly have social, economic, and political repercussions. Urban agriculture in terms of smart farming technology can be seen as a very reliable alternative to ensure that the administration meets the essential needs of such a magnificent urban population, such as food and drinking water. Drones in agriculture are giving farmers new options to boost crop yield by using improved agricultural apps and having access to information in real time. Once they have successfully finished their testing phase, drones will further improve the efficacy and efficiency of the agricultural industry by making it much easier to sow seeds, monitor crops, test the soil, and supply other essential components to the soil. In future this work will be extended to the successful implementation of various integrating technology in smart farming.

References

1. Nair, A., Gouripriya, J., James, M., Shibu, S.M., Shihabudeen, H.: Smart farming and plant disease detection using IoT and ML. Int. J. Eng. Res. Technol. (IJERT) NCREIS 09 (13) (2021)
2. Kalyani, Y., Collier, R.: A systematic survey on the role of cloud, fog, and edge computing combination in smart agriculture. Sensors 21(17) (2021)
3. Rangarajan, A.K., Purushothaman, R., Ramesh, A.: Tomato crop disease classification using pre-trained deep learning algorithm. Procedia Comput. Sci. 133, 1040–1047 (2018). ISSN 1877-0509, https://doi.org/10.1016/j.procs.2018.07.070
4. Wadumestrige Dona, C.G., Mohan, G., Fukushi, K.: Promoting urban agriculture and its opportunities and challenges—a global review. Sustainability 13, 9609 (2021). https://doi.org/10.3390/su13179609

5. https://government.economictimes.indiatimes.com/news/technology/use-of-drones-and-ai-technology-in-agriculture-improving-farmers-income-union-minister-narendra-singh-tomar/92993311

6. Balakrishna, K., Rao, M.: Tomato plant leaves disease classification using KNN and PNN. Int. J. Comput. Vis. Image Process. (IJCVIP) **9**(1), 51–63 (2019)

7. Wang, N., Zhu, L., Bing, Y., Chen, L., Fei, S.: Assessment of urban agriculture for evidence-based food planning: a case study in Chengdu China. Sustainability **13**, 3234 (2021). https://doi.org/10.3390/su13063234

8. Samundeeswari, K., Srinivasan, K., Paramaguru, N.: Analysis of soil nutrients for different crops using data mining techniques. In: AIP Conference Proceedings, vol. 2364, Issue 1. https://doi.org/10.1063/5.0062851

9. Jaber, M.M., et al.: Predicting climate factors based on big data analytics based agricultural disaster management. Phys. Chem. Earth Parts A/B/C **128**, 103243 (2022). ISSN 1474-7065, https://doi.org/10.1016/j.pce.2022.103243

10. Ghandar, A., Ahmed, A., Zulfiqar, S., Hua, Z., Hanai, M., Theodoropoulos, G.: A decision support system for urban agriculture using digital twin: a case study with aquaponics. IEEE Access **9**, 35691–35708 (2021). https://doi.org/10.1109/ACCESS.2021.3061722

11. Davies, J., et al.: Barriers to urban agriculture in Sub-Saharan Africa. Food Policy **103**(C) (2021). Elsevier

12. Xydis, G., Liaros, S., Avgoustaki, D.D.: Small scale plant factories with artificial lighting and wind energy microgeneration: a multiple revenue stream approach. J. Clean. Prod. **255**, 120227 (2020)

13. Food and Agriculture Organization of the United Nations, International Fund for Agricultural Development, World Food Programme, The State of Food Insecurity in the World 2015. In: Proceedings of the Meeting the 2015 international hunger targets: Taking Stock of Uneven Progress; FAO: Rome, Italy (2015)

14. Xianghui, T., Xiaoliang, X.: Urban agriculture and urban sustainable development. In: 2012 6th International Association for China Planning Conference (IACP), 2012, pp. 1–5 (2012). https://doi.org/10.1109/IACP.2012.6401979

15. Al-Kodmany, K.: The vertical farm: a review of developments and implications for the vertical city. Buildings **8**, 24 (2018)

16. Atzori, G., Pane, C., Zaccardelli, M., Cacini, S., Massa, D.: The role of peat-free organic substrates in the sustainable management of soilless cultivations. Agronomy **11**, 1236 (2021)

17. Kontothanasis, G.: Social practices of urban agriculture in the metropolitan region of Thessaloniki. Procedia Environ. Sci. **38**, 666–673 (2017). ISSN 1878-0296, https://doi.org/10.1016/j.proenv.2017.03.147

18. Deepthi, A.S., et al.: Integrated smart system for urban farming. In: 2021 International Conference on Advancements in Electrical, Electronics, Communication, Computing and Automation (ICAECA), 2021, pp. 1–4 (2021). https://doi.org/10.1109/ICAECA52838.2021.9675617

19. Yan, D., Liu, L., Liu, X., Zhang, M.: Global trends in urban agriculture research: a pathway toward urban resilience and sustainability. Land **11**, 117 (2022). https://doi.org/10.3390/land11010117

Disease Classification using CNN

Use of Machine Learning Algorithm for Analyzing Children's Health in COVID-19 Situation: Consideration of Organic and Inorganic Food Consumption

Dipti Nashine[1](✉), Rahul Chaudhari[2], and K. Nirmala[2]

[1] Atos Global IT Solution and Services Private Limited, Pune, India
dipti.nashine@gmail.com
[2] DYPIMCAM, Pune, India

Abstract. *People are becoming more fascinated with the term "organic," even if they are unaware of its exact significance or impact on a child's life.* An effort is made to map the organic food value of children, especially before and during the COVID-19 situation. As the health of children is an important criterion that needs to be monitored from an early stage of development for a better and healthier future, The effect of organic food on children is investigated.

Keywords: Machine learning · covid-19 · organic food · child health

1 Introduction

Children's health is always a major concern for all parents. During pandemic situations, parents have taken efforts to make their children healthy and safe. Most basic diseases that affect children under the age of five, such as cough, cold, seasonal fever, and viral infection, can be avoided by healthy children. Providing the right amount and quality of food is critical for improving children's nutrition. In this study, researchers look at the effects of organic and non-organic food consumption in children before and during the pandemic.

Statistical Data about Organic Food

i) Organic foods have a cadmium concentration that is 48% lower: According to Marcin Baraski et al.'s research and the article Higher antioxidant and lower cadmium concentrations and lower incidence of pesticide residues in organically grown crops: a systematic literature review and meta-analyses, organic crops and processed crop-based foods have higher antioxidant activity and higher concentrations of a wide range of nutritionally desirable antioxidants and polyphenolics, but low concentrations of pesticide residues [4].

D. Garg et al. (Eds.): IACC 2022, CCIS 1781, pp. 393–402, 2023.
https://doi.org/10.1007/978-3-031-35641-4_32

ii) There is a 48% lower chance that organic crops will test positive for cadmium. Cadmium is a heavy metal that accumulates in the kidneys and liver, and it's toxic. Apart from the lower cadmium content, facts about the benefits of organic food point out that organic crops are less likely to have detectable amounts of pesticide, based on an NCBI report

iii) Organic food consumption may reduce the risk of allergic disease and of overweight and obesity, but residual confounding is likely as consumers of organic food tend to have healthier lifestyles overall [5].

2 Literature Review

Many studies show that organic plant food has higher levels of vitamin C and phenolic compounds and lower concentrations of nitrate content and pesticides.

However, food from organically raised animals has a higher level of omega-3 fatty acids and conjugated linoleic acid. However, there is no conclusive evidence demonstrating a direct relationship between nutritional value and health effect. Through studies, it has been seen that there is a positive impact of an organic diet on fertility indices, food habits, weight, height, growth, and the immune system. The most recent human epidemiological studies show that eating organic food reduces the risk of allergies, but human intervention studies are unclear [1].

Agriculture is a traditional business in India. In ancient times, every farmer grew crops with natural pesticides and sewage sludge, and the crop was processed without the use of radiation or food additives. Hence, the nutritional values of food were higher. Now a days with the use of chemical fertilisers and pesticides have increased for economical reason. But it will affect the human body adversely.

Also, because of the excessive use of chemical fertilisers and pesticides, the fertility of the soil is reduced. Now we can see the adverse effect of insecticides and pesticides on the human body. According to data produced by the U.S. Department of Agriculture Nutrient Data Laboratory, foods grown in soils that were chemically fertilised were found to have less magnesium, potassium, and calcium content [2].

Age, income, and education may define organic consumers, but the correlation is not very significant. The high cost of organic food discourages consumers from purchasing it. Hence, growing organic food in domestic regions will drastically reduce the price of organic food. A growing interest in education may define organic consumers, but the correlation is not very significant. The high price of organic food is stopping the consumer from purchasing organic food. Hence, growing organic food in domestic regions will drastically reduce the price of organic food. A growing interest in organic food has prompted many studies comparing aspects of organic food because of human health, food safety, and environmental concerns, along with other sensory attributes such as nutritive value, taste, freshness, and appearance. Consumer perceptions about organic food are highly subjective [3].

3 Area Where ML and AI is Implemented During Pandemic

Many organisations have had to change their working styles as a result of the sudden outbreak of coronavirus. Many organizations survive pandemics, while others that are unable to cope with the epidemic struggle to survive.AI and machine learning have proven to be significant heroes in enabling organisations to scale and adapt to changing circumstances.

AI and ML play a major role in understanding how COVID-19 spreads, and analytics help in imposing some major actions like lockdown and curfews in many areas before the pandemic spreads more.

ML and AI play major roles in enhancing research and treatment work. In healthcare, accurate predictive analytics is more important.

AI aids in early detection and produces better results. It also provides solutions for contact tracing, prediction, and drug development, thus reducing the workload of the medical industry.

Food plays an important role in boosting a person's immunity, whether they have COVID-19 or not.One significant challenge was that one should protect us from covid-19 and one of the ways it can be achieved is by having good immunity. Organic food, according to researchers, helps boost immunity. According to the researcher, "There is evidence that this dietary approach can prevent COVID-19 disease or alleviate the clinical course and accelerate the process of creating specific immunity."

4   Organic Food and Covid Impact

The coronavirus has tremendously harmed many lives and areas, triggering a massive rethinking of: what people are eating, which type of food is being consumed, from where that food has been collected, what are the circumstances under which these foods are grown or cultivated, where the food is stored, and how it is prepared. People in urban areas are now more aware of the importance and benefits of a natural, balanced diet, which is boosting the demand for organic, sustainable food.

Children's food is always a matter of great concern. Parents always strive to find healthy options like organic vegetables, fruits, pulses, cereals, etc., which can be considered an improved option. Organic foods are composed of natural and organic ingredients that are cultivated as per the requirements of organic farming. Superficial or artificial preservatives are added to market foods to make them sustainable for longer intervals of time, which are not used in the case of organic food. Previously, organic vegetables were not widely available in the market, and even when they were, customers were unsure about their authenticity. Organic vegetables, pulses, and fruits are more expensive than regular fruits, vegetables, and pulses on the market. Many a time, fruit and vegetable sellers sell regular (not organic) stuff by the name of organic, and common people with less knowledge are cheated. In some cases, it has been found that people who consume original organic food have developed a taste for it, and they can even differentiate between original and artificial stuff. According to a study, people who substitute nonorganic food for organic vegetables and fruits notice a significant difference in flavour and taste. Organic market establishment is a challenging job. Growing organic food has long been a part of Indian culture. Researchers say that "the Indian organic market is yet to flourish." They even say that the supply is erratic and that sometimes the quality isn't that great.

The main aim is to live a healthy life without consuming pesticides and insecticides. as it has many health hazards. Many landowners grow their own vegetables and have a farm to counter-involvement within a short period of time. The pandemic has given people the opportunity to reconsider their decision to live a healthy lifestyle while eating organic food. Organically cultivated fresh fruits, vegetables, and food material without the addition of any compound products like pesticides, weedicides, insecticides, or fertilizers is the core concept behind organic farming. Farming has changed drastically over the years. If you're intent on eating correctly, it's great to lean towards fresh food from a genuine source. Apart from health benefits, there are environmental benefits to organic farming too.

Things to Remember While Purchasing Organic Food

Crisscross look of food: If food stuff is naturally and organically grown, it will definitely have different shades or shapes. For example, there is always a difference in shape, size, and even colour between an organic and regular apple.

Label reading is required, and before purchasing, one should look for any preservatives in the food. It has been observed that most of the preservatives are petroleum-based, which is not fit for eating.

The taste and smell: The smell, taste, and texture of organic food are completely different. There is an apparent sensibility in the flavours, such as fragrance, which is strong and can easily be detected in fruits, raw vegetables, pulses, and spices. Organic spices have a robust fragrance and flavour as they retain their oil content. For example, organic mustard oil taste has strong sensation that can be easily experience by our tongue even after having half teaspoon.

Authorizing: The government and private sectors provide licenses and verified documents for farming businesses. This retains faith in customers with respect to the product.

Farmers get a helping hand. Farmers are even getting financial support for producing organic food and getting monetary benefits after selling it. It shows their trust and faith in working with loyalty. Purchasing products from farmers can help them massively and protect their upcoming generations by maintaining their trust in farming. People's health improves when they consume organic products produced by farmers, so it's a win-win situation for both farmers and consumers.

5 Objective and Hypothesis

- To analyze the impact of organic food in child.
- To analyze impact sports, drinking water and electronic gadget exposure on sickness of children.

Hypothesis

H0: Children who plays sports in ground does not fall sick.
H1: Children who plays sports in ground fall sick.
H0: Organic food does not have significant impact on health.
H2: Organic food has significant impact on health.

5.1   Research Design

Methods used for Sampling: For this research, random sampling is used. Random sampling is one of the most widely used techniques for data collection. It is a sampling technique in which each sample has an equal probability of being selected. A randomly selected sample should be an unbiased representation of the total population. A biased selection will result in an error.

Data Collection

The random sampling technique is used, and for this research, secondary data has been collected from parents of children of different ages. The data contains 24 variables and 1438 samples, which were collected from different places by sharing a Google Form.

6   Implementation of Different Machine Learning Algorithm

Binomial Logistic Regression: A binomial logistic regression, which is also called logistic regression, helps in predicting the probability that an observation belongs to one of two categories of a dichotomous dependent variable based on one or more independent variables that can be either categorical or continuous. Here Binomial Logistic regression is implemented to predict the probability at which your child fall sick in year of getting sick during pandemic situation, where 3 independent variables were taken:

How much time child is playing sports in playground/sports ground?

How many glass of water child drinks in a day?

How much time child use to spend watching TV/Mobile/Kindle/Tablet/Laptop or any other electronic.

Kruskal Wallis H-Test: The Kruskal-Wallis test is a non-parametric alternative to the one-way ANOVA. Non-parametric means are used with the assumption that data comes from a specific distribution. The H test is generally used when the expectations for ANOVA aren't met. It is also called the one-way ANOVA on ranks, as the ranks of the data values are used in the test rather than the actual data points.

Interpretation says that the p-value is less than the significance level; hence we can reject the null hypothesis and conclude that not all the group medians are equal.

Here two variables are taken as: consumption of organic food and child falling sick in a year.

7   Experimental Result

Predictive analytics have great scope in the field of machine learning. Various algorithms are used based on the type of data. Structured algorithms are useful in this research because the data has input as well as output. For unstructured data clustering, classification algorithms are used. Some algorithms that are used in this research are

Binomial Logistic Regression is used to predict the likelihood of a child becoming ill when three variables are considered: time spent playing outside, amount of water consumed by a child per day, and exposure to electronic gadgets.

1. If a child plays sports in playground/sports ground and child drinks more water in a day and child is less exposed to electronic gadget child falls less sick. Accuracy found for this algorithm is 84.16% (Fig. 1).

Fig. 1. Accuracy of algorithm Binomial Logistic Regression

2. If a child eats organic food during the pandemic time, the fall sick for less no of time (Fig. 2).

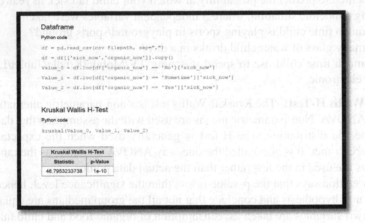

Fig. 2. p-value of Kruskal Wallis H-Test

STATISTICAL OBSERVATIONS

Based on the statistical data, it has been observed in Fig. 3 that there has been an 11% increase in the number of children wearing spectacles before the pandemic and now. There are many reasons that have been observed during the analysis. Some of these are:

- Exposure to the electronic gadgets has been increase, such as mobile, television, tablets, i-pods, electronic games.

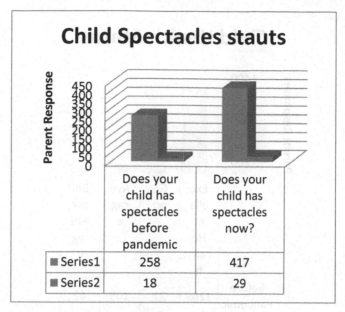

Fig. 3. Children Spectacles Status

– Because of pandemic children started attending online classes through mobiles, computers, laptops which increased their exposure to electronic device.

Based on the statistical data, it has been observed in Fig. 4 what parents think about their child's health. Prior to the pandemic, 1269 children had excellent health, which has now been reduced to 1221. Before the pandemic, 21 children were categorized under the "good" category, which is now reduced to 2. Whereas the average child's health improved from 105 to 196. And below-average health was also reduced from 42 to 18 children.

The reason that has been analyzed from the research says that children who have organic food, spend more time playing in playgrounds, and spend less time watching electronic gadgets have better health as compared to other children.

It has been observed, based on Fig. 5, that on the basis of statistical data, there is a 26% increase in the body weight of children during a pandemic, whereas 10% of parents believe it may increase during a pandemic. 64% of children have maintained their body weight during the pandemic.

Based on the analysis, it can be said that parents have engaged their wards in physical workouts like skipping, walking, running, skating, yoga, meditation, and cycling. Eating organic food, though in small portions, was significant.

Figure 6 depicts the habit of child getting up early in morning, based on the data it has been seen that 30% parent find it difficult to wake up their child in morning. 24% children feel fresh and enthusiastic for getting up in morning. 30% children get up with smiling face. Whereas it has been observed that 15% children get up with upset mood. 2% children cry for some time when they get up early in morning and then get settled.

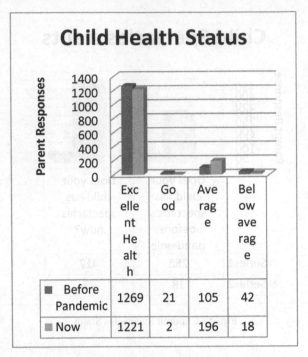

Fig. 4. Children Health Status

	Excellent Health	Good	Average	Below average
■ Before Pandemic	1269	21	105	42
▪ Now	1221	2	196	18

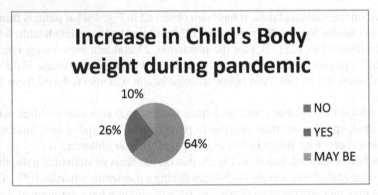

Fig. 5. Increase in Body Weight of Children during Pandemic

Researchers have found a significant impact of organic food on child mood and behavior. What children are eating and drinking during the day and the habits they have developed over the years can affect their health, behavior, and mood. It is important that parents encourage children to eat nutritious food.

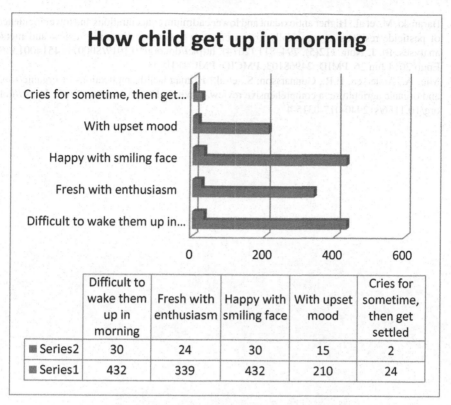

How child get up in morning

	Difficult to wake them up in morning	Fresh with enthusiasm	Happy with smiling face	With upset mood	Cries for sometime, then get settled
■ Series2	30	24	30	15	2
■ Series1	432	339	432	210	24

Fig. 6. Child's waking habit early in morning

8 Conclusion

The primary goal of this paper is to comprehend the significance of organic food in children prior to and during the pandemic. To maintain a child's health, they should be encouraged to participate in playground sports, drink plenty of water, sleep for adequate hours, and avoid excessive exposure to electronic gadgets. Based on literature review carried out during the research organic food has less pesticides and more nutritive value.

References

1. Huber, M., Rembiałkowska, E., Średnicka, D., Bügel, S., Van De Vijver, L.P.L.: Organic food and impact on human health: assessing the status quo and prospects of research. NJAS-Wageningen J. Life Sci. **58**(3–4), 103–109 (2011)
2. Puhalenthi, K., Vishnupriya, S., Rock, B., Pavithra, R. Supriya, A.S., Gayathri, K.: A study on awareness of organic food products in Trichy district. Int. J. Community Med Public Health **4**(12), 4490 4494 (2017)
3. Shafie, F.A., Rennie, D., Alam, B.P.: Consumer perceptions towards organic food. Procedia Soc. Behav. Sci. **49**, 360–367 (2012). https://doi.org/10.1016/j.sbspro.2012.07.034

4. Barański, M., et al.: Higher antioxidant and lower cadmium concentrations and lower incidence of pesticide residues in organically grown crops: a systematic literature review and meta-analyses. Br. J. Nutr. **112**(5), 794–811 (2014). https://doi.org/10.1017/S0007114514001366. Epub 2014 Jun 26. PMID: 24968103; PMCID: PMC4141693
5. Mie, A., Andersen, H.R., Gunnarsson, S., et al.: Human health implications of organic food and organic agriculture: a comprehensive review. Environ. Health **16**, 111 (2017). https://doi.org/10.1186/s12940-017-0315-4

Detection of COVID-19 from Chest X-Ray Images Using VGG-19 Architecture

Pooja Pradeep Dalvi(✉) ⑩, Damodar Reddy Edla ⑩,
and B. R. Purushothama ⑩

National Institute of Technology, Goa, Ponda, India
{poojadalvi,dr.reddy,puru}@nitgoa.ac.in

Abstract. Coronavirus disease (COVID-19) has been life threatening disease that harms the respiratory system of humans. Coronavirus that causes this disease is highly contagious and hence, detection of COVID-19 at preliminary stage is very necessary, so that we can control its further transmission. In this paper, VGG-19 is used for identifying the Coronavirus infected patients using their Chest X-rays. We use Chest X-ray images in our work since it is more affordable by common people than doing Computer Tomography (CT) scan. We use Nearest Neighbour interpolation technique for image preprocessing. VGG-19 model is used along with Adam optimizer for the task of COVID detection. We achieve 92% accuracy by using the pretrained VGG-19 and transfer learning approach. Experiments show that our model achieves higher accuracy than the VGG-16 model which gives 52% accuracy.

Keywords: COVID-19 · VGG-19 · Chest X-ray · Transfer learning · Adam Optimizer

1 Introduction

COVID-19 [1,2] causes infection in the lungs of the patients. It can even cause death if it is not treated properly and early. The virus that causes this disease, Coronavirus, is very contagious which can spread and replicate itself very fast. Hence, detection of COVID-19 at an initial stage is very crucial.

The real time reverse transcription polymerase chain reaction (RT-PCR) tests [2] are normally used for initial testing of patients, but due to the increase in patient count, these test kits are sometimes not sufficient. Hence, other detection mechanisms are being implemented for the diagnosis.

Researchers have been proposing many methods for the detection of COVID-19 using medical images like Chest X-rays or CT scan. In [3], the authors have implemented a model called 'DarkNet' for diagnosis of COVID 19. There are several deep learning models used for COVID-19 diagnosis such as ResNet152 [6], InceptionV3 [6,7], ResNet50 [6,8], ResNet101 [6], Inception-ResNetV4 [7], Inception-ResNetV2 [6,8], MobilenetV2 [8] DenseNet [7–9] and VGG16 [8].

© Springer Nature Switzerland AG 2023
D. Garg et al. (Eds.): IACC 2022, CCIS 1781, pp. 403–411, 2023.
https://doi.org/10.1007/978-3-031-35641-4_33

In [8], eight different convolutional neural networks are used for the detection of COVID positive patients using Chest X-rays and CT scan images. In [6], five different neural network models are used to categorize the Chest X-ray images into four categories based on the type of Pneumonia. In [5], an overview of digital image interpolation techniques is provided.

Most of the research mainly focus on appplying the convolutional neural networks on the dataset and getting the results. There is little contribution towards the data preprocessing steps involved before applying any deep learning model. Also, there has been little contribution towards using the VGG-19 architecture on Chest X-ray images. Hence, we first apply nearest neighbour interpolation technique and data augmentation technique for data preprocessing and then apply the VGG-19 architecture for classifying the Chest x-ray images. We used VGG-19 architecture because the pretrained VGG-19 neural network is already trained on ImageNet database and can classify the images into 1000 categories. Inorder to train the model to classify the medical images, we have used the transfer learning approach. We achieved an accuracy of 92% using our methodology.

The remaining part of the paper is organized as follows. VGG-19 architecture is described in Sect. 2. We provide an illustration of our methodology in Sect. 3. In Sect. 4, we elaborate the results obtained with our experiments. We conclude our paper in Sect. 5.

2   VGG-19 Architecture

In this section, we explain the VGG-19 architecture in depth. We have used this architecture in our methodology for detection of COVID-19. The abbreviation 'VGG' stands for Visual Geometry Group which is a group of researchers at Oxford who developed this architecture. It is called as VGG-19 because it has total 19 layers, consisting of 16 convolutional layers and 3 fully connected layers.

We have used pretrained VGG-19 architecture from the Tensorflow Keras package. This pretrained VGG-19 model has been trained for input images of size $224 \times 224 \times 3$. Hence, image preprocesssing needs to be done to resize the image to this size. The model consists of initial 2 convolutional layers with a max pooling layer, then again 2 convolutional layers with a max pooling layer, followed by 4 convolutional layers and a max pooling layer, again 4 convolutional layers and a max pooling layer, again repeating the 4 convolutional layers and max pooling layer, and finally 3 dense layers as fully connected layers. There are 4 convolutional layers at every stage to provide a hierarchical structure, so that the model can learn very deep features. The Fig. 1 depicts the detailed VGG-19 architecture.

The first two convolutional layers consist of 64 channels with kernels of size 3×3 with a stride of 1. This gives an output of size $224 \times 224 \times 64$. Then a max pooling layer is applied with kernel of size 2×2 and a stride of 1. This gives an output of size $112 \times 112 \times 64$. Then the next two convolutional layers consist of 128 channels with kernel size 3×3 and stride 1. This gives output of dimension $112 \times 112 \times 128$. Again, a max pooling layer is applied with kernel size 2×2. We get an output of size $56 \times 56 \times 128$. Similarly, the dimensions get iteratively updated by sets of convolutional layers and max pooling. Finally, we use Softmax activation function for classifying the image into COVID-19 or Normal.

Fig. 1. VGG19 architecture

3 Proposed Methodology

In this section, we explain our method in depth. Our methodology is described in the Fig. 2. The section consists of dataset and experimental setup, data pre-processing, VGG-19 model and Adam Optimizer.

Algorithm 1: Algorithm for our methodology

---

1. Collect Chest X-ray images of COVID-19 positive and Normal patients.
2. Divide the images into training and testing set.
3. Resize the images into dimension $224 \times 224 \times 3$ using Nearest Neighbour Interpolation technique. Normalise the pixel values in the range of 0-1.
4. Apply Data Augmentation technique of rotation to expand the size of dataset.
5. Import pretrained VGG-19 network and use transfer learning approach to train the network on our dataset.
6. Use Adam Optimizer to optimize the network for fast convergence.
7. Apply the model to classify the Chest X-ray images into Normal or COVID-19 positive patients.
8. Evaluate the model using performance metrics.

3.1 Dataset and Experimental Setup

We use Chest X-ray images from kaggle repository for our experiment. We use 2,100 images for training and 910 images for testing. We execute our methodology in Python using Google Colaboratory and GPU Processor.

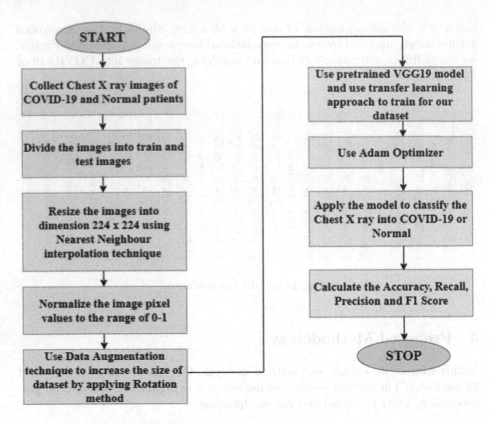

Fig. 2. Framework of our methodology

3.2 Data Preprocessing

We need to resize our images to dimension $224 \times 224 \times 3$ in order to meet the input requirements of our model. We use image interpolation technique to resize our images. Image interpolation is used to resize the image, thereby maintaining its quality. There are many interpolation methods like Lanczos, Nearest Neighbour, Bicubic and Bilinear. We use Nearest Neighbour interpolation technique in this work. In Nearest Neighbour interpolation technique, the closest value of the input pixel is given as the output pixel value. It selects the closest pixel values from the current pixel position to perform the interpolation.

The size of our dataset is too small for training a convolutional neural network. Hence, we use data augmentation technique to expand our dataset. We adopt the data augmentation technique of rotation, in which we rotate each image by a specific angle, in our case, 15°. This increases the size of our dataset. We normalize the image pixels in the range of 0–1.

3.3   VGG-19 Model for COVID-19 Detection

VGG-19 is a deep learning model which contains 19 layers. We have shown the detailed architecture of VGG-19 in Fig. 1. We have explained the VGG-19 architecture in the previous section. We use a pretrained VGG-19 network, which is pretrained using ImageNet weights. The network model is avaliable in the keras Application Programming Interface which is present in Tensorflow 2.0 and is an open source library in python. We add the fully connected layers on top of the model. At the end, we use Softmax activation function. We freeze the initial layers which have already been pretrained. This reduces the number of trainable parameters.

VGG-19 model consists of 19 layers, an improvement over VGG-16 model containing 16 layers. The increase in number of layers helps in better training of the model. In our methodology, we use the transfer learning approach since our dataset is not too large for training a deep learning model. Imagenet is a very giant dataset which consists of 1000 classes. Hence, we use the pretrained VGG-19 model on Imagenet using the Imagenet weights and then use the transfer learning approach to apply it on our dataset. On top of the pretrained network, we use average pooling, then flatten the output, use dense layer with ReLU activation function with a dropout of 0.25, again a dense layer with ReLU activation function and finally one fully connected dense layer with softmax activation function. The steps used in our methodology have been illustrated in the Fig. 3.

3.4   Adam Optimizer

'Adam' stands for 'Adaptive Moment Estimation' [4]. It combines the methods of AdaGrad and RMSProp optimization. We use Adam Optimizer to compile our model. This enhances the speed of convergence of our model. We achieve the results in a fewer number of epochs when we use Adam Optimizer. It is mainly used for faster convergence.

4   Results and Discussion

We used VGG-19 architecture for training our model. We used learning rate of 0.001, 40 epochs and batchsize of 32. The total number of model parameters were 20,550,722, out of which 526,338 were trainable and 20,024,384 were non-trainable. This reduction in trainable parameters is due to the transfer learning approach, wherein we train only the fully connected layers and keep the initial pretrained layers fixed.

The loss of the VGG-19 model on train and test data is shown in Fig. 4. It shows the loss of the model with respect to the number of epochs for train and test data. We see that the loss on train data is less than that on test data. This is because our model is slightly overfitted on our training set. The accuracy of the model on train and test data is shown in Fig. 5. We see that the accuracy increases as the number of epochs increases.

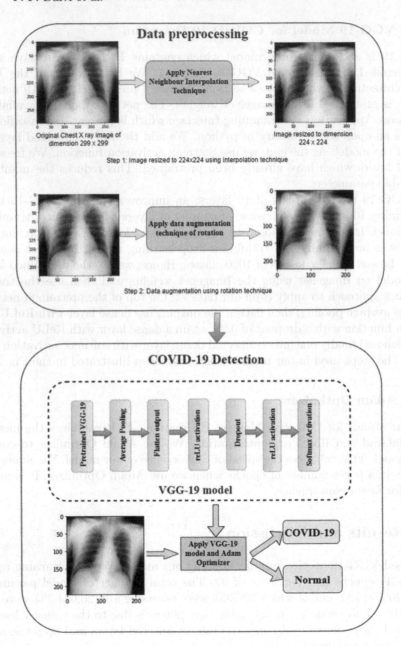

Fig. 3. Illustration of our methodology

Figure 6 displays the confusion matrix obtained after testing the model on test data. We see that out of total 450 COVID images, 439 were correctly classified as COVID and 11 were classified as Normal. Out of 460 images of Normal,

399 were correctly classified as Normal and 61 were classified as COVID. The Receiver Operating Characteristic (ROC) curve is shown in Fig. 7.

We evaluate our model depending on the values of Accuracy, Precision, Recall and F1 Score. Accuracy is defined as the percentage of number of images correctly classified to the total number of images. Precision is the percentage of number of images correctly classified as positive class (COVID in our case) to the total images classified as positive class (COVID). Recall is the percentage of number of images correctly classified as positive class (COVID) to the total number of images actually belonging to the positive class (COVID). F1 Score is the harmonic mean of precision and recall. We obtained Accuracy 92%, Recall 97.5%, Precision 87.8% and F1 Score 92.42%. We also implemented VGG-16 model on our dataset and achieved an accuracy of 50.55%. Our VGG-19 model with the transfer learning approach achieved higher accuracy than VGG-16 which achieved 50% accuracy on same dataset.

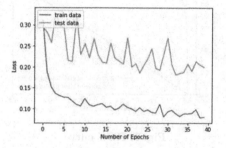

Fig. 4. Training and Testing Loss

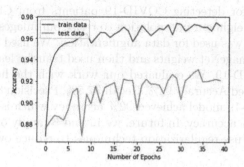

Fig. 5. Training and Testing Accuracy

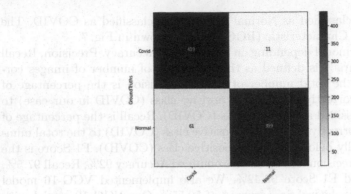

Fig. 6. Confusion matrix

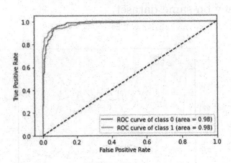

Fig. 7. ROC curve

5   Conclusion

In this paper, we presented a methodology using VGG-19 Architecture and Adam Optimizer for detecting COVID-19 patients from Chest X-ray images. We used Nearest Neighbour interpolation to resize our images in the dataset and rotation technique was used for data augmentation. We used a pretrained VGG-19 network with ImageNet weights and then used transfer learning approach for diagnosis of COVID-19. We evaluated our work with the help of performance metrics. We obtained Accuracy 92%, Recall 97.5%, Precision 87.8% and F1 Score 92.42%. Our VGG-19 model achieved 92% accuracy which is higher than VGG-16 model with 52% accuracy. In future, we intend to apply our methodology on larger dataset and use regularization techniques to reduce overfitting.

References

1. Wu, F., et al.: A new coronavirus associated with human respiratory disease in China. Nature **579**(7798), 265–269 (2020)
2. Huang, C., et al.: Clinical features of patients infected with 2019 novel coronavirus in Wuhan, China. Lancet **395**(10223), 497–506 (2020)

3. Ozturk, T., Talo, M., Yildirim, E.A., Baloglu, U.B., Yildirim, O., Acharya, U.R.: Automated detection of COVID-19 cases using deep neural networks with X-ray images. Comput. Biol. Med. **121**, 103792 (2020)
4. Kingma, D.P., Ba, J.: Adam: a method for stochastic optimization (2014). arXiv preprint arXiv:1412.6980
5. Fadnavis, S.: Image interpolation techniques in digital image processing: an overview. Int. J. Eng. Res. Appl. **4**(10), 70–73 (2014)
6. Narin, A., Kaya, C., Pamuk, Z.: Automatic detection of coronavirus disease (COVID-19) using x-ray images and deep convolutional neural networks. Pattern Anal. Appl. **24**(3), 1207–1220 (2021)
7. Albahli, S., Ayub, N., Shiraz, M.: Coronavirus disease (COVID-19) detection using X-ray images and enhanced DenseNet. Appl. Soft Comput. **110**, 107645 (2021)
8. Ahsan, M.M., Gupta, K.D., Islam, M.M., Sen, S., Rahman, M., Hossain, M.S.: Study of different deep learning approach with explainable AI for screening patients with COVID-19 symptoms: using CT scan and chest x-ray image dataset (2020). arXiv preprint arXiv:2007.12525
9. Hasan, N., Bao, Y., Shawon, A., Huang, Y.: DenseNet convolutional neural networks application for predicting COVID-19 using CT image. SN Comput. Sci. **2**(5), 1–11 (2021)

Covid Identification with Chest X-Ray Image Classification Using Convolutional Neural Network

Shikha Rastogi⬛, Neha Gupta⬛, Sarita Yadav$^{(\boxtimes)}$⬛, and Devansh Verma⬛

Bharati Vidyapeeth's College of Engineering, Paschim Vihar,
Delhi 110063, New Delhi, India
sarita.yadav@bharatividyapeeth.edu

Abstract. For one and half years when the whole world had been suffering from a pandemic and during this period different chatbots and virtual healthcare assistants came to help people to fight covid. The main problem was when RT-PCR techniques were used on a large scale for covid detection it was observed that the accuracy of the result had decreased and when its alternative CT-scan was thought to use to detect whether a person is covid positive or not then there was a chance that after a test of covid positive person his covid particles may be left in air which may cause a deviation of the result of next patient and maybe even transmission of it. The purpose of this study is to classify X-Rays images of lungs using CNN and other deep learning techniques to check whether the user is covid positive or not. (Fine-Grained visual recognition problem). This research paper further analyses the and proposes a transfer learning model which has been accomplished by pretrained VGG16 and ResNet50 deep learning models.

Keywords: X-Ray · RT-PCR · Res Net 50 · VGG16

1 Introduction

The year 2019 had a bright start but the winters were a lot colder than usual because a new virus had started spreading all over the globe with lightning speed from villages to cities and later engulfed the whole countries causing severe damage everywhere. Many people were caught by this deadly virus and lost their lives [15] and a stage came where global deaths because of it had a number which were an unimaginable number and the worst part is that still till this date it continues to grow and bring variations, just when the vaccine was rolled out a new variation came called omicron variant which speaks that the terror of this virus has yet to be gone. SARS-Co-V-2 is the virus that was the root cause of COVID-19 which stands for Corona Virus Disease 2019 and was fir5st reported out in laboratories of Wuhan, China in December 2019.

Bharati Vidyapeeth's College of Engineering.

When a proper WHO-certified vaccine was yet to be made a report showed that [9] artificial intelligence was a digital way to fight against covid 19 as it is well known that AI has shown off the charts results when dealing with complex tasks. The development of artificial intelligence in the following domains is exemplified through strategy games, speech recognition, image categorization, and so on: Black boxes are used to implement artificial intelligence and machine learning algorithms. [12], which means that the non-linear structure provides no information on how this prediction works because of the nesting. Apple's Siri, Amazon's Alexa, and Google Translate are all instances of artificial intelligence in our daily lives that make use of natural language processing (NLP) in translating into different languages [18]. Google and Microsoft have made significant investments in artificial intelligence in recent years, and they recognize that AI is the technology age's future. A study [14] in the United States stressed the role of computers and information technology. When it comes to health. Similarly, a study [4] developed an evolutionary model for classifying diabetes patients at high risk.

In this model, we have used image classification [8] which has become increasingly interesting in the study field. With the advancement of artificial neural networks and the creation of deep learning architectures based on artificial neural networks, such as the convolutional neural network, multiclass picture categorization and recognition [7] of objects belonging to many categories has become a reality. In terms of performance and complexity, every new machine learning framework has an edge over older ones. We have also used transfer learning which saves the information learned from one problem and applies it to a separate but similar problem. For example, the skills learned while learning to distinguish cats can be applied to identifying cheetahs. Transfer learning is a deep learning technique that involves training a neural network model on a problem that is similar to the one being solved. Transfer learning [20] provides the advantage of shortening a learning model's training time and lowering generalization error.

Karen Simonyan and Andrew Zisserman of the University of Oxford proposed the VGGNet Deep Convolutional Neural Network in their research paper 'Very Deep Convolutional Neural Networks for Large-Scale Image Recognition.' The name of their study group, 'Visual Geometry Group (VGG),' inspired the name of this model. VGG-19 is the term given to this convolutional neural network because it contains 19 layers in its architecture. The goal of this model was to reduce the number of parameters in a convolutional neural network while improving training time. VGG-19's architecture is depicted in the block diagram below. The major advantage of this network is that you can load a pre-trained version of it from the ImageNet database, which has been trained on over a million photos. A network that has been pre-trained can classify photos into thousands of different item categories. We will use this model on the CIFAR-10 image dataset, which has 10 object types, because of this advantage.

The goal of this research is to use CNN and other deep learning techniques to classify X-Ray images of the lungs in order to determine whether or not the user is covid positive. (Problem of fine-grained visual recognition). In the second section of the paper, the related works have been discussed and their short-comings and weak areas have been discussed which have been overcome in this model. The third section focuses on the methodology of the model concerning the core methodology, dataset, model selection, etc. the fourth section demonstrates the results and graphs which were obtained from our model and the final section is the conclusion.

2   Related Work

The World Health Organization (WHO) classified the COVID-19 outbreak as a pandemic on March 11, 2020, and the virus has spread fast in numerous countries throughout the world since then, killing people[people   [19]. COVID-19 is an acute respiratory infectious illness spread mostly through the lungs. The majority of COVID-19-infected individuals had previously come into contact with virus-contained surfaces, infected patients, or carriers of the virus. Patients had cold symptoms such as fever, cough, exhaustion, shocks, diarrhea, hemop-tysis, headache, shortness of breath, and other respiratory diseases. [1] Antigen detection methods, chest computed tomography (CT), COVID-19 biosensors, Real-time RT-PCR, and other procedures are popular methods used to diagnose covid-19. Among all of these techniques, the gold standard for diagnosing covid-19 is RT-PCR [2]. However, because RT-PCR is a time-consuming, complex, expensive, and manual technique, multiple studies have found that its sensitivity ranges from 30% to 60%, implying a decline in the accuracy of COVID-19 diagnosis in many situations[situations   [3]. Compared to RT-PCR, CT scan pictures show a higher sensitivity in identifying and detecting cases[cases   [5]. A software solution based on deep learning was developed for automatic COVID-19 detection on chest CT by Zheng et al.   [21] using 3D CT volumes to detect COVID-19. Also, a CTnet-10 model was proposed in   [5], and the model attained an accuracy of 82.1 percent for COVID-19 detection using CT scans.

However, CT scanner radiation can be problematic for individuals who need many CT scans during the course of their illness. Problems include the possibility of disease transmission while utilizing a CT scan scanner, as well as the technology's expensive cost, which can generate major complications for patients and healthcare systems. As a result, X-ray imaging is far more comprehensive and cost-effective in diagnosis than traditional diagnostic testing. A deep learning model was proposed in   [21] and the fundamental architecture of the proposed system was based on the Resnet-50 model. To boost the intensity of the CXR picture and reduce noise, image enhancement techniques were applied in the suggested system. COVIDXNet was introduced in   [23], a DL framework for detecting COVID-19 infections in X-ray images. Seven DL approaches were compared using a small dataset of 50 photos(e.g., MobileNetV2, ResNetV2, VGG19, DenseNet201, InceptionV3, Inception, and Xception). With a score of 91 percent accuracy, DenseNet201 performed the best. In   [6], by integrating computer vision and image analysis on Chest X-Ray pictures acquired from five open access data repositories, a deep convolutional neural network was presented specifically for the detection of COVID-19 patients. More than 13,870 patients were represented in that data, which included 9472 chest X-Ray images. However, the proposed model was far from ready for commercialization. In the study in [13] around 15 distinct deep transfer learning models were tested and their performance was analyzed to compare various transfer learning methodologies. The obtained findings demonstrated that the VGG series are the best models for the job.

3 Methodology

Classification of images can be done in numerous ways including techniques like supervised classification which uses algorithms like linear regression, logistic regression, random forest, decision tree, CNN, etc. [10] and unsupervised classification which works on anomaly detection, cluster analysis, etc. Further supervised classification algorithms can also be divided into Machine Learning and Deep Learning. In Deep Learning we use complex architecture while designing algorithm which resembles the functioning of a human brain, therefore it provides an advantage over machine learning, also studies [11] suggest deep learning algorithms are improving rapidly, especially in the field of medical imaging.

3.1 Dataset

Our dataset consists of more than 30 thousand Chest X-Ray images, which were developed by researchers from Qatar University and the University of Dhaka along with collaboration with medical doctors around the world, published on [2,16] and can be accessed from kaggle. The dataset contains folders having Covid +ve X-Ray images, Pnemoniatic (or other lung infection) X-Ray images, and Normal X-Ray images, along with the description of these images. This dataset contains more than 3616 Covid positive X-Ray images, 10192 Normal X-Ray images, and 1345 Other Pnemoniatic X-Ray images.

Model Selection. Custom CNN. Using the transfer learning approach [17] we have imported VGG16 and ResNet50 models and used them for classifying chest X-Ray images in our dataset, a study [22] shows this model yields high accuracy in the classification of medical images.

4 Result

4.1 VGG16

VGG16. VGG16 is one of the most preferred CNN architectures in recent times, study shows a depth explanation of VGG16. As its name suggests it has 16 convolution layers and a uniform architecture. A reason for its success is its

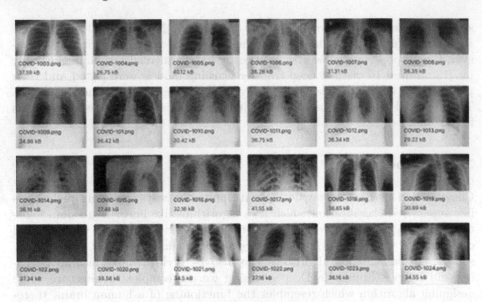

Fig. 1. Preview of the dataset

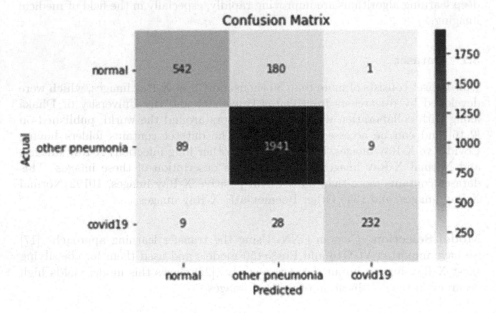

Fig. 2. Confusion matrix

huge number of parameters, i.e., it contains 138 million parameters. VGG16 with adam optimizer: Training Accuracy = 90 Training Loss = 0.22 Validation Accuracy = 89.75 Validation Loss = 0.29.

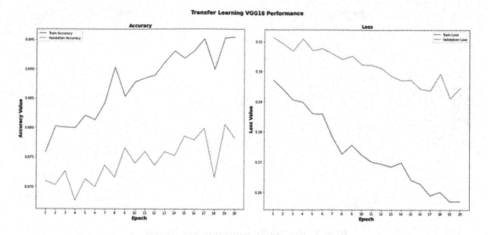

Fig. 3. VGG16 accuracy, loss graph

ResNet50. A Residual Neural Network (ResNet) comes in the category of Artificial Neural networks in which a network is formed by stacking residual blocks on top of each other. ResNet50 is a variant of ResNet that can work with 50 neural network layers. ResNet50 makes the use of residual blocks, Increasing the efficiency and minimizing error percentage with more neural layers (Figs. 1, 2, 3, 4, 5, 6 and 7).

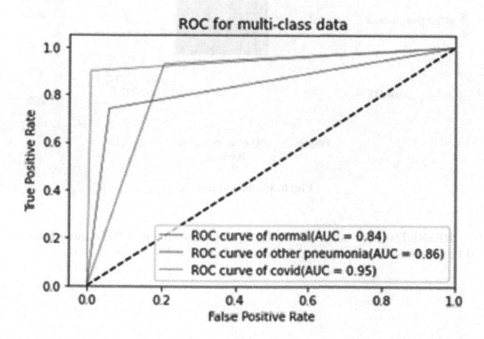

Fig. 4. ROC Curve

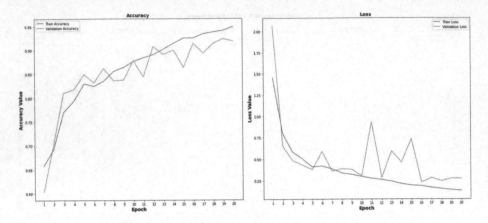

Fig. 5. ResNet50 accuracy, loss graph

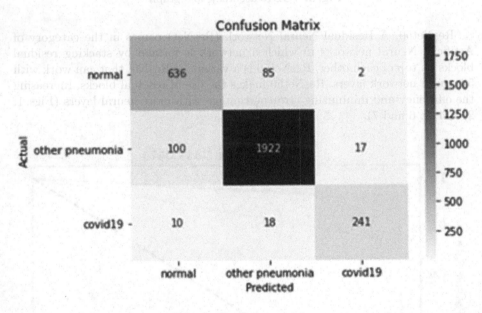

Fig. 6. Confusion matrix

RESNET50 with adam optimizer: Training Accuracy = 95Training Loss = 0.12 Validation Accuracy = 92 Validation Loss = 0.27

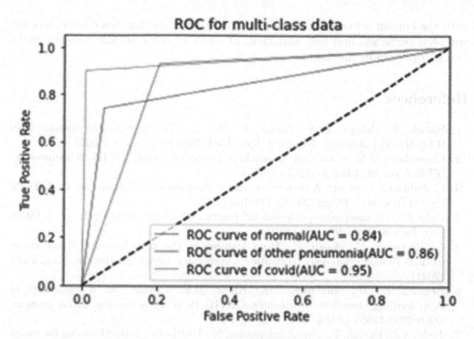

Fig. 7. ROC Curve

5   Conclusion

In this study, we proposed a few techniques for classifying Chest X-Ray images, whether it is covid positive or not. Firstly, our custom-made CNN model did not perform well with our dataset as it only yielded 65% accuracy. The model needed to be designed efficiently for better results and accuracy. Later we implemented a solution using the Transfer Learning approach, in which we used pre-trained VGG16 and ResNet50 deep learning models. We have imported these models from TensorFlow and used Adam optimizer, as well as SGD optimizer, and compared their results. VGG16 and SGD with Adam optimizer yield good accuracy, i.e., 90% and 95% upon testing with our dataset. There are a lot of future possibilities which can further enhance the model and can be used to make this a fully-fledged healthcare virtual assistant that not only detects and check COVID 19 but other lung-related diseases and chronic diseases also. As this is a medical application project so the accuracy of the project can be further increased to provide better results than the existing one. A much more advanced version of the project can be that as there are many variations of covid-19, this project can be further enhanced by studying the different variations of covid-19 and classifying the user with the report that which type of variation one has. CNN with ensample approach can improve the model performance for large datasets which is desirable. Also, the dataset has been compiled by us so the dataset can be further updated and similar changes can be made to keep the model updated with the current scenario because still a perfect vaccine for this disease has not yet been pertained and new variations of covid 19 come in like a snowy night and still pertain in the world.

References

1. Baloch, S., Baloch, M.A., Zheng, T., Pei, X.: The coronavirus disease 2019 (COVID-19) pandemic. Tohoku J. Exp. Med. **250**(4), 271–278 (2020)
2. Chowdhury, M.E., et al.: Can AI help in screening viral and COVID-19 pneumonia? IEEE Access **8**, 132665–132676 (2020)
3. El Jaddaoui, I., et al.: A review on current diagnostic techniques for COVID-19. Expert Rev. Mol. Diagn. **21**(2), 141–160 (2021)
4. Erdil, D.C.: A comparison of health informatics education in the USA. Int. J. Intell. Eng. Inform. **7**(4), 366–383 (2019)
5. Ghaderzadeh, M., Asadi, F.: Deep learning in the detection and diagnosis of COVID-19 using radiology modalities: a systematic review. J. Healthc. Eng. **2021** (2021)
6. Hemdan, E.E.D., Shouman, M.A., Karar, M.E.: Covidx-Net: a framework of deep learning classifiers to diagnose COVID-19 in x-ray images. arXiv preprint arXiv:2003.11055 (2020)
7. Joshi, A.J., Porikli, F., Papanikolopoulos, N.: Multi-class active learning for image classification. In: 2009 IEEE Conference on Computer Vision and Pattern Recognition, pp. 2372–2379. IEEE (2009)
8. Karkalos, N.E., Markopoulos, A.P., Davim, J.P.: Evolutionary-based methods. In: Computational Methods for Application in Industry 4.0. SAST, pp. 11–31. Springer, Cham (2019). https://doi.org/10.1007/978-3-319-92393-2_2
9. Khachfe, H.H., Chahrour, M., Sammouri, J., Salhab, H., Makki, B.E., Fares, M.: An epidemiological study on COVID-19: a rapidly spreading disease. Cureus **12**(3), 1–7 (2020)
10. Kotadiya, H., Patel, D.: Review of medical image classification techniques. In: Yang, X.-S., Sherratt, S., Dey, N., Joshi, A. (eds.) Third International Congress on Information and Communication Technology. AISC, vol. 797, pp. 361–369. Springer, Singapore (2019). https://doi.org/10.1007/978-981-13-1165-9_33
11. Latif, J., Xiao, C., Imran, A., Tu, S.: Medical imaging using machine learning and deep learning algorithms: a review. In: 2019 2nd International conference on computing, mathematics and engineering technologies (iCoMET), pp. 1–5. IEEE (2019)
12. Nguyen, T.T., Nguyen, Q.V.H., Nguyen, D.T., Hsu, E.B., Yang, S., Eklund, P.: Artificial intelligence in the battle against coronavirus (COVID-19): a survey and future research directions. arXiv preprint arXiv:2008.07343 (2020)
13. Organization, W.H., et al.: Coronavirus disease 2019 (COVID-19): situation report, 51 (2020)
14. Poole, D., Mackworth, A., Goebel, R.: Computational Intelligence: A Logical Approach (1998). Google Scholar Digital Library (1998)
15. Rahaman, M.M., et al.: Identification of COVID-19 samples from chest x-ray images using deep learning: a comparison of transfer learning approaches. J. Xray Sci. Technol. **28**(5), 821–839 (2020)

16. Rahman, T., et al.: Exploring the effect of image enhancement techniques on COVID-19 detection using chest x-ray images. Comput. Biol. Med. **132**, 104319 (2021). https://doi.org/10.1016/j.compbiomed.2021.104319, https://www.sciencedirect.com/science/article/pii/S001048252100113X

17. Saikia, A.R., Bora, K., Mahanta, L.B., Das, A.K.: Comparative assessment of CNN architectures for classification of breast FNAC images. Tissue Cell **57**, 8–14 (2019)

18. Samek, W., Wiegand, T., Müller, K.R.: Explainable artificial intelligence: understanding, visualizing and interpreting deep learning models. arXiv preprint arXiv:1708.08296 (2017)

19. Saxena, A., Singh, S.P.: A deep learning approach for the detection of COVID-19 from chest x-ray images using convolutional neural networks. arXiv preprint arXiv:2201.09952 (2022)

20. Schlüter, S., Sheppard, A., Brown, K., Wildenschild, D.: Image processing of multiphase images obtained via x-ray microtomography: a review. Water Resour. Res. **50**(4), 3615–3639 (2014)

21. Shah, V., Keniya, R., Shridharani, A., Punjabi, M., Shah, J., Mehendale, N.: Diagnosis of COVID-19 using CT scan images and deep learning techniques. Emerg. Radiol. **28**(3), 497–505 (2021)

22. Simonyan, K., Zisserman, A.: Very deep convolutional networks for large-scale image recognition. arXiv preprint arXiv:1409.1556 (2014)

23. Zheng, C., et al.: Deep learning-based detection for COVID-19 from chest CT using weak label. MedRxiv (2020)

Ocular Disease Recognition Using Convolutional Neural Networks

Abhinav Mangla⬭, Shafali Dhall⬭, Neha Gupta(✉)⬭, Shikha Rastogi⬭, and Sarita Yadav⬭

Bharati Vidyapeeth's College of Engineering, Paschim Vihar,
Delhi 110063, New Delhi, India
neha.gupta@bharatividyapeeth.edu

Abstract. In proposed work, we recommend a deep learning-based app-roach to ocular disease recognition, which includes diseases that affect the eye health of an individual. The proposed system tends to provide an economic and reliable method to aid in the early diagnosis of diseases such as diabetes, glaucoma, cataract, age-related macular degeneration (AMD), myopia, hypertension, and other diabetese model uses the Ocular Disease Intelligent Recognition (ODIR) dataset which is a structured ophthalmic data-base containing eye images with colour, age of 5000 patients. The annotations are done by trained human readers to eliminate any incorrect predictions due to mislabeled data. Computer vision and deep learning have the capability of detecting the abnormalities from high resolution fundus images. The pro-posed model is tried with different combinations of diseases and reaches a maximum accuracy of 93% when used for a single disease and an accuracy of 83% when used for a combination of multiple diseases. The proposed work is based on ODIR-2019 Dataset while the author uses Convolutional Neural Networks algorithm (CNN).

Keywords: ocular diseases · diabetes · AMD · hypertension · cataract · ODIR First Section

1 Introduction

Ocular diseases refer to the diseases that affect the eye health and vision in patients of all ages and demographics. While the consensus is that most ocular diseases affect the older population, younger and healthier individuals are also at risk of such diseases. Ocular disease recognition is generally performed using manual procedures. Thus, the process is inefficient and costly. It also leads to an increased work-load on the ophthalmologists and eye technicians since each procedure is complex and requires utmost concentration and time. Thus, there is a need for an automated and reliable process to perform these tasks. Delay in detection of ocular diseases can present some serious health risks including

Bharati Vidyapeeth's College of Engineering.

© Springer Nature Switzerland AG 2023
D. Garg et al. (Eds.): IACC 2022, CCIS 1781, pp. 422–433, 2023.
https://doi.org/10.1007/978-3-031-35641-4_35

a complete loss of sight. Patients with ocular diseases generally are not aware of any such abnormality and a diagnosis at a later stage is not as helpful since major damages have already taken place. Such diseases can only be successfully detected with regular medical screenings, but the procedures put a lot of strain on the clinical resources. According to reports by the World Health Organization (WHO), at least 2.2 billion people in the world are experiencing some sort of vision impairment. Of these, around a billion of the patients could be saved from permanent impairment if a proper diagnosis had been made available at an early stage. Early ocular disease recognition is a cost-effective and efficient method to prevent blindness caused by some diseases such as hypertension, diabetes, glaucoma, cataract, age related macular degeneration (AMD), and other abnormalities. Computer vision and deep learning technologies are capable of extracting minute details from high-resolution images and producing reliable predictions regarding the presence of ocular symptoms. Due to the fast rise in technology, many computer-aided systems (CAD) have been developed for such applications, but a majority of them are currently undergoing clinical trials and hence are not available in public domains. We present a complete review of the research already being done in this domain followed by a detailed explanation of our own system. The paper then proceeds to list the results of our experiments on real world images and its suitability in clinical environments.

We provide a novel HAR approach using convolution and recurrent neural networks in the suggested study (Conv-Rec). The raw image frames are processed by the Rectified Linear Unit (ReLU) [1] layer model as a convolutional layer in the proposed ConvRec architecture, and the information that is retrieved is then sent to the bi-directional recurrent network. The ODIR-2019 dataset served as the basis for training the ConvRec model, and it was these photos that were used to evaluate the model's performance.

2   Related Work

In this section, we explore the research undertaken and proposed by previous researchers working in the domain of ocular (related to the eyes) diseases. The sphere of detecting the presence of a disease by examining and processing the images of the eye of the patient has seen limited research [5]. Explores the various applications of iris recognition and the implications of an ocular disease on the recognition tasks. The re-searchers concluded that though such diseases do not have severe impacts on biometric recognition, some cases that may be the case. [23] discusses the use of iridology using machine learning to create a diagnostic model for type 2 diabetes. An impressive classification accuracy of 89.63% was obtained with a maximum specificity of 0.9687 and a maximum sensitivity of 0.988. These are promising results for non-invasive techniques to diagnose diabetes. Retinopathy for diabetes, glaucoma and AMD diagnosis is explored in [9] where the performance of a deep learning system is evaluated on a clinic based multi-ethnic population. The re-search concluded by saying that further research was needed in this domain to get better outcomes. A similar retinopathy-based approach was suggested in [27] where support vector machines and morphological image processing was used for automatic eye health diagnosis. Blood vessels, microaneurysms, exudates and haemorrhages were extracted from the raw eye images and passed on to the SVM for further classification. The method yielded a maximum accuracy of 94.11% for the moderate category. [3] proposes techniques for cerebral palsy rehabilitation and diagnosis in children. The project aims to monitor the progress of cerebral palsy in kids in the age range of 3–11 years. The technique showed a maximum accuracy of 94.17% with a maximum specificity of 0.98 and a sensitivity of 0.9165. Neural networks were used for the analysis. [11] presents a classification of five different kinds of classes of eye diseases using support vector machines. They achieved a sensitivity of 82% with a specificity of 88%. The aim of the work was to automatically detect normal, mild diabetic retinopathy (DR), moderate DR, severe DR and prolific DR. Diabetic retinopathy is one of the most common forms of visual impairment in the working class. A major factor in the prediction accuracy of a model is the availability of vast datasets with proper annotations and labelling. [3] focuses on classifying fundus images into diabetic and normal, hence ensuring the availability of usable datasets for ocular disease research. The classification was able to achieve an accuracy of 86%. Over the years, we are nearing the accuracy of human ophthalmologists, as depicted in [7]. It presents a review of multiple computers based automated diabetic retinopathy systems. The classification efficiency of different DR systems is discussed. It was concluded that the advent of digital systems has enabled us to keep a proper record of the progress of the patient. DiaNet [8] is a diabetes detection system which uses digital images of a person's eye to find out areas of the retina which indicate the presence of diabetes. The model is trained on a relatively small dataset and is still able to attain an accuracy of 84 The authors of [12] uses telemedicine for the diagnosis of ocular diseases. A trained reader analyses images obtained from remote cameras. The study focussed mainly on non-White ethnicities. [21] explores the domain of detecting glaucoma using computers since human observation is prone to errors. It was found that the computer aided detection was extremely successful and should be used extensively to aid clinics in diagnosis. A comprehensive review [10] of glaucoma detection systems covers multiple models with a maximum detection accuracy of 93.57% and an average accuracy of 85% among all existing systems. It also considers various approaches to glaucoma detection, which includes manual as well as auto-mated approaches [25] uses a neural network-based approach to glaucoma detection with an achieved sensitivity of 100% and specificity of 80%. The paper provides a cheap and efficient method for glaucoma detection as compared to the already prevalent OCT and HRT methods. Automated glaucoma detection using histogram methods [19] also generates promising results. A region of interest is selected, followed by the application of feature detection and Gabor convolution to get the desired results. Moving to cataract detection systems, [16] uses features such as Big Ring Area, Small Ring Area, Edge Pixel Count and Object Perimeter to classify the given image into three categories - normal, cataract and post-cataract using support vector machines for classification. The results are found to be extremely promising with a classification accuracy of 90%, sensitivity at 94% and specificity at 93.75%. Similarly, artificial neural networks

(ANN) [18] are used for cataract and post cataract eye images using backpropagation algorithms. The ANN classifier displays an average rate of 93.3% in classifying the images into normal, cataract and post cataract. The results were clinically significant. Cataract detection through the use of low-cost infrared cameras has been explored in [2]. Infrared images yield an accuracy of about 96% and hence is a reliable method for cataract detection. The domain of recognition of hypertension using eye fundus has not seen much research and progress. Multiple studies have indicated the inverse relation between increasing blood pressure (hypertension) and the narrowing of the retinal arteriolar diameter [28]. It was discovered that each 10 mm Hg increase in the blood pressure levels resulted in a 3 μm decrease in the retinal diameter. [6] aimed to explore and verify the facial features which are reliable indicators of hypertension in adults. It was found that cheek colour in men and nose and forehead colour in women were the distinct features related to hypertension. Age-related Macular Degeneration [4] can be detected using OCT (Optical Coherence Tomography) images. This method can outperform a transfer learning approach, put forward recently. It was also found that Support Vector Machines (SVMs) [14] provide a superior classification of eye fundus images into AMD/non- AMD class with an experimental accuracy of 93%. Thus, the research summarised above indicates that it is possible to get reliable results for ocular disease recognition from digital eye images. These results are accurate enough to be clinically significant and thus can provide expedited results at reduced costs. The summary also depicts that no reliable system has been proposed which can diagnose more than one image [22].

3   Proposed Methodology

Dataset. The dataset used for this system is the Ocular Disease Intelligent Recognition (ODIR) [13]. It contains eye images of around 5000 patients. Both left and right eye images of the patient are included. Each image is accompanied with the patient's age and the diagnostic keywords which have been written by an ophthalmologist. The dataset is properly structured and is collected from the patients across hospitals in China. Since different cameras were used for capturing the images, all images are of different resolutions. The data is a little unbalanced, for example, hypertension has less images compared to other diseases and the abnormalities extend to more than 10 different diseases. Despite these issues, ODIR still remains one of the best datasets for ocular diseases. The images are classified into 8 categories. The categories are: Normal (N) Diabetes (D) Glaucoma (G) Cataract (C) Age related Macular Degeneration (AMD) Hypertension (H) Pathological Myopia (M) Other abnormalities (O).

3.1   Data Pre-processing

The first step for preparing the data for training is to resize all the images to fixed dimensions, since all the images have large dimensions which are not fit for training. Instead of resizing each image at the time of training, we created a

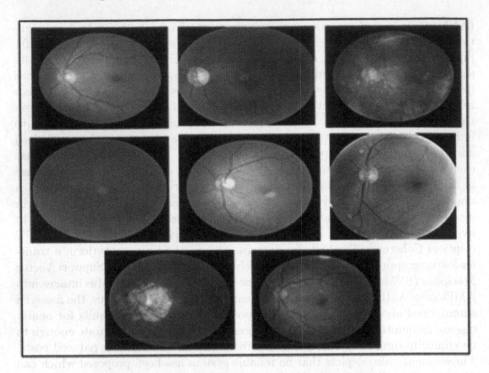

Fig. 1. Image 1: Normal, Diabetes, Glaucoma, Cataract, AMD, Hypertension, Myopia, Other Abnormalities Source: https://odir2019.grand-challenge.org/

separate directory where each image is resized only once and saved to save time and memory. The resulting dimensions should be small enough to prevent excessive memory and time usage but large enough for the results to be conclusive and image detailing should not be lost. The images were resized to 250×250 pixels. Following the resizing of the images, the next step was to get the labels right, since each eye can have a different disease. If the left eye has cataract and the right eye is normal, the diagnoses should be given differently. The dataset originally has been created by keeping a common overall label for both eyes. We mapped the appropriate label with the image. The label was stored in the name of the image. In this way, we do not need to create new files for labelling and renaming files is a very fast operation. Dusty and low-resolution images are then dropped from the dataset. The validation set is created by randomly selecting roughly 30% of all images in the dataset. This leaves a large portion of the images to be used by the training set and the validation set also gets enough representation to prevent any sort of bias [20]. One of the most important steps of data pre-processing is data augmentation. Since, the data is unbalanced and some classes are underrepresented, augmentation techniques are applied to balance the dataset. The techniques used include random zoom, random rotation, flip left-right, flip top-bottom, all these augmentation techniques are used, and the resulting images are saved in another directory. Special care is taken to keep the background noise to the minimum [29]. After completion of data augmentation, the TensorFlow [24] dataset object. An iterative learning process with a small batch size of 32 is used. A small batch size allows the weights to be updated at small intervals and yield better results. TensorFlow allows dataset shuffling which is beneficial to prevent over-fitting [30] (Fig. 1).

Performance Evaluation Metrics. F1 Score

The accuracy of a model on a dataset is gauged by the F-score, also known as the F1-score. It's employed to assess binary categorization schemes that label instances as "positive" or "negative". Recall The recall is determined as the proportion of Positive samples that were properly identified as Positive to all Positive samples. The recall gauges how well the model can identify positive samples. The more positive samples that are identified, the larger the recall.

$$\text{Recall} = \text{True Positive}/\text{True Positive} + \text{False Negative} \tag{1}$$

Accuracy It serves as a benchmark of how well the data can be classified by the classifier. The precision is provided by the following equation:

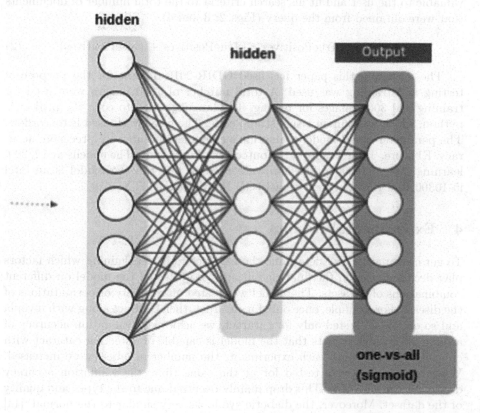

Fig. 2. Model Representation

$$Accuracy = \frac{TP + TN}{TP + FP + TN + FN}$$

Fig. 3. Accuracy Formula

$$F_1 = \frac{2}{\frac{1}{recall} \times \frac{1}{precision}} = 2 \times \frac{precision \times recall}{precision + recall}$$

$$= \frac{tp}{tp + \frac{1}{2}(fp + fn)}$$

Fig. 4. F1 Score Formula

Precision is defined as the ratio of the number of documents that are truly valuable to the user and fit his search criteria to the total number of documents that were obtained from the query (Figs. 2, 3 and 4).

$$Precision = TruePositives / (TruePositives + FalsePositives) \qquad (2)$$

The author in this paper has used ODIR-2019 dataset for the purpose of testing and training was used. A total number of 7000 images were used for training and 3000 images for testing. The language used to code the project is python, which was run on visual studio code. The framework used is tensorflow. The parameter-based model evaluation's essential measures are precision, accuracy, F1 score. Table 4 reports the outcomes of our study. The epochs at 12/200, learning rate at 0.0001, The hardware used to test run the model is an intel i5-10300H CPU @2.5 Ghz with a 16 GB RAM GPU - GTX 1650.

4   Experimental Results

To get clear results and determine the key factors in determining which factors play deciding roles in the final classifications, we tested the model on different combinations of datasets. The model was tested on a variety of permutations of the disease. For example, once only for cataract, then cataract along with myopia and so on. When tested only for cataract, we achieved a validation accuracy of around 93% which depicts that the model is capable of detecting cataract with clinical accuracy. With each experiment, the number of labels were increased. When all diseases were tested for at the same time, the validation accuracy dropped to around 50%. This drop mainly occurred due to the types and quality of the dataset. Moreover, the diabetic eye looks very similar to the normal [14] fundus and hence affects the overall accuracy to a large extent. Yet, it can be observed that the neural network is highly capable of classifying cataract and myopia and hence, has a wide array of clinical applications. For all the experiments, the same neural network architecture and parameters were used to provide a neutral environment for all the trial runs. Only the epochs were altered depending on the number of images in the dataset and to avoid any kind of overfitting (Tables 1, 2, Figs. 5, 6, 7 and 8).

Table 1. Results for different combinations

Class	Precision	Recall	F1 Score	Accuracy
N/C	0.9404	0.9406	0.9406	0.9406
N/D	0.5819	0.5819	0.5819	0.5819
N/C/M	0.8944	0.8808	0.8875	0.8795
N/C/M/A	0.8452	0.8315	0.8383	0.8325
ALL	0.4965	0.4875	0.4919	0.6052

Table 2. Model Comparison

Author	Accuracy	Precision	Recall	F1 Score	Dataset	Methodology
[15]	86.08%	-	-	-	ODIR-2019	ML-CNN
[26]	96.54%	95.71%	83.04%	89.7995	SD-OCT	DL-CNN
[17]	94.3%	91.5%	-	-	RFMiD	ML-CNN
Proposed	94.06%	94.06	94.06	94.06	ODIR-2019	ML-CNN

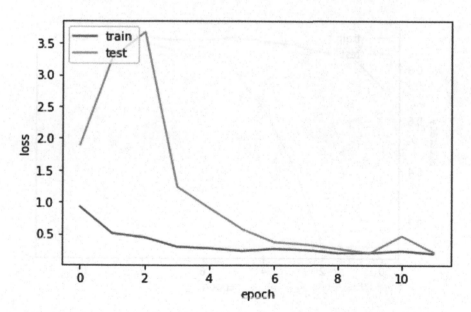

Fig. 5. Model Loss

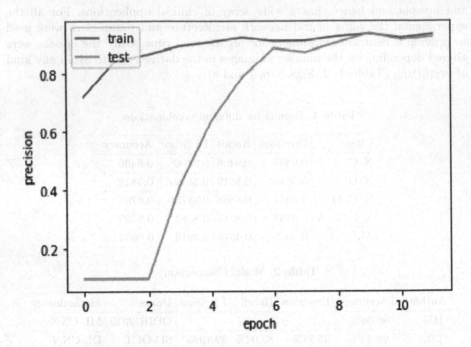

Fig. 6. Model Precision

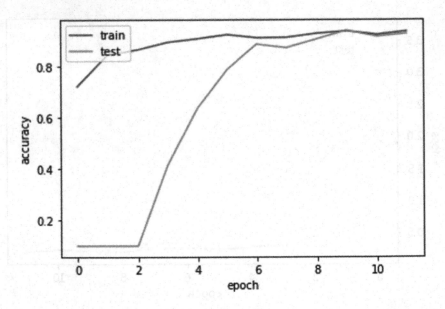

Fig. 7. Model Accuracy

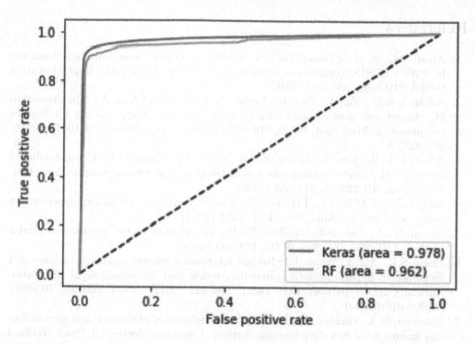

Fig. 8. ROC Curve

5   Conclusion

We have proposed a model which can detect multiple ocular diseases ranging from cataract to hypertension. The model is highly scalable and is made with the intention of expansion and room for improvement. With the availability of better and higher numbers of images, we can expect significant strides in this do-main. Early ocular disease recognition is an essential part of health technology and has the potential to better the lives of millions of people suffering from such diseases. If implemented properly, ocular detection can help numerous health institutions by saving testing costs and providing accurate, reliable results in fractions of the time. The applications of such a system are vast and hence, no slack can be cut when it comes to proper implementation. We have used TensorFlow libraries for the model which has good support for data augmentation. The ODIR dataset can be considered a "small" dataset when compared to datasets used in other deep learning applications. The number of images in this dataset do not seem to be enough to mark the distinct features of each disease. We have got significant results for cataract and myopia which is a testimony for the feasibility of the system. If better datasets are made and curated in the future, ocular detection accuracy will increase in leaps and bounds and help the healthcare sector.

References

1. Abadi, M., et al.: {TensorFlow}: a system for {Large-Scale} machine learning. In: 12th USENIX Symposium on Operating Systems Design and Implementation (OSDI 2016), pp. 265–283 (2016)

2. Acharya, R.U., Yu, W., Zhu, K., Nayak, J., Lim, T.C., Chan, J.Y.: Identification of cataract and post-cataract surgery optical images using artificial intelligence techniques. J. Med. Syst. **34**(4), 619–628 (2010). https://doi.org/10.1007/s10916-009-9275-8

3. Acharya, U.R., Lim, C.M., Ng, E.Y.K., Chee, C., Tamura, T.: Computer-based detection of diabetes retinopathy stages using digital fundus images. Proc. Inst. Mech. Eng. [H] **223**(5), 545–553 (2009)

4. Ang, L., Yim, M.H., Do, J.H., Lee, S.: A novel method in predicting hypertension using facial images. Appl. Sci. **11**(5), 2414 (2021)

5. Aslam, T.M., Tan, S.Z., Dhillon, B.: Iris recognition in the presence of ocular disease. J. R. Soc. Interface **6**(34), 489–493 (2009)

6. Chew, S.K., Xie, J., Wang, J.J.: Retinal arteriolar diameter and the prevalence and incidence of hypertension: a systematic review and meta-analysis of their association. Curr. Hypertens. Rep. **14**(2), 144–151 (2012). https://doi.org/10.1007/s11906-012-0252-0

7. Esfahani, M.T., Ghaderi, M., Kafiyeh, R.: Classification of diabetic and normal fundus images using new deep learning method. Leonardo Electron. J. Pract. Technol **17**(32), 233–248 (2018)

8. Faust, O., Acharya, U.R., Ng, E.Y.K., Ng, K.H., Suri, J.S., et al.: Algorithms for the automated detection of diabetic retinopathy using digital fundus images: a review. J. Med. Syst. **36**(1), 145–157 (2012). https://doi.org/10.1007/s10916-010-9454-7

9. Gupta, N., Gupta, S.K., Pathak, R.K., Jain, V., Rashidi, P., Suri, J.S.: Human activity recognition in artificial intelligence framework: a narrative review. Artif. Intell. Rev. **55**, 1–54 (2022). https://doi.org/10.1007/s10462-021-10116-x

10. Hagiwara, Y., et al.: Computer-aided diagnosis of glaucoma using fundus images: a review. Comput. Meth. Programs Biomed. **165**, 1–12 (2018)

11. Illavarason, P., Arokia Renjit, J., Mohan Kumar, P.: Medical diagnosis of cerebral palsy rehabilitation using eye images in machine learning techniques. J. Med. Syst. **43**(8), 1–24 (2019)

12. Islam, M.T., Al-Absi, H.R., Ruagh, E.A., Alam, T.: DiaNet: a deep learning based architecture to diagnose diabetes using retinal images only. IEEE Access **9**, 15686–15695 (2021)

13. Jais, I.K.M., Ismail, A.R., Nisa, S.Q.: Adam optimization algorithm for wide and deep neural network. Knowl. Eng. Data Sci. **2**(1), 41–46 (2019)

14. Kaymak, S., Serener, A.: Automated age-related macular degeneration and diabetic macular edema detection on oct images using deep learning. In: 2018 IEEE 14th International Conference on Intelligent Computer Communication and Processing (ICCP), pp. 265–269. IEEE (2018)

15. Khan, I.A., Sajeeb, A., Fattah, S.A.: An automatic ocular disease detection scheme from enhanced fundus images based on ensembling deep CNN networks. In: 2020 11th International Conference on Electrical and Computer Engineering (ICECE), pp. 491–494 (2020). https://doi.org/10.1109/ICECE51571.2020.9393050

16. Khunger, M., Choudhury, T., Satapathy, S.C., Ting, K.C.: Automated detection of glaucoma using image processing techniques. In: Abraham, A., Dutta, P., Mandal, J., Bhattacharya, A., Dutta, S. (eds.) Emerging Technologies in Data Mining and Information Security. Advances in Intelligent Systems and Computing, vol. 814, pp. 323–335. Springer, Singapore (2019). https://doi.org/10.1007/978-981-13-1501-5_28

17. Nair, V., Suranglikar, S., Deshmukh, S., Gavhane, Y.: Multi-labelled ocular disease diagnosis enforcing transfer learning. In: 2021 55th Annual Conference on Information Sciences and Systems (CISS), pp. 1–6. IEEE (2021)

18. Nayak, J.: Automated classification of normal, cataract and post cataract optical eye images using SVM classifier. In: Proceedings of the World Congress on Engineering and Computer Science, vol. 1, pp. 23–25 (2013)

19. Nayak, J., Acharya, U.R., Bhat, P.S., Shetty, N., Lim, T.C., et al.: Automated diagnosis of glaucoma using digital fundus images. J. Med. Syst. **33**(5), 337–346 (2009). https://doi.org/10.1007/s10916-008-9195-z

20. O'Shea, K., Nash, R.: An introduction to convolutional neural networks. arXiv preprint arXiv:1511.08458 (2015)

21. Park, D.W., Mansberger, S.L.: Eye disease in patients with diabetes screened with telemedicine. Telemed. e-Health **23**(2), 113–118 (2017)

22. Rajinikanth, V., et al.: Automated classification of retinal images into AMD/non-AMD class-a study using multi-threshold and Gassian-filter enhanced images. Evol. Intel. **14**(2), 1163–1171 (2021). https://doi.org/10.1007/s12065-021-00581-2

23. Samant, P., Agarwal, R.: Machine learning techniques for medical diagnosis of diabetes using iris images. Comput. Meth. Programs Biomed. **157**, 121–128 (2018)

24. Segall, R.S., Sankarasubbu, V.: Survey of recent applications of artificial intelligence for detection and analysis of COVID-19 and other infectious diseases. Int. J. Artif. Intell. Mach. Learn. (IJAIML) **12**(2), 1–30 (2022)

25. Shabbir, A., et al.: Detection of glaucoma using retinal fundus images: a comprehensive review. Math. Biosci. Eng. **18**(3), 2033–2076 (2021)

26. Tayal, A., Gupta, J., Solanki, A., Bisht, K., Nayyar, A., Masud, M.: Dl-CNN-based approach with image processing techniques for diagnosis of retinal diseases. Multimed. Syst. **28**(4), 1417–1438 (2022)

27. Ting, D.S.W., et al.: Development and validation of a deep learning system for diabetic retinopathy and related eye diseases using retinal images from multiethnic populations with diabetes. Jama **318**(22), 2211–2223 (2017)

28. Tripathi, P., et al.: MTCD: cataract detection via near infrared eye images. Comput. Vis. Image Underst. **214**, 103303 (2022)

29. Zhang, Z., et al.: A survey on computer aided diagnosis for ocular diseases. BMC Med. Inform. Decis. Mak. **14**(1), 1–29 (2014)

30. Zhou, Y., Wang, B., Huang, L., Cui, S., Shao, L.: A benchmark for studying diabetic retinopathy: segmentation, grading, and transferability. IEEE Trans. Med. Imaging **40**(3), 818–828 (2020)

Brain Tumor Segmentation from MRI Images Using Deep Learning Techniques

Ayan Gupta[1]($\boxtimes$), Mayank Dixit[1], Vipul Kumar Mishra[2], Attulya Singh[1], and Atul Dayal[1]

[1] Galgotias College of Engineering and Technology, Greater Noida, UP 201306, India
{ayangupta.19gcebcs080,mayank.dixit,attulyasingh19gcebcs121,
atuldatal.19gcebcs107}@galgotiacollege.edu
[2] School of Computer Science Engineering and Technology, Bennett University, Greater Noida, India
vipul.mishra@bennett.edu.in

Abstract. A brain tumor, whether benign or malignant, can potentially be life threatening and requires painstaking efforts in order to identify the type, origin and location, let alone cure one. Manual segmentation by medical specialists can be time-consuming, which calls out for the involvement of technology to hasten the process with high accuracy. For the purpose of medical image segmentation, we inspected and identified the capable deep learning model, which shows consistent results in the dataset used for brain tumor segmentation. In this study, a public MRI imaging dataset contains 3064 TI-weighted images from 233 patients with three variants of brain tumor, viz. Meningioma, glioma, and pituitary tumor. The dataset files were converted and preprocessed before indulging into the methodology which employs implementation and training of some well-known image segmentation deep learning models like U-Net & Attention U-Net with various backbones, Deep Residual U-Net, ResUnet++ and Recurrent Residual U-Net. With varying parameters, acquired from our review of the literature related to human brain tumor classification and segmentation. The experimental findings showed that among all the applied approaches, the recurrent residual U-Net which uses Adam optimizer reaches a Mean Intersection over Union of 0.8665 and outperforms other compared state-of-the-art deep learning models. The visual findings also show the remarkable results of the brain tumor segmentation from MRI scans and demonstrates how useful the algorithm will be for physicians to extract the brain cancers automatically from MRI scans and serve humanity.

Keywords: Image Segmentation · Brain Tumor · MRI scans · Convolutional Neural Network · U-Net · Attention mechanism · Residual U-Net · Recurrent and Residual U-Net

1 Introduction

The term "brain tumor" refers to a mass or proliferation of abnormal cells in the brain. And the human skull being a closed space leaves no room for such growth to prevail. Hence, this abnormal growth can lead to unexpected developments for the worse. Brain

D. Garg et al. (Eds.): IACC 2022, CCIS 1781, pp. 434–448, 2023.
https://doi.org/10.1007/978-3-031-35641-4_36

tumors occur in several varieties. Both benign and malignant brain tumors can begin in the brain as primary brain tumors and can also spread to nearby tissues, or, in the form of secondary brain tumors, cancer that started in another part of the body can move to the brain [1]. Imaging tests are vital in identifying if the tumor is primary or secondary. Magnetic resonance imaging (MRI) of the brain is the initial step in the tumor's diagnosis. MRI can create precise scans of the body using magnetic fields, as compared to the results from X-rays, which is also helpful in determining the size of the tumor which makes it the ideal method to identify a brain tumor as it also produces images that are more precise than CT scans [2]. Hence, we were obligated to use the dataset containing TI-weighted MRI scans of infected patients with three kinds of brain tumor: meningioma, glioma, and pituitary tumor. Deep learning is a kind of machine learning that uses neural networks to simulate how people learn subjects [3]. Deep learning makes it quicker and simpler to collect, analyze, and interpret vast amounts of data, which is very advantageous for those who are entrusted with doing so. We are using such deep learning techniques to perform image segmentation on MRI scans of the brain [4]. Image segmentation is the process of dividing up images into several segments and grouping those that belong to the same object class together. By segmenting an image, complexity of classification can be reduced and/or the representation of the image can be changed to make it more meaningful and clearer. These techniques are to be used to segment the MRIs in such a way that the tumor is recognizable as a part of the brain. The domain of medical image segmentation has been incentivized with the engenderment of Convolutional Neural Networks and encoder-decoder type architectures like U-Net, where the focus is specifically on preserving and generalizing localization of Regions of Interest. An architecture like U-Net preserves both the spatial and localized features of the input image in a highly optimized manner. Furthermore, techniques like Attention mechanism, Residual Blocks, Backbones, Recurrent networks and more, have also proved to work efficiently for segmentation related tasks. Our study seeks to do image segmentation on brain MRI data using deep learning techniques, for faster and more accurate cancer identification and localization in the brain. Patients, specifically over the age of 40 years, with brain tumors have a dismal survival rate, and many tumors even go unnoticed. It takes extremely little time to forecast a brain tumor when these algorithms are applied to MRI pictures, and higher accuracy makes it easier to treat patients where complicated cases usually require experienced medical personnel to locate the area of the tumor, compare affected tissues with nearby regions, and provide the final verdict. The radiologists can make speedy decisions thanks to these projections.

The major contribution of the paper is mentioned as below:

1) Segmentation of the MRI images using deep learning algorithms for better generalization capabilities.
2) Investigation of enhanced deep learning segmentation algorithms for brain tumors.

The rest of the paper is organized as Sect. 2 discusses the related literature present in the domain and motivation for doing this work. Section 3 presents the methodology used in the work for brain tumor segmentation. Section 4 provides the details of the deep-learning hyper-parameters and the evaluation metrics used in this work. Also, this section presents the statistical and visual result along with a discussion. Section 5 concludes the paper.

2 Related Works

Most studies show analysis on image data or classification techniques with remote segmentation techniques. Javaria Amin et al. [5] is an overview of the latest techniques used in deep learning that are being used for tumor detection. The paper delves deeply into the types of imaging involved for the brain, such as MRIs, CAT scans, PET etc. Different image segmentation techniques need to be used for different types of imaging methods. The paper also gives us an insight about the datasets publicly available, and the criteria by which each deep learning model used for image segmentation was evaluated. This research helped us identify that we are to use MRI imaging data for our own research and that deep learning models like U-Net and its variants would be best suited to get the most accurate results. Instead of using the resulting tumor segmentation masks, Getty N. et al. [6] recreated the capsule network architecture [7], refined the model parameters and MRI tumor images' preprocessing. It is stated that segmentation is not required for identifying the type of tumor, but the laborious problem of manually segmenting the tumor for localization and description still remains at hand. For mass detection in MRI scans, BrainMRNet, a deep learning model was developed by Toğaçar et al. [8]. Interestingly, an additional segmentation technique is also developed which determines the lobe area in the brain with higher concentration of two classes of tumors. Gunasekara SR et al. [9] present a comprehensive end-to-end systematic method for MRI-based tumor segmentation and detection of meningiomas and gliomas. A straightforward CNN algorithm is used to classify brain tumors, then a Faster R-CNN network is used to localize the tumor, and finally the Chan-Vese algorithm [10] is used to precisely segment the tumor. The final output was the precise tumor boundary for segmentation purposes for each given axial brain MRI. All three algorithms were linked in a cascade fashion. The suggested Faster R-CNN model is used to extract the bounding box, and then a segmentation approach is used to provide the tumor's precise contour. For early brain tumor detection, a brilliant approach was suggested by Suneetha and Rani [11]. The proposed method involves pre-processing the acquired brain MRI images using the Optimized Kernel Possibilistic C-means Method (OKPCM). To enhance the image, an adaptive Double Window Modified Trimmed Mean Filter (DWMTMF) is then employed. At last, the images are segmented using the region expanding method. Kadkhodai et al. [12] created an image enhancing model. Based on the intensities, the enhanced images are then segmented using 3D super-voxels. The study proposes a saliency detection-based feature employed with an edge-aware filtering technique which aligns the edges of the original image and saliency map further enhancing the border of the tumor. The output of their neural network is the segmented tumor. A proposition of Enhanced Convolutional Neural Network (ECNN) was put forth by Thaha et al. [13] accompanied by BAT algorithm as the loss function with the primary aim of presenting optimization-based segmentations. Small kernels used in the model enable deep architectural design and have favorable effects on overfitting, provided that lower weights are supplied to the network.

Ronneberger et al. [14] proposed an architecture with a symmetric pair of contracting path to collect context and an expanding path to enable exact localization. In certain categories, the study easily won the 2015 ISBI Cell Tracking Challenge. The work of Oktay et al. [15] learns to concentrate automatically on target structures of varying forms and sizes in medical imaging by combining the attention gate model with the U-Net architecture. According to experimental findings, Attention gates preserve computational efficiency while continuously enhancing U-Net's accuracy across various datasets. Zhang et al. [16], suggest the use of ResUnet in their research. This study proposes a neural network for semantic segmentation that blends residual learning with U-Net. This model has the advantage of making deep network training easy due to residual units and the quantity of skip links within the network that enable information flow. The concept is commonly used to partition medical images into different bodily areas and modalities [17, 18]. To overcome the difficulty of distinguishing healthy cells from tumor boundaries in the diagnosis of brain tumors, DeepSeg, a new deep learning architecture has been developed by Zeineldin et al. [19]. The system that was developed is an interactive decoupling framework in which the encoder part uses a convolutional neural network to do spatial information processing and the decoder part provides the full-resolution probability map from the generated map. The dense convolutional network (DenseNet), the NASNet using modified U-Net, and the residual network (ResNet) were just a few of the CNN models included in the study. For colonoscopic image segmentation, Jha et al. [20] developed ResUNet++, an enhanced ResUNet architecture that suggests methods to boost its sensitivity to the important elements, suppress the unimportant features, and give larger context. These methods include residual blocks along with attention mechanism, Atrous Spatial Pyramidal Pooling (ASPP), and squeeze and excitation blocks. Comparing ResUNet++ to other techniques, the outcomes for the colorectal polyps were better. The suggested models make use of the Residual and Recurrent Network, and U-Net in the paper of Md Zahangir Alom et al. [21]. These structures for segmentation problems provide benefits like aids deep architecture training, superior feature representation for segmentation tasks ensured by feature accumulation and improves performance for medical image segmentation with the same amount of network parameters [22].

With the review of the related work in the field of medical image segmentation, studies that use segmentation algorithms leave potential grounds for higher performance with fewer complexities. The problem of segmenting medical images has benefited from the development of U-Net architecture by using the capabilities of attention and recurrent mechanisms, different backbones, and residual blocks. It has shown more opportunities to improve the effectiveness of such an architecture for tumor segmentation.

3 Materials and Methodology

As presented in Fig. 1 our study follows the ensuing methodology for acquiring results from the input dataset. The dataset is initially preprocessed to provide appropriate data for the implementations. Images obtained from preprocessing are then partitioned into training, validation, and testing datasets. After determining the appropriate hyperparameters, the designated training and validation data are used to train the model. Using the inference on validation data, the model with best training coefficients is saved. Testing data is then utilized to gather inference using this model. Comparison between different methodologies using various metrics is performed.

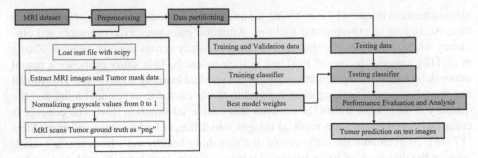

Fig. 1. Flow chart for conducting this work

3.1 Image Dataset

The brain T1-weighted CE-MRI dataset was obtained from Tianjing Medical University and Nanfang Hospital in Guangzhou, China, between 2005 and 2010 [23]. The dataset was first shared publicly in 2015 and saw multiple revisions, with the most recent iteration of the dataset released in 2017. The collection comprises 708 meningiomas, 1426 gliomas, and 930 pituitary tumors in 3064 T1-weighted, contrast-enhanced pictures, as depicted in Fig. 2, from 233 patients. Data fields for the tumor label, patient ID, image data, tumor boundary and mask data are stored in MATLAB file format. Further, a crucial preprocessing stage was required to appropriately use the data with Python.

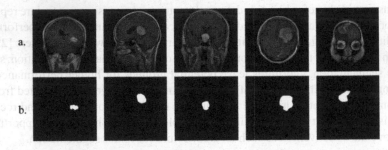

Fig. 2. Sample images of T1-weighted MRI dataset, a) MRI scans b) Ground Truth masks

3.2 Preprocessing Stage

Since the files were in MATLAB format, it was required to convert and preserve their contents as standard images so that our techniques could use them effectively without wasting memory by loading each mat file repeatedly. Using the SciPy module, the files with the "mat" extension were imported as dictionaries.

The data included fields such as tumor label: 1 for meningioma, 2 for glioma, 3 for pituitary tumor, patient id, image data: grayscale values with 3 channels in the form of an array, tumor border: a vector storing the coordinates of discrete points on tumor border; [x1, y1, x2, y2, ...] in which x1, y1 indicate planar coordinates of tumor border, and tumor mask data: a binary image with 1 indicating tumor region and 0 indicating non-tumor region. Image data and tumor mask data were extracted as NumPy arrays by iterating through the mat files. The values were normalized between 0 and 1. Using the OpenCV module, all the processed images are stored in "png" format and divided into train (2485 instances), validation (274 instances), and test (305 instances) sets.

3.3 Methodology

U-Net

U-Net is an architecture for a convolutional neural network that was developed mainly for image segmentation and offers advancements over CNNs, to deal with biomedical images where the goal is to not only categorize the infection but also to identify its location [14]. Prior to U-net, classification networks were unable to segment an image using pixel-level contextual information. U-net's adaptability led researchers to heavily include it in subsequent investigations using new imaging techniques. This research has grown steadily throughout the years, incorporating several imaging techniques and application fields [24].

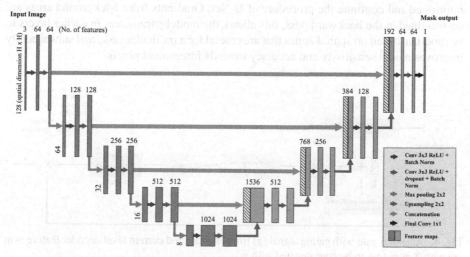

Fig. 3. U-net architecture for tumor segmentation

As presented in Fig. 3, the U-Net design can be seen as a pair of encoder-decoder networks with an expanding path that provides exact localization and a symmetric contracting path that collects contextual and spatial data, giving it a u-like shape. Each block of the contracting route, repeated for a few increasing filters, consists of two successive 3×3 convolutions, a ReLU activation unit and a max-pooling layer.

The U-Net's novel features may be found in the extending path, where, in each stage, the feature map is upsampled by 2×2 up-convolution. The contraction path's feature map from the matching layer is stacked onto the upsampled feature map to transport the encoder's high-resolution feature maps directly to the decoder network using skip connections. Then come two successive 3 × 3 convolutions, escorted by ReLU activation. This design not only exceeded the most effective technique at its imminence (a sliding window ConvNet) but was also simpler and quicker to train end-to-end with less input images.

Attention U-Net

Adding to the capabilities of U-net, the attention mechanism [15] intends to recreate the capability of humans to concentrate on relevant instances while ignoring others in the neural network and allocate more computing resources to important stimuli. The task is achieved using an attention gate which when added to the skip connection within the U-Net, provides localized classification resulting in more accurate and robust image classification performance and progressively suppresses highlight responses in unrelated background areas. As shown in Fig. 4, attention gate accepts input from the succeeding deepest layer feature map (better feature representation) and skip connection feature map from the contracting path (better spatial information). A sequence of operations like, adding the inputs after convolution to obtain aligned and unaligned weights (selective concentration), activation layer, single filter and stride convolution, sigmoid function for scaling weights and finally, resampling. The output and skip connection feature map are multiplied and continue the procedure of U-Net. Gradients from background areas are de-weighted in the backward pass, this allows the model parameters in earlier layers to be modified based on spatial zones that are crucial for a particular task, and subsequently improves model sensitivity and accuracy towards foreground pixels.

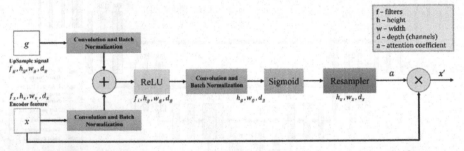

Fig. 4. Attention gate with gating signal (g) from encoder and current level decoder feature map (x) with $\hat{X}$ as output to be concatenated with x

ResUnet

He et al. [25] addressed in their study that a very deep architecture is difficult to train due to issues like vanishing gradients and adverse effects on the generalization power of the model. To overcome this predicament, they suggested using an identity mapping architecture for deep residual learning. The intuition to solve the degradation problem is to recognize that shallower networks perform better than the deeper networks and skipping extra layers can help us maintain the depth of layers and prevent degradation.

In this model, the layers give an output as H(x) = F(x) + x, where F(x) is residual (difference between output and input) and x being the identity skip connection as shown in Fig. 5. Hence, the layers in the residual network are learning the residual and not the true output which resolves the vanishing gradient problem and helps the system avoid lossy compression with identity mapping.

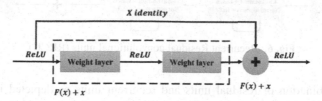

Fig. 5. Residual learning: a building block

Using the best of Deep Residual learning and U-Net architecture, Zhang et al. [16] came up with the Deep Residual U-Net architecture. ResUnet also consists of encoding path, skip connections and decoding path, where both the encoder and decoder units incorporate residual blocks for each level. Combining these crucial techniques, the network's training process is facilitated by the residual unit, and information spreads without degradation through the skip connections. Anita et al. [18] found in their study that, for lung segmentation, more discriminative feature representations can be extracted by a deeper residual network than a shallow network.

ResUnet++

ResUnet++ is based on the structure of ResUnet. In addition to that, it uses techniques like squeeze and excitation blocks, attention blocks, and Atrous Spatial Pyramidal Pooling (ASPP) [20]. This model begins with a stem block which is used to downsample the input image to ensure operations maintain low computational complexity and efficiency in results and passed onto the encoding path. Each encoder block's output is passed to the squeeze-and-excitation block which modifies the features and enhances the network's characteristic power. This leads to suppression of the redundant features and increased sensitivity for pertinent features [26]. Through the ASPP network, the output of the complete encoding block is passed [27] which connects the encoder to the decoder. It enlarges the field-of-view of the filters, by providing multi-scale information, to include a broader context. Before each decoder block, an attention block is used to improve the quality of features that improves the outcome. To obtain the final segmentation map at the end of the decoding path, another ASPP block is utilized followed by a 1 × 1 convolution with sigmoid activation.

Recurrent Residual U-Net (R2Unet)

Along with the structure of U-Net and the residual block technique, recurrent convolutions improve the model's capability to integrate context information to ensure better feature representation for segmentation. Keeping track of former input and current pixel information is necessary for recurrent blocks in order to anticipate future output. This helps in remembering and integrating context information which is most significant in semantic segmentation [28].

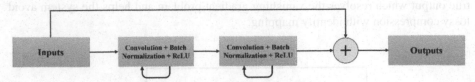

Fig. 6. Recurrent Residual convolutional units (RRCU)

The combination of residual units and recurrent units as depicted in Fig. 6 are extended to each block of the encoder and decoder component of U-Net architecture [21]. The residual unit helps in avoiding performance degradation by incorporating long/short skip connections over deep networks, and the recurrent unit can withhold reasonable dependencies among pixel values by considering contextual data. In blocks of both the encoder and decoder, recurrent convolutional layers (RCLs) with residual units are utilized in place of conventional forward convolutional layers, which aids in the development of a deeper and effective model. This segmentation approach demonstrates the efficiency of feature accumulation from one portion of the network to another and shows benefits for both training and testing phases.

4   Experimentations and Result Discussion

The experimentations were carried out on the Jupyter notebook platform. The collected data was preprocessed using SciPy to load MATLAB data and open-cv for normalizing the grayscale values and saving the images. The prepared data was trained on algorithms implemented using keras library and keras-unet-collection [29]. The experimental works, including training and testing, are carried out using the NVIDIA TESLA P100 GPU with 2 CPU cores, 16 GB GPU memory and 13 GB RAM. All models in our study are trained entirely from scratch without any prior weights. Only for U-Net and Attention U-Net, three different backbones are utilized to incorporate their salient features, viz. VGG-19, ResNet152 and DenseNet201.

4.1   Deep Learning Hyperparameters

The Table 1 presents the deep learning hyperparameters used in each of the tumor prediction algorithms which are kept the same for exact comparison.

4.2   Evaluation Metrics

A trained model's results should be summarized using metrics that are better at showing the model's segmentation skills. The precision (P) is calculated using $P = \frac{tp}{tp+fp}$, recall (R) is calculated using $R = \frac{tp}{tp+fn}$ which are used to calculate F1-Score represented by

Table 1. Hyper-parameters used for training of various deep learning models

Hyperparameters	Values
Learning Rate	0.001
Beta 1	0.9
Beta 2	0.999
Optimizer	Adam
Loss function	Binary Cross Entropy
Batch Size	32
Epochs	100

$F1Score = 2 * \frac{P*R}{P+R}$ and IoU is given as $IoU = \frac{tp}{tp+fn+fp}$. In the formulae, tp represents true positive, tn represents true negative, fp represents false positive and fn represents false negative. These metrics are often utilized for judging the performance of medical image segmentation [14, 15, 30] and are preferred over pixel accuracy as they are better at measuring the segmentation's perceptual quality [31]. For object segmentation, the dice score more accurately measures size and localization agreement [32].

4.3 Statistical and Visual Results

Based on the evaluation metrics, both statistical and visual results were gathered using the predicted output and ground truth which are provided below.

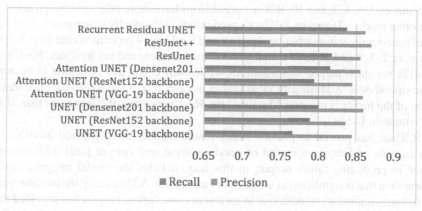

Fig. 7. Precision and Recall of all applied deep learning models for tumor segmentation

Based on the metrics, all the models quantitatively performed well. Table 3 and Fig. 7 findings show that U-Net and Attention U-Net are more accurate with DenseNet201 as the backbone. Primarily, it can be concluded from statistical findings in Table 3 that Recurrent Residual UNET (R2Unet) is the most effective model for segmenting

Table 3. Statistical results of various state-of-art deep learning models for tumor segmentation

Methodologies	F1 Score	Mean IoU
UNET (VGG-19 backbone)	0.8033	0.8322
UNET (ResNet152 backbone)	0.8116	0.8382
UNET (Densenet201 backbone)	0.8288	0.8507
Attention UNET (VGG-19 backbone)	0.8060	0.8342
Attention UNET (ResNet152 backbone)	0.8188	0.8434
Attention UNET (Densenet201 backbone)	0.8349	0.8553
ResUnet	0.8360	0.8562
ResUnet++	0.7969	0.8272
Recurrent Residual UNET	**0.8495**	**0.8665**

brain tumors from the test data. R2Unet (highlighted red in Table 3) outperformed other deep learning models according to all metrics except precision where ResUnet++ seems to perform better. For comparing qualitative results of the models, we chose 10 random samples from the test dataset as shown in Fig. 8. These MRI images exist in the form of three different planes, viz. Sagittal, Axial and Coronal planes. Compared to the ground truth and the outcome of various models having certain defects like under and over-segmentation and erroneous borders, segmentation predictions from R2Unet are almost perfect. Instance 3 from Fig. 8 shows that U-Net and ResUnet failed to detect the tumor, while Attention U-Net and ResUnet++'s predictions are under-segmented. R2Unet, conversely, delivered accurate segmentation with little disorder in the boundary. In instances 2, 5, 6, 7, and 10, R2Unet predictions have more fidelity to the ground truth than other models. However, R2Unet's predictions occasionally (instances 1, 4, 9) show slight over-segmentation whereas ResUnet and ResUnet++ predictions are more helpful. Instances 2, 3, 4 and 10 have simple ground truth shapes, and yet ResUnet, ResUnet++ and R2Unet show jagged segmentations while both U-Net and Attention U-net retain some smoothness. Additionally, other instances (1, 5, 6, 7, 8 and 9) make it clear that the shape of the tumor is preserved by ResUnet, ResUnet++ and R2Unet more than U-Net and Attention U-Net.

R2Unet has proved to provide better results among the compared models since it is capable of keeping a record of previous input and current pixel information to utilize in predicting future output; in this way, it helps the model integrate context information that is significant in semantic segmentation. Additionally, the introduction of the feature accumulation technique in recurrent convolutional layers has provided more robust feature representation vital for extracting low-level features especially pertinent to medical image segmentation.

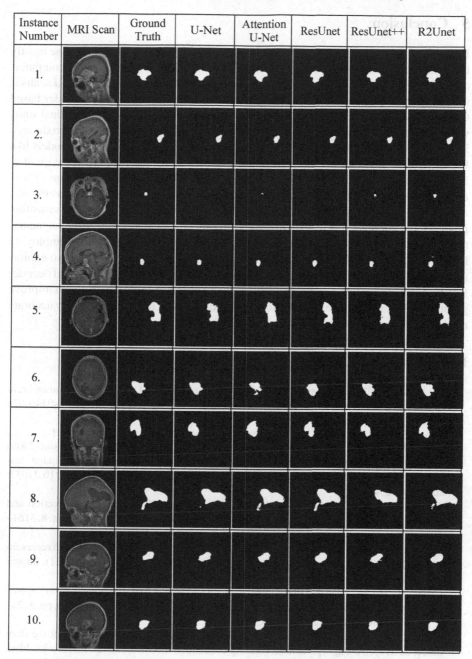

Fig. 8. Visual (Qualitative) results of various brain tumor segmentation models on T1-Weighted MRI scans

5 Conclusion

Detecting tumors is difficult and expensive in the modern world since it is done mostly through imaging and via specialists. This can be tackled by the means of computer-aided detection. In this work, the suitable model for tumor extraction from MRI scans is investigated. The results obtained from this work show that an encoder-decoder based Convolutional Neural Network architecture fused with Recurrent and Residual units when trained on a dataset of brain tumor MRI scans, using Adam optimizer, produces a F1 score of 0.8495 and an IoU of 0.8665, and outperforms other compared models like U-Net and Attention U-Net, deep Residual U-Net with its variants. Also, the qualitative results show consistent results for various representations of the MRI scans. These algorithms reduce the burden on the doctors and make healthcare more accessible and inexpensive for all. Our work helped us realize that residual block removes vanishing gradient, the attention mechanism provides a focus on essential features for segmentation. The accuracy of the suggested approach can be further improved by employing larger, more varied datasets, and various preprocessing techniques. We are also exploring other architectures that would bridge the semantic gap between encoder and decoder feature maps by creating dense skip connections on skip pathways which would improve gradient flow. Combining all these efforts, we look forward to creating a highly accurate model for tumor segmentation.

References

1. Ricard, D., Idbaih, A., Ducray, F., Lahutte, M., Hoang-Xuan, K., Delattre, J.-Y.: Primary brain tumours in adults. Lancet **379**(9830), 1984–1996 (2012). https://doi.org/10.1016/s0140-673 6(11)61346-9
2. Cancer.Net Editorial Board: Brain Tumor: Diagnosis. Cancer.Net, September 2021
3. Russell, S.J., Norvig, P.: Artificial Intelligence: A Modern Approach, 3rd edn. Pearson (2009)
4. Cai, L., Gao, J., Zhao, D.: A review of the application of deep learning in medical image classification and segmentation. Ann. Transl. Med. **8**(11), 713 (2020). https://doi.org/10.21037/atm.2020.02.44
5. Amin, J., Sharif, M., Haldorai, A., Yasmin, M., Nayak, R.S.: Brain tumor detection and classification using machine learning: a comprehensive survey. Complex Intell. Syst. **8**, 3161–3183 (2021). https://doi.org/10.1007/s40747-021-00563-y
6. Getty, N., Brettin, T., Jin, D., Stevens, R., Xia, F.: Deep medical image analysis with representation learning and neuromorphic computing. Interface Focus **11**, 20190122 (2021). https://doi.org/10.1098/rsfs.2019.0122
7. Afshar, P., Mohammadi, A., Plataniotis, K.N.: Brain tumor type classification via capsule networks. In: 2018 25th IEEE International Conference on Image Processing (ICIP), pp. 3129–3133 (2018). https://doi.org/10.1109/ICIP.2018.8451379
8. Toğaçar, M., Ergen, B., Cömert, Z.: Tumor type detection in brain MR images of the deep model developed using hypercolumn technique, attention modules, and residual blocks. Med. Biol. Eng. Comput. **59**(1), 57–70 (2020). https://doi.org/10.1007/s11517-020-02290-x
9. Gunasekara, S., Kaldera, N., Dissanayake, M.: A systematic approach for MRI brain tumor localization and segmentation using deep learning and active contouring. J. Healthc. Eng. **2021**, October 2021. https://doi.org/10.1155/2021/6695108
10. Getreuer, P.: Chan-Vese segmentation. Image Process. On Line **2**, 214–224 (2012). https://doi.org/10.5201/ipol.2012.g-cv

11. Bobbillapati, S., Areti, J.: A novel approach for brain tumor detection using DW-MTM filter and region growing segmentation in MR imaging. PONTE Int. Sci. Res. J. **74**, October 2018. https://doi.org/10.21506/j.ponte.2018.3.10

12. Kadkhodaei, M., et al.: Automatic segmentation of multimodal brain tumor images based on classification of super-voxels. In: Conference Proceedings: ... Annual International Conference of the IEEE Engineering in Medicine and Biology Society. IEEE Engineering in Medicine and Biology Society, October 2016 (2016). https://doi.org/10.1109/EMBC.2016.7592082

13. Thaha, M.M., Kumar, K.P.M., Murugan, B.S., Dhanasekeran, S., Vijayakarthick, P., Selvi, A.S.: Brain tumor segmentation using convolutional neural networks in MRI images. J. Med. Syst. **43**(9), 1 (2019). https://doi.org/10.1007/s10916-019-1416-0

14. Ronneberger, O., Fischer, P., Brox, T.: U-Net: convolutional networks for biomedical image segmentation. In: Navab, N., Hornegger, J., Wells, W.M., Frangi, A.F. (eds.) MICCAI 2015. LNCS, vol. 9351, pp. 234–241. Springer, Cham (2015). https://doi.org/10.1007/978-3-319-24574-4_28

15. Oktay, O., et al.: Attention U-Net: learning where to look for the pancreas. arXiv, abs/1804.03999 (2018)

16. Zhang, Z., Liu, Q.: Road extraction by deep residual U-Net. IEEE Geosci. Remote Sens. Lett. **PP**, October 2017. https://doi.org/10.1109/LGRS.2018.2802944

17. Venkatesh, G.M., Naresh, Y.G., Little, S., O'Connor, N.E.: A deep residual architecture for skin lesion segmentation. In: OR 2.0 Context-Aware Operating Theaters, Computer Assisted Robotic Endoscopy, Clinical Image-Based Procedures, and Skin Image Analysis, pp. 277–284 (2018)

18. Khanna, A., Londhe, N.D., Gupta, S., Semwal, A.: A deep residual U-Net convolutional neural network for automated lung segmentation in computed tomography images. Biocybern. Biomed. Eng. **40**(3), 1314–1327 (2020). https://doi.org/10.1016/j.bbe.2020.07.007

19. Zeineldin, R.A., Karar, M.E., Coburger, J., Wirtz, C.R., Burgert, O.: DeepSeg: deep neural network framework for automatic brain tumor segmentation using magnetic resonance FLAIR images. Int. J. Comput. Assist. Radiol. Surg. **15**(6), 909–920 (2020). https://doi.org/10.1007/s11548-020-02186-z

20. Jha, D., et al.: ResUNet++: an advanced architecture for medical image segmentation. In: Proceedings of the 2019 IEEE International Symposium on Multimedia, ISM 2019, pp. 225–230, December 2019. https://doi.org/10.1109/ISM46123.2019.00049

21. Zahangir Alom, M., Hasan, M., Yakopcic, C., Taha, T.M., Asari, V.K.: Recurrent residual convolutional neural network based on U-Net (R2U-Net) for medical image segmentation. arXiv e-prints, arXiv:1802.06955, February 2018

22. Khan, M.Z.: Recurrent residual U-Net: short critical review (2021)

23. Cheng, J.: Brain tumor dataset, October 2017. https://doi.org/10.6084/m9.figshare.1512427.v5

24. Siddique, N., Paheding, S., Elkin, C.P., Devabhaktuni, V.: U-net and its variants for medical image segmentation: a review of theory and applications. IEEE Access (2021). https://doi.org/10.1109/ACCESS.2021.3086020

25. He, K., Zhang, X., Ren, S., Sun, J.: Deep residual learning for image recognition, December 2015. http://arxiv.org/abs/1512.03385

26. Hu, J., Shen, L., Albanie, S., Sun, G., Wu, E.: Squeeze-and-excitation networks. IEEE Trans. Pattern Anal. Mach. Intell. **42**(8), 2011–2023 (2020). https://doi.org/10.1109/TPAMI.2019.2913372

27. He, K., Zhang, X., Ren, S., Sun, J.: Spatial pyramid pooling in deep convolutional networks for visual recognition. IEEE Trans. Pattern Anal. Mach. Intell. **37**(9), 1904–1916 (2015). https://doi.org/10.1109/TPAMI.2015.2389824

28. Liang, M., Hu, X.: Recurrent convolutional neural network for object recognition. In: 2015 IEEE Conference on Computer Vision and Pattern Recognition (CVPR), pp. 3367–3375 (2015)

29. Sha, Y.(K.): yingkaisha/keras-unet-collection: v0.1.13, January 2022. https://doi.org/10.5281/ZENODO.5834880

30. Kamnitsas, K., et al.: Efficient multi-scale 3D CNN with fully connected CRF for accurate brain lesion segmentation. Med. Image Anal. **36**, October 2016. https://doi.org/10.1016/j.media.2016.10.004

31. Eelbode, T., et al.: Optimization for medical image segmentation: theory and practice when evaluating with dice score or Jaccard index. IEEE Trans. Med. Imaging **PP**, 1 (2020). https://doi.org/10.1109/TMI.2020.3002417

32. Zijdenbos, A.P., Dawant, B.M., Margolin, R.A., Palmer, A.C.: Morphometric analysis of white matter lesions in MR images: method and validation. IEEE Trans. Med. Imaging **13**(4), 716–724 (1994). https://doi.org/10.1109/42.363096

33. Wilson, B.: Understanding the harmonic mean. UNSW CRICOS, 23 March 2006. http://groups.di.unipi.it/~bozzo/The%20Harmonic%20Mean.htm. Accessed 03 Oct 2022

Mammogram Based Breast Cancer Detection with Transfer Learning

Pema Wangdi, Dinesh Kumar$^{(\boxtimes)}$, and Hitesh Kag

Computer Engineering – Artificial Intelligence, Marwadi University, Rajkot, India
pema.wangdi108256@marwadiuniversity.ac.in, {dinesh.kumar, hitesh.kag}@marwadieducation.edu.in

Abstract. One of the primary and most prevalent causes of cancer in women is breast cancer. The occurrence of this condition has lately grown, and it is currently the most prevalent health problem. Breast cancer poses a major hazard to women, as it is highly morbid and lethal. Doctors find it challenging to develop a treatment strategy that might increase patient survival time due to the absence of reliable prognostic models. The greatest method for managing breast cancer outcomes is early detection. By facilitating suitable treatment and therapies, early detection of breast cancer increases the likelihood of survival. The digital mammography test aids in the early detection of breast cancer. A computer based automatic mammogram classification between benign and stages of cancers helps radiologist to prepare a diagnosis. For this purpose, deep learning based Convolutional Neural Network (CNN) models on Transfer Learning algorithms such as Dense Convolution Network (DenseNet201), Visual Geometry Group (VGG19), and Residual Network (ResNet50) is proposed in this paper. These models were applied on the dataset obtained from public shared data repository consist of about 7600 mammograms images. These models have performed accuracies of 96.77%, 97.99%, and 91.18% in DenseNet201, VGG19, and ResNet50, respectively. VGG19 model performs better in comparison with the other two models at epoch 40 in mammogram dataset.

Keywords: Breast Cancer · Deep Learning · CNN · Transfer Learning · DenseNet201 · VGG19 · ResNet50

1 Introduction and Related Work

In 2020, 2.3 million women were diagnosed with breast cancer and 6,85,000 women died worldwide, in fact till 2020, breast cancer was the most common cancer in the world with 7.8 million women were still alive those who had diagnosis before five years [1]. The study aims to offer a solution to the persistent issue of breast cancer. Complex patterns in the image dataset can be discovered using deep learning algorithms. The model may be trained to identify the existence of breast cancer cells and further classify them as benign or malignant based on the images in the dataset, allowing the doctor to treat the patient as necessary and preventing breast cancer-related deaths. One of the

© Springer Nature Switzerland AG 2023
D. Garg et al. (Eds.): IACC 2022, CCIS 1781, pp. 449–458, 2023.
https://doi.org/10.1007/978-3-031-35641-4_37

most effective techniques for identifying and diagnosing a patient's health is the CNN and transfer learning model for pre-trained data. Convolutional neural networks based on transfer learning algorithm analyze images using data that has already been created and made available. Based on real imagery, the algorithm is run to look for similarities and then make predictions using the images found.

In CNN models, we need to do feature extraction for each layer and those features are used to train the pattern classifier. However, in Machine Learning we need to do feature extraction separately to reduce the complexity of data and it is time consuming [2]. We then found it is the best to use deep learning algorithm with the best accuracy as we solely focused on mammogram dataset.

The large number of Deep Learning algorithms are being used to predict and diagnosis the breast cancer. Besides many machine learning algorithms used for diagnostic preparation in past years the focus has been in deep learning algorithms such as DenseNet201, VGG19, and ResNet50. In [4], authors demonstrated application of deep learning algorithms in Breast Cancer Wisconsin Diagnostics Dataset such as U-Net for image segmentation and CNNs for model accuracy and got an accuracy of 93.3%, 79.33%, 50% and 100% for ResNet18, GoogleNet, AlexNet and VGG16, respectively, showing VGG16 the best algorithm [3].

Similarly, three CNN models were proposed using a big dataset of 275,000: CNN model 1 with two convolutional layers of 32 and 64 kernel having dropout of 25% and reported 59% accuracy, CNN model 2 with triple convolutional layer of CNN exhibiting 76% of accuracy, and CNN model 3 architecture with 5-layers showed 87% accuracy [4].

The cancer is classified by AlexNet, YOLO, and Deep Belief Network (DBN) algorithms. All the algorithms used detection and data augmentation techniques. The AlexNet, using transfer learning algorithm got detection accuracy of 98.96% and classification accuracy of 95.64%. The YOLO algorithm is used to detect mass and fine tune model in pre-trained weight of ImageNet dataset. It detected and classified cancer with accuracy of 99.7% and 97% respectively. DBN is done without fine-tuned and got overall accuracy of 92.86% [5]. However, without using detection and data augmentation for all algorithm, the accuracy of detection and classification is comparatively low [5].

In this paper, a CNN based transfer learning model on mammogram dataset acquired from https://dphi.tech/challenges/75/data, consist of 7632 images with 8 different classes are proposed. Three different CNN models, VGG19, DenseNet50, and other are constructed whereby VGG19 showed the best accuracy in classifying 8 different imbalance classes. To the best knowledge of the author VGG19 is not used for the aforementioned dataset and therefore the results are also compared with other previously used CNN based transferring model such DenseNet19 and ResNet50.

This paper is structured as follows: Sect. 2 presents the dataset used in the study, in Sect. 3 the methodology for building the model is described, in Sect. 4 the experimental steps are showed, and finally, some conclusion is drawn in Sect. 5.

2 Dataset

Mammography is the technology that plays a vital role diagnoses breast cancer early as it can detect calcification part on breast. As a result, women can get early treatment and reduce the mortality. The breast cancer symptoms include: Loss of weight, change in skin color, pain and change in breast size (usually getting enlarge). For this, Deep Learning technique on CNN models like DenseNet201, VGG19 and ResNet50 are used to diagnose breast cancer on mammograms.

Doctors frequently use additional tests in order to identify or diagnose breast cancer. Doctors use mammograms to screen for breast cancer using X-images. Mammography is the most effective test available for doctors to detect breast cancer early, which can identify breast cancer up to three years before symptoms appear [6]. It reveals the breasts' density. Cancer risk is high in women who have thick/dense breast tissue as it is hard to differentiate between skin and cancer, a dense tissue on skin showing sample of images in Fig. 1.

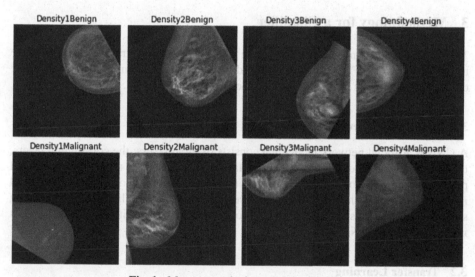

Fig. 1. Mammography images for each class

The mammography dataset of breast cancer contains train set and test set images. Each image has pixel of 224 × 224 with distinct labels of: 1) Density, and 2) Tumor. The dataset has four level of densities i.e.., Density1, Density2, Density3, and Density4 having each tumor (Benign and Malignant) shown in Fig. 2. Deep learning algorithms can detect whether the breast tissue is affected by cancer or not based on training model. The classification of cancer is:

a) Benign – it means that the tissue is not affected by cancer
b) Malignant – the tissue of breast is affected by cancer

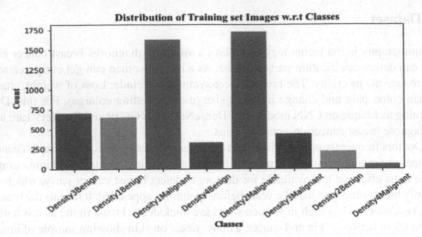

Fig. 2. Eight Classes of the Mammograms

3 Methodology for a Classifier

To classify breast cancer accurately, three CNN models with transfer learning were trained as shown in Fig. 3. It gives clear idea of how deep learning models are built, compile, and evaluate the performance of accuracy on testing set.

3.1 Convolution Neural Network

A CNN is artificial network model that consists of three layers: the convolution layers, the pooling layers, and the fully connected layers, widely used to recognize images and processing the pixel of an image [7]. It is the most reliable algorithm in the medical imaging system and hence its various traces can be found in almost all the imaging systems as per the research so far, also known for 'Transferability' which is the most import aspect of CNN [8].

3.2 Transfer Learning

The machine learning technique known as 'transfer learning', a model developed and trained for one task is then applied to another related activity [9]. It describes the scenario where knowledge gained in one context is applied to enhance optimization in another one. When there is a smaller amount of data than the initial dataset used to train the pre-trained model, transfer learning is frequently used [10]. It can extract useful spatial information from big datasets in various domains at the outset of training, it makes it possible to train models quickly and accurately overcoming cost and time consuming [11].

The idea of Transfer Learning comes from traditional CNN, which is not effective as it often gives overfitting [12]. The CNN needs to apply more preprocessing on dataset but Transfer Learning usually change the images resolution and resize the images size to 224×224 or 227×227 depending on selected pre-trained models (DenseNet201,

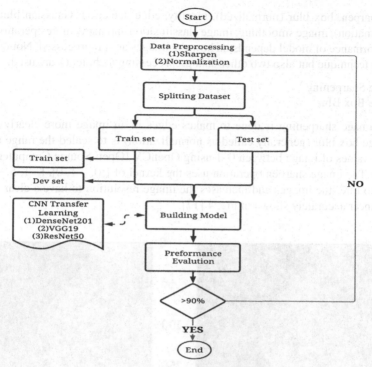

Fig. 3. Flowchart of CNN Models

VGG19, AlexNet, GoogleNet, ResNet50 and many more) [13]. So, it consumes less time on data preprocessing.

This paper proposes a system which uses a model based on DenseNet201, VGG19 and ResNet50 in which model trained on a base dataset i.e., ImageNet. Transfer learning is a reliable approach which allows learning features on ImageNet dataset and it can be able to adjust model to suits the new dataset [14]. TensorFlow is the most popular framework used in transfer learning, CNN pre-trained model [15].

4 Experiment

4.1 Data Preprocessing

In Fig. 2, the classes of mammograms shows that the data is imbalanced with the ratio of Density2Malignant to the Density4Malignant is more than 10:1. The classification on imbalanced data is done by sampling technique based on similar attributes into homogenous subgroup (strata) called Stratified Random Sampling. It uses test datasets to evaluate models particularly when the dataset is disproportionately large and imbalanced. The technique ensures that the model estimates accurate parameters and receives proper sample representation without losing an information.

Image preprocessing is a technique to remove the noise and enhance the quality or extract the useful information from the images. It usually includes operation like image sharpen, box blur (normalized), identity, edge detection, Gaussian blur 3×3 (approximation), image smoothing, image classification and many more operations [16]. The performance of model depends on how the images are preprocessed. Not only data balanced technique but also two other data preprocessing techniques are used;

a) Image Sharpening
b) Image Box Blur

The image sharpening is done to makes edges in an image more clearly defined and image box blur (generally called as normalization) is to scaled the range of pixel intensity values of image between 0–1 using OpenCV (Open-Source Computer Vision Library). The image sharpen operation uses the kernel of [[0, −1, 0], [−1, 5, −1], [0, −1, 0]] to filter the images and increases the image resolution to have a clear view or detect cancer accurately shown in Fig. 4 [17].

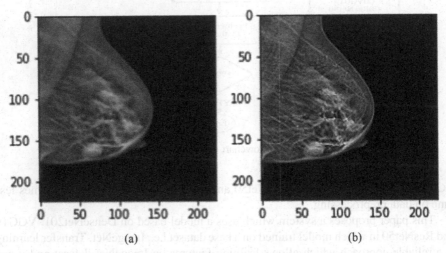

Fig. 4. Image Preprocessing: (a) - Before Preprocessing; (b) - After Preprocessing

4.2 Training the Model

After preprocessing, the hyperparameter optimization techniques like loss function, activation function, batch size, learning rate, and epochs are being used to tune the number of neurons in model to improve an accuracy. The activation function and loss function are the key parameter that optimize and enable networks to work on the models' performance [15]. Multi-classification model uses the loss function as cross categorical entropy and activation function as Softmax in output. However, the hidden layer use activation function ReLu as a standard function to avoid vanishing problem [18].

All the layers of DenseNet201, VGG19 and ResNet50 are not frozen implying that those layers learn via backpropagation as neural network does [19]. The process of updating weight during backpropagation is called as fine-tuning. It can avoid overfitting and increase model performance without losing training dataset although it takes too much time to run epochs. The regularization techniques; dropout is use to ignore selected neurons randomly while l2 regularization and batch normalization regularize the model performance [20]. The architecture of the transfer learning models with DenseNet201, VGG19, and ResNet50 are showed below in the Table 1, Table 2, and Table 3, respectively.

Table 1. DenseNet201 model summary.

Layer (type)	Output Shape	Param #
densenet201 (Functional)	(None, 1920)	18321984
batch_normalization (BatchNormalization)	(None, 1920)	7680
dense (Dense)	(None, 2048)	3934208
dropout (Dropout)	(None, 2048)	0
batch_normalization_1 (BatchNormalization)	(None, 2048)	8192
dense_1 (Dense)	(None, 8)	16392
Total params: 22,288,456		
Trainable params: 22,051,464		
Non-trainable params: 236,992		

Table 2. VGG19 model summary.

Layer (type)	Output Shape	Param #
vgg19 (Functional)	(None, 512)	20024384
batch_normalization (BatchNormalization)	(None, 512)	2048
dense (Dense)	(None, 2048)	1050624
dropout (Dropout)	(None, 2048)	0
batch_normalization_1 (BatchNormalization)	(None, 2048)	8192
dense_1 (Dense)	(None, 8)	16392
Total params: 21,101,640		
Trainable params: 21,096,520		
Non-trainable params: 5,120		

4.3 Result and Discussion

The model performance is evaluated based on accuracy and loss. It is not advisable to train with a training accuracy of 100% because the model will perform poorly and become overfit. If the model's accuracy in the dev and testing sets is 100%, the model is perfectly matched to the learning dataset. However, validation accuracy should never be

Table 3. ResNet50 model summary.

Layer (type)	Output Shape	Param #
resNet50 (Functional)	(None, 2048)	23587712
batch_normalization (BatchNormalization)	(None, 2048)	8192
dense (Dense)	(None, 2048)	4196352
dropout (Dropout)	(None, 2048)	0
batch_normalization_1 (BatchNormalization)	(None, 2048)	8192
dense_1 (Dense)	(None, 8)	16392
Total params: 27,816,840		
Trainable params: 27,755,528		
Non-trainable params: 61,312		

higher than training accuracy. The loss value represents model's errors, so, it measures how well or poor the model is performing. Those model with lower loss value does better job.

In common problem, the residual neural network perform better as it outperform shallower networks with technologically advanced and overcome the vanishing gradient problem in deep CNN model. However, being the technologically advanced does not mean that the model performs always better. There is a simpler model that outperform better in complicated dataset. Like that, VGG19 model (quite deeper network compare to residual network) is providing better results as compared to other algorithms. The Table 4 includes accuracy of training and validation set along with the number of epochs and time taken in training process. Evidently, VGG19 model yields the maximum performance shown in Fig. 5 while ResNet50 is the worst performing model in the applied networks.

Table 4. A model performance analysis with time.

CNN Models	Train Accuracy	Validation Accuracy	Epochs	Time (ms/step)
DenseNet201	99.65%	96.77%	40	852
VGG19	99.58%	97.99%	40	881
ResNet50	99.49%	91.18%	40	696

The limitation of this research is a computational problem. It needs high modern computational hardware equipped with GPU to classify the images. A supercomputer with GPU takes an average time of 852 ms/step, 881 ms/step and 696 ms/step for DenseNet201, VGG19 and ResNet50 respectively. However, the models cannot run in a device without GPU as it takes longer period (more than 10x in laptop) of time to run an epoch.

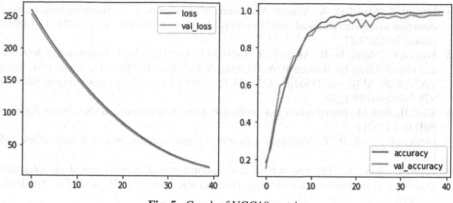

Fig. 5. Graph of VGG19 metrics

5 Conclusion

In this paper, a comparison of CNN models using transfer learning for classification of breast cancer to facilitate medical professional for definitive diagnosis that will eventually lead to reduce the mortality rate was performed. A data was classified into eight classes to classify cancer's type. The CNN models with transfer learning using mammography dataset performed significantly by showing accuracy of 96.77%, 97.99%, and 91.18% for DenseNet201, VGG19 and ResNet50, respectively. The VGG19 model performed the best with an accuracy above 97% among all the CNN models.

Some more deep learning models like semantic segmentation using U-Net and instance segmentation using Region-based Convolutional Neural Network (R-CNN) will be explored in the pursuit of finding masks (output label) with bounding box. This will increase the results more than the obtained one, besides explainable AI will be utilized in describing the medical significance of the outcomes in further research.

Acknowledgement. Authors would like to acknowledge the supercomputing facility established by Gujarat Council of Science and Technology (GUJCOST) at the Marwadi University, Rajkot, India. This work was carried out utilizing the PARAM Shavak supercomputer developed at the Center for Development of Advanced Computing (C-DAC).

References

1. World Health Organization WHO: Homepage, https://www.who.int/news-room/fact-sheets/detail/breast-cancer. Accessed 26 Mar 2021
2. Zhang, J., Humaidi, A., Al-Dujail, A., Duan, Y., Al-Shamma, O., Farhan, L.: Review of deep learning: concepts, CNN architectures, challenges, applications, future directions. J. Big Data **8**, 53 (2021)
3. Esraa, M., Essam, R., Tarek, G., Omar, S.: Deep learning model for fully automated breast cancer detection system from thermograms. PLOS ONE J. 15 (2022)

4. Narirul, S., Madallah, A., Yousef, A., Nasser, A., Muhammad, S.: Boosting breast cancer detection using convolutional neural network. Hindawi J. Healthc. Eng. **2021**, 11 (2021). Article ID 5528622
5. Hamed, G., Marey, M.-R., Amin, S.-S., Tolba, M.F.: Deep learning in breast cancer detection and classification. In: Hassanien, A.-E., Azar, A.T., Gaber, T., Oliva, D., Tolba, F.M. (eds.) AICV 2020. AISC, vol. 1153, pp. 322–333. Springer, Cham (2020). https://doi.org/10.1007/978-3-030-44289-7_30
6. Kim, H., Bae, M.: Breast cancer risk prediction using deep learning. RSNA, North America **301**(3), 1 (2021)
7. O'Shea, K., Nash, R.: An introduction to convolutional neural networks. ResearchGate 2–5 (2015)
8. Zhen, L., Sum, X.: The research of convolutional neural network based on integrated classification in question classification. Hindawi Res. Article **2021**, 4 (2021). Article ID 4276059
9. Larsen-Freeman, D.: Transfer of learning transformed. Lang. Learn. **63**, 107–129 (2013)
10. Hussain, M., Bird, J.J., Faria, D.R.: A study on CNN transfer learning for image classification. In: Lotfi, A., Bouchachia, H., Gegov, A., Langensiepen, C., McGinnity, M. (eds.) UKCI 2018. AISC, vol. 840, pp. 191–202. Springer, Cham (2019). https://doi.org/10.1007/978-3-319-97982-3_16
11. Kim, Y.G., Kim, S., Cho, C.E., et al.: Effectiveness of transfer learning for enhancing tumor classification with a convolutional neural network on frozen sections. Sci. Rep. **10**, 21899 (2020). https://doi.org/10.1038/s41598-020-78129-0
12. Gurucharan, M.K.: Basic CNN architecture: explaining 5 layers of convolutional neural network. upGrad's Knowledge Base, article (2022)
13. Zhang, Y., Satapathy, S., Zhang, X., Wang, S.: COVID-19 diagnosis via DenseNet and optimization of transfer learning setting. Springer Science+Business Media, LLC, part of Springer Nature, pp. 2–5 (2021)
14. Sharma, A., Sharma, K., Kumar, A.: Real-time emotional health detection using fine-tuned transfer networks with multimodal fusion. J. Neural Comput. Appl. 1–4 (2022)
15. Arrabelly, S., Huliet, S.: Transfer learning with ResNet-50 for malaria cell-image classification. In: Conference 2019, ICCSP, ResearchGate, pp. 1–4 (2019)
16. Zhou, W., Ma, X., Zhang, Y.: Research on image preprocessing algorithm and deep learning of iris recognition. J. Phys. Conf. Ser. ICCSCT **2020**, 3–5 (2020)
17. Paliwal, S., Sharma, V., Verma, B., Karsoulia, S.: Low resolution image enhancement of aerial image using scikit tools. Int. J. Sci. Eng. Res. **12**, 1–6 (2021). ISSN 2229-5518
18. Bansal, M., Kumar, M., Sachdeva, M., Mittal, A.: Transfer learning for image classification using VGG19: Caltech-101 image data set. J. Ambient Intell. Human. Comput. 4–8 (2021)
19. Lu, T., Han, B., Chen, L., Yu, F., Xue, C.: A generic intelligence tomato classifications using DenseNet-201 with transfer learning. Sci. Rep. 2–4 (2021)
20. Priyanka, K.: A review paper on breast cancer detection using deep learning. IOP Conf. Ser.: Mater. Sci. Eng. **1022**, 012071 (2021)

An Efficient and Optimized Convolution Neural Network for Brain Tumour Detection

Mohit Agarwal[1]($\boxtimes$), Lokesh Kumar Sharma[1], Suneet Kumar Gupta[1],
Deepak Garg[1], and Mani Jindal[2]

[1] Bennett University, Greater Noida 201310, India
26.mohit@gmail.com, {lokesh.sharma,deepak.garg}@bennett.edu.in
[2] Christ Deemed to be University Delhi NCR, Mariam Nagar,
Ghaziabad 201003, India

Abstract. Brain tumour is a life threatening disease and can affect children and adults. This study focuses on classifying MRI scan images of brain into one of 4 classes namely: glioma tumour, meningioma tumour, pituitary tumour and normal brain. Person affected with brain tumours will need treatments such as surgery, radiation therapy or chemotherapy. Pretrained Convolution Neural Networks such as VGG19, MobileNet, and AlexNet which have been widely used for image classification using transfer learning. However due to huge storage space requirements these are not effectively deployed on edge devices for creation of robotic devices. Hence a compressed version of these models have been created using Genetic Algorithm algorithm which occupies nearly 30–40% of space and also a reduced inference time which is less by around 50% of original model. The accuracy provided by VGG19, AlexNet, MobileNet and Proposed CNN before compression was 92.18%, 89.45%, 93.75% and 96.85% respectively. Similarly the accuracy after compression for VGG19, AlexNet, MobileNet and Proposed CNN was 91.34%, 88.92%, 94.40% and 95.29%.

Keywords: CNN · Compression · Brain Tumour · Acceleration

1 Introduction

Brain tumor is a very deadly disease and its timely diagnosis is needed by patients for their proper treatment [1]. Doctors use various laboratory tests including MRI scans to know the stage and type of tumour. These days images can be classified into different classes of diseases as needed for this research using Machine Learning and Deep Learning methods.

Due to advent of robotic IoT devices [?] a need is also felt for compression of heavy deep learning models. Hence Genetic Algorithm (GA) has been used in this research for the compression of these models without loss in performance by keeping track of model performance as nodes are dropped based on GA. It was

© Springer Nature Switzerland AG 2023
D. Garg et al. (Eds.): IACC 2022, CCIS 1781, pp. 459–474, 2023.
https://doi.org/10.1007/978-3-031-35641-4_38

found that models could be compressed from more than 200 MBs to less than 100 MBs.

As seen widely in existing research deep learning methods including Convolution Neural Networks (CNN) have been widely used by researchers [3–9]. Some research works also show the segmentation of diseases using special type of CNN models like SegNet, UNet etc. [10,11]. Similarly in several research works show the usage of Artificial Intelligence (AI) techniques for classifying and diagnosing medical images [12–14].

More recent works show the usage of deep learning methods and compression using meta heuristic approaches for image classification in different domains [15–21].

Sadoon and Ali [22] have proposed a 6 convolution layer CNN for classification of brain tumour in 1 of three classes (glioma, meningioma and pituitary). Authors have achieved an accuracy of 96.1% with the proposed CNN.

Matsui et al. [23] have used multimodal brain tumour data comprising of MRI images and numeric data such as age, gender, calcification etc. Authors have used this datatset and residual neural networks for classification of glioma into three classes: IDH-wildtype diffuse astrocytoma, IDH-mutant diffuse astrocytoma, and oligodendroglioma. Cross validation test accuracy of 68.7% was reported by the authors using this method.

Yang et al. [24] have used GoogleNet and AlexNet for classification of glioma into 2 classes: lower grade glioma (LGG) and higher grade glioma (HGG) and reported best cross validation test accuracy of 90.9% with dataset split into 80:20 ratio randomly using GoogleNet.

Ccinarer [25] have used wavelet radiomic features for classification of glioma into low grade glioma (LGG) and medium grade glioma (MGG) using deep learning and achieved a test accuracy of 96.15%.

The article's major contributions are:

– This research helps to diagnose brain tumours from MRI scans of patients.
– The paper also helps to compress pre-trained models using Genetic Algorithm.
– A multiobjective fitness function with accuracy and area under curve (AUC) was also designed for Genetic Algorithm.

The layout of rest of paper can be as seen in Fig. 1.

2   Material and Methods

2.1   Brain Tumour Disease Image Dataset

The brain tumour dataset was obtained from internet sources and comprised of 1321 Glioma tumour, 1339 Meningioma tumour, 1457 Pituitary tumour and 1595 normal brain MRI scan images. Sample images from each class is shown in Fig. 2. The red arrows depict the infected part of brain in three types of tumour.

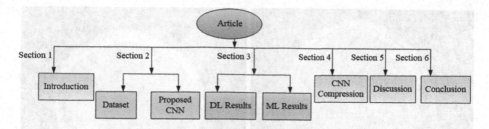

Fig. 1. Layout of paper.

2.2   Convolution Neural Network Architecture

The proposed CNN was developed with 3 convolution layers having 64, 32 and 16 hidden filters from input side. The size of filters was 3 × 3. Max-pool layers are present after each convolution layer. The 2-D layers are followed by a Flatten layer and then a Dense layer of 256 hidden nodes and finally an output softmax layer with 4 nodes for classification into 1 of 4 classes. The CNN architecture is shown pictorially in Fig. 3.

The hyper parameters used in CNN are given in Table 1.

Table 1. Proposed CNN model hyperparameters.

Hyperparameter	Description
CNN input size	256 × 256
Convolution layers	3
Max-pool layers	3
Dropout	.5
Activation function	ReLU, softmax
Learning rate	0.0001
Momentum	0.999
Number of epoch	100
Batch size	32

3   Results of Experimentation

All the experiments were conducted using NVIDIA supercomputer. The model was trained and tested using 3 pre-trained models and proposed CNN. The pre-trained models used were AlexNet. VGG19 and MobileNet. These were loaded with pre-trained imagenet weights and using transfer learning were trained on brain tumour dataset. The proposed CNN was trained from scratch and it was found its performance was best. This may be due to lot of redundant neurons in pre-trained models as only 4 output classes are present and these are designed for

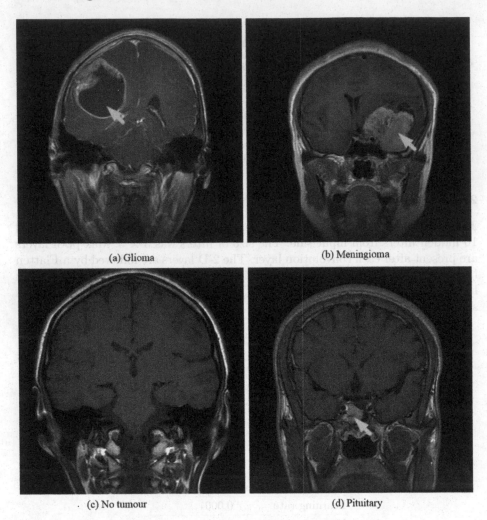

(a) Glioma

(b) Meningioma

(c) No tumour

(d) Pituitary

Fig. 2. Sample images of dataset showing 3 types of tumour and a normal brain MRI scan image. (Color figure online)

1000 class ILSRVC challenge. The comparison of accuracy of 3 transfer learning based models and proposed CNN is given in Fig. 4. As seen the proposed CNN gave best performance.

The activation images of 1st, 2nd and 3rd convolution layers is shown in Fig. 5, 6 and 7. The figures were created for a sample glioma infected brain MRI image.

3.1   Machine Learning

Seven Machine Learning classifiers namely: LR (Logistic Regression), k-NN (k-nearest neighbours), DT (Decision Trees), RF (Random Forest), SVM (Support

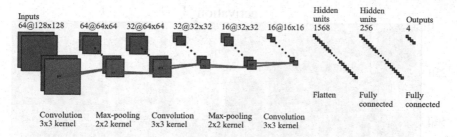

Fig. 3. Proposed CNN architecture.

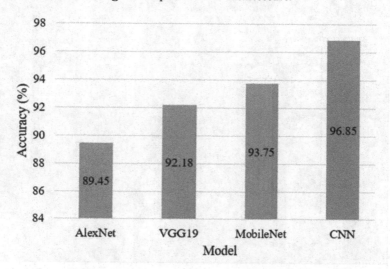

Fig. 4. Graphical view of performance of different CNN models.

Vector Machine), LDA (Logistic Discriminant Analysis), Naïve Bayes. Three different combination of features were using from following 4 set of features. The maximum accuracy was obtained using Random Forest with Hu, Haralick, HSV, LBP features of 93.18%. A brief description of feature set is as given below:

- HSV: These features convert the image to Hue, Saturation and Intensity Value (HSV) transform and make a histogram of the HSV values of whole image. Since these are close to human color perception they help to identify similar image features.
- Haralick: These features are based on texture of images and calculated using Gray Level Co-occurrence Matrix (GLCM).
- Hu-moments: These features calculate the translation and rotation invariant moments of objects in image.
- LBP (Local Binary Pattern): These features help to know texture of images by comparing any pixel by its surrounding 8 pixels in a circular fashion.

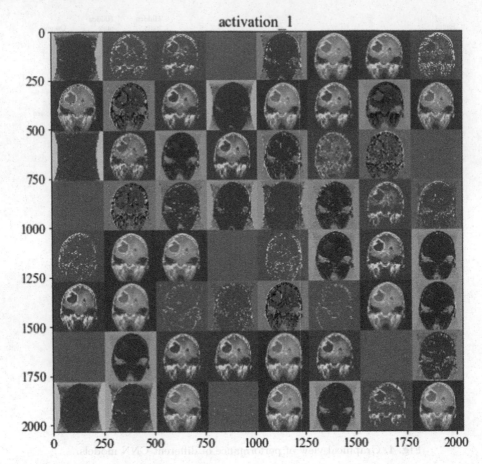

Fig. 5. Proposed CNN activation maps of a Brain tumour sample image from 1st conv2D layer.

This creates numbers between 0 to 255 and thus using these numbers for each pixel a histogram is formed.

The comparison of performance using various features combination is given in Table 2. The comparison of performance in form of ROC curves is also shown in Figs. 8, 9 and 10.

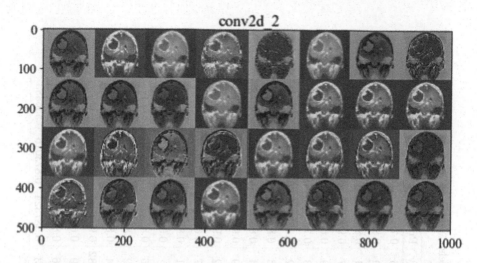

Fig. 6. Proposed CNN activation maps of a Brain tumour sample image from 2nd conv2D layer.

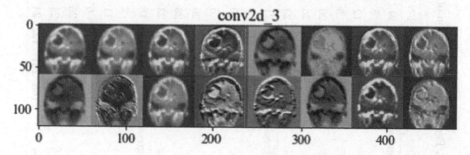

Fig. 7. Proposed CNN activation maps of a Brain tumour sample image from 3rd conv2D layer.

Table 2. Performance comparison of ML models.

Features	Model	TP	FP	TN	FN	Accuracy	Precision	Recall	F1-score
HSV, LBP	Logistic Regression	338	88	125	21	80.94406	0.793427	0.941504	0.861146
	KNN	375	51	141	5	90.20979	0.880282	0.986842	0.930521
	DT	364	62	134	12	87.06294	0.85446	0.968085	0.907731
	RF	386	40	141	5	92.13287	0.906103	0.987212	0.94492
	SVM	249	177	120	26	64.51049	0.584507	0.905455	0.710414
	LDA	338	88	120	26	80.06993	0.793427	0.928571	0.855696
	Naïve Bayes	156	270	123	23	48.77622	0.366197	0.871508	0.515702
HSV, Haralick, LBP	Logistic Regression	346	80	125	21	82.34266	0.812207	0.942779	0.872636
	KNN	376	50	142	4	90.55944	0.882629	0.989474	0.933002
	DT	388	38	136	10	91.60839	0.910798	0.974874	0.941748
	RF	388	38	141	5	92.48252	0.910798	0.987277	0.947497
	SVM	272	154	120	26	68.53147	0.638498	0.912752	0.751381
	LDA	354	72	123	23	83.39161	0.830986	0.938992	0.881694
	Naïve Bayes	159	267	123	23	49.3007	0.373239	0.873626	0.523026
Hu, Haralick, HSV, LBP	Logistic Regression	347	79	128	18	83.04196	0.814554	0.950685	0.87737
	KNN	373	53	144	2	90.38462	0.875587	0.994667	0.931336
	DT	375	51	135	11	89.16084	0.880282	0.971503	0.923645
	RF	393	33	140	6	**93.18182**	0.922535	0.984962	0.952727
	SVM	277	149	120	26	69.40559	0.650235	0.914191	0.759945
	LDA	357	69	122	24	83.74126	0.838028	0.937008	0.884758
	Naïve Bayes	165	261	122	24	50.17483	0.387324	0.873016	0.536585

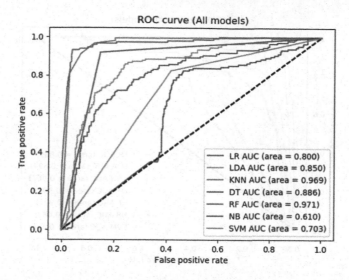

Fig. 8. ML classifiers ROC curve using HSV and LBP as features.

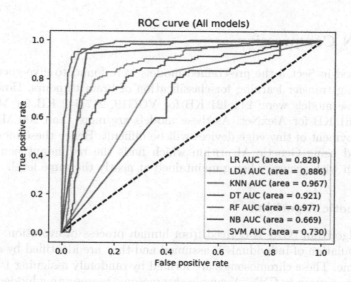

Fig. 9. ML classifiers ROC curve using HSV, Haralick and LBP features.

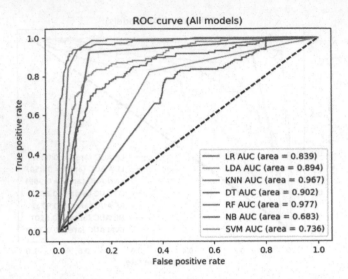

Fig. 10. ML classifiers ROC curve using HSV, Haralick, Hu moments and LBP as features.

4   CNN Compression

As discussed in Sect. 3 the pre-trained models were found to give good performance using transfer learning for classification of brain tumours. However the size of these models were: 211,421 KB for VGG19, 217,642 KB for MobileNet and 281,161 KB for AlexNet. As these models are more than 200 MB in size their deployment of tiny edge devices will be difficult. Hence these models were compressed using Genetic Algorithm which finds the redundant neurons and drops them with accuracy being maintained at nearly the same level.

4.1   Genetic Algorithm

Genetic algorithm (GA) is derived from human process of evolution. In this a initial population of individuals is assumed and they are identified by a distinct chromosome. These chromosomes are formed by randomly assigning 1 and 0 for each hidden neuron in CNN. A sample chromosome representing hidden neurons of VGG19 is shown in Fig. 11. Different colors show different hidden layers of VGG19 Here 1 is used to identify that neuron will be retained and 0 means it will be dropped. In next step chromosomes are allowed to exchange information with other individuals chromosomes and resultant chromosomes are called children chromosome. These child chromosomes are further subject to process of mutation in which randomly $\frac{1}{10}^{th}$ are selected and their bits are flipped to 0 if they are 1. Finally a fitness function is designed which checks fitness value of parent and child chromosomes and better chromosome is retained in population pool and with lesser fitness value are dropped. After several iterations chromosome with best fitness values can be obtained. The iterations stop when the change in fitness values <0.00001. The process of Genetic Algorithm is depicted in Fig. 12.

Fig. 11. A sample chromosome with random 0 and 1 for VGG19.

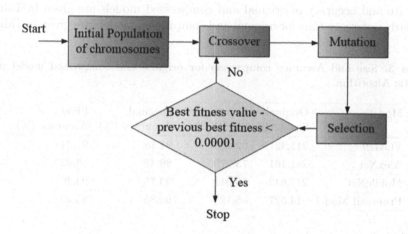

Fig. 12. Graphical view of GA flowchart.

The fitness function is multivalued objective function which depends on Accuracy and Area Under Curve (AUC) of the model. The accuracy generally help in knowing the performance of model but AUC also helps to evaluate performance when dataset is balanced. Since AUC takes only 2 classes, we use 4 values of AUC by keeping 1 class as positive and rest negative at one moment.

GA process application can narrow down to best chromosomes based on 5 objectives. The fitness function is as given by Eq. (1).

$$Maximize(X) = \frac{Accuracy}{100} + AUC_1 + AUC_2 + AUC_3 + AUC_4 \qquad (1)$$

Here X is the fitness value which needs to be maximized and AUC_1 is by taking glioma class as positive and rest negative, and similarly AUC_2 takes Meningioma class as positive and rest negative and AUC_3 takes only healthy class as positive and AUC_3 takes pituitary tumour class as positive and rest negative. The accuracy is divided by 100 to scale to similar values which AUC may take (0–1).

The equation for Accuracy is given by:

$$Accuracy = \frac{TP + TN}{TP + FP + TN + FN} \tag{2}$$

4.2   Compression Results

The size and accuracy of original and compressed models are given in Table 3. Similarly, inference time for original and compressed models are given in Table 4.

Table 3. Size and Accuracy comparison for original and compressed model using Genetic Algorithm.

Model	Original Size (KB)	Compressed Size (KB)	Original Accuracy (%)	Final Accuracy (%)
VGG19	211,421	92,206	92.18	91.34
AlexNet	281,161	73,279	89.45	88.92
MobileNet	217,642	50,011	93.75	94.40
Proposed Model	14,527	5,123	96.85	95.29

Table 4. Inference time comparison for original and compressed model using Genetic Algorithm.

Model	Original inference time (s)	Final inference time (s)
VGG19	119.33	27.18
AlexNet	38.19	22.76
MobileNet	88.97	35.87
Proposed Model	12.56	7.98

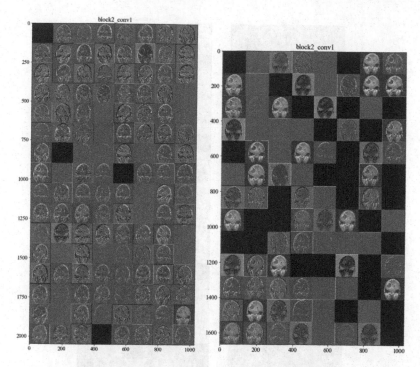

Fig. 13. Activation images for original model on top and compressed model at bottom for same sample image for 2nd block convolution layer of VGG19.

5   Discussion

As described in Sect. 4 the Genetic Algorithm helps to remove redundant neuron the activation images of original and compressed models were created and compared. It was found that several redundant neurons were dropped and dominant neurons were retained in compressed model. The accuracy does not drops in this process as fitness function depends on the performance parameters and thus best neurons are retained which can propagate the desired information to the final output softmax layer. The original model and compressed model activation images for 2nd and 3rd block convolution layers of VGG19 are compared in Fig. 13 and 14.

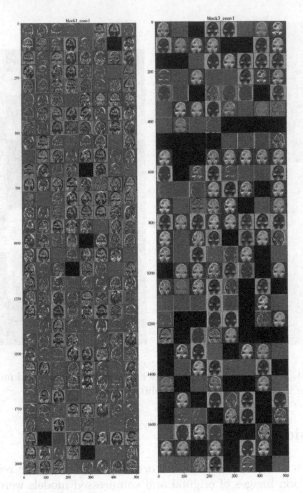

Fig. 14. Activation images for original model on top and compressed model at bottom for same sample image for 3rd block convolution layer of VGG19.

6   Conclusion

Brain Tumours pose a significant threat to human and if they could be diagnosed and treated early then they can be very helpful to such patients. Hence in this research deep learning, transfer learning and machine learning methods have been used to diagnose such disease from MRI images by using a training set of labeled images of these diseases. The best accuracy using transfer learning was 93.75% using MobileNet and best using proposed CNN was 95.85%. Similarly Machine Learning methods could give best accuracy of 93.18% using Random Forest with 4 set of features namely HSV, Hu-moments, Haralick and LBP. The second part of this research also helps to compress and accelerate the pre-trained models for their deployment on edge devices without much loss in performance. This study could be easily extended to other such human diseases in future.

References

1. Chattopadhyay, A., Maitra, M.: MRI-based brain tumor image detection using CNN based deep learning method. Neurosci. Inform. 100060 (2022)
2. Gupta, N., et al.: Economic data analytic AI technique on IoT edge devices for health monitoring of agriculture machines. Appl. Intell. **50**(11), 3990–4016 (2020)
3. Agarwal, M., Singh, A., Arjaria, S., Sinha, A., Gupta, S.: ToLeD: tomato leaf disease detection using convolution neural network. Procedia Comput. Sci. **167**, 293–301 (2020)
4. Agarwal, M., Gupta, S.K., Biswas, K.K.: Grape disease identification using convolution neural network. In: 2019 23rd International Computer Science and Engineering Conference (ICSEC), pp. 224–229. IEEE (2019)
5. Agarwal, M., Kaliyar, R.K., Singal, G., Gupta, S.K.: FCNN-LDA: a faster convolution neural network model for leaf disease identification on apple's leaf dataset. In: 2019 12th International Conference on Information & Communication Technology and System (ICTS), pp. 246–251. IEEE (2019)
6. Agarwal, M., Sinha, A., Gupta, S.K., Mishra, D., Mishra, R.: Potato crop disease classification using convolutional neural network. In: Somani, A.K., Shekhawat, R.S., Mundra, A., Srivastava, S., Verma, V.K. (eds.) Smart Systems and IoT: Innovations in Computing. SIST, vol. 141, pp. 391–400. Springer, Singapore (2020). https://doi.org/10.1007/978-981-13-8406-6_37
7. Agarwal, M., Bohat, V.K., Ansari, M.D., Sinha, A., Gupta, S.K., Garg, D.: A convolution neural network based approach to detect the disease in corn crop. In: 2019 IEEE 9th International Conference on Advanced Computing (IACC), pp. 176–181. IEEE (2019)
8. Agarwal, M., Gupta, S.K., Biswas, K.K.: Development of efficient CNN model for tomato crop disease identification. Sustain. Comput.: Inform. Syst. **28**, 100407 (2020)
9. Agarwal, M., Gupta, S., Biswas, K.K.: A new Conv2D model with modified ReLU activation function for identification of disease type and severity in cucumber plant. Sustain. Comput.: Inform. Syst. **30**, 100473 (2021)
10. Agarwal, M., Gupta, S.K., Biswas, K.K.: A compressed and accelerated SegNet for plant leaf disease segmentation: a differential evolution based approach. In: Karlapalem, K., et al. (eds.) PAKDD 2021. LNCS (LNAI), vol. 12714, pp. 272–284. Springer, Cham (2021). https://doi.org/10.1007/978-3-030-75768-7_22
11. Agarwal, M., Gupta, S.K., Biswas, K.K.: Plant leaf disease segmentation using compressed UNet architecture. In: Gupta, M., Ramakrishnan, G. (eds.) PAKDD 2021. LNCS (LNAI), vol. 12705, pp. 9–14. Springer, Cham (2021). https://doi.org/10.1007/978-3-030-75015-2_2
12. Agarwal, M., et al.: Wilson disease tissue classification and characterization using seven artificial intelligence models embedded with 3D optimization paradigm on a weak training brain magnetic resonance imaging datasets: a supercomputer application. Med. Biol. Eng. Comput. **59**(3), 511–533 (2021)
13. Agarwal, M., et al.: A novel block imaging technique using nine artificial intelligence models for Covid-19 disease classification, characterization and severity measurement in lung computed tomography scans on an Italian cohort. J. Med. Syst. **45**(3), 1–30 (2021)
14. Saba, L., et al.: Six artificial intelligence paradigms for tissue characterisation and classification of non-Covid-19 pneumonia against Covid-19 pneumonia in computed tomography lungs. Int. J. Comput. Assisted Radiol. Surg. **16**(3), 423–434 (2021)

15. Agarwal, M., et al.: Eight pruning deep learning models for low storage and high-speed Covid-19 computed tomography lung segmentation and heatmap-based lesion localization: a multicenter study using COVLIAS 2.0. Comput. Biol. Med. 105571 (2022)
16. Agarwal, M., Gupta, S.K., Biswas, M., Garg, D.: Compression and acceleration of convolution neural network: a genetic algorithm based approach. J. Ambient Intell. Hum. Comput. 1–11 (2022)
17. Agarwal, M., Gupta, S.K., Garg, D., Singh, D.: A novel compressed and accelerated convolution neural network for Covid-19 disease classification: a genetic algorithm based approach. In: Garg, D., Jagannathan, S., Gupta, A., Garg, L., Gupta, S. (eds.) IACC 2021. CCIS, vol. 1528, pp. 99–111. Springer, Cham (2021). https://doi.org/10.1007/978-3-030-95502-1_8
18. Agarwal, M., Gupta, S.K., Garg, D., Khan, M.M.: A particle swarm optimization based approach for filter pruning in convolution neural network for tomato leaf disease classification. In: Garg, D., Jagannathan, S., Gupta, A., Garg, L., Gupta, S. (eds.) IACC 2021. CCIS, vol. 1528, pp. 646–659. Springer, Cham (2021). https://doi.org/10.1007/978-3-030-95502-1_49
19. Yar, H., Hussain, T., Agarwal, M., Khan, Z.A., Gupta, S.K., Baik, S.W.: Optimized dual fire attention network and medium-scale fire classification benchmark. IEEE Trans. Image Process. 31, 6331–6343 (2022)
20. Skandha, S.S., Agarwal, M., Utkarsh, K., Gupta, S.K., Koppula, V.K., Suri, J.S.: A novel genetic algorithm-based approach for compression and acceleration of deep learning convolution neural network: an application in computer tomography lung cancer data. Neural Comput. Appl. 1–23 (2022)
21. Agarwal, M., Kaliyar, R.K., Gupta, S.K.: Differential evolution based compression of CNN for apple fruit disease classification. In: 2022 International Conference on Inventive Computation Technologies (ICICT), pp. 76–82. IEEE (2022)
22. Sadoon, T.A., Ali, M.H.: Deep learning model for glioma, meningioma and pituitary classification. Int. J. Adv. Appl. Sci. 8814 (2021). ISSN 2252(8814)
23. Matsui, Y., et al.: Prediction of lower-grade glioma molecular subtypes using deep learning. J. Neurooncol. 146(2), 321–327 (2020)
24. Yang, Y., et al.: Glioma grading on conventional MR images: a deep learning study with transfer learning. Front. Neurosci. 12, 804 (2018)
25. Çinarer, G., Emiroğlu, B.G., Yurttakal, A.H.: Prediction of glioma grades using deep learning with wavelet radiomic features. Appl. Sci. 10(18), 6296 (2020)

Brain Tumor Segmentation Using 3D Attention U Net

Siva Koteswara Rao Chinnam[✉][iD], Venkatramaphanikumar Sistla[iD],
and Venkata Krishna Kishore Kolli[iD]

Department of Computer Science and Engineering, Vadlamudi,
Guntur District, Andhra Pradesh, India
csrvictory@gmail.com

Abstract. Segmentation plays a significant role in the brain tumor analysis for
its early diagnosis and treatment planning. Manual segmentation of brain tumors
from MRI slices is a time-consuming procedure for cancer diagnosis. In subsequent therapy, brain tumor cells must divide automatically. Modern deep learning
architectures utilize attention approaches for computer vision and nerve translation to increase networks' spatial and channel-by-channel understanding. Existing approaches do not have powerful strategies for incorporating the details about
information on tumor cells and their environment. In this study, we considered
a deep learning model called "Attention based U-Net" based on boundary localization of brain tumor MRI scans. Models trained using U-Nets learn to put-
down unimportant areas, while starring major features that terminates the Usage
of explicit external organ/tissue localization modules. The segmented images may
predict survival rate and treatment responsiveness in further process. Multimodal
MRI scans were used to segment the glioma sub regions, which includes T1, T2,
T1CE and FLAIR modalities. The proposed Attention U-Net model segmented
the WT, TC and ET using the FLAIR modality and shown 95.56, 93.31 and 89.95
dice score respectively, over BraTS 2018.

Keywords: Brain Tumor segmentation · MRI · CNN · Attention U-Net · BraTS
2018

1 Introduction

Cancer is one of the deadliest diseases in which some abnormal cells spread uncontrol-
lably and extend to other parts of the body. This unusual growth of cells in the brain
is called a brain tumor. These include the most threating tumor types in the world.
About 350,000 new cases of brain tumors occur worldwide every year [1–3], and the
last 5-year survival rate for the brain is very less its about 36% while nearly 150 dissimilar types of brain tumors are recorded, in the main types of tumors are metastatic and
primary. Neoplasm emerges in the tissues of the brain or in the actual proximity of the
brain are known as primary brain tumors. Glial (glial cells) (structural or infrastructural
of the brain, including nerves, blood arteries, and glands) primary tumors are classified
as either malignant or benign. Tumors originate in different parts of the body (such as

D. Garg et al. (Eds.): IACC 2022, CCIS 1781, pp. 475–484, 2023.
https://doi.org/10.1007/978-3-031-35641-4_39

the Breast, Brain, Lungs) and spread to the brain through the bloodstream are known as metastatic or metastases brain tumor. Metastatic tumors are also called secondary cancers. Glioma, the most common primary brain tumor, caused by glial cell carcinogenesis in the spinal cord and brain. Gliomas, which are generated from glial cells that surround and support neurons in the brain, such as astrocytes, oligodendrocytes, and ependymal cells, account for about 33% of all brain cancers.

Gliomas grow in brain tissue and often mingle with normal brain tissue, they are called intra-axial brain tumors. Glioma symptoms include dizziness, headache, and personality and behavior changes. As a result, early detection, investigation, and treatment are critical for patients with a brain tumor to improve the treatment effect. MRI scans are useful in identification of shapes, sizes, localization and metabolism of brain tumors. While various modalities are combined to implement a unique knowledge on brain tumors, MRI is treated as a traditional technique due to its accurate soft tissue comparison. MRI generates weak signal for the analysis of gliomas in scientific medicine, due to the high-decision and clean comparison pixels of brain tissues. The four MRI modalities are T1, T1Gd, T2 and FLAIR. Each technique presents biological data about the tumor that can accurately depict the glioma's underlying structure. Brain tumor segmentation is difficult even with multimodal imaging because the pathogenic mechanisms involved in brain tumor genesis and growth are unpredictable. The accurate segmentation of distinct sub-regions of glioma using multimodal MRI scans, such as peritumoral edema, necrotic core, enhanced and non-enhanced tumor core [4], has crucial therapeutic implications for brain tumor analysis, projection, and treatment.

However, manual segmentation and analysis of structural MRI images of brain tumors is a tedious and prolonged work usually performed by a specialized neuroradiologist. Therefore, automatic cellular division of brain tumors has a significant impact on the diagnosis and treatment of brain tumors. Recent developments by applying deep learning models have proven effective in various semantic and medical image segmentation tasks. Most of them are grounded on a U-Net network architecture [5] with end-to-end segmentation, symmetric encoding and decoding paths, with high productivity and excellent achievement. In brain tumor segmentation, the 2-D nature of multimodal MRI poses demanding situations together with reminiscence and computation boundaries with sophistication imbalance while simultaneously employing the U-Net architecture. In this work, a deep study is conducted on the usage of a 2-D U-Net with diversification with the schooling and trying out strategies, community structures, and version parameters for brain tumor segmentation. 2-D U-Net segmentation is a structure primarily established on the Convolutional Neural Network (CNN), which has normal use to categorize labels. However, in clinical imaging, the preferred output must be extra than simply classification. It must include the localization of this installation to expect the elegance label of every pixel with the aid of using offering a nearby vicinity round that pixel as an input.

To generate a dense prediction of the entire image, Ronneberger et al. [5] proposed a U-Net with an encoder-decoder structure. Following that, an endless stream of U-Net variants based on the encoder-decoder architecture emerged, with convincing results. Oktay et al. [6] integrated the self-attention mechanism with 3D-UNet and effectively steered the network to represent global information using the attention gating module contained in skip links. However, none of these solutions can avoid the matrix multiplication framework, which has two issues: instability of the attention map and excessive computational complexity. Yu et al. [7] employ multi-scale information and global average pooling to tackle the problem of class inconsistencies implicitly. Furthermore, the boundary information is used to improve inter-class differentiation. Isensee et al. [8] used U-Net, a self-configuring framework that automatically adapts U-Net to a specific dataset and demonstrated strong performance with little changes to the traditional 3D U-Net by applying various BraTS-specific improvements. Jiang et al. [9] trained a two-stage cascaded U-Net, with the first stage producing coarse segmentation masks and the second stage refining the output of the first stage. To avoid overfitting, Ashtari et al. [10] presented a lightweight CNN for glioma segmentation, with low-rank limitations imposed on the kernel weights of the convolutional layers. Choromanski et al. [11] proposed Transformer as a linearly scalable alternative. FAVOR + provides an unbiased measure of attention while requiring just linear (rather than quadratic) time and space complexity. Except for the attention layers, the remainder of the baseline components are the same as those of Factorizer. Liu et al. [12] and introduced a Shifted Window (SW) Matricize operation, making the output feature maps smoother around boundaries. Sas et al. [13] suggested a robust segmentation model by combining the results of several CNN-based models, including 3D U-Net, 3D FCN, and Deep Medic. Zhou et al. [14] proposed using an ensemble of multiple CNN-based networks while taking multi-scale contextual information into account via an attention block. They employed a two-stage cascaded technique comprising U-Net models, with the first step calculating a coarse segmentation prediction that will be refined by the second stage. By processing the collected features at different resolutions, Xie et al. [15] proposed using a ViT-based model with deformable transformer layers between its CNN-based encoder and decoder. Hatamizadeh et al. [16] proposed the UNETR architecture, which connects a ViT-based encoder that directly uses 3D input patches to a CNN-based decoder. Using the MSD dataset, UNETR demonstrated promising results for brain tumor segmentation. The rest of the paper is organized as follows: Sect. 2 presents description of the proposed 3D Attention U-Net architecture. Section 3 presents experimental results and discussions. Finally, the conclusion is presented in Sect. 4.

2   Proposed 3D Attention-Net for Brain Tumor Segmentation

The topology of our proposed network is based on the U-Net represented in Fig. 1. The network is made up of two primary paths: the contracting route, which encodes the whole of the input image, and the expanding path, which restores the image's original resolution. In the encoder block a series of convolution blocks and max-pooling is applied. In a convolution block, there are two convolutional layers followed by Batch Normalization and ReLU activation. The framework of the proposed method consists of the following three main steps: preprocessing of MRI data, training the network, and applying the trained model to predict the brain tumor structure.

Preprocessing: Preprocessing the brain image before segmentation may increase the reliability of the image segmentation by eliminating the effect of irrelevant interference

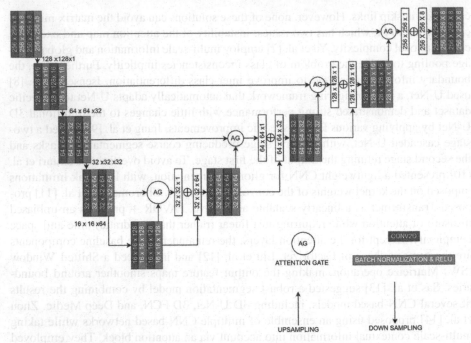

Fig. 1. Architecture of the proposed Attention U Net

information. The N4ITK technique is used on each MRI modality to correct the inhomogeneity of these images to remove the effect of no uniformity artefacts. Secondly, we normalize each modal picture independently and remove it from the mean and then divide it by the standard deviation to ensure a consistent intensity and contrast between the patient and the obtained image.

Convolution Neural Network: The convolutional layer's primary function in image segmentation is to concatenate kernels with images to produce feature maps that are mapped with kernel weight of the next layer. The application of nonlinear activation functions in neural networks allows to approximate the solution of any complex function. It is straightforward to create fuzzy recognition sample regions by combining the optimization solutions of many classifications into one optimization problem and improving the loss function to accomplish a multi-class classification. It is possible to acquire better flexibility and accuracy by combining basic classifiers that have been dynamically trained on data from multiple categories. There are three distinct types of tumors in this network: necrosis, edema, non-enhancing tumor, and tumor that are enhancing (TC, including necrosis, non-enhancing, and enhancing tumor). Increasing the number of network layers results in more abstract and detailed features leading to the enhancement of accuracy and reduction in error. But as the number of network layers' increases, the gradient disappears, resulting in the failure of convergence. During training, to solve the degradation issue, the preceding layer's information is passed between the network levels. The remaining networks help in training optimization and enhanced network model depth. Our deep learning network is depicted as shown in Fig. 1. In order to increase network training efficiency while decreasing overfitting, the following tactics are used.

Batch Normalization: Due to intensity variations in MRI, texture analysis may be seriously affected, resulting in inaccurate descriptions of tissues in the image. Prior to texture analysis, the image's spatial unevenness must be corrected to minimize these inaccuracies. Batch normalization (BN) normalizes the input values of each layer and solves the problem of input data layout drift during training. This balances the activation function with the numerical area to boost the gradient and to avoid gradient disappearance. Further, increasing the gradient of a deep learning network's convergence speed greatly saves training time. To get a zero-centered distribution, we subtract the batch mean from the activation input x during training.

To ensure the variance of the distribution for all activation inputs is 1, To ensure standardization effect, we transform the network and it was changed during backpropagation. Where α and δ are vector parameters.

Pooling and Activation Function: After the convolution layer, a feature extraction layer called "pooling" is used. Due to sliding the convolution window, the overlapping regions causes redundancy. To reduce this redundancy, Pooling is a useful technique. Pooling also represents image features at a higher degree of abstraction. To optimize the parameters, ReLU activation function is selected which is useful in solving gradient vanishing problem and also very fast in calculation.

Loss Function: The loss function is used to determine, how well our model fits the input data. To minimize the gap between predicted and ground truth, we used gradient descent approach. As, brain tumor samples are extremely imbalance, Dice loss is used. DSC is used as a measure of data similarity and is calculated as in Eq. 4:

Fine-tuning: To achieve the optative segmentation effect, the highly nonlinear loss function must be reduced to the minimum. For ease of implementation, lesser memory requirements and better computing efficiency, Adam (adaptive moment estimation) determines the adaptive learning ratio for the parameters, in line with the optimum method. When working with large amounts of data, the Adam method is a great choice since it is invariant to gradient diagonal scaling. There are two 3×3 convolutional layers, eight composite convolutional blocks, four pooling layer and five 1×1 inverse convolutions in the primary architecture of the suggested network model.

Attention: During training for image segmentation, focusing on just the relevant activations is called paying attention. i.e., the network is able to "focus" on certain areas of the image with better generalization.

Attention Gate: The attention gate takes two important inputs called vectors x and the vector g. U-Net architecture accepts a $256 \times 256 \times 8$ resolution input image and outputs a $256 \times 256 \times 1$ resolution image. The model's left side serves as an encoder, while the right side serves as a decoder. UNET employs a padded convolution layer. This allows you to use an image as input that is the same size as the output. The network has a U-shaped architecture with a reduced path and an extended path.

Attention 3D U-Net: Recognition of image segmentation is a way to emphasize only relevant activity during training. This reduces the computing wasted on the basic irrelevant activations and improves network generalization performance. The restored spatial information is inaccurate during up-sampling on the expanding path. To address this issue, UNET uses a jump connection that combines spatial information from the down-sampling path with the up-sampling path. However, this results in inadequate feature representation of the initial layer, resulting in many redundant low-level feature extractions. The attention gate takes two important two inputs called vectors x and the vector g taken from lower layer network Vectors come from deeper in the network, so they have smaller dimensions and better feature representations. In the image in the above example, the dimension of the vector x is $64 \times 64 \times 64$ (filter x height x width) and the vector g is $32 \times 32 \times 32$. The vector x undergoes a gradual convolution and its dimensions are $64 \times 32 \times 32$. The vector g undergoes a 1×1 convolution, so its dimensions are $64 \times 32 \times 32$. The two vectors are summed for each element. This process results in higher aligned weights and relatively smaller unaligned weights. The resulting vector passes through the ReLU activation layer and the 1×1 convolution, reducing the dimension to $1 \times 32 \times 32$. This vector goes through a sigmoid layer that scales the vector between ranges [0,1] and produces a factor of attention (weight). The closer the factor is to 1, the more relevant features are shown. The attention factor is up sampled to the original dimension (64×64) of the x vector using trilinear interpolation. The attention factor is multiplied by the original x vector element by element, scaling the vector according to its relevance. After that, it is usually passed over a hop connection (Fig. 2).

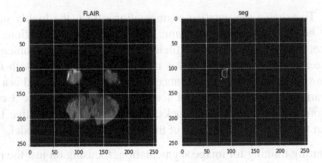

Fig. 2. Tumor Segmentation

The existing U-Net model is taken and fine-tuned so that it performs well with our Brats2018 dataset. The input to this network is $256 \times 256 \times 8$, and the output is the same size as the input, but with the segmented tumor from the original image. Convolution 2D, ReLU and max pooling operations are performed in each layer of the U-Net model. There are more activities going on internally, such as batch normalization and activation, which are common in ConvNet. U-Net model is equivalently separated into an encoder-decoder path and a contracting-expansive path.

Encoder (left side): It is made up of two 3 × 3 convolutions that are applied repeatedly. Following each conv is a ReLU and batch normalization. The spatial dimensions are then reduced using a 2 × 2 max pooling procedure. At each down-sampling stage, we double the number of feature channels while cutting the spatial dimensions in half.

The decoder path (right side) comprises an up-sampling of the feature map followed by a 2 × 2 transpose convolution, which reduces the number of feature channels by half. We also have a concatenation with the matching feature map from the contracting path and, in most cases, a 3 × 3 convolutional map (each followed by a ReLU). A 1 × 1 convolution is employed in the final layer to translate the channels to the appropriate number of classes. It is difficult to objectively evaluate the outcomes of various brain tumor image segmentation algorithms using the state-of-the-art. However, with the introduction of a widely recognized standard for automated brain tumor segmentation, the BraTS benchmark, it is now feasible to objectively compare multiple glioma segmentation approaches using this shared dataset. In this paper we have used BraTs 2018 dataset which is of 3 GB size. It contains multimodal 3D brain MRIs and ground truth brain tumor segmentations annotated by clinicians, with each case containing four MRI modalities (T1, T1c, T2, and FLAIR). There are three tumor sub regions annotated: the enhancing tumor, the peritumoral edema, and the necrotic and non-enhancing tumor core. The annotations were organized into three nested sub regions: total tumor (WT), tumor core (TC), and enhancing tumor (ET). The dataset contains 1689.nii files which are used for training and validating the model. Only the online evaluation tool allows for examination of testing data. The programme primarily displays results in the form of the well-known Dice Score, for three major tumor regions: total tumor (all tumor components), core tumor (all tumor components excluding edema), and active tumor (only active cells). Only dice scores are reported as performance indicators. For each tumor location, P1 represents the proposed method's segmented tumor area, while T1 represents the actual tumor area in the ground truth. The web programme then computes the dice score for each location using Eq. (1):

$$Dice = (2|P1 \cap T1|)/(|P1| + |T1|) \tag{1}$$

3   Experimental Results and Discussions

Kaggle is an online community platform that allows users to work with other users as well as search and share datasets. Kaggle datasets can be of varied sizes. Furthermore, some Deep Learning approaches need GPU assistance, which might lengthen training time. Colab is a platform for efficiently creating and running Python programs. It is mainly used for deep learning applications due to its many resources such as RAM, GPU and CPU [Colab]. It also provides a TPU (tensor processing unit) for processing tensors. Table 1 below provides detailed information about Google collaboration software and hardware specifications.

In this part, we compared the performance of our Attention U-Net model to that of some of the most recent models found and published in the literature, such as, SMU-Net [17], CGA U-Net [18], RES-Net [19] and V-Net [20]. In addition, to test the quality

Table 1. Software and Hardware specifications

Specification	Description
GPU	Tesla P100-PCIE-16GB
CPU	Intel Xenon CPU @2.30GHz
RAM	~25 GB
Disk space	~128 GB
Language	Python 3.8

Table 2. Model Comparison on BraTS 2018 Dataset

Ref	Dataset	WT	TC	ET
[17]	BraTs 2018	94.21	89.76	86.35
[18]		88.93	88.76	78.61
[19]		73.44	86.38	83.29
[20]		92.45	89.10	85.20
Proposed Method		95.56	93.31	89.95

of aspect modelling in this study, we created a conventional deep-learning model CNN (Table 2).

Adam Optimizer is used for the model building and the loss is binary cross entropy, with the batch size is 16, and model built with 100 epochs. Despite the large number of epochs, callbacks are used to prevent the model from overfitting the BraTS 2018 dataset. Callbacks give you better control over the training process, stop the model when a certain level of accuracy/loss is reached, and save the model as a checkpoint each time a successful epoch, over time. The Fig. 3 depicts the dice loss during validation process (Fig. 4).

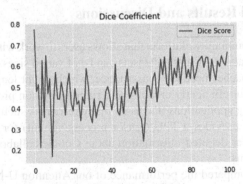

Fig. 3. Dice during validation

FLAIR   Prediction   Ground Truth

Fig. 4. Comparison between original images, Ground truths and segmented images

The experiment results of the proposed model are better when compared with other deep learning models and the segmented images are very close to the ground truths. Overall training dice score was 95.56%, 93.31%, and 89.9%. We can see that loss is reduced gradually, as a result training and validation accuracy was improved.

4 Conclusions and Future Scope

We demonstrated the advantage of an ensemble of 3D U-Nets for automated brain tumor segmentation over a single model. We derived a few basic variables from the segmentation findings and studied their relationships with overall survival. To improve performance of the proposed model for high accuracy and better predict survival, one needs to develop a new model with adaptive training for new samples or unseen samples without retraining the entire model from scratch.

References

1. Menze, B.H., Jakab, A., Bauer, S.: An adaptive-focus statistical shape model for segmentation and shape modeling of 3-D brain structures. IEEE Trans. Med. Imaging. **20**, 257–270 (2001)
2. Li, S., Tan, M.: Gene selection and tissue classification based on support vector machine and genetic algorithm. In: 1st International Conference on Bioinformatics and Biomedical Engineering (ICBBE), pp. 192–195 (2007). https://doi.org/10.1109/ICBBE.2007.52
3. Steen, R.G.: Edema and tumor perfusion: characterization by quantitative 1H MR imaging. Am. J. Roentgenol. **158**, 259–264 (1992). https://doi.org/10.2214/ajr.158.2.1729777
4. Saba, L., et al.: Brain MRI-based wilson disease tissue classification: an optimised deep transfer learning approach. Electron. Lett. **56**(25), 1395–1398 (2020)
5. Ronneberger, O., Fischer, P., Brox, T.: U-Net: convolutional networks for biomedical image segmentation. In: Navab, N., Hornegger, J., Wells, W., Frangi, A. (eds.) Medical Image Computing and Computer-Assisted Intervention – MICCAI 2015. MICCAI 2015. LNCS, vol. 9351, pp. 234–241. Springer, Cham (2015). https://doi.org/10.1007/978-3-319-24574-4_28
6. Oktay, O., et al.: Attention u-net: Learning where to look for the pancreas (2018). arXiv preprint arXiv:1804.03999
7. Yu, C., Wang, J., Peng, C., Gao, C., Yu, G., Sang, N.: Learning a discriminative feature network for semantic segmentation. In: Proceedings of the IEEE Conference on Computer Vision and Pattern Recognition, pp. 1857–1866 (2018)
8. Isensee, F., Jäger, P.F., Full, P.M., Vollmuth, P., Maier-Hein, K.H.: nnU-Net for brain tumor segmentation. In: Crimi, A., Bakas, S. (eds.) BrainLes 2020. LNCS, vol. 12659, pp. 118–132. Springer, Cham (2021). https://doi.org/10.1007/978-3-030-72087-2_11

9. Jiang, Z., Ding, C., Liu, M., Tao, D.: Two-stage cascaded U-Net: 1st place solution to BraTS challenge 2019 segmentation task. In: Crimi, A., Bakas, S. (eds.) BrainLes 2019. LNCS, vol. 11992, pp. 231–241. Springer, Cham (2020). https://doi.org/10.1007/978-3-030-46640-4_22

10. Ashtari, P., Maes, F., Van Huffel,S.: Low-rank convolutional networks for brain tumor segmentation. In: Crimi, A., Bakas, S. (eds.) Brainlesion: Glioma, Multiple Sclerosis, Stroke and Traumatic Brain Injuries. BrainLes 2020. LNCS, vol. 12658, pp. 470–480. Springer, Cham (2021). https://doi.org/10.1007/978-3-030-72084-1_42

11. Choromanski, K., et al.: Rethinking attention with performers (2020). arXiv preprint arXiv: 2009.14794

12. Liu, Z., et al.: Swin transformer: hierarchical vision transformer using shifted windows. In: Proceedings of the IEEE/CVF International Conference on Computer Vision (ICCV), October 2021, pp. 10 012–10 022 (2021)

13. Kamnitsas, K., et al.: Ensembles of multiple models and architectures for robust brain tumour segmentation. In: Crimi, A., Bakas, S., Kuijf, H., Menze, B., Reyes, M. (eds.) Brainlesion: Glioma, Multiple Sclerosis, Stroke and Traumatic Brain Injuries. BrainLes 2017. LNCS, vol. 10670. Springer, Cham (2018). https://doi.org/10.1007/978-3-319-75238-9_38

14. Zhou, C., Chen, S., Ding, C., Tao, D.: Learning contextual and attentive information for brain tumor segmentation. In: Crimi, A., Bakas, S., Kuijf, H., Keyvan, F., Reyes, M., van Walsum, T. (eds.) Brainlesion: Glioma, Multiple Sclerosis, Stroke and Traumatic Brain Injuries. BrainLes 2018. LNCS, vol. 11384. Springer, Cham (2019). https://doi.org/10.1007/978-3-030-11726-9_44

15. Xie, Y., Zhang, J., Shen, C., Xia, Y.: Cotr: efficiently bridging CNN and transformer for 3d medical image segmentation. arXiv preprint arXiv:2103.03024 (2021)

16. Hatamizadeh, C., Icek, O., Abdulkadir, A., Lienkamp, S.S., Brox, T., Ronneberger, O.: 3D U-Net: learning dense volumetric segmentation from sparse annotation. In: Ourselin, S., Joskowicz, L., Sabuncu, M., Unal, G., Wells, W. (eds.) Medical Image Computing and Computer-Assisted Intervention – MICCAI 2016. MICCAI 2016. LNCS, vol. 9901, pp. 424–432. Springer, Cham (2016). https://doi.org/10.1007/978-3-319-46723-8_49

17. Shehab, L.H., Fahmy, O.M., Gasser, S.M., El-Mahallawy, M.S.: An efficient brain tumor image segmentation based on deep residual networks (ResNets). J. King Saud Univ. Eng. Sci. 33(6), 404–412. King Saud University (2021). https://doi.org/10.1016/j.jksues.2020.06.001

18. Kermi, A., Mahmoudi, I., Khadir, M.T.: Deep convolutional neural networks using U-Net for automatic brain tumor segmentation in multimodal MRI volumes. In: Crimi, A., Bakas, S., Kuijf, H., Keyvan, F., Reyes, M., van Walsum, T. (eds.) BrainLes 2018. LNCS, vol. 11384, pp. 37–48. Springer, Cham (2019). https://doi.org/10.1007/978-3-030-11726-9_4

19. Pereira, S., Pinto, A., Alves, V., Silva, C.A.: Brain tumor segmentation using convolutional neural networks in MRI images. IEEE Trans. Med. Imaging 35(5), 1240–1251 (2016). https://doi.org/10.1109/TMI.2016.2538465

20. Ben Naceur, M., Saouli, R., Akil, M., Kachouri, R.: Fully automatic brain tumor segmentation using end-to-end incremental deep neural networks in MRI images. Comput. Methods Programs Biomed. 166, 39–49 (2018). https://doi.org/10.1016/j.cmpb.2018.09.007

Brain Tumor Detection Using Convolutional Neural Network

Uppari Sai Bhargavi, Shwati Tiwari, Aditi Mishra, Syed Hasan,
Sudhanshu Gonge(✉), Rahul Joshi, and Ketan Kotecha

Department of Computer Science and Engineering, Symbiosis Institute of Technology,
Symbiosis International (Deemed University), Pune, India
{uppari.bhargavi.btech2019,shwati.tiwari.btech2019,
aditi.mishra.btech2019,syed.hasan.btech2019,sudhanshu.gonge,
rahulj}@sitpune.edu.in, head@scaai.siu.edu.in

Abstract. The human brain primarily controls the humanoid system. Brain cancer is brought on by the persistent growth of brain tumors, which are brought on by the relationship between aberrant brain cell development and proliferation and human health. A big part is played by computer vision, which lessens the need for human judgment to produce accurate findings. The most dependable and secure magnetic resonance imaging (MRI) imaging techniques are CT scans, X-rays, and MRI scans. Every minute, MRI unearths objects. The application of several methods for detecting brain cancer using MRI is the main focus of our paper. Our paper's major objective is to apply the VGG16 model for the identification of brain cancer utilizing brain MRI. In this research, the noises that are found in an MRI image were removed using the bilateral filter (BF) during pre-processing. After that, convolution neural network (CNN) segmentation techniques and binary thresholding were used to reliably identify the tumor region. Datasets are used for training, testing, and validation. Using our machine, we were able to make a prediction about the subject's brain tumor status using our machine. The final results of our VGG16 model are that, it was successfully implemented with an accuracy of 92.31%, average precision 92%, recall 94% and f1-score of 92%.

Keywords: Brain tumor · Convolutional Neural Network · VGG16

1 Introduction

The brain is the most critical and fundamental of the several organs that comprise the human body. Brain tumors are among the frequent causes of mental illness. In simple terms, a tumor is a collection of out-of-control growing cells. Brain failure results from the proliferation of brain tumor cells because they gradually absorb all the nutrition intended for healthy cells and tissues. The location and size of the patient's brain tumor are currently determined by clinicians manually reviewing brain MR images of the patient. This is time-consuming and results in inaccurate tumor detection.

A lot of people lose their lives to brain cancer each year. An early detection and categorization technique for brain tumors is available. The tasks that include classifying

© Springer Nature Switzerland AG 2023
D. Garg et al. (Eds.): IACC 2022, CCIS 1781, pp. 485–493, 2023.
https://doi.org/10.1007/978-3-031-35641-4_40

cancers in clinical diagnosis are the most challenging. The technology under study in the project analyzes the MRI scans of various patients to find tumor blocks. Using a variety of techniques for processing images, such as feature extraction and image enhancement, and picture segmentation, it is possible to detect brain tumors in MRI scans of cancer patients. Image processing and neural network approaches improve the accuracy of detecting and categorizing brain cancers in MRI images.

The major objective of brain tumor detection is to detect the tumor. This can be helpful in instances where we require to be certain whether a tumor is present or absent. This system can recognize images of tumours and indicate whether they are positive or negative. This project explores a system that employs computer-based methods to analyze MRI pictures of various patients' tumor blocks using neural network techniques.

Now that the difficulties raised earlier have been addressed, we will synthesize our contributions and offer a framework for CNN-based satellite image classification.

Fully Convolutional Network: First, a fully convolutional architecture. In order to create the output classification patches, the CNN architecture's fully connected layer—which is connected to all of the previous layer's outputs—is first examined.

We draw attention to the fact that this architectural choice reduces accuracy and efficiency. Then, in order to construct the output classification maps, we suggest a new network architecture that is entirely convolutional and consists solely of convolution and deconvolution processes. By design, this architecture addresses the drawbacks of the earlier patch-based methodology. The neuronal connections are subject to more constraints with such a fully convolutional design than under a fully connected one, but the number of trainable parameters is decreased without losing generality. Reducing the number of parameters under reasonable assumptions frequently results in a simpler error surface and aids in locating better local minima, as has been shown repeatedly in the literature.

Two-Step Training Technique: We suggest a two-step approach to address the flaws in training data. In order to understand the generalities of the data set, we first train our CNN on brain tumor dataset. Second, we apply a tiny portion of manually labeled image to a few iterations of fine-tuning the resulting neural networks. We believe that after the network has been pre trained on a lot of imperfect data, its performance can be improved by "showing" it a tiny number of accurate labels. Our strategy is based on a deep learning technique that is frequently used: taking pretrained networks created to address one problem and adapting them to address another.

2 Literature Review

E. Irmak et al. (2021) in [1] explains how Histopathological examination of biopsy samples is still utilized in diagnosis and classification of brain tumors today and the existing approach is intrusive, cumbersome, and prone to human mistake. He proposes the use of deep learning in diagnosing brain tumor. M. Agarwal et al. (2021) in [2],discuss the disease Wilson's disease caused by copper accumulation in the brain and liver and proposed a CNN model to detect the presence of the wilson's disease. L.Saba et al. (2020) in [3] also created a model to detect Wilson's disease she along with VGG16 model uses MobileNet model to detect the presence of Wilson's disease. N.B. Bahadure et al. (2017)

in [4], explain the concept of brain tissues and how the brain's tissues were divided using MR images into healthy tissues including cerebrospinal fluid, tissues with tumors, white matter, and grey matter. Preprocessing is used. To increase the efficacy of skull stripping, a threshold-based method can be used. L. Kapoor et al. (2017) in [5], elaborates various methods that are components of Medical Image Processing and are prominently used in detecting brain tumors from MRI Images. Based on that research, the paper by L. Kapoor and S. Thakur was prepared, which includes a list of the many strategies now in use. Each technique is briefly explained as well. Of all the various stages involved in locating malignancies, segmentation is the most crucial. P. Gamage et al. (2017) in [6], concludes that the four categories are preprocessing, image segmentation, feature extraction, and image classification into which the process of finding brain cancers using MRI images may be divided.

Deepa. A. Singh et al. (2016) in [7], shows some recent studies as it relates to segmentation and detection of brain tumors are reviewed. It is explained how numerous scientists have used different methods to spot brain cancers in MRI images. One of the most prominent research fields was identified to be the automatically dividing and detection of brain cancers from MRI images. D. Somwanshi et al. (2016) in [8] describe the work that they have examined the different Entropy functions for segmenting tumors and identifying them from diverse pictures. Depending on the specified entropy, different threshold values can be reached. The segmented results are constrained by the different entropy functions, which in turn depend on the threshold levels. V. Shree et al. (2018) in [9] have proposed a study for the identification of using discrete wavelength changes, tumor areas (DWT). This study can be divided into three sections: tumor feature extraction using a gray-level co-incidence matrix (GLCM), tumor site segmentation using DWT, and picture enhancement using a filtering method. It is used to make things simpler and perform better overall. With the aid of morphological filtering methods, the sounds that could even be molded into a subsequent segmentation technique are repressed during the denoised phase. The PNN classifier is to be used to categorize the abnormality, and the accuracy is evaluated through the tumor region detection of brain MR images. The PNN classifier is trained using various datasets. K. Vinotha et al. (2014) in [10] recommended using the Fuzzy Support Vector Machine classification (FSVM) and Histogram Equalization (HE) approach in order to identify brain cancers. Histogram equalization is used to pre-process the brain MR image, and the MRF method is used to distinguish the anxious parts of the image from the overall image. The improved tumor segmentation accuracy of the MRF technique contributed to the overall performance of the proposal.

Minz et al. (2017) in [11] included development of an efficient technique for automatically classifying brain images that foresaw the application of the AdaBoost algorithm for mastering gadgetry. The proposed system comprises of three main parts. Pre-processing has been used to remove noise from the datasets, and photos have been converted to grayscale. The pre-processed image uses median filtering, segmentation, and thresholding.

3 Proposed Methodology

The automatic detection and classification of brain cancers is the key focus. MRI and CT scans are frequently used to assess the anatomical structure of the brain. Finding brain tumours is primarily done to aid in clinical identification. Our objective is to create a technique that ensures the detection of a tumor, resulting in a reliable way to detect tumors in MRI brain pictures. Approaches include edge detection, filtering, erosion, dilation, threshold, and tumor delineation methods. This project's objective is to take information about tumors from MR brain scans and present it in a way that is simple to grasp. This endeavor aims to provide users some useful information in a more appealing style, especially for the healthcare professionals caring for the patient. In this study, a method to create a cancer image that has been derived from an MRI brain image will be defined. The finished image will be able to divulge details about the tumor's boundaries as well as specifics about its size, shape, and location, all of which can be useful in a variety of circumstances. The team will have more information to draw from when deciding on the best course of treatment. A CNN model is used to detect whether a tumour is present in the supplied MR brain picture.

The aim is to develop a computerized method for enhancing, segmenting, and classifying brain tumors. The method is usable by medical specialists, including neurosurgeons. The technology will enhance the sensitivity, validity, and efficiency of screening for brain cancers by utilizing trend analysis, computer vision, and methods for image processing. Medical imaging projects' primary goal is to accurately and consistently extract data from the images with the fewest errors. The modeling and balancing of the stages enable progress of supplementary tools which are useful for prior detection or the tracking of cancer diagnosis and its position. The suggested system is made up of five parts. Dataset (input images), Pre-processing (image), data splitting, building the CNN model, and lastly, y classification. From the given dataset, one MRI image is taken as the input image out of several. During image pre-processing, both resize and label the image are encoded. The data has been split into two parts: i) 80 percent for training and ii) 20 percent for testing. Then, for further classifying the image according to the given input, it returns yes if the tumor is positive and no if tumor is not detected. This has been implemented using a model of CNN which is VGG16.

CNNs employ visual recognition and classification to find objects, identify faces, and perform other tasks. They are composed of neurons that can have their weights and biases learned. Each individual neuron gets a variety of inputs, weights them, then sends the result through an input signal to produce an output. They make use of multi-channeled visuals and are prompted by volume. CNNs are unable to distinguish between width and height-only flat pictures, which humans can see. The colored images having encoding of red-green-blue (RGB) combines three hues to generate a human-perceivable colored spectrum. The central component, also termed as the first layer, is the convolutional layer which is used to handle the majority of the computational labor. Filters or kernels are used to convolute data or images. In CNN, for increasing the non linearity we apply the rectifier function in the second step.and the activation layer makes use of ReLu (Rectified Linear Unit). Images are constructed from various nonlinearly related items. The pooling layer, which incorporates downsampling characteristics, comes in third. Every layer of the three-dimensional volume has it applied to it. At last, we have the fully connected layer which is used for flattening. For processing of the neural network, this entails converting an entire map grid of pooling feature into a single vertical. These features were merged into a model with the help of the fully connected layers. Finally, for categorizing the output, softmax or sigmoid has been used as an encoder.

4   Implementation

In this project we built a classifier that inputs MRI images and detects presence of brain tumor. The dataset [10] (Fig. 1.) comprises of 155 images with brain tumors and 98 images without them. After the dataset has been imported, we used the imread() and resize() functions to resize the images to 224 × 224 pixels.

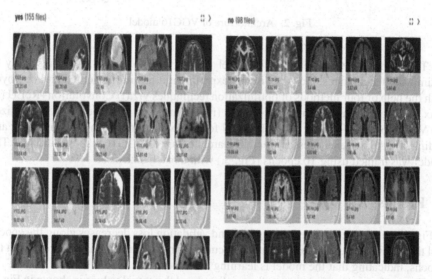

Fig. 1. MRI scans of Brain Tumor dataset [12]

The approach was as follows:

- Performing EDA on our dataset.
- Building a CNN model.
- Training and testing the developed model.

We then applied one hot encoding to the labels and normalized the MRI images to further split our dataset into train dataset and test dataset with a 9:1 ratio, making it a total of 228 training images and 25 test images. A convolutional neural network, as we have seen, is used for image recognition, segmentation, and classification. It primarily handles two tasks: executing feature extraction and predicting the images' class by using a fully connected layer that uses output of the convolutional layers. ImageDataGenerator is used for augmentation of the data through TensorFlow. It is useful when the data inputted is not sufficient. In order to increase the dataset size, various transformations like rotation, zooming, horizontal flipping, and more are carried out. In this case, we used the fill mode and rotation range transformations for filling the out of boundary pixels with the pixel closest to them and added a rotation of 15 degrees to the MRI images (See Fig. 2).

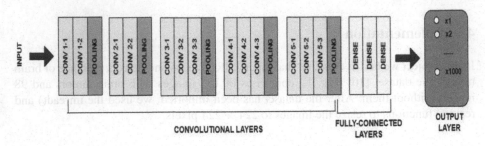

Fig. 2. Architecture of VGG16 model

The architecture of the VGG16 model is used and computed using a variety of optimization techniques. However in this experiment it has implemented and deployed with the help of four methods of optimization techniques viz.(i) Convolution+ReLU (ii) Max pooling (iii) Fully Connected+ReLU (iv) Softmax. In this research work utilized the VGG16 state-of-the-art network model for our project, removing the last layer and adding layers that were necessary for it.The architecture of VGG16 is shown in Fig. 3.The model was trained using 10 epochs (Fig. 3.) with a batch size of 8.

5   Results

In Fig. 3, we can see that the training loss and validation loss decreases along the epochs and the training accuracy and validation accuracy can be seen increasing throughout the epochs, indicating that the model is learning at a faster rate.

The confusion matrix between the predicted and the actual values is shown in Fig. 4. The model achieved an accuracy of 92.31% on the test dataset.

The obtained confusion matrix consists of four values such as -True Positive (TP) = 10, it implies that by the model 10 positive class data points have been classified correctly. False Negative (FN) = 0; it implies that by the model 0 data points of positive class have been incorrectly classified as the points that belong to the negative class. False Positive (FP) = 2; it implies that by the model 2 data points of negative class have been incorrectly classified as the points that belong to the positive class. True Negative (TN) = 14; it implies that by the model 14 data points of negative class have been correctly classified.

With accuracy of 92.31%, asverage precision of 92%, average recall of 94%, and average f1-score of 92%, the model outperforms all other approaches now in use. The comprehensive analysis of each class, which is represented by the words "YES" and "NO" in Fig. 5, can be found there.

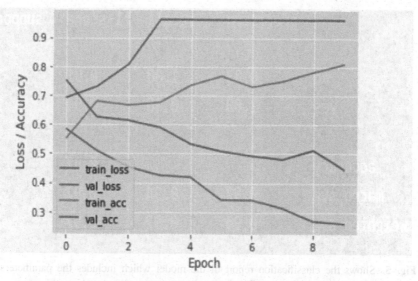

Fig. 3. Plot displaying the training loss and accuracy on our dataset

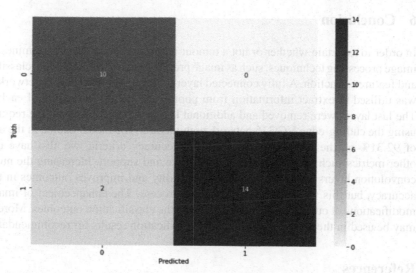

Fig. 4. Confusion matrix between the predicted and the actual values

	precision	recall	f1-score	support
no	0.83	1.00	0.91	10
yes	1.00	0.88	0.93	16
accuracy			0.92	26
macro avg	0.92	0.94	0.92	26
weighted avg	0.94	0.92	0.92	26

Fig. 5. Shows the classification report of the model which includes the parameters such as accuracy, f1-score, precision, recall and support.

6 Conclusion

In order to ascertain whether or not a tumour is present, this research examines various image processing techniques, such as image pre-processing, segmentation, classification, and feature extraction. A fully connected layer of a convolutional neural network (CNN) was utilised to extract information from photos and identify the class of each image. The last layers were removed and additional layers were added as per the requirement, using the cutting-edge VGG16 network architecture. The model hauled in the accuracy of 92.31% on the test data.Apart from the accuracy criteria, we also have used the other metrics such as recall, precision, f1 score and support. Increasing the number of convolution layers improves classification quality and improves outcomes in terms of accuracy, but this will lengthen the training process. The enhancement of images, the modifications of current datasets will improve the classification outcomes. More images may be used in the future to enhance the classification results for recommendations.

References

1. Irmak, E.: Multi-classification of brain tumor MRI images using deep convolutional neural network with fully optimized framework. Iran J. Sci. Technol. Trans. Electr. Eng. **45**, 1015–1036 (2021)
2. Agarwal, M., Saba, L., Gupta, S.K.: Wilson disease tissue classification and characterization using seven artificial intelligence models embedded with 3D optimization paradigm on a weak training brain magnetic resonance imaging datasets: a supercomputer application. Med. Biol. Eng. Comput. **59**, 511–533 (2021)
3. Saba, L., et al.: Brain MRI-based Wilson disease tissue classification: an optimised deep transfer learning approach. Electron. Lett. **56**(25), 1395–1398 (2020)

4. Bahadure, N.B., Ray, A.K., Thethi, H.P.: Image analysis for MRI based brain tumor detection and feature extraction using biologically inspired BWT and SVM. Int. J. Biomed. Imaging **2017**, 9749108 (2017)
5. Kapoor, L., Thakur, S.: A survey on brain tumor detection using image processing techniques. In: 2017 7th international conference on cloud computing, data science & engineering-confluence, pp. 582–585. IEEE (2017)
6. Gamage, P.T.: Identification of Brain Tumors using Image Processing Techniques. Gamage, University of Moratuwa (2017)
7. Deepa, Singh, A.: Review of brain tumor detection from MRI images. In: 2016 3rd International Conference on Computing for Sustainable Global Development (INDIACom), pp. 3997–4000. IEEE (2016)
8. Somwanshi, D., Kumar, A., Sharma, P., Joshi, D.: An efficient brain tumor detection from MRI images using entropy measures. In: 2016 International Conference on Recent Advances and Innovations in Engineering (ICRAIE), pp. 1–5. IEEE (2016)
9. Varuna Shree, N., Kumar, T.N.R.: Identification and classification of brain tumor MRI images with feature extraction using DWT and probabilistic neural network. Brain Inform. **5**(1), 23–30 (2018)
10. Vinotha, K.: Brain tumor detection and classification using histogram equalization and fuzzy support vector machine approach. International journal of engineering and computer science **3**(05) (2014)
11. Minz, A., Mahobiya, C.: MR image classification using AdaBoost for brain tumor type. In: 2017 IEEE 7th International Advance Computing Conference (IACC), pp. 701–705. IEEE (2017)
12. Chakrabarty, N.: Brain MRI images for brain tumor detection. Detection. https://www.kag gle.com/datasets/navoneel/brain-mri-images-for-brain-tumor-detection.2018

Web-based Tumor Detection and Classification Using Convolutional Neural Network

Kalab Kiros, Dinesh Kumar[✉], and T. Premavathi

Computer Engineering - Artificial Intelligence, Marwadi University, Rajkot, India
kalab.kiros108207@marwadiuniversity.ac.in, {dinesh.kumar,
premavathi.t}@marwadieducation.edu.in

Abstract. A brain tumor is a mass of abnormally developing cells in the brain or skull. There are around 120 different types of brain tumors based on the brain tissues that affect brain's normal functionality. Even benign (or noncancerous) brain tumors can be fatal due to their size or location. Unlike other types of cancer, primary brain cancer seldom spreads. When a tumor grows in size, it compresses and damages other areas of the brain. If the tumor is detected early enough, it can be treated, extending the patient's life. One of the most useful and important strategies is the use of Deep Neural Networks (DNN). In this paper, a convolutional neural network (CNN) to detect a tumor using Magnetic Resonance Imaging (MRI) images was employed. We were able to boost the diversity of our training set by making random (but realistic) alterations to the MRI images, resulting in a more robust training model. The data was then entered into the model for training and prediction. Based on the tumor identification results, the technique proposed an accuracy of 97.37% on the test data.

Keywords: MRI images · Brain tumor · Deep neural network · Convolutional neural network

1 Introduction

Meningioma, pituitary, and glioma are examples of primary tumors that begin in the brain. Alternatively, the tumor could be metastatic (cancer that began elsewhere in your body and has moved to your brain), such as breast cancer or skin cancer. Brain tumors are classified as benign (slow-growing and non-cancerous) or malignant (cancerous) (faster-growing and cancerous). CT or MRI brain scans are used to detect the majority of benign brain tumors [1]. Malignant brain tumors are cancerous growths. They typically spread into healthy brain regions and spread rapidly. Brain cancer can be fatal due to the changes it causes to the vital components of the brain. These tumors develop slowly, rarely penetrate neighbouring tissues or spread to other organs, and frequently have a boundary or edge visible on CT images. Metastatic (cancerous or spreading) tumors are uncommon in these tumors. The majority of benign brain tumors may be eliminated if caught early enough.

© Springer Nature Switzerland AG 2023
D. Garg et al. (Eds.): IACC 2022, CCIS 1781, pp. 494–502, 2023.
https://doi.org/10.1007/978-3-031-35641-4_41

Because of the size, form, location, and kind of brain tumours, manually detecting them is complicated, error-prone, time-consuming, and challenging [1]. The human brain is diagnosed using a variety of procedures, including CT scans and MRIs. One of the most prominent and significant technologies for diagnosing and analysing the human brain is magnetic resonance imaging (MRI) [2]. MRI, unlike CT-scan, creates an image using a magnetic field to create an image and there is no exposure to radiation which can sometimes be harmful. The image of unhealthy tissues is sharper with MRI.

In a traditional way of detecting the brain tumour, physician experts called radiologists analysed the MRI pictures [2]. Due to the noisy data in MRI pictures, radiologists find it difficult to examine them in a short amount of time. A Deep Neural Network (DNN), which is a Convolutional Neural Network, can be used to solve this challenge (CNN). A Convolutional Neural Network (CNN) is a type of artificial neural network used for image recognition and classification that is specifically designed to extract pixel input. It extracts picture attributes that enable for object categorization using various filters. In the realm of image categorization, CNN is widely employed.

The proposed technique uses TensorFlow to build CNN, which classifies brain MRI images into 4 labels meningioma, pituitary, glioma, and no tumour. Before classification the MRI images, the datasets are pre-processed, partitioned into training, validation and testing dataset, augmented and then finally trained with six convolutional and max pooling layers.

The entire paper is divided into five sections, excluding the abstract section: the second section contain previously related work, third section includes methodology while fourth section is to discuss results, and finally some conclusion and future work are mentioned in fifth section.

2 Related Work

A convolutional neural network model for brain cancer detection was presented in [3]. The first step was to improve brain magnetic resonance images in order to collect enough information for deep learning. The photos were then pre-processed to remove the background noise and get them ready for the next step. The presented approach classifies newly input images as malignant or normal using characteristics collected during training on previously processed MRI images. Backpropagation is used during training to reduce error and produced results in terms of accuracy and sensitivity as 95.55% and 96%, respectively.

The K-Means model and convolutional neural network are used in [4] to offer an automatic MRI Brain tumor identification approach based on a given brain MRI picture. The proposed methodology is divided into three sections. The first portion is centered on using a training database to build a deep learning network for BMRI anomalies detection and categorization as normal or tumorous brain. The white and grey matter pictures are extracted using the K-means algorithm in the second portion of the process. According to the deep learning network, the third phase is the classification of brain components as normal or tumorous situations. The proposed methodology successfully detects brain abnormalities based on the acquired results of brain tumours detection with an accuracy of 95%.

A Convolutional Neural Network (CNN) was utilized to identify a tumor in brain MRI pictures in [5]. CNN was the first to use images and Softmax function in Fully Connected Layer, which was utilized to categorize images, showed a detection accuracy of 98.67%. However, CNN's accuracy was found to be 97.34% using the Radial Basis Function classifier and found to be 94.24% using the Decision Tree classifier. Based on the outputs of the classifiers, the Softmax function showed the highest accuracy in the convolutional neural network, based on the outcome of model accuracy on image testing.

In [6], Deep neural network methods such as the VGG-16 architecture which is built from scratch and the convolutional neural network model are used to locate tumor regions in scanned brain pictures. It took brain MRI scans of 253 patients, with 155 tumorous and 98 non-tumorous MRI. The results of the VGG-16 architecture and convolutional neural network utilized are compared in this proposed work. Both methods were given useful outcomes. VGG-16, on the other hand, required more time for processing and storage than convolutional neural network but generates magnificent results.

The study presented in [7] intended to build a web application that uses CNN which is a deep neural network model to classify brain cancer into meningioma, pituitary and glioma according to the high precision T1 MRI. The web application can be used for decision support method in a hospital for brain cancer classification. Based on the investigational outcomes, all of the estimated performance accuracy for categorizing the brain cancer types on the training data are greater than 98%. When tested on the testing dataset, the performance measures are greater than 91%, with the exception of meningioma brain tumor's sensitivity and MCC metrics. The suggested model is capable of accurately categorizing brain cancer kinds when utilizing the generated performance measurements from the convolutional neural network model during the training step and evaluation.

Another related work was presented utilizing deep learning technique and includes a CNN-based model to categorize the Magnetic Resonance Images as "TUMOUR DETECTED" or "TUMOUR NOT DETECTED," in [8]. The model achieved an accuracy of 96.08% using 97.3 F-score. The model was consisting of convolutional neural network with 3 layers and only a few pre-processing actions to produce outcomes in 35 "EPOCHS".

It is believed that proposed approach provides more persuasive perceptions about how well brain MRI imaging performs at classifying brain tumours according to the above-mentioned data and results. The proposed work differs in its findings from the existing work.

3 Methodology

Here, we proposed a model which implements Convolutional Neural Network (CNN) which is category of deep neural networks with the TensorFlow framework.

3.1 Deep Neural Network

Deep neural networks are networks with an input layer, an output layer and at least one hidden layer in between which extracts high-level features from the given input dataset. It involves converting data into a more creative and abstract form. Compared to a conventional (traditional) neural network, the deep neural network is more sophisticated and inventive. DNN algorithms are able to analyze data, anticipate the future, think creatively, and recognize sounds and voice commands. They function similarly to the human brain.

3.2   Convolutional Neural Network (CNN)

CNN, also known as ConvNet is a deep neural network capable of taking an image as input, applying significance (biases and weights) to diverse components with in the image, and identifying them. These characteristics can be learned by Convnets. They are made up of several artificial neurons. Artificial neurons, like their natural counter-parts, are computational models which compute the summation of numerous inputs and produce an activation score. When you feed a picture into a Convolution layer, every network generates a number of activation functions that are forwarded on to the next phase or layer.

Convolutional Layer, Pooling Layer, and Fully-Connected Layer are the three primary types of layers that we employ while creating ConvNet architectures.

3.3   Model Description

The model was constructed on top of Keras and backed by Tensor Flow, a basic Python machine learning API, in the backend. The proposed model's procedure is described in the following phases (also see Fig. 1).

Step 1: Datasets are loaded and preprocessed
Step 2: The dataset is separated into three sections: training, validation, and testing datasets.
Step 3: Data cleaning and preprocessing performed
Step 4: Data augmentation
Step 5: CNN model is built
Step 6: Model evaluation

Dataset Description. The data for this study was obtained from Kaggle https://www. kaggle.com/masoudnickparvar/brain-tumour mri-dataset. It comprises 7022 RGB pic-tures of human brain MRI images classified into four classes: Glioma, Meningioma, no-tumour, and Pituitary (see Fig. 2). It contains 1621 glioma images, 1645 menin-gioma, 2000 no-tumour, and 1757 pituitary tumour images. Glioma tu-mours count for the most frequent central nervous system tumour in children and teen-agers and they exhibit a very wide variety of clinical behaviours [9]. The MRI images come in a variety of formats and sizes.

Image Preprocessing. As previously stated, the collection comprises photos in a vari-ety of formats and sizes. The goal of pre-processing is to improve the image's quality in order that we will be able to better evaluate it. We can reduce unwanted distortions and improve some aspects that are required for the application by pre-processing. A TensorFlow API: 'image dataset from directory' input pipeline is used in this work to

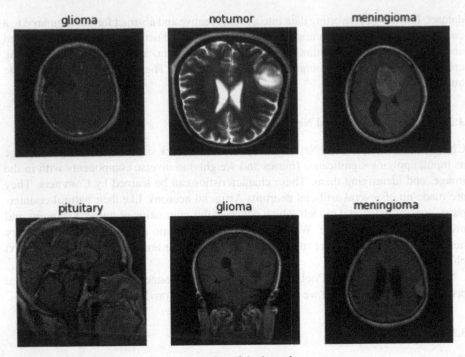

Fig. 1. Samples of the input images

create a dataset from image files in a directory, as well as resize and batch the photos into 256 × 256 form and 32 batch size, respectively. These inputs pipeline also generates batches of input images from subdirectories, along with integer labels for each image (0, 1, 2, and 3 as we used 'int' label encoder).

And then the dataset is divided into 80% training dataset, 10% testing dataset, and 10% validation dataset before it is fed to the model. A training step's preprocessing coupled to model execution in prefetching while the model is successfully completing training steps, the input pipeline is reading the data for step s + 1. As a result, the step time is reduced to the maximum (rather than the total) of the training and data extraction times. During model execution, a prefetching technique utilizing the tf.data API is employed.

Data Augmentation. Data augmentation is a regularization approach which prevents the model from overfitting during training. It is an approach which creates more diverse training datasets from the existing dataset so that the model will be introduced to different styles(version) of the datasets. It does not create new datasets, but rather modifies the existing training dataset using various techniques. Explicit data augmentation uses techniques like scaling, rotation, and flips to directly modify existing data into new samples. In this work, random rotating of images and flipping vertically and horizon-tally of images is implemented using TensorFlow's Sequential API.

CNN Model. A CNN model, which contains a pile of layers is fed the pre-processed picture. TensorFlow's Sequential API is used to build a model layer by layer. When

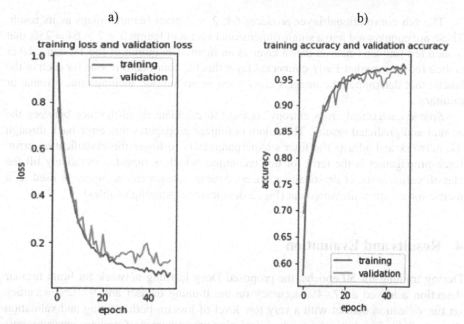

Fig. 2. a) Training loss and validation loss vs Epoch. b) Training accuracy and Validation accuracy vs Epoch

there is no layer sharing, a sequential API is acceptable. The input image makes up the input layer of the model. We have used 256×256 image size and 32 batch size for pre-processing the image. Each pixel has its own set of features. Six convolution layers (Conv2D) and Max Pool layers are employed in this study.

By sliding through the locations one by one, the first Conv layer applies 32 kernels of 3×3 size each to the source or input picture, generating a total of 32 feature maps. Feature extraction is the term for this procedure. The ReLU activation function takes these features and executes a threshold function. All negative values in the matrix are set to 0, while the rest are maintained. ReLu activates only the neurons with value greater than zero. And this makes ReLu more effective activation function. The output of 'ReLU' is applied to a 2×2 window size max-pooling layer, resulting in reducing the output to 127×127 image shape.

The output of the first pooling layer is sent into the next Conv layer. It consists of 64 filters, each with a 3×3 kernel size, that are passed to each of the 32 features collected from the 1st layer. To decrease the data to 62x62 pixels, same ReLU and Max Pooling algorithms are utilized.

The same principles are used in the third convolution layer, which employs 64 filters with 3×3 kernel sizes. After another cycle of ReLU, the data is transferred to the Max pooling layer, which provides 30×30 image size. Similarly, 64, 3×3 kernel size filters with Max-pooling and ReLu activation function is used for the 4th,5th, and 6th convo-lution layers. As a result, 14×14 pixels from the 4th layer, 6×6 pixels from the 5th layer, and 2×2 pixel data from the 6th layer are produced.

The 6th convolutional layer produces 64, 2 × 2 pixel features maps as its result. These are compressed into a single dimensional vector of length 2 × 2 × 64 = 256, that is then fed into a 64-neuron dense layer as an input. The output of the 1st dense layer is then fed into another Fully-connected layer that has four neurons, one for each of the labels, that determines the image's class, such as no tumour, meningioma, glioma, or pituitary.

Sparse categorical cross entropy' is used to calculate the difference between the ac-tual and predicted results. The Adam optimizer propagates this error back through the network and adjusts the filter's hyperparameters to lower the classification error. Back-propagation is the term for this technique, which is repeated iteratively till the classifi-cation error is drastically reduced. Sparse_categorical_accuracy is used as a metric for accuracy measurement (Fig. 3 demonstrates training profiles).

4   Results and Evaluation

During training for 50 epochs, the proposed Deep learning network for brain tumour detection achieved a 97.44% accuracy on the training dataset and 97.02% accuracy on the validation dataset with a very low level of loss on both training and validation datasets. Table 1 includes the number of training parameters, performance measures cost of training and validation processes.

Table 1. All model accuracy comparisons along with parameters.

CNN Model Performance Measures	
Training parameters	183,812
Train Accuracy	97.44%
Train Loss	0.0700
Validation Loss	0.0914
Validation Accuracy	97.02%
Test Accuracy	97.37%
Test Loss	0.0766

Change of training loss and validation loss according to the used epoch is plotted below.

After model training was performed the proposed model is evaluated and resulting an accuracy of 96.75% and 0.0766 loss on the test data which is better than some of the existing works that are mentioned in the related work section. Some outcomes of the image classifications are shown in Fig. 3.

Following the development of the proposed model, it was saved, integrated into a web page, and deployed on localhost using the Flask web framework. Flask is a Python package for quickly creating web pages.

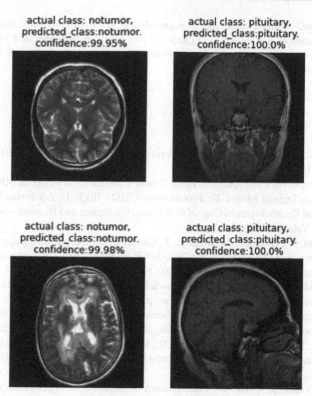

Fig. 3. Model evaluation

The functions listed below are available on the web page.

Step 1: Create an array from the input (uploaded) images.

Step 2: Submit an image to our algorithm to classify the MRI picture into glioma tumor, meningioma tumor, pituitary tumor and no-tumor.

Step 3: Show the tumor kind and the predicted picture.

5 Conclusion

In our research paper, the proposed model is based on Deep Neural Network which implements a Convolutional Neural Network with TensorFlow framework. Convolutional Neural Network was used to extract features from the given MRI images of the brain tumours (cancerous and non-cancerous). The extracted signals (features) are employed by CNN for detection and then classification. CNN is capable of detecting brain tumours. It is very useful for extracting features in medical MRI images. In this work, the Convolutional Neural Network model with six layers is used and successfully achieved a significant accuracy. This research aimed to show the importance of deep learning applications in helping radiologists to detect tumours without difficulty.

The future work will involve segmenting brain tumours to find where and how far the tumours parts have spread (active tumorous tissue).

Acknowledgment. Authors would like to acknowledge Marwadi University, Rajkot, India, for providing the resources and guidance to carry out this research. In addition, C3PC (Children's Cancer Care, Prevention, and Cure) Research Foundation is also being acknowledged for partial support in publishing this work.

References

1. Guan, Y., et al.: A framework for efficient brain tumor classification using MRI images. Math. Biosci. Eng. **18**(5), 26 (2021)
2. Yerukalareddy, D.R., Pavlovskiy, E.: Brain Tumor Classification based on MR Images using GAN as a Pre-Trained Model. In: Proceedings - 2021 IEEE Ural-Siberian Conference on Computational Technologies in Cognitive Science, Genomics and Biomedicine, CSGB 2021, Novosibirsk, Yekaterinburg (2021)
3. Raut, G., Raut, A., Bhagade, J., Bhagade, J., Gavhane, S.: Deep learning approach for brain tumor detection and segmentation. In: 2020 IEEE International Conference on Convergence to Digital World – Quo Vadis (ICCDW 2020), p. 5 (2020)
4. Kebir, S.T., Mekaoui, S.: An efficient methodology of brain abnormalities. In: 2018 International Conference on Applied Smart Systems, p. 5 (2018)
5. Siar, M., Teshnehlab, M.: Brain tumor detection using deep neural network. In: 9th International Conference on Computer and Knowledge Engineering (ICCKE 2019), p. 6 (2019)
6. Grampurohit, S., Shalavadi, V., Dhotargavi, R., Kudari, M., Jolad, M.S.: Brain tumor detection using deep learning models. In: 2020 IEEE India Council International Subsections Conference (INDISCON), p. 6 (2020)
7. Ucuzal, H., Yaşar, Ş., Çolak, C.: Classification of brain tumor types by deep learning with convolutional neural network on magnetic resonance images using a developed web-based interface. In: 2019 3rd International Symposium on Multidisciplinary Studies and Innovative Technologies (ISMSIT), p. 5 (2019)
8. Choudhury, C.L., Mahanty, C., Kumar, R., Mishra, B.K.: Brain tumor detection and classification using convolutional neural network and deep neural network. In: 2020 International Conference on Computer Science, Engineering and Applications (ICCSEA), p. 4 (2020)
9. Sturm, D., Pfister, S.M., Jones, D.T.W.: Pediatric gliomas: current concepts on diagnosis, biology, and clinical management. J. Clin. Oncol. **35**(21), 2370–2377 (2017)

Author Index

© Springer Nature Switzerland AG 2023
D. Garg et al. (Eds.): IACC 2022, CCIS 1781, pp. 503–506, 2023.
https://doi.org/10.1007/978-3-031-35641-4

Printed in the United States
by Baker & Taylor Publisher Services